KT-525-389

Religions in the Modern World

Traditions and transformations

Edited by Linda Woodhead

- Paul Fletcher
- Hiroko Kawanami
- David Smith

London and New York

BL50 — 11MAR03 — £17.99

First published 2002
by Routledge
11 New Fetter Lane, London EC4P 4EE

Simultaneously published in the USA and Canada by Routledge
29 West 35th Street, New York, NY 10001

Routledge is an imprint of the Taylor & Francis Group

© 2002 Linda Woodhead, Paul Fletcher, Hiroko Kawanami and David Smith,
selection and editorial matter; the contributors, their contributions.

Designed and typeset in Garamond and Frutiger by Keystroke, Jacaranda Lodge,
Wolverhampton
Printed and bound in Great Britain by TJ International Ltd, Padstow, Cornwall

All rights reserved. No part of this book may be reprinted or reproduced or utilised in
any form or by any electronic, mechanical, or other means, now known or hereafter
invented, including photocopying and recording, or in any information storage or
retrieval system, without permission in writing from the publishers.

British Library Cataloguing in Publication Data
A catalogue record for this book is available from the British Library

Library of Congress Cataloging in Publication Data
Religions in the modern world: traditions and transformations / edited by Linda
Woodhead . . . [et al.].
        p. cm.
    Includes bibliographical references and index.
    1. Religions. I. Woodhead, Linda.

BL80.2 .R417 2001
200–dc21   2001019142

ISBN 0–415–21783–0 (hbk)
ISBN 0–415–21784–9 (pbk)

SOUTH TRAFFORD COLLEGE
OF FURTHER EDUCATION

| 291 WOO | 85927 |
| BL50 | 11/3/03 |

IN MEMORIAM
NINIAN SMART 1927–2001

SOUTH TRAFFORD COLLEGE
OF FURTHER EDUCATION

Contents

LIST OF ILLUSTRATIONS

The following were reproduced with kind permission. While every effort has been made to trace copyright holders and obtain permission, this has not been possible in all cases. Any omissions brought to our attention will be remedied in future editions.

LIST OF TABLES

NOTES ON CONTRIBUTORS

Elisabeth Arweck completed her PhD in 1999 on the responses to New Religious Movements in Britain and Germany at King's College London, University of London. She is the co-editor of the *Journal of Contemporary Religion* and co-author (with Peter B. Clarke) of *New Religious Movements in Western Europe: An Annotated Bibliography* (Westport, CT, and London: Greenwood Press, 1997). She has contributed to *Dialog und Unterscheidung: Religionen und neue religiöse Bewegungen im Gespräch* (Berlin: EZW, 2000) and a jointly edited volume on *Theorising Faith* is forthcoming (with Martin Stringer). In April 2000 she became the Convenor of the BSA Sociology of Religion Study Group.

Peter Berger has been Director of the Institute for the Study of Economic Culture, Boston University, since 1985. He is the author of numerous books and articles in sociology and the sociology of religion. Recent publications include *A Far Glory. The Quest for Faith in an Age of Credulity* (New York, NY: Free Press, 1992), *Redeeming Laughter* (New York and Berlin: Walter de Gruyter, 1997) and (as editor) *The Desecularization of the World: Resurgent Religion and World Politics* (Grand Rapids, MI: Eerdmans Publishing Co., 1999).

Cathy Cantwell is presently a Research Fellow in the Department of Anthropology at the University of Kent at Canterbury (UKC). She has a PhD and publications in the field of Tibetan Buddhism, and her research interests include Tibetan ritual symbolism, tantric scriptures, Buddhist ethics, Tibetan ethnicity, Buddhism and ecology, and contemporary developments in Tibetan Buddhism.

She combines Buddhist and Tibetan textual studies with an anthropological training. She has taught widely in higher education, including (besides UKC) the University of Wales, Lampeter, the Open University (where she has been a consultant for new course materials on Buddhism), Roehampton Institute, London, Chichester Institute of Higher Education, and SOAS, London. She is a member of the International Association for Tibetan Studies, the UK Association for Buddhist Studies, the International Association for Buddhist Studies, the Association of Social Anthropologists, and she is on the editorial board of the *Buddhist Studies Review*.

Stephan Feuchtwang is a Senior Research Associate of the Department of Anthropology, London School of Economics. His area specialism is China and Taiwan. Together with a close colleague, Wang Mingming, who is in Beijing University, he has recently completed a book, *Grassroots Charisma in China*, to be published by Routledge (2001), on the theory of charisma and the recognition of authority based on life stories of rural leaders in Taiwan and the mainland. It is part of a larger project on the topic of local temples and festivals in modern China and whether they can be described as a form of public space quite different from Euro-American civil society. Decentred popular religion in the imperial state and what it suggests as a concept of religion as a collective representation are the subjects of the new edition of his earlier book *Popular Religion in China: The Imperial Metaphor* (Richmond, VA: Curzon, 2001), with the addition of a chapter on the transformations of popular religion in the People's Republic of China and Taiwan. He is now exploring the theme of the recognition of catastrophic loss, which in Chinese cosmology and possibly elsewhere is pre-figured in the category of ghosts. An outline of this theme has been published as a chapter in S. Radstone (ed.): *Memory and Methodology* (Oxford: Berg, 2000).

Charles Gore is Associate Lecturer in Sociology at the Open University and Visiting Lecturer in Social Anthropology at Birkbeck College, University of London. He has conducted field research in Benin City and Edo State in Southern Nigeria since 1986 with particular focus on Edo ritual and religion at grassroots level. He has published various articles relating to religion, ritual, media and art in the Edo State. Current interests are religion and ritual, visual anthropology, and approaches to popular culture and its relations to locality and the processes of globalization.

Wouter J. Hanegraaff (1961) is Professor of History of Hermetic Philosophy and Related Currents at the University of Amsterdam (Faculty of Humanities). He is the author of *New Age Religion and Western Culture: Esotericism in the Mirror of Secular Thought* (Leiden: E. J. Brill, 1996/Albany, NY: SUNY Press, 1998) and has published widely on various aspects of the study and history of Western esotericism and method and theory in the study of religions. He is co-editor of *Female Stereotypes in Religious Traditions* (with Ria Kloppenborg) (Leiden: E. J. Brill, 1995); *Gnosis and Hermeticism from Antiquity to Modern Times* (with Roelof van den Broek) (Albany, NY: SUNY Press, 1998); and *Western Esotericism and the Science of Religion* (with Antoine Faivre) (Louvain: Peeters, 1998). He is presently working on an annotated translation of the hermetic writings of Lodovico Lazzarelli (1450–1500) and a reception history of Swedenborg's *Arcana Caelestia.*

Howard L. Harrod is Oberlin Alumni Professor of Social Ethics and Sociology of Religion at Vanderbilt University. His publications include: *Mission Among the Blackfeet* (Norman, OK: University of Oklahoma Press, 1971, 1999); *The Human Center: Moral Agency in the Social World* (Philadelphia, PA: Fortress Press, 1981); *Renewing the World: Plains Indian Religion and Morality* (Tucson, AZ: University of Arizona, 1987); *Becoming and Remaining a People* (Tucson, AZ: University of Arizona, 1995); *The Animals Came Dancing: Native American Sacred Ecology and Animal Kinship* (Tucson, AZ: University of Arizona, 2000).

Jeffrey Haynes is Professor of Politics at London Guildhall University where he teaches courses on international and third world politics. His most recent relevant publications are: *Religion in Global Politics* (London: Routledge, 1998) and an edited book, *Religion, Globalization and Political Culture in the Third World* (Basingstoke: Macmillan, 1999).

Paul Heelas is Professor in Religion and Modernity at Lancaster University. During his university teaching career, which spans some twenty-five years, he has become increasingly concerned with how both religion and spirituality have been faring in today's world. Relevant publications are referred to at the end of Chapter 17.

Hiroko Kawanami is currently Lecturer in Buddhist Studies at the Department of Religious Studies at Lancaster University. Since 1986, she has done extensive fieldwork in Burma, Thailand and Japan, and has been involved in various educational projects for Buddhist nuns. Her interests focus on women and Buddhism, new Buddhist movements and modernity in Southeast Asia, religious transactions and anthropology of religion. She has written articles on contemporary Buddhist practices in both Japanese and English.

Robert Kisala is a Permanent Fellow at the Nanzan Institute for Religion and Culture, and Associate Professor at Nanzan University in Nagoya, Japan. He recently published a study of pacifism in the Japanese New Religions, *Prophets of Peace: Pacifism and Cultural Identity in Japan's New Religions* (Honolulu: University of Hawaii Press, 1999), and co-edited with Mark Mullins a volume on reactions to the violence perpetrated by Aum Shinrikyō, *Religion and Social Crisis in Japan: Understanding Japanese Society through the Aum Affair* (Basingstoke, Hampshire: Palgrave, 2001).

Seth D. Kunin is Senior Lecturer in Religious Studies at the University of Aberdeen. He received his doctorate in anthropology from the University of Cambridge and rabbinic ordination from the Leo Baeck College. He has written extensively on Jewish myth and culture from a structuralist perspective. His current research area is Crypto-Judaism, specifically in the American South West.

David Lehmann is Reader in Social Science at the University of Cambridge and was Director of the University's Centre of Latin American Studies from 1990 to 2000. His publications include *Struggle for the Spirit: Religious Transformation and Popular Culture in Brazil and Latin America* (Oxford: Polity, 1996).

Christopher Shackle FBA (b.1942) is Professor of the Modern Languages of South Asia in the University of London at SOAS. His publications on Sikhism include *An Introduction to the Sacred Language of the Sikhs* (London: SOAS, 1983); *The Sikhs* (London: Minority Rights Group, 1983, revised 1986); and *A Guru Nanak Glossary*, second edition (New Delhi: Heritage Publishers, 1995).

David Smith teaches Hinduism and South Asian Art in the Department of Religious Studies, Lancaster University. He is the author of *Ratnakara's Haravijaya: An Introduction to the Sanskrit Court Epic* (New Delhi: Oxford University Press, 1985); *The Dance of Siva: Religion, Art and Poetry in South India* (Cambridge: Cambridge University Press, 1996); and *Hinduism and Modernity* (Oxford: Blackwell, forthcoming).

David Waines is Professor of Islamic Studies, Department of Religious Studies, Lancaster University. He is the author of, among other works, *An Introduction to Islam* (Cambridge: Cambridge University Press, 1995) and has written extensively on medieval Islamic diet and medicine as well as on religious and political themes concerning the modern Islamic world.

Linda Woodhead is Senior Lecturer in Christian Studies at Lancaster University. Her research and writing focuses on the interpretation of Christianity and alternative religions and spiritualities in modern times. She is the editor (with Paul Heelas) of *Religion in Modern Times. An Interpretive Anthology* (Oxford, UK, and Malden, USA: Blackwell, 2000), editor of *Reinventing Christianity: Nineteenth-Century Contexts* (Aldershot: Ashgate, 2000) and *Peter Berger and the Study of Religion* (London: Routledge, 2000), and author of *Introduction to Christianity* (Cambridge: Cambridge University Press, 2002).

ACKNOWLEDGEMENTS

My first debt of gratitude is to my colleagues and assistant editors: Paul Fletcher, Koko Kawanami and David Smith. It was with them that the plan for this book was first hatched, and in conversation with them that its structure and shape were conceived. The four of us took responsibility for the initial round of commissioning and of communication with contributors. The commissioning of Part III, the final shaping of the book, and the editing of all the chapters was undertaken by me alone, and any flaws and errors must therefore be my responsibility. Since this book grows out of collaborative teaching at Lancaster University, I must also acknowledge debts to the Department of Religious Studies, to all colleagues there (especially Paul Heelas and Ian Reader for encouragement and advice) and to the founder of the Department, the late Ninian Smart. Lancaster's global and interdisciplinary approach to the study of religions has had a profound influence on this project.

My next debt is to the contributors to the book. In order to ensure coherence and a degree of uniformity in such a large volume, I often had to exercise a rather heavy editorial hand. Most chapters had to be revised and redrafted a number of times as the book took shape and its unifying themes and structures emerged. If the form of the book had been crystal clear from the outset, some of this work might have been avoided. But there would also have been loss, for the book has been shaped by the contributions of all those whose names appear on the contents page, and not only by the editors. I am grateful to them all, not only for their chapters, but for their ideas, their patience and their willingness to respond to 'just one more request for minor revision . . .' I hope they will be pleased with the end result.

The volume has also benefited greatly from the comments of referees in North America and the UK, including Dr Paul Ballard, Cardiff University; Dr Ron Greaves, Chichester Institute of Higher Education; Professor Bill Parsons, Rice University, Houston; Professor Irving Hexham, University of Calgary; Professor Brian Bocking, SOAS, University of London; Professor Philip Alexander, Manchester University; Professor David Sorkin, University of Wisconsin-Madison; Dr Simon Weightman, SOAS, University of London; Professor David Martin, LSE. Special thanks must go to Professor Brian Wilson and Cybelle Shattuck at Western Michigan University, who were closely involved in the whole refereeing process, and who offered extremely helpful comments not only on individual chapters, but on the shape of the book as a whole.

Finally, I must thank the staff at Routledge who commissioned this book (Adrian Driscoll, and his successor Roger Thorp), sent out contracts (Hywel Evans) and watched over its development and production. Of the latter, Moira Taylor's contribution has been outstanding and invaluable, and it is no exaggeration to say that this book would not have been possible without her. As Senior Textbook Development Editor at Routledge, she and I have often been in daily contact. She has overseen the collection and selection of illustrations, sought permissions, played a major role in designing the book and its layout, corresponded with contributors, sent chapters to referees, sorted out problems, co-ordinated the production process, and offered good advice whenever I needed it. What is more, she has remained cheerful, supportive and sweet-tempered throughout. Since the latter is true of my husband, Alan, I must – as always – thank him too.

Linda Woodhead,
Lancaster

Studying religion and modernity

Linda Woodhead

▌ STUDYING RELIGION

Religion is the subject of many different methods of investigation, but two have achieved particular prominence. The first centres round the concept of religious 'traditions' such as Hinduism, Buddhism, Christianity. These are treated as relatively self-contained and discrete entities which should be explored in terms of their most characteristic phenomena. The latter include distinctive personalities, events, beliefs, practices and rituals (thus this approach is sometimes referred to as 'phenomenological'). Scholarly access to these different internal dimensions of a religion is largely by way of texts; the raw materials of this mode of interpretation and analysis are normally scriptures and other written deposits of a religion.

The second approach to the study of religion makes less use of the concept of traditions and world religions, and is interested not only in religion in its own terms, but in religion in relation to wider society. It may consider, for example, how a particular form of religion relates to the nation state or to changing gender roles, or how religious decline can be explained in terms of wider social changes. Its data are derived from empirical research in 'the field' as much as from textual research. The scope and scale of such research vary considerably, as do those of the theory which flows from it. At one extreme this broadly sociological approach offers very general theories to account for widespread features of religion and society (theories of secularization, for example). At the other it is more ethnographic or anthropological, its aim being the detailed depiction of particular small-scale communities, cultures or other aspects of religious life.

The approach of this book

This volume aims to bring together these two broad approaches to the study of religion – and a whole range of possibilities which arise from their combination – in an original yet accessible textbook. Attention is paid to traditions as well as to the transformation and transmutation of traditions. Texts are taken seriously, as are fieldwork and empirical research. Religions are looked at in their own terms, as well as in relation to wider society and culture.

In order to ensure overall coherence in this integrative approach, chapters in the first two sections of the book are structured according to a common framework. This begins by setting forth the historical 'sources and resources' of a tradition, and goes on to consider how these have fared in modern times. Particular attention is paid to the interactions between religion and modernity. The latter refers to particular combinations of social, political, cultural and economic factors. Thus each chapter relates a major religious tradition to the wider sociocultural contexts and transformations of modern times. In particular, chapters consider whichever combination of the following topics are most relevant to the religion in question:

- politics (particularly the ways in which a tradition has adjusted to the rise of the modern nation state)
- economics (the impact of modern forms of economy, particularly global capitalism, on religion)
- gender (the interactions between changing gender roles and a tradition)
- colonialism (the impact of Western colonialism and subsequent decolonization on religious tradition)
- authority (the changing understandings of authority within a tradition, and how they relate to wider shifts in modernity such as 'the turn to the self')
- community (the fate of traditional religious communities and institutions in modernity)
- culture (the influence of modern culture – such as scientific rationality – on traditional beliefs, teachings, doctrines, ideas and self-understandings).

The chapters in Part II develop these themes and topics further and offer general reflection upon them. Such reflection makes reference to specific traditions, even when it is not primarily tradition-based. Themes like secularization and sacralization cut across traditions, as do topics like religion and politics and religion and globalization.

Rationale

There are a number of reasons why this volume has been designed to bring together approaches to the study of religion which have often been kept apart. All are related to contemporary debates within religious studies and related disciplines.

First, and most straightforwardly, both the approaches outlined above yield valuable and often complementary information and insights, and there can be considerable cross-fertilization between them. By bringing them into relation with one another we hope to give a fuller picture of religion than would otherwise be possible. The volume offers an informative account of religions on their own terms, whilst also showing how fruitful it can be to consider them in relation to wider social and cultural contexts.

Second, we acknowledge the insights of recent scholars who argue that the notions of 'tradition' and 'religion' have often been blunt instruments imposed by Western scholars on other cultures. More specifically, we agree that the use of these categories often assumes that Western styles of religion (particularly Protestant Christianity) provide the definitive model for all religion. On this model all religions are assumed to have a founder, a single set of authoritative scriptures and to be focused on a supernatural being. Similarly, they are believed to be clearly bounded and independent of wider society, culture and politics. Once these assumptions are made explicit, it quickly becomes clear that in relation to religion one size does not fit all. There are some traditions which have no founder and no single set of scriptures or teachings (many variants of Hinduism, for example), some which do not worship a supernatural being (many forms of Buddhism), and some which are so internally plural that it may not be appropriate to speak of a religion or a tradition at all. Equally, the crude imposition of these latter categories may obscure the fact that in many parts of the world religion forms an integral part of a total culture and society – so much so that it is not even distinguishable as a separate sphere. It is in recognition of this that a number of chapters in the first two parts of this volume focus not on traditions but on geographical areas (Chinese religions; Japanese religions; African religions). Such an approach acknowledges the interconnectedness of many forms of religion not only with their wider cultures, but also with one another (in China, for example, indigenous/vernacular Buddhist, Daoist and Confucian forms of practice are not separated by the clear boundaries that an exclusively tradition-based approach would expect – see Chapter 4).

Finally, we believe that there are particular developments in religion in modern times that destabilize an approach which focuses exclusively on traditions. For example, the New Age movement tends not to fit the model of a religious tradition, since it is not a discrete entity with identifiable 'external' authorities such as scriptures, a clear set of structures, and/or an identifiable hierarchy of leadership. Likewise, as Chapter 17 argues, 'detraditionalization' may be one of the most important of all the trends in contemporary religion, particularly in the West. The term refers to the process whereby faith is lost in the institutional and external elements of a religion, to such an extent that many men and women no longer describe themselves as religious at all. Whilst they distance themselves from religion and tradition, however, many are happy to speak of themselves as 'spiritual'. As with the New Age, authority is located in the self and inner life, not in 'externals'. Thus 'religion' and 'tradition' give way to more amorphous and individualized forms of spirituality. An exclusively tradition-based approach to the study of religion is ill-equipped to deal with such developments.

This volume has therefore been designed to offer students and general readers an introduction to the rich possibilities of the study of religion, by taking account of the latest work in the area, and by bringing together methods and approaches which have often been kept apart.

STUDYING RELIGION AND MODERNITY

The volume seeks to achieve its aims by considering religion in the modern world. Whilst it offers information about the historical sources and resources of a wide range of religions and spiritualities, its central interest is in their interactions with modernity. Such an approach makes it impossible to look at traditions in isolation from their wider contexts. Equally, it makes it impossible to look at the notion of modernity in isolation from religion, or from a purely Western perspective. Both religion and modernity may therefore be illuminated by being brought into relation with one another.

There is no universally agreed definition of 'modernity', for the concept is a contested one. Neither is there agreement about when modernity or the modern world began, for the dating of the modern period depends on what is to count as 'modern'. One of the most important reasons for this lack of clear definition and boundaries emerges from the pages of this volume: a focus on religion makes it very clear that the modern world comes in different guises and at different times in different parts of the world. Once one begins to take a religious and hence a global perspective, easy generalizations about modernity begin to fail, and the common (Western) assumption that all cultures and societies inevitably progress through uniform stages of development from the premodern to the modern (so repeating the experience of the West) becomes harder to defend.

One way in which this book deals with this issue is by allowing each chapter to state what counts as modernity for the particular tradition, area or form of spirituality with which it deals. Thus the chapter on Christianity considers the rise of the modern nation state to be decisive for the churches, and so dates modernity from the time of the French Revolution in 1789. By contrast, the chapter on Chinese religions speaks of a 'long modernity' in China which has had a thousand years of slow emergence and is characterized by the growth of commerce, monetary economy, contractual and share-holding agreements, long-distance trade and banking, cities of manufacture and commerce and luxurious consumption. This is contrasted with a more recent political or 'republican' modernity, characterized by the institution of a nation state and mass politics, both of which have had a much more dramatic effect on religious practices. And, as a final example, the chapter on Sikhism distinguishes between a modernity which is in effect an imposition of colonialism, initiated by the British conquest of the Punjab in the 1840s, and a later postcolonial phase which begins with Indian independence in 1947 and in which many aspects of the older modernity of the colonial period begin to be questioned and discarded in favour of new forms of traditionalized modernity or modernized tradition.

Such definitions and observations made from a global perspective serve as a corrective to assumptions which lie behind much talk of modernity. The global religious perspective reminds us that:

1 the West (Europe and then America) really became economically, technologically and possibly culturally dominant on the world stage only after 1800, and before that time other civilizations including Chinese and Islamic ones were often more advanced and powerful culturally as well as politically
2 modernization is not exclusive to the West, but can and did take place in non-Western cultures, often without Western stimulus
3 modernization may be a process internal to a particular society, or may be imposed from outside, most notably by colonial intervention (or by some combination of these two)
4 the Western experience of modernity and modernization cannot serve as the definitive model of 'evolution' and 'development' which is then imposed on all cultures and societies.

Instead of giving a single definition of modernity which implies that the latter is identical with the sociocultural changes experienced by the advanced economies of the West in the last two hundred years or so, it is therefore more helpful to think of modernity in terms of a number of different processes which may operate together or in some combination, in different parts of the world and at different times. These may be characterized as a series of profound changes or 'revolutions', which operate at political, economic, social and cultural levels. On the basis of the evidence presented in the chapters which follow, at least six emerge as particularly significant in relation to religion and spirituality worldwide.

1 Dominance of the nation state

There can be few if any cultures or religions which have not been profoundly affected by the rise of the nation state. Nations *per se* are not new (ancient Israel was a nation, for example) – what is new is the rise of the secular nation state with its extensive apparatus of control over a huge range of aspects of social and political life. What is also new is the way in which the nation state has become the almost universal unit of territorial control worldwide. Increasingly such states are constitutional, that is to say they exist to serve not those who rule but those who are ruled, and their power is checked in order to protect the freedom of their citizens. Only in the course of the twentieth century have truly democratic states developed, in which government is by representatives elected by all adult citizens. Many chapters in this volume remind us that the twentieth century has also witnessed the rise of the one-party state, in which a single party is established to govern, on the grounds that it is the legitimate expression of the will of its people (most communist and fascist regimes, for example). The 'triumph' of democracy is very recent, and may yet prove short-lived.

As the chapters which follow demonstrate, interactions between religions and nation states take many forms. Some states have been profoundly and violently hostile to religion. This has been particularly true of many communist states – see, for example, Chapter 2 on the way in which China tried to eliminate Buddhism in Tibet. On the other hand, some states and regimes have tried to win the support of religious leaders and devotees in the attempt to legitimize their rule, as Chapter 2 also shows in relation to Buddhism in Laos, Burma and Thailand. In the long run, the co-option of religion to support the state may prove a very mixed blessing for religion, since to become 'established' by this process is to lose independence and so become tainted and compromised in the eyes of many (as happened to some forms of Buddhism in Burma, and in relation to some Christian churches which co-operated with communist regimes). At the opposite extreme, religions may oppose the legitimacy or the policies of nation states. Thus the Catholic Church in Poland played a key role in the overthrow of communism in the late 1980s (see Chapter 7). An even more extreme example is provided by religious groups which organize themselves as religious alternatives to the secular nation state. The success of religious nationalism since the latter part of the twentieth century has surprised many commentators who believed that religion no longer had political significance in an era of nation states. In 1979, for example, the increasingly secular state in Iran was overthrown by Islamic nationalists, and religious nationalism continues to be a potent force in many other Islamic countries, as well as in India (Hinduism), Israel (Orthodox Judaism) and the former Yugolsavia (Roman Catholic Christianity, Orthodox Christianity, Islam) (for an overview see Chapter 15).

In Western Europe and the US, religion (preponderantly Christianity) has tended to accept the legitimacy of the nation state and democracy (at least since the twentieth century), and even to construct for itself a role as the defender of democracy (as in the case of Pope John Paul II, see Chapter 7). Yet even here, it remains capable of opposition, as the rise of the Christian 'New Religious Right' in the US in the 1980s demonstrated. Even where it tries to ignore the nation state and keep out of politics, religion is inevitably affected by the state's creeping dominance in many areas of social life. This process, known as 'social differentiation', gradually wrests control not only of political affairs, but of education, welfare and community organization from religious bodies, and may therefore lead directly to religion's diminishing influence in society. Or, to look at this process another way, religion becomes more a cultural than a political force, and more focused on regulation of private and domestic life than wider political affairs. The latter is true of two very vibrant forms of contemporary religion – Evangelical-Charismatic Christianity (see Chapter 14) and New Age spiritualities (see Chapter 11 and Chapter 17).

2 Colonialism and postcolonialism

Many chapters in this volume remind us that colonialism has been a second highly significant feature of the political landscape of the modern world. Colonialism is a modern variant of imperialism. Empires have always existed, and imperialism refers to the general process whereby states extend their power and dominion by force (usually military, but also political and economic). Colonialism normally refers to something more specific: the modern European expansion in which foreign territories were settled and ruled over by whites who controlled populations of indigenous peoples by legal and political means. (Arguably, non-Western forms of modern imperialism, for example Japanese, might also fit into the category of colonialism.) Western colonialism can be dated back to 1500 and the expansion of Spain and Portugal, but its decisive phase began three hundred years later when modernizing Western nations like Britain and France rapidly expanded their territories. In 1800 Western nations controlled 35 per cent of the world's land surface; by 1914 they were in charge of 84 per cent. By the 1970s, the vast majority of these empires had been dismantled and new independent nation states created in their wake.

The fates of religion and colonialism have been bound up together in at least two respects. First, colonial expansion had an impact on the religions of the colonizers, most notably upon Christianity. Colonialism was often accompanied by Christian mission. In some cases missions explicitly legitimated colonialism. More often, Christian missionary work supported the colonial enterprise implicitly (and often unintentionally) by acting as an agent of a cultural imperialism. At the same time, however, Christianity provided cultural resources (not least education) which would, in time, serve as resources which colonized peoples could deploy to win independence from foreign rule. Equally, Christianity itself has been appropriated by many colonized peoples in the postcolonial era, most notably in Latin America and sub-Saharan Africa. As a consequence, Christianity is now the largest of the world religions, and there are now more Christians in the Southern than the Northern hemisphere (see Chapter 7, Chapter 9 and Chapter 14). In addition, colonialism has been a major factor in what is sometimes called 'the Easternization of the West', the process whereby from at least the nineteenth century onwards oriental religions were absorbed into the cultural life of the West, often giving rise to new hybridized forms of religion and spirituality such as Theosophy (see Chapter 11).

Second, colonialism had a profound effect on religions within colonized territories. Amongst elites, it often generated reforming and revisionist activity as they sought to modernize their religious traditions to conform more closely to Western models. Various forms of 'reformed Hinduism' came into being, for example, as Westernized intellectuals in India sought to interpret Hinduism as a text-based, ethical, universal religion (see Chapter 1). In other cases, religions were revitalized as they became markers of colonized peoples' identity, and were mobilized to oppose colonialism (for an example of this development see Chapter 3 on Sikhism). Decolonization has also been highly significant for religions worldwide, and has led in many places to widespread religious resurgence. The two most vital and rapidly growing forms of religion in the postcolonial period – resurgent Islam and Charismatic Christianity – must both be understood in part in terms of their reaction to Western colonialism, Western-dominated forms of religion, and Western models of modernization.

3 Rationalization, cultural and economic

Rationalization refers both to cultural and broader socio-economic developments. At the cultural level it is associated with the rationalism of the eighteenth-century Enlightenment. This Western movement championed the application of reason (clear, distinct and universal ideas) informed by experience and experiment to all areas of life. As such, the rationalists became the theorists and apologists of both the human and the natural sciences. Whilst the rationalists themselves opposed 'reason' to 'tradition' and 'superstition', rationalism is not a wholly secular movement. Indeed, some of the early rationalists like some Deists or, later, Immanuel Kant (1724–1804) were devout Christians who wished to modernize their tradition. The most significant clashes with religion came in the West in the nineteenth century, when an evolutionary scientific view of life and the universe came into direct conflict with the biblical account of creation.

Not all forms of Christianity were equally challenged by these developments, just as not all religions have been equally challenged by scientific rationalism. As this volume illustrates, different accommodations have taken place. Most religions have been more than happy to appropriate modern technology to serve their own ends – for example, in disseminating their teachings via the mass media. As for science, some have claimed that its findings are entirely compatible with their own beliefs and teachings (Buddhism, for example, often stresses its own empirical credentials), whilst others have gone even further by claiming that their scriptures anticipated scientific findings (some forms of neo-Vedic Hinduism, for example). Another observable phenomenon is that whereby modern men and women compartmentalize their lives, living part of them in conformity with rational principles (in the laboratory, workshop or workplace), and others in conformity to non-rational or supra-rational beliefs and practices (asking invisible deities for worldly success, placing faith in alternative forms of medicine).

Rationalization also operates at the socio-economic level. It is most evident in the spread of rational–bureaucratic institutions and organizations which subject more and more spheres of life to rational control. These institutions are linked not only to the nation state, but also to the spread of the market economy and capitalism. The latter is a flexible, varied and rapidly changing form of economic organization which centres around:

1 a money-based economy with a developed banking system in which capital accumulation is possible, and in which a large proportion of capital is in the hands of institutions and corporations as well as private individuals
2 the separation of ownership from control, and the development of complex managerial hierarchies
3 the determination of individual and corporate activity by the overriding goal of profit
4 a competitive and free market regulating supply and demand
5 the division and specialization of labour (both between different trades, and within the manufacture of a single product)
6 the provision of labour by specialized and educated workers who are free agents, and the growth of a middle class
7 the global expansion of markets, commerce and production.

What is very clear from this brief description is that religion occupies little or no place in the capitalist scheme of things. Impersonal, rational calculation in order to maximize profit overrides and excludes any spiritual imperatives. Interestingly many of the chapters in this volume (some of which are silent about religion's relations with the economic sphere) also suggest that few religions in the modern world have been very active or effective in challenging the seemingly inexorable spread of capitalism. On the contrary, religion in the modern world seems to: (1) have aided capitalism (Max Weber's thesis about the compatibility of a Protestant work ethic with the spirit of capitalism, and the continuing ability of Evangelical-Charismatic Christianity to sustain the disciplines necessary for success in a capitalist economy); (2) have abandoned any attempt to interfere or influence the economic sphere (thus many devoutly religious people all over the world work in capitalist enterprises, without feeling that this contradicts or affects their religious commitment); (3) cope with capitalism by suggesting that religious practice can itself be a route to prosperity (most of the world's religions have prosperity wings). A number of chapters also illustrate (4) the ways in which religion can serve as a means of coping with the severe inequalities, disruptions, stresses and strains which capitalism brings in its train (see, for example, Chapter 9).

4 Universalism and difference

Rationalization favours the universal. Science seeks universal laws. The Enlightenment strove to uncover universal truths about human nature and the universal moral rules or 'categorical imperatives' by which all behaviour and all societies should be regulated. In the twentieth century, the modern world has been characterized by the spread of international human rights legislation. The notion of 'humanity' and 'the humanitarian' fits naturally with international action, for it assumes there is a common humanity which lies behind relatively inessential cultural differences. Global capitalism also tends to homogenize: to bring standardized methods, rules, forms of organization, opportunities, products. At the same time it commodifies; by making money the measure of all things, a powerful universal standard is set in place.

Religion has been widely affected by the processes of universalization. From the late eighteenth and nineteenth centuries onwards nearly all the world religions developed liberal wings which emphasized the rationality of their teachings, the universal laws they proclaimed, the freedom and equality of individuals, and the common humanity of all types and conditions of men (and sometimes women) – see, for example, the discussion of Reform Judaism in Chapter 6. There have also been several attempts to forge new universal forms of religion and spirituality which cut across all traditional differences and are capable of uniting humankind (in many ways the New Age movement falls into this category, see Chapter 11). Even those forms of religion which have remained loyal to their traditional differences have often been affected by universalizing and de-differentiating tendencies – where once different Christian denominations regarded each other as deluded and even diabolical, for example, today they are more likely to co-operate than to condemn one another. The growth of the ecumenical movement institutionalizes this tendency.

Yet the opposite process of differentiation is equally evident in modern society and modern religion. One of the most important functions of religion has always been that of marking boundaries and differences, and the late twentieth and twenty-first centuries have seen an intensification of this tendency at many levels. One of the most obvious examples is the way in which religion has been activated to mark and defend ethnic boundaries – the distinctiveness of a particular people. In some cases these boundaries may be coterminous with those of a real or desired nation state (as in religious nationalism), whilst in others they cut across the frontiers of modern political units (as in some forms of pan-Islamism and Charismatic Christianity, as Chapter 14 illustrates). The assertion of religio-ethnic difference may also take place within nation states, often couched in terms of a multiculturalism or pluralism which is hostile to the homogenizing effects of liberal secular democracies (see, for example, Chapter 10 on Native American religions).

Religion also plays an important role in marking gender boundaries. Many premodern religions constructed strong differences between the sexes, differences which universalizing tendencies in modern religion and culture have tended to undermine and challenge. Thus modern liberal forms of Christianity and Judaism, for example, have opened leadership roles to women for the first time in the history of these traditions. These egalitarian developments are, of course, reinforced by the wider cultural, economic and technological changes which have given women access to the public sphere and to choices once restricted to men. But the modern period has also witnessed a re-inscription of gendered difference in which religion has played a key role. As several chapters in this book show, one of the defining characteristics of conservative and Fundamentalist forms of Christianity, Judaism and Islam is their insistence on the integrity of the family unit, their delineation of women's role in relation to domestic functions, and their reassertion of male leadership. As Chapter 16 shows, however, women are not necessarily passive victims of this process of re-differentiation, not only because they have strategies of subversion, but because the sacralization of the family and the feminine may greatly enhance their power in otherwise male-dominated and macho societies.

5 Turn to the self and turn to life

Modernity tends to be corrosive of tradition – of authorities which lie outside the individual self and claim to be higher. The authority of the past, the authority of a clerical elite, the authority of established religious institutions and practices, and even the authority of a transcendent deity all come into question. Negatively, such detraditionalization represents what may be called a flight from deference. There is clear evidence that men and women in advanced industrial societies are less respectful not only of religious authorities, but of political authorities, the police, employers, the law, and other primary institutions. Many factors combine to cause this shift: universal democracy gives each individual the freedom and the right to choose those who govern; capitalism frees many people from 'given' places in the social and economic order and so from deference to 'one's betters'; increased wealth in a consumer society further enshrines the idea that we are free to choose what we want rather than being told what is good for us. More positively, detraditionalization may be understood as a turn to the self. Ultimate authority is ascribed to one's own reason, conscience or intuition. These become the judge and jury before which all other authorities must be tried. If something does not 'make sense for me', it will be

Figure 0.1 This photograph taken recently in Scotland illustrates the continuing force of a strongly traditionalized form of religion (Presbyterian Christianity) which insists that the demands of a transcendent God made known in the Bible override the demands and desires of the self and of life in the here-and-now. As such, Presbyterianism clashes with many of the priorities of modern social and cultural life. This may be the reason why such religion has been declining rapidly in Scotland since the 1960s

Figure 0.2 The increasing emphasis placed on the value of 'life' is evident throughout much modern culture. Opened at the beginning of a new millennium, this centre for 'life' in Newcastle-Upon-Tyne, UK, offers information about DNA and the genetic codes which many people hope will at last enable us to 'unlock the secrets of life'. As life here-and-now becomes a sacred value in society, religions which had previously placed more emphasis on preparing for 'after-life' come under pressure to adapt, whilst new forms of spirituality focused entirely on the enhancement of 'mind, body and spirit' win a ready audience

rejected – no matter how many other people believe it, or how hallowed a tradition it may be. In the end, I have to make up my own mind and (in the words of a theme tune of modernity) 'do it my way'.

Detraditionalization and the turn to the self obviously represent a challenge to traditional forms of religion which believe that they have possession of an authoritative truth which all men and women must obey. The traditional authority of religious communities, priests and monks seems particularly threatened, though many have shown a remarkable ability to adapt to changed circumstances (see Chapter 2 on the survival of Buddhist monasticism in modern times, or Chapter 7 on the reinvention of the role of the papacy). By contrast, the authority of authoritative religious texts seems, if anything, to have been strengthened in modern times – belief in the inerrancy of scripture is a defining feature of the many fundamentalisms which have come to birth across the world since the twentieth century, as well as of some New Religious Movements (on the latter see Chapter 12). Yet few conservative/traditional forms of religion in the modern world have been untouched by a turn to the self. Some of the most successful – like Charismatic Christianity – demonstrate a remarkable ability to combine a traditional emphasis on transcendent truth, with a much more modern emphasis on the importance of individual experience (in this case the experience of the Holy Spirit).

At the other end of the spectrum from highly traditionalized religions, we see the birth in modern times of new forms of self-religion which draw on traditional authorities only insofar as these resource the self. Some of these move so far away from tradition that they reject the title 'religion' altogether, and prefer the language of 'spirituality'. Interestingly, this volume suggests that such religions and spiritualities are not confined to the West (as in the New Age movement and some New Religious Movements), but are also found in many other parts of the world (see, for example, discussion in Chapter 4 of Chinese religions, and Chapter 5 of Japanese religions). Many self-religions also display a 'turn to life', that is to say, a concern with what religion or spirituality can achieve in the here and now, rather than in some higher afterlife. Indeed, a turn to life seems to be increasingly characteristic of many forms of contemporary religion, both traditional and detraditionalized, as Chapter 17 shows. Given that they have never drawn a sharp distinction between the earthly and the spiritual realms, and given that they have always had a strong focus on activating religion for immediate benefits and protection in the here-and-now, many indigenous forms of religion are already well adapted to this development, as several chapters in this volume show (see, for example, Chapter 4, Chapter 9 and Chapter 10). This may be one reason for the continuing vitality of many such religions – religions once dismissed by many Western scholars as primitive and destined to give way to higher and more evolved forms of religion and culture.

6 Secularization and sacralization

Finally we come to the characteristic of modernity which sociology of religion has always tended to put first: secularization. Many of the founding fathers of sociology believed that secularization was an inevitable concomitant of modernization. Despite agreement on this point, different reasons have been offered to explain why this should be the case. Four have been particularly important: (1) rationalization leads to the disenchantment of the world, and gradually squeezes out religion; (2) the process of differentiation leaves religions fewer and fewer social functions as other agencies take over roles like governance, education and welfare; (3) migration, urbanization and improved communications destabilize settled communities and social orders and the religions which were integral to them; (4) pluralization makes once taken-for-granted beliefs and practices and their claims to absolute and exclusive truth seem increasingly implausible. Whatever the reasons for secularization, the evidence from Western Europe, where churchgoing has declined throughout the twentieth century, but particularly since the 1970s, seems to support the secularization thesis. However, as many chapters in this volume demonstrate, secularization in Europe has not been matched elsewhere. This is obviously true outside of the West, where clearly religion remains a potent force in individual as well as social and political life, but it is also true in the US. Religious vitality can be seen both in the revitalization of many old traditions, and in the proliferation of new religions and spiritualities. 'Sacralization' is now as common a theme of reflections of religion in the contemporary world as is secularization, and unilateral theories of religious decline are increasingly being abandoned in favour of more nuanced 'mappings' of religion and secularity and the factors which explain them. Such themes are pursued in Chapter 13.

The reproduction below of a flyer for a book which channels *The Celestial Voice of Diana* serves as a reminder of the continuing and often surprising vitality of religion, even in the most (apparently) secular territories of Western Europe. One of the most remarkable aspects of the mourning for Princess Diana in September 1997 was the way in which both old and new forms of religion and spirituality were utilized to make interpretive and ritual sense of this tragic event. Thus the Church of England took charge of the funeral, and many mourners flocked to established churches to pay their respects or

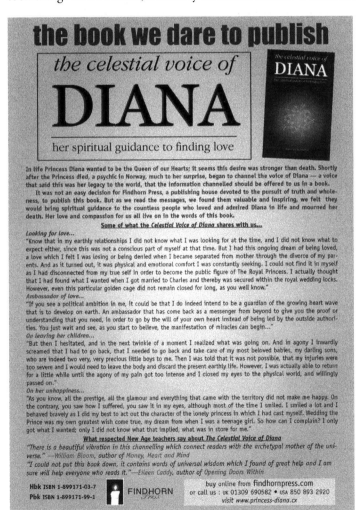

Figure 0.3 Findhorn Press leaflet advertising *The Celestial Voice of Diana: Her Spiritual Guidance to Finding Love*, a book which records the 'voice of Diana' channelled through a Norwegian psychic

leave flowers. But their words and tributes also indicated an ability and desire to use religious images and beliefs in new, post-traditional, deregulated ways (just as Diana had done in her own life). For some, as this flyer indicates, Diana became a celestial 'queen of hearts' who had exemplified and embodied a religion of loving kindness, and who was now in heaven offering help and guidance to the world. As her celestial spirit says: 'I do indeed intend to be a guardian of the growing heart wave that is to develop on earth'. Far from being straightforwardly secular or atheistic such evidence – together, more importantly, with that of the chapters which follow – suggests that the modern world may often be as vibrantly religious as ever, even if in some places the sacred is becoming partially detached from traditional containers and retainers.

Note on the use of italics and diacriticals: words which appear in the list of 'key terms' at the end of each chapter appear in *italic* in their first instance.

The use of diacriticals is at the discretion of the authors of individual chapters.

FURTHER READING

Studying religion

The development of a phenomenological approach to the study of religion owes much to the late Ninian Smart. See, for example, *The World's Religions*, second edition (Cambridge: Cambridge University Press, 1998). One of the most useful introductions to a sociological approach to the study of religion is Meredith McGuire's *Religion. The Social Context*, fourth edition (Belmont: Wadsworth, 1997). See also Richard K. Fenn (ed.): *The Blackwell Companion to Sociology of Religion* (Oxford: Blackwell, UK, and Malden, USA, 2001). Wilfred Cantwell Smith was a pioneer in thinking about the limitations of the concept of religion. See his *The Meaning and End of Religion: A New Approach to the Religious Traditions of Mankind* (New York, 1978). A more recent overview of this topic which takes account of the latest scholarship can be found in the chapter on 'Religion, religions, religious' by Jonathan Z. Smith in Mark C. Taylor (ed.): *Critical Terms in Religious Studies* (Chicago: University of Chicago Press, 1998, pp. 269–84).

Studying modernity

Stuart Hall and Bram Gieben (eds): *Formations of Modernity* (Cambridge: Polity Press in association with The Open University, 1992) is an extremely clear introduction to the topic in general rather than specifically religious terms. On the future of modernity and the idea of postmodernity see another book in the same series: Stuart Hall, David Held and Tony McGrew (eds): *Modernity and its Futures* (Cambridge: Polity Press in association with The Open University, 1992). *The International Encyclopedia of the Social Sciences* (New York: Macmillan, 1968) is a useful resource, with substantial entries on topics like modernization. It will be succeeded in 2001 by a new edition, *The International Encyclopedia of the Behavioral and Social Sciences* (New York and London: Elsevier).

Studying religion and modernity

Linda Woodhead and Paul Heelas (eds): *Religion in Modern Times. An Interpretive Anthology* (Oxford, UK, and Malden, USA, 2000) offers a framework and selected readings for thinking about the complex interactions between religion and modernity. A more tradition-based and phenomenological approach, though with reflection on cross-cultural issues, can be found in John R. Hinnells (ed.): *A New Handbook of Living Religions* (London: Penguin, 1998).

PART I
Traditions and transformations

CHAPTER 1

Hinduism

David Smith

INTRODUCTION

Hinduism, the primary indigenous religion of South Asia, claims to be the oldest living religion, and calls itself 'the eternal religion' (*sanatana dharma*). Its earliest scripture, the Veda, dates to approximately 1500 BCE; some features, such as goddess worship, and perhaps *yoga*, might go back to the Indus Valley civilization, around 2500 BCE. Traditionally it is held that the Veda is eternal and reappears at each new creation of the universe. At the beginning of the twenty-first century Hinduism has 800 million adherents worldwide, making it the third largest world religion.

The term Hinduism has only recently been adopted by Hindus themselves, and the word 'Hindu' is also of external origin, coming from the Persian word for those who live on the other side of the river Indus, i.e. Indians. With its multiple deities – traditionally 33 million – Hinduism could be seen as a cluster of religions rather than a single religion, but it is now usually presented as an all-inclusive polytheistic system, encompassing myriad forms and levels. Its extreme intellectual openness – when viewed as a whole – contrasts with the restrictions on behaviour brought about by the caste system. Hinduism's most influential philosophy distinguishes between *Brahman* – the highest absolute, formless consciousness about which nothing else can be said – and deities which have form, such as *Vishnu* and *Shiva*. The strength and vitality of the myriad strands of Hinduism make any clear and simple definition of Hinduism impossible, though fundamentalist and right-wing Hindus in India today may be seen to be mirroring Islamic certainty and authoritarianism while emphasizing Hindu difference from Islam. The efforts of some contemporary politicians notwithstanding, Hinduism has never been under the control of any central authority.

Buddhism and Jainism originated as reform movements within early Hinduism; both continued in symbiosis with Hinduism for many centuries, beginning by challenging the caste hierarchy and inspiring the development of coherent Hindu metaphysical systems (see Chapter 3). A third major indigenous tradition, Sikhism, emerged in the fifteenth century out of an amalgamation of Hindu, tantric Buddhist and Muslim ideas (see Chapter 6). Most of India was under Muslim rule from the fifteenth to the late eighteenth century, and there was some Islamic influence on Hinduism in north India; later there was some Christian influence during British rule (late eighteenth century–1947).

Early in the first millenium CE Hindu traders took Hinduism to Southeast Asia, but there it was replaced by Buddhism and Islam by the twelfth century, except in Bali. Hinduism spread again in the nineteenth century as Hindus migrated round the world, first to British territories as indentured labour and then as often highly skilled professionals, with North America the favourite goal from the 1960s. Nevertheless, as can been seen from Table 1, almost 95 per cent of Hindus still live in India.

In many ways Hinduism is the prime example of traditional religion, with continuous traditions such as the oral transmission of the Veda going back three thousand years, and animal sacrifice to goddesses perhaps far longer. Until the eighteenth century, under Islamic rule, the intellectual elite – the *brahman* caste – kept knowledge of *Sanskrit* religious and philosophical texts to themselves; little of Hindu thought was known to the West, and brahmans ignored both Western and Islamic thought. Paradoxically, the coming of British rule and British linguistic and archaeological investigations led to greatly increased knowledge about Hinduism not only in the West but also in India. British censuses of India led to an increased consciousness among Indians of the diversity of caste, and perhaps made caste into more of a system. Modernity came to India with the British, scientific education in English for the Indian elite being provided from the early nineteenth century. In the same period contact with the West prompted Hindu reform movements, influenced by Christianity and Western ideals of public service. Nevertheless, traditional Hinduism with its image worship and temple pilgrimage is as popular

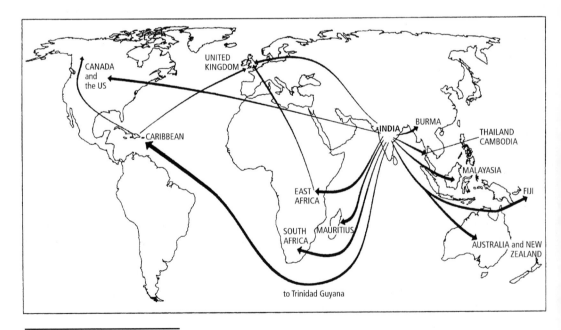

Figure 1.1 Map of Hindu migrations

Table 1.1 Largest Hindu populations		
COUNTRY	PERCENTAGE	NUMBER
India	79	751,000,000
Nepal	89	17,380,000
Bangladesh	11	12,630,000
Indonesia	2.5	4,000,000
Sri Lanka	15	2,800,000
Pakistan	1.5	2,120,000
Malaysia	6	1,400,000
US	0.2	910,000
Mauritius	52	570,000
South Africa	1.5	420,000
United Kingdom	1	410,000

Source: Adherents.com

as ever, and greatly reinforced by modern media. Practices such as child marriage and even live cremation of widows (*sati*) persist in parts of India even today. At the same time, it must be recognized that rational argument and debate have always permeated Hindu thought, and its tolerance of alien viewpoints and its generally rational cosmology make it possible to argue that Hinduism has always had some of the features now claimed by modernity.

This chapter will give a brief account of the historical features of Hinduism before turning to the present. We begin with the deities, rather than texts, for the deities have long been visually present in temple images, art, and many living incarnations, and do not depend solely on texts for their manifestation. A look at the many texts of Hinduism is followed by a summary of Hinduism in terms of self and society, concluding with consideration of gender. Much of this traditional Hinduism is still alive today, but we move next into specifically modern times by inquiring into the special relation of modernity and India, noting also the traditional Hindu interpretation of modern times – the worst of times, the *Kali* age. The socio-economic condition of India today is then summarized. Modern Hinduism is discussed in terms of six aspects. (1) Traditional Hinduism and its divinities thrive. (2) The 'reformed' forms of Hinduism produced by Western influence in the nineteenth century continue. (3) Gurus gain new importance and take Hinduism to the West. (4) Women's spirituality finds increased scope and expression. (5) Caste is still important, but the low castes gain influence, and the priestly caste declines. (6) Hindu nationalism, the idea that India belongs to Hindus alone, comes to the fore.

SOURCES AND RESOURCES

Deities

Traditional Hindus see themselves not as 'Hindu' but as *Vaishnava* ('worshipper of Vishnu'), *Shaiva* ('worshipper of Shiva'), or *Shakta* ('worshipper of the goddess'), though each of these terms has many subdivisions. Vishnu has ten incarnations, of whom *Krishna* and *Rama* are major deities in their own right. But whatever deity or deities are worshipped, the rituals, texts and beliefs usually have much in common. There is a common language of worship and practice within the branches of Hinduism. Each of the deities has its own iconography and mythology; but common to all is the fact that the divine reality has an explicit form, a form that the worshipper can behold – in images under worship in home and temple, and in dream and in states of possession. In addition to the three principal deities – Vishnu, Shiva and *Devi*, and the innumerable minor deities, regional and local, there is also Brahman the neuter absolute that is 'being, consciousness, and bliss', first mentioned in the Upanishads. The gods belong to a lower level of truth and are subsumed within Brahman along with everything else. Consciousness alone is the final reality, according to the non-dualist school of Vedanta called Advaita. A distinction is sometimes drawn between popular and philosophical Hinduism, but the fact that Shankara, the great non-dualist philosopher who commented on the Upanishads, is also held to have written fervent devotional hymns to a variety of deities shows that the distinction is easily bridged. The relative truth of the Hindu deities is readily seen by Hindus as shared by the gods of other religions, all of whom can be taken as aspects of the lower level of Brahman.

An essential notion in Hinduism is that of the chosen deity (*ishta devata*). None of the aforementioned deities is inherently supreme. The philosophically and mystically minded person might favour Brahman; most people will prefer to worship a tangible deity who can act upon the world. The deity a person chooses for him or herself is the supreme deity as far as he or she is concerned. Other than the universal Brahman, the deities are present in specific forms in specific locations. Their temples range from the vast city-temple of Shri Rangam in south India with its soaring gateway towers, to the pavement shrines of minor deities that flourish in every town. Every family has its home shrine with pictures or images of their deities, before which a lamp and incense burn. *Puja*, the loving offering of light, flowers, and water or food to the divine, is the essential ritual of Hinduism. For the worshipper the divine is visible in the image, and the divinity sees the worshipper. This interaction between human and deity, between human and *guru*, is called *darshan*, 'seeing'. Whenever they can, people go on pilgrimage to notable temples, and bring back pictures or images of deities. Tirupati, difficult of access in the mountains of Andhra Pradesh, is one of the most popular temples in India, and the richest. From the river Ganges, water is everywhere brought back to be used in rituals on special occasions. India is covered with sacred sites; India itself is a goddess, and the map of India is the primary image in some modern temples.

Divinity is found in human form as well as in divine images and divine texts. All of life forms a hierarchy in Hinduism, and human beings range from divine incarnations to the worthless products of many previous lives of sin. This variety is explained by the notion of rebirth. Rather than brief instances of one short life span, Hindus see themselves as the product of an infinite series of previous lives, all of which can bear upon the present. It follows that the range of variation of human character and ability is itself infinitely greater than could be achieved in a mere single lifetime. Both theory and tradition support the widespread belief in 'godmen' and 'godwomen', as the highest instances of gurus (religious teachers) are known. Most famous of all at present is Sathya Sai Baba, who is an incarnation of both the god Shiva and his consort *Shakti*. Semi-divine powers are claimed by many practitioners of yoga; the first canonical text of yoga, Patanjali's *Yoga Sutras* (c.400 AD), lists the *siddhis*, powers such as flying through the air and remembering one's past lives, that accompany the higher levels of yogic meditation. The priestly caste, the brahmans, intellectually and spiritually pre-eminent for many centuries, claim to be gods among men; their privileged position has been strongly contested by other castes, and saintly figures have featured among other castes since at least the coming of Islam to India. Deities also manifest themselves by possessing individuals. Possession may be voluntary, as in tantric ritual, or involuntary, as in festivals.

Texts

Hinduism's oldest text is the Veda, the earliest parts dated by scholars to approximately 1500 BCE, but held by the tradition to be eternal, seen anew by seers every time the world is recreated after its destruction. The variety of Hinduism relates to the variegated nature of the Indian social system with its many castes. A hymn in the oldest Vedic collection, the *Rig Veda*, describes the creation of the world from the sacrifice of a cosmic man: his mouth became the brahman or priest, his arms the warrior, his thighs the farmer, his feet the peasant. The great tradition of Hinduism, written in Sanskrit, the language of the Veda, is primarily the work of the brahman caste. The religious literature in Sanskrit is enormous, flowing from the Vedas, through the mystical Upanishads (*c.*700 BCE), the two epics – the *Ramayana* and the *Mahabharata* (texts finalized *c.*400 CE), and the mythological 'bibles' that are the Puranas (*c.*400–1600 CE). Most texts in medieval Indian languages continue the earlier tradition; there are also the teachings of innovative saints, first influenced by Buddhism (the Siddhas) and then by Islam, for example, Kabir (fifteenth century CE). All these texts, in varying degrees, are sacred and holy texts of Hinduism. The Vedas were learnt by heart by brahmans and passed on as an oral tradition. Many gurus pass on their teachings only as oral tradition; it is standard practice for the initiatory sacred syllable to be whispered in secret to the disciple by the teacher. The *Bhagavad Gita*, the teachings of the god Krishna on devotion and yoga, has become the best-known text of Hinduism, partly in response to the expectation of followers of other world religions that a religion should have a single scripture; but the *Bhagavad Gita* cannot be separated from the vast extent of the *Mahabharata* that contains it. In the *Bhagavad Gita* Krishna gives the warrior Arjuna divine sight so that he can see his true divine form, which is brighter than a thousand suns. But in all the Hindu sacred texts the gods make themselves known in visible form and are described by inspired sages (*rishis*).

The Vedas were the work of patriarchal pastoralists whose gods were mainly warriors. However, from around 400 CE the Sanskrit texts give increasing space to goddesses, and since the discovery of the Indus Valley civilization in the 1920s it is widely held by scholars that the agricultural society there from at least the third millennium BCE worshipped goddesses and perhaps practised yoga. The religion of the Vedic texts seems therefore to overlay a different culture that is only gradually revealed to us by the historical progression of texts. Yoga and the notion of rebirth, elements held in common with the heterodox religions of Buddhism and Jainism, almost certainly had a non-Vedic origin, and first appear in the Upanishads at the close of the Vedic period.

The Sanskrit tradition continued with the Puranas, some of which formed a kind of bible for particular sects. It is in one of these, the *Markandeya Purana* (*c.*500 CE), that the ancient goddess worship first resurfaces, in the section called the *Devimahatmya*. Here the goddess (Devi/Durga/Kali) appears as the supreme deity. Most famous is the *Bhagavata Purana* (*c.*900 CE), on which much Krishna worship is based. The rich mythology of the Puranas, itself of folk origin, is often omitted from formal presentations of their religion by Hindus, but nevertheless lives on, complemented by current folk and tribal mythology. From the Puranas arises the notion of the Hindu triad of *Brahma* the Creator, Vishnu the Preserver and Shiva the Destroyer. However, the four-headed Brahma, modelled on the Hindu priest, has never received exclusive worship in his own right. As noted above, Devi, who finds expression in all goddesses, is the third important deity, along with Vishnu and Shiva.

Also in Sanskrit is the extensive philosophical literature, principally in the form of commentaries on core texts. The qualified non-dualist Vedanta philosophy of Ramanuja (1017–1137), arguing that Brahman is Vishnu, and that the individual self finds salvation as a particle of that supreme reality, is more in accord with Hindu thought in general than the non-dualist Shankara, though Shankara's is the dominant philosophical system. Also of great religious significance are the systems of yoga, *samkhya* and *tantra*.

The next oldest Indian literature is that in Tamil, going back to perhaps 200 BCE. Texts in other regional languages are later, and until modern times are mainly derivative of Sanskrit texts. But there are hundreds of vernacular texts rich in religious significance – the poems of Kabir (*c.*1500) and the Hindi *Ramayana* of Tulsidas, *Ramcaritmanas* (*c.*1600), 'the bible of north India', to name but two. We should also note that the teachings of innumerable religious teachers (gurus) become the primary sacred text for their followers.

Self and society

Paralleling the profusion of divinities and texts, the caste system, which is an integral part of Hinduism, comprises thousands of different castes. One's caste (*jati*) has considerable influence on one's occupation and choice of marriage partner. The different castes form a hierarchy and are categorized under the four general caste categories (*varnas*) mentioned in the Veda, and in addition as a fifth category, the outcastes. Only relatively few castes are to be found in any one place. The dominance of the leading caste in any particular area does not necessarily relate to the *varna* hierarchy of brahman, warrior, farmer, peasant.

From the time of the Buddha, reformers have sought to abolish caste, but without success. Caste is explained for Hindus by the doctrine of *karma*. From the time of the Upanishads (*c.*700 BCE) Hindus have believed that one's actions (*karma*) determine one's future lives. One's condition in this life is thus morally justified because it is earned by previous actions. Caste is regulated by local caste councils, which have the power to set penalties for infringement of caste rules and even to exclude from a caste.

The *Laws of Manu* (*c.*200 CE) and other texts which set out Hindu *dharma* (the proper order of life) give detailed rules of life for the twice-born castes, so called because of the initiation or second birth that boys of the priest, warrior and farmer castes received. For males, there are four life stages (*ashramas*): student, householder, forest dwelling ascetic, and wandering ascetic. For females, there are ideally only two: girlhood and wifehood, though inevitably many wives become widows. For humans, as for gods, the proper and normal state is to be married. Having produced sons, a man may then retire to the forest with his wife to devote himself to religion, and if he so chooses thereafter give up all possessions, leave his wife, undergo a funeral ceremony, and end his life as a homeless wanderer, as a renouncer. In fact, this last stage may be undertaken at any time. Its adoption as the last of four stages is an instance of Hinduism copying the successful practice of the reform movements of Buddhism and Jainism.

Hinduism sets out very clearly a hierarchy of four goals for human beings. These are (1) sensory gratification (*kama*); (2) material well-being (*artha*); (3) religious behaviour (*dharma*), which leads to heaven or higher rebirth; (4) salvation, escape from rebirth (*moksha*). All four are legitimate goals. The fourth, and highest (*moksha*), involves the fourth life stage, that of the renouncer, though, as has been said, this life stage can in fact be undertaken at any time of life. The more spiritually advanced the person, the earlier it will be done. The renouncer leaves the caste system, dies to ordinary life and he alone is a complete individual, an autonomous self. The renouncer's view of the self is propounded by the samkhya philosophy. In samkhya the individual consciousness, which has the significant name *Purusha* ('the male'), has as its true goal the separation of itself from *Prakriti* '(mother) nature', and the analogy used for this liberation is that of a man who has been entranced by a female dancer but finally gets up and walks away.

In contrast to the spiritual self, the social self is enmeshed in society and family. A member of a caste, with duties and responsibilities to caste members, is usually also a member of a joint family, where parents and their married children share a single cooking fire. The social self necessarily has multiple roles, as son or daughter, husband, wife, daughter-in-law and so on. This multidimensional self, interlocked with many other selves, including its own previous existences, undergoes a series of life-stage rituals, that can begin with conception and continue even after death with the ritual feeding of dead ancestors. The self is polished and perfected by these rituals (*samskaras*) and ever more deeply embedded in Hindu culture (*samskriti*).

Gender

The biological difference of male and female is sometimes spoken of as the 'male caste' and the 'female caste'. Hinduism is patrilinear: families continue only in the male line. Daughters leave their natal families on marriage, and even as widows remain members of their husbands' families. Sons alone are required for the continuance of families. Daughters-in-law are not fully accepted family members until they have produced a son. At the same time, the mother of a son with her husband still alive is the most auspicious member of society. She nurtures and sustains not only her children but also her husband. Her status tumbles when her husband dies.

The auspicious married woman is a manifestation of divine power (*shakti*). A notable feature of Hinduism is the importance of goddesses (*Shakti*, Devi or 'mother'). Goddess temples, though generally very small, are more numerous than those of gods. Goddesses are invariably seen as powerful, and when unmarried as dangerous. Despite the patriarchal nature of Hindu society, women too are held to be powerful and at times dangerous.

Within society, two separate polarities are important. There is the distinction between purity and impurity and the distinction between auspicious and inauspicious. Raw nature, matter out of place, such as bodily fluids, which have left the body but are of the body, are impure: blood, afterbirth, semen, menstrual blood, dead bodies, all are impure. Culture, that which as it were rises above dangerous nature, is pure, as for instance are the Sanskrit language, vegetarianism and abstinence from sex. Impurity applies to women more than to men. The menstruating woman does not cook, does not enter a temple. Nor indeed does the priest whose wife is menstruating. But goddesses – in local or regional tradition – also menstruate. This fact of life is at the same time auspicious, for it means that the woman can give birth. Everything to do with birth and life is auspicious, whereas the barren woman and the widow are inauspicious.

According to the French anthropologist Louis Dumont, the caste system as a whole is to be explained by the opposition between purity and impurity. The brahman caste strives to maintain its purity by separating itself as far as possible from raw nature. The outcastes, who remove raw nature, impurity, from the higher castes by taking away their faeces, washing their clothes, dealing with dead animals and so on, are in a state of permanent impurity. These extremes of the opposition between pure and impure demonstrate the hierarchy that runs through all the caste system, each caste pure to those below it, impure to those above it.

INTERACTIONS WITH MODERNITY

India in modern times

Hinduism since the time of the *Mahabharata* has developed the notion of four world ages, going from good to bad. Dharma, visualized as the cow of righteousness, has four legs in the first and perfect age after creation, but then loses legs, so that at present she totters, notionally, on only one leg. The name of the current, and last, of the four ages (*yugas*), is *Kali yuga*. Religious change from previous ages, and indeed anything detrimental, is explained by the fact of our being in the Kali yug. This idea of deterioration, destruction of the world and then recreation in a continual cycle is the exact opposite of the Western Enlightenment notion of the perfectibility of mankind and the gradual move from superstition to rationality and from the premodern to the modern. It is important to note that Kali is the name of the worst throw of a dice, incarnate as Duryodhana, the villain of the *Mahabharata*, wherein the great battle marks the beginning of the Kali yuga. The name of Kali, the black goddess of destruction, is a different word and is spelt differently in Indian languages (Kâlî). In pictures around the end of the nineteenth century, the Kali yuga is presented as a ferocious meat-eating demon threatening to assault Mother India who is represented as a cow giving milk to her children. In the Kali age, forms of religion change, the Vedas are neglected, and new easy forms of salvation such as the tantras appear.

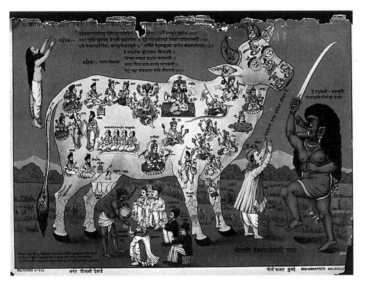

Figure 1.2 The personified Kali yug attacking the cow of Dharma, *c.* 1915. The cow has long been a potent symbol for Hindus. Milk and clarified butter (*ghee*) are key elements in Hindu vegetarian diet, and beef-eating Muslims and Christians have always been liable to be perceived as Hinduism's foes. From the nineteenth century cow killing has provoked Hindu riots, and cow protection societies have been expressions of strong anti-Muslim feeling

There are three key events in the history of India in modern times. The British takeover from Muslim rulers at the end of the eighteenth century, the formation of an independent and secular India and the rise of Hindu nationalism.

Colonial rule spearheaded by the British East India Company (a trading company) spread slowly at first from Calcutta, but the uprising in northern India in 1857, which used to be called the 'Indian Mutiny' by British historians, led in 1858 to the transfer of rule to the British government, and Queen Victoria became Empress of India. India gained independence on 15 August 1947, and was divided into India and Pakistan ('partition'). Another notable date is 1992 when Hindu nationalists destroyed the Ayodhya Mosque. Modern India has had to shake off the effects of long colonial rule, effects which include the exacerbation if not creation of Hindu–Muslim conflict.

Up to the eighteenth century India was prosperous, and enjoyed an important role in world textile trade. Europeans were impressed by the wealth and splendour of Indian cities. Conflict between rising Maratha power in the west of India and the crumbling Mughal empire in the centre allowed the British to take control from the east, and Bengal became modernity's bridgehead into India. The brahman middle classes in Bengal enthusiastically adopted Western thought, and took up subordinate roles in the administration of the country. English literature was eagerly studied, and forms such as the novel were adopted in Bengali and other modern languages of India. This burgeoning of indigenous literature contributed to the rise of Indian nationalism. The nation is sometimes said to be the nearest thing to divinity in modernity, with nationalism being modernity's religion, but in India the modern notion of the nation happily co-existed with traditional Indian forms. Kali, the black goddess of destruction, became the symbol of violent revolution. Bankim Chatterjee's novel *Anandamath*, 'the abbey of bliss' (1882), describes freedom fighters worshipping the goddess Kali as an essential prelude to ridding India of the Muslims and – in the original serialized version, though later removed – the British. The song *Vande mataram*, 'I praise the mother' from this novel became the anthem of the independence movement, but was not made the national anthem in 1947 because Nehru thought it too Hindu. The printing press, which did much to promote nationalism everywhere in the modern world, in India also served to spread traditional Hinduism, not only in texts but also in 'calendar prints', so called from the addition of calendars to the brightly coloured pictures.

▌ VANDE MATARAM

Mother, I bow to thee!
Rich with thy hurrying streams,
Bright with thy orchard gleams,
Cool with thy winds of delight,
Dark fields waving, Mother of might,
Mother free.

Mother to thee I bow,
Who hath said thou art weak in thy lands,
When the swords flash out in twice seventy million
    hands
And seventy million voices roar
Thy dreadful name from shore to shore
In our hearts that conquers death.

Thine the strength that nerves the arm,
Thine the beauty, thine the charm.
Every image made divine
In our temples is but thine.
Mother, I bow to thee!

Thou art Durga, Lady and Queen,
With her hands that strike and her swords of sheen,
Thou art Lakshmi lotus-throned.

Mother, mother mine!
Mother sweet, I bow to thee
Mother great and free!

      (Aurobindo's translation of the Sanskrit original of Bankim Chatterjee, verses 1, 3, 4, 6)

India's official national anthem is the first verse of the song *Jana Gana Mana*, composed by Rabindranath Tagore. Prime Minister Nehru objected to the popular choice *Vande mataram* because of its reference to image worship. Aurobindo's response was that the goddess Durga to whom *Vande mataram* paid homage was none other than Bharata Mata (Mother India) symbolizing Knowledge, Power, Greatness and Glory.

Sony Music in India celebrated India's fiftieth anniversary of independence in 1997 by issuing *Vande mataram* sung by the popular musician A. R. Rahman.

Hindus came to play a large part in the subordinate administration of British India, while Muslims stood apart, though praised for their martial ability by the British. Once it became clear that independence was inevitable, there was increasing rivalry between Hindu and Muslim elites. M. K. Gandhi (1869–1948), the Mahatma ('great-souled'), played an important role in reducing Hindu–Muslim conflict, and by his policy of non-violent action allowed the British Raj to end without violence between Britain and India. But Hindu and Muslim interests proved irreconcilable. Partition between Pakistan and India was hurried through by the British. Intercommunal murder took a million lives as Hindu/Sikh and Muslim crossed from one side to the other of the new border. Both countries, India and Pakistan, were deeply scarred by this traumatic event. India became a secular state, thanks to Nehru (Prime Minister 1947–64), with a population 20 per cent Muslim and 80 per cent Hindu.

The subsequent political history of India is that of conflict with Pakistan and a gradual crumbling of the founding ideal of the secular state which Nehru had cherished. Whilst refusing to recognize a 'state religion', Nehru gave a favoured role to minority religions, being especially concerned to make welcome those Muslims who had elected to remain in India rather than withdraw to Pakistan. A dynastic form of democratic leadership evolved, with Nehru's daughter Indira Gandhi (1917–84) becoming Prime Minister, followed by her son Rajiv Gandhi (1944–91). Rajiv's widow Sonia, Italian by origin, is currently head of the Congress Party. At partition, Kashmir had a Hindu ruler and a mainly Islamic population. Pakistan attempted to seize control but secured only half the state. The border remains in dispute, and tension is constant. Both sides possess nuclear weapons and threaten their use. The position of Muslims within India is difficult. The Bharatiya Janata Party forms the current government (1999–), having come to power by supporting Hindu nationalism. In particular, the party urged the destruction of the mosque which it claims was built on the site of Rama's birthplace at Ayodhya, and the rebuilding of the Rama Temple there. In the late 1980s the party organized a series of pilgrimages (*yatras*) across India in which the party's leader rode in a Toyota van adorned to look like the god Rama's chariot from the *Ramayana* – hence the term 'Toyota Hinduism'. The main political issues confronting India today have to do with status of Islam in a majority Hindu country, and the increasingly problematic notion of the secular state in a country where religion shows no sign of decline or loss of vitality. Note must also be made of increasing antagonism to Christianity by right-wing Hinduism, in respect especially of externally funded Christian missions.

Widespread poverty and corruption remain grave problems. But India is strong in natural resources, has a well-educated middle class and the largest number of scientific workers of any nation. Many professionals go abroad but return to India bringing new skills with them. India is particularly strong in computer software personnel and companies. India remains open to all modern ideas, while preserving its rich cultural heritage.

▌ HINDUISM AND MODERN SCIENCE AND TECHNOLOGY

It is not the British people who rule India, but modern civilization rules India through its railways, telegraph, telephone, etc. Bombay, Calcutta, and other chief cities are the real plague-spots of Modern India . . . India's salvation consists in unlearning what she has learnt during the past fifty years. The railways, telegraphs, hospitals, lawyers, doctors, and such like have all to go, and the so-called upper classes have to learn to live consciously, religiously, and deliberately the simple peasant life, knowing it to be a life giving true happiness.

(Mahatma Gandhi's *Confession of Faith*, 1909)

Gandhi's extreme position, product of his eclectic thought, has found favour neither with modern secular India nor with many traditional Hindus. Nehru declared that dams were to be the temples of the new secular India. Indeed, in his *Discovery of India* (1947) he admitted that the sculptures on south Indian temples made him 'feel uneasy'. Following the Soviet model, Nehru pushed the development of heavy industry and nuclear power. But the traditional Hinduism that Nehru hoped to move India beyond had no problem with science. Throughout the nineteenth century and up to the present there is no lack of educated Hindus who claim that modern science is developed from, or even replicates, the ancient science that can, according to them, be found in the Veda. Nearly all Hindus believe that Hinduism can be rationally and scientifically proven. They take the view that, leaving mythology aside, Hindu sacred texts are based on a rational understanding of the universe, and that Hindu teachings are generally confirmed by the findings of science. There are ecological protest movements in India, e.g. the group opposed to the Narmada Valley dam, but they are concerned with specific abuses rather than forming a general opposition to science and technology.

An important Government of India report on Hindu temples is typical in assuming the automatic efficacy of religious rites given properly qualified personnel, i.e. priests:

> [Temples are] occult laboratories where certain physical acts of adoration coupled with certain systematized prayers, psalms, *mantras* and musical invocations, can yield certain physical and psychological results as a matter of course, and if these physical processes are properly conducted, the results will accrue provided the persons who perform them are adequately equipped.
>
> (*Report of the Hindu Religious Endowments Commission*, 1962)

The following strands may be discerned in contemporary Hinduism, and are explored in what follows.

1 First and foremost, traditional Hinduism continues to thrive. Rather than fading away, gods and goddesses have been invigorated by film, television, video and cyberspace.
2 From the nineteenth century various Western-inspired reform movements have developed, which combine a universalist Vedanta with humanitarian social work. These are often classified as neo-Hinduism.
3 From the establishment of Islamic rule in thirteenth-century north India, there has been a steady rise in the power and influence of gurus, perhaps in compensation for the loss of Hindu kingship. New sects founded by gurus from the eighteenth century onwards continue to flourish (whereas sects founded earlier have simply become part of traditional Hinduism). Many gurus claim divinity for themselves, and some of these claims are widely accepted. Various forms of yoga, including tantra, have been strongly promoted in India and elsewhere by gurus.
4 There is increased scope for the expression of spirituality by women, but women generally continue to be subordinate to men in public life; male and female remain differentiated domains. *Sati* (widow's self-immolation on husband's funeral pyre) finds fervent supporters and opponents.
5 The power of low-caste Hindus, the Dalits, increases through their strength of numbers, and the status of brahmans continues to decline. Whether or not Dalits are Hindus is an important question.
6 Hindu nationalism reached a peak in the late 1980s but is still powerful and influential, dominating public discussion of religion.

Traditional Hinduism

> Rama incarnates in countless ways
> and there are ten millions of *Ramayanas*
>   (Tulsidas, *Ramcaritmanas*, 1.33.6)

Figure 1.3 A poster of Ram, Sita and Lakshman as depicted by actors who played these roles in the television serialization of the *Ramayana*

The television serialization of the *Ramayana* (1987–90, 91 episodes) and of the *Mahabharata* (1988–90, 94 episodes) strengthened the already secure position of the Hindu epics in public culture, for they have always been commemorated in festival and story-telling. Films about the gods and demons, known as 'mythologicals', are as old as Indian cinema, but the televising of the *Ramayana* struck a special chord in the nation. Televisions were treated as shrines, and airline schedules altered so that episodes were not missed. Another modern innovation is the combination of public recitation of sacred texts with the fire sacrifices (*yajna*) which have their roots in the Vedic sacrifice. Publishing and scholarship make ancient and medieval texts increasingly available. The practice of some brahmans learning a complete branch of the Veda by heart has not completely ceased.

Traditional Hinduism also flourishes in the several monastic traditions claiming to date back to the original teacher Shankara (Adi-Shankara) (*c*.700 CE), which continue to promote non-dualist (advaita) Vedanta. The most famous of these Shankaracharyas, as the monastic heads are called, was Chandrashekharendra, Shankaracharya of Kanchi (1894–1994), who had been supreme pontiff from the age of 13. The celebration of his 100th birthday, when he was showered with gold coins, was a national event. The current Shankaracharya at Kanchi, Jayendra Sarasvati, makes full use of modern technology, offering automated telephone advice and an elaborate website. On taking over as leader he said the new watchwords were 'culture of one's own land and technology from abroad' (*svadesa samskriti, videsa vijnan*). He has founded a university which offers advanced degrees in business administration, computer science and Sanskrit. A similar persistence, though with a lower profile, is to be found among the institutions of other forms of Vedanta.

Hindu nationalist determination to build a temple to commemorate Rama's birthplace at Ayodhya is an extreme example of the continuing strength of the traditional Hindu temple religion. The Hindu diaspora aspires to build fully traditional Hindu temples. The Swami Narayan Temple in Neasden, London, UK is an example in Europe of entirely traditional Hindu construction methods and materials. Traditional temples in India are renovated and expanded. In 1981 the temple of Dancing Shiva at Chidambaram in Tamilnadu was the first temple to allow dancing girls to perform since they were banned in 1947, but only on a concert platform in the courtyard, not before the deity. Apart from the exclusion of dance from forms of worship, the great Indian temples and their deities persist and thrive in modernity. On the local and regional front, animal sacrifice to goddesses is reduced, and buffalo sacrifice is rare, but tradition continues.

TANTRA

A major aspect of Hinduism that is also found in the Buddhist tradition is tantra, the radical and often antinomian sets of ritual practices that increasingly permeated indigenous Indian religious culture from the fifth century CE (see Chapter 3). Summed up in the aphorism 'Pleasure is liberation (*moksha*)', this initially crude worship of sexual union and the feminine principle appealed to court culture and was soon developed in sophisticated texts. These texts are often in the form of conversations between Shiva and Shakti, the divine feminine who is his consort. Incorporating the physiological teachings of Hatha yoga, tantra makes full use of the body to attain subtle and profound changes of consciousness. The body is said to contain centres of energy (*cakras*), from the base of the spine to the top of the head. Energy, in the form of a internal coiled snake (*kundalini*), rises up through the central subtle passage of the body to reach the thousand-petalled lotus at the top of the head, breaking through the *cakras* as it goes. The tantric practitioner sees his own self as a manifestation of the ultimate divinity, and mentally goes through the ritual of *puja* (worship) within his own imagination directed towards his own self. We see here most fully what is described in other chapters as the turn to the self (see, for example, Chapter 17). Tantras were first made known in English by Sir John Woodruffe in the early twentieth century. The authentic tantric systems of Kashmir Shaivism were taught by Swami Lakshmanjoo (1907–91), who had several eminent scholars as pupils. Ajit Mookerjee's book *Tantra Art* (1967) and the London Tantra Exhibition of 1971 aroused interest in the West that continues today, as numerous websites testify.

MODERN TRADITIONAL MOVEMENTS

Sikhism would be in this category had it not been so successful as to become a separate religion. Swami Narayan (1781–1830) founded the devotional (*bhakti*) movement in Gujarat that bears his name; and he is worshipped along with Krishna and Radha by his Gujarati followers around the world. Sikh elements including monotheism are present in another *bhakti* movement – the Radhasoami Satsang ('association') founded by Swami Shiv Dayal (1818–78). Here too Radha plays a part, a symbol of the individual soul in relation to God. A universal sound current carries the teaching of the living guru to his worshippers. Modern only in its missionary zeal and rapid worldwide spread is the otherwise traditional sect known as the International Society for Krishna Consciousness, the Hare Krishna movement. Founded by A. C. Bhaktivedanta (1896–1977), this devotional (*bhakti*) cult goes back to Chaitanya in the early sixteenth century and is based on the *Bhagavata Purana* and other texts of the great tradition. Western converts play a prominent part in the worldwide movement, adopting the dress and behaviour of orthodox brahmans. An American, initiated as Satguru Sivaya Subramuniyaswami (1927–), leads the dynamic Shaiva Siddhanta based in Hawaii. This movement is thoroughly authentic – its members are almost entirely Tamil Shaivas – but is most notable for its news magazine *Hinduism Today*, available on the Internet, which since 1979 has provided well-informed news coverage of Hinduism.

'Reformed' Hinduism

The term 'neo-Hinduism' has been applied to reformed Hinduism by Paul Hacker and others. According to Hacker, the ethical values of neo-Hinduism stem from Western philosophy and Christianity, although they are expressed in Hindu terms. Claims that Hinduism is a spiritual unity, that Hinduism is tolerant, that all religions are equal, are thus said to be the product of Hindu nationalism and are in fact the assertion of the superiority of Hinduism over all other religions. Hacker sees neo-Hinduism as beginning in the 1870s, with Bankim Chattopadhyaya, Vivekananda, Aurobindo, Gandhi, and Radhakrishnan as its most famous proponents.

Of the reform movements of the nineteenth century, the Arya Samaj (founded 1875 by Dayanand Saraswati) is the most active today. Its aim is a purified Hinduism with a ritual and ceremony that somewhat resemble procedures of Protestant Christianity, but are justified as a return to an original purity of Hinduism said to exist in the Vedic hymns. Those aspects of Hinduism that aroused censure in Westerners, such as child marriage and the practice of widow burning (*suttee, sati*), were repudiated. Unlike the earlier Brahmo Samaj (founded 1828 by Ram Mohan Roy) the Arya Samaj vigorously rejected Christianity, reflecting the growth in nationalism in the intervening years.

Still significant today are two figures from early modern Hinduism. The first, Saint Ramakrishna (1836–86), a priest in the large Kali Temple built at Dakshinesvar outside Calcutta in 1855 by a wealthy low-caste widow, is revered for his varied and intense mystical experience. He inspired the second, the charismatic organizer, Vivekananda. Vivekananda (1863–1902) founded the Ramakrishna order of monks, and preached a muscular Vedanta to India and the West. An important aspect of this movement came to be its taking up social work, and this Western inspired practical assistance thereafter comes to be a feature of many new Hindu movements. The Ramakrishna Mission has centres round the world, and publishes many key Hindu texts.

Aurobindo (1872–1950), at first a freedom fighter, was an independent thinker who claimed that his 'integral yoga' was the spiritual technique for the higher evolution of all mankind. India was the guru of the nations, and had been set apart by the Divine as the eternal fountainhead of holy spirituality. India was to send forth from herself the future religion of the entire world, the Eternal Religion which was to harmonize all religion, science and philosophies, and make humankind one soul.

Although Mahatma Gandhi is still the most famous Hindu of modern times, his idiosyncratic views were of political rather than religious significance. His defiance of modernity by advocating the spinning wheel in place of modern technology and his favouring of the Christian cross above all other symbols, separated him from many Hindus. While alive his charisma was unparalleled, but his fame is dwindling away in India. The name he gave outcastes, Harijans, 'children of god', is now rejected by them as patronizing, and in practice his doctrine of non-violence finds few takers.

Last in Hacker's list of proponents of neo-Hinduism is S. Radhakrishnan (1888–1975), President of India (1962–7), author of *The Hindu View of the World*, who found many Western parallels to Vedanta.

These thinkers have received much more attention in the West than has traditional Hinduism, but the introduction of the term neo-Hinduism is unfortunate in that it denies what is in fact the growth and change that has always been part of Hinduism, as well as undervaluing the part played by the natural development of non-dualist Vedanta. As Hacker admits, many educated Hindus have no problem in handling traditional and modern Hinduism simultaneously.

Gurus

Almost all Hindu spiritual teachers take from neo-Hinduism the proud assertion of the universality of Hinduism and, to a certain extent, the belief in the importance of social work, but many continue in other respects to teach only traditional spiritual practices. The title *swami*, 'lord', is usually prefixed to their names, and they often maintain retreats called *ashrams*. A standard procedure is the process of initiation (*diksha*) in which a disciple is given a secret Sanskrit phrase (*mantra*). Some teachers have established outposts in the West, but remain centred in India. A good example of hundreds if not thousands of such teachers is Shivananda (1887–1963) who founded the Divine Life Society. His work is continued by his disciples Chidananda (1916–) and Krishnananda (1922–). There are also Western successors such as the Canadian woman Swami Radha (1911–). A traditional mystic whose ashram continues but who has no successors was Ramana Maharshi (1879–1950), perhaps the best known and most respected of all Indian holy men in the twentieth century. The Ananda Marg founded 1955 by P. R. Sarkar (1921–91) is one instance of the murkier side of spirituality: maintaining tantric affiliations alongside welfare programmes, its members have also been involved in gun running and murder.

HINDU GURUS IN THE WEST

Among many gurus who brought forms of yoga to the West, important figures are Maharishi and Rajneesh. Maharishi Mahesh Yogi (1911–) founded Transcendental Meditation (TM). This technique of relaxed meditation on a personal *mantra* was especially popular in the 1960s, but TM centres are still found throughout the United States and Europe, where under the name of the Natural Law Party the movement puts forward candidates in democratic elections. Rajneesh (1931–90), later known as Osho, freely invented yogic and tantric practices; and the organization he started continues, sustained by video tapes of the master. Muktananda (1908–82) promoted as 'Siddha Yoga' his ability to make other people's *kundalini* rise; his movement, which like the two above mentioned organizations enthusiastically adopts modern business practices, is now led by a woman, Gurumayi Chidvilasananda (1955–). A more straightforward figure, and respected in India, is Satchidananda (1914–), a disciple of Sadananda, and founder of the ashram called Yogaville, in Ohio, who proclaimed Hinduism to America at the 1969 Woodstock music festival.

> The guru must be worshipped as God. He is God, he is nothing less than that. As you look at him, gradually the guru melts away, and what is left? The guru picture gives place to God Himself. The guru is the bright mask which God wears in order to come to us. As we look steadily on, gradually the mask falls off and God is revealed.
>
> (Vivekananda 'Discipleship', *The Voice of India*, November 1946, p. 170)

GODMEN AND GODWOMEN

Divinity is readily seen by Hindus to be present in special human beings; and gurus are often worshipped as gods by their followers. Various explanations have been given for the phenomenon of godmen. According to Max Weber the growth of guru worship, extreme forms of which can be traced back to the fifteenth century, relates to the replacement of Hindu kings by Muslim rulers, and the implication is that gurus took on the religious leadership role of the Hindu king. Another explanation is that where human relationships are organized by consideration of caste and family, choosing a guru is the only scope for free choice. The neo-Hindu explanation for the prevalence of gurus and guru worship would be that India is especially spiritual and the guru–pupil relationship is the primary expression of spirituality.

By far the most famous godman today is Sathya Sai Baba (1926–), whose pictures, smiling under a round mass of hair, and clad in an ochre robe, are everywhere in India. He backs up his claim to be an incarnation of both Shiva and Shakti by a wide variety of well-publicized miracles. He produces sacred ash magically from his hands or at a distance from pictures of himself, and for the favoured few jewels and watches. Apart from his miracles, his teachings scarcely differ from those of the *Bhagavad Gita*: one should be pure, one should do one's duty and dedicate one's actions to God in loving devotion. His divinity and miracles are accepted by many important Indians, and his charitable works are extensive, including hospitals and a university.

Figure 1.4 In this poster Sathya Sai Baba's universal divinity is here manifestly shared between himself, Jesus and Krishna

There are several instances of female gurus being accepted by their followers as manifestations of the Supreme Deity. Although veneration continues for medieval women saints such as Meera Bhai (late fifteenth century) who took nothing from their spouses, the first women gurus/saints in modern times tended to be wives of gurus who took over their husband's role after death or retirement, such as Saradamani (1853–1920), widow of Ramakrishna, and Mira Alfassa, 'the Mother' (1878–1973), wife of Aurobindo. A more modern phenomenon is women who are believed to embody the highest godhead. Instances are Anandamayi Ma (1896–1982), highly regarded by many important Indians; Ammachi, Amritanandamayi Ma (1954–), who touches and blesses individually vast crowds of devotees; Meera Devi (1960–) who does the same on a much smaller scale in Germany.

Gender

A remarkable feature of Hindu life both in India and abroad is the continuation even among highly educated people of arranged marriages. Love marriages are not unknown, and romantic love is a key feature of the ever popular Indian film industry; nevertheless most Hindus are content for their parents to find a marriage partner for them. Divorce is frowned upon: successful raising of children is the all important goal of marriage. The family continues through time as a living entity. Parents are looked after in their old age, and live with their children.

Although many Hindu women work outside the home, and middle class women are well educated, *Sita*, wife of Rama – who, as the *Ramayana* tells, faithfully followed her husband into the forest when he was banished by his father – remains a role model for many women. At the same time, many women play a vigorous role in public life, and the heroic goddess Durga also serves as a model. India has not only the late Mrs Gandhi, who at various times of crisis was identified with Durga in popular art, but also the female bandit Phoolan Devi (1963–) who worshipped Durga as well as identifying with her. After her surrender, having murdered the men who had raped her, she went on to become an MP (1996–99), and the film *Bandit Queen* (1995) told her story. India has a higher percentage of female members of parliament (the Lok Sabha) than does Germany.

Women play a leading role in domestic religious life. They usually tend the family shrine, and they maintain the well-being of their husbands and children by undertaking vows, usually to fast or otherwise offer devotion to their favourite deities. Grandmothers teach religious stories and rituals to their grandchildren. The active women's movement in India and its many organizations tend to be secular in character, but women dominate the Brahma Kumari religious movement. Founded by a man, Dada Lekhraj (1876–1969), it is run by women, and while expecting the end of the world to be followed by the rule of the god Rama, its members are active in many welfare projects. Celibacy is advocated, and a form of yoga is taught.

Outside the home, men retain nearly all the leadership roles, whether in religion or politics. In the world of cinema, popular with the population at large, especially young men, scenes of attempted rape are a regular feature, revealing the vulnerability of women, and showing male power both in the attempted wrong and the punishment of the wrongdoer by the powerful hero. The attempted stripping of Draupadi in the *Mahabharata*, prevented by her prayer to the god Krishna, is familiar to all Hindu women, and they sympathize strongly with her.

Hindu society is changing: there are more nuclear families, more education for women, more high level employment for women, and there is ever greater exposure to Western social models through film and television. Nevertheless, the biological difference between male and female mediated by the difference between what is called the male caste and the female caste, remains as apparent in society as ever. In many fundamental ways, modernity appears not to have significantly affected the role of gender in religion.

SATI

A notable event in this connection was the death on her husband's funeral pyre of a 19-year-old woman called Rup Kanwar in 1987. Thousands flocked to see this death, and many more later to venerate the site, while at the same time thousands protested against what they saw as a barbarous murder. This *sati* took place in Rajasthan, a rural region with a long tradition of *satis*, along with female infanticide and child marriages. No notice had been taken of occasional *satis* in the preceding decade. Progressive thinkers denied that there was any legitimate tradition of *sati*, and said that it was murder by the in-laws. All the men in the village were arrested and detained. Incitement to commit *sati* was made a crime with heavier penalties than murder. Nevertheless, many families in the higher castes of Rajasthan claim to have a *sati* somewhere in the family history, the dead widow becoming a beneficent deity who looks after the welfare of future generations of the family. Suicide by fasting or self-inflicted wounds was a regular practice in the nineteenth century by the bardic caste of western India, a tradition which Gandhi drew upon when he undertook his fasts to the death. In 1990 self-immolation by fire was a practice adopted by a dozen high-caste protesters against the implementation of the proposals of the *Mandal Commission Report on Backward Classes* to extend reservation of government jobs and education for low castes and tribespeople ('scheduled castes and tribes').

The case of Rup Kanwar brought out into the open the gulf that separated traditional minded Hindus from the Westernized urban elite. The Marwari merchant caste built dozens of *sati* temples; progressive thinkers pointed out the connection between *sati* and the infamous 'dowry deaths', numbered by the thousands in the big cities of north India, where brides who bring too little dowry are burnt to death in kitchen 'accidents' brought about by husbands and in-laws. *Sati* is a rare event, and is now proscribed by very severe legislation. Nevertheless *sati*, which figured largely in early European accounts of India, was legislated against by the British, and attacked by the Hindu reform movements of the nineteenth century, continues.

Sati is the name given to a wife's immolating herself upon her husband's funeral. Though illegal in India, it has happened as recently as November, 1999, in Mahoba, Rajasthan State. The event attracted far less publicity than the death of Roop Kanwar in the same fashion twelve years earlier, also in Rajasthan. But in both cases, reactions ranged from cries of 'murder,' to reverential awe at the widow's feat. In fact, police had to be posted at the Mahoba site to prevent a temple from being built upon it. The villagers protested the armed presence and, pointing to popular temples built in nearby areas to commemorate *satis*, demanded to know why they could not likewise honor their *sati*.

(*Hinduism Today*, May/June 2000)

Caste

One of the features of Hindu society which sits most uncomfortably with modernity with its broadly egalitarian, 'humanitarian' ideals, is caste. The untouchable leader, B. R. Ambedkar (1891–1956), strove for the removal of caste privileges such as participation in public festivals, temple entry, Vedic wedding rituals, and the wearing of the sacred thread. In 1932 his claim for untouchables to form a separate electorate, as was proposed for Muslims and Sikhs, led Gandhi to fast to the death until the claim was rejected. In 1935 Ambedkar declared that although he was born a Hindu he would not die a Hindu, and that untouchables could be free only outside the Hindu religion. Just before his death he converted to Buddhism, to be followed in this conversion by almost 4 million untouchables.

The caste system continues to be very important in respect of marriage, but the castes are no longer publicly admitted to form a hierarchy. People say that it is 'comfortable' to marry and socialize within their own castes; and caste associations have national political weight. The word 'community' is now sometimes used instead of caste. The former outcastes, the lowest castes, have given themselves the name *dalit*, 'the downtrodden'. Numbering 200 million, their voice is growing. The current President of India (1997–) is a Dalit, K. R. Narayanan (1920–). Despite extensive government legislation, caste remains an important and often contentious part of life for most Hindus in India.

Nationalism

REGIONAL NATIONALISM

India is made up of regions that are ethnically and culturally distinct. All are tinged to a greater or lesser degree by the Hinduism of brahmans, but that Hinduism is often rejected. To take one example: in the case of Tamilnadu, despite the strongly Hindu Chola Empire (ninth–thirteenth centuries CE) and post-Vijayanagara Nayak rulers (fifteenth–seventeenth centuries CE), Tamil language and literature both ancient and modern helped foster a strong sense of independent nationhood. With regard to theology, the Shaiva Siddhanta form of *Shaivism*, which had been a pan-Indian movement up to the thirteenth century, was declared on the basis of those of its texts in Tamil to be an indigeous Tamil and even non-Hindu religion. An anti-brahman independence movement was led by E. V. Ramaswami (1879–1973), who publically reviled Rama and took the demon Ravana as inspirational hero. Independence of India had meant the enslavement of the south by Hindu Delhi. However, despite continuing resistance to the imposition of the north Indian language Hindi, his political party under the popular leadership of M. G. Ramachandran (1917–87) – who as a film star had played the parts of gods – ended up supporting the Congress Party. MGR's sometime co-star and successor as Chief Minister of Tamilnadu, Jayaram Jayalalitha (1948–), enthusiastically backed Sanskritic culture: she herself has received public ritual bathing (*abhisheka*) as befits a deity. Her 1988 election campaign featured a film still of MGR as the god Murugan, son of Shiva, and herself as his divine consort. The Tamil nationalist opposition to Hinduism has here turned back to brahmanical Hinduism. Such variation and change continues in most regions of India.

HINDU NATIONALISM

A dominant part in Indian politics is played by Hindu nationalism. The Bharatiya Janata Party's unstoppable rise to power from the mid-1980s was brought about by its demand for the destruction of the Babri Mosque in Ayodhya and the rebuilding of the temple of Rama's birthplace. Although the secular Congress Party seemed the natural ruling power in India for three decades from independence in 1947, the rise of Hindu nationalism was almost inevitable. Hindu–Muslim tensions rose dramatically once it was clear the British Raj was about to end. While Gandhi attempted to form, or at least exemplify, a religion of love and sacrifice that ignored not only the realities of the modern industrial world but also the separateness of Hinduism, Islam and Christianity, many Hindus and Muslims saw themselves as belonging to separate nations. The widely used Indian term for this religious nationalism is 'communalism'.

Early Hindu nationalist thinkers were prominent in Bengal, the first home of the British Raj, and then in Maharashtra, the main industrial centre and also the region of the last Hindu conquerors, the Marathas, who defeated the Moghuls and ruled much of India prior to the British. Among the Marathas, brahmans were warrior kings as well as priests, and a succcession of Maratha brahmans played a leading role in the development of Hindu nationalism. B. G. Tilak (1856–1920) promoted as a national figure the Maratha hero Shivaji (1627–80) who initiated the defeat of the Moghuls, but while Tilak promoted the worship of Ganesha to strengthen the Hindu community in Maharashtra, V. D. Savarkar (1883–1966), terrorist and inspirational leader, made religion only one constituent part of being a Hindu. What counted for him was above all love of India, seen by him as the fatherland. All religions founded in India – Buddhism, Jainism, Sikhism – were Hindu. His nationalism was summed up in the new word Hindutva, 'Hinduness'. Savarkar argued that violent action was required to remove the conquerors of India.

In 1925 K. B. Hedgewar (1890–1940) founded the Rashtriya Svayamsevak Sangh National Volunteer Association (RSS), a uniformed organization designed to correct all those faults of Indian character that the British pointed to in justifying their own rule; and making Mother India a deity above all others. A related organization, the Vishva Hindu Parishad (VHP), was started in 1964 to assemble and give a common voice to as many Hindu religious leaders as possible. The demand was formulated that three notable Hindu temples should be rebuilt. Just after independence it had been agreed by the government that the famous Shiva Temple of Somanatha, many times destroyed by Muslims, should be rebuilt, though the rebuilding was not completed until 1995. But the new demand was very different, in that it called for the destruction of the mosques that had been built over the temple sites at Ayodhya, Mathura and Varanasi. To further such aims, a youth wing of the VHP was founded in 1967. Named the Bajrang Dal, 'Mighty Hanuman's Army', the power and energy of the unemployed youth of north India was harnessed and given direction. In 1954 the RSS, though its own aim was the regeneration of the Hindu character rather than politics, had played a large part in the formation of the Jan Sangh political party. This party had not done well, but in 1980 it was repackaged as the Bharatiya Janata Party. This group of right-wing organizations took the overall title of the Sangh Parivar. Separate but analogous was the Shiva Sena, the Army of Shivaji, founded by the Bombay politician Bal Thackeray (1927–). All these groups converged on Ayodhya, where in 1992 the mosque – said to be built over the temple of Rama's birthplace – was destroyed, despite all orders of government and supreme court.

In this significant event many characteristics of modern Hinduism and modern India are thrown into sharp focus. Right-wing movements such as RSS, with their uniforms and their military discipline, are an after effect of British colonialism, with its denigration of Hindu military prowess: these organizations want to demonstrate the strength of Hindus. Because of historical conflict and because of the ongoing dispute about ownership of Kashmir, Pakistan and all Muslims are perceived by Hindus of the extreme right as their enemy. The god Rama, *avatara* of Vishnu, already given new life by the televising of the *Ramayana*, is given a new iconography, as poised with his bow drawn ready to fire his arrow at the foe, with the elevation of the temple of his birthplace at his feet, yet to be (re)built. Previously, Rama had simply stood with his bow beside him, undrawn, ruler rather than warrior. Another innovation was a boy Rama, modelled on the much loved baby boy form of Krishna, a Rama who first showed himself, it is supposed, within the Ayodhya Mosque in 1948. Using the resources of modern technology, television, film, audio tapes of incendiary speeches, Hindu nationalist forces swept aside the restrictions of the secular state.

Hinduism has gained much from Islam over the centuries, expressed in the rich tradition exemplified by Kabir and other saints, but it is also the case that the recent upsurge in Hindu fundamentalism has been influenced by instances of contemporary Islamic intransigence. Right-wing Hindu intolerance of Islam and Christianity in India today has also to be noted. Enmity with Pakistan, especially because of ongoing conflict over Kashmir, fosters enmity with Islam and ill-treatment of Muslims in India. At the same time, resentment of former British colonialism continues, sometimes generalized into hatred of the West and of Christianity. All this is summed up in a popular New Year card by the well-known artist Balraj showing a giant Mother India calling the Indian (Hindu) people to arms with her furious lion beside her already pawing at the multiple dragons that are India's enemies, dragons whose snake-like bodies are marked with the American dollar sign, the Islamic crescent and the Christian cross.

LOOKING TO THE FUTURE

Most Hindus have not heard of the death of God. Hinduism's gods and goddesses are as alive as ever – in temples, in modern media, in human incarnations. It is impossible in a single chapter to do justice to the vigorous multiplicity of Hinduism. The controversial Indian novelist Salman Rushdie wrote that 'The selfhood of Indians is so capacious, so elastic, that it accommodates one billion kinds of difference'. This perfectly expresses the dynamic freedom that is the special heritage of India, despite all the constrictions that arise from communalism and caste.

Modern India has formed its own amalgam of tradition and modernity, indeed its own modernity. Indian government and Indian law are completely modern, fully rationalized, bureaucratized and secular. Hinduism likewise sees itself as modern and in accord with modern science, while at the same time accepting the plenitude and validity of human religious experience. The gods and goddesses are real because sacred texts describe them in detail and because people see, hear and touch them. Religious practices like yoga and tantra, based on esoteric understanding of the mind and body, are experientially proven. Hindu thinkers saw long ago the universe in terms of both the infinitely large and the infinitely small. Rather like the present day big bang theory, medieval Shaiva philosophers reasoned that the universe was produced in a split second from an infinitely small point, but go further by positing an infinite series of such creations.

Hinduism has spread round the world with the Indian diaspora and the limited activity of Hindu missionaries. Yoga and spiritual disciplines stemming from yoga have had worldwide success. Innumerable Hindu spiritual teachers are active round the world, even if their activities are small-scale. Hindu art and culture in the second half of the twentieth century at last began to be understood outside India. From the perspective of modernity, Hindu Puranic myths plainly bear upon the realities of the human psyche rather than a special version of history, and thus retain value even if not fully believed.

Hindu fundamentalism aside, Hinduism is thus generally at ease in the modern world. For Hindus the traditional values of the family are self-evidently valuable in whatever world we find ourselves, and caste continues as groupings of families. Indeed, so at ease is Hinduism in the modern world that it may be argued that in certain ways Hinduism is not only modern, but even intrinsically postmodern. If the postmodern world is characterized as the late-capitalist, post-industrial world of the Internet and cyberspace, a world of spectacle, sensation and simulation, then the Hindu view of the world as multi-levelled, infinitely varied and infinitely coloured, as bewitched by Krishna's flute, as the projection of the divine light of Shiva upon the wall of his own consciousness, as the pure consciousness of Brahman, is a view that is easily adaptable to this ethos, and is not threatened by any of the promised and threatened developments of modern science.

SUMMARY

- Traditional Hinduism continues into the modern world, and its rich complexity has to be understood for Hinduism today to be comprehended.
- Modernity was mediated to India by British colonialism. Salient features include the nation state and the dissemination of scientific rationality.
- One effect of the Western impact on Hinduism (particularly in the nineteenth and early twentieth centuries) is the rise of different forms of 'reform' or 'neo' Hinduism. Generally small-scale and elitist, such movements have nonetheless had a wider influence on Hinduism.
- At the same time traditional Hinduism persists in the modern world, in some cases revivified by

new media such as film and television. Hindu gods and goddesses, in the temple and in the home shrine, are as popular as ever. Gurus have also become increasingly important in modern times, teaching a wide variety of yoga-based techniques in India and the West.

- Caste sits uneasily with modernity, and gender roles often continue to follow traditional stereotypes. Feminized divinity continues to give scope for female spirituality.
- Hindu concerns dominate Indian politics, and the ideal of India as a secular state has been overturned.

KEY TERMS

ashrama   One of the four stages of life; the retreat or hermitage of a holy man or woman.

avatara   'Descent', the incarnation of the divine on earth, in divine or human form.

bhakti   Loving devotion to a deity.

Brahma   Four-headed male god, born from the lotus that arises from Vishnu's navel at the beginning of each cycle of creation.

brahman   Priest, member of the highest caste.

Brahman   Ultimate reality, the absolute that is pure consciousness; said by the Upanishads and the non-dualist Vedanta philosophy to be identical with the individual self.

darshan   Seeing, seeing a sacred image or person; also, philosophy, philosophical system.

Devi   Goddess in general; or supreme goddess.

dharma   The right way of life, in accord with cosmic truth. Hinduism is the eternal right way of life, the *sanatana* (eternal) *dharma*. *Dharma* in a more restricted sense is the third of the goals of mankind, meaning religious behaviour which leads to heaven or higher rebirth; in this sense it is inferior to *moksha*.

diksha   Ritual consecration, initiation.

Durga   Heroic saviour goddess, who kills the buffalo demon.

guru   Teacher, spiritual guide, godman.

jati   Literally 'birth' – caste, sub-caste.

Kali   The black goddess, fierce form of Parvati, destroyer of the universe.

Kali yuga   The fourth, worst, and final world age, endlessly recurring in the cosmic cycle of *samsara*. Kali here refers to the worst throw of a dice, sometimes personified as a male demon; and should not be confused with the goddess Kali (spelt Kâlî in Indian languages).

karma   Action; the personal consequences that accrue from action.

Krishna   The black or dark blue god, incarnation of Vishnu.

kundalini   The female serpent coiled at the base of the spine, raised by up by tantric yoga.

Lakshmi   Goddess of wealth and prosperity, wife of Vishnu.

mantra   Sacred word or formula.

moksha   Release, liberation of the self from rebirth.

Murugan   Son of Shiva and Parvati, Tamil form of Skanda.

Parvati   Goddess, wife of Shiva, mother of Ganesha and Skanda.

Prakriti   Mother nature.

puja   The act of worshipping a deity or holy person by offering light, flowers, food and water.

Purusha   'Male', the cosmic giant whose sacrificed body gave rise to the fourfold caste system; individual consciousness in the samkhya philosophy.

Rama   Hero of the *Ramayana*, husband of Sita, slayer of Ravana, incarnation of Vishnu.

samkhya   Philosophical system based on opposition of *Purusha* and *Prakriti*, consciousness and nature.

samsara   The eternal cycle of rebirth.

Sanskrit   The ancient language of the Hindu scriptures, still learnt by some brahmans. Belonging to the Indo-European family of languages, with strong resemblances to Greek, Latin, Celtic, Old German. Sanskrit words form a large part of the vocabulary of modern Indian languages.

sati (suttee)   Literally, 'a good wife' – a widow who joins the corpse of her husband on the funeral pyre and perishes in the flames; the act of so doing. After death, she is considered immortal and a family deity.

Shaiva   Religion, philosophy or devotee of Shiva.

Shaivism   The religion of Shiva.

Shakta   Relating to Shakti, the religion of Shakti, goddess worship.

Shakti   Feminine force, feminine divinity.

Shiva   One of the two great gods of Hinduism, the Great Yogi, the King of Dancers, husband of Parvati.

Sita   Wife of Rama, heroine of the *Ramayana*, ideal wife.

siddhi   Magic power acquired through yoga.

svami (swami)   Lord, master, usual title of a holy man.

tantra   Doctrine and practice based on secret ritual worship of the female and magical sounds.

Vaishnava   Religion, philosophy or devotee of Shiva.

varna   Literally 'colour' – the four caste groups of Priest, Warrior, Farmer and Peasant.

Vishnu   One of the two great gods of Hinduism, a kingly and warrior figure who periodically descends to earth to protect *dharma*.

yajna   Fire oblation, sacrifice.

yoga   'Joining' – self mastery, union with the divine; meditational practice and philosophy.

yuga   World age, of which there are four, endlessly repeating.

FURTHER READING

Overviews of Hinduism

Madeleine Biardeau: *Hinduism: The Anthropology of a Civilization* (Delhi: Oxford University Press, 1989). A masterly reading of what might be seen as the underlying structures of Hinduism, by a French Indologist.

Klaus K. Klostermaier: *A Survey of Hinduism*, second edition (Albany, NY: SUNY Press, 1994). Useful basic information.

Hinduism in the nineteenth century

J. N. Farquhar: *Modern Religious Movements in India* (reprinted Delhi: Munshiram Manoharlal ([orig.] 1914) 1967). Masterly survey up to 1913, but necessarily dated in treatment.

Kenneth W. Jones: *Socio-Religious Reform Movements in British India* (The New Cambridge History of India III, 1, Cambridge: Cambridge University Press, 1989). Includes an excellent account of the regional diversity of India.

Gyanendra Pandey: *The Construction of Communalism in Colonial North India* (Delhi: Oxford University Press, 1990). An explanation of the rift between Hinduism and Islam.

Hinduism and modernity

Vinayak Chaturvedi: *Mapping Subaltern Studies and the Postcolonial* (London and New York: Verso, 2000). Important essays on orientalism and postcolonialism in relation to South Asia.

Lloyd I. Rudolph and Susanne H. Rudolph: *The Modernity of Tradition* (Chicago: University of Chicago Press, 1967). The classic work on India and modernity. Good on Gandhi. Less directly concerned with religion but more up-to-date is the same authors' *In Pursuit of Lakshmi* (Chicago: University of Chicago Press, 1987).

David Smith: *Hinduism and Modernity* (Oxford: Blackwell, forthcoming). A study of classical and modern Hinduism in relation to modernity.

Contemporary Hinduism

Lawrence A. Babb: *Redemptive Encounters: Three Modern Styles in the Hindu Tradition* (Delhi: Oxford University Press, 1987). Excellent study of Radhasoamis, Brahma Kumaris and Sai Baba.

Robert D. Baird (ed.): *Religion in Modern India* (New Delhi: Manohar, 1995). A valuable series of essays on religious movements and individual thinkers, but for the most part only up to the 1950s.

Susan Bayly: *Caste, Society and Politics in India from the Eighteenth Century to the Modern Age* (The New Cambridge History of India IV, 3, Cambridge: Cambridge University Press, 1999). Excellent general account of caste.

Raymond Brady Williams (ed.): *A Sacred Thread: Modern Transmission of Hindu Tradition in India and Abroad* (Chambersburg: Anima Publications, 1992). Valuable well-balanced overview.

Diana L. Eck: *Banaras: City of Light* (Princeton, NJ: Princeton University Press, 1982). A fascinating and scholarly account of India's holiest city.

Geraldine Forbes: *Women in Modern India* (The New Cambridge History of India IV, 2, Cambridge: Cambridge University Press, 1999). A clear survey.

C. F. Fuller: *The Camphor Flame: Popular Hinduism* (Princeton, NJ: Princeton University Press, 1992). Invaluable, the best single book on modern Hinduism, though only dealing with the anthropology of traditional Hinduism. Clear and readable.

Paul Hacker (ed. W. Halbfass): *Philology and Confrontation: Paul Hacker on Traditional and Modern Vedanta* (Albany, NY: SUNY, 1995). Contains Hacker's account of neo-Hinduism.

Mary Hancock: *Womanhood in the Making: Domestic Ritual and Public Culture in Urban South India* (Boulder: Westview Press, 1999). A sophisticated account of the ideal of the auspicious married woman in relation to tradition and modernity in South India today.

Thomas Blom Hansen: *The Saffron Wave: Democracy and Hindu Nationalism in Modern India* (Princeton, NJ: Princeton University Press, 1999). A clear account of the politics of right-wing Hinduism.

Linda Johnsen: *Daughters of the Goddess: The Women Saints of India* (St Paul: Yes International Publishers, 1994). A popular and readable account of godwomen today.

Gerald James Larson: *India's Agony of Religion* (Albany, NY: SUNY, 1995). An overview of religion in modern India.

Lutgendorf, Philip: *The Life of a Text: Performing the Ramacaritmanas of Tulsidas* (Berkeley: University of California Press, 1991). A vivid account of the role of the Hindi *Ramayana* in the life of north India today.

T. N. Madan: *Non-Renunciation: Themes and Interpretation of Hindu Culture* (Delhi: Oxford University Press, 1987). Hinduism as the life of the householder rather than the ascetic.

Lise Mckean: *Divine Enterprise: Gurus and the Hindu Nationalist Movement* (Chicago: University of Chicago Press, 1996). A critical account, lacking in sympathy, but readable and very useful.

T. V. Sathyamurthy (ed.): *Region, Religion, Caste, Gender and Culture in Contemporary India* (Delhi: Oxford University Press, 1998.) Very useful collection of studies.

Arvind Sharma: *Hinduism for Our Times* (Delhi: Oxford University Press, 1996). Argues that the tolerance of Hinduism makes it uniquely valuable to the modern world.

CHAPTER 2

Buddhism

Cathy Cantwell and Hiroko Kawanami

▌ INTRODUCTION

Long established in Asia, Buddhism has become a fast-growing religion in Western countries today. The number of adherents worldwide in mid-1998 was estimated at around 357 million, and although it may not be easy to verify such estimates, these figures suggest that Buddhism ranks fourth amongst world religions. However, Buddhism has been affected by the impact of colonialism, capitalism, Marxism, and nationalism. Asian Buddhist countries have lost traditional systems of government and in some cases experienced communist rule or other political upheavals and social changes. Challenges have also resulted from new technology, different world views and transportation of Buddhism to different societies.

Buddhism remains dominant in Sri Lanka and some countries in Southeast and East Asia. It has survived or seen recent revivals in the Himalayan region, Tibet, China, Central Asia, pockets of east Bengal, south India and Indonesia. Late twentieth-century globalization has meant that the major Buddhist traditions all now have an international presence, and infringe on each other's territories. Buddhism has also become significant in North America and Europe. Many texts have been translated into European languages since the nineteenth century, and *Theravāda*, Tibetan, Zen, Chinese *Mahāyāna*, and Japanese Nichiren Shōshū Buddhist groups have mushroomed in the West. Meanwhile, both in Asia and the West, new forms of Buddhism have attracted growing numbers seeking spirituality compatible with contemporary life.

For Asian Buddhists, 'modernity' may imply experiences consequent upon their encounter with the West, their integration into modern economies and political systems, and the subsequent arrival of different world views and values challenging traditional outlooks and ways of life. In some cases, secular education, scientific knowledge and democratic ideas were introduced; all were a part of the modernity which stimulated local religious leaders to engage in reform or retrenchment. Secularization, mass literacy, urbanization, technological developments and growth in communications accelerated the process. Yet the timing of the Buddhist encounter with modernity, and the specific forms it took, varied significantly. In Sri Lanka, for example, modernity can be dated to British rule in the nineteenth century, whilst in Tibet it was postponed until the mid-twentieth century Chinese occupation.

This chapter focuses on southern Buddhism – South and Southeast Asian Theravāda (the way of the elders), and northern Tibetan Buddhism, concluding with a brief account of Buddhism in the West. Further discussion of East Asian Buddhism can be found in Chapters 4 and 5.

SOURCES AND RESOURCES

Origins and fundamental tenets

Siddhārtha Gautama (*c*.490–10 BCE) – who became the *Buddha*, one who had 'awoken' to the truth – was the founder of Buddhism. Emerging from the Indian *Renouncer movement*, which emphasized the abandonment of worldly life for the pursuit of spiritual enlightenment, his teaching of the 'four noble truths' drew attention to the unsatisfactory nature of existence. According to early sources, Buddha argued that everything is conditioned and subject to change, but people, ignorant of this reality, become attached to impermanent things. The only cure is the 'noble eightfold path', a set of methods encompassing morality, meditation and wisdom. The ultimate goal is enlightenment (*nirvāṇa*), freedom from the cycle of conditioned existence.

Buddhism developed a universalist ethical system: unlike the Vedic traditions, which tended to situate ethics according to the status of the actor (see Chapter 1), Buddhism held that there are universal values – especially that of the non-harming of living beings – which are equally valid for all people. In Buddhist thinking, rebirth in conditioned existence is dependent on laws of cause and effect (*karma*), which operate rationally and which are ethical in nature – morally good actions lead to positive results while evil actions lead to negative results. While encouraging ethical discipline for all, renouncers of household life were to develop meditation, mindfulness and wisdom in order to exhaust ignorance and craving, seen as responsible for conditioned existence, thus putting an end to the entire process and attaining the unconditioned. This approach was partly shared with other Renouncer groups. Specifically Buddhist elements included:

1 The idea that it is intentional action which generates results in a being's consciousness. This had implications for both individual conduct and relations between monks and laity. For instance, accidental taking of life might be seen as negative action influenced by confusion or carelessness, rather than entailing the full consequences of killing living beings. Thus, the stricter requirements for ascetics and layfolk in Jainism (a rival Renouncer movement which also had long-term success in India) were considered unnecessary in Buddhism.
2 The co-existence of perspectives which stressed the problem of ignorance and the corresponding need to develop wisdom, with perspectives stressing the problem of craving and the corresponding need to reduce the emotional defilements. Many of the variations in Buddhist practice are related to the relative importance given to these two perspectives.
3 The development of meditation techniques for calming the mind and for increasing mindful awareness, considered essential on the path to liberation; other elements of the Renouncer heritage, especially forms of asceticism, were comparatively neglected.

4   A conceptualization of the Buddhist Path as a 'middle way' between the extremes of worldly indulgence and asceticism, combining a strong commitment to renunciation with a simple lifestyle without ascetic tortures or avoidance of the wider community.

Many of these early characteristics continued to be central in Buddhism, although the tradition diversified in time, and underwent complex developments during one and a half thousand years in India. This period saw the rise of new forms of religious practice and the classical Hindu systems of philosophy; Buddhist schools developed in continual conversation with each other and with non-Buddhists. The Buddhist scriptural heritage was transmitted orally by schools of reciters until texts were written down around the beginning of the Christian era. It was codified in the separate but parallel collections of the early Buddhist orders, including sections on monastic discipline (*vinaya*), discourses (*sūtra*), and in the case of most (but not all) schools, Higher Teachings (*abhidharma*). The Mahāyāna (great vehicle) movement added a further set of *sūtras*, not recognized by all Buddhists. Initially small in India, the Mahāyāna had long-term historical significance.

Historical change and diffusion

Many Indian kings patronized Buddhism, but King Aśoka of the Mauryan empire played a crucial role in spreading Buddhism in the third century BCE to wider areas in Asia. Further diffusions of Buddhism were brought by the Mahāyāna teachings, which travelled to China and Central Asia from the early centuries CE, while large Mahāyāna scholastic centres of international fame thrived during the latter period of Buddhism in India, between the seventh and the twelfth centuries. In early Mahāyāna teachings, the actions of the compassionate *bodhisattva* (one on the path to Buddhahood, dedicated to saving others) were adopted as a religious path over spiritual endeavour focused on personal liberation.

■ SAMANTABHADRA'S ASPIRATIONS FOR PERFECTED DEEDS

Samantabhadra's aspirations, expressing the *bodhisattva* ethos, are well-known in Mahāyāna Buddhist countries. They conclude the *Avataṃsaka Sūtra*, a Mahāyāna sūtra which had a major impact on East Asian Buddhism. The extracts below follow Shenpen Hookham's translation from Tibetan.

May offerings be made in reverence to the Buddhas of the past
And those of the present in the worlds of the ten directions.
May those Buddhas-to-be proceeding towards Enlightenment
Quickly consummate all their wishes on the Path and become Buddhas.
May all the realms that there are in the ten directions
Become extensive and perfectly pure,
And each whole realm become utterly filled with Buddhas . . .

Throughout all my lifetimes as I pass from death to rebirth,
May I each time renew again my vow to live the life of renunciation.
Following the manner of training of all the Buddhas,
May I wholly complete the discipline of perfected deeds . . .
And never forget the aspiration of awakening to Buddhahood . . .

> May I relieve the suffering of the beings in the lower realms,
> Establishing them in happiness and acting for their benefit . . .
>
> May I be able to see in a single atom Buddha realms numerous as atoms,
> And then in each of these Buddha realms,
> Buddhas in number beyond conception,
> And each Buddha seated in the midst of his vast assembly of Bodhisattvas . . .
> I pray I may be able to perform the discipline of perfected deeds
> Before these endless Buddhas in the endless Buddha realms for endless aeons . . .
>
> By the power of miracles, swift and all-embracing,
> By the power of the universal gateway [the Mahāyāna],
> By the power of the all-good qualities of the perfected deeds,
> By the power of all-pervading love,
> By the power of seeds of goodness from all wholesome states and actions,
> By the power of unobstructed primordial wisdom,
> By the power of wisdom, skilful action and concentrative absorption,
> May I complete all the powers of Enlightenment.
>
> (*The Samantabhadra Charyapranidhana*, Shenpen Hookham, Oxford:
> Longchen Foundation, 1997)

The focus on compassion was combined with single-minded dedication to attaining wisdom, now summed up in the notion of *emptiness*. This complex teaching was elaborated at length in Mahāyāna philosophy, especially in the Madhyamaka school, which analysed the deceptive nature of all conceptual systems. On the other hand, the Yogācāra school in the fourth century integrated diverse Buddhist teachings, while emphasizing the centrality of the meditational experience of pure consciousness. More broadly, the Mahāyāna recognition of new sūtras as valid scripture, and the development of such philosophical and commentarial traditions in debate with the emerging Hindu philosophical schools, demonstrates the considerable dynamism and innovation in Indian Mahāyāna. This tendency later persisted to some extent, especially in Chinese Buddhist traditions. In contrast, the later Theravāda, which firmly established itself in Ceylon, consolidated a more conservative outlook.

A further development in Indian Buddhism was the Buddhist tantric or *Vajrayāna* tradition, using rich symbolic imagery and ritual practices, and based on the principle that the energies of aggression, passion and delusion may be used to overcome themselves. Pure in their true nature when not afflicted by ignorance, these powerful forces may be co-opted for the Buddhist goal of enlightenment, although safeguards were considered necessary to preclude misinterpretation. New esoteric scriptures called 'tantras' were revealed, and in time, Vajrayāna became rooted in major monastic centres in northern India, and travelled alongside other Buddhist texts and practices to various Asian countries.

By the thirteenth century, Buddhism had been eclipsed in its Indian heartlands, but it was firmly established through much of Asia, from Tibet to Japan. It spread not only in the form of religious scriptures but also in art, architecture and literature, which had profound impact on local cultures.

Most of the diverse forms of Buddhism which have survived into modern times can be categorized into three major groupings:

1 Southern Buddhism, practised in Sri Lanka and Southeast Asian countries, especially Thailand, Burma, Cambodia and Laos. The main thread holding this group together is Theravāda Buddhist practice. Theravāda derives from one of the ancient Indian Buddhist schools, and preserves the only surviving complete corpus of early texts in an ancient Indian language, *Pali*. It also draws on later commentarial works, including those of Ceylonese scholars during the first millennium CE.
2 Northern Buddhism, practised in Tibet, the surrounding Himalayan areas, and wherever Buddhism spread from Tibetan sources, such as parts of Central Asia, principally Mongolia. The Buddhism of this branch derives from later Indian Buddhism especially of the Pāla dynasty (Bengal, eighth–twelfth centuries CE), incorporating Buddhist monastic scholarship, Mahāyāna and tantric traditions. It preserves large collections of scriptural and commentarial texts in Tibetan, including a comprehensive set of translations from Sanskrit sources as well as a vast indigenous literature.
3 East Asian Buddhism, practised in East Asian countries such as China, Taiwan, Korea and Japan, in Vietnam, and in other countries with substantial ethnic Chinese populations. East Asian Buddhism mainly derives from the Mahāyāna traditions which were established in China in the early centuries CE, although the textual heritage in Chinese includes earlier Buddhist scriptures and a few tantras.

Organization and authority

Monasticism played an essential role in the consolidation and propagation of early Buddhism. Integral to Buddhism from the start, most Buddhist schools view monasticism as a superior way of life since it enables its members to avoid worldly concerns and concentrate single-mindedly on spiritual practice. The monastic code which governs Buddhist monks' and nuns' daily life and social relationships appears to have been codified at a very early stage in Indian Buddhism. Buddhist monks were trained to be socially presentable, to live an ethical life and accept lay support. Central to the Buddhist monastic code is the principle of combining aspects of the model of the other-worldly renouncer with that of the this-worldly householder brahmin priest. Buddhist monks, like ascetics, were to renounce household life, yet they were to serve the laity's religious needs by giving Buddhist teachings. The monastic community (*Saṅgha*) in its classic form, emphasizing monastic and lay interdependence, was the long-standing ideal of Buddhist organization.

In early Indian Buddhism, a number of discrete monastic orders developed on the basis of separate ordination lines, with minor variations in the list of monastic rules. These orders also came to be associated with certain doctrinal positions, but there was no insistence on adherence to these positions within each order. Rules governing the communal lives of monks seem to have derived from a model of republican government then current in parts of the region where Buddhism originated. Local Saṅghas were autonomous, united by common adherence to the monastic rule and the Buddha's teachings, not by hierarchical integration. Within each Saṅgha, ranking was based on seniority (dependent on time in the order) and gender, while decision-making was ideally by consensus, with provisions for majority voting. The small-scale, non-hierarchical structure of the Saṅgha persisted as an important feature, but it has frequently been modified by the integration of monasteries into wider political and socio-economic structures, which has generated increased cohesion and hierarchy in Buddhist monasticism.

Different models for religious practice stemmed from an early Buddhist opposition between town dwelling and forest dwelling monks. The alternative vocations of book duty and meditation duty are discussed in fifth-century Pali commentaries written in Sri Lanka. The ideal type of bookish monk would be resident in a permanent monastic institution, preserving and teaching the tradition as passed down, at first by oral transmission and later by written scriptures. Meditators, on the other hand, would be focused on gaining realization, often in reclusive forest retreats, wandering from place to place like the ancient renouncers. These two types can be seen as two distinct strands within the Buddhist tradition from the outset. Even before there were any books, the codified Buddhist monastic rule modified the strict ascetic codes for renouncers, encouraging the communal life of monasteries and association with the laity. These innovations appear to have been resisted by one faction of Buddhist monks; they won the concession that, although not binding on the whole community, various ascetic traditions would be allowable.

SOUTHERN BUDDHISM

Southern Buddhism is fairly uniform in accepting the canonical Pali scriptures and commentaries as its textual authority. It has a solid monastic tradition, and although there is no orthodoxy as such, Theravāda Buddhists take pride in practising a religious tradition seen as uncorrupted and close to the earliest forms of Buddhism. Conservative in outlook, the monks strive to preserve Theravāda doctrine and monastic tradition with minimal change. As a Buddhist, one accepts and places one's trust in the 'triple gem', *Buddha, Dhamma* (the teachings of the Buddha) and Saṅgha (the monastic community). The formula of 'going for refuge' to the triple gem, publicly recited, is indispensable for any Buddhist ritual.

The Saṅgha specifically refers to the 'noble', spiritually advanced community, which might theoretically include nuns and lay people. However, the monks pre-eminently came to symbolize the Saṅgha as the focus of people's worship. The monks' lifestyle is characterized by celibacy, detachment and monastic discipline which, especially in the Southern tradition, is valued above that of the ordinary lay person. The monks are thought to be in a privileged position to concentrate on the path to *nibbāna*, whilst the laity's main task is to work for better rebirths through merit-making activities. Traditionally, whilst monks are encouraged to study and meditate, lay followers are expected to observe the Five Precepts, feed the monks and perform regular worship. Lay devotees also take additional vows such as celibacy, fasting in the afternoon, and not taking alcohol or going to films on special days. In addition to such traditional duties, meditation is becoming an increasingly popular part of spiritual training. In countries such as Thailand and Burma, the custom of at least becoming a temporary novice or monk after twenty years of age, possibly for only a week to three months, is regarded as essential to attaining adult status. For a woman, however, the most prestigious and meritorious act is to send her son into the Saṅgha; a monk repays his parents with spiritual merit. The monastic community also provides education and social mobility for the bright and ambitious, especially from rural areas.

In the political realm, Southern Buddhism has long upheld the ideal of a 'righteous king' (*Dharmarāja*) who defends Buddhism and its moral principles of non-violence, tolerance and compassion. The ideal is enshrined in the historically based legend of King Aśoka (268–31 BCE), who promoted Buddhism in his empire. It incorporated a theme arising from accounts of the Buddha's life: that a universal ruler and universal spiritual teacher may in some senses be equated. Southeast Asian kings, taking up this theme, were consecrated as rulers of extraordinary grandeur, such as the thirteenth-century Khmer King Jayavarman VII, depicted as Bodhisattva Avalokiteśvara, and King Bodawpaya in seventeenth-century Burma, identified with Maitreya (Pali 'Metteyya'), the next Buddha-to-be.

The *Dharmarāja* model assumed that the king and monastic community were complementary, together maintaining stability. The king patronized the Saṅgha, ensuring its purity and strength, while the monks provided the country's spiritual foundation. The king was expected to administer the Saṅgha well. Failure justified removal, at least in theory if not practice; historically, religion was often subordinated to statecraft. To understand state control over the Saṅgha which has in some respects persisted to date, the following areas are important:

1 Monastic discipline was enforced by the ruling power, and corrupt monks were purged.
2 The state defined and enforced Saṅgha administration, appointing members to executive Saṅgha councils, and promoting monks supportive to the government.
3 The state protected lines of succession and ordination which would be, at least theoretically, traceable back to the Buddha, thus maintaining the Saṅgha's legitimacy.
4 The state became responsible for standards of Buddhist education, standardizing textbooks, and securing the quality of the state sponsored religious elite.
5 The state designated, regulated and controlled special areas for worship and religious constructions. Stūpas and pagodas containing relics of the Buddha were protected as symbols of kingship.

These provisions helped to ensure monks' upright behaviour, popular support for the Saṅgha, and long-lasting political stability. However, monks at times have been rebellious, manifesting their potential as an alternative power base. In recent Southeast Asian history, monastic communities without righteous patrons have had difficulties; but political rulers have not always been able to undermine the religious authority of the Saṅgha.

NORTHERN BUDDHISM: TIBET

In early Buddhism, doctrinal variations did not necessarily imply separate organization. The Mahāyāna movement spread within rather than institutionally separating itself from the early monastic orders. The same is generally true of Tibetan Buddhist monasticism; the monastic code followed everywhere is that of the Mūlasarvāstivāda, an ancient Indian order. Tibetan Buddhists also share Mahāyāna and Vajrayāna (tantric) practices and perspectives, while they are divided into monastic orders or loosely organized schools based on different lineages of Buddhist teachers, and not, in most cases, on strictly doctrinal differences. The main four traditions are the *Kagyu* (*bka' brgyud*), the *Sakya* (*sa skya*), the *Nyingma* (*rnying ma*) and the *Geluk* (*dge lugs*), but each of these major schools contains groupings within it, which may be to a greater or lesser extent autonomous. In this instance, the pattern of Buddhist monasticism is modified by the Vajrayāna stress on the *lama* (Tibetan *bla ma* = Sanskrit *guru*) – the Vajrayāna masters/gurus are the focus (although not always the chief administrators) of each monastery and wider tradition.

Certain doctrinal positions or specialisms in specific practices are associated with each school but, just as in the ancient Buddhist orders, there are no rigid sectarian boundaries. Movement between monasteries and study within institutions of different affiliation has never been uncommon and there has also been constant cross-fertilization of teachings at the highest level, senior lamas sometimes receiving teaching lineages of lamas from different schools. An old tendency not to consider a lama's education complete without some training from lamas of other schools, became prominent through the impact of the nineteenth century non-sectarian (*ris med*) movement, and even more so in the troubled contemporary situation. With the breakdown of formal mechanisms of social integration, there is increased concern for informal co-operation.

Cutting across the schools are three models of religious practice, each with precedents in Indian Buddhism: (1) the scholar monk; (2) the ascetic renouncer specializing in meditation; (3) the lay *mantra practitioner*, a tantric religious specialist. Frequently highly trained in Vajrayāna texts and meditation, lay mantra practitioners maintain a strict code of conduct distinct from the monks' code, and not entailing celibacy. Whilst different Tibetan schools have different emphases – some specializing in scholastic training, others on meditative retreats – the three types of practice are represented in each. There may also be movement from one pole to another at different stages of an individual's life, of a hermitage or even a monastic tradition. Meditators, responsible for exemplifying the goal, may repeatedly 'escape' from the world, only to find that they must cater for enthusiastic followers requesting the establishment of teaching centres, and the cycle begins again.

The third (lay) model of religious practice does not seem to have quite such ancient precedents in Indian Buddhism as the other two. In India we find a division of labour between monastics and layfolk, giving the laity important duties, but not generally the expectation of study and meditation focused on realization. Mahāyāna Buddhism introduced the theory that a lay person could work for, and even exemplify, the qualities of enlightenment, following the *bodhisattva* ethic to bring all beings to enlightenment. The idea that lay practice of *bodhisattva* virtues such as generosity and patience provides excellent potential for real spiritual progress is one which has persisted in lay traditions of practice in Tibetan Buddhism, but the model for the serious lay religious in Tibetan Buddhism is principally orientated to tantric traditions. Lay mantra practitioners may be considered to be of great religious stature, often preserving high status hereditary lineages, and in premodern Tibet sometimes inter-marrying with the aristocracy. Their religious training might include periods of retreat, pilgrimages and travel to visit religious masters, but the ideal type mantra practitioner would marry and live within a lay community, frequently serving the population with ritual skills. Many mantra practitioners were not of renowned stock or high status, and there were some entire communities of lay religious specialists.

Different kinds of religious institutions are associated with each of the three models: respectively, scholastic institutes within large monasteries, mountain hermitages and lay mantra practitioner communities or yellow householder (*gser khyim*) villages. Just as it is often impossible to draw clear lines between practitioners – since individuals may combine or shift between each type – so these religious institutions were rarely entirely separate. A hermitage might become a settled monastery; large monasteries might support retreat facilities and lay practitioners might participate in local monastic ritual. A monastery's reincarnate lamas (*sprul sku*) may be found in mantra practitioner families, and hereditary and monastic lineages may coincide in one individual. The three kinds of exemplary practitioners and institutions were all supported by the large-scale funding of religion at state and local level in Tibet. There was a higher proportion of monks than in other Buddhist societies, some recruited by government conscription as well as voluntary family donations of sons, and ordinary monks, who performed either ritual or administrative and other non-religious tasks, and who outnumbered trained scholar and meditator monks.

In premodern Tibet, there was often much stability in monastic institutions over generations, with long-standing local support backed by monastic land holdings and the political structure. Buddhist monasteries were almost everywhere central to sociopolitical organization in Tibetan speaking societies, although their exact role varied considerably owing to differences in social structure in different regions and at different historical periods. In politically centralized regions, large monasteries were part of the governmental administrative system. In contrast, in decentralized areas, monasteries helped to integrate local populations. Continuity of religious organization was provided by land owning monasteries which in various ways were part of the political system, but at the same time the Tibetan Buddhist emphasis on the lama generated some dynamism. As in the followings of Indian Hindu *gurus*, there was some individual and community choice in religious patronage; monasteries and hermitages might rise or decline according to the reputation of their principal lamas. Within the overall monastic structure, then, we find a multiplicity of religious authorities, summed up in the proverb, 'every district its own dialect, every lama his own religious practice'. A monastery needed its lamas, but its lamas would not always conform to the practices favoured by the monastic order concerned, and they might occasionally fulfil the ideal spiritual life pattern more successfully by escaping from the confines of their monastery.

In the Tibetan context secular authorities rarely entirely dominated religious authorities. The principle of the fusion of religious and secular authority (*chos srid zung 'brel*) was a powerful ideal in Tibetan society, drawing on pan-Buddhist symbolism of the righteous monarch (see above). The strength of the religious *vis-à-vis* secular authorities, except in instances of national submission of Tibetan religious authorities to foreign powers (Mongol and Manchu) which had few implications for religious organization, often contrasts with the situation that pertained in Southeast Asia.

Gender

There is no single Buddhist approach to gender issues. One significant strand emphasizes that in terms of spiritual attainment, women and men have equal capabilities and that women not only can but also in many cases have attained liberation. Such a perspective is found in a number of sources of different periods, including early Buddhist literature, Mahāyāna sūtras, and tantric writings. Furthermore, Buddhist doctrines do not differentiate between men and women since everyone, regardless of gender, status or age, is subject to old age, illness and mortality, and the suffering and impermanence which mark conditioned existence apply equally to all. There are stories of women and even children who attained enlightenment during the time of the Buddha. Many early Buddhist nuns, called *therīs*, were said to have attained liberation.

In premodern Asian societies, structures supporting female participation in the Buddhist Saṅgha persisted. Contemporary Buddhists seeking more egalitarian gender relations within the tradition have found inspiration in these aspects of early Buddhism. Nonetheless, the picture is modified both by doctrinal elements, which appear to qualify or contradict the theory of spiritual equality, and by organizational features which formally relegate women to a subservient status and restrict them from taking part in the decision-making of the Buddhist community. There are also statements in Buddhist scriptures which appear to be misogynist, such as the presentation of women as obstructers of men's spiritual progress or the notion that a woman's birth is an inferior one with less opportunity for spiritual practice. These are open to other interpretations. In societies where men have access to authority and wider choices, a negative judgement on women's fate might be seen as simply reflecting empirical reality. Furthermore, the religious literature is more likely to address men and hence we find the Buddhist emphasis on renunciation of sensual desires and worldly concerns expressed in terms of the problems with attachment to women more frequently than we find the reverse. Yet the distinction between recognizing *actual* gender inequalities and commenting on women's *innate* nature might not be obvious and such statements have been used to justify acceptance of the situation. Matters have been exacerbated by the organizational structure of the Saṅgha: the community was stratified by gender, so that even senior nuns were junior to all categories of monks, and the autonomy of nuns was restricted. This formal structure may help to explain the relative smallness of the nuns' order and its inability to survive long-term in most Buddhist countries. Individual ability or attainment was irrelevant in the ranking system, and thus a low status did not necessarily imply a deficient spiritual practice. Yet, it is clear that both in the past and the present, the weakness of institutions for female practitioners, coupled with higher valuation of monks in Asian societies, resulted in the nuns having fewer opportunities to receive instruction or to practise the Buddhist teachings.

INTERACTIONS WITH MODERNITY

Southeast Asia

Southern Buddhist countries mainly responded to colonialism and the forces of modernization both by reassessing their traditional religious identity and by strengthening the foundation of their monastic institutions. Also, Buddhist revival manifested as cultural resistance and political protest against foreign domination, with monks actively involved in the independence movements (against British rule) in both Sri Lanka and Burma. After independence, many Southeast Asian countries were directly affected by communism and the Cold War, and monastic communities became increasingly drawn into the ideological battle between communism and its alternatives. During the 1960s and 1970s Buddhism in Laos and Cambodia sometimes became a vehicle for local political factions advancing their political agendas. As the nation state has become increasingly dominant in Buddhist societies, education and welfare have ceased to be the exclusive preserve of religion, while patronage by kings and religious patrons has been lost. Yet the Saṅgha – as the only organization to have retained its position still equipped with a national network independent of state administration – has been expected to perform co-operative roles in nation building and social development. As monks sought new identities in a fast changing world, they came under increasing pressure to guide the public into a new era. Simultaneously, lay Buddhist activists have been gaining unprecedented importance in new Buddhist movements of a reformist and modernist hue.

▌ AWARENESS (APPAMĀDA-VAGGO)

The *Dhammapada* is an important and popular scripture in the Pali tradition. Contemporary Theravāda authorities recognize the second chapter, from which the extracts here are taken, to have special contemporary relevance.

The path to the Deathless is awareness;
Unawareness, the path of death.
They who are aware do not die;
They who are unaware are as dead . . .

Those meditators, persevering,
Forever firm of enterprise,
Those steadfast ones touch Nibbāna,
Incomparable release from bonds.

By standing alert, by awareness,
By restraint and control too,
The intelligent one could make an island
That a flood does not overwhelm.

Fame increases for the one who stands alert,
Mindful, and of pure deeds;
Who with due consideration acts, restrained,
Who lives dhamma, being aware . . .

Engage not in unawareness,
Nor in intimacy with sensual delight.
Meditating, the one who is aware
Attains extensive ease . . .

Among those unaware, the one aware,
Among the sleepers, the wide-awake,
The one with great wisdom moves on,
As a racehorse who leaves behind a nag.

(From J. R. Carter and Mahinda Palihawadana (trans.), *Sacred Writings, Buddhism: The Dhammapada*, New York: Quality Paperback Book Club, 1992)

Sri Lanka (Ceylon until 1972)

Sri Lanka is geographically part of South Asia, but has clear cultural links with Southeast Asia. Compared with Southeast Asian countries, Sri Lanka was subjected to foreign domination for much longer – ever since Portuguese traders arrived at the beginning of the sixteenth century. Although it remained independent during earlier periods of Portuguese and Dutch influence, the central Kandyan kingdom came under British rule in 1815. Christian missionaries and British rule challenged the *status quo* of Sinhala (Sri Lankan) Buddhists, and encouraged active involvement in religious dialogue and reassessment of religious and cultural identity. Buddhists had some success in debate with Christians in the late nineteenth century, arguing that Buddhism was neither backward nor superstitious, but rather a rational, indeed scientific, teaching.

An important Buddhist reformer, Anagārika Dharmapāla (1864–1933), founded the Maha Bodhi Society in 1891, and attempted to create a modern Sinhala-Buddhist identity. He was one of the main exponents of a new form of Buddhism often referred to as 'Protestant Buddhism', a term first coined by Obeyesekere in 1970 to refer to the 'protest' against Christian missionaries, coupled with the adoption by Buddhist revivalists in Sri Lanka of some of the traits and methods used by Protestant Christianity. Those sympathetic to this movement came largely from the English-speaking urban middle class whose religious orientation was liberal and modernist. They manifested a puritan streak, emphasizing moral discipline and meditation, and there was a shift of emphasis from traditional merit making (through offerings to monks) to individual responsibility. There also emerged a new type of Buddhist activism, which considered social engagement relevant for spiritual growth.

Involvement in the independence movement included even scholarly monks such as Walpola Rahula (1907–97), who became openly active in the mid-1940s, promoting religious patriotism and arguing that monks had a duty to engage in national politics for the welfare of the people. The period after independence in 1948 saw renewed enthusiasm and pride in the Buddhist heritage. Sri Lankan monks travelled abroad to teach and instruct in meditation, while eminent Buddhist scholars published influential writings in Buddhist philosophy. The EBP (Eksath Bhikkhu Peramuna) was formed in 1952, a monastic political party which, alongside populist grass root groups with lay and monastic leaders such as MEP (Mahajana Eksath Peramuna), became active in promoting Sinhala Buddhist nationalism.

However, not all monks supported the nationalist Sinhala political ethos. Some have opposed the fusion of Buddhism and nationalism, fearing that it fuels ethnic conflict with the (Hindu) Tamils. Others have considered social development and politics a distraction from spiritual development. Forest monks have revived the traditional ascetic ideal, retreating from human habitation and secular activities to concentrate on meditation. Their followers include many modernist lay Buddhists attracted to their ancient ideal and stoical discipline.

Laos, Cambodia, Burma

Buddhism in twentieth-century Laos, Cambodia and Burma demonstrates how relations with communist and socialist regimes have varied. In Laos, for instance, the government tried to control the Saṅgha more effectively by centralizing monastic administration and issuing monks with government identity cards to counter communist infiltration. The Pathet Lao revolutionary movement had infiltrated the Saṅgha from the 1950s by propagating anti-imperialist slogans and appealing to monks from rural and poorer areas. In response, in a strategy similar to that employed in Thailand, the government in the 1960s began to recruit and train monks to provide leadership for rural development and become the vanguard of anti-communist propaganda. Divisions within the Saṅgha (Thommayut and Mohanikay orders in Cambodia, and Thammanyut and Mahanikay in Laos, for example), representing a divide between urban elite and rural peasants, added to the polarization process.

The 1970s saw Buddhism dragged even further into revolutionary struggle. After Pathet Lao came to power in Laos in 1975, there were further efforts to find common ground between Buddhism and socialism. Monks were again used as propaganda agents to gain support for the communist regime, preaching that the two ideologies are compatible. Simultaneously, traditional Buddhist beliefs underwent scrutiny and those regarded as 'superstitious' by communist lights (including much of the cosmology) were purged. Even the traditional notion of *karma* was rejected during this time. The custom of feeding monks and donating to monasteries was regarded as redundant, so the only option for monks in Laos was to become part of the political agenda. Young monks were encouraged to join the revolution as teachers and health workers. Yet Buddhism was never targeted to the degree that it was in Cambodia; the party was relatively careful not to provide a focus for popular resentment.

In Cambodia, in contrast, the Khmer Rouge, a quasi-socialist movement advocating rural living and economic self-sufficiency, attacked Buddhism with devastating consequences during its short reign from 1975–9. Now called Kampuchea, the country came under the political control of the despotic leader Pol Pot. In their political campaign, the Khmer Rouge targeted Buddhism as foreign, unpatriotic and valueless. Monks were labelled corrupt and lazy and sent for re-education. Villagers were discouraged from offering donations or inviting monks to officiate rituals, so Cambodian monks were also deprived of traditional sources of income. In the revolutionary excesses, more than 60 thousand monks are said to have been killed or forced to disrobe. Buddhism went into considerable decline.

Since the late 1980s, however, reconstruction of monasteries and rebuilding of the ecclesiastical structure and system of monastic education has begun in both Laos and Cambodia. Especially in Cambodia where Buddhism came near to extinction, religious rebuilding began in earnest with the support of foreign aid. In recent years, the monastic community seems to be reclaiming its place as an essential institution, uniting the torn country and people. Buddhist monks have been active in the restoration movement and since 1992, a new non-partisan Buddhist activism has manifested in an annual peace march initiated by monk Maha Ghosananda.

Burma offers yet another example of relations between state and religion. The Burmese Saṅgha remained relatively unified despite British rule and the demise of the kingship in 1853, notwithstanding its history of fragmentation into sects and branches. Christian missionaries were active from the early nineteenth century, but interfaith dialogue and rigorous soul searching were less evident than in Sri Lanka. Nor did Burma produce prominent religious leaders such as Dharmapāla in Sri Lanka or scholar monks like Buddhadasa in Thailand to advocate new directions for contemporary spirituality. Yet the Saṅgha retained its traditional reciprocal relationships with the laity, commanding authority and respect, and providing a core for Burmese nationalism. It also maintained high standards of Buddhist scholarship among both monks and nuns, producing many famous meditation teachers in recent times.

The first Prime Minister of Burma after independence, U Nu (r.1948–62) cast himself in the role of an ideal Buddhist ruler, applying Aśokan ideals to his political policies. He promoted a type of Buddhist nationalism by implementing moral policies and hosting the Sixth Great Buddhist Council in 1954 to commemorate the 2,500th anniversary of the Buddha's death and enlightenment. However, his enthusiasm to revive the Buddhist ideal proved unable to accommodate the political realities of the time. In 1962, he was removed in the military coup led by General Ne Win. Although Ne Win's socialist government attempted to distance religion from politics, it did lay claim to the traditional role of precolonial Buddhist states, attempting to control the Saṅgha by introducing compulsory registration and removing anti-government monks from positions of influence. In 1980 the Saṅgha was reorganized

52

into a hierarchical structure parallel to that in the secular administration. Due to its isolationist policies, Burma remained secluded from the rest of the world. There were no public protests and monks withdrew from politics. Ironically, this period allowed the Saṅgha to consolidate the relationship with its lay congregation, providing them with a solid moral base, later to develop into a strong foundation to unite and counter political oppression.

It seems that one in every two monks participated in the demonstrations and public assemblies during the anti-government uprising in 1988. Although monks did not directly participate in violence, they were actively supportive of the pro-democratic movement and later of the NLD (National League for Democracy) led by Aung San Su Kyi which won the 1990 election. In the following two years, however, the military regime arrested hundreds of monk activists, forcing many to disrobe or escape to Thailand. This fuelled the Saṅgha and Burmese people to become even more defiant of the government, and later the same year Mandalay monks went on strike, overturning their begging bowls and symbolically depriving soldiers of the chance to acquire spiritual merit. Despite supervision of the Saṅgha by the Ministry of Religious Affairs, and the fact that the governing executive Saṅgha Council comprised senior abbots in a privileged position in relation to the state, the monastic community retained a degree of autonomy and its own national network of influence, maintaining independent links with its lay devotees in non-government sectors of society. Since the mid-1990s, the military government has made increased and explicit displays of donations to the Saṅgha, attempting to win back the favour of monks it had antagonized. Nevertheless, the Burmese Saṅgha has continued to serve as an alternative focus of defiance, using its influence that reaches down to the village level. Some even perceive the Saṅgha as the last hope in their struggle for democracy.

THAILAND

Thailand is the only Southeast Asian country that did not come under colonial rule, and it has been politically secure and prosperous since the late eighteenth century. The kingship has remained intact and lent Thailand stability, although it moved to constitutional monarchy and parliamentary government in 1932. The present King Bhumibol has exerted special authority at times of national crisis, and during the two attempted coups d'état in the 1980s, both of which failed to receive royal approval. In contrast to gradual development and social adjustment in Sri Lanka, Thailand has experienced rapid economic growth and major structural changes in the last forty years. With one of the world's fastest growing economies, the country has reaped some of the consequences in social and regional dislocation, inequality, corruption and disenchantment with the establishment. There have been social protests, and reformist Buddhist movements led by lay activists have emerged since the 1970s.

The state has played a major role in modernizing Thai Buddhism since the time of King Monghut (r.1851–68), conducting Saṅgha reforms, founding the Thammayut lineage, and introducing a new form of monasticism. King Chulalongkorn (r.1868–1910) continued his father's legacy in centralizing Saṅgha administration, uniting the sects and standardizing Buddhist education for monks. However, Buddhism seems to have changed most after Sarit Tharanat's government came to power in 1957, as he actively sought to strengthen national unity by bringing together traditional values associated with the king and Buddhism. Monks were trained for national programmes to promote community development in peripheral regions, and the government, perhaps fearing communist infiltration, sent them to minister to ethnic groups in the northern hills. The Saṅgha thus became part of the political programme for the promotion of national goals. In the process, monks who expressed opposition to government policies, such as the Mahanikay monk Phra Phimolatham, were labelled communists and expelled from the order.

Public regard for the Saṅgha in Thailand diminished as a consequence of the close relationship between the government, military, big business and the Saṅgha. Mounting disenchantment was expressed at the lack of spiritual direction provided by monks in a rapidly growing consumerist society. One consequence was that reformist Buddhist groups emerged in urban centres in the 1970s, representing a new movement motivated initially by urban middle class lay activists and students hoping to force the Saṅgha to overcome corruption and assert religious leadership. One of the most important religious reformers in the twentieth century was the monk Buddhadasa (1906–93), who integrated modernist rationalism and a distinctive forest tradition. His liberal interpretation of canonical texts attracted an educated elite following, and provided an ideological base for contemporary Buddhist activism. Although Buddhadasa was a 'career monk' who had received traditional religious education, he was remarkably critical of the Saṅgha and of the contemporary social situation. He rejected ritual practice and merit-making, and interpreted traditional concepts such as not-self, nirvāṇa, rebirth, and emptiness as moral principles for 'this' life. Although Buddhadasa's movement, Suan Mokkh (Garden of Liberation), was not supported by mainstream Buddhists, he left an important legacy of new directions for cultivating contemporary spirituality and promoting 'this-worldly' Buddhism.

A group directly indebted to Buddhadasa is Santi Asok, started by Phra Bodhiraksa in 1970. It manifested as a sectarian protest movement that came to Thai people's attention by repeatedly criticizing the national Saṅgha. The Asok movement presented a new Buddhist vision, replacing traditional ritual with hard work and stoical discipline, frugal communal living and agricultural self-sufficiency. In short, the members presented a radical moral critique of contemporary Thai society and the Saṅgha by living an alternative lifestyle. In contrast, other lay Buddhist groups attracted the rich and successful by embracing capitalist values and consumerist lifestyles. Thus Thammakai (Dharma-Body) led by Phra Thammajayo and Phra Thattajiwo and established in the 1970s, for example, advocated a type of visualization meditation through which it claimed followers could become even more successful in reaping the fruits of the capitalist economy.

In recent years, Buddhist lay social activists in Thailand such as Sulak Sivaraksa have fought against social injustice and environmental degradation. There are also activist monks, such as Phra Khru Man Nathipitak, who affiliated themselves with Sekhiya Dhamma Saṅgha founded in 1989, and participated in education and community development. These monks, addressing contemporary problems of deforestation, poverty, drug addition and AIDS, have been criticized for their close involvement in worldly affairs. However, many justified their involvement as duty to the community but distinguished themselves from the so-called development monks involved in state programmes of development. By contrast, the forest monk tradition continues, especially in the northeast, concentrating on meditation and traditional practices of magical protection and ritual, and resisting the hegemonic power of the national Saṅgha.

GENDER AND STATUS IN SOUTHEAST ASIAN BUDDHISM

In the Theravāda tradition the monks have been religious leaders and teachers, providing role models for Buddhist morality. The equivalent ordination lineage of female monks called *bhikkhunīs* apparently disappeared in eleventh-century Ceylon and thirteenth-century Burma, and since that time Theravāda nuns have been without official religious status. Although they shave their hair, fast in the afternoons and are celibate, contemporary nuns in the Southern tradition are seen as no more than 'pious lay women'. They observe eight to ten Buddhist precepts, which are equivalent to those observed by pious lay people on special religious occasions. Nonetheless, Buddhist nuns have been integrally involved in the monastic community, actively supporting the monks and novices. In Southern Buddhist countries today, there are approximately 5 thousand nuns in Sri Lanka, 8 thousand nuns in Thailand, 5 thousand nuns in Cambodia and Laos, and more than 25 thousand nuns in Burma. The fact that the number of nuns is so large and is increasing implies that, in practice, female renunciants perform important religious functions.

Figure 2.1 A nun collecting alms. Burmese Buddhist nuns who are completely dependent on the lay population for material support go for alms roughly twice every eight days according to the lunar calendar. They are given cooked rice and cash in contrast to monks who are given cooked rice and curry

Figure 2.2 Young nuns paying respect to their teacher. The seniority in the monastic community is decided not by age but by the number of rain retreats (once every year) spent as a monastic. They also pay respect to their preceptors and teachers who guide them throughout their career

Since the mid-1980s, the movement to restore the *bhikkhunī* lineage, initially instigated by Western Buddhist nuns and intellectuals, has been increasingly supported by local Buddhists. They assert that the female Vinaya lineage has survived in the Dharmagupta Vinaya preserved in East Asia, and thus the ordination procedure for Southern Buddhist nuns could theoretically be revived. In 1988, the first higher ordination was conferred on five Sinhalese nuns in Los Angeles with the support of the international Saṅgha, and since then these nuns have been in the vanguard of the new restoration movement. In 1996, ten Sinhalese nuns became *bhikkhunīs* in Saranath, India. However, once ordinations began on the island of Dambulla in Sri Lanka, opposition grew vociferous, and proponents of the *bhikkhunī* restoration were criticized for creating disunity in the Sinhalese Saṅgha. The difficulty for *bhikkhunīs* lies in the fact that their future remains in the hands of senior monks who influence Saṅgha opinion and the general public on whom they are dependent. Meanwhile, nuns in Thailand, Burma and of the Burmese lineage in Nepal are observing how the present situation in Sri Lanka may develop before making similar commitments.

From a social perspective, women in Southeast Asian societies (even in Muslim dominated Malaysia and Indonesia) have traditionally enjoyed high social status and economic independence. They are visibly active and a large proportion of them engage in market trade as family breadwinners. The bilateral kinship system and lack of emphasis on the family as a collective unit seems to have supported flexibility in gender roles, while marriage and child bearing do not reduce women's status. The situation, however, is gradually changing. The growth of the Chinese population has brought Confucian values to the region, in which women are subordinate within their husbands' families. Even if traditional advantages persist, high social standing does not seem to generate authority for women in the religious domain. On the contrary, according to their self-perception and religious ideology, economic power is not seen as a source of spiritual potency but more as a reflection of women's 'this-worldly' and materialistic nature. By the same token, motherhood is valued for Buddhist women, yet simultaneously depicted in vernacular texts as symbolizing attachment which binds them to the cycle of rebirth, restricting spiritual progress. Nevertheless, opting out of marriage and child bearing as a nun brings opposition and hostility rather than moral support.

The presence of contemporary nuns in Southeast Asia seems to challenge the cultural and religious ideal allowing males to renounce householder roles and become monks, whilst expecting females to look after the family and support the Saṅgha. A male is thought to have opportunities to steadily work towards enlightenment, but a female can only hope for a better rebirth. The nuns are anomalous in this scheme yet remain supportive of the Saṅgha. For example, in many Burmese monasteries, they are indispensable as treasurers and secretaries, accepting donation money and preparing ceremonies on behalf of the monks. Despite their position of influence, they are symbolically seen as spiritually inferior due to the frequent handling of a substance symbolizing 'worldly pollution'. The nuns also cook for and look after the welfare of monks and novices. By taking on subservient roles and merging their interests in the Saṅgha, however, they seem to have made their unofficial religious position acceptable. Whilst lay Buddhists are claiming more religious influence and questioning the traditional role of the Saṅgha, it seems crucial that the monks realize that the sustenance of the Saṅgha also relies on these nuns who protect the sanctity of monks from the encroaching influence of worldly corruption.

Tibet

THE IMPACT OF CHINESE COMMUNISM

In the first half of the twentieth century, Tibet was neither politically nor economically isolated. Lamas travelling to India arranged for religious works to be printed using modern printing presses, a development which would lead to wider readerships. The renowned Gelukpa scholar monk dGe-'dun chos-'phel, influenced by new social and intellectual contacts, composed untraditional literary tracts. However, the religious establishment as a whole, and especially the principal Gelukpa monasteries in the Lhasa area, exercizing a *de facto* veto over the government, strongly resisted socio-economic change, which they saw as threatening the dharma. Modifications to the sociopolitical structure were begun with the support of the Thirteenth Dalai Lama (1876–1933), but the changes were limited by monastic interests.

Thus Tibet's first large-scale encounter with modernity came with the Chinese communist invasion and occupation of Tibet from the early 1950s. Radical socio-economic upheaval, appropriations of wealth and attacks on monastic institutions were begun in eastern Tibet in the 1950s, and throughout Tibet after the abortive 1959 uprising, when about 100 thousand refugees escaped to India and surrounding countries. Forcible political and economic reorganization was justified in terms of a Marxist ideology infused with an imperialist emphasis on allegiance to the Chinese state, and by notions of Tibetan sociocultural backwardness and their need to be helped to progress by their Chinese masters. Matters were further exacerbated by the Chinese Cultural Revolution, in which even private religious expressions and Tibetan cultural traditions were suppressed. The entire monastic system and its socio-economic support structure was disbanded, many monks and nuns forced to disrobe, and even much of the textual heritage destroyed.

After the Cultural Revolution, which in the Tibetan case did not end until the early 1980s, the Chinese communist rhetoric of liberation from imperialism, feudalism and religion was toned down, and there were some liberalizations, permitting limited religious activities in a recognition that outright oppression of religion had been counter-productive. The change of policy was also fuelled by the hope that further economic integration into the People's Republic of China (PRC) would undermine Tibetan religious belief and practice without the need for costly forcible repression. Different factions within the Chinese government today remain divided over policies towards 'minority' ethnic groups and religions. One approach favours toleration towards religion and different ethnic cultural traditions so long as they provide no threat to national unity, and accept institutional state control. The other hardline approach points to the role of religion and ethnic traditions in resisting political and economic integration, and continues to see the outright suppression of religion as a necessity. This faction has been increasingly vocal and influential since 1995, and especially in the Lhasa and central Tibetan areas there has been some renewal of interference even in individual religious expressions.

Figure 2.3 Monks and lay people gather to hear the Dalai Lama (seated far right) talk, Dharamsala, India, 1996

From the outset, a major effect of Chinese persecution was to strengthen Tibetan concern to preserve their cultural heritage; Buddhism became a symbol of Tibetan ethnic aspirations. The remarkable success of the 'reconstruction' of Tibetan monasteries since the early 1960s by Tibetan exiles in the Indian subcontinent and beyond, and since the early 1980s by Tibetans in the PRC, must be related to the urgency of a people whose culture has suffered devastation. Yet while there is stress on recovering and preserving 'tradition', we are not dealing with conservatism. Indeed, a conservative rejection of modernity is not an option given the loss of Tibetan political and economic autonomy and of the traditional system for monastic support. Of necessity, contemporary monasteries are organized within an entirely different legal and economic framework from that which existed in premodern Tibet, and lamas must attract patronage not only from traditional sponsors, such as Himalayan Buddhists in the case of the exiled monasteries, but also from wider international sources, especially East Asian and Western Buddhists.

Thus the premodern pattern of a multiplicity of religious authorities and of various religious traditions cutting across monastic affiliations described above has become even more prominent in recent history, with neither the former Tibetan governmental apparatus nor the institutional centres of each monastic order retaining any effective socio-economic controls over individual lamas or monasteries. In the Indian subcontinent, the government-in-exile structure has brought some cohesion, but has had little effect on monastic organization. At the local level, Tibetans have attempted to keep alive some traditional connections between monasteries and communities. In exile, some of the monasteries represent groups of refugees from specific areas who have worked to rebuild their own monasteries. In Tibet, in similar efforts to re-establish relations between local monasteries and lay communities, Tibetans resist Chinese policies defining religion in terms of individual belief, but their success is inevitably restricted in a political climate in which the state will still not tolerate any threat to its monopoly of power. In some Himalayan Buddhist regions such as parts of Nepal and Ladakh, the effects of integration into the national economy and society has often reduced the political influence of traditional Buddhist institutions, while religious renewal has been encouraged by closer links with Tibetan exiled lamas and their new monasteries.

In terms of individual religious practice of the three types in Tibetan Buddhism (see above), opportunities for each were curtailed by the devastation of Buddhism in Tibet. The scholarly institutes were affected most severely; in Tibet, an entire generation was denied the option of scholastic training, and by the 1980s there were few surviving scholar monk teachers. Now, however, there is some revival of scholarly institutes and training. Meditation teaching was also severely disrupted, although meditation traditions are more able to survive without institutional backing. While open practice of long contemplative retreats was only possible outside the PRC until recent years, some meditation masters have gained renown through stories of their seemingly miraculous escape from persecution during the Cultural Revolution. Although no one was unaffected by the radical change enforced on Tibetan society, it would appear that the lay mantra practitioner religious practices were not altogether eclipsed, since their integration with lay life made them less obvious targets for anti-Buddhist persecution.

TRANSFORMATION AND RENEWAL OF TRADITION

The new international contexts in which Tibetan Buddhism must now survive, and indeed appears to thrive, coupled with weakening of traditional institutional regulation, have fostered an environment conducive to new and varied presentations of Buddhist teaching. Tibetan lamas now cater for Tibetans who receive modern education and may work in modern economies in the PRC, India and elsewhere, for Himalayan Buddhists, for Central Asian Buddhists involved in post-Soviet reconstructions of their own religious heritage, for Chinese and other East Asian Buddhists, for Western Buddhists with various cultural backgrounds. In some senses, Tibetan Buddhism has been rapidly catapulted from a premodern social context to one of postmodernity, missing out on some characteristic features of the encounter with modernity, such as gradual engagement with scientific rationality and modern nation states.

This does not mean that Buddhist doctrines are being radically reformulated or Buddhist practices changed beyond recognition. On the contrary, great efforts are put into the recovery of the scriptural heritage and the preservation of meditative and ritual traditions. Elaborate rituals with established written liturgies and ritual manuals remain central to monastic life, and there is considerable support for long contemplative retreats along traditional lines. Rather, creativity is evident in the ways in which tradition is interpreted to contemporary Tibetans and non-Tibetans, with variations in choice of practices, and an emphasis that teaching should relate to audience and situation.

In Tibet itself we currently find instances where (a) Buddhist revival steers a careful path between enhancing Tibetan identity and co-operating with the Chinese authorities, and (b) more confrontational approaches in which modern ideas concerning human rights and democracy are blended with Buddhism in opposition to the restrictions and ideology of the Chinese state. In the diaspora community there has been involvement in conversations with Western sympathizers on contemporary issues such as war and peace, environmental degradation and feminism. The Dalai Lama has written extensively in English, combining quite traditional Buddhist ethical perspectives with modern concerns.

In premodern Tibet, the Dalai Lama had been the head of state, a role which had not always entailed direct political involvement, but an active and politically skilled Dalai Lama could have a major impact on government. The Dalai Lama was an important figure of the Geluk tradition, which was politically and numerically dominant in Central Tibet, but his religious authority went beyond sectarian boundaries. While he had no formal or institutional role in each religious tradition, which was headed by its own high lamas, he was a unifying symbol of the Tibetan state, representing Buddhist values and traditions above any specific school. Furthermore, he was held in the highest esteem and treated with great devotion by Tibetans well beyond the political boundaries of premodern Tibet. This traditional function of a Dalai Lama as an ecumenical figure, holding together disparate religious and regional groups, has been enthusiastically taken up by the present Fourteenth Dalai Lama, who has worked to overcome sectarian and other divisions in the exiled community, and has become a symbol of Tibetan nationhood for Tibetans both in Tibet and in exile. At the same time, the Dalai Lama has expanded his constituency even further and become a major international representative not only of the Buddhist tradition, but also of ethical values which he sees as going beyond Buddhism and even beyond particular religions. As such, he has actively participated in international forums, has become widely respected globally, and has attracted popular support in Asian and Western countries.

▌ H.H. THE DALAI LAMA

I am a comparative newcomer to the modern world. Although I fled my homeland as long ago as 1959, and although my life since then as a refugee in India has brought me into much closer contact with contemporary society, my formative years were spent largely cut off from the realities of the twentieth century. This was partly due to my appointment as Dalai Lama: I became a monk at a very early age. It also reflects the fact that we Tibetans had chosen – mistakenly in my view – to remain isolated behind the high mountain ranges which separate our country from the rest of the world . . .

In the past, families and small communities could exist more or less independently of one another . . . This is no longer the case. Today's reality is so complex and, so clearly interconnected on the material level that a different outlook is needed . . . we cannot afford to ignore others' interests any longer . . .

Given today's reality, it is therefore essential to cultivate a sense of what I call universal responsibility. This may not be an exact translation of the Tibetan term I have in mind, *chi-sem*, which means literally universal (*chi*) consciousness (*sem*) . . . . What is entailed . . . is . . . a re-orientation of our heart and mind away from self and towards others . . .

It is a matter of common sense . . . There is no denying that our happiness is inextricably bound up with the happiness of others . . . Thus we can reject everything else: religion, ideology, all received wisdom. But we cannot escape the necessity of love and compassion.

(*Ancient Wisdom, Modern World: Ethics for a New Millennium,*
London: Little, Brown & Co., 1999)

Another recent development is the transportation of Buddhist ritual symbolism into environments foreign to its traditional contexts – for example, *maṇḍalas* constructed for cultural exhibitions, or monastic ritual dances performed in modern theatres. Tibetan lamas have encouraged the development of Internet sites to propagate and advertise their teachings, monasteries and new-style Buddhist centres, and popular books on Buddhist practice have appeared, written in English and with international sales, frequently simplifying traditional Buddhist practices to make them accessible to non-specialists. At the same time, the centre of gravity in Tibetan Buddhism remains with lamas based in monasteries in the Indian subcontinent and Tibet; these lamas have reservations about the value of relatively superficial explorations of the religion, and work for the establishment of more serious supports for Buddhist practice, such as long-term retreat facilities.

AUTHORITY IN CONTEMPORARY TIBETAN BUDDHISM

Different traditional understandings of what constitutes 'authentic' Buddhism live on; some are more problematic than others in adapting to postmodern contexts. One perspective emphasizes that the body of scriptures stemming from the historical Buddha constitute the ultimate authority as 'Buddha Word'. An alternative approach is more flexible, allowing for new scriptural revelations of 'Buddha Word' derived from ongoing visionary experiences of transcendent Buddhas. A collection of Indic Buddhist scriptures, the *Kanjur* (*bka' 'gyur*), considered to be the historical Buddha's actual words (but now shown by modern scholars mainly to derive from later Indian developments) was compiled in the fourteenth century. Conservative Tibetan scholars saw this as the only authentic 'Buddha Word', a view which often dominated politically influential scholastic traditions. Such a perspective can only persist today by ignoring modern scholarship. Whilst such conservatism remains common amongst the present generation of Tibetan lamas and their students, adherence to it does not appear to be a viable long-term strategy.

The alternative idea that new scriptures may be appropriate for different times was principally represented by the Nyingmapa (*rnying ma pa*) who follow the 'Ancient Tantras' (*rnying ma'i rgyud*). Many of these scriptures were rejected from the Kanjur because of non-Indic origins. The Nyingmapa still reveal new tantric scriptures (*gTer ma*) today. Nyingma *gTer ma* traditions were popular amongst the widespread small-scale monasteries and lay practitioner communities of the Nyingmapa, and also in some Kagyupa and Sakyapa circles. In principle, this more flexible approach to 'Buddha Word' is less threatened by modern historical findings, and new revelations by prominent mantra practitioner lamas are also playing a role in the dynamics of Tibetan Buddhist reconstruction.

The meditative traditions which can be found across the different schools may also have little problem with modern scholarship, since their 'truths' depend more on experience than on historical evidence. In practice, however, some lamas of these traditions may have as many reservations about modern academic work as the theoretically more conservative scholars, and this is especially the case amongst those meditator groups which emphasize faith above reason. The meditation vocation always had a central place in Tibetan Buddhism, and the idea that direct realization of enlightenment is a fruit of meditative endeavour and not of book learning remains powerful in Tibetan contexts. Today, it is also presented with some success to Western and other non-Tibetan pupils, some of whom may be happy to be spared the long study necessary to master the scholastic Buddhist traditions.

Despite the premodern mainstream scholastic acceptance of the idea of a closed canon of scripture, an important strand in Tibetan scholasticism emphasized the idea that the real essence of the 'Buddha Word' is to be defined in terms of its enlightening qualities, not in terms of historical authenticity. This was linked to a high valuation of the traditionally accepted works of interpretation and of Buddhist philosophy, which for many scholars were of greater value than the original scripture. Indeed, in Tibetan scholasticism, the main focus of the curriculum was the traditions of interpretation while the sūtras

Figure 2.4 Tibetan Buddhist monks at a monastery in Northern India in 1982, leading a procession beginning a public monastic ritual performance. The audience includes Himalayan Buddhists, Tibetans, local Indians and a few Westerners

were not directly studied, since they were considered difficult to understand, often appearing, at least superficially, to contradict one another. Logic and reasoning were given greater worth than mere scriptural citation, which was considered to have limited use without interpretation. Given the variety of messages in the sūtras, a typical concern of Tibetan scholars has been the re-ordering of classifications of Buddhist teachings in terms of whether they had final and definitive meaning, or merely provisional illustrative meanings that counteracted specific fallacies but were not illustrative of ultimate truth. Thus, although some of the assumptions of Buddhist scholastics, such as those concerning the historical origins of scriptures, are being challenged in today's world, the scholastic emphasis on reasoned argument and debate, and the scope for re-interpretation of scripture, means that not even the conservative wing of the scholastic tradition is as static or as closed to new approaches as it might at first appear.

Scholar monks and lamas today receive broader education than would be covered in traditional curricula, and not only do they have some modern education and foreign language training, but there has been some reworking of scholastic syllabuses. At the Central Institute of Higher Tibetan Studies in Sarnath, traditional and modern scholarship are combined in an institution in the Indian university sector, where scholars from different Tibetan traditions are represented and Sanskrit learning has been revived. There is scholastic interest in debates with Western and Indian philosophy, and some traditionally trained scholar monks have joined Western universities. While such exchanges may not be unproblematic for Buddhist scholarship, it seems likely that the traditions will be resilient enough to adapt and integrate more critical approaches to their textual heritage.

GENDER AND STATUS

Despite limitations on women's full participation in religious life, it would be a mistake to assume that women have entirely acquiesced in subservient roles in Buddhism. In the Tibetan case institutional restrictions often co-exist with active informal involvement. Women were unable to penetrate monastic hierarchies, and scholarly training, centred in high status monastic colleges, was not open to women. A small number of women from higher class and especially high status religious families were able to secure a good Buddhist education. But few nuns were well educated: nunneries, where they existed, were usually small-scale institutions, often junior partners to nearby monasteries. Nuns were generally expected to learn and recite prayers and rituals, not to study philosophy. Most nuns lived full- or part-time with their families rather than in nunneries, often having domestic duties. Yet, despite these impediments, at a local level vigorous nunneries might be established or expanded thanks to the efforts of determined nuns. Such cases were dependent on the inspiration and involvement of high status lamas and local community support. Women were not so constrained in the meditation traditions as they were in the formal authority structure of the Saṅgha and in scholarship. Some nuns made great efforts to travel to receive meditation instruction, and there was widespread acceptance of both male and female itinerant practitioners, who might spend extended periods visiting lamas, making pilgrimages and doing retreat. There were examples of women meditation adepts, a few of whom became teachers in their own right. Women were also often significant in lay hereditary teaching lineages. While the official lineage bearers were invariably men, women had informal importance, a fact which is reflected in the scriptural heritage of these traditions, which makes a female consort necessary to the success of a *gter ston* (revealer of tantric scripture), not for her reproductive powers but for her spiritual inspiration and abilities to generate auspicious conditions for the new revelation of scripture. In other traditions too, a woman could secure a good religious training and gain respect by marriage to a high lama, and might eventually be able to teach, although her status was essentially dependent on that of her husband.

Since the radical break in institutional continuity which marked the Chinese invasion of Tibet, there has been some reassessment of the roles of women in Tibetan Buddhism, especially amongst the exiles, who have greater involvement in the international community. There have been moves (supported by the Dalai Lama) to reintroduce the full nuns' ordination from East Asian lineages (see above) and to improve the economic position, education and status of nuns. Women are still largely excluded from monastic educational institutions, although since the 1980s some nuns in Dharamsala (the seat of the Dalai Lama and the Tibetan government-in-exile) have studied Buddhist philosophy, and elsewhere nuns' training has gradually improved. In contemporary Tibet, large numbers of nunneries have been re-established, and here too there appears to be some effort to provide nuns with reasonable training. Nuns in central Tibet have been in the forefront of political dissidence against the Chinese authorities, for which, like their monk counterparts, they have suffered imprisonment, torture and the closure of their institutions. Yet the rebuilding of nunneries continues.

While structural gender inequality in Tibetan Buddhism remains, many Tibetan nuns are cautious and unwilling to openly challenge monastic authorities. There is awareness that more confrontational approaches might be counter-productive and that women may gain more by relying on their lamas to help them expand their informal role rather than attempting to make radical structural changes. Not all cases of contemporary influential Tibetan Buddhist women have been affected by modern feminism. For example, a charismatic female meditation adept in 'Bri-gung, Tibet, has recently established herself in an apparently traditional position for a recognized emanation of the eighth-century female Buddhist saint Ye-shes mtsho-rgyal, and is active in recreating a nuns' community and revitalizing religious practice in the area.

East Asia

Buddhism in East Asia has co-existed with a number of religious traditions of the region such as Confucianism and Daoism in China, Shamanism in Korea and Shinto in Japan. Moreover, a prevalent undercurrent of indigenous folk practices and ancestor worship has added to its diversity and pluralistic orientation.

Buddhism in Korea and parts of China was affected by Japanese colonialism in the 1930s and 1940s, as Japanese Buddhist missionaries advanced into the continent to spearhead the campaign for imperial Japan. Korean Buddhism had experienced an orthodox revival towards the end of the nineteenth century, and many lay Buddhist societies were established, rekindling an interest in Buddhism amongst ordinary people. Later, with the Japanese occupation and presence of Japanese Buddhist missionaries, Korean Buddhists began to modernize and reform their Buddhist practice and tradition.

Although Buddhism in China declined since the thirteenth century, there were bouts of small-scale revival in the mid-nineteenth to the mid-twentieth century. Monasteries were closed and monks suffered poverty under communist rule, yet Buddhism survived the Cultural Revolution to a degree, and there has been renewed activity in certain regions since the late 1970s. In comparison, the contemporary Chinese government is more tolerant of Buddhism, which tends to be seen as useful for promoting ties with other Buddhist countries. Yet Buddhist institutions remain subject to state control, and the extent of tolerance varies (see Chapter 4).

Postwar Taiwan, originally set up as an alternative power base by the defeated nationalist China, has seen the most vigorous revival of Chinese Buddhism. Freed from traditional constraints of monastic lineage and Confucian pressures, lay Buddhists and nuns have been active in promoting new types of Buddhist movements emphasizing social welfare, education and meditation.

Meanwhile, in Japan, traditional Buddhism faced setbacks following its separation from the state in 1868, and the twentieth century witnessed some reaction to Buddhist monasteries and priests seen as overtly commercial, concerning themselves purely with funerary rites for the dead. With rapid urbanization and other postwar developments, politically inclined lay Buddhist organizations developed, along with new religions catering for the needs of the individual in contemporary society (see Chapter 5).

Buddhism in the West

The Buddhist tradition has not only faced radical sociopolitical and ideological upheavals in Asia. International migration of Buddhists and the conversion of Westerners have established Buddhism in Western countries, resulting in ongoing dialogue between Western convert Buddhists and traditional Buddhist authorities.

European intellectual curiosity in Buddhism dates from the mid-eighteenth century, but more general interest was initiated by scholars and philosophers who began translating Buddhist texts into European languages in the late nineteenth century. Active involvement in Buddhism became more common, a few Westerners becoming monks. The Theosophical Society, founded in 1875, had some involvement in the Buddhist reformist movement in Ceylon. Contemporary Sinhalese Buddhists are sceptical of their influence in Asia, but they certainly contributed to popularizing Buddhism amongst Western liberals and intellectuals and left a mark on the New Age movement in the West.

Buddhist teachings and traditions were brought to west coast America and Canada in the late nineteenth century along with immigrant labourers from China and Japan. Hawaii also became a major centre for Japanese Buddhism from the early twentieth century. Zen Buddhism gained particular popularity after the 1950s, partly due to the writings of D. Suzuki. The steady influx of refugees from Tibet after the 1950s, and from Vietnam, Laos and Cambodia in the 1970s, led to renewed interest in Buddhism, and the counter-cultural movements of the 1960s proved fertile ground for its diffusion. Almost all traditions of Buddhism were represented in America by then, as well as new Buddhist organizations such as Nichiren Shōshū (Sōka Gakkai) and other syncretic groups which became active in the latter part of the twentieth century.

Figure 2.5 Zen Buddhism was one of the first forms of Buddhism to attract interest and followers in the West. This picture shows Zen Buddhists in the US meditating in the temple on Furnace Mountain, Powell City, Kentucky, 28 June 1997

The popularity and rapid growth of Buddhism seem in part to have been a response to secularization, disenchantment with traditional churches and an increasingly pluralistic cultural orientation in the postcolonial, postwar period. More positive attractions of Buddhism have included an interest in its meditation traditions, its philosophy and psychological analyses of the human condition, as well as its empirical, experiential orientation. One significant strand in Buddhism is an emphasis on verifying the teachings for oneself, not only accepting them out of faith or respect for authority. In recent times, charismatic representatives of Buddhism, most notably the present Dalai Lama, have also been influential. Although Tibetan Buddhism was a late arrival on the Western scene, by the turn of the millennium it had became one of the most popular forms of Buddhism in the West.

It is difficult to generalize about which specific aspects of Buddhism appeal to Westerners. Cultural differences between Western societies together with the postmodern climate favouring diversity have meant that successful Buddhist groups range from those focused exclusively on formless meditation to those promoting elaborate ritual symbolism; from those which stress the centrality of reasoning in Buddhist thought to those which stress faith and devotion; and from those rooted in the renunciatory values of traditional meditator strands to those combining Buddhism with social and political activism. Asian Buddhism has always had such variants, but it is more usual, even now, for certain strands to dominate in specific regions, and for affiliation to owe much to family and community involvements. On the contrary, in the West, most Buddhists are first or second generation converts, exercizing personal choice in affiliation, often after some spiritual exploration. The myriad types of Buddhist practice we now witness in Western countries also range from new explicitly Western forms of Buddhism to branches of conservative Asian Buddhist traditions.

Even groups at the conservative end of the spectrum, however, such as representatives of the Thai Theravāda forest tradition who have established successful centres in southern England, cannot be entirely untouched by the radically different sociocultural context in which they must operate. Furthermore, the lack of formal institutional controls on the part of traditional Buddhist authorities over the development of Western Buddhist groups, coupled with limited public knowledge of Buddhist traditions in Western countries, encourage a situation in which groups with little formal support in Asia may thrive, and innovative reinterpretation of Buddhism is common. Some early twentieth-century Western enthusiasts for Buddhism now appear to have retained vestiges of colonial arrogance in criticizing traditional Buddhists as corrupt and in advocating a Buddhism purified of traditional

Asian practices. Some strands of contemporary Western Buddhism may be similarly ethnocentric, whilst others represent a more genuine dialogue between Western and Asian Buddhist approaches. In a context in which Asian Buddhists are themselves re-evaluating their religious practices and responding to the challenges brought by modernity and postmodernity, some of the developments centred on the contemporary West may even in time have profound impact on Asian Buddhism.

Perhaps the general comment which can be made with the most confidence is that as yet the monastic Saṅgha does not have the central place in the West that it usually does in Asian Buddhist countries. While there are increasing numbers of Western monks and nuns, they are not always the main representatives of Western Buddhist groups, nor central to their organization. It is difficult to say how far the present limited success of Buddhist monasticism in the West is a feature of limited resources for the support of full-time religious (a feature which could change in time with the further expansion of Buddhism), or of cultural values inimical to ways of life perceived as escapist or alien, or of urban lifestyles unsuited to monastic discipline, which have also contributed to a decline in monastic practice and the rise of alternative religious models in contemporary Asia.

LOOKING TO THE FUTURE

Once largely a religion of agrarian Asian societies, Buddhism has demonstrated vitality in surviving massive socio-economic change, in contributing to the development of new ethnic and cultural identities in Asia, and in adapting to numerous modern contexts internationally. Aspects of its heritage which fit well with postmodern environments include both its tolerance of diversity in social and kinship patterns and its teachings on the nature of mind, which underlie the Buddhist view that religious truth must be realized by each individual in a process of inner spiritual discovery.

The greatest challenge to Buddhism in modern times has undoubtedly been the loss of state and community support which were traditionally institutionalized in many Asian societies. Today, even where the Buddhist monastic Saṅgha retains an important place in society, it does not always represent the only or even the most influential voice on religious matters. Moreover, Buddhism has struggled to exist in the hostile environment of rapidly changing political regimes. Secular nation states in Asia, both communist and anti-communist, have alternately tried to control Buddhism, to eliminate it, or to harness it for the purposes of legitimation.

Besides coming to terms with political changes affecting monastic funding, organization, and education, traditional Buddhist authorities have also had to cope with dramatic social change, issuing (for example) in increasing lay demands for involvement in religious practice. And yet, despite adversity and rapid change, Buddhist monastic institutions have proved remarkably resilient. In some cases they have been revived in recent times, or taken the lead in religious and political developments. At times, as we have seen, they have been at the forefront of cultural and ethnic defence, and have even become agents of political action.

Buddhism's adaptability to postmodern conditions has been enhanced by a flexibility which stems in part from its own internal diversity. Buddhism's broad range of approaches to religious life stem from differences in the relative emphasis placed on morality, meditation or wisdom, and the contrasting models for religious practice. These variations characterized different traditions in the past, but today they facilitate flexibility, change and, increasingly, individual choice. Moreover, traditional attitudes of tolerance to alternative religious and philosophical viewpoints, so long as they promote well-being and reduce suffering, mean that contemporary representatives of Buddhist traditions have gained international respect by engaging readily in ecumenical dialogue.

Buddhism's survival in the modern world may also have been aided by the fact that, apart from its general ethical guidelines, it has little to say concerning 'correct' family or social relationships – these are 'worldly' matters, outside the proper scope of the religious tradition. Western cultural influences, together with socio-economic, environmental and political change in recent decades, have encouraged some rethinking of this approach. The new socially engaged movements within Buddhism are one result of this process. However, there seems little reason to anticipate the development of normative Buddhist teachings on family and social roles: not only would it be impossible to find agreement across different Buddhist schools, but the traditional flexibility seems a positive advantage in a world in which roles are continually being redefined in response to change. Equally, we find a number of quite different responses to political and environmental issues, ranging from withdrawal to activism – both can locate their authority in Buddhist scriptural sources.

At the same time, Buddhism does have well-developed perspectives on the psychology of individuals and methods for attaining liberation. There is the assumption that not only all humans but all living beings have much in common in terms of becoming attached to impermanent and unsatisfactory conditions as though they were stable and satisfying. Meditation techniques, many of which build on early Buddhist practices to generate tranquillity and insight, retain their traditional appeal, as well as seeming to fit with contemporary values stressing self-development and the cultivation of experience. The twentieth century has witnessed meditation practice moving out of the confines of the monastery to be taken up by the laity who are increasingly subject to the pressures of modern life. *Vipassanā*, a form of insight meditation that originally spread from Burma, has grown in popularity in Southern Buddhism and many meditation instructors have travelled to countries outside the confines of traditional Theravāda. Yet it is not only new lay urban forms of Buddhism which have been successful: the forest monk tradition with its overtones of ancient wisdom has attracted widespread support, including from the urban middle classes.

Buddhist scholarship, traditionally rooted in monastic learning, is increasingly challenged by the infringement of modern academic institutions and the perspectives of modern scholarship. Yet Buddhist philosophy has attracted some interest in global academic circles and there are instances of adaptations of the scholastic curriculum. A traditional assumption that the strength of Buddhism could be judged by the state of the monastic order may seem rather less relevant in today's world of lay meditation centres and the mass circulation of books on Buddhism, but it may be that it would be premature to dismiss it entirely.

Despite the very real setbacks which the Buddhist tradition has faced to its institutional position in Asia, far from witnessing the demise of a traditional religion uprooted from its socio-economic and cultural support systems, Buddhism has discovered both new and ancient sources of vitality on which to draw in its ongoing adaptations to modernity and postmodernity.

SUMMARY

- For Asian Buddhism, modernity and postmodernity have involved radical socio-economic changes which in many cases have severed Buddhism from its traditional institutionalized support systems.
- There is continuity in some aspects of monastic organization in the modern world: in presentations of Buddhist doctrine in terms of morality, meditation and wisdom; in traditional models for the religious path; and in the range and flexibility of religious practices.
- Changes in sociopolitical, economic, technological and communication systems have engendered rethinking and reworking of the religious heritage, including reassessments of monastic and

lay relations and roles, of Buddhist scholarship, gender relations and social and political involvements.

▌ Several new developments in Buddhism have been related to the internationalization or globalization of Buddhism: increased communication between Asian Buddhists as well as the expansion of Buddhism into Western countries.

▌ Key terms

Over time, the Buddhist scriptures in India were put into the language of the literate elite, Sanskrit, and were later translated from Sanskrit into other Asian languages. We have generally given the Sanskrit for Buddhist technical terms, although in specifically Theravāda or Tibetan contexts we have occasionally given the Pali or Tibetan respectively.

abhidharma (Sanskrit)/**abhidhamma** (Pali)   Higher Teachings, class of early Buddhist texts which systematized and expanded on the teachings given in the *sūtras*.

bhikkhunī (Pali)/**bhikṣuṇī** (Sanskrit)   Buddhist nun with full ordination equivalent to the Buddhist monk (*bhikkhu/bhikṣu*).

bodhisattava   One intent on attaining Buddhahood, in order to benefit all sentient beings and to bring them to enlightenment.

Buddha   The awakened one, who has put an end to emotional defilements and attained enlightenment.

Dharma (Sanskrit)/**Dhamma** (Pali)   The teachings of the Buddha, the true nature of reality.

Dharmarāja (Sanskrit)   'Righteous king', who rules in accordance with the *Dharma*.

Geluk (Tibetan *dge lugs*)   One of the principal Tibetan Buddhist schools, whose followers are the Gelukpa (*dge lugs pa*).

Kagyu (Tibetan *bka' brgyud*)   One of the principal Tibetan Buddhist schools, whose followers are the Kagyupa (*bka' brgyud pa*).

Kanjur (Tibetan *bka' 'gyur*)   A collection of Indic Buddhist scriptures compiled in Tibet.

karma (Sanskrit)/**kamma** (Pali)   Laws of cause and effect, which according to Buddhist thinking operate rationally and are ethical in nature.

lama (Tibetan *bla ma*/Sanskrit *guru*)   The teacher in Tibetan Buddhism.

Mahāyāna   The 'Great Vehicle', a Buddhist movement which developed around the turn of the Christian era, introducing new scriptures (*sūtras*) recognized as Buddha Word. It emphasized the compassion and wisdom of Buddhas and *bodhisattavas* intent on enlightenment, and both Northern and East Asian forms of Buddhism have grown out of the Mahāyāna heritage.

maṇḍala   A representation of the tantric vision of reality in terms of an enlightened deity or circle of deities, abiding in a pure Buddha realm: a focus for meditation which aims to transform ordinary reality into such an enlightened vision.

mantra practitioner (Tibetan *sngags pa*)   Lay tantric religious specialist.

nirvāṇa (Sanskrit)/**nibbāna** (Pali)   Enlightenment, the state of unconditioned existence and liberation from the cycle of rebirth.

Nyingma (Tibetan *rnying ma*) One of the principal Tibetan Buddhist schools, whose followers are the Nyingmapa (*rnying ma pa*).

Pali Ancient Indian language in which the Theravāda scriptures are written.

reincarnate lamas (Tibetan *sprul sku*) Tibetan teachers considered to be reincarnations of former Buddhist masters.

Renouncer movement Ancient Indian movement of renouncers (Sanskrit *śramaṇa*) who, in contrast to the Vedic tradition, stressed the renunciation of and liberation from worldly life. Early Buddhism sprung from this movement.

ris med (Tibetan) An ecumenical movement in nineteenth-century Tibetan Buddhism which has had much effect on contemporary Tibetan Buddhism.

Sakya (Tibetan *sa skya*) One of the principal Tibetan Buddhist schools, whose followers are the Sakyapa (*sa skya pa*).

Saṅgha The Buddhist community or order, often referring to the monastic order of monks and nuns. The noble Saṅgha consists of the spiritually advanced who are irreversibly established on the path to enlightenment.

sūtra (Sanskrit)/**sutta** (Pali) A discourse; class of the earliest Buddhist scriptures containing teachings attributed to the Buddha, later expanded in the Mahāyāna.

gTer ma (Tibetan) Revealed tantric scriptures, revealed by discoverers called *gter ston*.

Theravāda Way of the elders, the dominant tradition of Southern Buddhism.

therī Senior nuns in early Buddhism, many of whom were said to have attained liberation. Verses attributed to them were included in the early Buddhist corpus.

Vajrayāna Tantric Buddhism.

vinaya Class of the earliest Buddhist scriptures, on monastic discipline.

vipassanā (Pali) A form of insight meditation which has been popularized in contemporary Theravāda Buddhism.

FURTHER READING

Introductory

For introductions to Buddhism, see P. Harvey: *An Introduction to Buddhism: Teachings, History and Practices* (Cambridge: Cambridge University Press, 1990), a wide-ranging survey of Buddhist history, doctrines and practices, and R. Gethin: *The Foundations of Buddhism* (Oxford and New York: Oxford University Press, 1998), which introduces the fundamentals of Buddhist thinking and practice underlying the mainstream Buddhist schools. For an illustrated collection on Buddhism's history and relations with society, see H. Bechert and R. Gombrich (eds): *The World of Buddhism: Buddhist Monks and Nuns in Society and Culture* (London: Thames & Hudson, 1984). On Mahāyāna doctrine, see P. Williams: *Mahāyāna Buddhism: The Doctrinal Foundations* (London: Routledge, 1989).

Early Buddhism and Theravāda

On early Indian Buddhism and Theravāda in Sri Lanka, including modern developments, see R. Gombrich: *Theravāda Buddhism* (London and New York: Routledge & Kegan Paul, 1988). On revival of the forest monk tradition in Sri Lanka, see M. Carrithers: *The Forest Monks of Sri Lanka: An Anthropological and Historical Study* (Delhi: Oxford University Press, 1983), and on late twentieth-century religious practice in Sri Lanka, see R. Gombrich and G. Obeyesekere: *Buddhism Transformed: Religious Change in Sri Lanka* (Princeton, NJ: Princeton University Press, 1988).

Gender

For gender in Buddhism, see D. Paul: *Women in Buddhism* (Berkeley, Los Angeles and London: University of California Press, 1985). W. Pruitt (trans.): *The Commentary on the Verses of the Therīs*, by Ā. Dhammapāla (Oxford: Pali Text Society, 1988) gives accounts of renowned early Buddhist nuns. For an ethnographic study of contemporary Tibetan nuns, see H. Havnevik: *Tibetan Buddhist Nuns: History, Cultural Norms and Social Reality* (Oslo: The Institute for Comparative Research in Human Culture, Norwegian University Press, 1989). For an ethnographic study of contemporary Thai Buddhist women, see C. Kabilsingh: *Thai Women in Buddhism* (Berkeley: Parallax Press, 1991), and for Burmese Buddhist women, see Mi Mi Khaing: *The World of Burmese Women* (London: Zed Books, 1984).

Tibet

On Tibetan Buddhism, for historical developments and geographical variations, see G. Samuel: *Civilized Shamans: Buddhism in Tibetan Societies* (Washington and London: Smithsonian Institution Press, 1993). For an account of an early nineteenth-century meditator monk, see M. Ricard (trans.): *The Life of Shabkar: The Autobiography of a Tibetan Yogin* (Albany, NY: SUNY, 1994). For Buddhism and political protest in Tibet under Chinese rule, see R. Schwartz: *Circle of Protest: Political Ritual in the Tibetan Uprising* (London: Hurst & Company, 1994), and for religious practice in 1990s Tibet, see M. C. Goldstein and M. T. Kapstein: *Buddhism in Contemporary Tibet: Religious Revival and Cultural Identity* (Berkeley, Los Angeles and London: University of California Press, 1998). More advanced reading on traditional Buddhist scholasticism can be found in J. I. Cabezón: *Buddhism and Language: A Study of Indo-Tibetan Scholasticism* (Albany, NY: SUNY, 1994). For a Nyingmapa perspective, see D. Rinpoche: *The Nyingma School of Tibetan Buddhism: Its Fundamentals and History*, trans. and ed. G. Dorje and M. Kapstein (Boston: Wisdom Publications, 1991).

Buddhism in Asia

I. Harris (ed.): *Buddhism and Politics in Twentieth-Century Asia* (London: Cassell, 1999) provides a useful overview of the relationship between politics and Buddhism, and contemporary transformations of Buddhist traditions in Asia. For a descriptive analysis of contemporary Buddhist practices, rituals and rites of passage in Burma (Myanmar), Thailand, Laos, Cambodia and Sri Lanka, see D. Swearer: *The Buddhist World of Southeast Asia* (Albany, NY: SUNY, 1995).

Sikhism

Christopher Shackle

▌ INTRODUCTION

The development of Sikhism over the five centuries of its history has always been closely tied to its homeland, the Punjab in north-western India (see map on p. 79 below). From an original context in which Hinduism and Islam were the opposed dominant creeds, Sikhism had evolved through one particularly significant internal change of emphasis and organization as the ethnic religion of a significant local minority when it was subjected to the impact of modernity caused by the British conquest of the Punjab in the mid-nineteenth century. Over the next century this colonial context therefore largely conditioned the pattern of Sikh responses to the modern world. Only more recently has that pattern itself begun to be questioned.

Although statistically one of the world's smaller religions, Sikhism's recognized status as a world religion is to be associated with the large diaspora established over the last fifty years through emigration to several countries in the English-speaking world. The Sikh diaspora, comprising about 1 million out of the world total of 16 million, is proportionately much larger than that of other recognized Asian religions, and in the ongoing articulation of responses to postcolonial modernity its voice has become increasingly significant.

Table 3.1 Estimated distribution of world Sikh population

Punjab	13,000,000
Rest of India	2,000,000
UK	450,000
Canada	200,000
US	150,000
Rest of world	100,000

This chapter describes the evolution of Sikhism as falling into three overlapping phases, whose transitions are marked by the impact of two different kinds of modernity. Although itself marked by highly dynamic inner shifts of emphasis, the formative first phase lasting until the mid-nineteenth century is regarded as premodern. Initiated by the British conquest of the Punjab in the 1840s, the second phase is characterized by a largely successful set of redefinitions in the context of the notions of modernity and religious identity imposed by the dominant ideology of the colonial power closely associated with Victorian Christianity. Beginning after Indian independence in 1947, the third phase is the postcolonial age in which the more rigid formulations appropriate to the older modernity of the colonial period have come under growing internal question, particularly in the context of the very significant Sikh diaspora now increasingly acculturated to the acceptance of shifting fluidities characteristic of modern Western societies.

SOURCES AND RESOURCES

Sikhism provides a striking illustration of the general rule that it is typically through the interstices between existing faiths that new religions emerge. The late fifteenth-century Punjab embraced not only the internal religious variety always characteristic of the Hindu world, but also a powerful Islamic presence associated with a long established Muslim political authority. This dual context continued to the end of the premodern period to affect the evolution of Sikhism throughout its two formative phases, initiated respectively by the primary formulations of the First Sikh Guru Nanak (1469–1539), and the substantial redefinitions of authority and community effected by the Tenth Guru Gobind Singh (1666–1708).

The Nanak Panth

The broad alignment of Guru Nanak's teachings is with the *bhakti* movement of medieval north India. They are most nearly aligned with those of the Sants, the loosely associated group of teachers whose teachings were expressed in vernacular verse and are distinguished theologically by a soteriology based upon inward loving devotion to a formless divine principle rather than a personalized incarnation. Their social teaching is marked by an egalitarianism opposed equally to the qualitative distinctions of the Hindu caste hierarchy and to the value-laden religious differences between Hindu and Muslim. Guru Nanak is believed to have emerged from the direct experience of divine reality which initiated his mission with the words 'there is no Hindu, there is no Muslim' (*na ko hindu, na ko musalman*), signalling as a third way what was to become the Nanak *Panth*, the 'Path of Nanak', the community constituted by the Sikhs (*lit.* 'disciples') choosing to follow Nanak as their guide or guru, who were almost entirely drawn from Hindu backgrounds often similar to his own.

Powerfully organized in over nine hundred short verses, hymns and longer compositions of great beauty, Guru Nanak's teachings revolve around the path of salvation from the fate of unregenerate humanity, in which the domination of the psyche (*man*) by the impulses of the self (*haumai*) causes its subjection to the perpetual suffering of reincarnation. The key figure in the salvific path of alignment to the divine purpose is the guide, the true guru (*satiguru*), to whose inwardly heard voice God may graciously grant access in the case of those whose leading of a righteous life in this world allows the possibility of their being transformed from self-directed (*manmukh*) to guru-directed (*gurmukh*) beings, and thus of apprehending reality or truth (*sach*):

> If You bestow Your glance of grace, through grace we find the Guide
> This soul first passes many births, at last the Guide is heard
> No giver's greater than the Guide, all people mark this well
> The Guide once met imparts the Truth, to those who kill the Self
> The Guide who makes us grasp Reality.
>
> (*Asa ki Var M1 4, AG* 465)

Figure 3.1 The twentieth-century popular image of Guru Nanak

While similar to the teachings of the other Sants in their primary emphasis upon a spiritual psychology directed towards transformation of the self, Guru Nanak's hymns express a notably more positive attitude towards women, as in the verse 'Why speak ill of her from whom great kings are born?' (*AG* 473). Their similarly marked emphasis on the need to balance the spiritual with the practical and the ethical is summarized in a key extra-scriptural formula which adds to the primary injunction to maintain a loving meditation of the divine attributes (*nam japna*) the necessity of leading a productive daily existence (*kirat karni*) and practising the charitable sharing of surplus goods (*vand chhakna*).

Around the primary focal point of the divine Word (*gurbani*) of Guru Nanak's hymns access to the divine was provided by private devotion and by the singing of hymns (*kirtan*) in the congregation of the faithful which is the earthly exemplar of the heavenly congregation of the saints. Separate temples, later called *gurdwaras*, with their communal kitchens (*langar*) whose encouragement of inter-caste commensality may have been inspired by the example of the similar kitchens attached to Muslim shrines, date from this early period, when the Nanak Panth was subject to the authority of a succession of gurus, each of whom composed further hymns under the signature 'Nanak'.

The guruship had become hereditary within one family by the time of the Fifth Guru Arjun (d.1606), whose significant formalization and remodelling of the Panth included the construction of the Harimandir, the 'Golden Temple' at Amritsar which has ever since remained the spiritual centre of Sikhism. Guru Arjun was also responsible for the compilation of the Sikh scripture, the *Adi Granth* (1604), to which he is the largest single contributor. The *Granth* is is a massive collection written in the distinctive *Gurmukhi* script of hymns composed in a mixture of Old Punjabi and Old Hindi by the Sikh Gurus plus selected verses by other Sants. Although the Janamsakhis, the prose hagiographies of Guru Nanak compiled during this period, have always remained central to devotional understanding, they have never been accorded the special status enjoyed by the scripture as *gurbani*, whose canonization as a sacred book would seem in part to derive from the unique status accorded to the Qur'an in Islam.

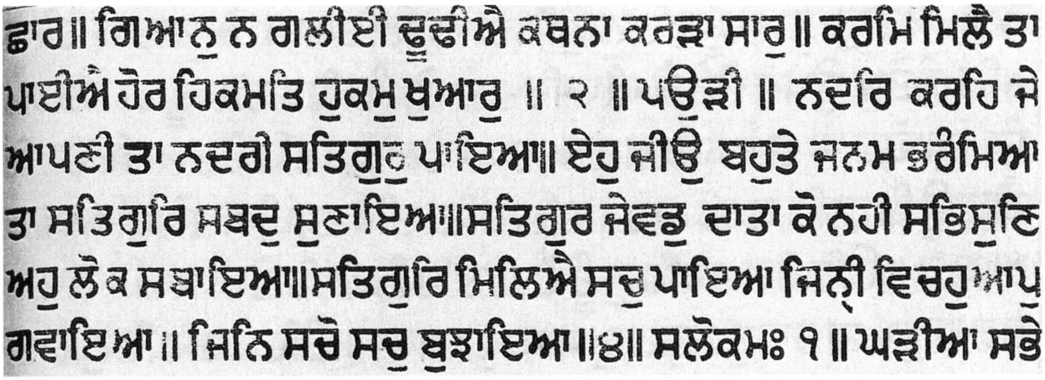

ਢਾਰੇ ॥ ਗਿਆਨੂ ਨ ਗਲੀਈ ਢੂਢੀਐ ਕਥਨਾ ਕਰੜਾ ਸਾਰੁ ॥ ਕਰਮਿ ਮਿਲੈ ਤਾ ਪਾਈਐ ਹੋਰ ਹਿਕਮਤਿ ਹੁਕਮੁ ਖੁਆਰੁ ॥ ੨ ॥ ਪਉੜੀ ॥ ਨਦਰਿ ਕਰਹਿ ਜੇ ਆਪਣੀ ਤਾ ਨਦਰੀ ਸਤਿਗੁਰੁ ਪਾਇਆ ॥ ਏਹੁ ਜੀਉ ਬਹੁਤੇ ਜਨਮ ਭਰੰਮਿਆ ਤਾ ਸਤਿਗੁਰਿ ਸਬਦੁ ਸੁਣਾਇਆ ॥ ਸਤਿਗੁਰ ਜੇਵਡੁ ਦਾਤਾ ਕੋ ਨਹੀ ਸਭਿਸੁਣਿ ਅਹ ਲੇ ਕ ਸਬਾਇਆ ॥ ਸਤਿਗੁਰਿ ਮਿਲਿਐ ਸਚੁ ਪਾਇਆ ਜਿਨੀ ਵਿਚਹੁਆਪੁ ਗਵਾਇਆ ॥ ਜਿਨਿ ਸਚੋ ਸਚੁ ਬੁਝਾਇਆ ॥੪॥ ਸਲੋਕਮਃ ੧ ॥ ਘੜੀਆ ਸਭੇ

Figure 3.2 Gurmukhi text of *Granth* passage translated above

The Khalsa

Following Guru Arjun's martyrdom by the Moghul authorities, much of the seventeenth century was marked by political and military conflict, both within the Panth as each succession to the Guruship provoked the secession of unsuccessful claimants with their followers and between Sikhs and the Moghuls, culminating with the execution in Delhi on imperial orders of the Ninth Guru Tegh Bahadur (d.1675).

His son Gobind, who became the Tenth Guru, instituted a major reorganization of the Panth through his foundation in 1699 of the *Khalsa*. This was designed as an elite brotherhood whose direct dedication to the Guru was formalized through initiatory baptism (*amrit*), and whose internal equality was symbolized by the addition of the Rajput titles *Singh* ('Lion') and *Kaur* ('Princess') to male and female names respectively. The emphasis on masculine features naturally associated with the strongly militant character of the Khalsa was underlined by the obligation on male members to bear the well-known *five Ks* as outward marks of membership.

The verse compositions associated with Guru Gobind Singh, many with militant themes, were gathered in a separate Khalsa scripture called the *Dasam Granth*, but this has always been secondary in importance to the *Adi Granth* for whose final recension he is believed to have been responsible. It was Guru Gobind Singh who before his death proclaimed the end of the succession of living Gurus and the transfer of the Guruship to the *Adi Granth*, thereafter given the honorific title of *Guru Granth*

Sahib, whose supreme status is underlined by the central position and numerous marks of ritual respect accorded to copies of the scripture in a *gurdwara*. In the absence of a Sikh priesthood, a parallel authority was considered to reside after the death of the last living Guru in the whole community as Guru Panth.

Not all the Sikhs of the Nanak Panth chose to become members of the Khalsa, with some choosing such alternatives as enrolment in one of the several Sikh ascetic groups while many continued in the traditional patterns of observance, distinguished from the Hindu co-members of their caste or family only by their devotion to the Gurus and the Granth. But in the wars which accompanied the progressive collapse of Moghul authority during the eighteenth century, it was the Khalsa which led the community, and formal meetings of its leaders were invested with the power to issue resolutions binding upon all Sikhs. Recruited primarily from the farmer caste of Jats rather than the business caste of Khatris from whom all the Gurus and most early converts had been drawn, the Khalsa emerged as a major military and political force in the Punjab.

Prescriptive codes of Khalsa conduct (*rahit*), including a ban on smoking tobacco, were drawn up during this period, and an abundant literature of heroism and martyrdom reinforced a spirit of militant opposition to Islam. In this still influential literature, it is the martial characteristics of the armed male Sikh warrior with his beard and turban which are repeatedly exalted. Rival Sikh warlords were eventually conquered by Maharaja Ranjit Singh, whose reign over the Punjab (1799–1831) in the name of the Khalsa marked the high point of Sikh political power, although Ranjit Singh's lavish patronage of Sikh institutions and religious specialists was never exclusive of other religions, and the absence of a proselytizing tradition accounts for the failure of Sikhism to expand with Ranjit Singh's territorial conquests beyond its traditional boundaries in the Punjab.

As in the case of all religions, understandings of the formative phases of Sikhism are themselves necessarily coloured by interpretations associated with modern viewpoints, but they may be understood as a process of evolution in which the kernel relationship of self to true guide leads from the living gurus and their *gurbani* to the scripture and the Khalsa. For this period at least, however, it would be misleading to conceive of the Khalsa as too tightly defined a community.

	NANAK PANTH	KHALSA
authority	*gurbani*	Guru Granth
	living gurus	Khalsa and Guru Panth
community	loosely defined adherence	baptismal admission
	Khatri prominence	Jat dominance
self	permeable boundaries with Hindu society	emergence of separate definition
		by five Ks and *rahit*
gender	relatively equalized status	powerfully masculine emphasis

Figure 3.3 Formative phases of Sikhism

INTERACTIONS WITH MODERNITY

Sikhism in the colonial world

While Ranjit Singh had successfully prolonged his independence by reorganization of the Khalsa forces on modern European lines, the full impact of modernity was only felt after the two Anglo–Sikh wars of 1845–9 when the Punjab became the last major conquest to fall to British colonial expansion in India. The subsequent development of Sikhism is intimately linked to the new status of the Sikhs as one of the many colonized groups subject to British imperial rule. Moreover, as a relatively small local minority even within the Punjab to which they were largely confined, the Sikhs were faced not only with the familiar general pressures of the direct challenge of the values and institutions of European colonial states on so many Asian religious communities, but also by the secondary challenges posed to them by other religious groupings as a consequence of the latters' own responses to modernity, particularly by a revived neo-Hinduism. The quite profound modern remodellings of Sikhism are primarily the consequence of responses evolved to cope with these linked challenges.

COLONIAL CHALLENGES TO TRADITION

The collapse of independent Sikh political authority left Sikh institutions variably well placed to cope with the challenges of the colonial state to traditional understandings. These challenges are best seen as having manifested themselves in the form of a whole set of linked category shifts, whose primary effect was upon definitions of community, but which in turn progressively influenced notions of authority, of the self and of gender. In the land settlements which followed the conquest, a number of leading Sikh landed families were confirmed in their estates, including the custodians of most major shrines and other religious leaders. The bulk of the Sikh population consisted of a rural population whose prime component was provided by the Jat farmer caste, from which the soldiery of the Khalsa had largely been drawn and who represented the British administration's ideal of the loyalist yeoman farmer.

Like most colonial powers governed by the divide and rule principle, the British were concerned with the mapping and definition of the peoples now subject to them and the determination of appropriate treatment for each group. As a religious minority with a demonstrable record of military prowess, the Sikhs were of particular interest to the imperial authorities. The British quickly defined them as a martial race whose loyalty was to be secured by privileged access into the army and whose separate status was to be rigidly underlined by making outward Khalsa observance a precondition of recruitment into the separate Sikh regiments.

Direct encouragement was thereby given to a shift from previous Indic patterns of highly permeable community boundaries to the operation of Western 'either/or' notions so characteristic of modernity. Later, access to the new economic opportunities provided by the colonial system, both in terms of internal emigration to new areas of the Punjab opened up for cultivation by canal irrigation or outside India to different parts of the empire again tended to be awarded along imperially defined community lines, and the Sikhs were well favoured in this process.

Simultaneously with this official reinforcement of separate definitions, all three indigenous religions of the Punjab were subject to the challenges posed by the modern and clearly successful Victorian Christianity of their new rulers, as particularly articulated by the missionary presence which was so prominent in the new educational system of the Punjab. These challenges provoked a series of responses

Figure 3.4 Ram Singh

ranging from conservative defences of tradition to more radical solutions which took on many of the concepts of modernity in order to reformulate new defences of tradition. One of the earliest and strongest responses of the latter type was the neo-Hinduism formulated by the Gujarati brahmin Dayanand Saraswati. Rejecting most of the features of traditional Hinduism condemned by its Western critics in the name of an absolutist scriptural authority quite newly conferred on the Vedas, his Arya Samaj gained rapid and long lasting support from the new Punjabi Hindu urban middle class. Initially its appeal extended even to some enthusiastic members of the much smaller Sikh middle class, but these rapidly became alienated by the characteristically aggressive line soon adopted by the Arya Samaj in its deprecation of the Sikh Gurus and its classification of the Sikhs as lapsed Hindus to be reclaimed for submission to Vedic authority.

SIKHISM AND COLONIAL MODERNITY

Intrinsically less bound by the elaborate orthodoxies and orthopraxies maintained by the religious specialists of both brahminic Hinduism and traditional Islam, the Sikhs with their emphasis upon lay reponsibility were in many respects well-placed to take advantage of the opportunities offered by a colonial system generally supportive of them as reliable soldiers and farmers. The inequalities of power between the British and Sikhs was however always going to ensure there would never be a perfect coincidence of interests between the British and the Sikhs, whose very lack of a centrally authoritative tradition of religious specialists was to condition the nature of their responses to the modernity introduced by the colonial system.

Thus a strongly hostile reaction to the colonial presence was formulated by Ram Singh (1816–85), the leader of the Namdhari sect, who combined calls for very strict observance of Sikh rituals with a boycott of the postal service and other colonial institutions. While exemplifying the heroic traditions of the Khalsa in his opposition to the British, his status was intrinsically discredited for most Sikhs by his claim to be the living Guru in direct descent from Guru Gobind Singh, in straight heretical contradiction to the central orthodox tenet of the latter's closure of the Guruship.

In accordance with the doctrine of the Guru Panth, it therefore fell to a lay leadership to articulate the main Sikh response to the general challenges of modernity while at the time mounting a defence against hostile takeover by the proponents of a revived Hinduism. Just like the Arya Samaj, the urban Sikhs who led this response adopted the modern forms of organization introduced by the colonial state, with the usual apparatus of elected officers, minutes and resolutions, in the formation of new lay associations. These were called *Singh Sabha*, the first being founded under aristocratic patronage in Amritsar in 1873, soon followed by the Lahore Singh Sabha (1879) whose more radical middle class membership's reformist agenda achieved the most successful articulation of a Sikhism adapted to modernity, which has until recently managed to dominate all subsequent understandings.

Figure 3.5 A nineteenth-century Sikh cavalryman

This reformulation was based on the ideal of the *Tat Khalsa*, the 'real Khalsa' as defined by the reformists to conform with the categories encouraged by the colonial state. This distinguished Sikhism from Hinduism as an ethical monotheism closely linked to a single scripture, the Granth as *Guru Granth Sahib*, whose unique authority unequivocally guaranteed Sikhism's separate status as a fully scriptural religion. In the absence of any systematic codification of prescribed Sikh practice comparable to the Hindu Dharmashastras or the Muslim Sharia, a crucial further underpinning of separate identity was provided by continual reference to the line of Sikh Gurus, the foundation of the Khalsa and the subsequent achievements of the Sikh Panth. A strictly linear religious history thus became a principal means of giving absolute primacy within the existing wide range of Sikh–Hindu practice and allegiance to the full Khalsa identity as the only real kind of Sikhism.

Ever wider adherence to this norm was encouraged by the Singh Sabha reformists' continual emphasis upon the outward marks of male Khalsa identity as palpable symbols of an inner moral fibre whose closeness to Victorian values was to be guaranteed by maximal distancing from many types of previously current ritual and practice which were now stigmatized as degenerate and as Hindu. The consequent ideal is well-captured in the words of Max Arthur Macauliffe, an ex-official who left government service in order to become the leading English associate of the Sikh reformists:

> To sum up some of the moral and political merits of the Sikh religion: It prohibits idolatry, hypocrisy, caste exclusiveness, the concremation of widows, the immurement of women, the use of wine and other intoxicants, tobacco-smoking, infanticide, slander, pilgrimages to the sacred rivers and tanks of the Hindus; and it inculcates loyalty, gratitude for all favours received, philanthropy, justice, impartiality, truth, honesty, and all the moral and domestic virtues known to the holiest citizens of any country.
>
> (M. A. Macauliffe, *The Sikh Religion*, 1909, 1, xxiii)

Besides its core programme of enforcing unambiguous notions of religious authority and community, the Singh Sabha movement led to cultural, institutional and political consequences of great significance for the understanding of Sikhism in the modern world. Culturally, great emphasis was laid upon the local identity of Sikhs, who had historically always remained closely linked to their regional origins in the Punjab. Thus in clear distinction from the Punjabi Muslims' espousal of Urdu as the chief cultural language of Islam in India and the Arya Samaj's strong support of Hindi, a core plank of the Singh Sabha programme was to encourage a congruence of religious and ethnic identity by for the first time developing Punjabi in the sacred Gurmukhi script as a vehicle for a modern literature. Since the Singh Sabha reformers were mostly lay activists lacking the specialist skills of professional theologians, their message was chiefly conveyed in writing by a few particularly creative figures like Vir Singh (1872–1957), whose imaginative works have been enormously influential in helping condition ideas of self and of gender.

Vir Singh

Figure 3.6

Well equipped by his learned family background and a modern education in the Church Mission School Amritsar, Vir Singh devoted sixty-five years of unremitting industry to the great task of conveying the message of a revived Sikhism. Possessing private means and distanced from the political activism to which most of his fellow reformers were drawn, Vir Singh concentrated upon the development of his outstanding gifts as a scholar, propagandist and creative writer in Punjabi.

Besides editing many older Sikh texts and compiling a lengthy scriptural commentary, Vir Singh founded the Khalsa Tract Society to produce pamphlets on Sikhism in imitation and rebuttal of Christian missionary tracts and himself wrote over one thousand of these. He also founded and for many years produced virtually single-handed the influential weekly newspaper *Khalsa Samachar*. A poet of considerable distinction, Vir Singh was the author of the first Punjab novels, beginning with *Sundari* (1898). This enormously popular tale set in the heroic age of the eighteenth century achieves a definitive portrait of idealized Khalsa womanhood in its eponymous heroine who is converted to Sikhism and helps a band of brave Sikh guerillas as cook and nurse before dying of the wound inflicted by a treacherous Muslim warrior.

It was however in the institutional and political spheres that the activist Singh Sabha programme was principally to work itself out. In the colonial period, the first major success in securing the validation of the Tat Khalsa agenda came with passing of the Anand Marriage Act in 1909 which prescribed circumbulation of the Granth by Sikh bridal couples in place of the traditional Vedic fire. A longer and more violent campaign to gain Khalsa control over the Harimandir and other major gurdwaras, fiercely opposed by the traditional custodians inimical to reformist Sikhism, was mounted by a new generation of activists under the banner of the *Akali Dal*. This finally resulted in the Sikh Gurdwaras Act of 1925 which handed the administration of these gurdwaras and their great assets to the *SGPC*, an elected committee dominated by the Akali Dal which is the single most important modern Sikh institution, acting not just in secular matters but also claiming a religious authority on behalf of the Panth over all matters not covered by the Granth.

Sikhism in the postcolonial world

As the modern world itself keeps changing, all processes of response to it must themselves necessarily be ongoing. The often troubled progress of reformist Sikhism in the postcolonial period since Indian independence in 1947 itself illustrates the rule that formerly very successful solutions may not always prove naturally adaptable to respond to altered questions. Definitions of authority and community were well devised by the Singh Sabha movement to maintain the independent development of a religion and its institutions in a colonial environment and to help lead these into the different circumstances of postcolonial independence. But they have proved less adequate to deal with the kinds of issues relating to self and to gender where pointers to a guided individual enrichment on the basis of a genuinely full equality of status for all humans are expected from religious thinkers in the Western societies where the Sikh diaspora is settled, as is also increasingly the case in a rapidly urbanizing and modernizing India.

ACTIVIST RESPONSES

When plans for Indian independence were seen to involve the partition of the Punjab on religious lines, there was some discussion of carving out a Sikh homeland to be called *Khalistan*. This came to nothing, but the massive transfer of Sikhs from areas awarded to Pakistan did result for the first time in a local Sikh majority population in some areas. This encouraged a determined Akali campaign disguised as a demand for a Punjabi-speaking state within the Indian Union for a Sikh-dominated Punjab. This was achieved by the separation of Punjab from Haryana in 1966.

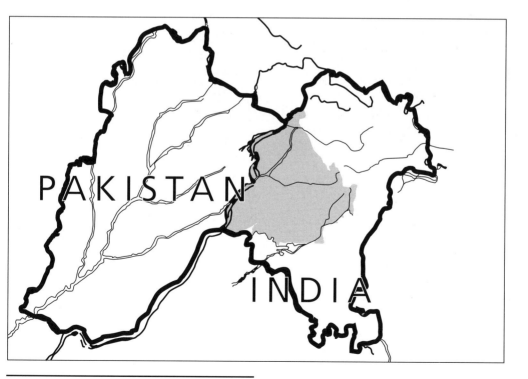

Figure 3.7   Map of historical and modern Punjab (shaded)

In the early 1980s, a combination of these traditions of successful action campaigns with the economic disruptions caused by the agricultural revolution and the increasing questioning in a Hindu-dominated India of the privileged position perceived to have been derived by the Sikhs from the former era resulted in increasingly violent confrontation between the central government of Mrs Indira Gandhi and groups of militant young Sikh activists. This culminated in 1984 with Operation Bluestar, the Indian army's sack of the Harimandir, which had become the armed headquarters of the charismatic Sikh preacher Jarnail Singh Bhindranvale, the subsequent assassination of Mrs Gandhi by her Sikh bodyguards and the consequent Hindu mob violence against Sikhs in many Indian cities.

As violence continued in the Punjab throughout the 1980s, backlash support for the Sikh cause was widespread in the new Sikh diaspora established from the 1950s in the UK and North America, for whom the renewed demand for an independent Sikh Khalistan, for all its lack of any very plausible religio-political programme, proved temporarily to have a particular appeal as a powerful focus for displaced loyalties. While this appeal has receded with the later reimposition of government authority in the Punjab and growing realization among younger Sikhs abroad that Indian solutions may not always be best suited to the situation of increasingly well-established independent overseas communities, the Punjab remains the homeland of Sikhism, with the Harimandir as its perceived focal point.

Figure 3.8 The Golden Temple at Amritsar

RETHINKING NEO-ORTHODOXY

The Tat Khalsa's successful formulation of a neo-orthodox Sikhism is summarized in the *Rahit Maryada*, an official handbook first published by the SGPC in 1950 which has remained the standard authority. This deals at some length with the individual life, under three headings:

> Study of the scriptures and meditation on God, including regulations for the prescribed daily devotions (*nitnem*) and the ritual of the gurdwara, with great emphasis on the centrality of the Granth.
> Living according to the Guru's teachings, embracing both ethical teachings and life cycle rituals.
> Brief instructions on the duty of active service to the community (*seva*).

A much shorter final section deals with the disciplinary rules of the Panth and the penalties (*tankhah*) to be imposed on those who transgress them.

The apparent disproportion in the code's treatment of the individual and the Panth should be understood as a consequence of the difficulty of enforcing disciplinary rules in a religion without a hierarchy of authoritative specialists, and the self – a conspicuously masculine self – is here conceived very much as a unit of the community and fully subject to the authority by which it is defined.

This community identity continues to rely heavily on the authority of its history to maintain its distinction in the shifting world created by the continual process of Indic religious creativity. Even movements of charismatic renewal led by teachers of impeccable Khalsa orthodoxy are often liable to excite the suspicion that they challenge community authority. These suspicions naturally apply still more strongly to movements drawing more widely upon the bottomless well of Indic religious resource so as to appeal to non-Sikhs as well as Sikhs. A notable example of this is the Radhasoami (Beas branch), with a Sikh leadership but owing a primary inspiration to the reinterpretations of yogic disciplines by the movement's Hindu founders.

Community boundaries are again called into question by the most significant modern proselytization movement, the Sikh Dharma or 3HO (Healthy Happy Holy Organization) founded by the Khatri Sikh known as Yogi Bhajan. Deliberately adapted to Western expectations, this has led to communities of American and Canadian Sikhs who have no intrinsic Punjabi background and differ from the standard pattern in such ways as their closer match with Hindu ascetic ideals in being practising vegetarians and wearing white clothes, and in the abolition of gender differences symbolized by putting women in turbans.

Such radical reformulations border upon heresy for most Sikhs who continue to be guided by the Tat Khalsa vision. But in recent decades some of the underpinnings of that orthodoxy, which relies so heavily upon the authenticity of historical tradition and scriptural text, are themselves coming to be questioned by modern scholarship in the fashion successively experienced by most world religions since the critical questioning of Christianity in the nineteenth century.

Since the dominance of orthodoxy in Sikh institutions in the Punjab extends to the universities there, it is unlikely that they would originate such questionings, which have instead come from outside. Particularly strong reactions were evoked by the New Zealand scholar W. H. McLeod with the publication in 1968 of his *Guru Nanak and the Sikh Religion*, which drew on the familiar techniques of biblical scholarship to question the amount of reliable historical information to be gleaned from a careful examination of the classic hagiographies of Guru Nanak, hitherto regarded very much as the Gospels had been in pre-nineteenth century Christianity. An enormous amount of energy has subsequently been expended by Sikh academics and others in attacking the work of McLeod and his pupils on this and subsequent aspects of early Sikh history. But as the history of Christian studies shows, victories in such matters are ultimately hardly to be gained by either side.

Similar questions are starting to be raised about the even more sensitive issue of the text of the Granth, whose central place in Sikhism was carefully reinforced by the reformers' preference for scriptural commentary over textual criticism. This hitherto unquestioned status of the *textus receptus* has long been reinforced by the standard pagination of the Granth, so that all editions contain the same 1,430 pages, much facilitating scholarly reference across its intrinsic organization by the musical modes to which the hymns are to be performed. Those seen to question the orthodox account of its compilation are liable to the kind of concerted attack which resulted in McLeod's pupil Dr Pashaura Singh being summoned from Canada to perform ritual penance at the Harimandir. Meanwhile, however, the work being done by several other Sikh scholars in the diaspora in the collection and critical study of early scriptural manuscripts seems certain to raise issues which may be difficult for some to square with inherited notions of religious authority.

LOOKING TO THE FUTURE

Since Sikhism is so very much a religion of the book, if never in the sense that this definition would have had for the Islamic authorities of Moghul times, it is continually to the Granth that the ongoing process of responses to modernity returns. Somewhat paradoxically, given the increasing distance from the language of the scripture in an English-speaking environment, this is perhaps especially true in the diaspora where the other institutions of orthodoxy are weaker than in the Punjab. Since it was in Guru Nanak's hymns that the self was first directly addressed, it is indeed natural that it should be from the Granth that fresh inspiration is being sought for the reconstruction of self and gender within a Sikhism looking to different definitions of authority and community from those formulated during the colonial period.

Very much in the first phases of discussion and formulation, this process may be expected to result in a major reformulation in the first decades of the new millenium. In keeping with the spirit of the new age, there is a new emphasis upon the musical and inward character of the *gurbani*. A creative indication of the way in which this process might be expected to develop comes from the music inspired by the Granth which draws upon both Eastern and Western sources which is starting to be produced by such artists as the Canadian Sikh classical violinist Parmela Attariwala.

As a pointer to another very important area in which such altered attitudes might be expected to occur attention may be drawn to the pioneering work of the American scholar Nikky Singh, who has

Figure 3.9 CD cover of Parmela Attariwala

drawn upon the insights of Western femininist theology to explore the implications of the Gurus' use of female poetic personae for the redefinition of understandings of gender in Sikhism, and who has produced the first gender neutral translation of *gurbani*.

Since it would be premature to forecast the exact direction of future changes, it is possible only to summarize the likely possibilities in diagrammatic contrast to the still dominant neo-Orthodox Sikhism of the Tat Khalsa.

	NEO-ORTHODOXY	NEW EXPECTATIONS
authority	justified by history	justified by truth
community	defined by ethnicity	defined by choice
self	externally fixed	internally chosen
gender	dominantly masculine	gender neutral

Figure 3.10 Challenges to neo-Orthodoxy

SUMMARY

- The dominant Sikh response to the modern world was conditioned by the need to enforce clear definitions of authority and community in the face of the double challenge of colonialism and of neo-Hinduism.
- The emphasis of this response, chiefly formulated by a lay Punjabi leadership and justified in terms of historic religious mission, was on securing institutional and political change in the Punjab.
- Further changes in the modern world, including the establishment of a very substantial Sikh diaspora in the West, are calling into question the adequacy of the earlier response and its underlying justifications, and are starting to provoke fresh responses.

KEY TERMS

Akali Dal (*lit.* 'army of the Immortal's followers')   The main Sikh political party.

five ks   The five marks of Khalsa identity (*panj kakke*), whose Punjabi names are *kes* (unshorn hair, whose natural concomitant is the turban), *kangha* (comb), *kirpan* (sword), *kara* (steel bracelet), *kachh* (undershorts).

Granth (*lit.* 'book')   The Sikh scripture, especially the *Adi Granth* (Original Book) first compiled by Guru Arjun and subsequently invested with supreme authority as the *Guru Granth Sahib*.

gurbani (*lit.* 'Guru's Word')   The Divine Word of the scripture.

gurdwara (*lit.* 'Guru's door')   Sikh temple.

Gurmukhi (*lit.* 'Guru-directed') The script of the Sikh scriptures used to write modern Punjabi in India.

Janamsakhi (*lit.* 'birth-witness') Prose hagiography of Guru Nanak.

Khalistan (*lit.* 'land of the Khalsa') Ideal Sikh homeland.

Khalsa (Persian *khalisa*, 'crown estate') The brotherhood founded by Guru Gobind Singh.

Panth (*lit.* 'path') The Sikh community.

rahit The Khalsa code of conduct.

SGPC ('Shiromani Gurdwara Parbandhak Committee') Committee which controls the historic gurdwaras of the Punjab.

Singh (*lit.* 'Lion') Rajput title affixed to names of Sikh males.

Singh Sabha (*lit.* 'Singh assembly') Sikh reformist association.

Tat Khalsa (*lit.* 'real Khalsa') The dominant definition of modern Sikhism.

FURTHER READING

Sources and resources

The classic English study by a close associate of the Sikh reformers, M. A. Macauliffe: *The Sikh Religion* (Oxford: Clarendon Press, 1909) is a frequently reprinted and still valuable guide to the compositions and traditional lives of the Sikh Gurus. W. O. Cole and P. S. Sambhi: *The Sikhs: Their Religious Beliefs and Practices*, revised edition (Brighton: Sussex Academic Press, 1995) is a useful general introduction written from a religious studies perspective, including helpful charts and the full English text of the *Rahit Maryada* (pp. 200–8). W. H. McLeod: *Sikhism* (London: Penguin Books, 1997) is a comprehensive general account with very full annotated bibliography.

Sikhism in the modern world

J. T. O'Connell *et al.* (eds): *Sikh History and Religion in the Twentieth Century* (Toronto: Centre for South Asian Studies, 1988) is a bulky collection of stimulating papers relevant to many of this chapter's themes. H. S. Oberoi: *The Construction of Religious Boundaries: Culture, Identity and Diversity in the Sikh Tradition* (Delhi: Oxford University Press, 1994) is a pioneering study of the nineteenth-century reformist transformation of many traditional features of Sikh society and practice. D. S. Tatla: *The Sikh Diaspora* (London: UCL Press, 1999) provides an overview of the diaspora and its responses to the Punjab crisis of the 1980s.

　　J. S. Grewal: *Contesting Interpretations of Sikh Tradition* (New Delhi: Manohar, 1998) is a balanced account by a senior Sikh historian of modern scholarship's challenges to traditional understandings and the reactions these have provoked. Many contemporary issues are addressed in papers by leading diaspora academics in C. Shackle *et al.* (eds): *Sikh Religion, Culture and Ethnicity* (Richmond, Surrey: Curzon, 2001). N.-G. K. Singh: *The Feminine Principle in the Sikh Vision of the Transcendent* (Cambridge: Cambridge University Press, 1993) is a pioneering study of Sikh scriptural and reformist texts from the feminist perspective which also informs her scriptural translations in *The Name of My Beloved: Verses of the Sikh Gurus* (San Francisco: HarperCollins, 1995). A. S. Mandair: *Religion and the Translatability of Cultures* (Manchester: Manchester University Press, forthcoming) offers the diaspora a fundamental rethinking of Singh Sabha assumptions.

CHAPTER 4

Chinese religions

Stephan Feuchtwang

▌ INTRODUCTION

This chapter will include as religions all traditions that transmit transcendental revelations about the world. They place everyday events in a time of greater scope – cyclical, ancestral, fateful, eternal, or providential – of both the living and the dead. Many of these traditions are written. Many others are purely ritual, handed down by experts and from elders to juniors, linked to but not dependent upon textual teachings and liturgies. But in cultures of writing, such as the Chinese, textual traditions dominate.

In the centuries of the modern era in China, the various textual traditions identified most closely with Chinese civilization have been grouped into three main teachings. They are those of Buddhism (Mahāyāna and tantric), Daoism, and the ancestral, calendrical and life cycle rituals prescribed in texts written by court officials or approved scholars and derived from writings attributed to Confucius and his followers. All three traditions are liturgical in the sense that they include services of offering and response between secular and transcendent subjects. In chronological order they start with the textual record of Confucius (551–479 BCE) teaching the importance of ritual. Next come the earliest texts of philosophical Daoism attributed to the mythical authors Lao Zi and Zhuang Zi about a century after Confucius's death. Full-scale rituals of Daoist religion were first instituted some time in the last two centuries BCE. Buddhist texts and rituals were introduced in the third century CE. Each has influenced the others. People resort to all three. All three teachings accommodate household cults, such as making offerings to the stove god before and after the turn of the year, or the handing down of cults of protectors of occupations and the even more numerous territorial protectors whose carnival-like fairs or festivals define every place in China. Chinese religion is unusual in at least two respects. One is the number of teachings that co-existed and influenced each other in China. The other is an internally creative *cosmology* and the personalization of its order and forces.

551–479 BCE	Confucius
fourth–third century BCE	Lao Zi and Zhuang Zi (authors to whom the first Daoist classics are attributed)
221 BCE	Unification of states under a single emperor
third century CE	Introduction of Buddhism to China
Tang dynasty (618–905)	A period of great openness during which all the main religions of the world entered China
	Consolidation of imperial bureaucracy
Song dynasty (960–1278)	A period of great commercial development. The neo-Confucian Orthodoxy was etablished, reinterpreting Confucius's ideas of ritual and self-cultivation
Yuan dynasty (1206–60 in northern China, 1280–1341 over all China)	Mongol rule, incorporation of Muslim regions
Ming dynasty (1368–1628)	Emergence of syncretic sects and lay religious communities. Introduction of Roman Christianity
Qing dynasty (1644–1911)	Manchu rule. Protestant missions
Republican rule (1912–)	Institution of a secular state
Cultural Revolution (1966–76)	Iconoclasm and suppression of all religious activities

Figure 4.1 Timeline

Modernity in China has had a thousand years of slow emergence: the growth of commerce, monetary economy, contractual and shareholding agreements, long-distance trade and banking, cities of manufacture and commerce as well as courts and the houses of the wealthy and their luxurious consumption. This is long-term modernity and it had distinct influences on religion in China. Much faster and more recent is political or 'republican' modernity, the institution of a nation state and mass politics. The movement for a constitutional state and the emergence of mass politics began only a century and a half ago in China. This is short-term modernity and has had a much more dramatic effect on religious practices. In what follows the present tense will be used to describe religion in China as it still exists at the beginning of the twenty-first century, persisting as traditions which in the courses of long- and short-term modernity have undergone many transformations and generated from within themselves many innovations. The past tense will be used to describe the imperial system, which ceased at the beginning of the twentieth century.

The great majority of China's population of 1.3 billion take part in rituals and festivals, many of them concentrated in the days around the turning of the lunar year, which belong to no particular teaching. In addition, there are the millions who belong to no religion and take part in no festivals at all. In part this is an effect of urbanization creating an environment without the pressure of local convention, and in part it is the effect of the spread of atheism during a century of republican revolution and states which are ideologically above religion, as are most other modern states (see Chapter 15). In China this spread has included strenuous campaigns of mass iconoclasm, particularly those of the decade of Cultural Revolution, 1966–76. But in the decades since the Cultural Revolution there has been an equally remarkable resurgence of religious activity. A small minority of the Chinese population adheres to what are now the dominant world religions of Islam and Christianity. But a minority in China is numbered in many millions, because its population is so large. Numbers of followers of any one tradition are difficult to estimate, and we must in China as everywhere else rely on statistics compiled by the largest institutions, either those of the state – which tend to underestimate – or those of the religious institutions themselves – which tend to overestimate. If we include all the population of those designated national minorities with an Islamic heritage in the territory of China then we can conclude that in 1990 there were 17.5 million Muslims in the People's Republic of China. The number is not growing by evangelism or conversion. In the case of registered and unregistered Protestants, estimates vary hugely, from 10 to 30 million in 1994, for example. But what everyone agrees is that there has been a remarkable growth, from some 3 million in 1982. There is a similar variation for Catholics, also growing to estimates in 1994 of between 6 and 10 million. For the non-congregational religions of Buddhism and Daoism, official numbers are the only ones available and they are totally misleading for they are only of the ritual practitioners themselves, and even they are outnumbered by unregistered practitioners.

This chapter will concentrate on Chinese vernacular religious traditions and the textual traditions of Confucianism, Daoism and Buddhism. These remain the largest religious traditions present in China. The chapter will first provide more detail on the historical traditions of religion and ritual in China. It will then deal with the 'long' process of modernization and of religious change. The last part of the chapter will concentrate on the 'fast' process of modernization, the politics of culture, and the facts of religious revival.

SOURCES AND RESOURCES

Indigenous traditions: Confucianism and Daoism

Chinese teachings are associated with their originating *sages*, such as Confucius or the legendary Lao Zi of Daoism. Many religions are similarly identified with a man or a woman said to be the first teacher, a prophet, a *patriarch*, or his mother. But usually there is a legitimating 'antecedent', believed to be the source of what they taught. That antecedent might be a force, such as Heaven or the Way in China or a divinity such as Jehova or Buddha, or the Unborn Venerable Mother who comes before all other teachings according to millenarian sects popular in China from the sixteenth century onwards. Shamanism and many other kinds of spirit possession and rituals of divination have also persisted in China, bound up with rituals and myths, but not confined to any of the named teachings. A number of cosmological terms, such as Tian (the celestial aspect of the cosmos, often translated as 'Heaven') and Yin and Yang (complementary forces of the universe), run through these *mantic* as well as the other Chinese religious traditions. Even so, there is serious debate about whether it is appropriate to write about 'Chinese religion' in the singular.

Confucianism is the search for a middle way in order to preserve social harmony in accordance with the ordering principle of Tian. Its social universe is a *patriarchy*, which is a veneration of ancestors and descent in the male line. The Confucian emphasis on ancestral veneration and on Tian as the ordering and moral principle informs the construction of ancestral altars within homes or, more communally, in ancestral halls of lineages and sub-lineages, and in the larger associations and halls of those who share the same family name. Within the family it stresses the core importance of filial father–son, elder–junior, male–female relations in the family. Beyond the family, it stresses reciprocity in personal relations of responsibility (*ren*), and the extension of filial duty (*xiao*) to the subjects of rulers. It is a prescription of family rituals, and in particular of death rituals. But it is important to note that death rituals performed in China also include major Daoist and Buddhist liturgies, along with those prescribed in the tradition associated with Confucius.

Confucianism in Chinese is called 'the teaching of scholars' (*rujiao*). It is both a teaching and a set of ritual practices. Its core textual canon consists of five books, only one of which – The Analects (Lun Yu) – is attributable to Confucius, but all of which are said either to be the sources or the transmissions of the tradition in which he is at once the greatest sage and its chief transmitter. The canon was fixed during the former Han dynasty (206 BCE–25 CE). Over the centuries since then this core and the texts added to it became the basis of a learning that made those with the material resources and ability to master it into scholar-administrators, usually called the *literati* or 'gentry' in Western accounts of China.

Daoism became its complement as a teaching about various disciplines for achieving perfection away from the politics of imperial administration. 'Perfection' is to achieve *immortality* by becoming one with the spontaneous, self-generating rhythms and forces of the universe called 'the Way (*dao*)'. The Way is a philosophical and metaphysical conception equivalent to the ancient Greek *physis* or 'nature' in modern English, an idea of the processes of generation and regeneration underlying the existence of things and their moral order. Daoist sages emphasized the Way itself, while Confucius and Confucian sages emphasized the principles of heavenly order.

Daoism generated a number of hermetic and lay liturgical traditions, the most widespread of which are traditions of exorcism and healing. Its textual corpus was turned into a canon by approved compilations under emperors who considered their regimes to be preordained by Daoist revelations. This canon is the result of revelations from past masters of the Way, ranging from metaphysics to instructions on how to control demons.

Emperors of China were themselves honoured as agents of heaven. They could bestow royal and feudal titles upon the dead, acknowledging them as sage and powerful objects, to be venerated by offerings of food and precious objects, verbal and written address. But this process of selection of gods from the dead, similar to the cults of saints in medieval Europe, had its base not in the literati but among the common people of China. For their own advancement as local leaders, Chinese literati sought imperial honour for gods already venerated in their home places.

Today, long after the end of this system of imperial honour, local gods with imperial titles again proliferate in China's towns and villages. They are deities whose human life energies and extraordinary deeds are considered to be effective after they have died, even though they are not associated with any particular teaching. Wealth gods, city gods, stove gods, door guardians and local temple gods can all be identified by a personal name and the history of the person bearing that name. Worship of the most popular deities has spread throughout China. Each has a centre and a temple in a place where the hero or heroine or their parents lived, and there are frequently disputes over which is the original place and therefore which is the source temple and main destination of pilgrimages.

Imported traditions and heterodoxies

All the great religions of the world have existed in China at some time or other. In the past 2 thousand years Buddhism, Manichaeism, Christianity, Islam, and Judaism have entered China and been transformed and indigenized in the process. Manichaeism and an early Eastern Christianity were introduced in the seventh century by land from Central Asia and by sea through south-eastern ports. They affected various syncretic movements, but have ceased to exist as separate traditions, though they could be revived. Similarly, Judaism has ceased to exist as a practice except for a few hundred who profess to be Jews and do not eat pork. Roman Catholicism from the sixteenth century, Protestantism from the eighteenth century onwards, but none of the Eastern Orthodox traditions of Christianity, have spread throughout China, and there are now many Chinese-born Protestant movements. Likewise, in every province there are Muslim families. But Islam entered China largely by the Chinese empire's Western expansion into Central Asia, particularly when it came under Mongol and Manchu rulers in the thirteenth and the seventeenth centuries. It exists mainly as the religion of non-Chinese people in its Western provinces.

Of the imported traditions, Mahāyāna Buddhism (see Chapter 2) has had by far the greatest influence. Its entry to China in the first two centuries of the common era, along the Central Asian trade routes, began to have profound effects after it was adopted by emperors during a period of disunity between 311 and 589 CE. Asceticism and monastic organization were among its chief influences. But

Figure 4.2 Domestic religion combines all three teachings of Confucius, Buddhism and Daoism as well as vernacular deities, in this case Guan Di who is popular throughout China. This is a print of the pantheon of deities to be pasted up for the year at New Year above a household altar shelf in Hebei province (Qing dynasty). The main deities, from top to bottom, are the three Buddhas of past, present and future, the three Pure Ones of Daoism, the Jade Emperor, ruler of Heaven, and his six subordinates, and the red-faced God of War and Commerce (Guan Di), who is also a god of wealth. He is flanked by heavenly marshals and is seated behind a tablet inscribed with the characters for 'True rulers of the three realms and ten directions'. Similar prints are pasted up now in rural households all over China

their slow spread throughout China was always in tension with the more consistent orthodoxy of family, lineal reproduction, worldly responsibility, the unworthiness of begging, and the imperial suspicion of the danger of vagrants to social order. Tantric Buddhism and its clergy, called lamas, were introduced to China in the seventh century. It took from Hindu religion an emphasis on ritual action, called *tantra*, which had something in common with the magical rites of Daoism, but it spread mainly with Tibetan influence in the south-western regions of China and as the religion of Tibetan and Mongol rulers of China.

Some monarchs arranged disputations between the masters of opposed teachings. In addition, to enhance the cosmological power of their persons as well as the legitimacy of their reigns, several of them employed masters of one or other of Daoist alchemists, Roman Catholic scientists or Buddhist monks, such as Matteo Ricci, and arranged for the collection of their teachings.

Outside such authorized accommodations there was a continual process of intermingling and a proliferation of teachings. Traditions maintained as distinctive also absorbed elements of other traditions. At the same time, proliferation and mixing have been a source of political concern for all

Figure 4.3 Vernacular religion is vivid and demonic. Zhong Kui, whose fearsome ugliness and warrior skills could command and quell demons, was depicted on doors to ward off malign influences from the Tang dynasty onwards until and including today, throughout China. This is a print to be pasted on the door of a rural house.

the regimes of China, including today's. Most unauthorized teachings were open and not rebellious, but some did purport to be a secret knowledge superseding all others, and this fuelled state suspicion of conspiracy with the result that there are many more records of secret societies with rebellious intent than actually existed. The best known is the White Lotus movement, which is still described as an extremely widespread teaching in the singular by those who rely too much on official records. White Lotus has in fact been shown by Barend ter Haar (1992) to be a hostile official label for quite distinct syncretic teachings and rituals, combining Buddhist, Daoist and Confucian elements, from the fourteenth century to the present day.

Most dangerous among heterodoxies were those in which a living person assumed an imperial title, ordinarily bestowed by the ruling emperor on humans-become-gods. Such heterodoxies were intrinsically rebellious and usually millenarian, promising a new age. They claimed a pedigree which was so often repeated that it can be called a paradigm. In this paradigm without a textual tradition or a sage, the world is seen as chaotic, a battlefield of demonic powers into which someone who can command them by secrets revealed through dream, vision or spiritual possession will bring about a new order. The secrets include treasures such as a peach and pennants coloured red and numbering nine, a sword, and a protective amulet that can be multiplied. The demon commander is a new emperor who has entered into a blood covenant with a bestowing divinity to save the world, in which humans are like hungry ghosts and are prey to the violent depredations of monster devils. The police in modern China still prosecute several cases a year of such imperial imposters. They are haunted by the historical memory of how in the past some have become heads of great movements of rebellion, such as the syncretic Chinese Christian movement for Great Peace (Taiping) which captured and formed a regime over many provinces of China from 1854 to 1864.

Human agency and the cosmos

In Chinese cosmology, human agency participates in the ordering of the universe by Li ('rites'). One of the most common Chinese definitions of a rite is that it makes the invisible visible. Through the performance of rites at the proper occasions, humans make visible the underlying order, focus, link, order and move the social, or human, in correspondence with the terrestrial and celestial realms to keep all three in harmony. This procedure has been described as 'centring'. Centring was the duty of the Son of Heaven, the emperor. But it was also done by all those who conducted state, ancestral and life cycle rites, and in another way by Daoists who conducted the rites of local gods as a centring of the forces of the universe upon a well-defined locality.

All the different rituals conducted by officials of the Board of Rites, by Daoists or by local experts in the siting of graves and buildings according to the art popularly known as *fengshui*, convey a dynamic cosmology. In this cosmology the universe creates itself out of a primary chaos of material energy, organized into the cycles of *Yin* and *Yang*, and formed into objects and lives. Yin is the receptive and Yang the active principle, seen in all forms of change and difference such as the annual cycle (winter and summer), the landscape (north-facing shade, south-facing brightness), sexual coupling (female and male) and sociopolitical history (disorder and order). At the height of Yin, there is a growing nucleus of Yang, and similarly every state of Yang dominance harbours a reflux of Yin. Humans are merely one among the myriad things formed out of this primary organization of material energies, or breaths, called *qi*. But since they can cultivate and centre them, human actors are themselves central.

The two cosmic principles of Yin and Yang are never personalized, but in a widespread usage they distinguish the invisible world of those who have died (Yin) from the visible world of the alive and corporeal (Yang). Dreaming and other kinds of communication with the dead have been described as meetings of Yin and Yang. The practical concept of force that establishes responsive communication between the Yin and the Yang worlds is *ling*. *Ling* is the magical power of gods or demons multiplied by their appearance in visions during trance, or by location through a ritual of inspiration into the objects which represent them. It is a power like that of uncanny intelligence, which is indeed one of the translations of the Chinese character for *ling* offered by dictionaries. *Ling* is a divine reciprocation for offerings and pledges of devotion to a deity or demon, an effective power sought to bring about such things as recovery from illness or success in gambling. At a more abstract level, it is a concept of the exemplary force of a sage, such as Confucius. Even more abstractly it has also been expounded as an attribute of the cosmological interplay between order and disorder.

Other forces could be conceived as universal or spontaneous, and at the same time personified and responsive. The state cults of the imperial dynasties included, at the highest and most elaborate level of sacrificial rites, temples for the veneration of the imperial ancestors and open altars for offerings to Heaven, Earth, the heavenly bodies, Winds-Rain-Thunder-and-Clouds, Mountains and Rivers, Land and Grain. Like ancestors, they were represented by inscribed tablets and addressed with imperial titles. Similarly, in Daoism and Buddhism the most supreme and abstract concepts and positions in Chinese cosmology are also personalized. The three pure points of the universe, the central one of which is that of primary origin, are personalized as Heavenly Worthies and as lords of the Three Treasures by Daoists. In Buddhism, enlightenment, salvation and post-apocalyptic paradise are identified with three Buddhas: Sakyamuni, Amithabha and Maitreya (whose Sanskrit names are transliterated into Chinese). And in sixteenth-century lay Buddhist and syncretic teachings, a myth and doctrine of the Unborn Venerable Mother was 'revealed' as the personalization of the creative origin itself of the million things. She is the matriarch of a heavenly realm of spirits from which humans have been exiled and to which they may hope to be returned in the new Maitreyan age.

Daoist recluses in monasteries or hermitages on mountains and other Daoist masters in their domestic altar rooms, which they treat as holy mountains, cultivate perfection by a discipline that concentrates cosmic forces. Their inner alchemy (*neidan*) takes them on a spiritual journey back to the original state of the cosmos transcending life and death. Buddhist recluses, particularly those in the Chinese Buddhist school of *Chan* Buddhism, similarly purify themselves in hermitages or monasteries by meditation and the reading of scriptures. But whereas Daoists seek to perfect their inner nature and thus attain oneness with the totality surrounding them, Buddhists seek to rid themselves of the emotional entanglement which is the self and to achieve enlightenment and the spiritual release described as Buddhahood. Transcendence in both cases is beyond the person, yet the states of immortality and Buddhahood are pictured as human bodies clothed and arranged in commanding and dignified postures.

At the more disorderly end of the cosmos, Daoist priests conduct rituals of adjustment for the refurbishing or opening of temples, which include dances with swords to command deities who are military heroes to bring demons under control. In lesser rituals they issue talismans of similar command to rid clients of malign influences. The fiercest and most malign demons are not human ghosts. They are monsters such as the Hound of Heaven, or the White Tiger, or another one of the 108 baleful stars. Exorcizing them is not to destroy, but to control them, putting them in their places where their forces are no longer baleful. There is certainly non-human agency in Chinese religious cosmology, even in this demonic, most popular and vivid imagery. But command over it is human. This imagery of command over demons is most evident in the territorial guardian carnivals and processional pilgrimages to regional temples that define every place as part of a sacred landscape. It is the vision of an imperium as seen by commoners. On the other hand, those in positions of authority within the system of actual imperial or indeed republican rule decry the popular festivals, meat offerings and feasts as carnal, wasteful and superstitious, and stress the more civil, ascetic and abstract nature of the cosmos. They scorn as wild and heterodox the vernacular spirit-mediums producing written or spoken voices of deities and the recently dead. The latter are demonstrative, theatrical productions in trances whose contents are not remembered by the medium, whereas elite inspiration occurs in solitude and is remembered by its medium. Demons and human ghosts, or gods with great force but without the virtues and accomplishments of Confucian, Daoist or Buddhist merit, are among the most popular objects of attention for changes of luck. But even literati, who scorned such amoral practices, sought inspirational visions of gods and immortals by going into trance, ink brush in hand, in the hope that what they wrote would disclose the questions of imperial examinations they were about to sit.

Death rituals work the other way around, from personal to cosmological status. They deal directly with the demonic aspects of human being. All three textual traditions are involved. In rites of encoffinment, burial and commemoration, all human beings are treated as ghosts. If neglected or abandoned, they are hungry and trapped in the places where they met their death and can be very harmful to those who pass by. Death rituals deal with three aspects of human being. They seal off the demonic and corporeal aspects, by burying the body whose bones convey the forces gathered by the site of the grave. They honour and elevate what is conceived as an ancestor on the one hand and on the other they intervene on behalf of a soul that needs salvation into the Buddhist Western Paradise. The ancestor is installed as a name on to the domestic altar of its descendants, to be honoured on its deathday and on standard occasions for the veneration of ancestors. The soul must be released from a purgatory pictured in both Daoist and Buddhist scrolls, prints and temple murals. It is as lurid in its inventions of torment and torture as that of Christianity (see Figure 4.4).

The gaining of merit, by virtue of the soul's children employing Buddhists or Daoists to recite scriptures and intercede on behalf of a soul, is solemn and repetitive. But attached to it is a much more theatrical enactment of the mythic stories of those who, like the dutiful son Mu Lien rescuing his dead mother or the merciful first Emperor of the Tang dynasty, crossed from the Yang to the Yin world. The fact that they made the crossing shows the way to intercede on behalf of what would otherwise be an eternally trapped or forgotten soul. The performances of their crossings include comic enactments of the wiles of bribery and cajoling needed to find a way past guardian monsters and officious gatekeepers.

Figure 4.4 Hell Scroll (see also note on page 104)

Many people have observed that the imperial imagery of the Yin world is an idealization of the bureaucracy and courts of Chinese dynastic rule. But it differs markedly from the actual imperial administration in its gender and in its stress on military command. Imperial authority and the orthodoxy of ancestral veneration were strictly male and stressed descent in the male line, whereas the celestial pantheon included very important female deities. The most important and widespread god of intercession, for the dead, for women wanting children, and for the sick, was originally a Buddhist divinity who in Chinese history was transformed from a male into a female deity. This is the bodhisattva or *pusa* (one who has achieved buddhahood but chooses to remain in merciful attachment to the world) who in Sanskrit is called *Avalokitesvara*. In China he was merged with the legendary Miaoshan, a princess who incurred her father's rage by her choice of an ascetic, unmarried life until her death. She then returned to life to save him from severe physical and moral sickness by the sacrifice of her eyes and arms for him to eat as medicine. As a deity she is the female Guanyin, often known in English as the Goddess of Mercy. Her depiction is usually benign, but many Buddhist temples portray her other aspect as a much more majestic and commanding deity with a thousand arms and with her feet literally stamping authority on the monstrous dragon of the waters which is the realm of demons. Daoists honour her, as well as Buddhists. She is one of the gods whose worship has spread throughout China and epitomises the mix of vernacular and textual traditions in Chinese religion.

INTERACTIONS WITH MODERNITY

Modernity in the long term

The gradual modernization of China over a thousand years brought with it a synchronic development through mutual influence of the three traditions of Confucianism, Daoism and Buddhism. Central in this development was the process whereby Buddhism was indigenized or sinicized by being brought into relation with Confucianism and Daoism. Other syncretic movements also arose which combined all three traditions in different ways. All these developments were closely related to political, economic and social changes affecting China during this period.

By the tenth century, the increasing power of the imperial bureaucracy had already reduced the privileges of a landed nobility and augmented those of the literati and with them of Confucian orthodoxy. The growth of commerce and manufacture was beginning to provide new channels of social mobility and achievement of high status through mercantile wealth and the education of children, with the result that the next generation could be admitted into the ruling class of literati.

After a series of introductions of different kinds of Buddhism from the fourth century onwards, two main schools of monastic Buddhism persisted. They were much affected by a preference for vivid imagery, internal alchemy, a genealogy of patriarchs, and a lay following. Land and wealth donated to Buddhist monasteries enabled their donors to avoid taxation until the Emperor Wu-tsung (841–7) ordered the biggest of the periodic imperial attempts to control their independent power by confiscating their land and emancipating their slaves. From then onwards, the imperial state controlled the number of large monasteries where monks could be ordained. In alliance with these large monasteries it sought to control the far greater number of smaller temples of Buddhist families. A novice joined a 'tonsure family' headed by a monk, one of whose 'sons' inherited the temple and looked after his grave and soul tablet. Together with the large monasteries these made up the Chinese Saṅgha, the body of Buddhism. Beyond monastic orders there was a steady spread of the popularity of Buddhist deities like Guan Yin, which from the twelfth century spread beyond any particular textual or monastic order. Between these popular deities and the monastic orders were organizations of lay Buddhists who sought the blessings of bodhisattvas honoured in the temples of the monastic orders.

One of the two Chinese orders that persisted is that of the Pure Land, both monastic and lay. It is a discipline of ascetic vows, learning what the patriarchs of the order said. For lay followers it is simplified into the practice of repeating the name of Amithabha (O-mi-to-hu) in greeting, parting and any other opportunity, in order to escape the cycle of rebirths and be born into the Pure Land as a place rather than as a state of mind. Gatherings of lay Buddhists for the recitation of Omitohu called themselves White Lotus meetings, after the floating bloom which symbolizes purity and transcendence from muddy underwater roots.

The other Chinese school of Buddhism is Chan, a monastic order that included productive labour, rather than begging for alms, and a highly ritualized discipline to induce sudden enlightenment. The state of enlightenment, provoked by the master's impossible paradoxes and quizzical gestures, is a non-activity, a plunge into the state of nothingness that precedes all distinctions.

Buddhist and Daoist monks earn material rewards as well as spiritual merit by performing scriptural readings and rites of sacrificial offering for the laity. Buddhist specialities are merit-making for the dead, as souls and as ghosts, and the charitable care of the forgotten dead in the seventh month festival of the release of hungry ghosts to be fed and clothed by offerings transformed by rhetorical hand gestures (*mudra*) and the appropriate scripture of alms giving. Daoists also perform these rituals, as well as their own speciality of the *jiao*, a great offering for cosmic adjustment and harmonization of sacred places and their territories involving their whole population over a period of three or more days.

As the Chinese empire in the Song dynasty (960–1278 CE) reached heights of commerce and civil culture unrivalled in the world, Confucianism became the confirmed state orthodoxy. But it was very different from that of Confucius. It is for good reason called neo-Confucianism, since it incorporated Buddhist and Daoist ideas and disciplines of the purification of self. Inner reality became a source of authority, but in relationship with the outer world of others. It was a relationship tense with the problems of not accomplishing the required calm and oneness with others, covered over with decorum and strategies of indirection. Thomas Metzger has analysed this stance as an anxiety quite different from but equivalent to Protestant ascetic worldliness, an anxious predicament of Confucian self-cultivation combined with worldy involvement in conflict and corruption.

Emphasis on *Li*, centring, was always central to Confucianism. But Li had begun as a term for royal and noble sacrifices to ancestors and to deities and then was extended to all the manners and protocols of the court and nobility. Now the scope and meaning of Li was broadened to a cultivation by the whole population of the dispositions, inclinations and emotions essential to the appreciation and performance of ritual. To perform Li is to cultivate an ideal of human responsiveness, not only to other humans and their stations in the imperial and patriarchal order but also to the rest of the world and its harmony. This was the ideal and the ideology of the ruling literati of China. But their acts of cruelty, ruthless careerism and indulgence in the pleasures of eating, sex and drugs led to accusations of hypocrisy.

Vernacular literacy and commerce spread and their networks of communication deepened from the fourteenth century onwards (Ming and Qing dynasties) presenting many challenges to the moral authority of the literati and to the administration of the empire. The latter was undergoing a demographic explosion, putting extra strains on the comparatively small staff of the imperial civil service. Local gentry became increasingly powerful. They extended the notion of family and kinship to tax protected clients. Many among the rest of the rural population, over taxed and thrown into debt, had no alternative than to allow their land to be expropriated. They became bondservants and labourers for the commercializing gentry. Against this, replacing the disappointed expectations of local ties of benevolence and compassion, new kinds of association were created, under the patronage of reform minded gentry. Among such new associations were syncretic religions bringing together neo-Confucian teachings, a Buddhism of lay leaders independent of monasteries, and Daoist healing and meditational techniques. Many of their leaders were evangelists giving public lectures, publishing moral tracts and keeping moral ledgers by which the merit and demerit of their followers' actions could be recorded and their prospects of salvation calculated. The Confucian priority of filial duty was retained but placed in a larger Buddhist context of karmic retribution. At the same time, the effort and discipline of classical learning and ritual were undermined by doctrines of spontaneous enlightenment.

Eventually, in the seventeenth century, against such popular moral cultivation, there was a Confucian reaction. High ranking and disillusioned or dismissed officials and some of the highest degree holders in the lower Yangtze River region formed the Donglin Academy for reform of the gentry and the practice of good administration. In order to deny authenticity to the many new sectarian associations, they demanded return to the canonized classics and the virtues they proclaimed.

The new stress on what had originally been written by a sage was accompanied by the development of an apparatus of careful textual scholarship to authenticate what was and was not written by the claimed master. In the same vein, empirical observation of astronomical and other changes, using whatever new instruments had been developed in China or brought from Europe, was another way of establishing authenticity and the superiority of the scholarly elite. In this way, the preservation of the authentically ancient came into tension with the observations of anomalies and irregularities. Great sophistication was required to justify ancient cosmology. Scholars themselves drew the parallel between inevitability of corruption leading to necessity for reform of the human heart–mind, which includes rectification of social custom, and observations of anomalies leading to the necessity for a rectification of cosmology. Communications between the lowest and highest levels of the imperial bureaucracy maintained the prestige of this new metaphysics. They funnelled suspicion of every new movement of lay Buddhism and syncretic association. Corruption and extortion, large-scale persecution of peaceful associations, and the rebellions of millenarian sects against their persecution spread wide a sense of insecurity.

In this atmosphere, several bouts of mass fear flared, word passing like prairie fire of spells being posted on doors and weird shapes flying into people's houses and causing disaster. Such panics had occurred before, but in the sixteenth century for the first time they were attributed to individual magicians who were Buddhist monks, Daoist priests, carpenters, puppeteers, peddlers, or beggars, precisely the travelling objects of official suspicion and persecution. The internalization of agency and authority into magicians and imperial imposters paralleled the internalization of dignity, agency and authority in Orthodox neo-Confucianism.

Panics of mass fear indicated political crisis and growing numbers of those dislocated by debt and into beggary, refugees from flood, drought, banditry and the depredations of imperial troops. Another indication of political crisis was the increasing mobilization of local militia, organized as martial arts bands displaying the forces of the generals and soldiers of a local protective deity. Now they took part in uprisings to bring about a new age and to overthrow the rule and power of strangers, such as the Manchu dynasty or the missionaries of European business and religion, and any others branded as spies by local residents.

LAY COMMUNITIES

Buddhist monasteries and the imperial state together tried to bring under control one of these movements of new teaching, a movement whose followers took ascetic vows (*zhaijiao*). Their number grew into a proliferation of branches from the sixteenth century onwards. These lay Buddhists accused the tonsured Saṅgha of corruption, mocked them in popular stories and declared themselves to be separate and better. They formed their own, lay Saṅgha, combining married life with fasts, obedience to key precepts such as not to indulge in malicious or salacious talk, nourishing life in the Daoist and Chan Way, cultivating the neo-Confucian Way of Heaven, and studying precious scrolls revealed and derived ultimately from the Unborn Venerable Mother. They met in congregations for the recital of memorized passages from both orthodox *sutras* and precious scrolls and made donations for the printing and distribution of the scrolls and the building of assembly halls. Their congregations included both women and men, which was a scandal for Confucian orthodoxy. More scandalous yet, biographies of model women who had renounced marriage, and the stories of female deities who had done the same, encouraged one strand of this movement in which women formed communities equivalent to nunneries except that they earned their own livelihood by silk manufacture.

Religious communities for the less literate included meetings of the pupils of masters of meditation, the circulation of breaths (*qi*) and other exercises to recover from illness, to nourish one's nature (*xing*) and strengthen one's destiny (*ming*), an inner visioning of the colours, directions, forces and processes of the cosmos. Often this strengthening had a martial character. The most famous of these networks of masters and pupils stretched from the Shaolin Buddhist monastery, but there were many others.

The most common 'religious' communities by far were, however, not these voluntary Buddhist and syncretic associations, but those formed by neighbourhood temples in cities, village ancestral halls and local, rural temples. Their endowments of land furnished the means to perform annual festivals, provide special meals and meeting places for the elderly, and in the case of ancestral trusts elementary schooling for lineage children. In many instances temples or halls were village corporations through which the use of such common property as land and inshore waters was distributed, or market concessions and standards of weight and measure were managed. In all instances, in addition to these sources of income, the collection of dues from households paid for the refurbishing of local hall or temple, and for the procession and theatre of annual festivals. To donate to temple and festival was a work of public good by local residents along with the building of bridges and opening of roads. Rotation of responsibility for paying respects to the smallest Earth God could, for instance, carry with it responsibility for maintaining paths and bridges.

Republican modernity

In the end, though, it was not a millenarian uprising nor a combination of local temple militia but a republican movement for self-strengthening progress that abolished the imperial state, its cosmological rites and its neo-Confucian orthodoxy. From 1912 the political parties and the new armies, first of nationalists and warlords, then communists, fought a devastating civil war interrupted by eight years of Japanese invasion and occupation (1937–45). The nationalists led by Chiang Kaishek could claim the most direct inheritance of the republican overthrow of the last imperial dynasty in 1911, but had become extortionate, corrupt and indebted to military and financial support from the US. The communists led by Mao Zedong emphasized socialism, land reform, self-reliance and anti-imperialism. But both were republican and had two things in common: the claim to represent 'the people' rather than a celestial mandate to rule harmoniously, and the desire to promote mass literacy and a scientific education. Both imported from Europe via Japan a suspicion of religion, a desire to separate state from any form of religion and a secular and constitutional definition of religion as an organized institution of beliefs and textual authority. They also carried forward the imperial state's suspicion of lay religious communities and movements and condemnations of the carnal, theatrical and martial festivals of local temples. But of course the condemnation of superstition in twentieth-century China is implemented by governments with far larger apparatuses of policing than those of the imperial state. Among them are the Religious Affairs Bureaux with which every religious institution has to register on the mainland, if it is to avoid the potential danger of being harassed or persecuted.

The new word *zongjiao* used to import the category 'religion' combines 'ancestral tradition' with 'teaching'. Institutions that fit this category, such as monasteries and churches, so long as they are patriotic, are registered and granted the religious freedom pronounced by the state's constitution. In the People's Republic (mainland China) everything else is liable to be categorized as 'superstition' (another European category). 'Superstition', or 'errant beliefs' (*mixin*), is a term used in the 1997 Criminal Code of the People's Republic alongside older categories of legal prohibition on forming secret societies and using heterodox teachings to organize movements which cause unrest or cover other criminal and sexually licentious acts.

In practice the notion of superstition has been used to condemn aspects of popular culture that do not suit the ideals of a project of secular modernization. But since modern governments claim popular legitimacy, compromises have to be made. Modernity's ideologues swing between condemnation of religion, and treating popular religion either as a way of promoting modern civilization or as heritage and local custom to be preserved. Religious buildings and spectacles can be an attraction to tourists and to the nostalgia for their origins of urban and overseas visitors. In either case, the general trend has been for overt hostility to religion to diminish as religious activities are reflected in the mirror of legitimation by the agencies of a secular state.

Yet the corrosive effects of the nation state on religion in China are evident. Damage has been inflicted in numerous ways, both direct and indirect. In the mid-twentieth century the communist state of the People's Republic of China on the mainland and the nationalist state on the island of Taiwan redistributed the land, not only of private but also of corporate landlords. A main material foundation of religious communities was thereby removed. The building and repair of large and small temples and the holding of festivals were forced to rely only on subscription and donation, perhaps an appropriately populist basis for sacred communities. Yet the main cause of decline in religious activities has not been the confiscation of land but mass destitution – caused by war, civil war and economic disaster. The converse has also been true – prosperity has been a spur to religious activity, though not always to revival of earlier forms of rite and organization. But in addition to the effects of disruption, destitution and prosperity, direct political action did have a decided effect on the mainland. From 1953 the collectivization of land and the state administration of industry in collective units of work and home created a monopoly for socialist political culture. This had the effect of making religious teachings and practices private and marginal. Then, in the culmination of a series of campaigns against religion, the Cultural Revolution campaign against old habits, ideas, customs and culture in 1966 and 1967 destroyed or forced them underground.

The Cultural Revolution can itself be viewed as a secular or civic religion, and a ritualization of revolution. Its mass campaigns are still remarkable for the intensity of political rituals that were of a new, congregational kind, and represented the culmination of a politics of mass mobilization first introduced for the redistribution of land through peasant associations. They were at a greater level of frequency and of a longer duration than any other rituals performed by Chinese people and they affected everyone. This 'civic religion' was reinforced through education. Citizens were imbued with ideals of service to the people and mass participation in revolutionary transformation, and were constrained by the necessity for discipline and deference to the leadership of the Chinese Communist Party (CCP), which became personalized in the figure of Mao. Children's dances and songs became rituals, performed in schools and in public displays. Everyone learnt and then knew by habit the gestures of selfless determination, the distant gaze into an Eastern sunlit future, the indomitable fury of the downward gesture defeating enemies of the Chinese popular masses, and the ardent look toward the leadership of Mao and the Communist Party. Youth from the city volunteered for immersion in the countryside to propagate devotion to Maoist socialism. They competed with each other for hard work in the fields and for the honour of being viewed as paragons of selflessness. They set up daily study sessions, and broadcast several times a day from village loudspeakers to praise instances of good political attitude and work performance and to criticize laggards. Production improved. So did material well-being, reduction of pilfering and respect for the idea of acting as part of a collective. Other meetings dramatized stories of the longer distant past, before land reform, where those who had suffered most learnt to recite their bitterness and bring tears to the eyes of listeners. As at the Jewish Passover, all shared a meal of bitter herbs.

Maoist socialism as expounded and recited during the Cultural Revolution eventually exhausted its ideological credibility as campaigns became too frequent and too patently harnessed to vengeance and advancement by activists. This civic religion was gradually replaced by a socialism couched not so much in terms of discipline, self-sacrifice and collective action as in terms of advancing people's material livelihood. Religious buildings were returned and fevers of enthusiasm for various religious and quasi-religious teachings occurred, particularly those of *qi* exercizes promoted by various masters, some accepted by officials as scientific (*kexue*, both natural and historical knowledge), others viewed as a danger to society.

But one lasting effect of the political rituals of mass mobilization is the habit of congregational participation with overtones of egalitarian comradeship and mutual support. This may be one reason for the increase in the numbers of Christian meeting points and churches. Asked about their experiences from land reform to the end of the decade of Cultural Revolution, people often speak of chaos, fear and hunger. But in relation to the present, the same speakers remember those years as a time of security and straight dealing to be contrasted favourably with the self-seeking party of the post-Mao state. Mao has become a means to criticize the present regime.

LOOKING TO THE FUTURE

There are now a great many religious teachings and rituals practised in China, each claiming to be a tradition and having its own sanctity. Inflecting these traditions, it is possible to distinguish three different religious tendencies or styles, all of which can be found in any one religious tradition. One tendency is individual or family oriented, seeking changes or maintenance of fortune, personal health and lineal reproduction. A second is to identify a teaching with the Chinese nation or civilization, or an ethnic identity within it, and to maintain or establish institutions and liturgy accordingly. The third is to meet in congregations and seek to strengthen the intimate bonds of community.

In both Taiwan and the mainland, the intensity of material incentives and engagement in global economic competition has brought about a ruthless cynicism on the one hand and a search for spiritual healing and justification on the other. Sources of moral regeneration in a chaotic and corrupt world are sought as before from responsive deities in local temples. Millenarian teachings and communities and imperial imposters thrive among those excluded from material advancement. But other, newer senses of religious community, not confined to a place or to traditional paradigms, have also emerged.

Freed from the assertion of imperial canonical, ritual and cosmological authority, religious traditions and movements in China now renew themselves under another kind of authority. Many forms of Chinese religion today – despite widely varying emphases – are characterized by a national or local identification and seem under a compulsion, both externally imposed and internalized, to locate themselves within a grand historical narrative of the Chinese people or peoples. At the same time they assert an alternative and transcendental authority. It may be an authority within the cosmology of the Way of *qi*, Yin and Yang and *ling*, or reformulations of syncretic Buddhism and neo-Confucianism. It may be the joining of new transnational foundations of Buddhist, Christian and Muslim teachings. It may be the wish to escape all political involvement by withdrawal into communities of mutual spiritual support, such as house churches and meeting points. But few escape politicization, not least because they are always subject to governmental surveillance or supervision.

In the decades after Mao, economic inequalities have grown, and self-interest and cynicism are perceived to be on the increase. New spiritual groupings for healing and moral order seem to offer some compensation and even a space for protest in the face of these discontents. They are still, however, viewed with grave suspicion by the government, as the following news item indicates:

> The approach of the year 2000 has given rise to a number of millennial groups which are outside the mainstream and are singled out by the government for suppression. In June of 1999, the head of the Religious Affairs Bureau spoke of a 'government crackdown on a small number of cults which threaten the social and public interest'. Among groups singled out by the government to be closed down are the 'Shouters [a sectarian Christian movement]', the Disciple Group, the Holistic Group, the Bei Li Group and the Yi Guan Dao [the Way of Basic Unity, a syncretic movement of the three teachings with elements from other religions, formed in the first two decades of the century in northern China, spreading throughout the mainland and Taiwan. It was disbanded and suppressed on the mainland and in Taiwan for forty years. But in Taiwan it is now a recognised religion].
>
> (From the website of the International Committee for
> Religious Freedom, December 1999)

Mass exercises take place as part of a new communist tradition. Public health posters for physical and spiritual civilization include pictures of young people doing them. Dancing with fans and drums, which stems from a north Chinese festival procession tradition, was also once officially promoted. It is now popular in several neighbourhoods of large cities but officially frowned upon. Old people conduct group exercises in the strengthening of their *qi*, or can be seen ballroom dancing early in the morning for similar reasons. All these have become popular. Meetings in parks and other open spaces for *qi* exercises are increasing with the increasing number of retired people, organizing themselves, helping each other, exchanging views of the world. But when they are not in regulated surroundings such as schools, they are looked upon with suspicion and anxiety by government agencies, because they hark back to the mass movements of the Mao era or even further back to the Taiping kingdom of the nineteenth century.

> One of the movements stemming from the popularity of Qigong (exercising to enhance *qi* energies) is the Great Method Of the Buddhist Wheel (Falun Dafa) that emerged and grew rapidly in the late 1990s following the books and recordings (audio and video) of a Master Li Hongzhi. He lives in the US after being exiled in 1997. In February 2000 it was pronounced personally by President Jiang Zemin to be the biggest danger to the security of the People's Republic because of the steadfast continuation of protests by its followers against wrongful arrests despite concerted police actions starting in April 1999. An interpretation of its impact is given in the following extract.
>
> Differences with traditional groups are for instance the absence of rules and rites of daily worship, the degree of self-consciousness about outside critics long before the persecutions since April 1999, the centrality of writing, the use of modern technology, the unusual fusion of essentially Daoist inspired Qigong with a Buddhist cosmology derived from books. There are no references, however, to Buddhist divine figures in any central position, nor is any mention made of the Eternal Mother

cosmology that is so central to a number of new religious groups and traditions of the late imperial period. Li Hongzhi is explicitly against the Yiguandao (Unity Teachings) in his *Zhuan falun* II, pp. 86–91 (although I do not get the impression that he is very familiar with this or other traditional Chinese new religious groups' actual teachings and practices). Commonalities are the focus on healing (at least in the early phase) and moral behaviour as an explanatory paradigm for all kinds of personal and societal problems. On the other hand, we find a similar stress in pre-1976 PRC (Maoist) propaganda and political campaigns, which is quite relevant given Li Hongzhi's background in propaganda activities.

(From Barend ter Haar's website on the Falun Gong, December 1999)

In Taiwan, where the government of the Nationalist Party has been transformed into a far more open, tolerant and multiparty regime, religious activities are far less strictly supervised. But culture, including religious culture, is the subject of intense rivalry between the main political parties for community development and loyalty, and for establishing a sense of Taiwanese identity. Another new development is the rise of Buddhist foundations, enormously wealthy on the basis of donations. Their teachings emphasize action in the world such as flood and earthquake relief, the building of hospitals, universities and museums.

Nothing like this is possible on the mainland. Here selected Daoist and Buddhist seminaries are training a small, controlled number of monks and ritual experts. They are, as in imperial times, part of a system of religious control and supervision. But beyond their influence, Daoist and Buddhist practitioner families have revived their own traditions in several regions of every province by pooling resources, bringing out such manuscripts as they had managed to keep and sharing what they could recall of their liturgies. In all provinces of China, temples and ancestral halls have been rebuilt, usually with the endorsement of local officials. New cults have been added, including for instance in southern Fujian the cult of Che Gong, a protector of motor vehicles, and in the northern province of Shaanxi the Three Sages: Mao, his premier Zhou Enlai and General Zhu De. But in some regions and in most large cities, local cults and festivals have not been revived. This may be because of the presence and vigilance of officials still committed to the project of scientific modernization and party atheism. It may also be because the time elapsed since the destruction of religious institutions is now so great that they are no longer part of living memory. But in these places, as elsewhere in China, over and beyond the revival of local festivals, congregational religion (Buddhist or Christian) is growing, forming communities of followers of a faith which does sometimes coincide with a locality, but need not.

Gender considerations appear to have a bearing on the growth of congregational forms of religion. Local temple and rural domestic forms of rite and festival are not congregational, and here males dominate public roles on special occasions. Women merely watch theatrical performances and furnish offerings to deities and ancestors. But Christian and Buddhist congregational meetings are public settings in which women have in recent centuries not only participated, but assumed positions of leadership. Both forms of religion have been revived and prospered – and this feminization may well turn out to be a feature of future religious practices in other traditions, as it is increasingly in town and city dance and *qi* exercise groups. Female drum and musical bands have also been formed in some villages and towns, where in the past they had been exclusively male preserves. The participation of young women, in groups opposite groups of young men, singing karaoke in towns and large villages is a parallel development.

Patriarchy, associated with Confucius, continues to be strongly associated with the veneration of ancestors. Rather ambivalently, the heritage of Confucius as a historical figure and a sage, condemned to eradication in a campaign during the last years of the Cultural Revolution decade, is now officially sponsored and recycled as the distinctively Chinese national and civilizational spirit of global humanity, and is related to the remarkable growth of the Chinese economy. Philosophical studies of Confucian thought are published. His home and the temple to him in Qufu, Shandong province, are well kept and visited by high officials for the annual celebrations of his birthday.

Confucius's is one of a number of national shrines and birthdays of legendary and historical figures of Chinese ethnic nationality, starting with the mythic founder of the Chinese race, the Yellow Emperor. But more numerous are the memorials to twentieth-century founders such as Sun Yatsen, leader of the first Republic in 1911, and the monuments, birthplaces and dwellings during their military campaigns of Mao, Deng Xiaoping and other selected heroes of the communist revolution. In the same spirit, minority nationalities in China have also built shrines to heroes of their own ethnohistory, such as the great Mongol Emperor Genghis Khan in Inner Mongolia. The revitalization of Islam among the northwestern peoples of China, and the politicoreligious reverence of the Dalai Lama among Tibetans in China participate in the same cycle of ethnic nationalism. But of course they are far more problematic to the leaders of the Chinese Communist Party than their own promotion of the cult of the Yellow Emperor.

Beneath all these religious and quasi-religious institutions are religious activities of domestic and personal life. Ancestors are revered in most households, led by their older members, particularly when families get together during the longest annual holiday at the turn of the lunar New Year, officially called the Spring Festival in partial denial of its traditional religious importance. When new houses are built for married sons ceremonies are performed for the breaking of the earth, the raising of the roof beam, and completion, to ward off malign influences and bring blessings. The expertise of *fengshui* masters is sought for the orientation of houses in villages and graves in cemeteries. Recent studies indicate increased resort to *fengshui* masters, other kinds of diviner and spirit mediums for cures to ill-health, exorcizing dwellings and other rites for changes of fortune. *Fengshui* is practised along with the popular exercises to increase *qi* stress self- and family-centred accumulation of benign energies and defence against the malign. Daoists are more closely linked to local cults of deities and to territorial communities, warding off their demons and ghosts. Nevertheless this new development indicates a sense of self in a less territorially defined world, and the possibilities of movement through it and change for oneself within it. On the other hand, the new, more congregational religious communities create environments for mutual care and transcendent principles of judging wordly conduct, including the self-centerd exploitation of the world and its energies, and the conduct of political leaders and local officials. But as before in China, these new, less localized senses of transcendent self and community are not exclusive. Their followers often also participate in revitalized local cults and festivals, employ Daoist ritual experts and express national political pride.

▌ SUMMARY

▌ There are three main written religious traditions in China: (1) ancestral veneration, filial duty, reciprocity and the importance of rites, associated with the teaching of Confucius; (2) the disciplines and rituals of harmonization with the cosmic order, called Daoism; (3) Mahāyāna Buddhism and the rituals and disciplines of merit making for reincarnation and salvation from purgatory.

▌ These three traditions are eclectically mixed, and have influenced each other deeply in the course of the millennium of 'slow modernity' from the tenth century under an established imperial bureaucracy and its literati. The traditions are also mixed with a great number of vernacular traditions and local cults and festivals.

- Running through both written and vernacular traditions are a number of cosmological principles and their personifications as deities. They include Tian (celestial order), the internal creativity of the universe out of its own origin, human agency in the harmonization of celestial and earthly orders, the complementarity of Yin and Yang, effective and communicative response beyond death between Yin and Yang, and the potential for both order and disorder in human demonic power and material energies, benign and malign.
- The imperial state sought control and legitimation through the authorization of religious orthodoxies and the accompanying suspicion of what it had not authorized.
- Since at least the sixteenth century there has been a growth of lay religious communities, evangelical and syncretic, but the most common lay religious communities were those based on ancestral graves or halls and on local temples, a great many of which have recently been revived after their destruction in the Cultural Revolution (1966–76).
- 'Short modernity', characterized by the rule of secular, modernizing and atheist states, has seen the establishment of much stronger powers of supervision over religious teaching and activity, often with secularizing consequences.
- At the end of the twentieth century this was accompanied by ethnic nationalization of Chinese and non-Chinese traditions, drawing local traditions into national narratives.
- Simultaneously there has also been an increase in contrasting religious styles. One of them is congregational religion, Buddhist and Christian, in which women predominate. They may develop into large-scale non-governmental organizations of poverty relief, education and other kinds of charitable engagement in the world.
- The other style is self- and family-centred consultation of spirit media, or by *fengshui* and exercises to accumulate and strengthen *qi* to change luck and cure spiritual and physical sickness.

Note re Figure 4.4: This is one of a set of scrolls that a family of Buddhists in northern Taiwan used in the 1960s for merit-making ceremonies after death. At the top in the centre is the last, tenth court of purgatory whose president is the Prince of Karma (the turning to new life through death according to a ledger of merit and misdeeds committed in each previous life). Everything is labelled, to help the mourning family and its neighbours familiarize themselves with the afterlife. To his left is the Gate of the Wheel of Karma of human ghosts whose rebirth is shown in the incense smoke rising from the cylinders on the shelf. To his right is seated a benevolent old woman, the Buddhist goddess Meng So. Immediately below are virtuous people being led up to rebirth. Further below are four hells, showing human ghosts tormented by demons and labelled by the misdeed for which they are there. Some of them are: in the upper two mountains, cruelty and plotting to injure others; in the Ox-goring Hell, killing oxen; in the Hell of the Tree of Double-edged Swords again plotting against others, and for harming their *fengshui*.

KEY TERMS

chan A Chinese monastic form of Buddhism.

cosmology A transcendental context of life, which places it in a universe of forces and an order of things.

fengshui The art of selecting an auspicious site for dwellings, graves and important buildings, and for laying out gardens and cities.

immortal   One who has achieved perfection through inner alchemy and achieved unity with the Way (*dao*), transcending life and death. Stories of immortals, particularly those of a set called the Eight Immortals, tell of their funny, robust, licentious and heroic deeds.

Li   Rites, manners, and protocol; observance of the right way of doing things; making the invisible visible.

ling   The uncanny power to respond, of a sage, a deity or a demon.

literati   Those who had been educated in the classics of the canon of scholars, whose greatest transmitter was Confucius, and who had passed at least the lowest level of the examinations testing their knowledge of these classics to qualify for entry into the imperial civil service.

mantic   Of or concerning divination, possession or prophecy.

patriarch   A Buddhist sage who has taken on the teaching of a previous patriarch, sometimes by a claim to being his reincarnation.

patriarchy   The senior male monopoly of public authority, including authority over a family.

qi   Material energies or breaths.

sage   A person whose wisdom and teachings have been passed on and paid the highest respect.

FURTHER READING

General

Christian Joachim: *Chinese Religions: A Cultural Perspective* (Englewood Cliffs, NJ: Prentice-Hall, 1986).

Sourcebook

Gary Seaman and Laurence Thompson: *Chinese Religions: Publications in Western Languages*, Volume 3: 1991–5, (Ann Arbor, MI: University of Michigan Press, 1988).

Cosmology and divination

John B. Henderson: *The Development and Decline of Chinese Cosmology* (New York, NY: Columbia University Press, 1984).

Richard J. Smith: *Fortune-Tellers and Philosophers: Divination in Traditional Chinese Society* (Boulder, CO: Westview Press, 1991).

Daoism

Judith Bolz: *Survey of Taoist Literature: Tenth to Seventeenth Centuries* (Berkeley, CA: Institute of East Asian Studies, University of California, 1987).

Kristofer Schipper: *The Daoist Body* (Berkeley, CA: University of California Press, 1993).

Confucianism

Chow Kai-wing: *The Rise of Confucian Ritualism in Late Imperial China* (Palo Alto, CA: Stanford University Press, 1994).

Patricia Buckley Ebrey: *Confucianism and Family Rituals in Imperial China: A Social History of Writing about Rites* (Princeton, NJ: Princeton University Press, 1991).

Thomas A. Metzger: *Escape from Predicament: Neo-Confucianism and China's Evolving Political Culture* (New York, NY: Columbia University Press, 1977).

State cults

Angela Zito: *Of Body and Brush: Grand Sacrifice as Text/Performance in Eighteenth-Century China* (Chicago and London: University of Chicago Press, 1997).

Buddhism

Holmes Welch: *The Practice of Chinese Buddhism, 1900–1950* (Cambridge, MA: Harvard University Press, 1967).

Holmes Welch: *The Buddhist Revival in China* (Cambridge, MA: Harvard University Press, 1968).

Christianity

Kim-Kwong Chan and Alan Hunter: *Protestantism in Contemporary China* (Cambridge: Cambridge University Press, 1993).

Richard Madsen: *China's Catholics: Tragedy and Hope in an Emerging Civil Society* (Berkeley, CA: University of California Press, 1998).

Islam

Dru Gladney: *Muslim Chinese: Ethnic Nationalism in the People's Republic* (Cambridge, MA and London: Harvard University Press, 1991).

Popular religion

Stephan Feuchtwang: *Popular Religion in China: The Imperial Metaphor* (Richmond: Curzon Press, 2001).

Philip A. Kuhn: *Soulstealers: the Chinese Sorcery Scare of 1768* (Cambridge, MA: Harvard University Press, 1990).

Steven P. Sangren: *History and Magical Power in a Chinese Community* (Stanford, CA: Stanford University Press, 1987).

James Watson and Evelyn Rawski (eds): *Death Ritual in Late Imperial and Modern China* (Berkeley, CA: University of California Press, 1988).

Syncretic teachings and millenarianism

Barend ter Haar: *The White Lotus Teachings in Chinese Religious History* (Leiden: E. J. Brill, 1992).

Barend ter Haar: 'China's inner demons; the political impact of the demonological paradigm' (*China Information* 11 (2/3), 1996: 54–88).

David Johnson *et al.* (ed.): *Popular Culture in Late Imperial China* (Berkeley, CA: University of California Press, 1986). See the chapters by Judith Berling, Susan Naquin and Daniel Overmyer.

The Cultural Revolution and its rituals

Richard Madsen: *Morality and Power in a Chinese Village* (Berkeley, CA: University of California Press, 1984).

Japanese religions

Robert J. Kisala

▌ INTRODUCTION

In contrast to the situation in many of the European countries and some other areas of the West, where we see relatively high levels of at least nominal religious affiliation and low levels of participation in religious rites, religion is Japan in marked by almost universal participation in certain rites and customs but low levels of self-acknowledged affiliation to a religious group. It has become commonplace to say that Japanese are born Shinto, marry as Christians and die Buddhists, a phrase that indicates both the high level of participation in religious rites of passage as well as the eclectic nature of Japanese religiosity. Note is also often made of the fact that nearly 90 per cent of the Japanese observe the custom of annual visits to ancestral graves, and 75 per cent have either a Buddhist or Shinto altar in their home. However, surveys consistently show that only 30 per cent of the population identify themselves as belonging to one of the religions active in Japan – this despite the fact that the religions themselves claim an overall total membership that approaches twice the actual population of 126 million. This is mainly due to the fact that much of the population is automatically counted as parishioners of both the local Shinto shrine and the ancestral Buddhist temple.

Although identified today as the major religious traditions of Japan, Buddhism and Shinto have been so closely intertwined throughout much of Japanese history that the forced separation of the two at the beginning of the modern period in the mid-nineteenth century resulted in a great upheaval in Japanese religious practice that, some have argued, continues to have repercussions today. In addition, these religious traditions have been combined with elements of Daoism and Confucianism from China, issuing in a kind of common or popular religiosity that is not easily contained in any one religious tradition. Christianity, introduced to Japan in the fifteenth century by the Catholic missionaries who accompanied the Spanish and Portuguese explorers, was actively persecuted throughout the early modern period (seventeenth century to mid-nineteenth century), and small groups of 'hidden Christians' continue to preserve a secret faith tradition that they trace back to the time of persecution. Reintroduced in the modern period, Christianity has had little success in attracting members in Japan, with less than 1 per cent of the population belonging to one of the Christian churches. Christian influence is generally acknowledged as greater than those membership numbers would indicate, however, especially in the fields of education and social welfare.

The modern period has seen the proliferation of new religious movements in Japan, to the extent that the country has sometimes been called a veritable religious museum and laboratory. Some of the new religions trace their roots to the end of the early modern period in the first half of the nineteenth century. Groups from this period are often based on folk religious practices and the experiences of a charismatic founder, and they can be described as attempts to revitalize traditional cultural elements in the face of the influx of Western influences during that century. Another wave of new religious movements emerged in the immediate postwar period, attracting much media attention in Japan as well as abroad. These movements were often Buddhist-based lay movements, and some of them have been successful in attracting followers numbering in the millions. Part of the reason for their success lies in the fact that they offered the increasingly urban population a means to perform the traditional ancestor rites in the home, independent of the Buddhist clergy and temples that they left behind in the move to the cities. Finally, a third wave of new religions has emerged since the 1970s, mirroring religious developments predominantly seen in the West. These movements emphasize personal spiritual development, and encourage the adoption of ideas and practices from a wide range of religions in order to contribute to that development.

Given this religious ferment, it is hard to describe Japan as a secular society. However, many Japanese would prefer to see themselves as secular or unconcerned with religion. In a recent survey, for example, only 26 per cent of the respondents in Japan described themselves as religious. In part this is due to the controversy surrounding some religious groups, particularly the new religions that have become so prominent in the modern period. The already poor image of these groups was further damaged by the terrorist activities of Aum Shinrikyō in the mid-1990s, contributing to the rise of an anti-cult movement in Japan. However, the attitude towards religion in Japan is also a function of fundamental differences in the understanding of 'religion' as compared to the West, differences that arise from the history of religion in that country.

Modernity, as it is understood in Japan, is closely associated with the country's contact with the West. What is commonly referred to as the early modern period followed the arrival of Portuguese and Spanish explorers in the sixteenth century, and was marked by the attempt to limit contact with the West during the two-and-a-half century Tokugawa Shogunate (1603–1867). The modern period was ushered in by the collapse of that regime in the face of the forced opening of the country by American and other Western powers, leading to a mad rush to catch up with the West economically, technologically and militarily. The desire to build a nation strong enough to avoid Western colonization contributed greatly to emergence of Japanese nationalism and Japanese colonialism, and impacted on religious developments during this period. Government attempts to separate Buddhism from Shinto and establish Shinto as the moral and spiritual basis for Japanese nationalism provided the background against which religion as a concept was debated and understood. In addition, the effects of industrialization, urbanization and the affluence of the postwar period are especially apparent in the emergence of new religious movements, where the changing face of Japanese society is reflected in the development of first rural movements that emphasized an egalitarian solidarity, then urban mass movements and finally a turn to the self in post-1970 movements. Despite the official attempt to identify a native Japanese religious tradition alongside various imported traditions, Japanese religious

Figure 5.1 The Daibutsu, or Great
Buddha, at Kamakura, cast in the
thirteenth century

history is marked more by the eclectic use of religious elements from various traditions, a tendency that
continues in the religious movements of the modern period.

SOURCES AND RESOURCES

Buddhism was probably gradually introduced into Japan through Korea by means of migration from
around the fifth century CE. The date usually given for the official introduction of Buddhist images
and scriptures to the Japanese court is 552 CE, or perhaps 538 CE. This presentation was supposedly
made by the ruler of a Korean clan allied to Japan, shortly before the loss of a Japanese colony on the
peninsula. Prince Shōtoku, who administered the government of Japan from the end of the sixth century
to the early seventh century, is credited with adopting Buddhism as the religion of the court, under the
influence of the Soga clan, avid supporters of the religion.

The Buddhism introduced to Japan was predominantly Chinese Mahāyāna Buddhism, and from
the seventh century groups of Japanese monks were sent to China for training. Of the myriad Buddhist
texts, particularly important for Japanese Buddhism already from this period was the *Lotus Sutra*.
Literary-critical analysis indicates multiple authorship of the sutra, and the text was largely complete
by the late second or early third century CE, although Chapter 12 was probably added in the sixth
century. The sutra consists of twenty-eight chapters, and purports to be the final teaching of Sakyamuni,
the historical Buddha. It can be divided into two parts. The first half of the sutra, Chapters 1 to 14,
expound the idea of the 'one vehicle', or the supremacy of Mahāyāna, the 'large vehicle', over monastic
forms of Buddhism. Here use is made of the concept of 'expedient devices', or *hoben* in Japanese, to
explain the limited nature of previous teaching as an attempt by all means to open humanity's eyes to
Buddhist truth, but it is only now that the final teaching of universal salvation can be given. The second
half of the sutra elucidates the idea of the eternal Buddha, existing from the eternal past and being born
into this world to bring humanity to the truth of salvation. The historical Buddha preaching the sutra
is just one of these appearances of the eternal Buddha.

This sutra has had profound influence not only on Japanese religious ideas, but also on Japanese art
and literature. As the sacred text of some of the new religious mass movements in the postwar period,

it continues to play a role in contemporary Japanese culture. Other sutras that have been particularly important in Japanese Buddhism include the *Garland Sutra* (*Kegon-gyō*), centring on the idea of the *bodhisattva*, one who seeks to attain Buddhahood by working for the enlightenment of all beings; the *Kannon Sutra* (*Kannon-gyō*, actually Chapter 25 of the *Lotus Sutra*) exalting the salvific grace of the bodhisattva Kannon; the *Essence of Wisdom Sutra* (*Hannya shin-gyō*) presenting the wisdom of the teaching of *ku*, or emptiness; the *Nirvana Sutra* (*Nehan-gyō* or *Daihatsu nehan-gyō*) explaining the eternal presence of the Buddha and the inherence of Buddha nature in every living being; the *Mahavairocana*, or great illumination, *Sutra* (*Dainichi-kyō*) and the *Diamond Peak Sutra* (*Kongō chō-kyō*), both presenting esoteric teachings; and the three canons of Pure Land Buddhism, the *Buddha of Infinite Life Sutra* (*Muryōju-kyō*), the *Meditation on the Buddha of Inifinite Life Sutra* (*Kanmuryōju-kyō*) and the *Amida Sutra* (*Amida-kyō*), offering a means to rebirth in the Pure Land through faith in the name of Amida.

The following is an extract from Chapter 10 of the *Lotus Sutra*, extolling the surpassing merit of this particular sutra. This passage is fundamental to the belief that faith in the power of the sutra is sufficient for salvation, central to Nichiren Buddhism and many of the postwar new religions.

At that time the World-honoured One addressed the eighty thousand great leaders through the Bodhisattva Medicine-King (saying): Medicine-King! Do you see in this assembly innumerable gods, dragon-kings, *yakshas, gandharvas, asuras, garudas, kimnaras, mahoragas,* human and non-human beings, as well as *bhikshus, shikshuṇīs,* male and female lay devotees, seekers after śrāvakaship, seekers after pratyeke-buddhahood, seekers after bodhisattvaship, or seekers after buddhahood? All such beings as these, in the presence of the Buddha, if they hear a single verse or a single word of the Wonderful Law-Flower Sutra and even by a single thought delight in it, I predict that they will all attain to Perfect Enlightenment.

(Translation by Bunnō Katō, Tokyo: Kosei Publishing Company, 1971)

It was also under Chinese influence that the early histories of Japan, the *Record of Ancient Matters* (*Kojiki*) and the *Chronicle of Japan* (*Nihon shoki*), were compiled. Both of these works cover events from the mythical age of the native Japanese gods up to the late seventh century. Although they diverge on some details, together these works provide the mythical basis for the foundation of the nation as well as the imperial line, and thus they are central texts for the development of *National Learning* (*Kokugaku*) thought, a nativist intellectual movement in the eighteenth century, as well as state Shinto in the modern era.

Confucian and neo-Confucian texts are also sources for Japanese religion. Confucian learning entered Japan in much the same way as Buddhism, introduced through Korea from around the fifth century. The neo-Confucian revival reached Japan in the thirteenth and fourteenth centuries, primarily through Zen monks who had studied in China and made their monasteries centres for Chinese studies. While such study was largely limited to political, religious and military elites throughout much of Japanese history, Confucian and neo-Confucian teachings were popularized in the early modern period, largely through the efforts of itinerant preachers, and have had considerable influence on religious thought in the modern period. In addition to the *Analects* and the *Classic of Filial Piety*, prescribed as part of an official curriculum for members of the court in the eighth century, the *Book of Changes*, the *Elementary Learning* and the *Great Learning* have also been given a level of importance in Japan. Native Japanese Confucian works, such as *A Chronicle of Gods and Sovereigns* (*Jinnō shōtō* and the *Chronicle of Great*

Peace (*Taiheiki*), both from the fourteenth century, emphasize the Confucian virtues of loyalty, benevolence and courage, important in the development of *bushido*, or the 'warrior ethic'.

In addition to these traditional texts, some of the new religions have developed their own scriptures, often based on the private revelation of their founder or some other charismatic personality within the group. Although believers of the particular groups are generally the only ones familiar with these texts, works of the founders of some of the earlier new religions, the *Ofudesaki* (*The Tip of the Writing Brush*) of Tenrikyō or the *Reikai Monogatari* (*Tales of the Spirit World*) of Ōmotokyō are somewhat more well known. In addition, despite the small number of followers that the Christian churches have been able to attract in Japan, the Bible is generally well known, and its teachings have clearly had some influence on the doctrine of some of the new religious movements.

BUDDHIST SECTS AND BUDDHIST SAINTS

Buddhism in Japan is organized around several major sects, most of which trace their development to Buddhist schools in China. Ritsu, Kegon, and Hossō are among the earliest of the sects, active in Japan during the Nara period (710–94 CE). Ritsu was established by Ganjin (Chinese *Chien-chen*, 688–763 CE), a Chinese monk who introduced procedures for the ordination of Buddhist clergy into Japan. As its name implies, Kegon takes as its text the *Garland Sutra* (*Kegon-gyō*), while Hossō is based on the Yogācāra tradition, offering the practice of yoga as a means to enlightenment.

Introduced during the Heian period (794–1185 CE), Tendai and Shingon have both played major roles in the development of Buddhism in Japan. Tendai, founded on Mount Hiei in present-day Kyoto by the monk Saichō (764–822 CE), is the Japanese expression of the Chinese T'ien-t'ai school. Both venerate the *Lotus Sutra* as the central Buddhist text, and teach the value of meditation as the means to enlightenment. A monk who had studied in both the Hossō and Kegon sects, Saichō retreated to a hermitage on Mount Hiei shortly before the capital was moved to present-day Kyoto. There he became familiar with the writings of the T'ien-t'ai founder, Chih-i, and in 804 travelled to China to study T'ien-t'ai doctrines. While in China he also became acquainted with Chan (Japanese *Zen*) meditation and esoteric tantric practices, which were incorporated in Tendai in Japan. Saichō emphasized the concept of a universal Buddha-nature inherent in all beings and a consequent egalitarian view of salvation. Later, under the influence of Kūkai, the founder of the Shingon sect, the idea of 'original enlightenment' (*hongaku*), the belief that all beings already exist in a state of enlightenment, also became a central tenet of Tendai doctrine.

Hongaku thought has played a major role broadly throughout the schools of Japanese Buddhism, and remains an essential element of Japanese religiosity today. It is an egalitarian concept; there is a popular expression in Japanese that even the 'grasses and trees' possess Buddha nature. It is non-dualistic; particularly in religious discourse one will often see opposites combined with the word *soku*, meaning 'at the same time'. In recent years it has been the focus of controversy as a result of the work of so-called 'critical Buddhists,' who blame the concept for an unreflective tolerance and inability to make moral judgement that they identify with Japanese Buddhism, and Japanese culture in general.

Kūkai (774–835 CE), more popularly known by the posthumous name of Kōbō Daishi, founded his sect on Mount Kōya, near present-day Nara. Kūkai was born into an aristocratic family on the island of Shikoku, and as a young adult took up the study of the Confucian classics prescribed for training as a government bureaucrat. After a conversion to Buddhism, however, he abandoned his studies and started practising physical austerities on various mountains, with the aim of attaining extraordinary powers. Such ascetics were called *ubasoku*, indicating an unordained Buddhist priest; *hijiri*, a saint or

Figure 5.2 Rows of Jizo Bosatsu, a bodhisattva especially popular as the saviour of the spirits of dead children. These statues are purchased for *mizuko kuyo*, a memorial service usually associated with aborted fetuses

holy man; *onmyoji*, a practitioner of Yin–Yang Daoism; or *shugenja*, a mountain ascetic. The mixture of Buddhist, Daoist and folk religious beliefs and practices exhibited by these men is one of the important streams of Japanese religiosity, and the belief that extraordinary powers can be obtained through the practice of physical austerities is another characteristic of Japanese religiosity up to the present day, as seen in the emphasis on the attainment of psychic powers in some of the latest new religious movements.

Like his contemporary Saichō, Kūkai also travelled to China in 804, but his study was more limited to the esoteric mantra tradition, the meaning of the Japanese word 'Shingon'. There he was initiated into several esoteric rituals as yet unknown in Japan, and ordained as a master of this tradition. Kūkai also emphasized the universally inherent Buddha nature, as well as the dissolution of dichotomies and oppositions through the awareness of the mutual relation and interdependence of all phenomena. One of the tenets of the Shingon school is the attainment of Buddhahood in this life, or in the body, just as it is (*sokushin jōbutsu*). In the belief that this was realized by Kūkai himself, his presence is still venerated on Mount Kōya.

Kūkai, or Kōbō Daishi, has become a legendary figure in Japanese religiosity, invoked not only within the Buddhist tradition, but also, for example, by some of the founders of new religious movements without clear Buddhist ties. In another form of popular religiosity, he is associated with pilgrimages in Japan, most famously with that to eighty-eight temples on his native island of Shikoku. In his lifetime he was also favoured by the court. Although in the early years after the capital was moved to present-day Kyoto Saichō's Tendai school was in ascendancy with the court, from early in the ninth century it was Shingon esotericism that predominantly enjoyed the court's favour.

Both Saichō and Kūkai were open to the introduction of native Japanese religious elements into their schools of Buddhism, a trend that became increasingly noticeable in this period, and is yet another characteristic of Japanese religion. It became common to construct *jingūji*, or shrine-temples, where Buddhist rituals were performed within Shinto shrine precincts, often by the same clergy. Doctrinally, the idea of *honji suijaku* was promoted, identifying the Shinto *kami* as local manifestations of buddhas or bodhisattvas. Counter movements were also present, especially in the early modern period, but this Buddhist–Shinto amalgamation was dominant until the forced separation of the two at the beginning of the modern period in the mid-nineteenth century.

The twelfth and thirteenth centuries saw the emergence of several new Buddhist schools, one of them of native Japanese origin. Political and social instability towards the end of the Heian period ushered in an era of *de facto* military rule that was to last until the modern period. This instability contributed to the popularization of the Buddhist concept of *mappō*, or the final, degenerate age. In this final age former practices were deemed to be no longer effective, and thus new ways to salvation were sought. Although many of the schools that emerged at this time had their roots in Tendai, they differ from the older school in that they concentrate on one aspect of Tendai belief and practice rather than presenting a synthesis of varying Buddhist traditions.

The Japanese *Pure Land* school (*Jōdoshū*), whose founding is attributed to the monk Hōnen (1133–1212), illustrates well these characteristics. Orphaned as a youth, Hōnen was sent to a nearby Tendai temple, where his potential was noticed, leading to his acceptance at the main temple on Mount Hiei and ordination at the age of fourteen. Apparently dissatisfied with the political intrigues at the main temple, then deeply involved in the larger power struggles in the capital, Hōnen sought refuge in a small retreat at the foot of the mountain, a centre of Pure Land practice. Pure Land, also imported from China, had been popularized in Japan from the tenth century as part of the Tendai synthesis. It preached salvation by faith in Amida, a bodhisattva known for the *hongan*, or 'original vow', to postpone his own enlightenment until all beings had been saved. Through the invocation of Amida's holy name, the *nenbutsu*, the believer is assured of rebirth in the Pure Land, or Land of Bliss, there to await enlightenment. The *nenbutsu* was used as a means of meditation, or occasionally as a kind of charm to ward off evil, but in Hōnen's teaching it became the supreme act of faith, replacing attempts at attaining salvation through meditation or the study of Buddhist texts. In this way Hōnen introduced the distinction between salvation through one's own efforts (*jiriki*) or salvation by faith in Amida's mercy (*tariki*), and the latter was deemed to be the only effective means in the degenerate age of *mappō*.

Shinran (1173–1261), a disciple of Hōnen, was exiled along with his master in 1207, at the instigation of the Tendai establishment on Mount Hiei. A monk since the age of nine, Shinran married and fathered six children during his exile, finding religious meaning in the abandonment of monastic rules – the single-minded pursuit of salvation through faith in Amida rather than through one's own efforts. Following Shinran's example, clerical marriage had become all but the norm not only in the True Pure Land sect, which Shinran is considered to have founded, but throughout Japanese Buddhism by the early modern period, although the legal prohibition was only removed in 1872. With the exception of the True Pure Land sect, however, clerical celibacy continues to be the official norm, making the role of the priests' wives rather ambiguous; although accepted as a fact of everyday life, and even essential to the running of the temple in many cases, they are occasionally not even allowed a place in the family grave after death, since their marriage has not been recognized.

In contrast to the emphasis on salvation through faith alone in the Pure Land schools, other schools that emerged in this period continued to promote meditation as the means to enlightenment. The dominant Zen schools of Rinzai and Sōtō were both also founded by Tendai monks, Eisai (1141–1215) and Dōgen (1200–53) respectively. Seeing the need for a religious revival on Mount Hiei, Eisai went to China in 1168, and again almost twenty years later, retracing the steps of the monks from the ancient period that had founded the established Buddhist schools. While he emphasized Zen, particularly after his second visit to China, he did not abandon the other Tendai beliefs and practices, but continued to preach devotion to the *Lotus Sutra* and perform esoteric rituals. However, his efforts still elicited opposition from the Tendai establishment, leading him to seek support from the military rulers in Kamakura who had gained ascendancy at the end of the twelfth century. Eisai is also credited with the introduction of the tea ceremony, and the Rinzai school that he founded is perhaps best known in the

West for the use of *kōan*, cryptic statements or paradoxes used as an aid to meditation or the gaining of intuitive knowledge.

Born almost sixty years after Eisai, Dōgen also studied Tendai at Mount Hiei, but he was attracted to Zen at an early age. He travelled to China in 1223, where he attained awakening under a Zen master. He returned to teach the sole practice of *zazen*, sitting meditation. Establishing a monastery in the mountains near the Japan Sea coast, Dōgen instituted a rigid daily order for his monks, centred on the practice of *zazen*. After Dōgen's death, however, Sōtō Zen was popularized among the provincial samurai and the peasantry, especially through the development of funeral and memorial services for the dead, with which Buddhism is identified in Japan today.

The final school that emerged at this time was Nichiren, named after the monk who was its founder. Nichiren (1222–82), the son of a fisherman from the area north of Kamakura, was ordained a monk at a nearby Tendai temple before making his way to Mount Hiei in 1242. Not limiting himself to the Tendai tradition, he also studied at Mount Kōya and ultimately became convinced that all of the Buddhist schools were incomplete and false. With a self-appointed mission to preach true Buddhism, he advocated faith in the *Lotus Sutra* alone, and promoted the chanting of the *daimoku*, a phrase in praise of the sutra. Attributing an increase in natural disasters and political unrest to the propagation of false faiths, in 1260 he presented a treatise to the military government in Kamakura entitled *Risshō ankokuron* (*Treatise on Pacifying the State by Establishing Orthodoxy*). As a result of this critique of the establishment, he was exiled the following year, and after a pardon in 1263 he was once again exiled in 1271. The only native Japanese school of Buddhism, the Nichiren sects are characteristically nationalistic and exclusivist, preaching that only faith in the one true religion can guarantee peace and stability. Through its popularization in the modern period, when it was linked with a rising nationalistic fervour, it has become an important religious resource for some of the mass new religious movements that emerged in the postwar period.

It is the monks and male mountain ascetics who have traditionally been highlighted in speaking of the Buddhist traditions in Japan. Ordained nuns, however, have played a role at key stages in the history of Japanese Buddhism. It was a nun by the name of Zenshin-ni who was the first Buddhist ordained in Japan, and it was nuns who first went to China to study. The first temple in Japan was a nunnery. In the early modern period, Sōtō Zen nuns did a better job of preserving the tradition of meditation while their male counterparts were largely engaged in the performance of funerals and memorial rites, and in this way they contributed to the Zen revival in the modern period.

The Japanese Buddhist traditions described here are perhaps more properly referred to as schools rather than sects or independent religious groups throughout much of Japanese history, for, as we have seen, it was not uncommon for monks to study several of these traditions. However, occasional rivalries, even conflicts, between the schools cannot be ignored, and despite an overall atmosphere of religious plurality – not only among the Buddhist traditions themselves but also with Daoist, Confucian and native Shinto beliefs and practices – the emergence of an exclusivist tradition in Nichiren Buddhism is also an important element of Japanese religiosity. It was in the early modern and

Figure 5.3 The monks of Nipponzan Myohoji, a New Religious Movement in the Nichiren Buddhist tradition, chanting at a ceremony held at the Tama Dojo, west of Tokyo

modern periods that the Buddhist traditions increasingly took on the aspects of sects, as a result of government policies. In the early modern period, to enforce the prohibition against Christianity, everyone was required to be affiliated with a Buddhist temple for the purpose of funeral and memorial rites. This introduced a parochial system previously unknown to Buddhism, and served to institutionalize Buddhism as the purveyor of funeral rites, as well as the tool of government control. And in the modern period local temples were required to have clear affiliation with a major temple that served as headquarters for one of the Buddhist groups, further clarifying allegiance along sect lines. In present-day Japan, Pure Land groups (including True Pure Land) claim both the largest number of temples and believers, with Zen following in number of temples but Nichiren groups second in number of believers.

INTERACTIONS WITH MODERNITY

The emergence of modern Shinto

Usually described as Japan's native religion, Shinto is a complex reality, reflecting in its concrete and historical expression several interwoven strands. Even today many Japanese would not consider Shinto a 'religion', but would rather describe it as a set of traditional customs without a doctrine, reflecting the official point of view in the prewar period, which has been upheld in court cases concerning the separation of religion and state in the postwar period as well. The term 'Shinto' itself was not in popular usage before the end of the early modern period. In the intellectual history of Japan, the term became important in the National Learning school, where it was used in contrast to Buddhism and Confucianism in order to legitimate it as a distinct, native Japanese religion. It would appear that the term Shinto was first used to refer to a distinct religious tradition in the fifteenth century at the earliest, when the Yoshida Shinto movement emerged to challenge the concept of *honji suijaku*, or the incorporation of the Shinto kami in the Buddhist pantheon.

Shinto incorporates belief in nature spirits, the veneration of clan ancestors, local and national cults surrounding heroes or warriors, as well as mythological beliefs in the foundation of the nation and the imperial lineage. Activities at local shrines centre around festivals to mark the seasons or to celebrate the particular kami venerated there. Some of the larger shrines, particularly those at Ise and Izumo, were better able to resist the trend towards amalgamation with Buddhism, thus providing some institutional continuity that indicates the preservation of an independent religious tradition. Clearly, however, it was in an atmosphere of Buddhist and Confucian thought, and in opposition to these traditions, that the organized Shinto traditions developed.

Both popular and intellectual influences led to the emergence, or perhaps more accurately the creation, of a Shinto institution in the modern period. From the early modern period pilgrimages to the shrine at Ise were popularized. Often local confraternities were formed to provide monetary support for a number of pilgrims annually, and the pilgrimages were occasionally raucous affairs. Intellectually, it was the development of the National Learning school that contributed greatly towards the establishment of the modern Shinto institution.

National Learning is at once a literary, political and religious movement whose foundation lies at least partly in a reaction to the increasing influence of Confucian ideas and scholarship in the early modern period. National Learning evolved from the philological study of Japanese classical literature and ancient writings whose purpose was generally to identify peculiarly Japanese cultural traits or a distinctive Japanese mentality. This study can be traced back to Keichū (1640–1701), a Buddhist monk of the Shingon sect who took up the study of the *Man'yōshū*, an anthology of eighth-century poetry. Keichū insisted that in order to understand the ancient classical literature one had to allow one's mind to become unfettered by intellectual concepts so as to come in touch with the naive emotions of a direct, human response, a primitivism that is reflected in later National Learning writings.

Another early influence on National Learning was Kada no Azumamaro (1669–1736), a descendant of a family of Shinto priests who focused his study on ancient documents as well as literary works. He opened a school for Japanese studies in Kyoto and had a direct influence on Kamo no Mabuchi (1697–1769), also from a family of Shinto priests. Like Keichū, Mabuchi took up the study of the *Man'yōshū*, finding there an honest and direct expression of emotion without the artificiality he thought had been introduced by foreign, specifically Buddhist and Confucian, influences.

Motoori Norinaga (1730–1801), usually acknowledged as the central figure of this movement, came to National Learning through a study of Keichū's work, later becoming a disciple of Mabuchi. Norinaga completed a study of the *Kojiki*, a foundational text of Japanese mythology from the eighth century, that had been started by his mentor. Continuing in the primitivist tradition of his teachers, Norinaga propounded his belief that in order to understand the text one needs a sensitivity to the appearance of objects and events in the human and natural world and the emotions that they arouse, unfettered by Confucian or Buddhist doctrinal interpretations. Norinaga believed that the *Kojiki* text was a factual record of the activity of the gods and people in ancient times, and that it reflected a natural moral sense. He maintained that ancient Japanese texts do not contain the word *michi*, or 'way' in the sense of a correct moral path, because the ancients had a natural feel for what was right, and were in this way superior to the Chinese, who were in need of the moral guidance supplied by Confucian principles.

In another work, the *Naobi no mitama*, Norinaga develops at length this idea of Japanese cultural superiority, identifying stability as the basis of that superiority. Relying on Japanese mythology, Norinaga states that Japan is the land of the appearance of Amaterasu Ōmikami, the central native goddess, and that the land is ruled by the emperor, the descendant of the goddess. For that reason, he argues that the rule of the emperor is in fact the rule of the gods, as it was, unchanging from ancient times, and that in turn is why Japan is referred to as the Land of the Gods. In foreign lands, namely China, there is no end to revolution and unrest, with people of lower status trying to seize power from those above. In Japan, however, the emperor's reign continues unbroken, and the people follow naturally that order as it has been established in ancient times, ensuing in profound peace. If there is unrest in Japan it is a result of the fact that people have tried to learn foreign ways and have allowed their spirit to become separated from the spirit of the emperor. This situation can only be corrected if people are loyal and obedient to their superiors and do what they know naturally to be right; they are endowed with this natural ethical sense because all share in the spirit of the gods that is the foundation of Japanese culture.

Although the ideas of cultural superiority based on the perceived presence of an unparalleled stability and innate morality did not originate with Norinaga or National Learning, their codification in this school had a direct influence on important intellectual developments in the immediate early modern period. The Mito school, named after a domain north of present-day Tokyo where it was located, actually combined National Learning trends with Confucian thought to propose a plan for governing the nation in the face of increasing threats from abroad, based on the development of a common religious tradition to strengthen social cohesion. After Japan's self-imposed isolation was broken by the arrival of US gunboats in 1853, leading to the restoration of imperial rule in 1868 and the beginning of a rush to modernization in the mid-nineteenth century, the Mito synthesis provided a blueprint for the new government's religious policy. Buddhist elements were forcibly removed from Shinto shrines under the banner of *shinbutsu bunri*, or the separation of the gods and buddhas; a state agency for the administration of Shinto shrines was established, indicating the unity of ritual and government, or *saisei itchi*; a hierarchy of shrines was established, with Ise at the top, and new national shrines dedicated to the imperial family or war dead were constructed; a new set of national holidays, centring on imperial commemorations or dates associated with the mythical establishment of the nation, and commemorative rites to be performed by the emperor were prescribed; the official recognition of the Buddhist parish system, initially instituted by the early modern military government, was removed, and although the Buddhist temples were not directly targeted by the central government, widespread destruction of Buddhist statues and other treasures by mobs protesting against the temples' links with the previous government was allowed.

Devotion to State Shinto, as the new religious establishment was known, was made a duty incumbent on all citizens of the country. When a new constitution was promulgated in 1889, including the guarantee of religious freedom, State Shinto was defined as a set of traditions and rites that transcends 'religion,' thus allowing for government patronage and the enforcement of universal participation in State Shinto rites. Formation of a civic creed was further enhanced by promulgation the following year of the Imperial Rescript on Education, a succinct statement of the national myths surrounding the imperial establishment and a Confucian code of conduct that emphasized filial piety, harmony, benevolence, self-cultivation, obedience, and loyalty. The Rescript was committed to memory, recited by schoolchildren, and venerated alongside the portrait of the emperor and other Shinto symbols.

> The Imperial Rescript on Education is a succinct summary of the official ideology promoted in the Meiji period as the moral and spiritual basis of the Japanese nation. It emphasizes the unbroken rule of the imperial line and the common Confucian morality of filial piety, right relationships, benevolence, and self-cultivation. The official translation of the rescript reads as follows:
>
> Know ye, Our Subjects:
>
> Our Imperial Ancestors have founded Our Empire on a basis broad and everlasting and have deeply and firmly planted virtue; Our subjects ever united in loyalty and filial piety have from generation to generation illustrated the beauty thereof. This is the glory of the fundamental character of Our Empire, and herein lies the source of Our education. Ye, Our subjects, be filial to your parents, affectionate to your brothers and sisters; as husbands and wives be harmonious, as friends true; bear yourselves in modesty and moderation; extend your benevolence to all; pursue learning and cultivate arts, and thereby develop intellectual faculties and perfect moral powers; furthermore advance public good and promote common interests; always respect the Constitution and observe the laws; should emergency arise, offer yourselves courageously to the State; and thus guard and maintain the prosperity of Our Imperial Throne coeval with heaven and earth. So shall ye not only be Our good and faithful subjects, but render illustrious the best traditions of your forefathers. The Way here set forth is indeed the teaching bequeathed by Our Imperial Ancestors, to be observed alike by Their Descendants and the subjects, infallible for all ages and true in all places. It is Our wish to lay it to heart in all reverence, in common with you, Our subjects, that we may all thus attain to the same virtue.

State Shinto was abolished by decree of the occupation forces in 1945, and many of the local as well as former national shrines are now independently affiliated with the Association of Shinto Shrines (*jinja honchō*). Since the 1970s, however, there have been repeated attempts to grant formal status to Yasukuni

Shrine in Tokyo as a national memorial to the war dead. Yasukuni Shrine's predecessor was established in 1869 to enshrine the spirits of those who died fighting to restore imperial rule, and subsequently the spirits of those who fought in Japan's wars throughout the modern period have also been enshrined there. In 1978 the spirits of those executed as a result of the Tokyo War Crimes Trial were also added to the shrine. Other controversies have involved the use of Shinto rites to mark the construction of government buildings, visits to shrines by government officials and the use of public money to pay the customary fees on those occasions, as well as the use of Shinto rites in conjunction with the installation of the present emperor in 1989 and 1990. Japanese courts have consistently ruled in favour of the government on these occasions, arguing that these actions are more a matter of custom than religion. In a recent case, however, the court prohibited the use of public funds to pay for a Shinto service, and observers noted that the court in this case seems to be following public opinion, since there seems to be less support for such actions in recent years.

Although more than 80 per cent of the population will visit a Shinto shrine during the New Year holidays, smaller shrines have in recent years found it difficult to continue their festivals, because fewer young people, needed to carry the portable shrines that are central to these events, are either present or willing to participate. However, more famous festivals, such as the spring and summer festivals in Tokyo and the northern region of the country, or the naked-man festivals held in winter at various locales, continue to draw crowds in the tens of thousands.

New Religious Movements in the early modern period

The creation of a national religious ideology as a vehicle to promote cultural identity could only be maintained by the use of increasingly oppressive force, and ultimately failed when that force could not be sustained following the defeat of the nation in 1945. Other religious movements that emerged at the same time that State Shinto was being created ultimately proved to be more effective and long-lasting means to preserve cultural identity in the face of the massive importation of foreign cultural items. These movements can be identified as the first of three major waves of New Religious Movements that largely define the contemporary Japanese religious scene.

Tenrikyō, founded in 1838, is generally recognized as one of the oldest of the Japanese New Religious Movements. Its founding is traced back to the possession experience of Nakayama Miki, a farmer's wife living in the area of Nara, the ancient capital. Having already lost two daughters to disease, a *yamabushi*, or mountain ascetic, was called to cure the injured foot of Miki's son. Since the shamaness, or *miko*, who would normally accompany the *yamabushi* and acted as his medium could not come, Miki took her place. After falling into a trance, Miki was possessed by a god who revealed his name as Tsukihi, literally sun and moon. Tsukihi declared through Miki that, 'I have come to save all of mankind. I wish to receive Miki as the shrine of God.' This incident was followed by numerous other possession episodes, subsequently without the aid of the *yamabushi*. At the direction of Tsukihi, later also called Oyagami, meaning 'God the Parent', Miki began to give alms to the poor, to the extent that the Nakayama family, once wealthy landowners, was left destitute. Miki took up sewing to support the family, and from the 1850s began to gain a reputation as a healer and miracle worker, after which time this new faith began to grow.

In 1869, the year following the institution of the new imperial government, Miki, who is supposed to have been illiterate, took up writing and composed the *Ofudesaki*, the record of Oyagami's revelation, one of Tenrikyō's scriptures. In the *Ofudesaki* the centre of the universe is revealed as lying precisely in the Nakayama residence, found in an area called Yamato, traditionally seen as the birthplace of Japanese civilization. Today Tenrikyō headquarters is located on this spot, and visitors to Tenri City are greeted with the words 'Welcome home!' indicating this is the place of birth for all humankind.

Tenrikyō teaches that it is the will of God the Parent that all human beings enjoy *yōki gurashi*, translated as 'joyous life'. The doctrine is based on the principle of fundamental equality, teaching that, 'All people of the whole world are equally brothers and sisters. There is no one who is an utter stranger' (*Ofudesaki* XIII, 43). Eventually all of humankind will partake in this 'joyous life' together here in this world, a paradise that is to be inaugurated after an indeterminate number of rebirths of those now living. All people are called to participate in the final establishment of this joyous life by reflecting now on the cause of their suffering, in order to understand their *innen*, or karma. Karma – in Tenrikyō doctrine the good or bad effects of past actions, either in this life or previous lives – is the cause of all experience. Reflecting on karma should lead to a reform of life, to wipe away the dust that accumulates on the heart or spirit, in Tenrikyō 's idiom. Tenrikyō teaches that there are eight 'dusts': miserliness, covetousness, hatred, self-love, grudge-bearing, anger, greed, and arrogance. The attitude of reform, or sweeping away this dust, is expressed through *hinokishin*, a word that is used to describe activity that ranges from service to the church to various volunteer activities, including international aid and development work.

> The *Ofudesaki* is the written record of the revelation received by Nakayama Miki, the founder of Tenrikyō. The following text, from the opening passage of the book, describes God's purpose in making this new, and final, revelation: to realize the joyful life that has been ordained from the time of creation for all people.
>
> > Looking all over the world and through all ages, I find no one who has understood My heart. No wonder that you know nothing, for so far I have taught nothing to you. This time I, God, revealing Myself to the fore, teach you all the truth in detail. . . . When I, God, reveal Myself and teach you everything in detail, all people of the world will become equally cheerful. As I hasten to save all of you equally, I will set out to cheer up the minds of the world. If your minds become cheered up step by step, rich harvests will prevail all over the world, and every place will become prosperous.
> >
> > (From the *Ofudesaki*, Part I, 1–3, 7–9. Translation by Tenrikyo Headquarters, Tenri: Jihōsha, 1971)

Tenrikyō is representative of many of the new religions in its optimistic view of human nature, its emphasis on moral self-cultivation, the affirmation of benefits in the present world, and its use of elements common in Japanese religiosity in developing its own doctrine. The case of Nakayama Miki also illustrates one role that women have traditionally played in Japanese religiosity, that of a shaman-like practitioner, a role that has become more prominent in some of the new religions.

Tenrikyō and other new religions that emerged at this time in Japanese history served two social functions. Their emphasis on solidarity within an essentially rural society – through the preaching of a universal equality, mutual help activities such as *hinokishin* in Tenrikyō , and emphasis on individual moral reform – helped to cushion the impact on the agricultural sector of the economic changes that had begun to occur already in the latter part of the early modern period. Second, they helped to preserve a sense of cultural identity in a rapidly changing society, as seen for example in Tenrikyō 's belief that the centre of the universe lies precisely in the cradle of Japanese civilization. Indeed, many of the new religions emerging at this time were located in the area around Nara and Kyoto, the ancient capitals of the country. This sense of cultural identity sometimes took the form of xenophobia. This is perhaps most pronounced in Ōmotokyō, a group founded in the last decade of the nineteenth century by Deguchi Nao, a woman who, like Miki, was prone to episodes of possession. Nao is said to have proclaimed in a trance that, 'Japan is the way of the gods, but foreign countries are the lands of the wild beasts, ruled by devils, where only the strong survive.' She goes on to say that, under the influence of these foreign cultures, 'Japan is likewise becoming a land of wild beasts. Because the country can't survive like this, God has revealed himself and will reform the world.'

In this way Ōmotokyō perhaps possessed a stronger sense of mission that led it to openly oppose the central government, and as a consequence it was crushed completely by the authorities in the 1930s. Tenrikyō and the other new religions of this period were co-opted by the government, changing their doctrine in line with the official State Shinto ideology and eventually achieving recognition as Sect Shinto groups.

The urbanization of Japanese society and the postwar new religions

While it is difficult to give an accurate count, there are perhaps up to one thousand New Religious Movements active in Japan. The vast majority are small, local groups; national, or international, movements like Tenrikyō , which has over one million believers, are relatively few. Nearly all of the mass movements, such as Sōka Gakkai with perhaps nine million members, or Risshō Kōseikai with over six million, are postwar urban forms of Buddhism, and they comprise the second wave of New Religious Movements in Japan.

Risshō Kōseikai was founded in 1938 but enjoyed a period of tremendous growth in the postwar years, like most of the religions in this group. The founder, Niwano Nikkyō, was himself born in a rural village in north-west Japan, and emigrated to Tokyo while still a teenager. In Tokyo he became engaged in various small businesses, and was exposed to a myriad of folk divination techniques before joining Reiyūkai, a lay Buddhist movement in the Nichiren tradition. He quickly made a convert of Naganuma Myōkō, and in 1938 both of them broke with Reiyūkai to found their own group. Risshō Kōseikai incorporated some of the divination practices that Niwano had picked up, and Myōkō played a shaman-like role in the early development of the religion. Thus, while Risshō Kōseikai displays some elements of popular folk belief, in doctrine and practice it is a Buddhist-based group, revering the *Lotus Sutra*, chanting the *daimoku*, and encouraging daily prayers in front of the family Buddhist altar in the home.

Like its predecessor Reiyūkai, Risshō Kōseikai offers its believers a means to venerate the ancestors in the home, without the assistance of a Buddhist priest – an important religious development in reaction to the urbanization of Japanese society. Early in the twentieth century more than 80 per cent of the Japanese population was engaged in agriculture. By 1935 the urban population stood at 30 per cent, a figure that rose to 50 per cent by the end of the war. By 1977, however, more than 80 per cent of the population lived in cities, reversing the situation of only sixty years before. For many people this meant that their ties with the local Buddhist temple were completely severed by the move to the city. Interestingly enough, the observation can be made that Japanese urbanization has led to a considerable religious revival. Whereas in the past the main tie to the local Buddhist temple centred on annual memorial rites, for which a Buddhist monk was summoned and paid, the lay Buddhism that emerged in postwar urban Japan not only encouraged daily practice at home, but also resulted in more active and sustained participation in communal religious functions. A central practice here is the *hōza*, a combination of group counselling and faith witnessing carried out by the believers, often on a weekly or monthly basis.

The postwar new religions serve a function in enhancing social cohesion comparable to that of the first-wave new religious groups. The postwar groups act as a bridge, both religiously and socially, between rural and urban Japanese society, providing an entirely new way to perform the requisite memorial rites for the ancestors, as well as becoming the focus of community for many people in the impersonal urban milieu. They also share much in common with the earlier new religions in terms of a doctrinal emphasis on moral self-cultivation and the enjoyment of benefits in the present world. Although women often play a major part in the establishment of these movements and in encouraging others to join the group, their governing structures continue to reflect the male dominance seen throughout Japanese society.

Figure 5.4 The naked man festival at Konomiya Shrine in Inazawa near Nagoya. The festival is held every year in February

New Age religions

As in much of Europe and North America, in the last twenty years in Japan one can see a new interest in mysticism and the occult that is normally summed up under the term New Age. This new religious ferment is often characterized as eclectic, individualistic and result oriented. Through the use of certain techniques, either meditation or body work or some combination of the two, it is believed that one can achieve a personal transformation, resulting perhaps in a higher level of consciousness or the attainment of psychic powers. While often one participates in this movement by purchasing books that amount to training manuals at the local book shop, or at best through a loose association or 'network' of fellow practitioners, in Japan a number of organized religious groups incorporating these characteristics have become popular since the 1970s.

Agonshū is representative of this latest wave of New Religious Movements. Although Agonshū was founded in 1978, it has its roots in a group called Kannon Jikeikai, founded by Kiriyama Seiyū in 1954. Kiriyama was born Tsutsumi Masuo in 1921, and came to religion after failing in business and an arrest for violation of alcohol tax laws. He was ordained a Shingon sect priest in 1955 and practised a religion based on fasting and cold water austerities, common to mountain ascetics in Japan. Around 1970 he abandoned these austerities and instead adopted the *goma* fire ceremony of esoteric Shingon Buddhism as his group's primary rite. He began to publish on spiritist and esoteric themes at about this time, and some of his books on the development of psychic powers became bestsellers. In late 1978 he came upon the *Āgama Sutra*, purportedly predating both Mahāyāna and esoteric Buddhism, and this became the basis of faith in Agonshū, as he renamed his religious group.

In Kiriyama's teaching, misfortune is caused by karma from previous lives, or by the curse of ancestors who have been unable to attain Buddhahood, a common belief in Japanese religiosity that encourages the performance of memorial rites in order to help one's ancestors achieve this goal. In Agonshū this was done especially through the practice of *senzagyō*, a forty-minute memorial service to be performed in the home for one thousand days in succession. In 1986, however, Agonshū received a relic of the Buddha from the President of Sri Lanka, and thereafter *senzagyō* was declared unnecessary, replaced by simple veneration of the relic or its representative in the home.

Kiriyama has consistently shown a sensitivity to popular culture, moving from esoteric Buddhism through an interest in psychic powers to the discovery of early Buddhism as religious tastes changed through the 1970s. He was also the first religious leader to take up the prophecies of Nostradamus, which have enjoyed a high level of popularity in Japan since the publication of a volume interpreting the prophecies in 1973. Apocalyptic thought connected with the prophecy of some kind of disaster that was to occur in 1999 is one characteristic of many of the groups that emerged in this period, and contributed to the violent actions of Aum Shinrikyō, the group that released sarin poison gas on the Tokyo underground in 1995.

Asahara Shōkō, the founder of Aum Shinrikyō, was himself a follower of Agonshū in the late 1970s and early 1980s. He went on to found his own independent yoga school, teaching the practice of yoga for the purpose of attaining psychic powers. Incorporating elements of Hindu with Tibetan Buddhism, Aum Shinrikyō's faith and practice focused increasingly on the role of Asahara as the guru essential to the spiritual development of his followers. Vague ideas of a cataclysmic destruction, based on the Nostradamus prophecies, were present from early on in the group, and these were developed and played an increasingly important role as Asahara and some of his followers resorted to violence both within the group as well as directed at outsiders.

Movements from this period are at least in part a result of contemporary cynicism and ennui. In the 1970s and 1980s Japan achieved a level of economic development that would have been unthinkable a generation before. The 'oil shock' in 1973, however, introduced a period of relatively low growth, which made future advancement, for both the individual and society, less certain. This trend was further exacerbated by the collapse of the 'bubble economy', based largely on stock and land speculation, and the decade-long recession in the 1990s. With economic or social advancement thus stymied, individual spiritual development has perhaps become more attractive. In addition, the failure of the 1960s student protest movement encouraged a turning inward: what could not be achieved through social protest was now sought through personal transformation, the reformation of society one person at a time.

The following is a promotional blurb taken from *Initiation*, published in English by Aum Shinrikyō in 1988. It identifies some of the religious elements that were incorporated in the group by its founder, Asahara Shōkō, promising the attainment of superhuman powers through the development of an innate spiritual capacity. The role of the guru in the training of the members is also emphasized. Shaktipat, for example, was a rite through which it was believed that Asahara transferred power by placing his hand on the forehead of the believer.

AUM Supreme Truth, founded by Shoko Asahara, is an organization to promote one's spiritual growth, ultimately toward the state of absolute freedom and happiness, and the betterment of society. It provides the Yoga Tantra System to its members, which is a unique training method consisting of several Eastern practices: Yoga, Tantric Buddhism, Primitive Buddhism, and Daoism.

Three Initiations are the core of the training method. They are *Earthly Initiation*, which purifies your *consciousness*; *Astral Initiation*, which purifies your *subconscious*; and *Causal Initiation*, which purifies your *super-subconscious*. Not only that, through these initiations you can develop various kinds of superhuman powers.

Earthly Initiation is given through oral instruction of a secret meditative and breathing technique. Astral Initiation is the input of the master's divine energy into a trainee by such means as Shaktipat. Causal Initiation imprints the perfectly purified mind of the Guru into a trainee. These three initiations purify your mind and help you to realize your True Self.

You can advance your practice in various ways, such as attendance at intensive seminars, on-going classes, weekly workshops, astral music meditation meetings, and home practice with our teaching materials. A free introductory lecture if provided every Sunday, and a free brochure is also available.

Shoko Asahara believes that it is quite rare for one to meet with the path to the truth, and hopes that you will seize this opportunity. The path to the truth is the path to supreme bliss and freedom.

(*Initiation*, New York: AUM US Co., 1988, p. 231. Punctuation and grammatical changes have been made to the translation where necessary.)

LOOKING TO THE FUTURE

In a recent survey, when asked about their confidence in seventeen social institutions, only 13 per cent of the respondents in Japan indicated some level of trust in religious groups, putting religious institutions at the bottom of the list. This result reflects a high level of distrust towards religious groups across the board. Indeed, in popular discourse, Buddhism is usually identified with the lucrative funeral industry, and its priests are criticized for their married state and meat-eating habits; Shinto suffers for its identification with the militaristic state; and new religions are seen as often dangerous frauds. In such an environment those affiliated with a religious group often feel that they have to hide their religious beliefs in order to be accepted.

Despite this low level of religious affiliation and considerable distrust of religious organizations, three-quarters of the population profess some kind of belief in a higher power, whether that be described as God, spirit or life-force. A similar number feel it is important to have a religious funeral service, and 80 to 90 per cent participate in annual rites such as the New Year's visit to a shrine or memorial services for the ancestors.

Religion is a difficult concept in modern Japan, because it is identified with religious organizations and is often divorced from religious sentiments and activities. In the wake of the Aum affair, one influential religious studies scholar, Yamaori Tetsuo, attributes these developments to the forced separation of Buddhism and Shinto at the beginning of the modern period and the introduction of the idea that one must choose an exclusive religious affiliation, an essentially Christian point of view. Yamaori argues that free participation in beliefs and rites of the various religious traditions present in Japan is the more proper expression of Japanese religiosity.

Thus we can expect that the Japanese will continue to be born Shinto, marry Christian and die Buddhist, all the while bearing a certain amount of reserve regarding all of these institutions. A certain number will continue to find meaning in some New Religious Movement, perhaps moving through affiliation with several movements in search of an answer to illness, discord or poverty. And New Religious Movements, drawing on diverse traditions that offer spiritual attainment and benefits in this life, will continue to emerge. The more difficult question, however, is whether these movements as well as the more traditional religious institutions will be able to find a moral voice in Japanese society and contribute positively to public discourse on important questions of ethnic and gender discrimination, individual rights and public ethics, war and peace.

SUMMARY

- Japanese religiosity is characterized by low levels of self-initiated affiliation with a religious institution but high levels of participation in religious rites and practices.
- Throughout much of Japanese history, Buddhist, Shinto, Confucian, and other religious elements have been combined, forming a kind of common religion that is still characteristic of Japanese religion today.
- In the modern period, a large number of New Religious Movements have emerged, providing a means to express traditional religious beliefs and practices in ways adapted to the changing modern situation.

KEY TERMS

bodhisattva One who seeks to attain Buddhahood by working for the enlightenment of all beings; the Buddhist model of compassion.

Buddha nature A sharing in the state of enlightenment, inherent in all beings.

daimoku Chant in praise of the *Lotus Sutra*.

hongaku thought The concept of 'original enlightenment,' the belief that all things already exist in a state of enlightenment.

hongan The 'original vow' of Amida to bring all beings to rebirth in the Pure Land.

honji suijaku Buddhist concept that identified native Japanese gods as local manifestations of Buddhas or bodhisattvas.

Jiriki Salvation through one's own efforts.

kami Native Japanese gods.

kōan Cryptic statement or paradox used in Rinzai Zen as an aid to meditation or the gaining of intuitive knowledge.

mappō Buddhist concept designating the final, degenerate age.

National Learning (Kokugaku) Japanese nativist movement in the early modern period.

nenbutsu Chant in praise of the name of the bodhisattva Amida.

Pure Land Land of Bliss, for those awaiting enlightenment.

saisei itchi The unity of rites and government, expressed in the support of State Shinto by the government in the modern period.

shinbutsu bunri The separation of Buddhism and Shinto, enforced at the beginning of the modern period.

sokushin jōbutsu The attainment of Buddhahood in this life.

Tariki Salvation through reliance on another power.

zazen Sitting meditation; Zen.

Zen Meditation practice common to many of the Buddhist schools, but emphasized especially in the Rinzai and Sōtō schools.

FURTHER READING

General

For general works on religion in Japan see Tamaru Noriyoshi and David Read (eds): *Religion in Japanese Culture: Where Living Traditions Meet a Changing World* (Tokyo, New York, London: Kodansha International, 1996); Shigeyoshi Murakami (trans. H. Byron Earhart): *Japanese Religion in the Modern Century* (Tokyo: University of Tokyo Press, 1980); Winston Davis: *Japanese Religion and Society: Paradigms of Structure and Change* (Albany, NY: SUNY Press, 1992); and Ian Reader: *Religion in Contemporary Japan* (London: Macmillan Press, 1991).

Buddhism in Japan

On Buddhism in Japan see Koyu Sonoda and Yusen Kashiwahara (eds): *Shapers of Japanese Buddhism* (Tokyo: Charles E. Tuttle, 1994); George J. Tanabe, Jr. and Willa Jane Tanabe (eds): *The Lotus Sutra in Japanese Culture* (Honolulu: University of Hawaii Press, 1989); Richard K. Payne (ed.): *Re-Visioning 'Kamakura' Buddhism* (Honolulu: University of Hawaii Press, 1998); and Jacqueline I. Stone: *Original Enlightenment and the Transformation of Medieval Japanese Buddhism* (Honolulu: University of Hawaii Press, 1999).

State Shinto

Helen Hardacre: *Shintō and the State 1868–1988* (Princeton, NJ: Princeton University Press, 1989).

Japanese new religions

On Japanese new religions, see the first chapter of Helen Hardacre: *Kurozumikyō and the New Religions of Japan* (Princeton, NJ: Princeton University Press, 1986). Several works are available on individual new religious movements: Winston Davis, *Dojo: Magic and Exorcism in Modern Japan* (Stanford, CA: Stanford University Press, 1980); Helen Hardacre: *Lay Buddhism in Contemporary Japan: Reiyūkai Kyōdan* (Princeton, NJ: Princeton University Press, 1984); H. Byron Earhart: *Gedatsu-kai and Religion in Contemporary Japan: Returning to the Center* (Bloomington, IN: Indiana University Press, 1989). See Mark R. Mullins: *Christianity Made In Japan: A Study of Indigenous Movements* (Honolulu: University of Hawaii Press, 1998) for a study of Christian-based new religions and discussion on some characteristics of Japanese religiosity. See Robert Kisala: *Prophets of Peace: Pacifism and Cultural Identity in Japan's New Religions* (Honolulu: University of Hawaii Press, 1999) for an analysis of postwar Japanese pacifism in several new religions and discussion of the role of religion in Japanese society.

Contemporary Japanese religiosity and practice

Robert J. Smith: *Ancestor Worship in Contemporary Japan* (Stanford, CA: Stanford University Press, 1974); Ian Reader and George J. Tanabe, Jr: *Practically Religious: Worldly Benefits and the Common Religion of Japan* (Honolulu: University of Hawaii Press, 1998); and Helen Hardacre: *Marketing the Menacing Fetus in Japan* (Berkeley, CA: University of California Press, 1997).

Aum Shinrikyō

Ian Reader: *Religious Violence in Contemporary Japan: The Case of Aum Shinrikyō* (Richmond: Curzon Press/Honolulu: University of Hawaii Press, 2000) and Robert Kisala and Mark Mullins (eds), *Religion and Social Crisis in Japan: Understanding Japanese Society through the Aum Affair* (Basingstoke, Hampshire: Palgrave, 2001).

Judaism

Seth D. Kunin

INTRODUCTION

The Jewish people number some 15 million worldwide. Almost half of these, approximately 7 million, live in the US. The majority of Jews both in the US and the rest of the world are secular: they maintain some type of Jewish identity but have little or no strong connection to Judaism as a religion. Of the 6.8 million Jews who live in the US, less than a third are members of one of the movements into which modern Judaism is divided. The memberships of the three main movements are: 355 thousand Orthodox, 760 thousand Reform and 890 thousand Conservative. Some percentage of the remaining Jews will align themselves with the Reform movement, which is in some sense the default movement of American Jewry. Outside of the US, the numbers of Orthodox Jews outweigh those of the other movements, due in part to the fact that outside America Orthodoxy tends to be the default position taken by Jews who have no other strong alignment.

Judaism is a complex cultural system which in its modern incarnations can be viewed through a number of different, interrelated and sometimes contradictory categories: religious affiliation, ethnicity, nationality, (vague) secular identity, civilization. Each one of these categories reflects a different way of categorizing groups in the modern world. None are mutually exclusive, though in most cases individuals or groups will emphasize one of the elements above the others. They reflect the fact that in the modern context 'Jewishness' constitutes only a partial aspect of individual and group identity that must compete or co-operate with other often more dominant cultural constructs.

During the last two centuries, the period in which a significant number of Jews began their encounter with the Enlightenment and modernity, there has been interplay between Judaism as religion, Judaism as a nation and the pressures of *assimilation*. All the modern Jewish movements are products of these forces,

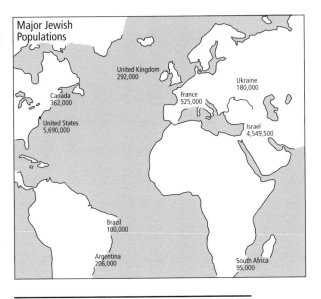

Figure 6.1 Map of major Jewish population distribution

Major Jewish Populations

United Kingdom 292,000
Ukraine 180,000
Canada 362,000
France 525,000
United States 5,690,000
Israel 4,549,500
Brazil 100,000
Argentina 206,000
South Africa 95,000

and represent attempts to respond positively or negatively to them. Each of these forces, at least in part, is distinctive of modernity. The compartmentalization of Judaism as a religion reflects the influence of the Enlightenment model of religion as something private and separate from other aspects of cultural and national identity. The development in the nineteenth century of political *Zionism* and the notions of race or peoplehood is a direct outgrowth of Romanticism and its notions of nationalism. The pressure for assimilation, although in part a response to living within increasingly dominant modern sociocultural frameworks, is also a reflection of the progressive development of liberalism and concepts of rational secularism.

Judaism in modern times can roughly be divided into five religious and two secular streams. The religious movements include: Reform (also called Liberal or Progressive), Reconstructionist, Conservative (also called Mesorati), Orthodox (also called Modern or neo-Orthodox) and Ultra Orthodox (including the Hasidic communities). The secular streams include the various forms of political Zionism, many or which are or were anti-religious, and secular Jews who sometimes have only vague ethnic associations with Judaism. In addition to these divisions, there is an additional divide between *Ashkinazic* and *Sephardic* Jewry. Ashkinazic Jews descend from the Jews of Central and Western Europe. Sephardic Jews descend from the Jews of Spain and Portugal and Islamic countries. This chapter focuses primarily on the Ashkinazic community as it is this community (as well as small pockets of Sephardic Jewry in the UK and the US) which historically has most strongly responded to issues of modernity. In recent years, however, due to the role of Sephardic Jews in Israel, the Sephardic community has played an increasingly significant role in defining the State of Israel and therefore aspects of wider Jewish identity as well.

All of these streams can be seen as inheritors of a much less strongly defined and perhaps more heterogeneous historical tradition dating back to the first or second millennium BCE. Although some of the religious groupings might claim to be continuations of this earlier cultural form with little or no transformation, and thus the exemplar of authentic Judaism, it seems more likely that all the recent streams are products of or responses to modernity with roots going back to the Enlightenment. Each of these streams responds to the challenges of modernity by emphasizing or de-emphasizing the elements of religion, nationalism and assimilation.

SOURCES AND RESOURCES

Judaism as a religious tradition has its roots in the second and first millennia BCE. The diversity of the traditions which ultimately developed into Judaism is reflected in the diversity of sources which were redacted to create the Torah, the first five books of the Bible, and the other sections of the Hebrew

Bible. This diversity, in different forms, continued until 70 CE, the time of the destruction of the Second Temple in Jerusalem, after which Judaism was increasingly shaped by the *Pharisees, sages* or *rabbis* in a form which became to a large degree normative. This 'rabbinic' tradition established the foundation of all subsequent forms of Judaism.

The tradition established by the sages was primarily based on a legal tradition, *halakhah*, encapsulated in the *Mishnah* (200 CE) and the *Babylonian Talmud* (700 CE). This tradition worked through the interaction of models of interpretation with an authoritative set of legal sources. Although the sages also addressed non-legal questions, *aggadah*, they were primarily interested in establishing a context of accepted behavioural patterns. The legal tradition that developed covered a wide range of activities and spheres. It included, for example, discussions of ritual purity, family law and torts. Issues of belief and dogma – beyond certain basic conceptions of monotheism – were secondary, with a much greater degree of interpretation and individual or communal diversity. The emphasis on the *halakhah* remained the foundation of Judaism into the modern period, and the law continues to be debated and discussed.

The *halakhah* is divided into two main categories – the Written and Oral Torah. The Written Torah includes the first five books of the Bible and was believed to have been given in written form to Moses on Sinai. The Oral Torah minimally includes the Mishnah and Talmud and maximally includes all *halakhic* discussions as an unfolding, expanding tradition. The Oral Torah was believed to have been given by God to Moses in oral form on Sinai. During the past centuries, it was encapsulated in several legal codes, culminating in the *Shulkhan Aruch* (1542) which remains the cornerstone of traditional Judaism. The Orthodox and Conservative approaches to Judaism arise from differing interpretations of the possibilities of change within the *halakhic* system (see below). It should be emphasized that in spite of some traditions' view that the *halakhah* is unchanging, it has in fact constantly changed and developed and continues to do so today particularly in response to issues raised by Judaism's encounters with modernity.

Alongside the legal tradition the *aggadic* tradition developed in many different directions. The most significant of these included mysticism and philosophy. These also laid the basis for some of the directions taken by Judaism in response to modernity – for example the Orthodox Hasidic community (established in the eighteenth century) emphasizes (alongside the *halakhah*) the mystical tradition and has its roots in the mystical response to the expulsion of the Jews from Spain in 1492. Likewise, the Reform movement can be viewed as a continuation into modern times of the philosophical tradition. It draws on philosophy, particularly that of Kant, as the basis of its understanding of action and (in part) of God. The philosophical emphasis is even more important as the basis of Reconstructionist Judaism.

Several themes from the Biblical and historical tradition became major mythological motifs which shaped rabbinic Judaism and continue to shape all modern forms of Judaism. Historically, the most significant of these has been the concept of covenant, and the associated concept of redemption. These motifs are particularly encapsulated in the exodus narrative (recorded in the book of Exodus in the Bible) which tells of both the redemption from Egypt and the acceptance of the Commandments on Mount Sinai. This account became one of the significant paradigms for interpreting God's role in history. Its influence can still be seen – for example – in the way in which some Jewish communities and thinkers interpret the foundation of the State of Israel in the modern period.

A second motif of almost equal significance is based on the historical events surrounding the destruction of the Temple in Jerusalem. Here the motif is one of the power of God in destruction and punishment. Although this motif, which often focuses on punishment of Israel, has its roots in a biblical concept of reward and punishment and is first articulated in respect of the destruction of the First

Temple by the Babylonians, it is most strongly developed in relation to the destruction of the Second Temple by the Romans and the *diaspora* (dispersion, migration) which followed. In modern times this motif has been used as a model for the interpretation of the periodic persecution of Jewish communities culminating in the Holocaust (the systematic persecution and extermination of Jews by the Nazi regime in Germany during the Second World War). Indeed, in many ways the Holocaust has become the prime exemplar of this motif in modern times, so much so that the latter has become a new lens for re-understanding persecution and anti-Semitism.

The Holocaust has also become a significant motif in its own right. Its symbolic and theological effects have been felt throughout the second half of the twentieth century. As suggested, it has become symbolic of anti-Semitism and persecution of the Jewish people both linking into and surpassing or superseding past persecutions. It also has had a significant impact on all subsequent Jewish theologies. This is most clearly seen in respect to interpretations of evil and theodicy (explanations of evil and suffering). After the Holocaust many theologians could no longer accept older understandings of suffering as God's judgement, particularly as this would make Hitler and the Nazis God's tools. Many new theodicies have thus been suggested. They have included: arguments about the 'death of God', denials that God acts in the world through miraculous intervention or even revelation, and an emphasis on the reality of unrestrained human free will. Other scholars have suggested that the Holocaust simply reveals the limitations of human understanding. In practical terms, the Holocaust has become for many the basis for a new emphasis on the importance of Jewish survival – often survival for its own sake. The theme may also be expressed in the terms of resistance to giving Hitler a 'posthumous victory'. Such ideas of survival, resistance and anti-Semitism often inform thinking about Zionism and the problem of diaspora. Their impact is various. As well as encouraging the formation of a separate Jewish state (Israel), they may challenge notions of messianic communal progress, or re-emphasize Jewish particularism.

A final historical motif that has been re-activated by particular pressures of modernity is that of the promised land – originally part of the covenant myth (in the Hebrew Bible God grants the promised land to Israel so long as they remain faithful to the covenant with God). For most of the last two thousand years – during which time Israel has been dispersed, in diaspora – this mythological complex has played only a minor role, often associated with messianic speculations. But it has been revitalized in the nineteenth and twentieth centuries, and has developed in association with modern (Romantic) concepts of nationalism into Zionism. Although not all modern Zionists believe in a divine basis for the modern State of Israel, the biblical depiction of God's promise of the land clearly provided a strong religious and emotional tie to a specific geographic location, and continues to provide political and religious motivations for many Zionists.

Thus the events of the twentieth century have added new mythological ways of understanding past and present in Judaism. Zionism and the Holocaust (particularly a Zionist interpretation of the Holocaust) have been two essential shaping motifs. Some Zionist thinking sees the return of all Jews to the State of Israel as the culmination of Jewish history, and the return to normality as a nation. All events of the past, particularly those of the diaspora, are interpreted in this light. The model focuses on periods of persecution – culminating in the Holocaust – as the result of living in diaspora. It suggests that the only way to resolve this problem – the relation of Israel to the other nations – is to transform Israel, to make it a nation like any other nation, living in a land of its own.

This chapter examines how different forms of Judaism have attempted to respond to these motifs and the forces of modernity. Although the different movements reacted in various ways, some positive and some negative, all were forced to respond to modernity in some fashion. The political position of the Jews made this inescapable. Since most Jews prior to the foundation of the State of Israel in 1947 dwelt within host European societies, the rise of modernity in general and the modern state in particular was experienced at first hand. Equally, the migration of many Jews to American in the twentieth century placed them at the heart of the current lead society of the modern world. The chapter as it develops focuses most strongly on the Reform movement, not because it is the most significant, but because it most consciously and clearly articulates the issues raised by modernity.

INTERACTIONS WITH MODERNITY

Moses Mendelssohn and the Jewish Enlightenment

The philosophy of Moses Mendelssohn marks the beginning of the Jewish encounter with the seventeenth-century Enlightenment, and may be regarded as the precursor of the Jewish encounter with modernity. Whilst it is true that Spinoza (1632–77) was an earlier and more significant Enlightenment philosopher, his influence on Judaism was less direct. This was due both to the radical nature of his philosophical arguments and to his ultimate excommunication by the Jewish community of Amsterdam. Mendelssohn (1729–86) marks the transition from a traditional Talmudic scholar to an Enlightenment philosopher; his work was influenced by that of Spinoza, Leibniz, Hobbes and Locke. His achievement also marks the beginnings of the wider integration of Jews into Western European culture, and the introduction of ideas from that culture into the wider Jewish community in both Western and eventually Eastern Europe.

In regard to the wider transformation of Judaism in the context of early modernity, the most significant of Mendelssohn's philosophical works is *Jerusalem Or, On Religious Power and Judaism*. This work was intended both as an argument against compulsion within religion, and as a demonstration that allegiance to Judaism was compatible with full participation as citizens of European nation states. *Jerusalem* is divided into two parts. The first examines the relationship between the political and the religious and establishes the foundations of political philosophy. The second is a defence of Judaism. It argues that in terms of its core beliefs Judaism is a religion of reason; in arguing this Mendelssohn was situating Judaism within the Enlightenment search for the rational basis of all religion. For Mendelssohn the revealed and particular aspect of Judaism was its law, which was binding on Jews alone. As such Judaism was a religion of law rather than dogma. In arguing this, Mendelssohn drew a distinction between Judaism and Christianity. Unlike Christianity, which imposed a set of religious dogmas on its adherents, Judaism permitted its adherents freedom of belief. Its spirit was 'freedom in doctrine and conformity in law'. None of its laws, however, were coercive or dogmatic. In effect, Mendelssohn was arguing for the existence of the separate historical religions, thereby opposing the view that all religions should be merged into a homogenized form of Christianity presented as the universal religion of reason. His work thus presents a strong argument for the inclusion of Jews as citizens within European states, and lays the groundwork for the significant change in the social and political status of the Jewish people in Europe in the late eighteenth and nineteenth centuries.

Mendelssohn cannot simply be viewed as a reformer due to his arguments for the maintenance of Jewish law, and his commitment to the maintenance of the law. Yet in some respects his thought opened up cracks in the tradition. Amongst his innovations were the rejection of excommunication and of the right of the religious community to exercise force and compulsion, and his views about the laws of burial – these changes became touchstones for arguments between traditionalists and modernists. Mendelssohn's work also signals the beginnings of important changes within the Jewish community, and in the relation of that community to a new world of nation states. He can be seen as an exemplar of the possibilities of Jewish participation in modern European culture and thought. His contribution led to the development of the *Haskalah* or Jewish Enlightenment, which sought to introduce European thought and culture to the Jewish community. As such Mendelssohn became a symbol for reform and 'liberalism' – a new freedom of belief in religious matters.

The Haskalah: the Jewish Enlightenment

The *Haskalah* marked a change in many aspects of Jewish cultural life. At its simplest it was a movement of Jewish writers influenced by European literary forms. But it also had wider ideological goals, and sought to transform almost every aspect of Jewish life from education to communal organization. It viewed the Jews, particularly of Central and Eastern Europe, as remaining in a form of medievalism and challenged them to confront and absorb the best elements of modernity.

The initial period of the *Haskalah* was led by disciples of Mendelssohn. They championed a return to Hebrew and rejected *Yiddish* – the traditional language of the Jewish community of the time – as a degenerate form of German. They also respected biblical Hebrew rather than the later rabbinic Hebrew. This stance related to their rejection of traditional Jewish education which emphasized the study of rabbinic texts, particularly the Talmud, almost to the exclusion of any other subject. The reformers viewed rabbinic forms of Judaism as degenerate compared with the purer and earlier biblical form. Like liberal Christians, they sought a return to a purer, more historically authentic faith. Such a project ultimately became one of the building blocks for Reform Judaism as it developed in the nineteenth century. In terms of language the *Haskalah* initially emphasized Hebrew and subsequently emphasized the use of German – the emphasis on German and the vernacular language of the country of residence also became one of the hallmarks of Reform.

The *Haskalah* played a provocative and oppositional role in relation to the development of Orthodox Hasidism in modern times (the Hasidic community is discussed in greater detail below). As the *Haskalah* moved into Eastern Europe and Russia, its opposition to medievalism often translated into a rejection of Hasidism with its emphasis on mysticism and its charismatic leaders, the *tzadikim*. Its satires often singled out Hasidism for ridicule. One effect was to engender a fierce mutual opposition between the two tendencies in modern Judaism, and to precipitate Hasidic opposition to modernity. The opposition is reflected in many Hasidic tales in which the *Maskil* (disciple of the *Haskalah*) is depicted as an opponent.

Like the ideas developed by Mendelssohn, the *Haskalah* can be seen as transitional. It represented the beginnings of the transformation of the Jewish community through its encounter with modernity. It laid the foundation for many of the religious trends that came to fruition in the middle of the nineteenth century. On the one hand, as missionaries of modern values and culture the *Haskalah* influenced the early Reformers who sought to create a Judaism that was consonant with modern values and culture. On the other hand, by its opposition to traditional values and the Hasidic community, it helped create a strong association between modernity and the rejection of traditional Judaism and thereby strengthened Orthodox Judaism's suspicion and hostility towards modernity.

The beginnings of modern Jewish movements

This section of the chapter examines some of the developments in the eighteenth and nineteenth centuries that led to the rise of many of the movements which now constitute modern Judaism. It argues that all of the movements arose as responses, either positive or negative, to the Enlightenment and modernity. Each of the movements is examined in somewhat greater detail in later sections of this chapter.

REFORM

In *Leviathan* Saul Ascher (1767–1822) laid the philosophical cornerstone of the Reform movement in Judaism. Unlike Mendelssohn who saw Judaism as a revealed law, Ascher argued that the defining feature of Judaism was its religious faith, not its political or legal constitution. This emphasis on faith, in effect, made Judaism equivalent to other European religions – a theme constantly returned to by modern Reform Judaism. By separating it from its political and practical basis, Ascher placed Judaism among other 'religions', and saw it as compatible with the cultural and political life of modern Europe. Unlike traditional Judaism which treated all aspects of Jewish law and tradition as equally authoritative, Ascher selected or emphasized certain practices as essential while ignoring or de-emphasizing others. He focused on the subjective personal aspects of religion, emphasizing the importance of personal satisfaction and happiness. He saw the law as a means to these ends, thus opposing those who emphasized the communal aspects of religion and who saw faithful observance as the fulfilment of God's will and thus an end in itself. Ascher also emphasized a concept of history which underpins all modern forms of Judaism, that is, as a process of development with the implication of unfolding spiritual progress. Many of these themes, particularly the concept of religious subjectivity, underpinned the ideas of the Reform movement and are still significant features of it. Ascher's arguments also provided a philosophical basis for the changes which were subsequently introduced by both his contemporaries and successors.

The origins of the Reform movement lie not only in the cultural transformations associated with the dawn of modernity (notably the rise of the Enlightenment), but also in the political changes which characterized early modern Europe – most notably the rise of the nation state and individual freedoms. During the latter half of the eighteenth century and the first half of the nineteenth the Jewish community in Western Europe experienced a significant transformation in status. As the period progressed Jews were increasingly given political freedom – a transformation marked by the move from protected, semi-autonomous minority to citizen (or subject). The French Revolution and the Napoleonic period marked one of the key points in this transformation. With increasing access to political and cultural life and decision-making, Jewish communities, particularly in what was to become Germany, began to develop forms of Judaism more in keeping with their new found status.

Although the process of reforming synagogue practice had been progressing since the late eighteenth century in Amsterdam, a more structured programme of reform did not occur until the nineteenth century, under the leadership of Israel Jacobson (1768–1828). It is perhaps significant that Jacobson was a lay rather than a rabbinic leader. The process began in Westphalia and continued in Berlin. Among the changes which were initially instituted was a transformation in the form of service, moving from one which was perceived to be less decorous, and thus out of keeping with wider

Figure 6.2 Israel Jacobson

cultural forms, to a form of service which was more highly structured and characterized by European ideas of decorum. Some of these changes included a reduction of physical rituals, for example the procession, and changes in the content and structure of the service, for example minimizing active congregational participation. After his move to Berlin, Reform services were held in the homes of Jacobson and Jacob Baer. These services added to the changes already instituted in Westphalia. The new additions included the use of German elements in the service alongside the Hebrew, removal of the partition between men and women and the removal of repetitions within the service. The process was also occurring in Hamburg with the establishment of the first Reform Temple in 1817.

By the mid-nineteenth century the process of reform moved from a focus on forms of worship and life to include areas of belief and self-perception. Thus in the prayer book reforms of that period we find removal of concepts of messianic ingathering, bodily resurrection and Zionist hopes. The removal of the messianic ingathering was tied to two separate concepts: (a) a transformation of the concept of messiah from the traditional model of an actual political and spiritual leader who would bring about a transformation in the world and gather all Jews back to Israel to a concept of messianic age which would be brought about through the inexorable progress of humanity; and (b) the rejection of the notion that Jews would be returned to Israel as an end to the negative condition of diaspora. Reformers considered diaspora to be a positive state and wanted to emphasize their ongoing commitment to the European states in which they lived. These priorities led them to be hostile to Zionism. They saw Zionism as a statement of Jewish separatism and the desire for a nation set apart. The reformers chose to define Judaism as a religion not a people or nation and thus with no need of a national home or end to diaspora. Likewise, the concept of bodily resurrection offended their ideas of rationality. In many prayer books it was either removed or changed to reflect belief in the immortality of the soul.

Abraham Geiger (1810–74) was another intellectual and rabbinic leader of Reform during this period. He introduced or emphasized several themes which remain characteristic of the Reform movement. He emphasized the historical nature of Judaism and thus the contingent nature of its practices and beliefs. He also emphasized Judaism's universal message – a theme that also has been very influential in changes in the language of prayer. One of Geiger's most significant emphases was the ethical nature of Judaism and the concept of ethical monotheism. For him the key unifying theme of Judaism was not observance but morality. This concept was enshrined in the notion of prophetic Judaism – an emphasis on the ideals proclaimed by the prophets rather than the observances taught by the rabbis.

ORTHODOX

The self-consciousness of other parts of the Jewish community developed to a large degree in response to the rise of reform and the Reform Movement. Thus, Orthodoxy came into existence as a self-conscious movement in opposition to the innovations that were being developed by the reformers. The two main early centres of Orthodoxy were Hungary and Germany, both areas in which the *haskalah* and the reformers had made significant inroads. In Hungary the major figure in the development of the movement was Rabbi Mosheh Sofer (1762–1839). The form of Orthodoxy that he espoused rejected any changes in tradition. To some extent he also rejected any real accommodation with the wider culture. One of the key aspects of self-conscious Orthodoxy was the view of the past and tradition as unchanging and uniformly authoritative. The approaches to community and Zionism found in Hungarian Orthodoxy also reflected this rejection of modern values. Rabbi Sofer supported settlement of Israel with the hope of establishing a Jewish community that was separated from the corrupting secular

Figure 6.3 Samson Raphael Hirsch

influences of the modern world. The Hungarian community also expressed their separatist values through the maintenance of an autonomous communal structure – which continued and was legally sanctioned in the latter half of the nineteenth century.

A second model of Orthodoxy developed in Germany in the middle part of the nineteenth century. Samson Raphael Hirsch (1808–88) was the leading figure of this approach. Although Hirsch, like Sofer, accepted the unchanging authority of *halakhah* (Jewish law) he took a different approach to modernity. His approach can be summed up in the statement: *Torah im derekh erets*, 'Torah [Jewish law] and the way of the world'. He believed that modernity and emancipation of the Jewish community could complement and enhance the Jewish mission, the core of which was leading a life according to God's will. The maxim was meant to suggest that Jews should take advantage of the modern world, especially its knowledge, but not allow this to undermine the commitment to Torah. The two worlds were not meant to be joined together or seen as equal partners, rather the two are meant to co-exist, with Jewish values and traditions ultimately being the arbiter for participation and acceptance of modernity. Like other German Jews, Hirsch de-emphasizes aspects of Jewish nationalism or national aspirations. He saw exile as having a positive rather than a negative value.

Rav Abraham Isaac Kook (1865–1935) offered a third approach to Orthodox Judaism that was different from those proposed by both Sofer and Hirsch. Although he was aware of trends in modern philosophy, his approach was more inwardly focused and placed an emphasis on traditional Jewish mysticism. He emphasized that the world was in a state of spiritual disharmony which was mirrored by the exile of Israel from her land. He argued that the return of Israel from exile would bring about a transformation both in the human and spiritual realms, and result in the redemption of all humanity. Kook was very strongly associated with Jewish nationalist aspirations. He saw Zionism as a yearning of the Jewish soul to fulfil its spiritual destiny. Thus even secular Orthodox was a sacred mission in spite of its own self-perception. On this basis Kook was more receptive and supportive of secular Zionism than other Orthodox leaders of his time. Kook prefigures some of the trends at the end of the twentieth century – this is most clearly seen in his synthesis of mysticism with aspects of modernity creating approaches that co-exist with modernity and to some extent validate aspects of it.

To a degree the approaches of Kook, Hirsch and Sofer have all had a lasting impact on Orthodox Judaism. Hirsch's position became mainstream for the Orthodox movement, for example, particularly in the US and the UK for much of the twentieth century. During the latter half of the century, however, there seems to be a shift in focus among many Orthodox communities to a stance which is more similar to that of Sofer (see below).

CONSERVATIVE

Like Orthodoxy, Conservative Judaism arose as a response to the process of reform. Unlike Orthodoxy, however, it had its roots among reformers both in Germany and the US. The process of reform was not a unified one; it had both traditional and radical wings. Rabbi Zachariah Frankel (1801–75) represented the traditionalist wing. He argued for a slower process of reform, with change focused on the less significant features of Jewish life and practice. The main split between Frankel and the reformers occurred respecting the use of Hebrew in religious services. Although both parties to the argument agreed that some German would be used as well as Hebrew, Frankel objected to the view that the maintenance of Hebrew was advisable rather than necessary. The argument over language was symbolic of a deeper argument over the nature and significance of tradition.

Frankel introduced a concept which was to become the cornerstone of Conservative Judaism: that of positive, historical Judaism. This concept included two, perhaps paradoxical, elements. It suggested that in order to understand Judaism one must examine the historical development of the tradition. Such historical consciousness was both modern and conservative. It forced an acceptance that the tradition had undergone a continuous process of change and development, and a recognition that this process of change would continue. It also, however, emphasized that Judaism is an organically integrated authoritative whole that develops over time. History and tradition should be a major element in shaping any decision for reform. Frankel also introduced a related concept – the wishes of the community. Change and tradition should reflect the needs of a community at a particular time; it should not run ahead of them due to the desires of individual reformers who embraced modern ideals and values wholesale. Through these two tenets Frankel sought to achieve a creative balance between tradition and reform with a strong emphasis on historical continuity.

The rise of Conservative Judaism in the US was influenced by Frankel's approach. Like Frankel, the founders of the movement started within the reformist camp and found themselves uncomfortable with the pace and level of reform. Two rabbis, Alexander Kohut (1842–94) and Sabato Morais (1823–97) led the split in the US. Both Kohut and Morais argued against many of the changes proposed by the radical reformers, while supporting a slower process of reform. The split in the US led to the establishment of the Jewish Theological Seminary of America, which became the foundation of a distinctive movement. This process was completed and given final form with the appointment of Solomon Schechter to head the seminary in 1901. Schechter helped establish the institutional structures of Conservative Judaism and likewise gave the concepts fundamental to Conservative Judaism an intellectually coherent form. He emphasized the historical development of Judaism as both a reforming and conservative tool, and argued for the need to respond to the consensus of the community, which he called 'catholic Israel'. Schechter argued that it was this communal force throughout Jewish history that was both the motive force for change and for continuity. By community he was not referring to all Jews, but the core of committed Jews – who unconsciously kept, dropped or transformed practices through time.

Reform Judaism

The platforms

Since the nineteenth century the Reform movement has responded to the changing faces of modernity at almost every level of practice and belief. Although in recent years there has been a trend back towards more traditional patterns, in general the trajectory has been towards transforming Judaism in line with Western cultural values and understandings. Many of these changes are highlighted in three main 'platforms' that have punctuated the history of the movement. Although all three are products of the American Reform movement, they have been reflected and influenced trends in the Reform or Progressive movements worldwide.

The Pittsburgh Platform of 1885 marks the first self-conscious statement of the American Reform movement, and the point at which the American Conservative movement was born via those rabbis, particularly Kohut and Morais, who rejected the changes and values found in the platform. The platform reflects changes in beliefs and practices. Several significant changes or expressions in the statement indicate the reformers' attempted synthesis of Judaism with modernity. The first section of the platform speaks of God as the 'God-idea'. It is possible that this formulation reflects the influence of neo-Kantian thought. Although Hermann Cohen's (1842–1918) significant discussion of Judaism in neo-Kantian terms, *Religion of Reason out of the Sources of Judaism* was not published until 1919, the Pittsburgh Platform does seem to be influenced by similar ideas. This is also seen in an emphasis on ethical monotheism which was also characteristic of Cohen's position. Moreover, the statement about the 'God-idea' reflects a universalist view of Judaism and other religions. While it recognizes the spiritual value of all religions' search for the infinite, it views Judaism as the highest expression of that search. The second statement of the platform affirms the value of the Bible as a record of Judaism's relationship with God and as a source of morality. It also, however, accepts the historically contingent nature of the text. It suggests that the Bible is a product of its own time – focusing primarily on the conflicts between modern science and the miracles and other non-scientific views found in the text. It argues that these forms are clothing for the message, but not the message itself. Another key change in belief is found in relation to the messiah. Rather than looking forward to an actual messianic figure, the platform looks towards a messianic age. One of the significant aspects of this change is an acceptance of nineteenth-century notions of progress. The platform views the modern era as the beginning of the messianic age. This change also reflects a general trend in reform which values the modern age as the acme of human progress. One additional change in belief is found respecting the fate of human beings after death. Traditional Judaism believed that there would be a bodily resurrection that would precede judgement. The platform rejects both bodily resurrection and heaven and hell. It argues instead for the immortality of the soul.

Several sections of the platform also reflect significant changes in both practice and the attitude towards Jewish law. The third section posits that the law was only binding during the period in which the Israelites lived in Palestine. During that period it served to prepare the people for their mission. Today, however, only the moral law – which was seen as being based on reason – remains binding. The other ceremonial aspects of Judaism should only be retained if they 'elevate or sanctify our lives'. Any rituals which are in conflict with modern values or aesthetics should be rejected. These themes are more specifically emphasized in the fourth section. It rejects food, purity and clothing rules as being obstructions rather than aids to spiritual elevation. These sections illustrate a key trend in reform thinking which emphasizes morality as being the heart of Judaism and sees ritual practice as being a means to that end, and to that of individual spiritual elevation, rather than being a significant end in itself. Yet the platform also emphasizes the sense of mission which was characteristic of the early stages of the Reform movement. It suggests that Judaism and its daughter religions of Christianity and Islam have the mission of spreading ethical monotheism. The platform concludes with a statement reflecting the liberal values which have been characteristic of the Reform movement. It specifically mentions the gap between rich and poor and the need to create a society based on justice.

The Pittsburgh Platform thus lays out many of the key themes that would remain central to the Reform movement during the twentieth century. In terms of belief it offered a rationalist and more transcendent view of the 'God-idea' and viewed all religions as coming from the same infinite source. It emphasized the notion of progress and encapsulated it in the concept of the messianic age. In terms of practice, it enshrined a more instrumental view of the law, seeing it as a means to a moral or spiritual end. It also enshrined the view that the law is historically contingent and that groups or individuals have the right to judge the law based on modern values and aesthetics, and that only the universal moral law was binding.

The Columbus Platform of 1937 reiterated and clarified many of these ideas. It, however, moves back from some of the more extreme positions taken by the earlier reformers, for example, that of the God-idea, critical discussion of the rabbinic tradition and the positive statement regarding Zionism. It does, however, retain the key trajectories of reform. This is particularly seen in the emphasis on morality, particularly twentieth-century liberal values. It also continues the rejection of the binding nature of Jewish law and emphasis on spiritual elevation and inspiration.

In 1976 the Reform movement celebrated one hundred years of reform in America with a new statement of Reform principles, 'Reform Judaism – A Centenary Perspective'. One of the most significant changes indicated by the document was a change in attitude towards modernity. Due to the Holocaust, the movement no longer expressed the same attitude towards progress and modernity. The Holocaust also caused a new emphasis on survival, which found expression throughout the text. It expressed a much more positive attitude towards Zionism – this reflected a clear change in the Reform movement's attitude that initially occurred at the conclusion of the Second World War. Though the Centenary Perspective retained a universalistic emphasis on values and mission, the central focus on liberal values also dropped out. The text as a whole is much more inward looking and focused on the needs of the Reform Jewish community. It offers a new understanding of the relationship with modernity, emphasizing the uncertain nature of the individual's experience of the modern world, and using uncertainty as an explanation for the increasing diversity within the Reform movement. Arguing that the Reform movement is open to any 'position thoughtfully and conscientiously advocated', the Centenary Perspective reflects the increasing emphasis on individual conscience, choice and diversity which had developed during the course of the twentieth century.

ONE HUNDRED YEARS: WHAT WE HAVE TAUGHT

We celebrate the role of Reform Judaism in North America . . . We also feel great satisfaction at how much of our pioneering conception of Judaism has been accepted by the household of Israel. It now seems self-evident to most Jews: that our tradition should interact with modern culture; that its forms ought to reflect a contemporary aesthetic; that its scholarship needs to be conducted by modern critical methods; and that change has been and must continue to be a fundamental reality in Jewish life. Moreover, though some still disagree, substantial numbers have also accepted our teachings: that the ethics of universalism implicit in traditional Judaism must be an explicit part of our Jewish duty; that women should have full rights to practice Judaism; and that Jewish obligation begins with the informed will of every individual.

(From 'Reform Judaism – A Centenary Perspective')

These three documents reflect several elements of continuity and development in the Reform project. There is a continued emphasis on universality and a positive attitude towards other religions, particularly Christianity and Islam. There is also a clear rejection of Jewish law as obligatory. Although the early documents do not highlight the mechanisms for change, the element of autonomy is clearly emphasized in the Centenary Perspective. It is not unlikely that this emphasis reflects a greater emphasis on the individual and individual spiritual needs and aspirations (a detraditionalization and 'turn to the self'), which has developed in the twentieth century. There are also several areas where the more recent documents reflect a retreat from the stances taken in the early stages of the movement, for example, a more positive revaluation of ritual and retreat from strong statements of liberal/individualistic values which reflect a more inward-looking movement, increasingly concerned for the survival of Judaism.

AUTHORITY AND THE INDIVIDUAL

As seen in the Centenary Perspective, Reform Judaism emphasizes the role of the individual – reiterating the position initially taken by Ascher. Religion is seen as serving both individual and communal needs, and though the importance of ritual gains fresh emphasis, it is left to each person to be responsible for their own ritual practice. The emphasis on autonomy means that there can be great diversity in practice within the movement based on individual choices and needs. In actuality, however, there is a greater degree of acceptance of authority in the movement. Most individuals do not exercise their responsibility to create their own Jewish life.

The degree of conformity found among Reform Jews was much more marked prior to the 1960s and 1970s. Until that time several factors combined to support conformity of ideas and practice rather than diversity: an acceptance of the value of a universal reason, social conformity and a greater sense of social cohesion and mission. In the 1960s this consensus began to break down with an increase in individualization and perhaps a broader relativization of values. It is also likely that the philosophy of Martin Buber (1878–1965), with its emphasis on the divine–human (individual) encounter and rejection of traditional forms of religion, also played a part in this process. Although the diversity found is still limited to a relatively small group of Reform Jews it plays a key role in challenging the movement's identity and in the 1990s has led to a move towards various forms of spirituality and mystical practices.

Authority in the Reform movement is vested at several levels. Within most communities there are both lay and rabbinic structures. The lay leaders are primarily managerial, leaving most religious direction to the rabbis. The congregation elects the lay leadership. The rabbinic role is variously interpreted. Some rabbis emphasize the teaching aspect of the role, seeing themselves as facilitators rather than leaders, whilst others take a stronger role in shaping the ritual life of both the community and individuals within it. Most fall between these two poles. In all cases, however, it is important to note that the rabbi is an employee hired by the congregation and working for them on a contractual basis. This type of relationship shapes the interaction between the rabbi and congregation and may prevent the rabbi from moving in directions that are uncomfortable to the congregants or the congregational leaders.

The Reform movement in the US is also highly organized in its institutional structures. Since the foundation of the movement in the nineteenth century three institutions have been dominant. The Hebrew Union College-Jewish Institute of Religion (HUC-JIR), with four campuses in New York, Cincinnati, Los Angeles, and Jerusalem – trains the rabbinic and other professionals for the movement. The Central Conference of American Rabbis (CCAR) is the organizational body of Reform rabbis. The CCAR has provided many of the communal aspects of religious input into the movement, publishing the prayer books used by Reform synagogues and making statements on aspects of religious practice and belief – the Columbus Platform and the Centenary Perspective were both produced by the CCAR. The third institutional body, the Union of American Hebrew Congregations (UAHC), is the congregational organization of the movement. Since its inception it has had both rabbinic and lay leadership. Of the three organizations in recent years the latter has tended to be the most influential in shaping religious policy. Similar structures are found in other parts of the Reform movement worldwide, though only the UK has a fully independent rabbinical seminary, the Leo Baeck College.

GENDER

One of the most significant changes instituted by the Reform movement almost since its inception has been a move towards the equalization of the roles of men and women in Judaism. This change accelerated over time and reflected changes in the status of women in Western society during the course of the nineteenth and twentieth centuries (see Chapter 16). As in many aspects of the Reform approach to tradition, its decisions regarding women reflect the view that where modern values come into conflict with Jewish tradition, the tradition should be changed in line with the modern values.

In Reform temples today no distinction is made between male and female roles. Men and women sit together during all types of services and events – with the exception of some women's services, often regarding the new moon, which have been introduced by women in response to the desire to have rituals which reflect their particular needs. Rituals that were once limited to men such as *Bar Mitzvah* have been extended to women (*Bat Mitzvah*). Women can also fulfil all ritual roles within the community. These roles include both congregational participation in ritual and all professional roles. In 1972, HUC-JIR was the first seminary to ordain a woman as rabbi. Although the possibility of women rabbis had been debated and in principle accepted earlier in the century – and a woman, Regina Jonas, had served as a rabbi – it was only in the late 1960s that the college accepted a woman as a candidate for ordination. Today there are an increasing number of women rabbis, though none have yet been appointed as a senior rabbi of a flagship congregation. The other Reform seminaries followed the lead of HUC-JIR and women now serve as rabbis within all parts of Reform Judaism. Women are also found in other professional roles within the Jewish community including temple administrators, cantors and religion school directors.

Figure 6.4 Women from the Jewish Community of Great Neck, New York, dance with a Torah specially commissioned and brought to the only existing synagogue in Oswiecim, Poland, where the Auschwitz death camp was built, during a joyful ceremony on 30 August 1999. The ceremony and the Torah restored the synagogue's religious character

RECENT DEVELOPMENTS

Reform Judaism, like other forms of liberal religion, is currently struggling to maintain its numbers and identity. During the past thirty years the movement has participated in many initiatives, some on its own and some in co-operation with other movements, to enhance Jewish practice and identity. It has also gone through many internal changes trying to fit the needs of a changing constituency. Many of the changes have been highlighted above. Thus, the shift in focus from liberal, social and political concerns to internal and spiritual concerns, which was seen in the Centenary Perspective, is even clearer in the most recent position statement of the CCAR. This change is seen particularly in the introduction of a wide range of forms of experience-based spirituality which have become increasingly common in Reform temples. The most visible of these are healing services which range from the calling out of names to the laying on of hands. The spirituality and mystical elements which have been introduced also indicate a move away from the rationalism which was the hallmark of classical Reform.

In part some of these trends are a response to the challenges posed by New Age religion. A New Age Judaism has arisen on the periphery of the mainstream movements. It tends to have weak boundaries and exhibits the modern phenomena of 'spiritual shopping' and 'networking' characteristic of the New Age. Such spirituality offers a more experiential or mystical form of Judaism. Many Reform and Conservative Jews, both as movements and more significantly as individual congregations, are responding to this external challenge by introducing similar practices and ideas. It will be interesting to see whether these changes alienate the parts of the Reform movement that still accept the notions of rationality which were fundamental to modernism rather than the more subjectivized experience which is fundamental to postmodernism.

Yet there is an additional trend in the Reform movement today which moves towards the opposite side of modern religious practice – a move towards the recreation of stronger religious structures. This is found in a move away from individual autonomy to a new Reform *halakhah*. While it is true that this pressure has been present through much of the twentieth century, it has made its mark primarily in the latter half of the twentieth century. This is seen in the increasing number of traditional practices that are followed by Reform congregations. The trend towards a neo-traditionalism was particularly highlighted in the preparatory documents, which led up to the CCAR's position statement of 1999. Although the final document watered the emphasis down, the trend towards a much more structured definition of Reform practice and ideology is clearly present. This trend is also found in the progressive movements of the UK. Both Reform and Liberal Judaism have become increasingly traditional and to some extent have tried to establish basic (sometimes extensive) sets of practices and beliefs that identify a progressive Jew. Very often this trend is accompanied by rejections of relativism and the need to re-establish baseline values.

Conservative Judaism

Conservative Judaism has responded to many of the same influences as the Reform movement – as well as to Reform itself. The key difference between Reform and Conservative Judaism, however, lies in their differing attitudes towards Jewish law. As mentioned above, the Reform movement has often been willing to set aside Jewish law if it conflicts with modernity. The Conservative movements, however, place greater emphasis on the significance and authority of tradition. Conservative Judaism, as suggested above, recognizes that Judaism undergoes a continuous process of change and thus accepts that modern values and norms will shape the Judaism of the future. It also argues for the importance of continuity and considers Jewish law and the legal processes which have shaped it as the key source of that continuity. This somewhat paradoxical dual emphasis has meant that the changes instituted by the Conservative movement have been introduced more slowly than in Reform and have required the validation of the Jewish legal process. Nevertheless, during the past century the Conservative movement has made many of the same changes to tradition as has the Reform movement – for example equalizing the roles of men and women. Often the difference is one of process and attitude towards the law rather than one of final content and judgement.

The most recent and comprehensive statement of Conservative beliefs, *Emet Ve-Emunah*, was produced by the Conservative movement in 1988. The text was written by a commission and attempted to encapsulate a consensus of the beliefs found in the movement. As a consensus document it tends to attempt to present a moderate position which will satisfy the different wings of the movement. In those areas where consensus is impossible it presents the alternative positions. This type of process and result are characteristic of the Conservative movement as a whole. As the document covers a wide range of ideas, we will only touch on a few of them here. Many – such as the discussion of messianic expectations and a largely relativist understanding of the value of other religious traditions – are broadly similar to those found in the Reform movement. The document also mirrors the Reform concern for social values and includes a strong statement expressing the need for social change and justice.

The document opens with a discussion of Conservative theology, 'God in the World'. The first part of the section illustrates the diversity of belief within the movement. It offers two main divergent theological positions. The first presents a traditional depiction of the divine. It states that many people within the Conservative movement see God as being the supernatural power who controls and rules the world. It emphasizes, however, that there are many different reasons why people believe and many different ways in which human beings encounter God in experience. This position is in part shaped by the thought of Abraham Joshua Heschel (1907–72) who argued for a more traditional, mystical or experiential understanding and relation to God. The second position is closer to the thought of Mordechai Kaplan (1881–1983), who argued for a non-supernatural and non-personal understanding of the divine. This position suggests that God is not a supernatural power who can be encountered, but rather a source of meaning or perhaps the moral–logical structure of being. This second position is perhaps even more extreme than would be found among most Reform Jews. The discussion concludes with a validation of diversity of belief. It ties the many different understandings of god to God's elusive nature.

The most important part of the first section of the statement, and perhaps the document as a whole, deals with the Conservative understanding of Jewish law. It emphasizes the importance of the law on several grounds: as an expression of God's will for the Jewish people; as a continuing way of encountering God; as a key feature of Jewish identity, and as an important means of preserving the Jewish people. There is also a discussion of tradition and development within the law. Both the need to maintain continuity with the past and the need to make appropriate changes as change in values and social contexts are highlighted, as is the necessity of change and of standing firm. Decisions need to be taken on a case-by-case basis and in dialogue with the legal tradition. It is asserted that the rabbi in a congregation is the primary source of religious authority – his authority derives both from training in Jewish law and the ordination process. Two further loci of authority are also identified: the Committee on Law and Standards and the Rabbinical Assembly. These two groupings of rabbis are viewed as the ultimate arbiters of Jewish practice within the movement (and are discussed further below).

The State of Israel is a further topic that attracts extensive discussion in *Emet Ve-Emunah*. In general the text is very positive towards Zionism and highlights the importance of the role of Israel to Jews in the diaspora. Not surprisingly, the document particularly emphasizes the importance of religious

Figure 6.5 A two-month-old donkey is carried into a synagogue of the Hasidic 'Toldot Aharon' community in Jerusalem, 13 September 1998, during a ritual 'Peter Chamor', where a first-born donkey is given to the cohen (Jewish priest) as a gift from followers. The donkey is usually exchanged then with a kosher animal or with money

pluralism in Israel, specifically focusing on the rights of non-Orthodox Jewish religious movements. This issue is increasingly significant to all non-Orthodox movements, none of which are recognized by Israeli law. To an extent the text presents the State of Israel as the cultural and religious hub for Jewish people in diaspora. In spite of this emphasis, however, it echoes the Reform documents in affirming the value of diaspora. Thus it offers a bi-polar model for Jewish life, which values both the diaspora and Israel as creative centres for the continuation of a creative Jewish spiritual and cultural existence.

The last section of the document covers a range of issues that relate to living a Jewish life. The two most significant of these are the section on women and the concluding section on the 'Ideal Conservative Jew'. While the statement on women strongly advocates the equality of men and women, there is also a degree of equivocation. It is emphasized that since the earliest days of the movement men and women were not seated separately, and that the ceremony of *Bat Mitzvah* (Daughter of the Commandments) was instituted first by the Conservative movement. Yet the conclusion of the section highlights the ongoing debate in the movement regarding women's participation in ritual. It states that some believe that women should be allowed to participate fully in ritual and to become rabbis and cantors, while others believe that women can best express their spirituality in more traditional roles. It is emphasized that whichever position is taken, the Jewish law remains the necessary validation for views on gender roles.

The final section of the statement presents an image of the ideal Conservative Jew. The image is shaped by the challenges of living a Jewish life in the modern world. It is recognized that the holistic pattern of Jewish life, which preceded the Enlightenment, is no longer part of most people's experience. A return to this traditional pattern is impossible; what is advocated is a creative forum in which both Judaism and modernity can 'reshape each other'. Three elements are seen to be essential: first, a commitment to Jewish practices and concerns and the adoption of a Jewish perspective on all matters; second, the need for a continuous process of learning; third, a view of Jewish life as a constant process of open striving which is constantly enriched through engagement with the Jewish tradition.

▮ THE IDEAL CONSERVATIVE JEW

Throughout most of its history, Jewish life was an organic unity of home and community, synagogue and law. Since the Emancipation, however, Judaism has been marked by increasing fragmentation . . . Participating in a majority culture whose patterns and rhythms often undermine our own, we are forced to live in two worlds, replacing whole organic Judaism with fragments: ritual observance or Zionism, philanthropy or group defence; each necessary, none sufficient in itself.

Facing this reality, Conservative Judaism came into being to create a new synthesis in Jewish life . . .

Three characteristics mark the ideal conservative Jew. First, he or she is a *willing* Jew, whose life echoes the dictum, 'Nothing human or Jewish is alien to me.'

The second mark of the ideal Conservative Jew is that he or she is a *learning* Jew.

Finally, the ideal conservative Jew is a *striving* Jew.

Given our changing world, finality and certainty are illusory at best, destructive at worst. Rather than claiming to have found a goal at the end of the road, the ideal Conservative Jew is a traveller walking purposefully towards 'God's holy mountain.'

(From *Emet Ve-Emunah*)

INDIVIDUAL AND AUTHORITY

As suggested in this discussion of *Emet Ve-Emunah*, Conservative Judaism places a stronger emphasis on rabbinic authority than is usual in Reform Judaism. This authority, however, is restricted to decisions regarding Jewish law, tradition and practice. Conservative Jews fully participate in modern life and accept the value placed on the individual and notions of individual choice. Nonetheless, due to its emphasis on the Jewish legal tradition, rabbis in their capacity as scholars (or students) of Jewish law are the primary source for information about *halakhic* practice. The traditional term used by the Conservative movement to describe this aspect of the rabbinical role is *mara d'atra*, 'master of the place', emphasizing that the rabbi is the primary authority for his or her community.

The hierarchy of legal authority, however, moves beyond the individual rabbi to the movement, or at least a committee of rabbis representing the movement, that is the Committee on Jewish Law and Standards. The committee represents all sections of the movement. Its voting members are all scholars of the Jewish legal tradition. It also includes lay members, chosen by the congregational arm, who participate in discussions but are not allowed to vote. A key feature of this process is that although it seeks consensus it will occasionally produce a range of opinions, reflecting divergence of views within the committee. Where there is a unanimous decision taken by the committee, the decision is binding on all Conservative rabbis and communities. If, however, there are several different opinions, it is left to the individual rabbi to select the position that he or she finds most convincing.

WOMEN

Like the Reform movement, the Conservative movement has changed its attitudes on gender roles in line with changes in the wider cultural context. From the early part of the century the separation between men and women during services was removed – allowing them to sit together. As the century progressed the movement opened a greater number of doors to women's participation. Thus, in 1955 it allowed women to have *aliyot*, to participate in the rituals surrounding the reading of the Torah during a service; in 1973 it allowed women to be counted as part of the *minyan*, the minimum number of people, ten, needed for a public religious service; and finally in, 1983, the Jewish Theological Seminary decided to admit women to be trained as rabbis.

In many ways the current position taken by the Conservative movement is not dissimilar to that of the Reform movement. The key difference is one of process. The Reform movement viewed the status of women in tradition as going against modern ethical values; it therefore made the changes it saw as necessary to redress this problem. The Conservative movement saw the same conflict but needed to work within the Jewish legal system to make the necessary changes – this process meant that in some cases they were not able to go as far or as quickly as many would have liked. Due to its decision-making process, however, there is some diversity of practice with regard to women's participation. Several of the decisions that opened ritual participation to women also produced minority positions that opposed women being granted these rights and responsibilities. Thus there are communities that will not allow a woman rabbi to serve them. Outside the US congregations in the Conservative tradition tend to be more traditional regarding women's roles in ritual life.

Orthodox Judaism

▌ RELIGION ALLIED TO PROGRESS

Now what is it that *we* want? Are the only two alternatives either to abandon religion or to renounce all progress with all the glorious and noble gifts which civilisation and education offer mankind? Is the Jewish religion really of such a nature that its faithful adherents must be the enemies of civilisation and progress? . . . We declare before heaven and earth that if our religion demanded that we should renounce what is called civilisation and progress we would obey unquestioningly, because our religion is for us truly religion, the word of God before which every other consideration must give way . . .

There is, however, no such dilemma. Judaism never remained aloof from true civilisation and progress; in almost every era its adherents were fully abreast of contemporary learning . . .

In truth, if only most Jews were truly Jews, most of the factors would disappear which to-day bar many an avenue of activity to them.

(P. Mendes-Flohr and J. Reinharz (eds): *The Jew in the Modern World*
Oxford: OUP, 1980, p. 179)

Orthodox Judaism is a much more heterogeneous grouping than the other movements discussed above. Indeed, there is really no such thing as the Orthodox 'movement', but rather many separate groups or alignments sharing some basic tenets and differing widely in other areas. The main ideas that bind Orthodox Jews together are: the historicity of the revelation on Sinai and the acceptance that both the Oral and Written Law are eternally binding and essentially unchanging. Most Orthodox reject modernity where it impinges on or challenges aspects of Jewish tradition. Thus, most Orthodox rabbis will not accept the findings of archaeology or critical analysis of the Bible, particularly if they challenge the Mosaic authorship of the Torah.

Within the Orthodox community there are a wide range of responses to other aspects of modernity. These responses resemble those of the three Orthodox figures discussed above – Sofer, Hirsch and Rav

Kook. Most Orthodox Jews accept the position presented by Hirsch. They find a creative synthesis between their Judaism and modernity, taking advantage of what modernity can offer them (such as technology) without compromising their heritage. Where there is a conflict between Judaism and modernity they accept the Jewish view rather than that of modernity. There were also an increasing number of Jews in the late twentieth century moving towards the position presented by Sofer. They were increasingly hostile to modernity, particularly to ideas of relativism and pluralism, and were looking for more authoritarian and clearly bounded forms of Jewish thought and practice. The term *Haredim* is sometimes used for this community. In Israel this form of Judaism has increasingly mixed with extreme forms of Zionist thought. This group is very strongly represented by settlers on the West Bank and among those Israelis who challenge any moves towards regularizing Israel's relations with her neighbours and the Palestinians. The mystical form of Judaism offered by Rav Kook is finding its way into many forms of Judaism today. It has its mainspring in the Hasidic community (which historically preceded Rav Kook) but is also found in other groups who are looking for more spiritual and less rational forms of Jewish expression.

The *Haredi* model of Judaism, in both its political and religious respect, has increasingly been that accepted by Sephardic Jews in Israel – particularly those who came to Israel after 1948 from countries in the Arab world. Many individuals from the Sephardic community have been attracted to the messianic aspirations of the *Haredi Yeshivot*. Due to its size, and to discrimination against Sephardic Jews by the secular Ashkinazic Israeli establishment, the Sephardic community has developed a strong bounded identity which is increasingly powerful in Israeli politics. The agenda of the Sephardic parties and political blocs often is shaped by right-wing religious and political tendencies.

These *Haredi Yeshivot* have also been very attractive to large numbers of young Jews from Western Europe and more particularly from the US. These Jews, often coming from secular or non-traditional backgrounds find in *Haredi* Judaism a clarity and surety which seems to have been lost in those forms of Judaism which have responded positively to modernity. These Jews reflect a growing trend in many Western countries of individuals who reject the more liberal forms of Judaism in search of a firmer foundation against the tides of modernity and postmodernity. In an age of relativism these forms of Orthodoxy make strong claims to moral superiority and authority which are an increasingly loud voice within Jewish communities throughout the world.

Hasidic Judaism, which forms part of the right wing of Orthodoxy, develops the strongest opposition to modernity. It tends to take a strongly fundamentalist view of tradition and emphasizes the mystical aspects of religion as the most significant part of human experience. Over the last three hundred years the Hasidic community has developed a wide range of methods for maintaining strong boundaries. These methods of boundary maintenance include particular forms of dress, highly centralized communal structures and an extreme emphasis on food rules. In addition, the Hasidic community refuses to participate in secular education and very few of its members, if any, participate in secular higher education. Some Hasidic communities also reject the use of television or other public media in order to control the flow of secular influences.

One of the most interesting trends in Judaism in the latter half of the twentieth century was the successful missionary activity undertaken by one of the major Hasidic dynasties, the Habad under its *rebbi* (leader) Rabbi Menahem Mendel Schneerson. This missionary activity was only aimed at the Jewish community – as the Habad saw it they were bringing Jews back to Judaism. The goal of this activity was primarily mystical. They believed that by bringing Jews back to Judaism they were causing transformations in the supernatural realm that would bring about the coming of the messiah. Many of the Habad Hasidim hoped that their rebbi would turn out to be the messiah. Non-Hasidic Jews were also influenced by this activity and a significant number became part of the Habad community or associated to related communities. Whilst this move towards traditionalism and rejection of modernity can be understood in part as a response to R. Schneerson's charisma, it also reflects a trend in many areas of modern religion towards more authoritarian structures with strong well-defined boundaries, combined with personal charismatic leadership (see Chapter 14). Like other fundamentalist groups, the Habad have made very effective use of television and other forms of media to carry their message to a wide audience.

INDIVIDUAL AND AUTHORITY

Although most modern Orthodox Jews participate in social, economic and cultural aspects of modern life, and thus accept something of the value placed on the individual in modern times, within their formal religious structures there is little or no place for individual autonomy. All aspects of religion are believed to be clearly stated in an eternal body of law which has a greater authority than individual choice. The authority to interpret the law is vested in the rabbis, who were traditionally seen as judges within the Jewish legal system rather than pastoral leaders. Although the pastoral aspect of the rabbinic role is also emphasized in Orthodox Judaism, it is this role of judge which has been reactivated.

In many Orthodox Jewish communities today, however, there are no formal hierarchical rabbinic structures – the exception being countries like the UK which has a Chief Rabbi of part of the Orthodox community. Certain rabbis who are recognized as being great scholars are looked to as the supreme arbiters of Jewish law. Different communities will look to different scholars. They will follow the scholar who reflects the part of Orthodoxy or the part of the Jewish community (for example, Sephardic, of Spanish origin, or Ashkinazic, Central or Eastern European origin) from which they come. The decisions made by these scholars are considered to be binding on their generation – future scholars may take different decisions that will then be binding on their generation.

The Hasidic Jews place the greatest emphasis on the authority of their leaders. Unlike other Jewish communities whose rabbis gain their position through education or selection by a community, the leader of a Hasidic community, the *rebbe* or *tzadik* gains his position through birth. He is seen as being a spiritual conduit through which his followers, his Hasidim, gain a connection to God. His followers will look to him not only for decisions about Jewish law and practice but also for guidance on almost any aspect of their lives.

WOMEN

Most modern Orthodox women are fully integrated into modern Western culture. Many have university degrees and work in a wide range of professions. Within their Jewish practice, however, they are excluded from most ritual activities. Essentially, women are excluded from any public ritual activity that might include men. In the synagogue women are separated from men sometimes by a partition or a gallery. No Orthodox community allows women to become rabbis. Within traditional Judaism a woman's primary place of activity is the home and she is seen as being responsible for maintaining purity in the home and educating young children. Many women express the idea that men and women each have their own equally important sphere of activity.

In recent years some Orthodox women have been exploring ways in which they can participate more actively in ritual activities outside the home. One possibility that they have explored is having a religious service only for women – in which case they can do most of the necessary ritual activities. Although in the US some Orthodox rabbis permitted this, in the UK it was ultimately forbidden.

Among the Ultra-Orthodox and the Hasidim, women's participation in wider society is much more restricted. They tend not to have received higher education and usually do not work outside of the community. In these communities women's activities are much more centred on the home than are those of the modern Orthodox Jews. Due to the emphasis on tradition and differentiated gender roles within these communities, such women are not publicly challenging the restrictions on their religious activity.

LOOKING TO THE FUTURE

This chapter has highlighted some of the responses, including acceptance or rejection, by Judaism to modernity.

- Within the Reform, Conservative and modern Orthodox communities most individuals have had to find some way of accommodating their religious beliefs and practices to modernity. Some type of synthesis is clearly necessary as all of these communities wish to participate to a greater or lesser extent in modernity.
- The Reform community has done this by privileging modernity over Judaism and modern Orthodoxy has attempted its synthesis by privileging Judaism over modernity.
- The Conservative movement has tried to find a balance. Although it changes and develops in response to modern values and norms it maintains continuity via the *halakhic* process.
- Only those communities that reject modernity, the Ultra-Orthodox and the Hasidim, are able to try to develop patterns of life, which exclude modern values and ideas.

It is appropriate to ask if these attempts at accommodation have succeeded in offering forms of Judaism which are meaningful in the beginning of the twenty-first century. The demographic numbers presented at the beginning of the chapter suggest that they have not succeeded for the majority of Jews – more than 50 per cent of American Jews are secular. In the course of the twentieth century an increasing number of individuals rejected the mainstream forms of Judaism. They moved, in line with more general trends in modern religion, in two directions: some have moved to more authoritarian and structured forms of Judaism, and others have moved to a much more diffuse version of religion – a Jewish version of 'spiritual shopping'. These developments have begun to pull the mainstream movements in both directions. On the one hand, modern movements are learning from the spirituality movement and have added more individualistic, spiritual elements to their religious practice, on the other certain parts of the movements are moving in more traditionalist, authoritarian directions, publicly disavowing aspects of universalism and most clearly rejecting the notions of relativism which were characteristic of the modern period.

SUMMARY

- Jewish legal and historical tradition have supplied many themes and motifs which are central in modern reconstructions of Judaism, not least those of law, covenant, exodus and redemption; divine destruction and punishment; the promised land; the Holocaust.
- The three most important movements in modern (religious) Judaism are Reform, Conservative and Orthodox.

- The Reform movement has a particularly important place in the story of Judaism's interactions with modernity, not only because it was highly permeable to modern ideas and institutions, but because the other main movements of modern Judaism were often reacting to reform.
- Judaism's initial interaction with modernity begins in the eighteenth century with Moses Mendelssohn. Mendelssohn began the process of trying to recreate or rethink Judaism in response the ideas and philosophies of the Enlightenment. Although he was seen by later movements as heralding the beginnings of reform, many of the issues which he addressed were fundamental to the other Jewish movements as well.
- The three major movements of Reform, Conservative and Orthodox Judaism are distinguished by their responses to many of the challenges posed by modernity, such as individualism, authority and the role of women. An underlying issue concerns identity, conceived in terms of Jewish particularism versus accommodation to Western philosophies and Western ways of living.
- Contemporary Judaism is as deeply divided as at anytime in its history. Extreme Orthodoxy flourishes alongside a growing liberalism – the latter even showing some affinities with movements like New Age. Whilst the former tries to exclude modern values and ideas, the latter embraces them.

KEY TERMS

aggadah   Rabbinic texts discussing non-legal questions.

Aliyot   The rituals of being called up to the Torah during a religious service.

Ashkinazic   This term is used to describe Jews of European origin other than Spain and Portugal – usually referring to Jews from Central or Eastern Europe.

assimilation   The process through which a minority culture loses or merges its identity with the majority culture.

Babylonian Talmud   The most authoritative text of Jewish law, written as a commentary or application of the Mishnah, edited in approximately 700 CE.

Bar Mitzvah   Ceremony celebrating a boy's becoming an adult. The *Bar Mizvah* occurs when the boy is 13 years of age.

Bat Mitzvah   Ceremony celebrating a girl's becoming an adult. The *Bat Mizvah* occurs when the girl is either 13 or 14. This ceremony was first introduced by the Conservative movement and is now also practised by Reform congregations.

Diaspora   This term refers to the settlement of Jews outside of Israel. It is often associated with the concept of exile.

Enlightenment   Western cultural movement of the seventeenth and eighteenth centuries which emphasized the importance of rationality. Often viewed as the dawn of modernity.

Halakhah   The Jewish legal tradition.

Hasidism A mystical, revivalist branch of Ultra-Orthodox Judaism, which emerged from Eastern Europe in the eighteenth century.

Haskalah Eighteenth- to nineteenth-century movement of Jewish Enlightenment which sought to spread Enlightenment ideas to European Jewry.

Mara d'atra A Hebrew term which is used to indicate that a rabbi is the primary legal authority in his or her community. It is used by the Orthodox and Conservative movements.

Minyan The minimum number of people need to conduct a public religious service – ten men for Orthodox Jews and ten men or women for Conservative Jews.

Mishnah The first code of Jewish law based on the discussions of the rabbis edited by Rabbi Judah HaNasi in approximately 200 CE.

mysticism An experience or knowledge of God based on experience rather than reason. Jewish mysticism is often encapsulated in the term *Kabbalah*.

Pharisee A member of a devout Jewish sect which flourished from the second century BCE to the early second century CE. Pharisees may have been the forerunners of Rabbinic Judaism.

rabbi Term meaning teacher, or leader, used to designate religious functionaries. Role is gained through education and ordination. Sometimes translated as 'sage'.

rebbe Term meaning 'My rabbi', used to designate the leader of a Hasidic community.

Reconstructionist Judaism A form of modern Judaism, which denies the existence of a supernatural God, it grew out of the Conservative movement based on the teachings of M. Kaplan.

sage See **rabbi**.

Sephardic Jews who are believed to be descended from Jews from Spain and Portugal, the majority of whom were expelled in 1492. The term also includes Jews from non-European communities, for example, Yemen or Iraq.

Shulkhan Aruch A major code of Jewish law written by Joseph Caro (1488–1575).

Torah The first five books of the Hebrew Bible also called the Five Books of Moses.

tzadik Term, literally meaning 'righteous man,' used to describe the leader of a Hasidic community or sect. Equivalent to the term **rebbe**.

yeshiva Institution of higher learning for the study of Torah.

Yiddish Language related to German and Hebrew which was spoken by all Jews in Central and Eastern Europe.

Zionism   The political movement established in the nineteenth century with the aim of building a Jewish homeland in Palestine.

FURTHER READING

Judaism in the modern world

Robert Seltzer: *Jewish People, Jewish Thought* (New York: Macmillan, 1980) is one of the best one-volume histories of Judaism which includes both historical and philosophical analysis. It includes an extensive discussion of the response of Judaism to the Enlightenment and modernity. Arthur Cohen and Paul Mendes-Flohr (eds): *Contemporary Jewish Religious Thought* (New York, NY: Free Press, 1987) presents a comprehensive set of essays examining modern Jewish concepts, movements and beliefs.

Reform Judaism

One of the best histories of the Reform movement is found in Michael Mayer: *Responses to Modernity: A History of the Reform Movement in Judaism* (Oxford: OUP, 1988). Eugene Borowitz: *Reform Judaism Today* (New York, NY: Behrman House, 1983) provides a readable discussion of Reform Jewish thought by a major thinker within the modern Reform Jewish movement.

Conservative Judaism

Moshe Davis: *The Emergence of Conservative Judaism* (Philadelphia, PA: Jewish Publication Society, 1963) provides a comprehensive analysis of the early development of the Conservative movement. Neil Gillman: *Conservative Judaism* (West Orange: Behrman House, 1993) provides an approachable discussion of the history and theology of the Conservative movement. It includes a very useful selected bibliography.

Orthodox Judaism

Norman Lamm: *Torah Umadda: The Encounter of Religious Learning with Worldly Knowledge in Jewish Tradition* (New York, NY: Aronson, 1990) presents a statement of Orthodoxy's response to modernity. Jonathan Sacks: *Tradition in an Untraditional Age* (London: Vallentine Mitchell, 1990) presents a view of modern Orthodoxy which is moving towards a more traditionalist inward-looking form of Orthodoxy written by the Chief Rabbi of the United Synagogue in the UK. Jerome Mintz: *Hasidic People* (Cambridge, MA: Harvard, 1992) provides an anthropological account of the Hasidim.

Zionism

Walter Laqueur: *A History of Zionism* (New York, NY: Schocken, 1972) provides a useful history of Zionism and Zionist thinking.

CHAPTER 7

Christianity

Linda Woodhead

INTRODUCTION

Christianity is the largest of the world's religions, and the most extensive across the globe. Estimates of the total Christian population of the world at the beginning of the twenty-first century put the figure at around 2 billion, or 32 per cent of world population. Its status as a truly global religion is fairly recent. At the beginning of the modern period Christianity was largely confined to the Northern hemisphere. Rapid expansion of Christianity in Latin America, Africa and parts of Asia has gathered pace during the course of the twentieth century, and is shifting Christianity's centre of gravity from the developed to the developing world. At the same time that it has been growing in the Southern hemisphere, Christianity has also been declining in many parts of the North – particularly in Western Europe (see Chapter 13). This, of course, has only served to accelerate the shift in numbers and vitality from North to South.

Despite these developments, Christianity remains the dominant traditional religion of both Europe and the US. As such, it has been more intimately bound up with the rise of modernity than any other faith – so much so that some theorists (like the sociologist Max Weber) have argued that Christian (particularly *Protestant*) culture had an 'elective affinity' with modernity and played an important part in its rise. To many non-Western religions, modernity appears as a foreign import. The situation is rather different for Christianity which has been the dominant religion of the West throughout the modern period. Modernity arose within Christian countries and cultures, rather than coming to them from the outside. Indeed in some cases – as where Christians came as missionaries to non-Christian cultures – Christians were agents and spokespeople of modernity (see, for example, Chapter 10, on Native American religions). As this chapter will show, there is no single pattern of Christian interaction with modernity. Whilst the revolutions of modernity were inescapable for

YEAR	1800	1900	1980	2000
Population (millions)	902.6	1619.9	4373.9	6259.6
Christians (millions)	208.2	558.1	1432.7	2019.9
% Christian	23.1	34.4	32.8	32.2

Table 7.1 Graph of Christian profession as percentage of world population

Source: David B. Barrett (ed.): *World Christian Encyclopedia* (Nairobi, Oxford, New York: Oxford University Press, 1982, p. 3)

Christianity, different forms of the latter related to them in different ways. Some (like 'fortress Catholicism') resisted; some (like liberal Protestantism) embraced modern progress; some (like *Evangelicalism*) came into being as traditional forms of Protestantism were reshaped by the forces of modernity.

After surveying the historical sources and resources of Christianity and its three major traditional divisions (Orthodox, Roman Catholic and Protestant), this chapter considers modern Christianity in terms of its different interactions with modernity. It considers, in turn, how the *Roman Catholic* church, the Protestant churches and the Orthodox churches have developed in modern contexts. The chapter concludes by identifying certain key trends in Christianity in modern times, and using them as a basis for speculation about possible future developments.

SOURCES AND RESOURCES

Christianity can be thought of as a reservoir of beliefs, stories, laws, symbols, rituals, practices, patterns of relating, and social institutions. Together these constitute the sources and resources of the religion. Different periods, contexts, circumstances, groups and individuals activate different resources from the Christian reservoir. As a result, Christianity displays both continuities and discontinuities in different places and different times. Over more than two thousand years it has manifested such a variety of forms that some observers prefer to speak of 'Christianities' rather than 'Christianity'. Modernity has only exacerbated this diversity; as this religion begins the third millennium of its existence, its plurality is as great as at any time in its history. So long as its reservoir continues to provide the resources for men and women to make sense of their lives and times, and to connect with the divine, it flourishes.

Three clusters of resource are particularly important for Christians: the Bible, the figure of Jesus Christ, the institutions of church and tradition. They may be called the key authorities in Christianity. As we shall see, different branches of Christianity are differentiated by the ways in which they understand and activate their relative importance.

The Bible and the Jewish connection

All forms of Christianity accept the authority of the Bible, though this may mean very different things in different types of Christianity. Like Christianity itself, the Bible is not simple or unitary. It does not have a single author, a single style, or a single message. Rather, it is a collection of different books and genres including historical chronicles, genealogies, stories, myths, prophecy, laws, poetry, proverbs,

154

gospels, letters, and apocalyptic literature. The oldest documents of the Bible probably date back to the fifth century BCE, though they may contain traditions from as early as the eleventh or twelfth centuries BCE; the latest documents in the Bible date from the first century CE.

The diversity and richness of the Bible are partly explained by the fact that it is made up of not one but two collections of scripture: the Hebrew Bible (the Jewish scriptures, which Christians refer to as the Old Testament), and the New Testament. The former is in the Hebrew language, the latter in *koine* ('common') Greek. The *canon* of the Christian Bible was not settled and closed until the late fourth century CE. Even then, there has been persistent disagreement among Christians about a number of disputed books, which some Christians regard as scriptural and others as *apocryphal*. Generally speaking, Roman Catholic Christians accept a greater number of books as canonical than do Protestant Christians.

For all its diversity, however, many Christians have read the Bible as having a certain narrative unity. It begins with the book of Genesis, which tells how the world and humankind were created, and ends with the book of Revelation which tells how God will bring creation to a glorious climax at the end of times. In between, the Bible tells of God's persistent attempts to reform and redeem the human race through his chosen people Israel, and of Israel's repeated failures to respond to the divine initiative. For many Christians, the turning point of this story comes with the sending of God's Son, Jesus Christ, to save the world and usher in the end times. Christians have thus tended to view themselves as the 'new Israel' and the heirs of God's promise to the Jews – this belief is one factor in the *anti-Semitism* which has sporadically characterized Christianity's relations with Judaism.

Jesus Christ

It was their belief that Jesus had been raised from the dead (resurrected) that convinced his first followers of his unique status. Many Jews in Jesus's day cherished the hope that God would send a messiah to save Israel. This saviour would be raised from the dead as a sign that God's rule on earth had been inaugurated. Set in this context, Jesus's resurrection seemed to prove that he was the messiah, that God had decisively intervened in history, and that the end times were at hand. Just a few decades after Jesus's death the apostle Paul, some of whose letters are preserved in the New Testament, was articulating these beliefs, and ascribing to Jesus the unique status not only of 'Christ' (the Greek word for messiah), but the 'Son of God', 'Lord' and 'second Adam' sent to redeem the world. It was not only Jesus's resurrection, however, which made (and continues to make) him special in the eyes of Christians. His life and teaching as recorded in the New Testament also have great authority. As we shall see below, some modern Liberal Christians have little interest in Jesus's resurrection or miracles, and emphasize his humanity and inspired teaching rather than his divinity. These represent just some of the many ways in which Christians have come to think about Jesus Christ.

In the attempt to secure unity, early Christianity attempted to articulate Jesus's status in a systematic way, particularly through its councils (meetings of bishops) and the creeds they produced. These statements of belief (such as the Nicene Creed of 325 CE) were designed to establish the limits of orthodoxy, and those who disagreed with them were branded 'heretical'. By the time the process of credal definition came to an end in the eighth century CE, an understanding of God as Trinity had emerged as distinctive of Christianity. This doctrine enabled Christians to explain how the one God could be the omnipotent Creator, could take human form as Jesus, and could be present to his people at all times in the Spirit. The doctrine states that God is 'triune': Father, Son and Holy Spirit. According to orthodox doctrine, God is fully present in all three of these 'persons' of the Trinity – no one is any less divine than another. Nor are they separate gods ('tritheism'): the Trinity is one substance (*homoousios* in the original Greek), in three different instantiations (*hypostases*). In many ways the creeds have served to set the boundaries and limits within which Christian thought must work, though they have never been able to secure the unity which those who drafted them hoped they would secure.

The church and its diversity

The institution of the church dates from the time, shortly after Jesus's death, when Christians first began to meet together to worship, pray and reflect on their faith. It was a radical experiment in a new form of godly community. Christianity is thus a communal religion. Until modern times it would have been thought impossible for an individual to be a Christian on his or her own, without belonging to a community. Christians, like Jews, believe they are a chosen people, and wish to live as a new society. It is only in modern times that some forms of Christianity have become more individualized, as this chapter will illustrate. Christianity is also a universal religion. Unlike Judaism, which is tied to a particular people and locale, it aims to bring the whole of humanity into its ambit, and so into God's (universal) kingdom. Despite this universalism, Christianity has split into a number of different branches. Of these, the three largest groupings are:

1 Roman Catholic
2 Orthodox
3 Protestant

Jesus did not lay down any guidelines whatsoever for the formation of a church or a new religion. At first Christianity was composed of many competing communities and groups which took different forms and had different scriptures and beliefs. By the second century CE a dominant form of sacramental and sacerdotal Christianity was emerging, which claimed for itself the titles catholic (universal) and orthodox. It tried to suppress other forms of Christianity as heretical. It quickly spread from Palestine around the Mediterranean into Europe, Africa, the Middle East, and parts of Asia. (Despite this some major churches, such as the Nestorian churches in Asia and the Monophysite churches in North Africa, split off from 'catholic' Christianity and remain separate to this day.) Historical circumstances, including the expansion of Islam, led to a separation between the church in the West (centred on Rome) and that in the East (centred on Constantinople). The latter evolved into the Orthodox (or Eastern Orthodox) church, and the former into the Roman Catholic church. The split between the two was formalized in 1054, though it had developed for several centuries before that. The Roman Catholic church is monarchial with a single leader, the Pope, whilst the Orthodox church is made up of a number of autonomous churches with their own leaders, all of which are in communion with one another. Orthodox Christianity has always been marked by its sense of unchanging continuity with the past and its reverence for tradition.

The origins of the Protestant churches lie in dissatisfaction and protest against the Roman Catholic church in the West which came to a head in the early sixteenth century and eventually resulted in the creation of a number of churches or denominations which, despite their many differences, are grouped together under the Protestant label. The largest Protestant groups (in order) are the Lutherans (founded by Martin Luther), the Presbyterian or Reformed churches (founded by John Calvin), the Baptists, and the Methodists. Anglicans also constitute a large worldwide communion, but although it has its origins in the Reformation, the Anglican church often emphasizes its Catholic as well as Protestant roots. There are also many smaller Protestant denominations as well as many independent Protestant churches.

One of the chief differences between these different groupings in Christianity lies in their understanding of authority. For the Orthodox churches, the tradition of the church – including its liturgy and its earliest writings and creeds – has primacy. For Catholics, the church, its sacraments and tradition are central, and these come to a focus in the figure of the Pope. By contrast, Protestants tend to attribute greater authority to scripture than to tradition, and to have a less hierarchical understanding of authority in the church. In modern times, both Protestantism and Catholicism have also developed liberal wings, which emphasize the authority of individual reason and experience alongside scripture and the church. An even more recent development is Charismatic or Pentecostal Christianity (again cutting across both Protestantism and Catholicism, though with more direct links to Protestantism), which attributes authority to both the Bible and direct experience of the Holy Spirit. The following diagram offers a (highly simplified) picture of the primary locations of authority in traditional (premodern) and in modern Christianity. The remainder of the chapter offers fuller exploration and explanation of the main varieties of Christianity in modern times.

Table 7.2 Primary authority in types of traditional (premodern) Christianity

TYPE OF CHRISTIANITY	AUTHORITY
Orthodox	church, tradition, liturgy
Catholic	church, tradition, Pope
Protestant	scripture, church

Table 7.3 Primary authority in types of Christianity in the modern world

CHURCH	AUTHORITY
Orthodox	church, tradition, liturgy
Catholic	
a conservative	church, tradition, Pope
b liberal	reason, experience
c charismatic	Holy Spirit, scripture
Protestant	
a evangelical	scripture
b liberal	reason, experience
b charismatic	Holy Spirit, scripture

INTERACTIONS WITH MODERNITY

Roman Catholicism

FORTRESS CATHOLICISM AND THE STRUGGLE WITH THE MODERN STATE

Of all the transformations of modernity, the one which has had the greatest impact on Christianity has probably been the rise of the modern state. And of all the churches, the one which has been most radically affected by this revolution has been the Roman Catholic church. The reason is simple: for over a thousand years, the Catholic church had attempted to maintain a political dominance in Europe. Even though it did not directly rule most of the region, it played a key role in giving legitimacy to the changing regimes which did. The church continually attempted to assert itself as the highest authority in political, economic and social matters. It believed it had the right and the duty to regulate every aspect of the lives of those who lived in Christendom.

The rise of the modern state was a direct challenge to the church's assertion of political power. At the heart of the modern state lies the revolutionary idea that government should be not by God, nor by his clerical representatives, nor even by divinely appointed rulers – but by the people. Once this idea became established, the centuries-old link between state and church began to dissolve. No longer could a particular religion be imposed on a people by the state; rather, they must be free to practise the religion of their choice. The threat which this posed for the Catholic church became very apparent in France after the Revolution of 1789, when a new constitution subordinated both monarchy and church to the state. The papacy reacted angrily, and continued to attack the rise of the modern state and the associated ideals of liberty and democracy throughout the nineteenth century, as the *Syllabus of Errors* (a list of the errors of the modern world condemned by the church) makes very clear.

■ THE SYLLABUS OF ERRORS CONDEMNS THE MODERN STATE AND LIBERTIES

Syllabus of the principal errors of our time . . .

15 Every man is free to embrace and profess that religion which, guided by the light of reason, he shall consider true . . .
24 The church has not the power of using force, nor has she any temporal power, direct or indirect . . .
44 The civil authority may interfere in matters relating to religion, morality and spiritual government . . .
77 In the present day it is no longer expedient that the Catholic religion should be held as the only religion of the State, to the exclusion of all other forms of worship . . .
80 The Roman Pontiff can, and ought to, reconcile himself, and come to terms with progress, liberalism and modern civilization.

(Pope Pius IX, 1864. In Henry Bettenson (ed.): *Documents of the Christian Church*,
Oxford: Oxford University Press, 1989, pp. 273–4).

One way in which the Roman Catholic church reacted to its loss of social and political power was by attempting to consolidate control over its own followers. From the mid-nineteenth century to the 1950s, Catholicism developed a fortress mentality, attacking modernity and setting its face against an increasingly secular world. The declaration of papal infallibility in 1870 was part of this strategy. So too was the development of a particular style of Catholic piety centred around reception of the sacraments of baptism and the eucharist; regular confession; veneration of the saints, in particular Mary; devotion to the Pope and reverence for the clergy and religious orders. More than ever before, the Catholic church strove to maintain unity, even uniformity. Such unity was embodied in the person of the Pope who, in a world of rapidly improving communications, now became a figurehead for Catholics across the globe. Unity and centralization were also achieved by the introduction of new rationalized forms of organization, training and bureaucracy (a case of the church borrowing the tools of modernity in order to revivify a premodern institution). Thus Popes surrounded themselves with ever-larger staffs in the Vatican, and clergy training was organized and standardized across the world. The unity of the thought world of fortress Catholicism was achieved by elevating the medieval theologian Thomas Aquinas (1225–74) to the status of official theologian of the church. In 1879 Pope Leo XIII gave official approval to this development. As a result, 'neo-Thomism' became the official theology of fortress Catholicism, with all courses in Catholic colleges and seminaries based on Aquinas's teachings.

Despite their fundamental hostility to modern nation states, the modern Popes and their clerical advisers and diplomats worked tirelessly to achieve the best possible position for Catholicism in the modern world. The church entered into numerous agreements ('concordats') with modern rulers and governments designed to safeguard Catholicism's work and liberties within as many territories as possible. Such agreements often established the church's right to maintain Catholic schools and colleges, protected the status and property of the church and its clergy, and allowed Roman Catholicism to be practised freely and openly. The church was determined that the nation state should not squeeze it out of existence – the violence and repression suffered by the church in the French Revolution and its aftermath haunted the Catholic imagination.

Fortress Catholicism's efforts to protect its interests were not, however, confined to Europe and North America. It was also engaged in a highly active and influential drive to establish its presence across the globe. The missionary impulse in Catholicism was not new; from the sixteenth century onwards the church had sent missionaries to Latin America and Asia in order to win converts. Such mission developed hand in hand with the expansionist strategies of the powerful Spanish and Portuguese empires, and served the interests of both church and empire. The nineteenth century saw a revitalization and reconfiguration of this missionary impulse. In some cases Catholic mission went hand in hand with the new colonial enterprises of modern Catholic nation states (as, for example, in the Belgian Congo in Africa). Often there was competition with Protestant mission, which in turn was tied up with the empires of Protestant nations like Britain and the Netherlands (see below). But Catholic missionary work was not confined to Catholic countries, and it was aided as much by new communications as by colonialism. In most cases the agents of Catholic mission were clergy or religious (monks and nuns). Indeed the huge expansion of Catholic religious orders in the nineteenth century was often stimulated by the mission impulse – many orders were formed or reformed with world mission as their prime objective. Catholic missionaries worked in every part of the globe; their greatest impact was in Latin America, sub-Saharan Africa, China and the Philippines.

VATICAN II AND THE PARTIAL LIBERALIZATION OF MODERN CATHOLICISM

The end of fortress Catholicism came with Vatican II (1962–5). This council of almost 3 thousand bishops and a number of theologians was set up to consider ways in which Catholicism could open itself to the modern world without losing its distinctiveness. When he summoned the council in 1959,

Pope John XXIII spoke of his desire for *aggiornamento* ('bringing up to date') in the church; and in his opening speech in 1962 he said that one must distinguish between the 'deposit of the ancient doctrine of the faith', and the way in which it is presented. Whilst remaining fairly conservative about many fundamentals of the faith, Vatican II thus opened the door to some significant changes including:

▪ a less hierarchical and clericalized understanding of the church; a new model of the church as the whole 'people of God'; emphasis on greater participation by laity
▪ use of vernacular languages rather than Latin for the church's liturgy
▪ greater openness to other churches and religions
▪ an acceptance of every individual's right to freedom in matters of personal decision, including religion
▪ acceptance of the legitimacy of the modern state and democracy.

In view of the Roman Catholic church's bitter opposition to democracy and the nation state throughout the nineteenth century, the latter change is particularly significant. In many ways Vatican II overturned the *Syllabus of Errors*. What it had once regarded as error it was now prepared to revisit and, in some cases, rehabilitate. Both critics and supporters of the council alike saw it as representing a partial liberalization of the church.

The radicalism of Vatican II can be overstressed. In many ways the council's conclusions were highly conservative – especially when contrasted with the new permissiveness of the time (the 'swinging sixties'). Whilst the Christianity which emerged from the lengthy deliberations of the council made some adjustments to modern times, the adjustments were selective and qualified. The most complete adjustment was to the modern political revolution – the rise of the nation state and modern democracy (though it is worth noting that Roman Catholicism did not, and still has not, accepted the legitimacy of democracy in its own institutional arrangements). There was also some adjustment to the market economy – though Vatican II, like the so-called 'social encyclicals' which had preceded it, was also keen to criticize the harsh, destructive and anti-human tendencies of capitalism. Interestingly, the strongest resistance of Vatican II and official church teaching since has been to one important aspect of the modern social revolution – the emancipation of women. Vatican II was followed swiftly by *Humanae Vitae*, Pope Paul VI's encyclical which confirmed an absolute ban on the use of all artificial forms of contraception. The church has been equally adamant in its ban on abortion, its opposition to homosexuality and its refusal to entertain the possibility of women's ordination. These prohibitions are linked not only to an uneasiness about women's equality with men, but to a strong positive affirmation of the value of the 'traditional' nuclear family in which men and women have complementary roles, and women's responsibility for care and nurture is particularly stressed.

Vatican II also represented a qualified accommodation to the modern cultural revolution. Its accommodation was most obvious, and most influential, in the way in which it affirmed the possibility of Catholics embracing modern scholarship and its methods – both historical and scientific. Vatican II gave its blessing to a new era of scholarship in which Catholic New Testament scholars were freed to embrace the methods of historical criticism of the Bible, and Catholic theologians freed to engage with modern philosophy and sociology and move beyond the rigid limits of neo-Thomism. Three major trajectories of Catholic theology resulted which emphasized: (1) a return to the sources; (2) a turn to the self; (3) political and social liberation. Whilst the first is the more conservative, all three illustrate the way in which Catholic theologians have drawn on modern culture in the course of a broader attempt to explore and re-present their Christian heritage in terms which make sense in the modern world.

Trajectory 1, the 'return to the sources', was guided by the idea that in order to tackle theological problems, whether they be old ones like the relationship between scripture and tradition, or new ones like the ethical problems of industrial society, the church needed to enrich its thinking by recovering the whole of its spiritual and intellectual heritage. The best-known exemplars of this trajectory are the theologians Henri de Lubac (1896–1991), Yves Congar (1904–95), and Hans Urs von Balthasar (1905–88). De Lubac is most well-known for his work on the interpretation of scripture and on the nature of the church, but he also wrote on other topics, like modern atheism. Yves Congar was mainly interested in the theology of the church, understood widely, as including topics like the role of the laity and ecumenism. He is best known for his rehabilitation of the Holy Spirit in theology, and his trilogy *I Believe in the Holy Spirit* is the most substantial work on the Holy Spirit by any Catholic theologian of the twentieth century. Its production coincided with a revival of interest in the Holy Spirit among theologians of many different traditions, and also among many ordinary Christians (see section on Charismatic Christianity below). Like Congar, von Balthasar also wanted to mine the full riches of the Catholic tradition. The last decades of his life were devoted to three vast works, each in several volumes: *The Glory of the Lord*, *Theo-Drama* and *Theologik*. In each of them he emphasizes that theology must be rooted in prayer, the Christian life and the full richness of the available sources. But these sources, for von Balthasar, include poets, novelists and dramatists as much as philosophers and theologians. Thus the earlier parts of *The Glory of the Lord* (fundamentally a study of the most neglected of God's attributes, beauty) include studies of (for example) Dante and Gerard Manley Hopkins as well as of theologians like St Bonaventure and St Anselm. Similarly, *Theo-Drama* begins with a history of the theatre since the ancient Greeks, as a prelude to the development of the main theme, which is that God has taken the drama of human existence, described by von Balthasar as 'the drama of salvation', and inserted it into his own play – which, nevertheless, he wishes to play on our stage. Thus we have a play within a play, and God is the hidden director in the world's drama.

Trajectory 2, the 'turn to the self', draws not only on Christian sources, but on the broad trajectory in modern culture and society which makes the self and its experience the starting point of reflection and action. In philosophy the work of Descartes and Kant focused the preoccupation of modern European philosophy on the self, consciousness and fundamental human experience. Some Catholic theologians have attempted to appropriate this shift by bringing it into relation with God, suggesting that the human mind may by its very nature be open to God, because he is, as it were, on the horizon of any experience or reflection. The most ambitious development of this line of thought is found in the work of Karl Rahner. Rahner argues that human beings are self-transcending: i.e. that in their constant questioning, in their pursuit of truth and goodness, and in the humbler virtues of courage, hope and openness to the future, they are always going beyond where they are and reaching out. Rahner sees all this as a dynamism of the human spirit, directed towards God: for in our self-transcending we are opening ourselves, whether we realize it or not, to divine grace (which, from the other side, is God's self-communication). Since all those who open themselves to God's grace are related to Christ, they may be described as in some sense Christian. This, in essence, is Rahner's famous thesis of 'Anonymous Christianity'.

LIBERATION THEOLOGY AND THE GLOBALIZATION OF CATHOLICISM

Whilst the influence of political theologians like J. B. Metz on Liberation Theology should not be neglected, this third trajectory of modern Catholic theology takes us beyond the West. For Liberation Theology is a movement which arose in Latin America in the late 1960s, and which has subsequently spread to other parts of the developing, Third or Two-thirds world. As such, it is just one symptom of the increasingly global nature of modern Catholicism. In the mid-1980s, Catholicism was estimated to comprise approximately 840 million people. Of these, around 277 million lived in Europe, 352 million in South America, 64 million in North America, 70 million in Africa, 71 million in Asia, and 6 million in Oceania. In the year 2000 it was estimated that 70 per cent of all Catholics were living in the Southern part of the globe.

The emergence of Liberation Theology is often dated to a meeting of the Latin American bishops at Medelín in Colombia in 1968. The meeting was called in order to discuss the application of the teaching of the recently ended Vatican council to Latin America. In the event it concentrated especially on social, political and economic issues. It denounced the oppression, injustice and institutionalized violence endemic in this part of the world, and it called on the church to endorse a 'preferential option for the poor'. This approach has been articulated systematically and became well-known through the work of Latin American Catholic theologians like Leonardo Boff, Gustavo Gutiérrez and Jon Sobrino. Liberation Theology does not regard itself as one branch of theology among many, but as a precondition for any theology. It also sees itself as an example of what all theology should be – i.e. contextual theology, a theology that is alive to the needs of a particular society at a particular time and uses the Gospel to answer those needs. It criticizes European and North American theology for being confined mainly to universities and seminaries, and so cut off from the life of ordinary Christians and issues of political and social justice. Hence Liberation Theologians claim that praxis (i.e. practice guided by theory) is primary, and that theology is a 'second step'. Thus Gutiérrez argues that it is only if one has an open heart and a commitment to the welfare of the poor that one can truly come to know Jesus Christ.

Liberation Theology is far more than merely an intellectual movement. Its aim is to become a grass-roots movement of the poor who read the Gospels together and are struggling to realize the Kingdom of God here on earth. The institutional outworking of this ideal are the 'base communities' (CEBs – *communidad(e) eclesial de base*) which have developed in many parts of Latin America. Connected to Roman Catholic churches, and often facilitated by a priest, these are small groups of lay people who meet regularly to pray, talk and work together, with the aim of tackling oppression and changing society according to Christian ideals.

Whilst the Liberation Theology movement has had – and continues to have – considerable success, particularly in Latin America, it also faces some serious challenges. Support from Rome and from Pope John Paul II has been qualified, not least because of the fear that such theology owes too much to Marxism, and that its political agenda may lead it to neglect core Christian teachings and values. In Latin America itself, the movement is also challenged by two powerful competitors – indigenous spiritualist and healing cults, and the rapidly-growing Pentecostal movement (see below). In contrast to both these movements, and despite its emphasis on lay involvement, Liberation Theology can seem a somewhat elite movement led by academics and clergy and subject to control by a hierarchical church based in Rome.

In some respects then, Roman Catholicism in Latin America (as in Africa and Asia) may still be burdened by its colonial connections. Thus one of the most important debates in twentieth-century Catholicism has concerned the 'indigenization' of Christianity in non-Western cultures. The debate centres round the question of the extent to which Catholicism can and should borrow from the non-Christian cultures it 'converts'. A major step in indigenization was the ordination of non-Western and non-white clergy and bishops, which took place from the beginning of the twentieth century (in advance of many Protestant churches). Another step has been the integration of indigenous elements of culture into church worship and life subsequent to Vatican II (for more on this tendency see Chapter 14). But there are limits to how far the Catholic church can go in these directions without losing its identity

Figure 7.1 Pope John Paul II delivers his traditional *urbi et orbi* ('to the city and the world') blessing to the faithful from the central balcony of St Peter's Basilica during the traditional Easter Sunday celebrations at the Vatican, Sunday, 7 April 1996. John Paul II has been particularly successful in carving out a new global mission for the Papacy and the Roman Catholic church in the changed circumstances of the modern world

and undermining its control. Those who feel it has not gone far enough may be attracted to other religions or other forms of Christianity. Without doubt the most important competitor to the Roman Catholic church in the Southern hemisphere is now Pentecostal Christianity, a form of Christianity for which indigenization is not an issue, since (a) it has no old-established, Eurocentric tradition to uphold, and (b) it has no formal, sacramental priesthood, being a movement not just for the people but of the people. Yet in recent times there have been some signs that Roman Catholicism is itself beginning to adopt Pentecostal features, in Latin America in particular.

Despite being the 'Bishop of Rome', the modern papacy has endorsed and actively encouraged the shift in Roman Catholicism from being a Eurocentric to a global religion. The long reign of Pope John Paul II (enthroned in 1978) has been particularly notable in this regard. Building on the work of his predecessors, John Paul II has carved out a new, truly international role for the papacy. From being the opponent of modern democracy at the beginning of the nineteenth century, the papacy became its defender on a world stage at the end of the twentieth. As the extract from one of his speeches reprinted below makes clear, John Paul now views himself as guardian and defender of the rights of the human

Table 7.4 Relative size of major Christian groupings, 1985	
Roman Catholic	872,104,646
Protestant	277,912,513
Orthodox	169,648,520
Non-white indigenous	94,796,927
Anglican	51,100,061

Source: David B. Barrett (ed.): *World Christian Encyclopedia* (Nairobi, Oxford, New York: Oxford University Press, 1982, p. 14).

person. Polish by birth, his role in the opposition to and eventual overthrow of communism in Eastern Europe in the 1980s was considerable. Helped by his personal charisma and astute exploitation of the possibilities of modern mass media like television, Pope John Paul II has managed to maintain a high profile for the Catholic church and to win it considerable respect throughout the modern world. Decline in Catholic attendance in the West has been more than matched by vitality outside the West, and Roman Catholicism remains by far the largest of all the Christian denominations at present (See Table 7.4 on page 166).

▮ POPE JOHN PAUL II DEFENDS HUMAN LIBERTY AND RIGHTS

It is interesting to compare the following statement by Pope John Paul II with the denunciation of the modern state and human liberty in the *Syllabus of Errors* (see above). In a little over a century the Roman Catholic church has shifted from attack to defence. In doing so it has successfully come to terms with the rise of the modern state and carved out a new role for itself as a global defender of human rights and what Pope John Paul II calls a 'culture of life'.

Humanitarian interference in defence of victim peoples
The emergence of the individual is at the base of what is called 'humanitarian law'. Interests exist that transcend the State: they are the interests of the human person, his or her rights. Today, as yesterday, human beings and their needs are, alas, despite the more or less binding texts of international law, still threatened . . . The principles of the sovereignty of states and of non-interference in their internal affairs – while retaining all their validity – cannot, however, be used as a screen behind which one may torture and assassinate . . . the Holy See [Rome and the Papacy] is pledged to remind the world in the international appeals in which it often takes part, [that] the organization of societies only makes any sense if it has the human dimension as its central concern, in a world made by human beings and for human beings.

(Pope John Paul II: *Agenda for the Third Millennium*,
London: Fount Paperbacks/HarperCollins, 1997, pp. 203–4.)

Orthodoxy

One of the many differences between Roman Catholicism and Orthodoxy concerns their understanding of church–state relationships. From the early medieval period onwards, Roman Catholicism developed an understanding of church and state as separate realms. Each had its own area of discretion, but ultimately the church had supreme authority. Thus church and Pope had both the right and the duty to legislate for affairs in the temporal as well as the spiritual realms – for economics and education as much as worship and doctrine. By contrast, the Orthodox churches accepted the supreme authority of the state – whether in the person of an emperor or an impersonal state apparatus. Whilst Orthodoxy believes that church and state should work harmoniously together for the good of their people, it is has therefore been more willing to accept the state's right to legislate in all matters including church belief and organization. This tendency has been reinforced by Orthodoxy's conciliar structure. Instead of having a single focus of authority like the Pope, Orthodox Christianity is composed of a number of autocephalous (self-governing) churches which run their own affairs and are identified with an empire or nation state. (Historically four patriarchates had primacy in Orthodoxy: Constantinople (now called

Istanbul), Alexandria, Antioch and Jerusalem. The largest autocephalous churches today are (in order) Russia, Romania, Greece, Serbia and Bulgaria.)

These historic differences help explain the different pathways of Roman Catholicism and Orthodoxy in modern times. Given its tradition of supremacy over the state, it is not surprising that Catholicism was deeply threatened by the rise of the secular state, nor, perhaps, that it now adopts a critical, prophetic role in relation to politics. By contrast, Orthodoxy's long tradition of co-operation and subordination to the state helps explain why it has generally offered little resistance to the powerful and even tyrannical forms of secular power it has had to endure. In the vast majority of cases (with notable exceptions like Greece and Cyprus), these regimes have been communist. Russia, for example, was the first communist state, as well as the largest Orthodox country. Faithful to Marx's teaching that 'religion is the opiate of the people', the Communist Party of the Soviet Union launched a sustained offensive against religion during the seventy or so years it was in power from 1918 until the late 1980s. The offensive against the churches was most brutal in the inter-war period; Orthodox property was seized, clergy and believers were persecuted, and the church was not allowed to elect a new Patriarch. In 1919 there had been some 46,000 churches in Soviet territory; by 1939 no more than a few hundred 'registered' churches were allowed to remain open. Significantly, however, the events of the Second World War led Stalin to realize how important the church could be in mobilizing support for the nation, and the church was once again allowed to exist – albeit as a *de facto* department of the state. After the Second World War, the state also made use of the church for propaganda purposes; clergy were used to spread a favourable image of communism abroad, and to promote the Soviet concept of peace in international gatherings. In 1961 the Russian Orthodox church became a member of the World Council of Churches. Despite this, the Khrushchev regime launched a new anti-religious offensive in the Soviet Union. From 1959 to the 1980s, institutional Christianity was allowed to exist only in a drastically limited and emasculated form.

Despite – or perhaps because of – its treatment at the hands of the Soviet regime, the Russian Orthodox church seems to have played little or no part in the collapse of communism in the late 1980s. The same is true of Orthodox churches in other communist territories, such as the Balkans and Eastern Europe, but cannot be said of Catholic or Protestant churches. Thus the Catholic church was a powerful force in organizing resistance to communism in Poland, whilst the Lutheran evangelical church in East Germany played a role in the overthrow of communism there, and the revolt against the infamous Romanian communist leader Ceaucescu began in a Reformed church.

For Orthodoxy then, modernity has been encountered as an almost entirely negative and destructive force. Partly because of its traditional form, Orthodoxy found itself lacking the resources with which to resist secular nationalism. The violent nature of the assault on Orthodoxy by secularizing states nipped in the bud a number of reforming initiatives which were beginning to take shape at the beginning of the twentieth century. The growing influence of Marxism had led to a quest to bring Orthodox values to bear on pressing social, cultural and even political questions, and to free the church from its long subjection to the state. But the revolution of 1917 brought such initiatives to an abrupt halt, and forced leading figures of the Russian religious renaissance of the twentieth century into exile in the West. Several, like Vladimir Lossky (1903–58) and Georges Florovsky (1893–1979), championed the reinterpretation of the patristic (early Christian) heritage. Others, like Sergii Bulgakov (1871–1944), developed a sophiology (doctrine of Holy Wisdom), whilst Nikolai Berdyaev (1874–1948) blended Orthodox and modern Western philosophical themes to develop a widely influential and quasi-mystical account of human freedom and potentiality. The nature of the church, humanity, creation. and (more recently) the Trinity have been key themes in modern Orthodox thought, whose influence has probably been greater in the West than in Orthodox lands.

The historical and political circumstances which prevented Orthodoxy from modernizing in its own territories also had the effect of enabling it to keep alive premodern traditions to a greater degree than the Western churches. Most Orthodox churches remain hierarchical, patriarchal, worship-centred, deeply reverent of the past, and closely linked to a continuing and prestigious monastic tradition. As such, Orthodoxy now exercises considerable appeal to many in the West who are disenchanted with modernity and the modernization of the churches and who seek a more 'authentic' religion. As a consequence there have been a small but significant – and increasing – number of conversions to Orthodox churches in the West.

In formerly communist countries, the newly liberated Orthodox churches are also tending to revert to traditional roles. In many cases they have been active in supporting the resurgent forms of (sometimes xenophobic) nationalism which have developed in the wake of communism. The most notorious example has been in Serbia, where the Serbian Orthodox church has played an important role in legitimating aggressive Serbian expansion. In Russia the Orthodox church has also become a rallying point for many who wish to defend Russian identity against the whole range of threatening forces unleashed by the collapse of communism – economic and political instability, the breakdown of law and order, the incursions of Western culture and Western goods. The Orthodox church has also become extremely defensive about the proselytizing activities of other religious groups in Russia – ranging from the Roman Catholics to the Baptists to New Religious Movements. It has campaigned, with partial success, for the repeal of a law passed in 1990 offering toleration to all forms of religion. The pluralism which is such a notable feature of most modern Western nations sits uneasily with the traditional ideals of Orthodoxy. In Greece there has been greater accommodation with pluralism, though the Orthodox church there is still recognized as the 'established' church. It is still unclear what accommodations Orthodoxy will make with modernity in the course of the twenty-first century. But given Orthodox churches' remarkable ability to survive the onslaughts of modernity, it will not be surprising that they remain wary of any easy accommodation or capitulation now.

Figure 7.2 Greek Orthodox priests bless Greek soldiers assembled in an army camp in the northern Greek town of Gianitsa before taking off for Kosovo, 11 June 1999. The soldiers were part of a NATO peacekeeping force. In the former Yugoslavia, Orthodox priests of the Serbian church were also giving their blessings to the Serbian nationalism which was a factor in fuelling the civil war which these troops are flying out to control

Liberal Christianity

Liberal Christianity serves as a reminder of just how diverse Christianity's interactions with modernity have been. In contrast to the conservative wings of the Roman Catholic and Orthodox churches, which have generally tended to view modernity with suspicion and to accept its revolutions only partially, gradually and hesitantly, liberal Christianity not only embraced modernity more wholeheartedly, but viewed itself as an integral element in the process of modernization.

Unlike Roman Catholicism or Orthodoxy, liberalism is not a church or denomination, but a movement within many of the mainline churches, both Catholic and Protestant. We have seen above, for example, that Vatican II represented a partial liberalization of the Roman Catholic church. Supporters of the council who wanted to implement and extend its reforms (for example, by campaigning for a greater role for women in the church) belong to the liberal wing of the church, whilst those who wished to limit its reforms belong to more conservative wings. In many cases, liberals and conservatives will worship together in the same church. Liberal Protestantism is slightly different in that there may be whole denominations which have a liberal stance (Unitarians and Congregationalists, for example), but here too there are mainline Protestant churches (like the Anglican church) which contain both liberal and more conservative members and constituencies. In historical terms Protestantism has a closer connection with liberalism than Roman Catholicism, for it was within the Protestant tradition in Europe and North America that Liberal Christianity first developed. Liberal Christianity remains a predominantly Western movement, and a relatively 'intellectual' one. In many ways liberalism represents a particular theological interpretation of Christianity, albeit one which often has a strongly activist agenda.

The first anticipations of liberal Christianity appear as early as the sixteenth century, when reformist Christians like Erasmus (c.1469–1536) and the Deists (late sixteenth to seventeenth centuries) began to champion a purified version of the Christian faith which would strip Christianity of what they believed to be its superstitious, oppressive and divisive elements (rituals, dogmas, clericalism, for example), and leave only its essential teachings (rational love of God and humanity). These ideas later helped inspire the Enlightenment of the eighteenth century, and so played a significant role in the rationalist cultural revolution of modern times (see Introduction). Equally, Liberal Christianity was closely connected with the Romantic cultural revolution of the later eighteenth and early nineteenth centuries. The so-called father of Liberal Theology (or even of modern theology), Friedrich Schleiermacher (1768–1834), was an important figure in the German Romantic movement. The Romantics (artists, poets and novelists as well as philosophers and theologians) accepted some aspects of the Enlightenment project, including its suspicion of traditional religion and its exaltation of the freedom of the individual, but reacted against its belief in the authority of reason. In place of reason, the Romantics privileged feeling, sensibility and emotion. In this vein, Schleiermacher interprets the insights of the Christian religion so that it appears as that to which Romanticism aspires, but without knowing it. In *The Christian Faith* (1821–2, revised 1830–1), Schleiermacher presents religion as a determination of 'feeling', but now defines it as a 'feeling of absolute dependence', over and against the feeling of relative dependence with which we are related to the world and to others. This feeling of absolute dependence is 'immediate self-consciousness', and it is 'God-consciousness' – for Schleiermacher the terms are equivalent. In this way he aimed to move the Protestant faith away from the cultural margins in modern Europe, and place it at the centre.

By the latter part of the nineteenth century it seemed possible that Schleiermacher's dream would be realized – especially in the world of Anglo-Saxon Protestantism, and in the US in particular. The last decades of the nineteenth century up until the First World War represented the heyday of Liberal Christianity. Many Americans, particularly those belonging to the rapidly expanding and increasingly influential white middle classes, wove liberal Protestantism into their proud sense of national and self-identity. They saw America as leading the world in social, political and cultural terms, and liberal Protestantism as the religion which undergirded such progress. One reason why liberalism could be viewed in this way was that it was so open to the revolutions of modernity. As its name suggests, it actively embraced the institution of the secular nation state which seemed to enshrine its ideals of political and religious freedom. Equally, it had no difficulty in accepting the findings of modern history and science, including the historical criticism of the Bible and the Darwinian theory of evolution which shook many more conservative Christians. Since Liberal Christianity had always respected the rights and abilities of human reason and conscience, it was happy to follow where they led. Its strategy was not to reject or reinterpret science in the light of the Bible, but to reinterpret the Bible and Christian belief in the light of science.

The outcome tended to be a strongly humanistic reading of Christianity, often focused on the historical figure of Jesus Christ. This religious humanism generally included the following elements: (a) a strongly ethical and activist concern (religion must be about deeds as much as beliefs); (b) a humanistic rhetoric and conceptuality (religion is about service of one's fellow humans); (c) an anthropocentric characterization of the Godhead (God is a loving Father); (d) a positive valuation of human ability, human worth and human potential; and (e) an optimistic belief in the natural progress of humanity and human society. Such humanism fitted an increasingly differentiated culture and society in which the church's functions were being taken over by the state and other agencies. As the church's ability to pronounce on the laws of the natural world shrank along with its activities in the public realm, so it began to emphasize its expertise in the more restricted realm of the 'human'. This emphasis was reinforced by a wider universalistic 'turn to the human' in modern culture which was reflected in secular and political liberalism and their discourses of human liberty and human rights. It was influenced by social and economic changes like the spread of capitalism and democracy which saw an increasing stress being placed on the equal value of each and every individual.

Figure 7.3 'All You Need is Love' – an advertisement produced by The Churches' Advertising Network in the UK. The design shows company executives posed as the twelve disciples in the *Last Supper* by Leonardo Da Vinci. The advert aims to challenge those involved with 'mammon' with a message about the importance of love – a theme which unites all Christians, but has a particularly central place in Liberal Christianity. The gender bias may be more striking in this contemporary re-rendering than in the original painting

In some of its versions, nineteenth-century humanistic Liberal Christianity appeared to lack any critical cutting edge. It seemed to be a religion that undergirded the comfortable aspirations of imperialistic Western nations, and legitimated the interests of their new middle classes. Yet the humanistic and activistic stress of Liberal Christianity also generated a 'social gospel' teaching at the end of the nineteenth century which was often radical in its condemnation of social, political and economic complacency. Intellectually the social gospel was inspired by the work of theologians like Albrecht Ritschl (1822–89) who searched for the essence of Christianity and found it in ethical action directed to establishing the Kingdom of God which Jesus had proclaimed. It also developed as a response to changes and disruptions in the rapidly developing urban–industrial societies of the time. It is thus no coincidence that one of the earliest versions of the social gospel – English Christian socialism – dates from 1848, a year of revolution, protest and unrest in many parts of Europe. In that year the Anglicans F. D. Maurice, Charles Kingsley and John Ludlow met to plan a Christian response to the Chartist agitations for democratic political reform. These European influences quickly fed into the developing social gospel movement in America. Here too the social gospel often commenced with an attack on individualism: individualism in existing Christianity and individualism in capitalist society. Against such individualism it set a new social vision which must transform both church and society. As the most influential American spokesmen of the social gospel, Walter Rauschenbusch (1861–1918), put it: 'We are emerging from the era of individualism. The principle of co-ordination, co-operation and solidarity is being applied in ever-widening areas and is gaining remarkable hold on the spirits of men'. Rauschenbusch based his theology on Jesus's preaching of the Kingdom of God, a kingdom which Rauschenbusch believed could not be confined to another world but which must involve the 'harmonious development of a true social life' here and now. At an institutional level the social gospel's greatest success lay in the establishment of social agencies or commissions in many mainline Protestant denominations. The burgeoning *ecumenical* movement was also part and parcel of a new social concern stimulated by the social gospel, and the foundation of the (American) Federal Council of Churches played an important part in spreading its message – as, later on, did the World Council of Churches (founded in 1948).

The common perception is that the twentieth century witnessed a sharp decline in the fortunes of Liberal Christianity. This view is supported by the evident decline of many mainline Liberal Christian denominations in Europe and America (for example, Anglicans and Lutherans), a decline which accelerated after the 1960s. By contrast many smaller, more conservative Protestant denominations appear to have fared much better. There appear to be a number of reasons for such liberal decline, not least the increasing challenges faced by the ideas and constituencies which Liberal Christianity once legitimated (Western colonial cultures; the interests of the white, Anglo-Saxon middle classes; evolutionary optimism; confidence in the power of science and human reason). At the same time, Liberal Theology suffered a crisis of confidence in the wake of attacks by 'neo-orthodox' theologians like Karl Barth (1886–1968). In Barth's view Christian liberalism paid more attention to man than to God. It was a form of 'culture Protestantism' which baptized the sociocultural *status quo* whilst losing sight of the radical message of the Gospel.

▌ KARL BARTH ON THE OTHERNESS OF GOD

In this passage Karl Barth overturns the presuppositions of Liberal Theology – that there is a natural relation or affinity between God and humanity – by insisting on the otherness of God.

> The Gospel is not a religious message to inform humanity of their divinity, or to tell them how they may become divine. The Gospel proclaims a God utterly distinct from humanity. Salvation comes to them from him, and because they are, as human beings, incapable of knowing him, they have no right to claim anything from him. The Gospel is not one thing in the midst of other things . . . The Gospel is the Primal Origin of all things, the Word which, since it is ever new, must ever be received with renewed fear and trembling.
> (Karl Barth, *The Epistle to the Romans*, Oxford: Oxford University Press, 1933, pp. 28–9)

Yet Liberal Christianity is far from dead. An important recent study of Christianity in the US, for example, suggests that Christians of a broadly liberal persuasion may still form a small majority in the north American churches (Ammerman, 1997). Nor is liberalism confined to Protestant churches; we have also noted above the liberalizing tendencies of Vatican II, and the continuation of a liberal tradition in the Roman Catholic church (to some extent even in the Christian humanism of the otherwise conservative John Paul II – see the extract above). Equally, it is hard to dispute the triumph of many liberal ideas even in fairly conservative Christian circles, ideals such as: free churches in a free state; the acceptance of the legitimacy of modern science and historical criticism of the Bible; a stress on the equal value of all human beings, male and female; an emphasis on the overriding importance of love.

Neither has Liberal Theology died out. Liberal Protestant theologians as diverse as Rudolf Bultmann (1884–1976), Dietrich Bonhoeffer (1906–45), Paul Tillich (1886–1965) and Jürgen Moltmann (1926–) have attempted to bring the Gospel into conversation with modern culture and the experiences of modern men and women. Since the 1960s the influence of Liberal Theological thought has also been discernible in the rise and vitality of feminist theology, and (arguably) as an influence within Liberation Theology as well. The latter two movements are linked insofar as both take the concrete experiences of oppressed peoples as the starting point of theological reflection, and human dignity as a key principle. Writing from the late 1960s onwards, feminist theologians have privileged women's experience, and criticized earlier theology (including the Bible) as the product of male experience. Whilst some feminist theologians, including the early pioneer in this area, Mary Daly, have come to abandon Christianity as irredeemably sexist and to style themselves 'post-Christian', others like Rosemary Radford Ruether have attempted to change theology and reform the church from within. Ruether's liberal credentials are evident in the way she uses the category of human liberation as a key interpretative tool, in similar ways to many Liberation Theologians.

Evangelicalism

Evangelicalism is a broad movement within Protestant Christianity which has gathered up many of the most distinctive emphases of the sixteenth-century Reformation and developed them into a form of Christianity which has flourished in the context of modernity. As such it is not a church or denomination, but a widely influential current of Christianity (there are, for example, Evangelical Anglicans, Lutherans and Presbyterians). An Evangelical style of Christianity first emerged clearly in Europe and America in the eighteenth century in movements like Methodism, and it has staged periodic revivals ever since. Its identity as a pan-denominational movement became clearer and more self-conscious throughout the course of the twentieth century, partly in reaction to secular culture, and partly in reaction to what it regards as the easy accommodation to such culture by Liberal Christianity. The most extreme and anti-modern wing of Evangelicalism emerged early in the twentieth century in North America under the banner of Fundamentalism, and broke from the broader current of Evangelical Christianity after 1957.

▌ METHODISM AND THE ORIGINS OF EVANGELICALISM

Evangelicalism grew directly from a number of movements in earlier Protestantism. From the Reformation it took its central doctrines of biblical authority, personal trust in God's saving work (faith), and salvation through Jesus Christ. From Puritanism it took a concern with individual moral and spiritual development nurtured through self-examination and self-discipline and exemplified in thrift, hard work, self-control, independence, charity, and loyalty to family and church. The most immediate precursors of Evangelicalism, however, were the revivals and awakenings of the eighteenth and early nineteenth centuries in both the Anglo-Saxon world and continental Europe. On the continent Pietism was the most important of the proto-evangelical movements, in Britain and North America the Methodism which emerged from the personal quest for holiness of John Wesley (1703–91), his brother Charles (1707–88), and like-minded university friends, most notably George Whitefield (1714–70).

Like Pietists, the Methodists organized themselves into small groups in which they could exhort, examine, encourage and discipline one another; developed a strong missionary emphasis; encouraged Bible reading, personal devotion, and intense religious feeling; and attempted to renew existing Protestant churches from within. In a style which would become typical of Evangelicalism, Methodists also emphasized the importance of a deeply felt experience of conversion. In 1738 John Wesley recorded his own conversion in a now famous entry in his journal:

> In the evening I went very unwillingly to a society in Aldersgate Street [London], where one was reading Luther's Preface to the Epistle to the Romans. About a quarter before nine, while he was describing the change which God works in the heart through faith in Christ, I felt my heart strangely warmed. I felt I did trust in Christ – Christ alone for salvation; and an assurance was given me that He had taken away my sins, even mine, and saved me from the law of sin and death.

Wesley's conversion echoes the great Protestant Reformer Luther's experience, and the Lutheran influence is important. Yet Wesley developed the doctrine of justification by faith in a new way by placing much greater emphasis on the 'assurance' which accompanies it, and by insisting that it involves not merely an imputation but an attainment of righteousness. Methodism spread rapidly in both the US and Britain in the eighteenth and early nineteenth centuries, and fed the growth of the broader Evangelical current which emerged at the end of the nineteenth century and grew throughout the twentieth.

Evangelicalism has a paradoxical relationship with modernity. On the surface it often appears hostile. Evangelicals tend to be sharply critical of many features of the modern world, particularly in the area of personal morality. Thus they stridently oppose the breakdown of the family signalized by rising divorce rates, tolerance of homosexuality and the abandonment of traditional domestic roles by women. Fundamentalists go even further, by opposing any teachings and practices which they regard as contrary to biblical teaching – even if these have the backing of science (the theory of evolution being the most obvious example). Instead of looking to the modern world for inspiration, Evangelicals look back to Jesus and the early church (as portrayed in scripture). Yet Evangelicalism comes to birth in the modern era, and fits extremely well with other features of the modern world. Unlike Roman Catholicism or Orthodoxy, for example, it easily accommodates the modern secular state, for it is far more concerned with winning individual souls for Jesus than with winning political influence. Likewise, Evangelicalism makes an easy alliance with capitalism – indeed it seems actively to promote the virtues which make capitalism possible – like hard work, honesty and frugality.

At the heart of Evangelicalism lies a series of fairly simple and straightforward affirmations. Two are particularly important: first, that salvation comes through a conversion in which the individual enters into personal relationship with God's only Son, Jesus Christ, and is saved through the latter's saving ('atoning') work on the cross; second, that the Bible has a unique authority in human life. Evangelicalism, in other words, manages to hold together two very different elements. On the one hand, it recognizes a tangible and irrefutable source of authority in the Bible, and thus gives its followers clear rules for the guidance of their lives. On the other hand, it has a tendency to be experiential because of its stress on the importance of an overwhelming conversion experience. These two elements, it seems, make Evangelicalism attractive to many modern men and women, for it is able both to provide guidance in a pluralistic and rapidly changing world, whilst at the same time accommodating a typically modern 'turn to the self' and 'turn to experience'. Evangelicalism also fits the modern context by virtue of being more individualistic and egalitarian than Roman Catholicism and Orthodoxy; it offers to bring each individual into relation with God without the mediation of church or clergy (though in practice membership of a church is important to most Evangelicals).

These characteristics are closely bound up with a distinctively Evangelical way of reading the Bible. Many Evangelicals and Fundamentalists read the Bible as a unified account of salvation history. According to this reading, scripture tells the story of God's work of creation from the beginning of time (the creation of the world in the book of Genesis) to its end (Christ's return to earth in the book of Revelation). The whole of history is seen as converging towards its climax – the sending of Jesus Christ to save the world by his cross and resurrection, followed by his final return to claim his chosen people (those who have been converted). Evangelicalism thus divides up history into a number of divinely ordained periods or 'dispensations'. The contemporary world lies in-between the dispensation of Jesus Christ and his second coming. As a result, Evangelicals tend to feel intense pressure not only to ready themselves for Christ's return, but to convert others. Nothing less than eternal salvation is at stake, for only those who have accepted Christ in their hearts and been 'born again' will be saved when he returns, whilst all others will be damned – hence the powerful Evangelistic dynamic from which this form of Christianity derives its name. It was because Darwin's theory of evolution challenged this dispensational reading of history that many Evangelicals were so troubled by it, and it was for the same reason that they reacted with hostility to historical criticism. Today the majority of Evangelicals accept both Darwin and historical criticism, whilst continuing to read the Bible as a unified narrative of a history focused on Jesus Christ. Fundamentalists distinguish themselves by their refusal to accept either Darwinian science or historical criticism of the Bible.

As we have seen in the previous section, the nineteenth century was the great Protestant century in which the two most powerful nations in the world – Britain and North America – affirmed and tried to export the virtues of industry, sobriety, frugality, domesticity, sentiment, and order. (Evangelicals embarked on world mission with as much enthusiasm as Roman Catholics.) In the pre-Darwinian era liberals and Evangelicals had not fully distinguished themselves, and they shared many core beliefs and values. The pulling apart of these two tendencies since the end of the nineteenth century has tended to favour Evangelicalism, for whilst liberal churches have declined, Evangelicalism has shown greater vitality. Evangelicalism's success in the late modern world seems to be related to the way in which it has shown itself able to adapt to changing conditions whilst maintaining certain core affirmations. Although it insists that it still preaches the same changeless Gospel truths, it has tended to become open to the findings of modern science, less concerned about denominational, national and racial difference, less exclusivistic, and less optimistic about the possibilities of Western superiority and inevitable progress. Evangelicals (and Fundamentalists) have also shown themselves to be remarkably adept in utilizing new media in spreading the Gospel. All these tendencies have been evident in the career of the unofficial leader of twentieth-century Evangelicalism, Billy Graham. Yet traditional emphases have also remained, including reliance upon scripture and an emphasis on the importance of conversion, evangelism and the atoning work of Christ.

Perhaps the most significant of all the shifts to affect Evangelicalism since the 1960s has been the gradual absorption of Charismatic influence. The effect in the West has been a new emphasis not on the biblical pole of Evangelicalism, but on the experiential pole. Many Evangelicals have found a new place in their faith for the Holy Spirit and the exciting signs and wonders which accompany it. By the beginning of the twenty-first century, much Evangelicalism in the West could more accurately be termed 'Charismatic-Evangelical'. But it is outside the West that the Charismatic upsurge has been most dramatic (see below).

Evangelicalism has produced a huge literature for its highly literate audience, but much less academic theology than Roman Catholicism or Liberal Christianity. It has tended to favour biblical commentaries and spiritual literature designed to meet the practical needs of ordinary Christians trying to conform their lives more closely to Jesus Christ. The thought of Karl Barth (1886–1968) – the most influential of twentieth-century Protestant theologians – cannot be squarely located in the Evangelical camp, yet many of Barth's central themes would be welcomed by Evangelicals. Like them, he was generally hostile to Liberal Christianity, insisted that the Bible was God's word, that it proclaimed God's Kingdom, and that it threw light on God's relation to the world. Barth, in other words, wished to restore transcendence to Christianity. Whilst stressing the 'otherness' of God in his early dialectical theology, Barth also came (in Evangelical fashion) to put much more emphasis on the humanity of God in Christ in his later work (most notably the multi-volume *Church Dogmatics*). Whilst influential amongst many Protestant clergy and academics, however, the complexity of Barth's thought, some of its more Calvinistic themes, and its far from literalist approach to the Bible, mean that it has not been as widely influential within Evangelicalism as have more popular authors like C. S. Lewis. Barth's influence within modern academic theology, however, has been profound.

Global Charismatic upsurge

It is some indication of the widespread significance of Charismatic Christianity at the turn of the twentieth century that so many chapters in this book discuss it: Chapter 9, Chapter 13, Chapter 14 and Chapter 17. In addition, the discussions of both Roman Catholicism and Evangelicalism above inevitably ended by drawing attention to the impact of recent Charismatic influence. In the opinion of David Martin, one of the leading scholars in this area, Charismatic Christianity and resurgent Islam represent the two most vital and rapidly spreading forms of religion in the world today. Martin estimates that as many as a quarter of a billion people may be involved in the Charismatic upsurge worldwide. Whilst Charismatic renewal has affected churches in the West, both Protestant and Catholic (see above), its greatest impact has been in the so-called developing or Third World, particularly Latin America and sub-Saharan Africa. It is also notable in the Philippines, the Pacific rim (above all Korea), China, and parts of Eastern Europe, notably Romania.

Pentecostal Christianity arose at around the same time as Fundamentalism (the start of the twentieth century) and the two movements have much in common, including hostility to mainline and Liberal Christianity, similar ways of reading scripture, belief in scriptural inerrancy, strict moral teachings, and belief in the imminent second coming of Jesus. What differentiates Pentecostalism, however, is the supreme importance it places on possession by the Holy Spirit. Most Pentecostals agree that 'baptism in the Spirit' is the pivotal Christian experience which differentiates those who have been 'born again' from those who are still in slavery to the world, the flesh and the devil. The lives of those who have been saved in the Spirit are marked by powerful 'signs and wonders' including glossolalia (speaking in tongues, a humanly incomprehensible 'language' believed to be inspired by

God), prophecy, healing and exorcism (casting out demons). Services of worship in which these 'charismata' (gifts) are experienced lie at the heart of Pentecostal life, and greater weight is placed on them than on correct doctrinal belief, social action, reception of the sacraments, or obedience to church hierarchies. Much traditional Christianity is regarded by Pentecostals as a matter of empty ritual and dry 'externals' which lack the dynamism of the living Spirit of God. Pentecostals trace their heritage back to the early Christian communities described in Paul's letters and to the 'Pentecost' described in Chapters 1 and 2 of the Acts of the Apostles when the Holy Spirit descended on the first Christians. They believe that they are restoring the pristine, primitive and powerful religion of the New Testament.

In many respects, Pentecostal Christianity is a religion of the margins. In the West it originally flourished amongst those who found themselves peripheral to mainline churches and affluent white middle-class society. Elsewhere it flourishes in nations and societies which have experienced the marginalization which first accompanied colonization, and which now results from the pressures of participation as unequal partners in a rapidly evolving global market economy. Pentecostalism had several, near simultaneous points of origin. In 1906 the Asuza Street Apostolic Faith Mission in Los Angeles (a Western margin of the US) became the centre of a Pentecostal movement which quickly spread to other parts of the world. Asuza Street was founded by the black Christian preacher William Joseph Seymour, and Pentecostalism owes much to the vibrant non-literary forms of Evangelical Christianity which had developed amongst blacks in America. At much the same time, Pentecostal-style Christian revival was also burgeoning in Wales – another western margin, though this time of Great Britain. In sub-Saharan Africa, Pentecostal-style independent churches were founded from the 1920s onwards by indigenous leaders marginalized by white-led colonial churches. They included the Zion churches in South Africa, the Aladura movement in Western Africa, and the Church of God on Earth through the prophet Simon Kimbangu in Central Africa. Pentecostalism was introduced to Latin America as early as 1910, but has grown most dramatically since the late 1940s. Pentecostalism is characterized by a huge variety of church styles, ranging from large denominations to small independent churches, some of the latter housed in tents, shops or garages.

Though the two terms may be used interchangeably, Pentecostalism generally refers to the first phase of Charismatic growth and the earliest denominations it spawned (the Pentecostal churches), whilst

Figure 7.4 This photo of a Charismatic church in Kampala which meets in a tent illustrates several features of Charismatic Christianity in the Third World: the ease with which new churches can be set up (in shops, garages, fields, tents); the poverty of many of those involved in the movement; and the mobility, ubiquity and rapid spread of the movement (many similar churches can be found not only in Uganda, but across Africa)

the label Charismatic is more often applied to later, post-1960s developments. As has been noted above, this later Charismatic upsurge has not only given rise to a plethora of new churches, but has profoundly affected some of the mainline Christian denominations as Pentecostalism has moved from the margins to the mainstream. There are now Pentecostal Catholics as well as Charismatic Anglicans, Baptists and Methodists. Some scholars have linked Charismatic renewal in the West with the 1960s hippy counter-culture, since they share a common emphasis on the importance of personal experience in religion. The former differs, however, in having a much stronger social/institutional framework provided by a church, and much clearer and stricter moral rules and disciplines. As Chapter 17 shows, churches which combine the latter features with an emphasis on individual experience tend to be those which are currently displaying most vitality both in the West and elsewhere.

This ability to combine features of tradition with features of modernity may be a major factor which helps explain the success of Charismatic Christianity. It offers a remedy for the fears generated by a rapidly changing world in which social and moral order appears to be breaking down, whilst leaving behind those features of traditional religion which modern men and women find hardest to accept – hierarchies of power, formalized rituals, lack of participation. By offering the gift of the Holy Spirit to all men and women without distinction, Charismatic Christianity is also profoundly egalitarian and helps engender a new self-confidence in those who have previously been marginalized. Its lively and colourful services of worship do not demand high levels of literacy, education or culture, and its cohesive and mutually supportive congregations offer aid, education, care and welfare for all who participate. By bringing the spiritual realm into such direct contact with the material world, Charismatic Christianity shares features with many indigenous religions (see Chapter 9), and may take over some functions of the former, including exorcism and healing.

Interestingly, Charismatic Christianity appears to attract at least as many women as men, despite the fact that positions of leadership are nearly always reserved for the latter. One explanation may be that, despite this exclusion, Charismatic Christianity offers the empowerment that matters most (the gift of the Holy Spirit) to both sexes, and in practice opens roles of considerable responsibility to women (for example, healing and prophecy). Another reason may be that, like the Evangelical tradition from which it flows, Charismatic Christianity affirms the pre-eminent value of the family and of the mother's role within it, and domesticates and tames men by affirming the womanly values of care, love and responsibility (see Chapter 16 on Women and religion).

LOOKING TO THE FUTURE

The most obvious way to think about the future is to extrapolate on the basis of present trends. In relation to Christianity, the following seem particularly significant:

1 Secularization. According to many sociologists, secularization is one of the most characteristic aspects of modernization, and Christianity, as the religion most closely involved with Western modernity, has been most affected. If we look at Western Europe in the modern period, the reality of secularization is very apparent. In most cases secularization is quite recent, having gained pace throughout the twentieth century, and particularly since the late 1960s. In France, for example, weekly Mass attendance dropped from about one-third of Catholics in the 1950s to about 15 per cent at the end of the 1970s. Yet rates of secularization are very variable. In the US, for example, rates of church-going are much higher than in Europe (some estimates put them as high as 40 per cent). There are other important variations too. In Europe some countries (like Sweden) are much more secular than others (like Northern Ireland). And within different countries, some forms of Christianity (like

Figure 7.5 Early Christianity was accused by its detractors of being a religion for women and children. Its appeal may, if anything, have increased in modern times as the pressures of 'feminization' have affected a religion which already emphasized the importance of domestic life and 'womanly' virtues. Nevertheless, the church is often criticized by feminists for its patriarchal language, imagery, and forms of leadership

Evangelicalism) are doing much better than others (like liberalism). One conclusion must be that the strength or weakness of Christianity is very much a factor of particular circumstances, including its effectiveness in sustaining ethnic or national identity, aiding social and economic advancement, competing with other religions, and negotiating the changes associated with modernity.

2 Globalization and postcolonialism. Not only do rates of secularization vary in the West, they vary even more across the globe. In many parts of the non-Western world, Christianity has expanded rapidly since the second part of the twentieth century. This may be viewed as a second phase of Christian globalization. The first was associated with missionary activity and was bound up with Western colonialism. The second is postcolonial, and has seen much more rapid growth of Christianity. Unlike the first phase it is much more indigenous. Today few Western Christians continue to believe that they have a superior culture, or a superior form of Christianity, which they must impose on other nations. Non-Western Christianity is growing in confidence and in some cases exporting ideas and energy back to the West. This may well change the face of Christianity, as Western priorities become less and less determinative of the future of Christianity.

3 Compromises with modernity. All traditional, premodern forms of Christianity have been forced to react to modernity and, in most cases, to make compromises with certain aspects of it. Most of these compromises have involved some surrender of power, particularly in the economic and political spheres. Thus the Roman Catholic church, for example, had to surrender its ideal of overall control in Europe (Christendom), and recognize the legitimacy of modern states. In the social and cultural realms, this surrender has not always been as great. Many forms of Christianity have vigorously defended their particular doctrinal and moral teachings against the onslaughts of 'secular modernity', whilst others (notably Liberal Christianity) have been more open to change. Broadly speaking Christianity

has been able to maintain more power in relation to personal and domestic life than public life, especially in the West.

4 The feminization of Christianity. The differentiation of Christianity and its gradual and partial exclusion from the political realm (especially in the West) have also tended to result in Christianity becoming more feminized. There are more female churchgoers than male, and women are often more actively involved in the church's life. Similarly, Christianity tends to focus on 'feminine' issues and values such as love, gentleness and relationship. Charismatic Christianity, the fastest spreading form of contemporary Christianity, has been very successful in attracting women. As women have increasingly taken up public as well as domestic roles and become more economically independent, however, the gender profile of Christianity has begun to be challenged. For a start, the exclusion of women from clerical roles began to be questioned, and many Protestant denominations have decided to ordain women for the first time (Roman Catholic and Orthodox churches still oppose women's ordination). In addition, as we have seen above, women have begun to write feminist theology and to question some allegedly patriarchal biases in Christian thought and practice. At the moment these developments are concentrated in the West; given the preponderance of women in Christianity worldwide, its ability to retain their loyalty under the changing conditions of modernity will be crucial to its survival.

5 Detraditionalization and the flight from deference. Nearly all forms of Christianity in the modern world have been affected by a series of interlinked developments whereby a readiness to trust and obey external forms of authority has gradually been eroded in favour of a greater reliance on individual reason, experience and choice. The process may be called 'detraditionalization', because one of its symptoms is a decline in respect for the past and for tradition. The process is also referred to by some observers as the 'turn to the self' (see Introduction). In general it leads to a gradual democratization of the churches, whereby each individual becomes responsible for his or her salvation, and the authority and prestige of the clergy diminishes. At its most extreme, the turn to the self leads to a complete rejection of the church, and to the belief that one may be a Christian on one's own, without any institutional support. Thus at the end of the twentieth century some people continue to call themselves Christians, though they never go to church. Detraditionalization is also observable within tradition, as new forms of Christianity which are more open to individual experience gain ground – Charismatic Christianity being the most striking example.

6 A 'turn to life', whereby belief in the greater reality and importance of 'the next life' than this life begins to fade may be an accompanying trend. In Christianity it may be evident (for example) in the rapid decline in monasticism in the twentieth century; in a diminishing emphasis on hell, purgatory and damnation; and in a tendency to emphasize Christianity's ability to change lives dramatically in the here-and-now – as in the typical Charismatic–Evangelical emphasis on conversion and perfectibility, and in the rise of new forms of 'prosperity Christianity' both in the developed and developing world.

SUMMARY

- The historical sources and resources of Christianity include the Bible, Jesus Christ and the institution of the church – each of which has been interpreted in widely varying ways over more than two millennia of Christian history.
- Christianity in modern times may be divided into five main divisions: mainline conservative Roman Catholic, Orthodox, liberal, Evangelical, Charismatic. Since the mid-twentieth century the centre of gravity of Christianity has shifted from the Northern to the Southern hemisphere.

▌ Each of these five divisions has interacted differently with the interconnected revolutions of modernity. Roman Catholicism and Orthodoxy have generally been most resistant, liberalism the most co-operative. Evangelicalism and Charismatic Christianity have both opposed aspects of secular modernity (particularly in the sphere of culture and morality), though they themselves arise out of the interaction between modernity and Protestant Christianity.

▌ Most Christians accept the authority of Bible, tradition, church and experience, albeit in varying combinations and with different emphases. A major shift in the twentieth and twenty-first centuries has been towards a greater emphasis on experience, in combination with one or more of the traditional authorities.

▌ Key terms

anti-Semitism   Hostility or prejudice against Jews.

apocalyptic   A genre of literature which reveals things normally hidden, particularly things having to do with the heavenly realm and the world to come (the Greek word *apokalupsis* means 'revelation' or 'unveiling').

apocryphal   Documents whose canonical status is disputed, i.e. which not all Christians accept as part of the canon of biblical scripture.

autonomy   Self-regulation, independence.

canon   From the Greek word meaning measuring rod or rule, the term refers to the books which were officially accepted within Christianity as authoritative.

Catholic/Roman Catholic   The largest of the Christian churches whose leader, the Pope, resides in Rome.

Charismatic Christianity   An offshoot of Evangelicalism which has spread rapidly across the world throughout the twentieth century. Places particular emphasis on the gifts of the Holy Spirit. See *Pentecostalism*.

Christology   The study of Christ; the attempt to articulate his nature and significance.

conciliar   Concerning a council; ruled by an ecclesiastical council.

council   An ecumenical or general council is a meeting of all the bishops of a church, advised by theologians, to formulate church teaching or to take measures to reform the church.

denomination   A branch or grouping within Christianity (such as Methodism, Roman Catholicism).

ecumenical   Seeking Christian unity, unity of all the churches.

Evangelicalism   A pan-denominational movement within modern Protestantism which emphasizes the authority of the Bible and experience of the Holy Spirit.

Fundamentalism   The strictest form of Evangelicalism which stresses the inerrancy and infallibility of the Bible.

heteronomy   Opposite of autonomy; being regulated or governed by others or external duress.

monarchial   Ruled by a single individual (like the Pope).

Liberal Christianity   A self-consciously 'modern' form of Christianity which stresses human goodness and freedom and is open to reform in the light of modern change.

liturgy   Prescribed form of public worship and the formularies for it.

mainline churches/denominations   The largest denominations with the most influence in mainstream culture (especially Western culture) – such as the Roman Catholic, Lutheran, Anglican and Methodist churches.

Orthodoxy   The conciliar Eastern churches which separated from the Western (Catholic) church in the eleventh century. Sometimes called Eastern Orthodoxy.

Pentecostalism   Often used interchangeably with 'Charismatic' Christianity. Used in a stricter sense, Pentecostalism refers to the first phase of the Charismatic movement (up to the 1960s/1970s).

Protestant   The churches which split from the Roman Catholic church at the Reformation.

sacraments   Sacred signs and rituals which convey God's grace (for example, the water of baptism, the bread and wine of the eucharist, and the rite of ordination).

sacerdotal   Having to do with priests, the priestly hierarchy or the priestly office.

social encyclicals   A series of official documents issued by the Roman Catholic church since the end of the nineteenth century which applied Christian teaching to the social conditions of the modern world.

FURTHER READING

General

There is no definitive introduction to Christianity in the modern world. The best option for the student wishing to begin study of this topic is to consult the most reliable studies of Christianity in particular areas in modern times. On Christianity in the US see the relevant sections of Sydney E. Ahlstrom's *A Religious History of the American People* (New Haven and London: Yale University Press, 1972). On Christianity in Western Europe see Hugh McLeod's *Religion and the People of Western Europe 1789–1970* (Oxford: Oxford University Press, 1991). For the rest of the world see the relevant sections of Adrian Hastings (ed.): *A World History of Christianity* (London: Cassell, 1999). See also Linda Woodhead: *Introduction to Christianity* (Cambridge: Cambridge University Press, 2002) the second half of which offers an introductory overview and interpretation of Christianity in the modern world.

Roman Catholicism

The collection edited by Thomas M. Gannon, SJ: *World Catholicism in Transition* (London and New York: Macmillan) offers an overview of the state of Catholicism in every part of the world in the 1980s, and contains a useful introductory survey article by David Martin. Bill McSweeney's *Roman Catholicism: The Search for Relevance* (Oxford: Blackwell, 1980) is a lively and controversial survey of the development of Catholicism in the modern period in relation to its wider sociopolitical contexts. A useful overview is provided by Roger Aubert: *The Church in a Secularised Society* (The Christian Centuries Volume V, New York, Ramsey, NJ, Toronto: Paulist Press and London: Darton, Longman & Todd, 1978).

Orthodoxy

Two useful recent surveys of modern Orthodoxy are: Sabrina P. Ramet: *Nihil Obstat. Religion, Politics, and Social Change in East-Central Europe and Russia* (Durham and London: Duke University Press, 1998) and Nathaniel Davis: *A Long Walk to Church. A Contemporary History of Russian Orthodoxy* (Boulder, CO: Westview Press).

Liberal Christianity

There is surprisingly little literature on Liberal Christianity, and no general introduction to the subject. Liberal Christianity in the latter part of the twentieth century is the subject of Robert Michaelsen and Wade Clark Roof's valuable collection of essays *Liberal Protestantism: Realities and Possibilities* (New York, NY: Pilgrim Press, 1986). Wade Clark Roof and William McKinney's *American Mainline Religion. Its Changing Shape and Future* (New Brunswick and London: Rutgers University Press, 1987) also contains much relevant information. Nancy Ammerman's findings on the current state of liberalism in America are summarized in her chapter 'Golden rule Christianity. Lived religion in the American mainstream'. In Donald G. Hall (ed.): *Lived Religion in America: Toward a Theory of Practice* (Princeton, NJ: Princeton University Press, 1997, pp. 196–216).

Evangelicalism

By contrast, there is no shortage of books on Evangelicalism. George Marsden's *Understanding Fundamentalism and Evangelicalism* (Grand Rapids, MI: Eerdmans, 1991) offers an accessible introduction to the topic. David Bebbington's *Evangelicalism in Modern Britain A History from the 1730s to the 1980s* (London and New York: Routledge, 1993) is a major historical survey which treats Evangelicalism as an Anglo-American movement and sheds a great deal of light on its relation to the wider culture. There are a number of illuminating empirical studies of late twentieth-century Evangelicalism including James Davison Hunter's *Evangelicalism: The Coming Generation* (Chicago and London: University of Chicago Press, 1987) and (on a Fundamentalist church) Nancy Ammerman's *Bible Believers. Fundamentalists in the Modern World* (New Brunswick and London: Rutgers University Press, 1987).

Charismatic Christianity

Vinson Synan's *The Holiness–Pentecostal Tradition: Charismatic Movements in the Twentieth Century*, second edition (Grand Rapids, MI/Cambridge, UK: Eerdmans, 1997) surveys the holiness movement,

Pentecostalism and recent Charismatic renewal. David Martin's *Tongues of Fire,*(Oxford, UK, and Cambridge, MA: Blackwell, 1990) is a classic interpretation of the Charismatic upsurge in Latin America. His *Global Pentecostalism* (Oxford, UK and Cambridge, MA: Blackwell, 2001) provides the most up-to-date survey of the worldwide Charismatic movement.

Theology

On modern Roman Catholic theology see Adrian Hastings (ed.): *Modern Catholicism: Vatican II and After* (London: SPCK, 1991). This is a useful collection of essays on the council and on subsequent developments in the church. Chapter 14, by John McDade, 'Catholic Theology in the Post-Conciliar Period', is especially helpful. On modern Orthodox theology see Nicolas Zernov: *The Russian Religious Renaissance of the Twentieth Century* (London: Darton, Longman & Todd, 1963). On modern Protestant theology see Alasdair I. C. Heron: *A Century of Protestant Theology* (Cambridge: Lutterworth Press, 1980). Heron offers a readable and trustworthy overview of Christian thought from the Enlightenment to recent times. Also useful as an introduction is David F. Ford's *The Modern Theologians: An Introduction to Christian Theology in the Twentieth Century,* second edition (Oxford: Blackwell, 1997). This is a comprehensive collection of essays that provides solid introductions to all the major figures and movements in twentieth-century Christian thought. Alister McGrath (ed.): *Blackwell Encyclopedia of Modern Christian Thought* (Oxford, UK, and Cambridge, MA: Blackwell: 1995) is a useful and reliable reference work.

Acknowledgements

I would like to acknowledge the invaluable assistance of my colleagues Paul Fletcher and Patrick Sherry in writing and revising this chapter.

Islam

David Waines

▌ INTRODUCTION

The number of Muslims worldwide is estimated to be in excess of 1 billion, making Islam the largest faith community after Christianity. Of this number the overwhelming majority would identify themselves as Sunni Muslims whilst about 15 per cent follow a variety of Shi'a Muslim persuasions (see below). The Arabic word *islam* means the willing recognition of and active submission to the guiding command of the One God, Allah. Whoever acts in this manner is called a *muslim*, one who acknowledges and submits to the sole, unique God. The Islamic tradition or *din* (pronounced 'deen', a word which conveys the sense of obedience closely related to islam) is founded upon the guiding command of Allah as contained in the Qur'an. Muslims hold the Qur'an to be the word of God delivered to Muhammad (c.570–632 CE), God's elected messenger. The revelations were received in just over a twenty-year period, first in Mecca, the Prophet's birthplace, and later in Medina where the first community was established. Both these cities are in present day Saudi Arabia and are regarded by all Muslims as the central holy places of their faith.

From rather inauspicious beginnings in Arabia, Islam made a surprisingly rapid impact upon the contemporary map of the Middle East. Within a century of the Prophet Muhammad's death, Muslims governed throughout the Middle East and North Africa as far west as the Iberian peninsula (present day Spain and Portugal). In the East there were Muslim outposts in the Indus valley (northwest India) and expeditions which reached as far as the great wall of China. It naturally took much longer for mature, 'mass' Muslim societies to evolve in these areas. In regions such as Egypt some three hundred years elapsed before Muslims became a majority displacing the previous majority Christian population

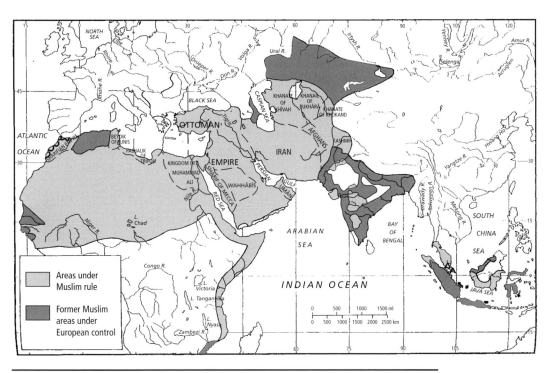

Figure 8.1 The Muslim world in the mid-nineteenth century, showing areas under European control

through conversion. Significant Christian and Jewish communities nevertheless continued to exist and flourish in the Middle East throughout the premodern period. These traditional heartlands of Islam remained fairly stable until about 1200 CE when a new phase of expansion commenced, although balanced to a lesser extent by territorial losses. By 1500 CE Muslims had been defeated and driven from the Iberian peninsula by the Christian reconquest supported by the Pope in Rome. By this same date Muslims under the banner of the Ottoman Turks had captured the capital of the Eastern Orthodox church, Constantinople. The city was renamed Istanbul, and by its capture Muslims secured a foothold in Europe which subsequently included the Balkans and parts of Hungary and Austria. The Ottomans also absorbed Syria, Egypt and much of North Africa and became the guardians of the holy cities of Arabia. Another formidable Muslim dominion, the Moghul empire, was about to emerge in India while Muslim traders, preachers and holy men during the years 1200–1500 CE had been slowly spreading Islam eastwards from India to present day Malaysia, Indonesia and the Philippines. There even appeared a small and thinly scattered Muslim presence in China. During this same period Islam also became firmly established in parts of sub-Saharan and East Africa. Apart from the Ottoman and Moghul empires, a third great dominion emerged from 1500 onwards in Iran where, wedged between the two former Sunni powers, the Shi'a Muslim Safavid dynasty established itself. Shi'ism has since then grown into the predominant expression of Iranian Islam to the present day.

The worldwide Muslim community (*umma*) achieved its greatest territorial extent in the late seventeenth century. The most significant change in the *umma*'s premodern configuration has been the emergence in the twentieth century of Muslim communities throughout Western Europe and North America. As yet small, they are formed almost exclusively by immigrants from former European colonial territories. For example, the largest non-Christian religious minority in Britain today is comprised chiefly of Muslims from the Indian subcontinent. This phenomenon is the result of significant population movements from East to West. An even more recent development has been the emergence of independent Central Asian Muslim republics, like Tajikistan and Kirgizstan, formed out of the collapse of the former Soviet Union.

'Modernity' is generally understood to refer to developments in Western Europe which commenced during the eighteenth century. It is also widely assumed that since such developments, especially those relating to science and technology and the challenge they posed to religious authority, did not occur elsewhere at this same time, non-European areas of the globe could therefore only truly 'modernize' once they adopted and followed European patterns. This model of modernity, however, can lead to important eighteenth-century religious developments in non-European cultures becoming obscured or ignored altogether. In the case of Islam, religious reform thought in the eighteenth century, while not entirely overlooked, has not been sufficiently appreciated for its influence on nineteenth-century Islamic movements which, consequently, have then been interpreted as simply 'anti-Western' and therefore 'anti-modern' developments since they occurred at the very time when much of the Muslim world was succumbing to overwhelming European political domination. On the other hand, Islamic thought and movements of the eighteenth to nineteenth centuries must be given their due as providing critiques of and tentative or partial solutions to clearly perceived problems of internal moral and spiritual decay in Islamic societies. With reference to the non-European world, one has often to become sensitive to observing and imagining modernity-as-tradition. These problems will be looked at in detail in this chapter following an initial discussion of the sources of the Islamic tradition.

SOURCES AND RESOURCES

Scripture and tradition

The two major sources of the Islamic tradition are the Qur'an and a body of literature known as the Traditions of the Prophet (*hadith*) which contain the Prophet's *sunna*, his 'way' or 'path'. Described in its own terms the Qur'an appears in many ways distinct from the scriptures of other communities such as the Hebrew Bible of the Jews and the Christians' New Testament. The word *qur'an* means 'recitation', which emphasizes its essentially oral character, intended to be read aloud and listened to. Moreover, the Qur'an is seen as the literal and immutable word of Allah, the Arabic word *al-ilah* meaning 'the god' (Qur'an, Chapter 18: verse 27; also 10:15). Next, it is a guidance to all peoples, confirming the essential message of previous revelations (Q 6:92). Muslims believe these scriptures are either incomplete (Q 4:44) or had become corrupted by the earlier communities (Q 2:174) who distorted their original meaning (Q 5:16–18). The Qur'an is, therefore, the culmination and completion of God's guidance to the world.

▌ EXCERPT FROM THE GABRIEL HADITH

[The second Caliph] Umar ibn al-Khattab said: One day when we were with God's messenger (Muhammad), a man wearing very white clothing and black hair came up to us. No mark of travel was visible on him, and none of us recognised him. Sitting down before the Prophet, he said, 'Tell me, Muhammad, about submission (*islam*).' He replied, 'Submission means bearing witness that there is no god but God and that Muhammad is God's messenger, that you perform the ritual prayer, pay the alms tax, fast during Ramadan and make the pilgrimage to the House (in Mecca), if you are able to go there.' The man said, 'You have spoken the truth.' We were surprised at his questioning the Prophet and then declaring he had spoken the truth. He then said, 'Now tell me about faith (*iman*).' The Prophet said, 'Faith means that you have faith in God, His angels, His books, His messengers, and the Last Day, and that you have faith in divine destiny, both its good and its evil.' Again remarking that he had spoken the truth, he said, 'Now tell me about goodness and right action (*ihsan*).' The Prophet replied, '*Ihsan* means that you should worship God as if you see Him, for even if you do not see Him, He sees you.' When the man went away, I waited for a while and the Prophet asked me, 'Umar, do you know who the questioner was?' I replied, 'God and His messenger know best.' He said, 'That was (the angel) Gabriel. He came to teach you your religion.'

[This famous Tradition describes the 'surrender to God' (*islam*) in terms first of the ritual 'pillars', then as the inner faith (*iman*) in God and His final judgement, and lastly as pious behaviour (*ihsan*) in all aspects of one's daily life as though acting in the presence of God.]

The relationship between the message and the messenger, the Prophet Muhammad, is often misunderstood. As the Qur'an is held to be the eternal word of God, the message is logically and existentially prior to an earthly messenger; hence the Qur'anic message should properly be viewed as the manifestation of the divine, somewhat in the manner that Christians regard Jesus Christ. As such, the Qur'an presents a kind of self-portrait of God as lord of all creation, as lord of history, past and present, and as lord of the last judgement.

Through Muhammad God disclosed his will, nature and the purpose of creation. As a vehicle of the divine message, the Prophet became the second source of spiritual authority for Muslims. This was expressed in the *sunna* or 'way of the Prophet', the sum of his exemplary words and deeds. Unlike the Qur'an, a single volume about the length of the New Testament, the *sunna* is found in a large corpus of multivolumed works. Six such works, compiled in the late ninth and early tenth centuries are considered as genuine, authoritative sources of information concerning all aspects of the Prophet's life. These works could be described as containing the early Muslim community's collective memory of the Prophet. The information is preserved in the form of stories, anecdotes or simply personal observations, each called a *hadith*, or Tradition. These might be attributed either directly to the Prophet himself or to his close companions relating what they knew about him, about life in the early Muslim community or even about the days in Arabia before the Prophet's mission. The collections of *hadith* helped to clarify and extend Muslims' understanding of the Qur'an, since Muhammad was held to be the first interpreter of the revelations he had received. Moreover, they kept alive the memory of God's messenger who in turn became an exemplary model for Muslims to follow in their own daily lives.

In the generations following the Prophet's death an informal group of experts emerged, each specialized in one or more areas related to the relevance and application of the Qur'an and Traditions to the evolving life of the Muslim community. Collectively, this scholarly elite was known as the *ulama* (singular, *alim*) whose task it was to shape the religious ethos of the community based upon these twin foundations. Fields such as Qur'an commentary, *hadith* analysis, history, law, theology, ethics, grammar, lexicography, and medicine developed. Some of these early scholars were converts, or descendants of converts from Christianity, Judaism or other faiths, which explains the presence of influences from these sources in the early Islamic scholarly disciplines. Popular storytellers and preachers instructed and entertained audiences of ordinary folk with morality tales for their edification and guidance. The story of Joseph and his brothers, for example, is uniquely narrated in the Qur'an as 'signs for seekers after truth' (Q 12:7). The storytellers drew from the annals of all the ancient prophets, which included Adam, Abraham, Moses and Jesus, because they contained 'a moral for those of understanding' (Q 12:111). Some storytellers were later charged with inventing and disseminating false Traditions, albeit from the most pious of motives, in order to instil in their audiences the proper awe and reverence for the faith.

Community, authority and the self

The Sunni Muslim understanding of community (*umma*) and authority is reflected in its historical experience. The Prophet Muhammad founded the first Muslim community in Medina and guided it until his death after which leadership fell to a series of four caliphs (singular, *khalifa*) from among his close companions, including his cousin and son-in-law, Ali. This period of nearly forty years (622–61 CE) came later to be regarded as one in which the community was 'rightly guided', living in practice as closely in tune with the divine command as was humanly possible. Thereafter, rapid expansion and internal divisions endangered, according to some, the community's spiritual well-being. In response, they adopted a more ascetic style of life than common piety required which evolved into the spiritual expression known as *Sufism*.

▌ QUR'AN 24:35 'THE LIGHT VERSE'

God is the Light of the heavens and the earth. The similitude of His light is as a niche wherein is a lamp. The lamp is in a glass. The glass is as it were a shining star. (The lamp is) kindled from a blessed tree, an olive of neither the East nor the West, whose oil would almost glow forth (of itself) though touched by no fire. Light upon light. God guides to His light whom He will, and speaks to humankind in allegories, for God is the Knower of all things.

[This verse, a favourite among Sufis, is seen as describing the immanence of God to His creatures.]

The notion of a pristine community comprising the first two or three generations of Muslims is reflected in Prophetic Tradition. Muhammad was reported to have said that after him the community would become divided into seventy-three sects, only one of which would be saved from eternal damnation. When asked which that would be he said: 'Those who follow me and my Companions.' This widely known Tradition was understood to mean that salvation, individual and collective, would be attained by following the guidance of the Qur'an and the Prophet's example expressed in the *sunna*. The Sunni (from the word *sunna*) community adhered to the *shari'a* (sacred law) as expounded in detail by the founders and their followers of four main schools of legal thought and practice. The law was derived from the material sources of the Qur'an and the *sunna*. Vigorous debates during the law's development were decisively resolved in favour of the experts in *hadith* who claimed the *sunna* had equal status with the Qur'an. In addition, legal scholars came to accept as binding the consensus of opinion on a legal matter arrived at within their own school or that of the broader community. Finally, decisions could also be made employing the rational tool of argument by analogy. The religious law covered two domains

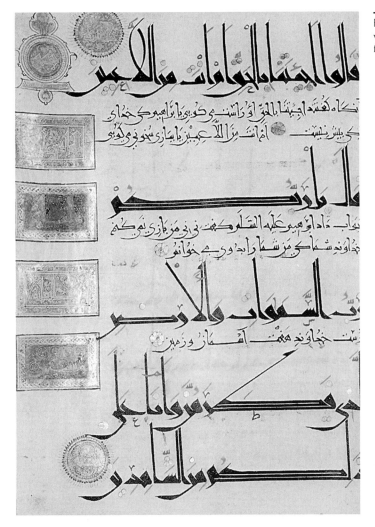

Figure 8.2 Qu'ran, Kufic Arabic script with interlinear Persian paraphrase, fifteenth century

of activity, the relationship of the individual with God in worship, and the relationship of individuals with each other in social matters which included, among other fields, what today would cover family, commercial or criminal law.

One significant dissident group became known as the supporters of Ali, or the Shi'a. They held that legitimate leadership of the community had been designated by the Prophet to lie solely with the family of Ali and his male descendants, known as the twelve *Imams*. (Another dissident group, the Isma'ilis, held that the line of *Imams* ended with the seventh in the line.) The Sunni caliphs, excluding Ali, were regarded as usurpers. The Shi'a would in time claim their *Imams* were divinely designated and possessed an infallible knowledge of the divine will expressed in the Qur'an. Shi'a understanding of the law is based upon the Qur'an and the Prophet's way as taught by the Imams, beginning with Ali. The twelfth and last Imam who 'vanished' around 900 CE, is believed by the Shi'a to be alive and his return is awaited to restore justice on earth prior to the day of judgement. The doctrine of the Imams is the key to the division between Shi'a and Sunni. This has led one modern observer to describe them as two parallel orthodox perspectives of the Islamic revelation which, in their formal, outward aspects, cannot converge. Conciliation is possible, however, both in daily life and at the inner spiritual level of Sufism. Differences notwithstanding, both Shi'a and Sunni Muslims base their sense of community upon acceptance of the Qur'an and his Prophet.

From this brief account, three levels of authority can be described: first, ultimate authority rests unquestionably with God who provides guidance for all humankind. Second, during Muhammad's lifetime, authority over his community was derived from his role as messenger of God (*rasul allah*). These two aspects are summed up in the Muslims' confession of faith, considered as the fundamental pillar of Islam, that 'There is no God but Allah and Muhammad is His Messenger'. To this the Shi'a add '. . . and Ali is the friend of Allah'. All Muslims would accept the Qur'anic injunction that 'if you have a dispute concerning any matter, refer it to Allah and the Messenger if you truly believe in Allah and the Last Day' (Q 4:59). The third level of authority is social, vested in those who possessed the requisite knowledge of the Qur'an and *sunna*, and a deep personal piety. This applied to the Sunni religious scholars and, following the disappearance of the twelfth and last Imam (c. 900 CE), to those of their Shi'a counterparts who were expert in the law (*mujtahids*). According to the Sunni axiom 'scholars are heirs of the Prophets' and among the Shi'a the saying is that 'jurists are heirs of the Imams'. Thus religious authority in Islamic societies is diffuse and scattered, entrusted to individuals recognized within their own communities for the qualities mentioned, and at times for their aura of holiness alone.

The Muslim sense of community is reinforced by the other rituals or 'pillars' of the faith. For example, the daily prayers (*salat*) are performed in the direction of Mecca, the focal point of community worship. The annual pilgrimage (*hajj*) to Mecca, at least once in a Muslim's lifetime should conditions permit, brings together a microcosm of believers from around the world. Fasting (*sawm*) during the month of Ramadan is a time of spiritual renewal for the individual as well as the community; and finally, the giving of alms (*zakat*) is a spiritual form of community welfare.

Each of these ritual acts also defines the status of the self, for every Muslim is ultimately responsible for his/her own salvation before God without resort to either intermediary or redeemer. Each individual possesses an innate sense of the divine and a need for guidance and, therefore, must choose to follow or reject God's will and await his just dispensation at the last judgement. Unique in the order of creation, man and woman have been entrusted with building a moral social order on earth, a fearsome burden itself which can be achieved only by constant personal struggle (*jihad*) aided by God's mercy and compassion. Here the self and community are inextricably linked. The proper fulfilment of each is sought in an enduring 'remembrance of God'. The link is alluded to in the Qur'anic verse 'The successful are those who can be saved from their own selfishness' (Q 59:9). Another approach to the creator–creature relationship is that of the Sufi who strives, through various spiritual exercises, to live the words of the famous *hadith*, to 'worship God as if you see Him, for even if you do not see Him, He sees you'. Striving for a vision of the divine did not necessarily entail withdrawal from community concerns. Whether Sufi or not, every Muslim as *muslim* (one who has submitted to God) strives for a life of balanced, integrated moral action called *taqwa*, a term often rendered as 'piety' but is more properly understood as guarding oneself against the harmful consequences of one's own conduct.

The Muslim experience of community, prior to the modern era was, in an interesting sense, never exclusively Muslim. As the youngest of the monotheist traditions, Islam's roots in the Jewish and Christian traditions were acknowledged insofar as biblical figures like Adam, Abraham, Moses and Jesus were accepted as part of God's long prophetic chain culminating in the mission of Muhammad. Jewish and Christian minority communities of the Middle East, North Africa and the Iberian peninsula, therefore, lived in treaty relationship within Muslim dominions which allowed them generally peaceful pursuit of their own religious beliefs and practices. In India, Muslim rule confronted

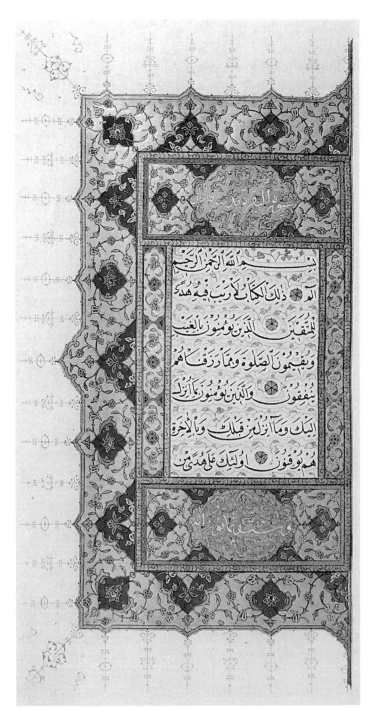

Figure 8.3 Qu'ran, copied by Shaykh
Hamdullah, Ottoman Turkey, 1495

numerically superior Hindu communities which ensured the latter continuing vitality despite conversions to Islam particularly from among the lower castes. Muslim experience of 'the other' was, nevertheless, a unique premodern experiment in pluralism.

INTERACTIONS WITH MODERNITY

Islam and the modern world: the eighteenth century

Following upon the ravages of the Mongol invasions of much of the Middle East and northern India in the thirteenth century and a series of plagues in the fourteenth century, the *umma* entered upon a phase of gradual recovery. As already noted in the Introduction, the sixteenth and seventeenth centuries witnessed the rise and consolidation of formidable empires under Ottoman, Safavid and Moghul rule. By the beginning of the eighteenth century weaknesses had already begun to appear in these once impregnable dominions.

The story of Islam from 1700 CE onwards has often been discussed in terms of the 'decline of Islam' versus the 'rise of the West' or as the struggle between 'tradition' and 'modernity'. The complexity of historical reality cannot simply be reduced to simple contrasting descriptive terms such as these.

It was evident that political corruption and military defeat were damaging the very core of these Muslim imperial structures allowing local, provincial authorities to rise to prominence. Moreover, weakness at their centres occurred at a time of increasingly aggressive commercial and trade policies on the part of major private international trading companies which had been established in Britain, France and the Netherlands a century earlier. In the long run European economic expansion overseas would be converted into direct political control over Muslim lands. This resulted from the need of these Western nations to protect their own rapidly growing economies at home which were increasingly dependent upon these overseas links. Yet during the eighteenth century European economic penetration alone had little or no impact upon Muslim religious developments, which were directed specifically at socio-moral revival of Muslim societies and reorientation of the Sufi tradition.

Such internal Muslim developments arose out of local conditions but achieved notice well beyond the areas of their immediate influence. The dissemination of revival ideas occurred in traditional ways, first via the annual pilgrimage to Mecca and second in the practice of religious scholars (*ulama*) travelling over vast distances to gather knowledge from famous teachers elsewhere and exchanging views on current conditions within the *umma*. Moreover, the holy cities of Mecca and Medina were themselves centres of study for scholars from near and far. For example, of the dozen or so most prominent teachers between 1650 and 1750, apart from those born in Mecca and Medina, there were scholars who had come from as far away as India, Iraq and Morocco.

One of the greatest figures of the eighteenth century was the Indian Shah Wali Allah (1702–62). He was born in Delhi and was accepted into the reforming Naqshbandi order of Sufis by his father who had undertaken his son's early education. While on pilgrimage to the holy cities of Arabia, he became immersed in the study of *hadith*. On returning to India his chief concerns were the decline of Moghul power and disunity within the Indian Muslim community. Over the centuries Sufism in the Indian context had acquired un-Islamic accretions and superstitions derived from Hindu influence. Wali Allah condemned practices like auto-hypnotic visions, orgiastic rituals and saint veneration bordering on worship. Drawing upon the work of his great predecessor Ahmad al-Sirhindi (d. 1648) he attempted to 'purify' Sufism and then to reconcile the various strands of contemporary practice into one that reflected both the Indian spiritual environment and the need to regenerate Islamic forces. A profound study of the *hadith* (Prophetic Traditions) led Wali Allah to highlight points of agreement between the four Sunni schools of law and to insist that blind imitation of the teachings of any single school damaged community welfare. In effect, the only unquestioned sources of authoritative guidance were God and his messenger.

A second important figure was Muhammad ibn Abd al-Wahhab (1703–92). He was born in central Arabia, at the time nominally under the suzerainty of the Ottoman sultan. Like his contemporary Wali Allah, he studied in Mecca and Medina where he too underwent a rigorous study of *hadith*. This forcefully brought home to him the gulf between the ideal community expressed in the Traditions and the sorry state of Arabian society he saw around him. His thought was also influenced by a major puritan of an earlier era, Ibn Taymiyyah (d. 1323). Between Abd al-Wahhab and Wali Allah there were points of agreement but more profoundly, points of difference. Both accepted the Qur'an and *sunna* as binding sources for a Muslim's faith and law. Moreover, each rejected blind imitation of generations of medieval legal scholarship which, over the centuries, had thoroughly examined these sources. But whereas Abd al-Wahhab insisted that there was no human guide for a Muslim other than the Prophet, Wali Allah allowed, within proper limits, the guidance of a Sufi master so long as the relationship did not involve the disciple's veneration of his teacher. Abd al-Wahhab also stressed the transcendence of the One, Unique God, while Wali Allah accepted the possible vision of a more accessible, immanent God. Their greatest point of disagreement was over Sufism, although each had studied with prominent Sufi masters. Abd al-Wahhab roundly denounced practices including the seeking of intercession with God from the 'spirits' of dead holy men and women and the excessive devotion at their tombs since prayer 'for' the dead could easily degenerate, he thought, into prayer 'to' the dead. Wali Allah, on the other hand, strove to purify Sufism, bringing those practices broadly agreed as acceptable and its individualist form of spirituality more firmly into the domain of the sacred law (*shari'a*).

In brief, these revivalist programmes attacked the world-negating attitudes and 'superstitions' of medieval Sufism. Reformed Sufi orders shifted the emphasis away from popular ecstatic practices and stressed as well the need for the social and moral reconstruction of Muslim societies. The significance of the study of *hadith* was a renewed focus upon the role of the Prophet as a model for moral conduct at both the individual and collective levels. Indeed, recent research into reformed Sufi orders suggests a desire to reform society through the efforts of individual renewal reminiscent of the Christian Pietist movement which began in seventeenth-century Europe (see Chapter 7). Revivalists challenged the acceptance of the opinions of the medieval legal schools as fixed and final. Instead they insisted on *ijtihad*, or the effort to rethink for oneself the meaning of the original message contained in the Qur'an and *sunna*. They intended also to reflect the moral dynamism of early Islam, thereby attacking the debilitating burden of a predeterministic, fatalistic outlook produced by popular religion. Political involvement, therefore, was a logical corollary of their religious views as they vigorously assailed social and economic injustices. For example, the Wahhabiya became the dominant religious force in Arabia when it allied with the political forces of the Sa'ud family and established the first Sau'di polity in 1773. Shah Wali Allah was himself not directly involved in the Indian political scene but his influence was evident in the activities of his son and grandson in the early nineteenth century. Militant revivalist movements emerged elsewhere across the *umma* from West and North Africa to Indonesia and China. The chief weakness of the revivalist programmes, it has been observed, was the belief that the sacred law could (and, of course, should) be more or less literally implemented in all ages. This presented an obstacle to creative rethinking of the social content of Islam. Nevertheless, revivalist groups did represent an important expression of self-analysis and criticism of contemporary Muslim societies.

Meanwhile, in Shi'a Iran, the power of the Safavids came to an end in 1722. By the end of the eighteenth century they had been replaced by the Qajar dynasty which ruled until 1925. An unsettled interregnum during which the new ruler, Nadir Shah (1736–48), attempted for political reasons to transform Shi'ism into a fifth Sunni legal school, proved a passing episode without lasting consequence. Despite the political instability witnessed throughout the century, the Shi'a tradition preserved its vitality and, ultimately, its predominance. An important, ongoing controversy between two groups, the Akhbaris and Usulis ended in victory for the latter. The core of the dispute was about whether scholars could exercise their independent judgement (*ijtihad*) in deriving fresh insights from the Qur'an and the Traditions of the Prophet and the teaching of the Imams. The Akhbaris denied this, claiming solutions to all questions could be found solely within these sources alone. The Usuli position, emphasizing *ijtihad*, stressed the *mujtahids'* role as spiritual guides in helping the community to cope with changing times in the absence of the last Imam. In effect, the *mujtahids* became agents or representatives of the last, vanished or hidden Imam. The Usuli triumph helped religious scholars consolidate their social position in Iranian society, with their own financial resources and a growing sense of independence from all central political authority. Among Sunni reformers, as we have seen, *ijtihad* was also urged, although in their societies this never had the consequence of the *ulama* securing a collective role independent of political power.

Examination of the eighteenth-century Islamic experience has shown vigorous revival movements emerging within contexts of weakening political and social structures. These movements significantly established an Islamic agenda which influenced future reform strategies in an era of the increasingly direct impact of Western ideas, values and institutions upon Muslims throughout the *umma*.

The 'long' nineteenth century: colonialism and modernity

The nineteenth century in modern Islamic history was an unusually long and troubled one. Symbolically it begins with the invasion of Ottoman Egypt by Napoleon Bonaparte in 1798. The French occupation, although short lived, was a clear signal of the Ottoman Empire's waning fortunes. The symbolic end of the period is 1920, when Britain and France divided the remaining Ottoman territories of Iraq, Syria and Palestine between themselves. Throughout the long century European colonialists managed to occupy or directly influence almost the entire Islamic world. Of the three great medieval Muslim empires, the Ottoman and Moghul were totally dismembered; only Iran emerged relatively intact but subject nevertheless to pressure from both Britain and Russia. Muslim inhabited territories in sub-Saharan Africa and in modern day Malaysia and Indonesia also fell under European control.

Set in this framework, modernity and Muslims' responses to it raise problems which are different in significant ways from the course of modernity in Europe itself. Understood as a cluster of social, political, economic and cultural institutions and values, modernity was experienced in Europe and North America as an internally generated transformation. As part of that process some European nations, notably Britain, France and the Netherlands, built vast imperial networks overseas in Asia. These nineteenth-century imperial structures enjoyed advantages possessed by no premodern empire. Developments in science and technology, transport and communications, together with commercial and industrial transformation of the home economies gave these countries unprecedented power of expansion overseas. 'Modernity', therefore, was experienced in Muslim lands within a power relationship between themselves and their new non-Muslim rulers. Even territories which did not come under direct European control, like modern day Saudi Arabia and Turkey, were nonetheless confronted with the same powerful challenges of the modern era.

The experience was by no means all negative. Until the 1880s, thoughtful Muslims who had acquired first-hand experience of European countries, admired those features which were most conspicuously lacking in their own societies. These observers recognized that parliamentary governments stood in stark contrast to their own despotic, dynastic regimes. They also acknowledged that European charitable societies, dedicated to ameliorating the plight of the poor and disadvantaged, were superior to the

Figure 8.4 Great Mosque, Jenné, Mali, built *c.*1907

equivalent traditional Muslim institutions which had fallen into widespread neglect. At the same time the implications of secularization for religion in their own societies were not grasped.

Gradually the mood in educated Muslim quarters changed. A new sentiment of nationalism arose and the desire for independence from European rule. This goal was fed in part by growing Muslim resentment at the double standards exercised by the European 'civilizing missions' towards their colonial possessions. Enlightenment values of equality, democracy and human rights were often distorted and devalued in their application by European imperial rulers to subject peoples. A complicating factor was religion. In Europe, modernity was experienced as the challenge by the secular nation state to the traditional religious authority of the church. But for their part, Muslims experienced Europe's power over themselves as Christian power. This was exercised most clearly in the expansion of Christian missionary activity encouraged by European governments. Missions provided education in the 'new European knowledge' and health care. These provisions were widely welcomed. The explicit missionary objective to convert Muslims was, on the other hand, stiffly resisted. Muslims drew parallels with the era of Christian Crusades against Muslims in the Middle Ages. Missionary propaganda attacked the character of the Prophet as sensual and violent and dismissed the Qur'an as his own incoherent composition. Apart from the crudity of such methods, the major obstacle to the missionary programme was the Muslims' own understanding of Jesus as one of God's great prophets and exemplary model of love, but not as the missionaries' Son of God or redeemer of humanity. Nonetheless, Protestant scripturalist views influenced modernist Muslim thinking as we shall see below.

The legacy of European colonial rule was mixed: Muslims willingly accepted the real material benefits of modernity such as science and technology, but were more suspicious of and ambivalent towards certain values like individualism and democracy. Individualism went against the Muslim sense of community and family, while democracy compromised the sovereignty of God. Moreover, in a few notable cases the violent end of colonial rule contributed to the subsequent politicization of Muslim religious movements. Three such traumatic examples of the colonial endgame were in Algeria, Palestine and India. In Algeria, France had implanted a huge colony of French settlers on vast tracts of prime agricultural land, dispossessing the local population. Only a bloody eight-year war brought about Algerian independence in 1962, which left the country on the verge of economic ruin. Britain promoted the idea of a Jewish national home in Palestine against the wishes of its inhabitants. The creation of the State of Israel in 1948 was built upon the destruction of Palestinian society and the creation of hundreds of thousands of refugees. Finally, in the wake of Britain's hasty retreat from India in 1947 two nations, India (Hindu majority) and Pakistan (Muslim majority), divided the subcontinent in bitterness and enmity at the cost of hundreds of thousands of lives and the displacement of as many more.

The association of colonialism with Christianity had further consequences. In the minds of modern Muslim reformers, social change could not entail secularization or the trivialization of religion manifested in the removal of its interest in politics, economics or social problems. The policies of the colonial powers promoted secular institutions in their overseas domains. Two key institutions were education and the law. While private mission schools were allowed to flourish, colonial governments' overall control of education further encouraged the marginalization of Islamic knowledge. Likewise, Muslim legal systems were reformed and largely replaced by the introduction of European codes (especially, French, Swiss and German) lock, stock and barrel. In both cases it meant that those trained in traditional Islamic knowledge, the *ulama*, were disenfranchised and replaced socially by a new secularized Muslim elite. This process occurred earlier in India than in the Middle East, although in Iran the *mujtahids* maintained their social and economic base for a longer time. Politically, the new secularized elite formed the governing circle in all the independent nation states of the postcolonial period.

On the question of the place of religion in modern society, a gulf by then existed between the visions of the *ulama* and the secularists. Towards the end of the nineteenth century there slowly emerged an uncoordinated group of modernist reformers – they could hardly be called a 'school of thought' – who were at once acutely aware of their society's modern needs and also for a public debate about Islam's present and future role. They built upon the work of their medieval and early modern predecessors, but rather than seeking to recapture an ideal past looked to a better, modern future. Their impact touched both the more culturally sensitive secularists and the enlightened wing of the *ulama*.

Muslim responses: tradition and modernity

Religious debate and controversy throughout the twentieth century were fluid, a good example, perhaps, of 'tradition-in-modernity'. Some religious movements viewed over time seem to defy simple labelling, making analysis more complicated and terminology meaningless when applied rigidly. An example may help illustrate the problem.

The Deobandi movement began in India with the foundation of its first school in 1867. Some of its founders had close connection with *ulama* linked to the family of Shah Wali Allah and to Delhi College established and run by the British. The goal of the Deobandi school was to provide instruction in the faith and graduates to carry on the work at a moment when traditional support for Muslim education in India had collapsed. British policy was openly hostile to the Muslim community, holding it responsible for the Indian uprising against imperial rule a decade earlier. The six-year curriculum emphasized the study of Traditions (*hadith*), individual responsibility for correct belief and practice, together with spiritual transformation along sober Sufi lines. The school, however, borrowed many institutional features from British example, including formal exams, an annual convocation, and a system of raising public contributions through mail and money orders. Students from all India, Central Asia and Afghanistan were attracted to the school whose members remained politically quiescent until just before outbreak of the First World War. This apolitical strand gave rise since the 1920s to a significant international movement which today is well established among Muslim communities in Europe and North America. Among the various available labels, how may one best characterize this many sided movement: traditionalist, fundamentalist, modernist, or secularist? While inevitably described as fundamentalist, in fact it shares features with all four categories. The application of any single label can be misleading, as important features may thereby be overlooked. In the Deobandi movement, tradition and modernity seem in league with one another. Recent studies on Islam in the modern world employ a number of designations for different movements. While the term 'fundamentalist' seems to lack rigorous analytical power when used of Islamic contexts, in a very broad sense 'modernist' Muslims may be said to seek to modernize Islam, while more radical reformers, sometimes called 'Islamicists' (another unfortunate term), seek to Islamize modernity.

Since it is impossible to deal with every twentieth-century development across the vast breadth of the Muslim world, in what remains of this chapter, the central question of religious authority and its implications for Muslim society will be highlighted. Debates on this issue have occurred in many countries and contexts, but it is those in India (and latterly Pakistan), Egypt and Iran which will be dealt with.

Modernist reform: nineteenth and twentieth centuries (Sunni and Shi'a)

SUNNI DEVELOPMENTS

Two figures stand out as the major Sunni reformers in the Muslim world: the Indian Sayyid Ahmad Khan (d. 1898) and the Egyptian Muhammad Abduh (d. 1905). Both confronted direct British imperial rule over their lands, of India since 1857 and of Egypt since 1882. Abduh supported a protonationalist uprising in the Egyptian army which led to British occupation and as a result he spent some years in exile. Ahmad Khan was employed in the British East India Company. In the wake of the revolt against British presence in 1857, he strove to reconcile the Indian Muslim community with British rule and assure the British of Muslim loyalty to them. He was knighted in 1888. Each received a traditional Islamic education, and had early close relations with Sufi spirituality, while in their middle years each became acquainted with Europe first-hand. All these influences informed their efforts towards social reform focused especially upon education. Ahmad Khan founded the Muhammadan Anglo-Oriental College; it would become the first secular university for Muslim students in India. Abduh, from his position as the highest religious authority in Egypt, strove to reform the religious courts, religious endowments and the 1,000-year-old al-Azhar University. He also conceived the idea for a

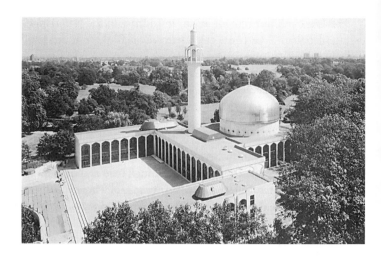

Figure 8.5 Central Mosque, London

complementary secular university, eventually founded after his death. Both men also conveyed their ideas through the modern medium of newspapers which they founded or edited themselves.

The modernist agenda set out two interrelated goals. The first was to provide a way forward out of Muslims' current spiritual malaise and material decadence by demonstrating the compatibility of Islam with the values of the modern world. The second was to counter the Western perception of Islam as destructive and irrelevant to the modern world, and to challenge assertions like that of Lord Cromer, onetime governor of Egypt, that 'Islam reformed is no longer Islam'.

Traditionally, the state of contemporary life had been judged on the basis of norms which were, in theory, ultimately grounded in the Qur'an and *sunna*. Modernists, on the other hand, approached the Qur'an and *sunna* from the rational norms of nineteenth-century natural science. Like their eighteenth-century predecessors, modernists argued that fulfilment of their task entailed returning to Islam's original sources. But where the revivalists had tended to read the sacred texts in a literal fashion, modernists sought to capture their essential spirit and to distinguish a universal, immutable core from features deemed valid only for a particular time or place.

The modernist position implicitly involved a reassessment of the authority of the past. Like their eighteenth-century predecessors, they rejected *taqlid* (the authority of the medieval law schools), advocated *ijtihad* (independent rethinking) and *hadith*-based reform. Modernists, however, were far more radical in their reassessment of the *hadith* and *sunna*. Ahmad Khan expressed his view of Islam in the following revealing aphorism: 'the Qur'an is the Word of God, nature is the Work of God'. No modernist ever questioned the fundamental precept of Islam that the Qur'an was the eternal word of God. It provided the principles by which the individual and society were governed just as nature followed its own laws also created by God. From here Ahmad Khan was led to deny miracles as they contravened God's natural and immutable order. The Qur'an, he argued, did not support the view that some events could violate the laws of nature. Therefore, incidents recorded in the Qur'an which traditionally had been accepted as miraculous needed to be rationally reinterpreted: Moses's escape across the Red Sea (Q 26:63) by smiting the waters with his staff meant simply he had found a fordable path across it at low tide. Abduh fully upheld the natural order of cause and effect but argued more cautiously that miracles could not rationally be demonstrated to be impossible.

The nature of the Traditions (*hadith*) was quite another matter. Ahmad Khan questioned and finally rejected the supposed authenticity of almost the whole corpus. He dismissed the classical methods of *hadith* criticism and argued for new, rational methods of assessment, allowing only a handful of Traditions dealing with spiritual matters as relevant and binding on contemporary Muslims. For his part, Abduh expressed a slightly more cautious scepticism toward the Traditions but did open the way for personal judgement to determine which Traditions to accept or reject. Significantly, their positions meant that rather than interpreting the Qur'an in the light of Traditions, revelation could be understood solely on its own terms. In other words, Tradition literature and the *sunna* it contained no longer held equal status with the Qur'an but were subordinate to it. This approach did not belittle the stature of the Prophet in modernist eyes, but meant that the large amount of *sunna*'s minute detail which touched upon worldly matters was now judged to have been relevant only for the lifetime of the Prophet. Moreover, in a somewhat 'Protestant' fashion, the modernists implicitly proposed that each Muslim could search for scripture's meaning for him/herself.

Neither thinker worked out the implications of his position for the traditional understanding of the religious law (*shari'a*) and its application to public life. If the authenticity of *hadith* were questioned, severely affecting the scope of the *sunna*, the second most important foundation of the law was placed in peril. Both Abduh and Ahmad Khan appeared to be saying that rather than blindly adhering to the accumulated medieval corpus of the law, 'pure' and 'pristine' Islam had to be rediscovered by seriously adopting the Qur'anic proposition that 'God does not alter what is in a people until they alter what is in themselves' (Q 13:12). This verse became the banner of all modernist thought. It meant that rather than indiscriminate, literal acceptance of the past, Muslims had to shape their future based upon what might be called the public interest or welfare in order to meet the dramatically new circumstances of the modern era. The concept of 'public interest' or 'equitable preference' was known and discussed in the medieval legal literature. Critics of the modernist position represented by Ahmad Khan and Abduh and their followers, argued that its application in modern times was still subject to traditional legal norms and had to be supported and applied according to the four legal sources including the *sunna*. For example, both men concluded from close examination of the Qur'an alone that the traditional practice of polygamy was unjustified and monogamous marriage had always been God's clear intention. A more recent application of the principle has been in the banking system which is based upon the giving and taking of interest, a practice forbidden in Islamic law. The notion of Islamic banking rationalizes 'interest' as 'dividends' received by an investor from joint participation with the bank in its investment schemes.

The early unsystematic body of modernist ideas expounded by Ahmad Khan and Abduh may appear to have an air of unreality about them. Discussion over the nature of the *sunna* and prophetic authority was unlikely to affect the current reform of law along European lines in India and Egypt. British policy and secularist Muslims alike opposed building the modern state upon the medieval *shari'a*. Debate continued nonetheless. The supporters and detractors of *sunna* endorsed contrasting views of the purpose and scope of revelation. If the *sunna* was a form of revelation, it was eternal and immutable, embracing every area of individual and communal life in a fixed pattern of norms. Opponents of the *sunna* asserted that God revealed only the general principles of guidance in the Qur'an, leaving mankind to work out the details by reason themselves; hence each generation must draw its own conclusions from the Qur'an in tune with the circumstances of its day. Underlying this controversy is a contest over who possesses the proper authority to interpret the Qur'an. The traditional religious leadership (*ulama*) claimed their expertise in the *sunna* was indispensable to true Qur'anic interpretation while the more technocratic, modern educated Muslim held that his understanding of the world best enabled him to make the Qur'an relevant to modern conditions. Even secularists have attempted to justify the separation of the spheres of religion and politics by referring to the Prophet's model Medinan community as secular.

In the climate of debate stimulated by modernist ideas over a return to the sources and their relative authority, one writer, thinker and activist took the controversy on to new terrain by advocating an Islamic state. Sayyid Abu al-Ala Mawdudi (d. 1979) was born in India and moved to Pakistan after the partition of the subcontinent in 1947. Educated by his father at home and then largely by his own efforts, his career was dedicated to writing especially as editor of a religious journal, the main instrument for dissemination of his views, from 1933 until his death. He also set out his teachings in a six-volume commentary on the Qur'an; together with his many other publications, he became one of the most widely read Muslim authors of the late twentieth century. He was founder and head of a political–religious movement from 1941 for the promotion of Islamic principles. He initially opposed the creation of Pakistan as he believed it would be run along secular European lines rather than built upon an Islamic foundation. His radical movement subsequently campaigned for Pakistan to become an Islamic state subject to sacred law.

Mawdudi attempted to steer a middle course between those who rejected *hadith* altogether, and their opponents who held that *sunna* was part of revelation. He defended the necessity of the *sunna* for the stability of Islam, but demanded flexibility which would allow for adaptation to change. Simply put, he adopted the jurist's approach to Traditions by closely examining their content and relevance to a given context rather than the technique of *sunna* experts who stressed the vital importance of the good character and reputation of the transmitters of *hadith*. Critics charged that Mawdudi's method was arbitrary by introducing an excessive degree of subjectivity to *hadith* criticism leading, in effect, to an unrestrained freedom in Qur'an interpretation. Secularists dismissed his blueprint for an Islamic state and society as puritan and totalitarian. Mawdudi described it as a 'theo-democracy' in which God remained sovereign but the people elected a temporal ruler who, like everyone, was subject to the divine law. His views influenced those of his Egyptian contemporary, Sayyid Qutb (d. 1966). Both men deeply held the conviction that Muslims should conduct their entire lives according to God's law.

Traditional Islamic notions of authority are associated with the understanding of community (*umma*) as we have seen in an earlier section. The ideal triad of one God, one law and one community may have long since ceased to be historical reality, but Muslims everywhere still retain a sense of belonging to the domain of Islam where Muslims control their own affairs. European colonial encroachment seriously challenged this sense of belonging. Calls to revive Islamic unity and solidarity to withstand European pressures have been widely popular but short lived and ultimately ineffective. The modern era introduced the powerful symbol of the secular nation state as competitor to the traditional informal view of the *umma*. A response characteristic of the modern era was the creation in 1962 of the Muslim World League based in Mecca. Its purpose is to co-ordinate affairs affecting Muslims throughout the *umma*, develop missionary work and to discuss matters of Islamic jurisprudence and social welfare.

SHI'A IRAN

Iran witnessed the most spectacular development anywhere in the modern Islamic world in the 1979 revolution led by religious leader Ayatollah Khomeini. Out of the collapse of the Pahlavi regime of Muhammad Reza Shah, the Islamic Republic of Iran was born, the most evident contemporary example of 'modernity-as-tradition'.

Shi'a scholars (*mujtahids*) had gained in power throughout the nineteenth century consolidating their claim that certain experts among them could act as deputies of the last, hidden Imam who had vanished a thousand years earlier. Although some scholars chose to remain politically quietist others threw their moral authority against attempts at European intervention in Iran and the corrupt misrule of the Shahs. Between the years 1906–11 many became involved in, both for and against, the social movement known as the Constitutional Revolution. This raised the fundamental problem of whether authority rested in a humanly created law or the *shari'a* and whether sovereignty ultimately resided in the people rather than God. The same dilemmas had confronted the Sunni modernists treated above, but their responses were muted and ineffectual by comparison to those of their Shi'a counterparts. This was due to the *ulama*'s historically less assertive role before political authority and their inability to build independent financial resources coupled in more recent times with the more controlling presence of a colonial power, as in India and Egypt.

The Constitutional Revolution ended the days of the Qajar dynasty to be replaced by the rule of a military leader who styled himself Reza Shah, founder of the new Pahlavi dynasty. His aim was Western-style modernization in the spirit of the secular reforms of his neighbour Kemal Ataturk in Turkey. These involved wholesale legal changes, the importation of European criminal, civil and commercial codes and administrative centralization along French lines. Reform, however, went in tandem with political repression and a frontal attack on the influence of the *mujtahids*, policies also pursued by his son and successor Muhammad Reza Shah. Leading scholars wrote and preached against rising secularism and the growing climate of nationalism, but remained aloof from direct political combat until the early 1960s when Khomeini called for the overthrow of the Shah. He was arrested and exiled in 1963 where he remained until his triumphant return in 1979.

Figure 8.6 Worshippers on the steps of the Faisal Mosque, Islamabad, Pakistan

Khomeini's radical interpretation of one strand of Shi'a thought produced his thesis for an Islamic government. In the absence of the twelfth Imam and uncertainty as to the date of his return – and further given the present state of corruption and despair in Iran – responsibility for its affairs could not be entrusted to tyrannical rulers like the Shah. Citing passages from the Qur'an and Prophetic Traditions he concluded that only those with knowledge of the sacred law, the jurists (*mujtahids*), could regulate Muslims' daily affairs and ensure the community's salvation. In other words, the jurists would assume all the tasks the Prophet Muhammad had performed. However, Khomeini's views provoked dissension among the *mujtahids* when he proposed that only one, the leading jurist or 'the source of emulation' (i.e. himself), was owed obedience by everyone including all other jurists. Khomeini's own interpretation of supreme spiritual and political leadership survived in practice until his death in 1989, although changes were introduced into the Iranian constitution before that time.

Observers' fears, Western and Muslim alike, that Iran's example would spill over and ignite revolution in other Sunni countries have proved unfounded. Whether the regime survives and adapts or is overthrown, it nevertheless sets a challenge in one sense for all developing, modernizing Muslim countries. The challenge is to what extent and in what ways Islam will be and remain authoritative as divine guidance in the lives of Muslims into the new millennium.

GENDER AND PRESENT TRENDS

Earlier it was noted that the Muslim understanding of community and the self are closely related, even intertwined. This was illustrated by the daily prayer when Muslims around the *umma* worship in the direction of Mecca. Individually each Muslim worships alone before God while collectively prayers are offered from the community's spiritual heart, the birthplace of the Prophet. All Muslims, men and women, pray as equals in the eyes of God. Men and women congregate as equals to perform the annual pilgrimage in Mecca. The Qur'an (33:35) describes this spiritual relationship: 'Those who surrender themselves to God and are believers in the faith; who are devout, sincere, patient, humble, charitable, and chaste; who fast and keep constant remembrance of God – on these both men and women, God will bestow forgiveness and a rich reward.' Or again, God's promise to all is the same in that 'I will deny no man or woman among you the reward of their labours. You are the offspring of one another' (Q 3:195). The spiritual equality of men and women has been traditionally agreed and accepted. Questions of social equality, on the other hand, have throughout this century been a deeply contested field. The complexity of the issues is nowhere more evident than in debates on laws affecting family life and the role of women within it.

The family is the microcosm of society. A medieval view of Islamic society proposed that harmony and stability could be achieved ideally through the ruler's holding together the disparate but unequal segments of society in just and equitable balance. Likewise a harmonious and stable family can contribute to the greater good of the whole when the relationship between its parts (comprising adult males, females and children) is based upon equity. The goal was sincere while nevertheless frankly acknowledging the patriarchal dominance of the husband within the family, thereby privileging male power. Traditional legal doctrine and thought upheld a system of roles and rights in matters of marriage, divorce and parental responsibilities based on gender. Jurists agreed that the Muslim marital relationship was one of complementarity but not of equality. As recent studies of some pre- and early-modern Islamic societies have shown, the interpretative ability of the jurists and the discretion of the judges allowed them to respond flexibly and with independent judgement to concrete cases brought before them. They worked to prevent or correct abuses when male privilege threatened the harmony and stability of the family. The legal process they oversaw was one of negotiation and judicial discretion. With no conscious sense of paradox, they strove to uphold the gendered social system, but attempted to modify it in part, always from their sense of responsibility to dispense justice for all, men, women and children, under God's law.

> . . . There is more Qur'anic legislation pertaining to the establishment of justice in the context of family relationships than on any other subject. This points to the assumption implicit in much Qur'anic legislation, namely if human beings can learn to order their homes justly so that the human rights of all within its jurisdiction – children, women and men – are safeguarded, then they can also order their society and the world at large justly. In other words, the Qur'an regards the home as a microcosm of the ummah and the world community. It emphasises the importance of making it 'the abode of peace' through just living.
>
> (Riffat Hassan, feminist scholar)

Modernist thought has sought in several ways to reduce customary male privilege within the family: by arguing that the Qur'an's true intent supported monogamous marriage, not polygamy; by raising the minimum age of marriage for young men and women and thereby abolishing child marriages; by restricting the male right of divorce and increasing the grounds upon which women may sue for termination of marriage and by adjustment to the traditional laws affecting the custody of children in the event of dissolution of marriage. Profound structural changes in modern Muslim societies – among them the promotion of equal education for girls and boys and economic pressures forcing women on to the job market, male migration in search of better work opportunities – have further eroded the age-old patriarchal edifice. Positive results in practice, however, have been very unequal from one country or region to the next throughout the *umma*. Debates about the place of religion in the modern state, the very nature of that state, the place of the family in modern society and the very nature of the family, the role of men and women within life's private and public spheres – all are being conducted along a spectrum ranging from pure secularists at one end to advocates of religious purity at the other. Both extreme positions and those occupying the middle ground today and for the indefinite future seek answers to the same two questions: first, 'How does God speak?' through the Qur'an and *sunna* or by His Word alone; and second, 'Who may speak for God?' that is, who is best equipped to interpret His will and command for the modern era.

   At the present juncture it would be rash to speculate on the future course of developments within the richly diverse religious world of Islam. For example, having once judged that religions in general were past their 'sell by' dates, Western observers now write of their ubiquitous revival or resurgence. Looking back over the recent past, we might conclude that in the case of Islam, it had been there all the time although observers had not, perhaps, been alert enough to notice. The lesson, surely, is that as the future unfolds we should remain attentive to what Muslims say and do.

SUMMARY

▍ Although Islam is today spreading in Europe and North America, Muslims historically have belonged overwhelmingly to the non-Western world. The experience of 'modernity' for Muslims, therefore, was bound to differ from that experienced by Christians in the West.

▌ Islamic revivalist movements in the eighteenth century set the tone of later modernist developments in a call for a 'return to the sources' and the use of independent judgement towards them.

▌ Modernist reformers confronted European colonialism and the modern values and institutions which it brought; the debates in response throughout the twentieth century reflect historical change on the patterns of 'tradition-in-modernity' and/or 'modernist-as-tradition'.

▌ KEY TERMS

din Faith tradition, used in the Qur'an to refer to the beliefs and practices of a people.

hadith A Tradition or report, being the source for the sunna of the Prophet.

hajj Pilgrimage to Mecca once in a lifetime if a believer is able; one of the obligatory religious duties for all Muslims.

Imam Title of each of the line of twelve religious leaders of the Shi'a who are the source of authority in their community.

ijtihad The use of one's personal effort to arrive at a legal decision not found in the Qur'an or *sunna*.

jihad Internal, personal struggle in the faith; in a more general 'holy war'.

khalifa Caliph, leader of the Sunni community.

mujtahid Used among both Sunni and Shi'a communities meaning a jurist qualified to exercise his individual effort (*ijtihad*) in arriving at legal decisions.

rasul allah Messenger of God, referring to the Prophet's role as deliverer of the Qur'an.

salat One of the five daily prayers required of all Muslims.

sawm Fasting during the month of Ramadan, one of the obligatory duties for all Muslims; according to tradition, the Qur'an was revealed in this same month.

shari'a The sacred law in Sunni Islam based upon four sources, Qur'an, *sunna*, consensus and analogy; the major law schools are known as Maliki, Hanbali, Hanafi and Shafi'i.

Sufism (or **tasawwuf**) The way of inner spirituality in Islam, generally referred to as 'mysticism'.

sunna The model behaviour of the Prophet collected and recorded in *hadith* reports; one of the sources of the four Sunni schools of law together with the Qur'an, consensus and argument by analogy.

taqwa Piety, or guarding against the consequences of one's behaviour.

ulama (singular, *alim*) Learned class of scholars in religious matters.

umma Community; worldwide community of Muslims.

zakat Alms or purification tax, one of the obligatory five pillars for Muslims.

FURTHER READING

Islam and modernity

D. W. Brown: *Rethinking Tradition in Modern Islamic Thought* (Cambridge: Cambridge University Press, 1996). Excellent discussion of modern Muslim debates on authority.

J. L. Esposito (ed.): *The Oxford Encyclopedia of the Modern Islamic World* (Oxford: Oxford University Press, 1995). The leading reference work on Islam in the modern world.

G. Nonneman, T. Niblock and B. Szajkowski (eds): *Muslim Communities in Europe* (Reading: Ithaca Press, 1996). Covers communities in both Eastern and Western Europe.

F. Rahman: *Islam and Modernity: Transformation of an Intellectual Tradition* (Chicago: University of Chicago Press, 1982). The now classic work by a leading Muslim thinker.

A. Rippon: *Muslims: Their Religious Beliefs and Practices*, vol. 2: *The Contemporary Period* (London: Routledge, 1993). A useful introduction to the impact of modernity on Islam.

J. O. Voll: *Islam: Continuity and Change in the Modern World* (Syracuse, NY: Syracuse University Press, 1994). A good general introduction which attempts universal coverage of Islam from the eighteenth century.

Politics and law

D. F. Eickelman and J. Piscatori: *Muslim Politics* (Princeton, NJ: Princeton University Press, 1996). Explores how the politics of Islam unfold in the daily lives of Muslims.

H. B. Hallaq: *A History of Islamic Legal Theories: An Introduction to Sunni Usual al-fiqh* (Cambridge: Cambridge University Press, 1997). Contains a very good chapter on modern developments.

M. Z. Husain: *Global Islamic Politics* (New York, NY: HarperCollins, 1995). Deals with various categories of Muslim revivalists.

Gender

C. F. El-Solh and J. Mabro (eds): *Muslim Women's Choices: Religious Belief and Social Reality* (Oxford: Berg, 1994). Presents a cross-cultural perspective of Muslim women's experiences and choices.

Mai Yamani (ed.): *Feminism and Islam: Legal and Literary Perspectives* (Reading: Ithaca Press, 1996). On Muslim women and their efforts to improve their status through a re-reading of their rights in Islamic law.

Religion in Africa

Charles Gore

▌ INTRODUCTION

This chapter considers African religious traditions and transformations in modern sub-Saharan Africa. Comprising a land mass more than three times the size of the US, this region south of the geographical barrier of the Sahara desert is characterized by a great diversity of religious ideas and practice found in a wide range of societies. There is also the major presence of the two world religions, Christianity and Islam, which both have long historical trajectories in certain areas of sub-Saharan Africa. These world religions are often portrayed as part of the modern world – especially as the twentieth century has seen mass conversion to these religions, associated initially with the changing social conditions produced by colonialism. Localized forms of religious expression are often distinguished as 'traditional' or 'indigenous' in contrast to these world religions to reflect their claims to precolonial antecedents and legitimation (despite the fact that some may have originated in the twentieth century). These indigenous religions include a complex and variable range of social phenomena which do not easily match or correspond to Western institutional and conceptual categories of the religious, political, economic, judicial and social. Whilst the focus of this chapter is on indigenous religions their range in Africa is such that it will only be possible to consider a few salient regional examples that illustrate major themes, issues and debates.

According to the provisional World Bank African Development Indicators (1998/1999) in 1997 sub-Saharan Africa had a total population of 613.71 million. Both Islamic and Christian missionaries make competing claims as to the numbers of adherents in sub-Saharan Africa, and for this reason such

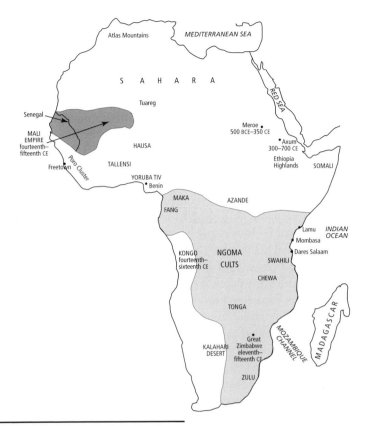

Figure 9.1 Map showing distribution of African religions

figures are unreliable. The numerically similar totals that they claim may suggest that the total population is divided, at least nominally, into approximately equal numbers affiliated to Islam and Christianity with a very small number asserting sole affiliation to indigenous or traditional religions. This approximate ratio gives an insight into affiliations to these two world religions as membership is exclusive between one or the other. A range of other world religions also have adherents in sub-Saharan Africa including Bhuddism, Rosicrucianism, various forms of Hinduism, Scientology and others. Although not significant in overall numbers of adherents, some of their iconography, ideas and practices can have a more widespread impact. A far more complex picture emerges in relation to indigenous religious ideas and practices, since these often co-exist, complement or overlap with an affiliation to one of the world religions. Thus an individual can be characterized as participating in both a world religion and in traditional forms of worship, depending on the various particular social contexts in which an individual finds him- or herself.

'Modernity' is a much debated term in conceptualizing social change as well as economic development, but it is usually linked to the emergence of the European nation state and its bureaucratic infrastructures as a political institution. For this reason with regard to sub-Saharan Africa, modernity can be related to the colonial annexation of territories imposed on Africa by the competing European nation states. These divisions were outlined in the Berlin conference of 1884–5 at which European nations agreed between themselves to separate spheres of influence in claiming such territories. However, it needs to be noted that many African economies were already linked to Europe through prior mercantile capitalism in complex ways, the most tragic and inhumane example being the mass trafficking of Africans across the Atlantic ocean.

These colonial partitions engendered radical changes in political organization, territorial demarcations and the development of social and economic infrastructures that articulated new but unequal linkages with the European colonizing nations, together with the imposition of bureaucracies that managed these new territorial units. An imperialist desire for monopolistic economic control and increased exploitation of commodity resources (required by the manufacturing processes of European industrialization) allied to the ideological justifications of spreading Christianity and European civilization fostered an intense competition between the European powers. This colonial partitioning of Africa is commonly described as 'the scramble for Africa' and took place in the last two decades of the nineteenth century.

Once territory was seized – despite armed resistance in many instances – the major administrative structures of the European colonies were gradually set in place. These developed differently in relation to territories used for permanent European settlement, which allowed for direct control of all resources, and territories that were not settled by Europeans. Large areas of Africa, particularly in West and equatorial Africa where environmental health conditions were seen as particularly inimical to Europeans, were not utilized for settlement, and in these a policy of rule through existing African political hierarchies was developed – most explicitly by the British in the colonial doctrine of indirect rule codified by *Lord Lugard* and published in the 1920s. However, European administrators lacked detailed knowledge of precolonial forms of governance, were subject to manipulation by competing local African interests, and imposed hierarchial colonial orderings that suited their imperialist and bureaucratic interests rather than corresponded to precolonial conditions.

Although territorial partition of Africa had for the most part been completed by 1904 (with some readjustments at the end of the First World War), consolidation was uneven and varied greatly between colonies. In general terms, colonialism centred on the expropriation of labour and land in order to extract the economic resources of the colonies. In more concrete terms, colonialism involved the introduction of standardized currencies regulated by the colonizing nation; development of new transport links; and the emergence of new or expanded urban centres that attracted migrants from rural areas. It was accompanied by the emergence of new social groups and formations equipped with the skills required by the colonial enterprise. Although locked into unequal political, economic and cultural relations with the dominant colonizing nation, these relations also linked the African colonies to the processes of modernity, albeit along trajectories specific to African contexts.

The 1940s saw the rise of nationalist movements in Africa, and decolonization commenced with Ghana (the former Gold Coast) gaining independence in 1957. However, in many of the settler colonies throughout Africa the tide of nationalism was resisted, often encouraging armed struggle such as the Mau Mau uprising in Kenya against the British in 1952. Independence was conceded to most colonies by the mid-1960s, although the Portuguese colonies remained obdurate until the mid-1970s. Zimbabwe and South Africa remained notable exceptions shored up by their large European settler communities, and economically through their greater integration into the world economy – here independence was not gained until 1980 and 1994 respectively. With decolonization came an increased drive for modernization as planned programmes of national economic self-development were implemented in many of the newly independent African nation states. However the economies of these new nation states were still structured by their origins as dependent colonies fashioned to extract the maximum resources for the benefit of the colonizer. One consequence has been the perpetuation of often unequal economic relations to the world markets as part of the postcolonial experience.

This chapter opens with a look at the three main forms of religion present in sub-Saharan Africa: indigenous religions, Islam and Christianity. It also considers the significance of the Western missionary movement in Africa. In its central sections it explores the most salient features of indigenous African religions in the modern world, highlighting how indigenous religious beliefs and practices have been transformed or shaped by the impact of modernity. The chapter then considers the place of Islam and Christianity in modern sub-Saharan Africa and the ways in which both religions have been aligned to their African contexts, before turning to a consideration of recent changes and innovations in religion in Africa.

SOURCES AND RESOURCES

Indigenous religions

In the localized forms of indigenous religion found in sub-Saharan Africa, there is an emphasis on participation in religious or ritual activities which usually precedes the acquisition of religious knowledge. The specialist esoteric religious or ritual knowledge is often restricted in access and gained only by induction into long apprenticeship or initiation. In contrast to the world religions which are exclusive in terms of affiliation (one cannot be a Christian and a Muslim), indigenous religious frameworks are often open ended, allowing individuals to acquire and accumulate various and different forms of religious experience according to need and inclination. Moreover, few indigenous religions separate out material from spiritual experience (unlike Judaeo-Christian traditions which often draw a contrast between the material and spiritual). In indigenous African religions the two spheres are considered interdependent, such that events in the material world are predicated on relations to the spiritual world – but open to individual, and sometimes contested, interpretation. As a consequence much indigenous or traditional religion centres on the well-being of the community or social grouping through explanation, prediction and control of events. Although it is possible to extrapolate coherent or systemized doctrines and cosmologies of a particular community (such as the classic example of the anthropologist *Griaule*'s exploration of the religion and cosmology of the Dogon peoples of Mali in conversations with Ogonmetilli [1965]), this emphasis on the experiential means that such abstractions or rationalizations of cosmology are not necessarily shared by all members of community (although there may be the insightful reflections and interpretations of a particular individual). Analysis which gives undue emphasis to such systemized abstraction overlooks the dynamism, creativity and innovation available within African religious processes.

Many of these localized indigenous forms of religion and ritual rely on oral traditions, which makes it difficult to chart their historical trajectories and the ways in which change has taken place. But this feature gives much flexibility in adapting to changing social circumstances, migration and diverse physical environments. Religious ideas and practice can vary from adjacent community to community, but others spread over wide geographical areas and cross social, linguistic and ethnic divides. Similarly, even where religious ideas differ between communities and different societies, many of the assumptions upon which they are based are shared over wider regional areas. What varies is the way in which they are articulated within different societies that can range in organization from kingdoms and empires to petty chiefdoms to less hierarchical and non-centralized communities. But a defining characteristic in the twentieth and early twenty-first centuries is that all these different sociopolitical formations are now situated within postcolonial African nation states with their hegemonic bureaucratic infrastructures.

Islam and Christianity

Historically the geographical barrier of the Sahara did not preclude the diffusion of the world religions of Christianity and Islam. Islam spread southward along the trans-Saharan trade routes from the eighth century CE onwards, with conversion taking place on a reciprocal basis between trading partners (a process whereby an individual conversion to Islam occurred as a personal choice within a primarily non-Islamic society as a means of securing trust and economic credit with an external Islamic trading partner). But by the fourteenth century CE the rulers of the empire of Mali in the northern savannah (that stretched between the upper regions of the rivers Senegal and Niger) had embraced Islam. A record of a stay in Cairo in the fourteenth century CE during a pilgrimage to Mecca by one of its greatest rulers, Mansa Musa, describes that his lavish expenditure in gold caused a devaluation of money at that time. Christianity spread from lower Egypt reaching Meroe and Axum by the fourth century CE, and then to Ethiopia in East Africa where it has maintained a historical continuity up to the present day with the Orthodox Ethiopian Coptic church as the official state religion. Christianity was also disseminated by European mercantile traders and missionaries from the fifteenth century CE onwards; they followed the Atlantic sea routes along the West and Central African coast, occasionally gaining an insecure and temporary purchase in some societies. A notable success was the adoption of Christianity by Mbanza Kongo, the ruler of the Kongo kingdom in Central Africa in 1491, along with many of his elite followers. Despite the political disintegration of the kingdom in 1665 and the disappearance of Christianity by the beginning of the eighteenth century CE, Christian iconographic elements such as the crucifix were incorporated into local religious practices, and are evident up to the present day.

Along the East African coast there arose a series of trading centres incorporating a mix of Arabian, African and Indian populations that linked Eastern Africa to the Indian Ocean with the importation of iron goods in exchange for gum, spices, ivory and horn. These trading centres became a conduit for the spread of Islam from the eighth century CE onwards resulting in the emergence of a relatively homogenous mercantile coastal corridor up to the present day (that did not preclude political and social diversity). By the eleventh century CE this corridor stretched from the Somali coast in the north to what is now Mozambique in the south, having in common shared social and economic ties underpinned by Islam and the Swahili language.

The missionary impact

Though Islam and Christianity have had a longstanding presence in certain areas of sub-Saharan Africa, the nineteenth and twentieth centuries have seen an intensification and expansion of their influence. In relation to Christianity this expansion was initiated by European missionary activity. In 1787 a Christian settlement was established on the coast of Sierra Leone for Africans liberated from slavery as well as, among others, loyalists of Afro-American descent who had fought on the side of the British in the American War of Independence. This founding of a Christian settlement inspired the modern missionary movement to evangelize among the indigenous peoples of sub-Saharan Africa. Various mission societies were set up by different Christian denominations including the prominent Protestant *Church Missionary Society (CMS)*. Christian missionaries (who were prominent in the successful drive to abolish the slave trade in the nineteenth century) were active along the coast of Africa throughout the nineteenth century following in the footsteps of the coastal trading enclaves of the European nations that had developed in their pursuit of trade for commodities from the interior such as rubber and palm oil. Much of the programme of conversion of peoples of the interior was left to African missionaries –

the most notable example being Bishop Samuel Ajai Crowther of the CMS who travelled extensively into the interior of what is now southern Nigeria to proselytize. At least initially, successful conversion mainly began with the marginalized or outcast in indigenous societies.

In many ways colonialism and mission went hand in hand. In the drive for conversion missions imparted education as part of the Christianizing process. Education offered many useful skills relevant to the colonial state which gave an added momentum to conversion to Christianity. However the concomitant hierarchial imperialist ideologies that accompanied the establishment of the colonies also saw the replacement and subordination of African ministers by European missionaries as Christianity was institutionalized as a religion allied to the colonial state. In time this exclusion would precipitate the establishment of independent African churches headed by Africans. Such churches attracted congregations drawn from the growing urbanized African populace which had acquired literacy and the attendant clerical skills required by colonial bureaucracies. These congregations embraced the modernity expressed in the innovation of Christian religion, while at the same time rejecting European churches and developing Africanized forms of worship which subsequently dispersed to rural populations.

However the relationship between mission and colonialism was often more complex. The agendas of the European missionaries who wished to recreate African society within the framework of the Christian faith did not always coincide with the colonial project. The high costs of imposing martial law on African societies meant that colonial administrators in the interests of civil order, where expedient, supported indigenous political hierarchies such as those based around the institution of sacred kingship. In effect colonial administrations utilized and co-opted such indigenous institutions to govern even where the latter were legitimated by indigenous religious ideas and practices abhorred by missionaries. But other religious leaders, not recognized by the colonial authorities as part of traditional kingship or chieftaincy, were carefully monitored for the threats they posed to civil order. In more extreme instances they were dealt with through military intervention (as, for example, in the British suppression of the charismatic prophets of the Nuer indigenous religion in the Sudan during the 1920s). Similarly, the emergence of African-led Christian and Islamic institutions which successfully recruited through mass conversions was also closely monitored. Missionaries, particularly from non-conformist denominations, were sometimes placed in an ambiguous position in relation to colonial authority when they defended the interests of their converted communities against the depredations of state or other opportunist exploitation. A striking example is found in the brutal atrocities and exploitation of populations in the Congo Free State in Central Africa controlled as a personal dominion by King Leopold of the Belgians: these abuses were highlighted in print by an Afro-American Presbyterian missionary, William Sheppard, from 1900 onwards. Their exposure would ultimately precipitate a Congo mass reform movement in Europe and its handover to the Belgian state in 1908.

Further evidence of the important link between Christianity and colonialism is provided by the fact that the colonized in some areas, such as Senegal or in large parts of the Yoruba-speaking areas of Nigeria, adopted Islam as a means to assert alternative forms of identity. Islam provided access to different resources of moral power and legitimacy, that had long been a component of their societies, and challenged the coercive colonial hierarchies of secular power and authority. In colonies where rapid mass conversion to Islam took place the colonial authorities often discouraged Christian missions as a direct threat to civil order. Indeed the Islamic emirates which developed in the Hausa-speaking areas of what is now northern Nigeria in the first half of the nineteenth century as a result of the great reformist movement (which sought to purify Islam of elements deemed pagan), led by the Islamic cleric Sheik Uthman Dan Fodio, were held up by Lord Lugard and the British colonial administrations as an ideal exemplar of an indigenous political hierarchy that the colonial indirect rule policy could utilize.

Islam and Christianity continued to make inroads in the conversion of the populations of Africa in the twentieth century, penetrating all areas of the continent. Islamic and Christian missionaries generally sought to undermine local indigenous religious ideas and practices and aspired to provide universal religious frameworks for adherents in their place. In their conjunction with the particular historical trajectories of the colonial enterprise their effect was also to help implement major social reorderings. In the postcolonial order they became key institutions within the new secular nation states of sub-Saharan Africa. None of these developments, however, have meant the disappearance or exclusion of localized forms of 'indigenous' or 'traditional' religious experience, nor resulted in the syncretization or merging of local indigenous beliefs with the world religions. Much more common has been a compartmentalized positioning of individuals in relation to both indigenous religions and Christianity or Islam. This overlapping accommodation and dialectic with the world religions underlines the dynamic and creative qualities of religious experience in Africa.

INTERACTIONS WITH MODERNITY

The modern period in sub-Saharan Africa has witnessed the transition from precolonial forms of social organization to their subjection within colonial structures of domination, to the emergence of autonomous nation states. Although independence has been achieved, these nation states are still locked into capitalist economic formations shaped by the needs of Western societies and their transnational corporations. As a result sub-Saharan nation states are often unable to control the economic flows out of their territories, and any consequent political instability can engender conflict and political violence as well as the accumulation of debt in relation to the international banking community. Such factors in turn contribute to a weakening of the state and its bureaucracies as the principal means of organization of these nation states. However this retreat or transformation of the state provides a postcolonial space for the emergence and shaping of alternative and multiple identities that draw on the diverse histories and cultural resources available from the post-independent, colonial and precolonial periods. Religious repertoires in sub-Saharan Africa establish continuities with the past as well as positioning themselves as part of the processes of African modernity.

In considering such religious repertoires here, themes and topics are selected to highlight key characteristics associated with 'indigenous' or 'traditional' religious ideas and practice – although it needs to be noted that many of these are innovative in the twentieth century and do not necessarily have the historical continuity with precolonial Africa that they may claim, even though seemingly legitimated in this way as 'traditional'. Exploration of these themes begins in relation to the individual and kinship, and then moves outwards to take account of the social orderings of institutions as they articulate and shape relations of power and authority within contemporary society. Account is also taken of some of the major studies and debates relating to the interpretation of these phenomena.

Ancestors, elders and community

In many African societies conceptualizations of the ancestors play an important role in structuring religious experience and social life – so much so that African kin groups are sometimes described as communities of both the living and the dead. Ancestors are distinguished from other cults of the dead by virtue of being named forebears with specific genealogical relations to a particular grouping of descendants which is mediated by collective rituals. They can reward and punish the living lineage members, a power that underpins the authority of elders who ritually mediate on behalf of the ancestors through their closer proximity in terms of age.

The role of the ancestor can vary considerably from society to society. One example of the way in which ancestor worship relates to social organization comes from the classic study by Fortes (1987) of the Tallensi-speaking people of northern Ghana. Their society is organized without forms of centralized authority, and they practise subsistence farming focused on a family unit of a father, his wives and the adult sons and their wives. These family units are organized into *patrilineages* descended from a single common ancestor. There is little material wealth and consequently little differentiation in material terms between one individual and another. However ritual and jural authority is vested in the men who have the status of fathers and during their lifetime their offspring have no independent economic, jural or ritual rights except through the father. The relationship between father and sons is marked out with ritual prescriptions of behaviour that ameliorate the conflictual tensions between the generations, which also tend to increase as the sons marry and become fathers themselves. Fortes observes that in Tallensi society all events are dependent on the ancestors to whom shrines are established and suggests that the ancestors encapsulate an idiom of 'parental' relations of absolute authority over the succeeding generations which can only be accessed through the father.

However this is mediated by the capability of individuals to discover through divination and dreams knowledge of their prenatal destiny, which is given by special relations with particular groupings of ancestors unique to each individual. Prior to birth the individual appears before a remote supreme being to choose certain ancestors who provide guidance throughout life. Fortes suggests that this plurality of ancestors, both in their absolute relations of power and in their individuated configurations, provides complex and resourceful means for individuals in Tallensi society to negotiate success and adversity as they pass through the succession of rigidly ascribed statuses during the course of their lives.

This theoretical model was taken up by Horton (1983) who develops it further to argue that there is a correlation between the spiritual agencies available in a society and the forms of social organization of that society. He compares the near exclusive control of the ancestors in Tallensi society (linked to its rigidly ascribed statuses) with the wider range of roles available in other societies, including the Kalabari of the Nigerian riverine delta where he conducted most of his research. Kalabari society depends on fishing along the swamps and creeks which are accessible to all male members within a community's domain. In each community there are a variable number of lineages of differing size organized on the basis of a dual system of marriage, whereby high bride price affiliates the children to the father's group, while low bride price affiliates the children to the mother's group. As a consequence descent can be traced through the male and female lines from a lineage founder. However the different lineage founders within the community are considered to be unrelated so that village unity is organized through territorial isolation, political autonomy, an age-grade system that shapes collective identity, and a shared cultural repertoire centring most notably around masquerade displays (Horton, 1963).

Some settlements such as New Calabar have been historically expanded as a series of canoe houses. These consisted of closely knit trading and war canoe teams that ruled through an elected head who was often comparatively young and chosen for his abilities in trade and war. The heterogeneous diversity of recruited members (some were slaves purchased from the Atlantic trade) of these expanded houses was overcome by creating fictitious descent that represented its organization in notional terms of a lineage with the founding ancestor. As houses expanded, successful and ambitious traders could apply to establish their own canoe houses. In Kalabari society, whether fishing settlement or city state, there was and is considerable scope for self-advancement of individuals by using an advantageous choice of economic trading partners and networks. Women are able to trade equally successfully and, although not able to intervene directly in the public political arena, gain much influence through the profession of divining in which they are possessed by water spirits.

The individual in Kalabari society can thus choose among a diversity of roles and routes to economic and social success which, according to Horton are represented in the spiritual agencies available. In Kalabari society there are both the founding heroes of the community that protect the entire community, as well as the founding ancestors who sustain the unity and prosperity of their particular lineages. These ancestors are able to reward harmonious living with success, and punish disruptive conduct that endangers the lineage with sickness and misfortune. However, in Kalabari society individuals can also draw on the powers of the water spirits that reside in the creeks who bring economic success in return for human devotion. These water spirits are sited in the natural world rather than in the human community (such as the ancestors and founding heroes), and engage in particular relations with an individual. As among the Tallensi, Kalabari individuals are considered to appear before a remote supreme being prior to birth to make prenatal choices. Here, however, there are more options open to individuals from which to choose a particular course for their future life with a greater variety of spiritual agencies to assist them. Moreover, if they fail in their personal life there are rituals through which they may revoke their choices and replace them with a new set of goals. In contrast to the Tallensi where only men choose guardian ancestors, both men and women in Kalabari society choose and develop relationships with spiritual agencies emphasizing the wider spectrum of social and economic possibilities available for both genders. These spiritual agencies, rooted in the social world and also the natural world, are thereby linked to the achieved statuses of Kalabari society where individual initiative, skill and effort play a crucial role in their successful attainment.

In the late twentieth century such conceptualizations of the ancestors still form an important part of individual and collective identity. They define and validate particular corporate kingroups who are obligated to mutual support (with the threat of punitive sanctions from the ancestors) in relation to wider social groupings. The often predatory nature of the nation state in the late twentieth century with little or no provision of social security for its citizens underlines the necessity of this mutual support provided by the kingroup (however constituted) in order to guarantee personal security. The delineation of the ancestors within the social environment also contributes to collective claims to ownership of land in precedence to later incoming migrant groups and is often utilized in maintaining particular ethnic identities. Furthermore, claims to ownership of land, buttressed by ancestral claims, often shape and mediate the ways in which the nation state regulates and distributes land resources in relation to local communities (a contentious political and social issue in resource rich areas – as is demonstrated in the civil disturbances of the oil bearing regions of the delta areas of Nigeria in the 1990s).

Masquerade, spirits and embodiment

In many societies in Africa relations between the living and the spirit world are enacted through masquerade performance. Here relations with the spirit world are embodied in the masquerade figures. Masquerade performances usually, but not always, entail some form of masking and, through whatever means, establish a social or dramatic distancing of the masquerade performer. A convention of most masquerades is that the identity of the individual performer remains secret and participation in masquerade usually requires access to restricted or initiated knowledge that marks out the boundaries of a collective membership.

Throughout most of sub-Saharan Africa masquerade is differentiated on the basis of gender, being a male organization from which women are excluded – although representations of women often appear among the masquerade forms. The masquerader is recognized as an embodied agency from the spirit world vested with the appropriate social, political and spiritual powers. Masquerade often enacts a collective as opposed to personal authority within the community that can be used beneficially or punitively. But in some contexts it is also used to criticize those in power without the fear of retribution. This is possible because such commentaries emanate from the collective authority of the spirit world and not from identified, and therefore vulnerable, individuals in the community.

One of the most well-known masquerade complexes is the Poro secret society cluster which is found in various forms throughout the petty chiefdoms of Sierra Leone and Liberia. All boys are taken into the bush to be initiated at puberty by the great spirit Poro, who originated deep in the forest and is assisted by lesser spirits who appear masked among the community (unlike the spirit of Poro which is only heard and always remains unseen). The boys spend two or three years in the bush removed from village life (although this period of time has now become greatly reduced to coincide with public holiday periods). During this seclusion they are circumcised and instructed into the social skills necessary for adult life. At the end of the initiation period they return to the community as newly born male adults with a new status within their households. The Poro society as an institution structures social life in the community but also provides arbitration in disputes and regulates trade both within and between communities and chiefdoms. It provided a focus of resistance to the imposition of colonial rule and facilitated the organization of widespread opposition to its regimes.

This Poro masquerade cluster is complemented by the Sande secret society which initiates girls into women's life such that there is an alternating cycle of ritual time constituted between the Poro and the Sande. For three or four years the Poro society manages the initiation of all the boys of appropriate age and publicly regulates the community and land. However after an interval the Poro society formally withdraws into the forest and the women's Sande society emerges to initiate the young girls who are removed to the Sande forest groves. It similarly regulates the community and land, albeit for a somewhat shorter period of time of about two or three years. The Sande secret society to which all women belong originates through a mythological charter between the first founders of the community and the autochthonous nature spirits whose land they occupied. This co-operation (which guarantees the fertility of the land and the safety of the community) was secured by ritual marriage of women of the founding lineages to these nature spirits. The members of each Sande lodge are characterized as the wives of their particular nature spirit. These spirits appear as masquerades in the community to enforce the social relations with which they are concerned. Exceptionally these masquerades are performed by women, both masked and unmasked, in contrast to most other areas of Africa (d'Azvedo, 1973). Gender differentiation is still assiduously maintained but in this context it is the men who are excluded from women's affairs.

Masquerades and other local cultural forms such as art and dance have been adopted by the nation state and utilized in secularized presentations in national and regional sponsored festivals that outline local variations of identity within the processes of nation building. They have also been appropriated for international presentation of 'African Heritage' in national sponsored projects of tourism. However the forms of legitimacy and power embedded in the constitution of masquerade ideas and practice have also been, on occasion, more overtly co-opted to support the repressive politics of authoritarian regimes. In Malawi in Central Africa the one-party regime of the Malawi Congress Party (MCP) led by life President Dr H. Kamuzu Banda (which lasted some three decades until the beginning of the 1990s) utilized Nyau, the male secret society of the Chewa-speaking people to political ends (Englund, 1996). The Nyau society and its masquerades which feature public displays of animal masquerades within the rural communities had dispersed and been adopted by the other ethnic groupings throughout Malawi. At national level the Nyau was used as a cultural display during public political rallies and was directly associated with President Banda as a Chewa-speaker. In the one-party state of President Banda party membership was mandatory and fees were collected by the Malawi Young Pioneers, a paramilitary arm of the MCP. Where resistance was encountered fees would be collected by Nyau masqueraders in the middle of the night. The significance of the Nyau spirits as predatory animals and their role in mortuary rituals inspired fear in villagers. Nyau was used both in the coercion of party membership and also as a means of enforcing attendance at local and regional political rallies where, prior to commencement, Nyau masqueraders would round up the community to ensure full attendance and participation. The legitimacy and authority of the MCP were thus embedded at village level both in the overt politics of the party and also in the shared religious traditions of the rural communities where the political hierarchies of the one-party system were expressed in local idioms of power, even though the majority of the community were Christian. Though Christianity is dominant throughout Malawi, active membership of Nyau masquerade does not exclude participants from practising as Christians.

Masquerade can have a more ambiguous relationship with the governing elite as Nunley (1987) shows in his research on the Ode-lay masquerades of Freetown, Sierra Leone. Freetown has a diversity of social groupings in part due to its initial founding as a settlement for liberated slaves as well as a coastal cosmopolitan metropole. Many of these social groups have their own forms of masquerade and at the appropriate times these parade about the town in procession. These include many forms of Yoruba masquerade introduced by resettled Yoruba speakers such as Egungun ancestral masquerades and the hunting societies, as well as (among others) Poro, Sande and Kono masquerades introduced from the interior of the country. However there also developed urban forms of masquerade from the 1950s and 1960s onwards known as Ode-lay. These are organized along the lines of Egungun masquerade and Yoruba hunting societies that provide access to the powerful spiritual and medicinal protections of the society. Membership is drawn from the marginal and socially excluded youth within the urban environment.

Figure 9.2 Youth masquerade at Enugu, a twentieth-century town in eastern Nigeria, a New Year and Easter ceremony where youths learn contemporary traditions of urban masquerading

Members of Ode-lay societies often illegally occupy squatting settlements and sometimes engage in criminal and semi-criminal activities, including drugs and robbery. Their masquerades draw on local and international sources such as urban gang identities (reflected in their names, such as Bloody Mary or Firestone). They appropriate selective tenets and music of Rastafarianism in order to fashion an urban and cosmopolitan identity that cuts across the markers of ethnic identity with which the more 'indigenous' masquerades are associated. The Ode-lay masquerades adopt contemporary forms and materials in their physical appearance, although they still draw on the aesthetic and religious conventions of masquerade. They use an eclectic repertoire of imagery drawn from futuristic films (such as in the robot masquerade) as well as international films from Hollywood and India. They also use modern materials (including gas masks) with which to construct the masquerades, while vinyl records are included among the sacrifices made at the beginning of masquerade processions. These youthful urban societies are often sponsored by members of the political elite as a means of identifying with particular areas and their constituencies. But the sometimes violent conflicts that occur between rival societies during parades – as well as their marginality and association with criminality outside the bounds of society – has led to their public banning within Freetown.

The civil war that started in Sierra Leone in 1991 curtailed much of the urban masquerades. However insurgents in their abduction of boys and girls to military training camps in inaccessible forest continue to utilize concepts of initiation during the transition from childhood to adult maturity (when the Poro and Sande masquerade seizes the uninitiated child). The child disappears into the forest to re-emerge with a new social identity as part of a rebel army, often wearing eclectic adornment associated with masquerade and its associated protective medicines which highlight their new means of enforcement over civil populations.

Spirit possession and cults of affliction

It is not only through the effacement or transformation of an individual's identity in masquerade that spiritual agencies are made visible in the social world. In many parts of Africa individuals develop personal relations with such agencies and are possessed directly by them. Among the Tonga in the Zambesi valley in Zambia authoritative spirits, Basungu, are often the deceased important male members of the community who possess men. These chosen individuals become prophetic diviners and rainmakers able to mediate between the spirit and material worlds and their shrines become an important focus of community worship. Tonga women who are constrained within a domestic environment, on the other hand, are possessed by marginal non-ancestral spirits known as Masabe who demand and are satisfied with gifts bought out of the wages of their husbands from a cash economy from which they are excluded access (Lewis, 1971).

However in other societies, such as among the Yoruba- and Edo-speaking peoples in southern Nigeria, a pantheon of deities possess male and female devotees of their respective cults. In Benin City individuals can set up shrines to particular deities who intervene in their lives through initiation, with each deity having its own distinctive set of knowledge that remains exclusive to those that have initiated (Gore, 1998). Some charismatic individuals are recognized to have particularly strong relations with the deities, and develop large public followings of devotees and clients. They are possessed by the deities who are encouraged to manifest through music and dance in the course of worship. During such possession devotees and clients are able to consult directly with the deity who is able to advise them in speech or song about the difficulties they face. These public performances also provide the possibility for the recruitment of new devotees; on occasion uninitiated onlookers will be possessed by a particular deity under the guidance of the chief priest or priestess, indicating which deity has possessed them through the form of dancing and music to which they respond. Onlookers who become possessed are encouraged to initiate, as the deities are considered to be calling them.

There is a reciprocal relationship between the deity and devotee such that the devotional impulse to glorify the deity increases its fame which in turn reflects back on the devotee. Moreover a devotee can acquire different deities and, if one proves inadequate, is able rely on others. This empirical validation or rejection enables innovation and creativity in the range of possibilities of religious experience. These priests and priestesses in Benin City have developed their personal shrines through their own charismatic capabilities. The expanding population of Benin City combined with the cash economy in the twentieth century enable these priests and priestesses to sustain their full-time activities with the establishment of large-scale followings that support them economically. Moreover the economic independence provided by the urban cash economy has created a framework in which women, who in precolonial times were excluded on account of their gender from many areas of religious ritual, have been able to take up roles as full-time priestesses and assert their religious authority underpinned by the legitimacy provided through possession by the deities.

Figure 9.3 Two women who have just started their initiation into the deity Olokun, god of the sea and fertility, in Benin City, Nigeria

Possession often has political significance. In pre-liberated Zimbabwe, for example, the royal ancestral spirit mediums associated with particular regions of the country played an important role in the liberation struggle conducted from neighbouring countries (Lan, 1985). Liberation forces moving through regions of Zimbabwe had to contend with both the security forces and the political difficulties of relating to areas with which they had no social or ethnic connection. Regional spirit mediums in Zimbabwe publicly recognized the liberation fighters as spiritually legitimated representatives of the ancestral owners of the land. They conferred various ritual injunctions on the fighters within the borders of Zimbabwe including abstinence from sex, prohibitions on the killing of wild animals in the forest, and the eating of certain foods. These marked them out as contemporary agents of the ancestors who therefore must be supported by rural communities rather than excluded as unknown strangers. This made a powerful contrast with the European colonizers who had taken most of the land but had none of the legitimacy that derived from the moral order which these spirit mediums underpinned. The liberation forces successfully positioned themselves as part of this moral order to mobilize support from local populations. In the independence parades at the end of the war the ancestors who had helped secure victory in the liberation struggle were displayed prominently in banners and referred to in political speeches. The legitimacy of these ancestors was now mobilized to endorse the new nation state of Zimbabwe.

Personal adversity or misfortune experienced by the individual is often interpreted in terms of the intervention of deceased human or spiritual agencies. One means of resolving such adversity is through induction of the afflicted individual into cults that venerate the particular spiritual agency involved. These interpretations of affliction and healing situated within frameworks of cults, specialized communities and networks, usually accompanied by a therapeutic dimension, are found throughout Central, Southern and Eastern Africa. In seeking to understand their range and variation, this categorization of 'cults of affliction and healing' is used by Janzen (1994) as a model for extended regional and historical comparisons. Many, but not all, of these cults are known as *Ngoma*, a linguistic term distributed from the Atlantic coast of Angola and the Congo to the Indian Ocean coast of Kenya and Tanzania. Ngoma describes the single membrane wooden drum which is a central feature in the music and dance in such rituals, often in conjunction with other musical instruments (although in Southern Africa Ngoma refers exclusively to the singing, divining and the diviners of these cults). Cults of affliction provide a therapeutic redress for afflicted individuals through which social situations are mediated and notions of personhood reconstituted by the ritual processes of affiliation to the cult, often entailing such individuals becoming diviners and healers themselves. In colonial and postcolonial Africa these cults with their emphasis on redressing affliction and adversity have proliferated as sources of revitalization and renewal within the constraints of the nation state, which has tended to limit their regional spread through the maintenance of national boundaries.

Sacred kingship

In many kingdoms in Africa the principles underlying relations between the living and the ancestors underpin the constitution of kingship where the ruler's ancestors represent the ancestors of the entire kingdom. In South Africa with the emergence of the Zulu kingdoms in the eighteenth century, it was through the king and his ancestors that all the Zulu-speaking members of the kingdom were united as members of a single polity. The king officiated on behalf of his ancestors at the great first fruit ceremonies and in war rites or during exceptional circumstances such as at the advent of drought. He possessed important exclusive therapeutic medicines and controlled all the rainmakers of the kingdom.

Other parts of Africa developed similar forms of ritual–political authority. Benin City is the urban centre of the Edo kingdom in southern Nigeria ruled by the Oba of Benin, the descendant of a dynasty dating from at least the fourteenth century onwards. In the Edo kingdom rights of inheritance pass from father to eldest son upon the accomplishment of funerary rites during which the son incorporates his father into the ancestral shrine. The ritual relations of the Oba of Benin to the spirit world are exercised not only on behalf of his family but also for all the various groupings of the kingdom and so encapsulate the relationship between the living and the dead as defined within the idiom of the family and its ancestors.

The king's ritual and political authority are based not only on his office and the institutions that underpin it but are also vested in the actual person of the Oba. He is regarded as the reincarnation of previous Obas and embodied with their spiritual attributes. During the coronation the new Oba undergoes a series of ritual events which redefine him as a unique and singular social category separate from all his subjects (including his close kin) over whom he has the sole power of life and death. Similarly, in the many court rituals that surround the Oba of Benin his actual person is ritually sanctified

Figure 9.4 Oba of Benin attended by a retinue of chiefs and priests at the festival of Igue where the person of the Oba is renewed for the coming year, thereby renewing the kingdom also

as the embodiment of the kingdom – as can be seen during the annual festival of Igue when his body is physically fortified with medicines (during the ceremony an attempt is made to ritually shake him but he remains immobile demonstrating the strength of the kingdom). However in the twentieth century after an interregnum of seventeen years until 1914 the Obaship has been articulated within the infrastructures of first the British colonial administration and then the Nigerian nation state. It acquired a strategic importance during the years of military rule of the 1980s and 1990s as the sole representative of legitimate rule drawing on precolonial traditions and endorsed by the local Edo-speaking population. The military regime ensured that its actions were publicly endorsed by traditional rulers such as the Oba of Benin.

While such metaphysical and political kingship is often described as 'divine kingship' this shorthand term of reference does not indicate the complex ways in which an exclusive and unique social category is vested in the singular office and person of the ruler. It is through the articulation of sacred kingship that a hegemony of seamless political and ritual power centred on the ruler is constituted as an organizational principle underpinning a kingdom (albeit that the ways in which it is configured varies from kingdom to kingdom). In the twentieth century these precolonial antecedents are often utilized to inscribe a local ethnic identity within the context of the nation state.

Witchcraft and the ambivalence of power

Veneration of ancestors as spiritual beings is unknown in some African societies, as among the Tiv of central Nigeria. In many such societies ancestors are simply deceased forebears through which lineage is traced. It is the living who are able to act in the world through their physical efforts but also through spiritual prowess. In certain contexts, however, this prowess is considered ambiguous in that the benefits it provides can also be detrimental to others, causing physical and spiritual harm which are often defined in terms of an illegitimate use of power. This is characterized as witchcraft, although how it is defined can vary from society to society.

Among the Tiv all individuals who have exceptional talents or skills are presumed to have this spiritual prowess or power. This is accompanied by a physical analogue known as Tsav which grows in the heart region as individuals become older. However it can also grow unnaturally through the harming and killing of other human beings. In these cases it is believed that malign individuals meet at night in order to eat the human flesh of kin offered up by members of these covert groups. Consequently Tsav is used to describe powerful individuals who act legitimately on behalf of the community as well as witches organized for clandestine and evil purposes who act illegitimately for private gain at the expense of the community. As such it becomes an idiom for describing the ambivalence of power.

An important contribution to the understanding of witchcraft was made by Evans-Pritchard's seminal analysis of witchcraft in the Azande kingdoms of the Sudan (Evans-Pritchard, 1937). In this society witchcraft is hereditary, although when a guilty witch is discovered he or she is always considered (for one reason or another) not to have been part of the patrilineage. As with the Tiv, there is also the concept of a physical analogue (in the body, located near the liver) for witchcraft activities which is sometimes revealed at post mortems. Both men and women can be witches (as well as certain categories of wild animals) and witchcraft usually works through close proximity to the victim. Evans-Pritchard suggests that witchcraft plays an important part in understanding the causes and consequences of events that occur in Azande society, especially misfortune. As an example he describes how granaries often collapse due to the predations of termites. This is a commonplace event which needs no further explanation. However, if people were sitting underneath it at the time of collapse and suffer injury, the intersection of two events (the people sitting and the collapse) is explained through the malign actions of witchcraft rather than in terms of random chance.

In order to identify and counter the effects of witchcraft the Azande use different forms of divination. The most well-known of these is the poison oracle operated by married men in which poison is administered to a fowl and questions are asked while its movements are closely observed prior to its death or survival. Usually two fowls are used and a clear verdict on a situation depends on one fowl surviving in response to the questions posed and the other dying. Women are excluded from using the poison oracle which is considered a key resource for married men in discovering their wives' adultery. Moreover, bridewealth offered in marriage alliances resides with the senior men of a narrow group of patrikin (brothers and their offspring) and it is these groups who own poison oracles. As a consequence the poison oracle plays an important role in concentrating political power, controlling marriage alliances and structuring gender relations. The poison oracles of princes and rulers are extremely prestigious and decisions that affected the entire kingdom were often based on the outcome. Though an important means of political and social power, colonial and postcolonial rule have removed much of the judicial aspect of the poison oracle except in localized situations.

Conceptualizations of witchcraft can be applied in varied social contexts within a society. Among the Maka of the Cameroons in West Africa, for example, witchcraft at village level is a powerful means of levelling inequalities between villagers through the pressure it exerts to share communally the fruits of individual success rather than risk witchcraft attacks (Geschiere 1997). Witchcraft is also used in the client–patronage relations that villagers seek to maintain with successful members of the urban elite who control the resources of the nation state and to whom they are connected through kinship and common place of birth. There is constant pressure on elite members of a village to redistribute wealth and employment opportunities through the conduit of client–patronage relations with the ultimate sanction of witchcraft if they prove recalcitrant. The urban elite are unable to sever their relations with their close kin in the village setting even though they often regard their natal villages as hostile environments because of this potential threat of witchcraft. As a result they often redistribute a large proportion of their income and use the state apparatus to provide roads, schools, hospitals and other state provisions for their local communities.

Similarly the political contestation between members of this urban elite within a one-party system leads to sudden and extreme shifts of political fortune for individuals, which are also couched in the idiom of witchcraft. The successful elite claim personal skills of witchcraft in order to survive the intense political competition – and these assertions increase their prestige. The forms of witchcraft they have control over are popularly represented as urban and modern with powerful abilities garnered from other ethnic groups and ritual specialists rather than simply relying on the more local and rural village forms of witchcraft articulated in their own communities. This reflects the capacity of the ruling elite to order the hierarchy of unequal power in patron–client relations. Witchcraft provides a potent mode of discourse about the acquisition of power, legitimate and illegitimate, and a means to critique the ways in which it is exerted within a moral economy. Witchcraft is a fluid category dependent on the context in which it is applied and the variable ways in which it is configured within different societies.

Africanization of the world religions

The consolidation of the colonial territories in Africa at the beginning of the twentieth century underpinned the development and spread of institutional frameworks of missionary Christianity, although for some colonized peoples Islam afforded an alternative identity with which to contest

European colonial hegemonies. Mass conversion to both Christianity and Islam began to take place among many peoples in Africa where the world religions had not been much in evidence before. Such conversion was often related to the emergence of new social groupings which were responsive to conversion. They developed in the urban areas with the clerical skills required for administering the colonial enterprise. They were also linked to social change among rural populations where the introduction of new transport infrastructures accompanied changing modes of production (such as the introduction of commodity crops for export) and expansion of various mass communication media.

Although mass conversion can be linked to social change engendered by the processes of colonization, other complex – and much debated – factors were also at play. In an influential analysis, Horton (1975) notes that mass conversion to Christianity and Islam took place in relation to the changing boundaries of social life. He describes precolonial African cosmology as two-tiered between a remote supreme being and lesser but more active spiritual agencies. He suggests that the lesser agencies underpin events and processes in the microcosm of social life within the local community and environment whereas the supreme being underpins events and processes in the wider world. Horton's analysis, sometimes described as 'intellectualist', argues that where the way of life of a community is restricted to the local boundaries of the microcosm far more emphasis is placed on the lesser active spiritual agencies whereas the remote supreme being remains in the background. When these boundaries of the local microcosm weaken or shift to include events and processes of the wider world (because of trade, enclosure within colonial systems of administration or other reasons) the supreme being comes to feature more prominently. Horton argues that in these weakening circumstances of the microcosm where there is already a shift in emphasis towards the supreme being, this provides a catalyst for mass conversion where the dissemination of Christianity and Islam is already taking place (with their emphasis on a universal God). However the differentiation necessary between the social worlds of the microcosm and macrocosm for this model of explanation is questioned by examples of some local shrines and cults with their emphasis on lesser spiritual agencies (in both precolonial history and the twentieth century) which have extended beyond the local microcosm to include large regional areas within their influence, often providing networks of personal security and trade for diverse social groupings.

Missionary Christianity and orthodox Islam both emphasize salvation achieved in the next world and so present a contrasting model of religious experience compared with the processual emphasis of African indigenous or traditional religion with its focus on explanation and control of events, utilizing an open-ended range of spiritual resources. The contrast is sometimes described as between salvational and structural modes of religion; however with the Africanization of these world religions, these distinctions become blurred and interpenetrate. The processes of mass conversion to Islam and Christianity at the beginning of the century led to new and dynamic forms of religious innovation and organization that developed to meet African concerns and contexts, leading to the Africanization of the world religions. Among the Yoruba-speaking areas in south-western Nigeria, for example, conversion to Christianity contributed to the formation of a new regional Yoruba ethnic identity coalesced from the heterogeneous cluster of city states and dialects in the region. The dissemination of the Bible as a textual resource translated into an indigenous language by converts fostered the regional acceptance of a standardized Yoruba language over its range of dialects, some of which are mutually unintelligible (Peel, 1989). As happened in many parts of Africa, however, conversion to Christianity was followed by disillusionment with the control maintained by European mission churches which marginalized African clergymen, who had often been at the forefront of the drive for conversion. Many left the mission churches to form independent but orthodox churches.

In southern Nigeria the new administrative subordinate class with the literate skills acquired from the mission schools and inculcated in Christianity utilized the text of the Bible to mediate the often acute tensions and evident contradictions generated by colonization. They initially formed prayer bands in the Yoruba-speaking areas, which developed into the *Aladura churches*, and began to articulate radical religious innovation through the use of visions, prayer, and healing rituals in comparison to the mission and more orthodox African churches (Peel, 1968). The development of such indigenous churches occurred elswhere in Africa as in the case of the Zion churches of Southern Africa. Such churches were not simply a form of resistance to colonial hegemonies but rather created an autonomous space in which to form sacred communities that were aligned to what might be called the modernities of contemporary life. There was a rejection of what was now defined as pagan worship as a prior religious form that was no longer appropriate although the problems it mediated were still relevant. For example, notions of witchcraft and its effects within the community were still salient but the modes of action through which such concerns were addressed were situated within a new radical Christian context, such as the Aladura churches. Though the dependence on charismatic religious leaders led to fission and the formation of new churches up to the present day, these processes provide a means of renewal and revitalization that aligns itself with the ongoing processes of modernity.

Conversion to Islam under the European colonial regimes in the twentieth century also led to new adaptations. In Senegal in Western Africa, for example, the charismatic Islamic religious leader Cheik Amadu Bamba became a focus for religious resistance to the French administration at the beginning of the twentieth century. He was educated in the traditions of the longstanding Sufi brotherhood of the Qadiriyya prevalent in West Africa. Although his religious teachings always advocated peaceful resolutions to conflict, some of his followers supported more forceful political action which resulted in the French authorities exiling him first to Gabon and subsequently to Mauretania. This merely increased his charismatic appeal as a martyr and attracted increasing numbers of adherents who formed the independent Islamic brotherhood of the Mouride with its own litany and clerical hierarchy. With the introduction of the commodity crop peanuts by the colonial regime, the Mouride brotherhood further increased its power and political influence through its development of new farming communities in the semi-arid and more remote regions of Senegal. They comprised impoverished adherents who cultivated the new crop and contributed a tithe of their earnings to the brotherhood. The Mouride brotherhood underpinned the agricultural transformation of the rural economy in Senegal and its making into a modern nation state, as reflected in the close ties maintained between the Mouride clerical hierarchy and the governing elite after independence.

However, the introduction of Christianity and Islam into new areas of Africa in the twentieth century did not curtail or hinder innovations in other forms of religious experience that are usually described as 'indigenous' or 'traditional'. Often there is an affiliation with one or other of the world religions as well as an overlapping participation in these other forms of religious activity. Janzen (1994) describes how the city of Dar-es-Salaam on the Indian Ocean coast of East Africa lies within the Swahili regional corridor that runs along the coast with its longstanding traditions of Islam. Yet Ngoma cults of affliction and healing are also found here and are patronized by the coastal Islamized peoples as well as by migrants from the interior. However Ngoma in Dar-es-Salaam can be utilized for therapeutic or entertainment purposes and this provides an ambiguity in defining its relation to Islamic doctrine. Janzen gives an example of two Islamic healers to demonstrate this ambiguity; the first uses Ngoma rituals as a medical healing rite which consequently does not compromise his Islamic devotion whereas the second, a Sufi adherent (with an alternative repertoire of prayers, singing and dancing that is therapeutically available), considers it a pagan religious ritual and therefore unacceptable.

Recent renewal and innovation

<small>INDIGENOUS: BWITI AND MAMI WATA</small>

In the twentieth century New Religious Movements have developed that appropriate elements from the world religions but also creatively maintain continuities with 'indigenous' or 'traditional' prior beliefs and practices. They are reconfigured and transformed so as to mediate or incorporate the localized conditions of modernity as they impact on their community or society. A notable example is the Bwiti religious movement researched by Fernandez (1982) among the Fang-speaking peoples in the Gabon in Central Africa. The Fang are an uncentralized patrilineal society that traces descent from founding ancestors of clans and is organized into segmented lineages. The smallest unit in Fang society is the family household of the father, his wives and children living in villages with a number of other families. As a people they had slowly migrated southwards from the savannah to the tropical rainforest with a history that in different contexts reads either as conquering newcomers or fleeing refugees. With French colonization these villages which had tended to relocate periodically became fixed spatially within its bureaucratic infrastructures (for which they supplied a flexible labour force). Prior to colonization the focus of religious activity was the ancestor cult with the reliquaries of bones and skulls of its deceased male members located in the men's council house where all important matters of village life took place, watched over by the benign protective guardianship of the ancestors. Although the cult had become discredited as uncivilized by the impact of mission Christianity, these ideas still had a powerful influence in the lives of villagers. Anti-witchcraft cults periodically swept through the Fang-speaking region, in part a response to a perceived divisive individuation engendered by access to the cash economy of the colony that undermined the communal egalitarian basis of village life. Among these cults was one known as Mademoiselle of Ndende who was a white female spirit originating in the river and equated with the Virgin Mary of Christianity. Her devotees offered protection against witchcraft on condition reliquary bones (described by them as 'fetish' objects) were dug up and destroyed to be replaced by a shrine devoted to her. However the impact of her cult was, in the main, transient in the village communities.

From the 1920s onwards a new and innovative religious movement of renewal started to develop. Known as Bwiti among the Fang peoples, it sought to reconstitute an egalitarian but communal social life through the organization of chapel houses, which were formed by a constant process of fissioning rather than the establishment of a hierarchy. Leading members of Bwiti were often mission educated and literate. During initiation into Bwiti, large quantities of Eboga, a psychotropic drug derived from the rainforest, are ingested causing vivid hallucinations and psychomotor disturbances. These experiences are structured through what Fernandez describes as the religious imagination of the Bwiti movement as an enactment of creation – a journey which resonates with their mythic history of migration. In the course of this journey initiates encounter the supreme being and Jesus Christ, who is represented as an indigenous healer, as well as ultimately the ancestors who impart to them experiential but esoteric knowledge of communal one-heartedness that restores an egalitarian understanding with which to relate to all members of the chapel house and the wider community. These experiences are integrated within Bwiti into complex rituals of worship using dance and song. They take place during the night focused around a central post that is a conduit between the physical and spirit worlds. Although there is considerable adoption of Christian liturgy and imagery, members do not consider themselves Christian. Bwiti is a renewal and revitalization of the ancestral cult articulated within the modern world, of which Christianity is a feature. Bwiti and many similar prophetic movements in Africa dynamically appropriate Christian motifs to indigenous idioms and discourses to obtain a legitimacy similar to that perceived in the orthodox Christian hegemony from which they are marginalized.

However not all religious innovations draw on the past. Mami Wata is a new riverine deity found throughout West and Central Africa and depicted as a fair-skinned female with long flowing hair and often represented with a fishtail (to underline her links to the water spirit world). The term Mami Wata derives from pidgin English, which is used as a common language over wide areas, and was initially used to describe and compare differing riverine female deities from different localities. In the twentieth century she has developed as an autonomous female deity who is able to bestow great wealth and riches on her devotees or wreak severe suffering on those who displease her. She is represented as seductive, and associated with notions of irresistible female sexuality, often maintaining a sexual relationship with her devotees in the spirit world. She is considered cosmopolitan and characterized as fast living and independent. She has all the consumer goods of this urban lifestyle, including sunglasses and fast cars. When possessed by her, devotees sometimes smoke cigarettes and play popular musical instruments such as the harmonica or guitar instead of the traditional musical instruments appropriate to other deities. Mami Wata is prominent in popular discourses featuring in books, films and songs in describing the qualities of independent urban women. Similarly she is utilized through her association with extreme unexpected riches in discourses on the illegitimate acquisition of unexpected wealth, especially relevant where patrimonialism is often exercised by the governing political elite who are able to extract extreme wealth from the government infrastructures.

Evangelical and Pentecostal churches have vigorously attacked the followers of indigenous or traditional forms of worship as pagan idol worshippers. They single out Mami Wata in particular as exemplifying all paganism's demonic evils and dangers through her lure of uncontrollable female sexuality that destroys the spiritual community which these churches seek to create. However these church communities often marginalize single and divorced women who are seen as a potential threat to the spiritual harmony of married life. Mami Wata offers an empowering autonomous role model for such women. It underlines and legitimates control of their own individual sexual, reproductive and economic capacities and frees them from being determined by kinship or marriage, while at the same time sanctioning the personal pleasures of modern urban consumption.

Figure 9.5 Priestess playing the harmonica while possessed by Mami Wata

Evangelical and Charismatic churches

Evangelical and Pentecostal churches have spread rapidly throughout Africa in the late twentieth century. They have promoted themselves using mass media techniques, inspired by the example of similar churches in the US. They often aspire to an international programme that reflects the global possibilities of conversion for their organizations which build up a network of associated branches – although their dependence on charismatic leaders leaves them prone to a certain amount of fission. These Evangelical and Pentecostal churches are distinguished by a common set of religious ideas and practices that include baptism in the Holy Spirit, speaking in tongues and healing through personal prayer. The use of exorcism from the devil and demonic forces is central to their concept of personal deliverance afforded through the intervention of the church and its spiritual community which shields the individual from the malign forces that pervade wider society. These churches place an emphasis on situating themselves as modern and vigorously oppose what they consider the idolatrous customs of the pagan past, albeit that they share many of the same concerns such as witchcraft which is articulated in terms of these demonic forces. It is through this positioning against demonic forces that they distinguish themselves from the more orthodox churches from which they attract many of their followers to offer a more radical approach in addressing an individual's spiritual and material needs.

The prosperity gospel many churches disseminate aspires to the success and material benefits of the consumer world brought about through the personal intervention of God on behalf of the individual. Consumption is consequently valorized as the reward of the individual who has achieved deliverance within the spiritual community of the church. The success of these churches is reflected in the size of congregations, the conversion rallies held and the use of the latest technologies to promote their church. This emphasis on material success in the modern world also provides the ideological framework for worshippers to redefine and reduce the collective obligations (and economic costs) of extended kinship in order to replace it with the spiritual community of the church to which they belong and so focus on a more individuated sociality. (For more on the charismatic upsurge see Chapter 8 and Chapter 14.)

Figure 9.6 Evangelical church that highlights its prosperity gospel in its roadside sign

ISLAMIC RENEWAL

Islam has undergone dynamic renewal and revitalization from precolonial times to the present day, through processes of reform and purification in which elements of Islamic practice deemed idolatrous are rejected. Islam provides a religious context underpinned by the legitimation of a new orthodoxy through which to challenge established hierarchies of authority and transform them into a new social and religious order. With the emergence of independent nation states from the colonial states a renewal of international links within the Islamic world has taken place, particularly between sub-Saharan Africa and the Middle East. The pilgrimage to Mecca which all Islamic adherents are encouraged to take has now been mobilized in sub-Saharan Africa through modern means of mass transportation. Links have been further strengthened with the core centres of Islam through the establishment and sponsorship of Islamic institutions including schools and hospitals.

The dominance of the *Wahhabi* Islamic movement founded in the eighteenth century by Muhammad ibn' Abd al-Wahhab in the Arabian peninsular, and in particular Saudi Arabia, has resulted in the dissemination of Wahhabi-inspired teachings which advocate a return to the primary teachings of the Qur'an and a complete rejection of the longstanding culturally mediated interpretations of it found in the Islamic Sufi brotherhoods in sub-Saharan Africa (see Chapter 10). Furthermore, the successful resistance of Islamic nation states to the encroachments of Western capitalism and its attendant secularization has served as a model for Islamic activist groupings who wish to turn the secular nation state into a religious theocracy under the guidance of Islamic law. These diverse reformist Islamic movements challenge the longstanding Islamic institutions of sub-Saharan Africa and resort to the use of the mass media of print and cassettes to pass on their teachings, especially effective when met with hostility or repression. Such Islamic renewals and the means by which they disseminate their messages align them as modern religious mass movements which attract a broad grass-roots base of support that includes radical intellectuals and Islamic scholars as well as both the urban and rural disenfranchised, among whom the young feature prominently.

In northern Nigeria from the 1970s onwards the reformist Yan Izala movement has spread rapidly. Emphasizing doctrinal understanding, Arabic literacy and strict ritual practice, it rejects Sufi or Islamic brotherhood derived influences as non-Islamic. In addition it criticizes these brotherhoods for endorsing the high expenditure involved in marriage and other social customs which reinforce the economic and status divisions in society. This movement has recruited poorer farmers, the socially disadvantaged and young men who are keen to limit these expenses which they find financially onerous (Loemeier, 1997). The adoption of Yan Izala also provides a means to limit socially necessary costs by restricting the boundaries of sociality to other adherents of the movement and thereby excluding the fulfilment of social obligations of distant kin affiliated to other forms of Islam which are categorically rejected as non-Islamic. It advocates better (if separate) education for Muslim women and modern schools and aligns itself as a progressive movement that offers a modernity with which to challenge the *status quo* of the longstanding Sufi brotherhoods. It has been castigated by the latter for the ways in which its teachings have created deep-seated divisions and conflicts within communities and families.

LOOKING TO THE FUTURE

The capacity of religion to renew and innovate in sub-Saharan Africa means that it continues to be an important resource in associational life, generating new forms of community that provide a means for local empowerment even in the most marginalized of social contexts. Where military rule or government elites control the resources of the nation state, the religious imagination at grass-roots level can offer alternative visions of society. Often this is a positive force. As Gifford (1998) has argued, for example, Christianity in Africa can offer the possibility of democratization by offering a vision of an alternative social order as well as by generating its own institutional frameworks to structure local social communities in more democratic ways. However religion can also have a negative impact where it is adopted to empower conflict, such as in the case of the Lord's Resistance Army in northern Uganda which continues to wage an unwinnable war on the nation state (with the potential threat of its fragmentation), and which is led by the charismatic Joseph Kony who organizes his army as a form of cult guided by his possession by spirits. Religion can also mediate the articulations of the grass-root communities to the institutions of the nation state. An example of this is the way in which the South African government in its AIDS awareness programmes has also made use of the Ngangas, traditional healers, to give advice on AIDS prevention during their divination and healing consultations, thereby creating local idioms for the communication of information.

A striking trend in religion in Africa is the way in which it continues to be exported to other continents, especially the Americas and Europe, as part of the processes of globalization. It has travelled historically with the dispersion of the African diaspora through the Atlantic slave trade up to the end of the nineteenth century. The varied religious resources drawn from the heterogenous slave social groupings, articulated in differing ways with the dominant Christian system, often led to translations between the African spiritual agencies and the saints of Christianity in religions such as Santeria of Cuba, Candomble and its variations in Brazil, and Vodou of Haiti, among other examples. With continued migration from these societies (particularly to the US) throughout the latter part of the twentieth century, African religions have dispersed further. Moreover the rejection of a Eurocentric Christianity and the adoption of African religion by Afro-Americans have seen a massive increase in affiliation to these religions, supplemented by its spread to other communities in both South and North America who have no claims to it by descent, literal or figurative. Arguably religions characterized under the rubric of traditional African religion have now attained an international status that qualifies them as members of the world religions.

Similarly, the Africanization of Christianity with the emergence of independent churches and their dynamic forms of worship which energize and personalize ritual are currently being exported to both the US and Europe. The methods of recruitment through conversion rallies are gaining worshippers outside of their migrant groups and helping reshape the practices of Western Evangelical churches. Likewise Orthodox or mainstream denominational Christian constituencies in Africa (both Protestant and Catholic) with their rising numbers of followers are becoming an increasing influence in determining the directions of Christianity as a religion in the twenty-first century (see Chapter 8).

SUMMARY

- There is a great diversity of indigenous religions in sub-Saharan Africa but there is also the long-standing presence of Christianity and Islam in particular areas since the fourth century CE and, at least, the ninth century CE respectively.
- Indigenous religions found in sub-Saharan Africa include a complex and variable range of social phenomena that do not easily correspond to Western institutional categories of the religious, political, economic, judicial and social.
- Indigenous religions emphasize participation and are also open ended in that they allow individuals to acquire alternative forms of religious experience from different sources and according to need

and inclination. They focus on the well-being of the community or social grouping and for this reason often emphasize explanation, prediction and control of events.

▎ Mass conversion to Christianity and Islam took place at the beginning of the twentieth century in response to the consequences of colonialism and the impact of missionaries, although at this time in some areas Christianity was embraced as a resource associated with the modern benefits of colonialism whereas in other areas peoples converted to Islam (which often already had a long-standing presence) as a means of resistance to these hegemonic colonial encroachments.

▎ Mass conversion to the world religions of Christianity and Islam did not result in the disappearance or exclusion of indigenous localized forms of religion nor a syncretization of indigenous and the world religions; but rather there is often a compartamentalized positioning of individuals in relation to both indigenous religions and either Christianity or Islam.

▎ The dynamic and creative forms of religious experience deriving from sub-Saharan African social and cultural contexts, characterized by renewals and revitalizations, have resulted in the Africanization of the world religions in sub-Saharan Africa.

▎ The Africanization of Christianity is helping to shape its worldwide forms both in its Orthodox Protestant and Catholic denominations and also its more radical Evangelical modes, while sub-Saharan African forms of Islam are engaged in closer international links with the rest of the Islamic world, especially Northern Africa and the Middle East.

▎ Indigenous religions of sub-Saharan Africa, which were carried across the Atlantic to the Americas with the African diaspora to develop new forms, have expanded enormously (and contrast with a Eurocentric Christianity); they also attract new adherents who have no claims to them by descent, literal or figurative.

KEY TERMS

Aladura churches Aladura churches are independent African churches formed in the Yoruba-speaking areas from the beginning of the twentieth century onward. They emphasized the efficacy of prayer and healing to directly effect change in the spiritual and material circumstances of individuals as well as introducing African religious practices such as the use of drumming that had been previously rejected by the European missionaries.

Church Missionary Society (CMS) The Anglican missionary society was founded in 1799 to spread the Christian gospel overseas, specifically to lands where Christianity was not present. The first CMS missionaries reached Sierra Leone in 1804.

Griaule, Marcel One of the most prominent French anthropologists working principally in Francophone Africa between 1928 and 1956 who is famous for his long-term project to understand the complex culture of the Dogon peoples of Mali, particularly under the tutelage of a Dogon elder, Ogotemmeli.

Lord Lugard British administrator who developed and codified the British system of colonization which utilized the precolonial authority and hierarchies of chieftaincy and kingship to rule the colonies.

Ngoma Linguistic description of drumming that plays a central part in the range of cults of healing and affliction that have a wide regional currency in Southern and Eastern Africa.

Patrilineage Kinship group tracing descent through the male line.

Wahhabi Islamic groupings, associated with the contemporary ruling elites of the Arabian peninsula, that follow the eighteenth-century teachings of Muhammad ibn' Abd al-Wahhab. They advocate a direct return to the teachings of the Qur'an with condemnation of all innovations and religious practices, such as venerating saints' tombs or the mystical aspects of the Sufi religious orders which are classed as non-Islamic.

FURTHER READING

Introductory

Thomas D. Blakely, Walter E. A. van Beek and Dennis L. Thomson (eds): *Religion in Africa: Expression and Experience* (New Haven, CT: James Currey/Heinemann 1994). A series of indigenous, Christian and Islamic case studies that suggest how wide ranging and diverse religious experience is in sub-Saharan Africa.

Louis Brenner: 'Religious discourses in and about Africa'. In K. Barber and P. F. de Moraes Farias (eds): *Discourse and its Disguises: The Interpretation of African Oral Texts* (Centre of West African Studies Series 1: University of Birmingham, 1989, pp. 87–105). An important discussion of how to understand the framings of religious ideas and practices in sub-Saharan Africa.

P. Geschiere: *The Modernity of Witchcraft: Politics and the Occult in Postcolonial Africa* (Charlottesville, VA, and London: University Press of Virginia, 1997). An explanation of the persistence of witchcraft as a key idea for conceptualizing social and political relations among the Maka and the Cameroons as a response to modern exigencies as experienced within the articulations of the postcolonial nation state.

Christianity and Islam in Africa

Paul Gifford: *African Christianity: Its Public Role* (Bloomington and Indianapolis IN, 1998: Indiana University Press). A survey of the ways in which Christianity has emerged in relation to the state and civil society in the late twentieth century.

Robin Horton: 'On the rationality of African conversion: part 1' (*Africa* 45 (3), 1975, 219–35). A seminal discussion of why mass conversion to the world religions has taken place in sub-Saharan Africa.

Donal B. Cruise O'Brien: *Saints and Politicians: Essays in the Organisation of a Senegalese Peasant Society* (Cambridge: Cambridge University Press, 1975). In-depth analysis of the processes of conversion to Islam in Senegal in opposition to the imposition of French colonial hegemonies.

John D. Y. Peel: *Aladura: A Religious Movement among the Yoruba* (Oxford: Oxford University Press, International Africa Institute 1968). A comprehensive study of the rise of the Aladura movement in Nigeria and its relations to mission Christianity.

John D. Y. Peel: 'The cultural work of Yoruba ethnogenesis'. In M. Chapman, M. Mcdonald and E. Tonkin (eds): *History and Ethnicity* (ASA Monograph 27: London: Routledge, 1989, pp. 198–215).

An analysis of the interaction between emerging articulations of ethnic identity and the missionary project.

David Westerlund and Eva Evers Rosander (eds): *African Islam and Islam in Africa: Encounters between Sufis and Islamists* (London: Hurst, 1997). An important discussion of the Islamic reformist movements in Africa and their interaction with the more longstanding forms of Islam already present, with case studies.

Indigenous religions in Africa: general

E. E. Evans-Pritchard, *Witchcraft, Oracles and Magic among the Azande* (London: Oxford University Press, 1937). Evans-Pritchard's seminal discussion of how the Azande use witchcraft, oracles and magic to structure and order social events. He demonstrates the importance of such concepts in explaining the chains of causation by which this fortune befalls individuals (where no other forms of explanation can be found) and how this provides an alternative model of determinancy which contrasts with Western models of random chance in accounting for events.

James W. Fernandez: *Bwiti: An Ethnography of the Religious Imagination in Africa* (Princeton, NJ: Princeton University Press 1982). An in-depth comprehensive study of the development of an indigenous religion in Central Africa in the twentieth century which makes accommodations with the presence of Christianity to reshape and restructure the precolonial cosmology.

Meyer Fortes and Robin Horton: *Oedipus and Job in West African Religion* (Cambridge: Cambridge Press, 1983). A cross-cultural comparison and exploration of the relations between religious cosmologies and social organization in selected societies in West Africa.

John M. Janzen: 'Drums of affliction: real phenomenon or scholarly chimaera?' In Thomas D. Blakely, Walter E. A. van Beek and Dennis L. Thomson (eds): *Religion in Africa: Expression and Experience* (New Haven, CT: James Currey/Heinemann, 1994, pp. 160–81). A review of how cults of affliction and healing can be used to understand religious movements regionally and historically.

Ian M. Lewis: *Ecstatic Religions* (London: Pelican, 1971). Overview of how spirit possession is articulated in a wide range of societies including sub-Saharan Africa.

Various case studies

Warren d'Azvedo: 'Mask makers and myth in western Liberia'. In Anthony Forge (ed.): *Primitive Art and Society* (Oxford: Oxford University Press, Wenner-Gren Foundation, 1973, pp. 126–50).

Karen Barber: 'How man makes gods in West Africa: Yoruba attitudes towards the Orisa' (*Africa* 51 (3), 1981, 724–45).

Harri Englund: 'Between God and Kamuzu: the transition to multi party politics in central Malawi'. In R. Werbner and T. Ranger (eds): *Postcolonial Identities in Africa* (London: Zed Books 1996, pp. 105–35).

Meyer Fortes: *Religion, Morality and the Person: Essays on Tallensi Religion* (Cambridge: Cambridge University Press, 1987).

Charles Gore: 'Ritual, performance and the media in urban contemporary shrine configurations in Benin City, Nigeria'. In F. Hughes-Freeland (ed.): *Ritual, Performance and the Media* (London: Routledge, 1998, pp. 66–84).

Marcel Griaule: *Conversations with Ogotemmeli* (Oxford: Oxford University Press, International Africa Institute 1965).

Robin Horton: 'The Kalabari Ekine society: a borderland of religion and art'. *Africa* 33, 1963, 94–114.

Robin Horton: 'Social psychologies: African and Western'. In M. Fortes and R. Horton (eds): *Oedipus and Job in West African Religion* (Cambridge: Cambridge Press, 1983, pp. 41–82).

Igor Kopytoff: 'Ancestors as elders in Africa'. *Africa* 41, 1971, 129–42.

David Lan: *Guns and Rain: Guerillas and Spirit Mediums in Zimbabwe* (London: James Currey, 1985).

Kenneth Little: 'The political function of the Poro: Part 1'. *Africa* 35 (4) 1965, 349–65.

Roman Loemeier: 'Islamic reform and political change'. In David Westerlund and Eva Evers Rosander (eds): *African Islam and Islam in Africa: Encounters between Sufis and Islamists* (London: Hurst, 1997, pp. 286–307).

Joseph N. Nevadomsky: 'Kingship succession rituals in Benin. Part 3: the coronation of the Oba (*African Arts* 17 (3), 1984, 48–57).

John W. Nunley: *Moving with the Face of the Devil: Art and Politics in Urban West Africa* (Urbana and Chicago, IL: University of Illinois Press, 1987).

CHAPTER 10

Native American religions

Howard L. Harrod

▌ INTRODUCTION

This chapter describes the religions of Native Americans who lived on the Northern Plains of North America. It was these peoples who became the 'true Indians' in the modern American and European imagination. It is suggested that indigenous traditions and rituals shaped the responses of Native American peoples to changes introduced by contact with Europeans, and that these responses cannot therefore be fully understood without taking religion into account. In this context 'modernity' refers to the processes of colonialization and conquest that took place in both North and South America, and associated social, political and cultural changes. The complex responses of Native American people to modernity are understood to begin with the voyages of Christopher Columbus (1492–1504) and to continue into the present. It will be shown that contemporary responses of native people to the continuing pressures of the majority society in North America are also deeply implicated with religious beliefs and practices. Sometimes these are associated with older indigenous traditions; sometimes they represent a synthesis of elements from Christian, modern Western, and native traditions.

The chapter begins with an account of the oral traditions and ritual processes that constituted the identity of Native American groups on the Northern Plains during period between 1750 and 1850. It will be seen that these societies often responded creatively to social changes engendered by encounters with Europeans, and that these responses are best understood against the background of indigenous traditions and ritual practices. After 1850 the economic and political autonomy of peoples on the Northern Plains were seriously undermined by the destruction of the buffalo and the people's conquest and confinement to reservations. During the late nineteenth century and through the twentieth, these peoples continued to face the enormous pressures consequent upon attempts to coerce assimilation

Figure 10.1 Selected groups on the Great Plains according to early observers

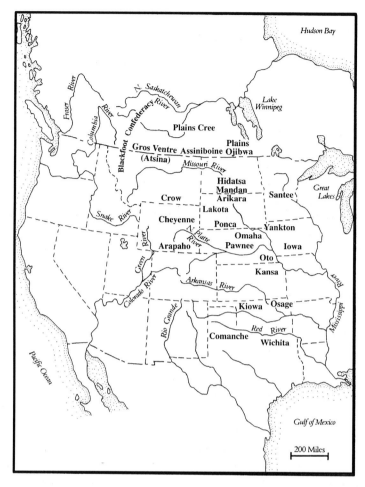

into North American society. The fact that some of these peoples have nonetheless maintained their ethnic identities is astonishing. This suggests that the preservation of cultural identity, together with recurring rhythms of cultural renewal, cannot be fully understood without taking into account the role of religious traditions and ritual practices.

SOURCES AND RESOURCES

The Northern Plains and its peoples

The Great Plains stretch eastward across North America from the Rocky Mountain front. In the present-day US, the northern portion of this larger region includes the states of Montana, North and South Dakota, Wyoming, and the northern portion of Nebraska. Rich in animal life, particularly buffalo, this area was homeland to a number of distinct groups. The names by which they became known in Europe and America – *Blackfeet, Crows, Cheyennes, Arapahoes, Lakotas* – evoke the images of horse mounted, buffalo hunting, tipi dwelling nomads which continue to pervade popular culture and consciousness in both Europe and the US.

These romantic images not only conceal the complex humanity of past North American Indian peoples; they also obscure the many varieties of historical experience on the Northern Plains. All of the peoples mentioned above, for example, had migrated to the area at different times. The earliest of these migrations may have begun in the late sixteenth century and continued into the seventeenth century. In the course of their movements they developed cultural adaptations that enabled them to flourish in their new homelands.

Not all the residents of the Great Plains were as modern, however. Often forgotten are older residents of the Northern Plains, peoples who migrated to the region much earlier, and who took up residence in many locations on the great Missouri River system. In the area that is now North Dakota, for example, village peoples elaborated a way of life of considerable cultural depth, which included a very successful dual economy based on gardening and hunting. They lived in highly visible energy efficient earth lodge villages along the Missouri River and its tributaries. Perhaps the most famous of these peoples were the Mandans and Hidatsas, some of whose ancestors may have migrated to the Northern Plains as early as the twelfth or thirteenth century. These people became known to French fur traders by the mid-eighteenth century, were encountered by Lewis and Clark at the beginning of the nineteenth century, and were made highly visible in the paintings of George Catlin and the Swiss artist Karl Bodmer. Both Catlin and Bodmer lived among these peoples in the 1830s. Also well known were village peoples further to the south such as the *Pawnees* and their kinsfolk the *Arikaras*. Village people were no less adaptable than the more recent arrivals and they were able successfully to maintain their cultural identities in the face of often overwhelming odds, such as the periodic epidemic diseases that engulfed the Northern Plains.

Religion and social change

The continents that became known to Europeans in the fifteenth century as the New World were thus inhabited by peoples possessing very diverse cultures and languages (it has been estimated that in North America there were some fifty-nine different linguistic families). Archaeological and ethnographic evidence has established that these populations encountered one another, migrated to new environments, made war on one another, and responded to environmental changes. These were far from the static 'timeless' cultures of the European imagination. Social change was an essential ingredient within the pre-Columbian world, and the coming of the Europeans merely inaugurated a new phase of such change.

The scale of the threat posed by the Europeans was, however, enormous. The European colonizers introduced new diseases and strange new animals, engaged in the systematic conquest of native peoples, and sought to subject them to the cultural values and religions of Europe. The impact of Christian missions, both Protestant and Catholic, on native peoples cannot be overemphasized. Mission activity was often intertwined with military and imperial power and, later in the nineteenth and twentieth centuries, with systematic policies of forced acculturation in the US and Canada.

The impact of European culture and religion on Northern Plains peoples unfolded through a series of complex historical events. But because the approach of Europeans was gradual, the perceptions of some Northern Plains peoples concerning their own power and autonomy continued well into the middle of the nineteenth century. For example, in 1859 the Indian Agent on the Blackfeet Reservation in the US reported that 'The Blackfeet say they are a great and powerful people, but the whites are few and feeble' (US Department of the Interior, *Annual Report of the Commissioner of Indian Affairs*, 1859), Despite such perceptions, the Blackfeet had been impacted, often indirectly, for a very long time before this statement was made. They had indirect and then direct contact with English fur traders pushing west from Hudson Bay early in the eighteenth century, and later in the century with French fur traders from Montreal.

While perhaps not perceived by the Blackfeet as significant, changes introduced in their material culture and social life by the fur trade can be traced historically. In response to the demands of European traders, Blackfeet gradually began processing such items as buffalo robes and pemmican for an increased external market. Without realizing the full implications of their actions, the Blackfeet were gradually drawn into a national and international market network. Even though their material culture expanded, they were impacted negatively by the liquor that was often used as a bargaining tool by the traders. As the eighteenth century wore on, more material and cultural changes would ensue. Guns reached the Blackfeet from the north, and horses came to the Northern Plains as a consequence of raiding and trading with the Spanish in the southwest. The horse and gun revolutionized Northern Plains cultures and created a brief period of relative affluence and cultural vitality that continued until the destruction of the buffalo in the nineteenth century. Along with the destruction of the buffalo, the spread of epidemic diseases across the Northern Plains in 1781, 1837 and 1869 placed great strain on these cultures. The Mandans, for example, were almost exterminated by the epidemic of 1837 while the Blackfeet lost almost one-third of their population.

Cultural responses to social and economic change introduced by Europeans were very seldom separated from the religious frameworks within which native peoples interpreted their experience. Understanding this fact requires some elaboration of Native American religious traditions since religion played such a central role in the formation of individual and social identity as well as the production of social change in these societies. It was through religious experiences that individuals on the Northern Plains came to a sense of personal identity; and religious practices provided essential aid to persons in each of their life stages. Furthermore, it was through the symbolic boundaries established by religious traditions that particular groups distinguished themselves from other societies in their environment; and it was through shared religious practices that this sense of separate identity as a people was maintained and periodically renewed. The energies released in religious experiences and practices provided not only a sense of identity and continuity, but also enabled individuals and societies to respond creatively to the emergence of novelty in their environment. Whether novelty was imposed as a direct or indirect consequence of European presence, pressures from other Plains societies, or as a result of conflicts internal to the group, religion played an essential role in determining the direction and shape of social change. If individual and social identity became threatened, religious experiences and practices were central to any successful social reconstruction. If the threat was traumatic, such as the spread of epidemic diseases, religious energies sometimes played a creative role in projecting a new or drastically reorganized social identity.

A sense of social continuity and identity was evoked in the experience of Northern Plains peoples through their participation in religious meanings that were embodied in powerful reservoirs of shared memory. These shared memories were richly textured and included explanations of how the land that dominated everyday experience took shape; interpretations of how humans as well as animals and other powerful beings came into existence; and narratives about how the special identity of the people was formed.

Origin traditions

Origin traditions provided an account of the rise of landforms prominent in the experience of Northern Plains peoples. According to these traditions, particular landscapes arose as a consequence of the exploits of one or more creator figures. In these traditions creator figures were often not clearly distinguished from another ubiquitous presence: the *trickster*. Sometimes appearing as a coyote or in the form of another animal, trickster figures were often involved in the creation or transformation of the world. In some traditions they exercised their powers alone, while in other traditions they worked in co-operation or in tension with the creator or creators.

Tricksters in these traditions exuded a gross physicality. Their appetites were barely if ever under control. They roamed the world seeking an easy meal, engaging in sexual trickery and exploitation, or enduring the consequences of their own foolishness. They often violated the moral order that was normative for the groups in which they appeared. Perhaps for this reason their negative examples were sometimes used to socialize children in appropriate forms of behaviour. Despite these morally ambiguous qualities, trickster narratives were extremely widespread and popular among Northern Plains societies.

In many Northern Plains origin traditions, such as the Blackfoot case, diving birds or animals brought earth from below primal waters and assisted creator figures in their work. Out of this earth the land was formed, sometimes taking shape in relation to the four cardinal directions. The creator figure also shaped the more specific features of a people's particular environment. In *Mandan* and *Hidatsa* societies, for example, the experienced environment was dominated by the Missouri River and its tributaries, as well as by more concrete landmarks, such as the buttes and breaks along the streams and rivers. In addition there were animals such as the buffalo, bear, deer, and elk; and there were plants, such as beans, corn, squash, and sunflower seeds. Another extremely important plant, central to religious practice all across the Northern Plains, was tobacco.

These animals and plants were not only regarded as food sources; they also appeared to the people in their visions and dreams. They were in the world of everyday experience as concrete plants and animals, but in their dream forms they transcended the world of everyday life. When they appeared in the dream or vision world it was usually in the form of persons who possessed extraordinary powers essential for the people's lives. And when they were encountered as the animals and plants of the everyday world, they were believed to possess consciousness and purpose and to form their own societies to which the human world was related.

In many of these origin traditions, humans were represented as flourishing in the land, having been provided by the creator with an abundance of plant and animal food. Animal skins were made available for clothing, and lodges could be constructed either out of these materials or from the earth and wood that were readily available in the stream and river bottoms. Life was rich, but suffering also came to humans, and death was the final outcome. Northern Plains traditions accounted for death in many ways. In some instances death became the human fate as the result of a wager between a creator figure and another powerful person, as in the Blackfoot case of a wager between *Old Man* and *Old Woman*. Sometimes the dead remained in communication with the living, as was the case in Mandan culture. And in many traditions the ancestors were believed to travel to a land of the dead; there they followed an existence that was much the same as their earthly lives. In some traditions, particular features of the land of the dead were portrayed as opposite to the world of the living. For example, ancestors might hunt at night in the land of the dead while they slept during the day.

The primordial order of gender relations was sometimes alluded to in these traditions. In some instances males and females were portrayed as initially living apart. Then through various means they were brought together, marriage arose and children were born. Some traditions described a normative division of labour between males and females, although many traditions were incomplete or unclear at this point. Often gender relations were more specifically shaped by traditions and ritual practices that surrounded two main economic activities, hunting and agriculture. In many instances there were persons who formed a third gender in Northern Plains societies. If these persons were male, they performed many of the roles that were usually assigned to females; and if they were females, they might go to war or perform other roles that were usually assigned to males. Sometimes these third gender roles involved same-sex relations, gay and lesbian behaviours, but in other instances sexual expression seemed to be lacking. In either case, these persons often played important religious roles in these societies.

Ritual objects and practices

Along with religious traditions, religious practices were also central to the people's lives. They enabled individuals and societies to act appropriately toward plant, animal and other life sources in their environment. 'Appropriate' ritual action issued in an abundant harvest or a successful hunt, providing nourishment essential for life. Religious practices were also important for ensuring good health, for overcoming the powers that caused illness, and for healing the wounds that were common occurrences in both everyday life and in war. Religious practices were also employed to neutralize the power of enemies or to overcome them in the case of conflict.

In all of these contexts, religious practices on the Northern Plains usually took the form of ritual processes that released the power believed to reside in religious objects known as *bundles*. Bundles were believed to originate in the vision experiences of a contemporary individual or a predecessor, or to arise as the result of a gift from a culture hero. Bundles were composed of a variety of things: pipes, earth paints, plant materials such as sweetgrass and sage to be used as incense, animal and bird skins, as well as stones, animal bones, and other materials. These items were wrapped in one or more animal skins and secured by leather thongs.

In a ritual sense, Northern Plains peoples believed that bundles were alive and that their power could be released into the world through effective ritual action. This belief was based on the view that other-than-human persons, such as Otter, Buffalo, Elk, or Corn, had given their special powers to an individual in a vision or had mediated these powers through a *culture hero*. These powerful others had specified what should be in

Figure 10.2 A Northern Plains bundle

particular bundles, how they were to be cared for and how their rituals were to be enacted. If the ritual action was performed correctly, then a hunt would be successful, a wound would be healed, an enemy overcome, or rain would fall on a thirsty garden.

There were, generally speaking, bundles that were associated with the well-being of groups or even the entire society; and there were bundles that were related to the needs of particular individuals. Since the needs of the individual were not clearly distinguished from those of society, the functions of these two classes of bundles often overlapped. Smaller bundles that assisted hunters or protected individuals during battle were common; some of the larger bundles that related to the needs of the group performed these functions as well.

Bundles that were powerful for hunting and for gardening, as well as the rituals that enacted their power, expressed in a more concrete manner the relationship between genders in Northern Plains societies. Male culture heroes or male animal persons often gave hunting bundles to men, although there were exceptions to this rule. And agricultural bundles were associated in some societies with female culture heroes, although there were important exceptions to this rule as well. Ritual knowledge surrounding these important life activities drew a symbolic boundary between the genders and created a division of labour between them.

Because bundles were associated with important cultural values within Northern Plains societies, they tended to be resistant to change. And because they were given by other-than-human persons to individuals who were members of particular groups, their origin traditions and rituals tended to become a deep part of the self-understanding of the people. Along with religious traditions that embodied the actions of creator figures, bundles and their ritual processes became formative for Northern Plains world experience. In many instances, the religious traditions along with their other-than-human figures became dramatized in the rituals of specific societies.

Bundles were focused not only upon important life activities, but were also central to other more complex rituals that released energies believed to be efficacious for the society as well as the individual. The various Sun Dances on the Northern Plains often had one or more bundles at the core of their ritual processes. For example, the Blackfoot Natoas Bundle was a central ritual object in the historic *Okan* or Sun Dance ceremony. The Mandan *Okipa*, a ritual of great complexity, as well as the *Sacred Arrow* ceremony of the Cheyennes, were focused around bundles that were essential to their meaning as well as to their success. These more elaborate societal rituals often dramatized the migration traditions of the group, their creator and culture hero traditions and their special homelands. In this manner, the symbolic forms enacted in these rituals deepened and sustained that identity of the people.

Bundles were in the possession or under the care of ritually and religiously qualified persons. Such individuals were bound by the rules that surrounded these living realities, and they were custodians of knowledge and the ritual processes by means of which their power was released. Social power in Northern Plains societies was acquired through religious experiences and through ownership or control of religious powers released through bundles. Persons who were ritually and religiously qualified occupied a higher status and exercised more social power than those who were recipients of the religious energies released. These ritually and religiously qualified persons were often elevated to positions of political leadership; they gained wealth as a result of gifts that were given as payment for exercising their ritual knowledge in bundle openings; and they were often prominent leaders in major religious ceremonies.

Because of the close relationship between religious experiences, religious practices and social power, resistance to change and impulses towards preservation of religious continuity were common in Northern Plains societies. Yet change did occur. Whether a bundle was owned or kept by a qualified individual there had developed elaborate rules in most of these societies that governed the transfer of bundle ownership and its power. Generally, the movement of bundles and their power was structured either by kinship or by an exchange of property between two unrelated individuals. If the control of major bundles was based in kinship patterns, then they might be inherited, following either the father's or the mother's line, depending on the societal pattern. No matter what the pattern of descent, the ritual knowledge that released the bundle's power was carefully guarded and passed systematically to the appropriate kinsperson or family group. In this system of bundle ownership, both the individual owner or keeper and the family group were recipients of the social status and

Figure 10.3 A ceremonial pipe that might be in a Northern Plains bundle

power associated with the bundle. There was an attempt on the part of these family groups to keep their social power and influence intact. These patterns of transfer were characteristic of the Mandans, for example. If bundles were transferred from one unrelated individual to another, the extended families still participated in gathering the horses, material goods and food necessary for the exchange. The family also shared in the social influence that accompanied bundle ownership. In these cases there was also an attempt to control access to social influence and to transfer to those who were qualified by virtue of their religious experiences and their social status. Such processes of transfer were characteristic among the Blackfeet.

Religious experience

Dreams and visions, as well as induced suffering and physical deprivations, prepared Northern Plains people for religious experiences. Since there was such a close relationship between religious experience and social status, the quest for visions and dreams, as well as for honourable occasions to endure suffering, were prominent features of these societies. The life chances for young men and in some groups for young women were vastly enhanced by a successful vision quest, although the quest for power did not necessarily end with youth but often continued throughout an individual's life. The Sun Dances and other ritual processes provided occasions for individuals to endure the suffering that was often a prerequisite for religious experience.

The most rigorous forms of induced suffering involved fasting and the sacrifice of flesh and other body parts. During many Northern Plains Sun Dances, as well as during the Mandan Okipa, male dancers were pierced on each side of their chest and sometimes on each side of their back. Skewers were inserted into these cuts and individuals were suspended from the rafters of the ceremonial Okipa Lodge in the case of the Mandans. Among the Blackfeet, Lakotas and other groups, individual dancers attached thongs to the chest skewers. These thongs were then tied to the centre pole of the Sun Dance enclosure. The dancers would usually fast and refrain from drinking water during the course of the ceremony, and would dance until the skewers were torn from their flesh. In some instances they would attach a number of buffalo skulls to skewers on either side of their back, dragging the skulls until their flesh was torn and they were released. During these periods of intense suffering, individuals often had rich, life changing vision experiences. Sometimes these visions were believed to be beneficial for the flourishing of the group as well.

In some Northern Plains societies, powerful dreams or visions, combined with appropriate suffering, might qualify individuals to become bundle owners, but there were social controls that governed such experiences in these societies. Older persons who were religiously or ritually qualified and who were or had been bundle owners became gatekeepers who interpreted the meaning of dreams or visions to younger persons. Control over the interpretation of dreams and vision experiences provided some limitations on both who and how many persons could share in bundle ownership and the social privileges that followed from such ownership. No matter what the patterns of ownership and transfer were, the power of major bundles circulated throughout most Northern Plains societies. This power, focused as it was around core values having to do with essential life activities, was finally believed to be of benefit to all and could not for this reason be dominated by any

Figure 10.4 A Northern Plains Sun Dance lodge

one individual or group. Even though there were occasional examples of individual or group aggrandizement, there were social pressures that militated against such egoistic tendencies.

INTERACTIONS WITH MODERNITY

Interpreting social change

Social continuity within Northern Plains societies was maintained by shared world pictures and common religious practices that were specific to each group. These world pictures arose out of cultural symbols that embodied the activities of powerful others who transcended, yet who at the same time gave rise to, the world of everyday experience. Images of origin and destiny funded the sense of identity among peoples and maintained cultural boundaries between groups. If social continuity was constituted and maintained by such powerful symbols, how is social change to be understood and what is the role of religion in social change, especially that brought about by European colonizers and modernizers?

European contact brought not only new cultural items, such as iron pots, guns, and horses, but also epidemic diseases and powerful but alien cultural values. What is needed is a view that emphasizes the significance of religion for understanding the responses of Northern Plains societies to such threats and the appearance of novelty in their environments. In addition, we need to understand how a sense of continuity was maintained in the experience of people faced by dramatic social change. The essential point is that cultural interchange, whether between Europeans and Northern Plains societies or among Northern Plains societies, did not always lead to an experience of fundamental social change. A sense of continuity was often maintained in the experience of many groups because their cultural identities, grounded in traditions of origin and evoked in ritual processes, were reinterpreted. The process of reinterpretation functioned to preserve a sense that the world experience and the basic identity of the group were intact.

When novelty, threat, or perceived danger appeared in Northern Plains social worlds, traditional methods of interpretation came into play. Seeking visions was the socially legitimated method for dealing with both internal and external threats. Religiously qualified persons, such as bundle owners or keepers, sought counsel through their dreams and visions. The results of these experiences motivated interpretations of the meaning of novelty or threats and also suggested modes of response that were viewed as being in continuity with self-understanding of the society. From this perspective, social change needs to be interpreted in relation to the creative responses of human agents as they struggled to reconstitute their worlds.

Because dreams were so pervasive in these societies, individuals who were at the margins of the group and who were lacking in social power might make their contributions through this avenue as well. There were many narratives in the oral traditions, for example, that told of powerful dreams and visions that arose in the experience of socially marginal, often anonymous, individuals. Sometimes the experiences of these individuals became important sources of social innovation. But for the majority of dream experiences, the successful legitimation of new interpretations required the co-operation of past and present bundle owners. If such legitimation occurred, then the reservoirs of memory that mediated a sense of continuity in social life and that maintained the symbolic boundaries that constituted the identity of the group were reshaped.

Given these complexities, social change needs to be understood from at least two perspectives. On the one hand, interpreters of the Northern Plains have rightly focused on traumatic or externally induced social changes as a characteristic and pervasive feature of these societies. On the other hand, looked at from within these societies, many Northern Plains peoples experienced continuity more predominantly than change. Reinterpretation sometimes led to an expansion of tradition rather than to a sense of rupture and social crisis. It is essential to understand these societies from both of these perspectives.

There were also times when Northern Plains societies endured experiences of social transformation that led to the formation of a new identity. In these cases, the same patterns of religious leadership, religious experience, and social legitimation that have been discussed were employed as groups moved towards a new social identity. The outcome, however, may not have been the expansion of shared traditions, but rather the construction of new traditions that became, over time, socially routinized and taken for granted. For example, the Cheyennes moved from their earlier homeland in the present day state of Minnesota to a semi-sedentary background on the Missouri River, and finally to the Northern Plains. In their case, the emergence of a new social identity was dependent on the appropriation of reinterpreted origin and culture hero traditions. In this case, the culture hero led the people to a new homeland, bringing them the gift of a bundle focused on hunting and war rather than agriculture.

The groups who lived on the Northern Plains became identifiable peoples through creatively constructing shared social meanings that led to the emergence of specific societies. But these societies did not construct their social identities out of nothing. Even the older occupants of the area, such as the Mandans, had a history and came from other places, experiencing social changes and perhaps significant transformations in the course of their migrations. The construction and maintenance of their identities as peoples was historically emergent, and the sense of continuity that they possessed had more the quality of a moving equilibrium than of stasis or the realization of an unchanging social essence.

While the importance of colonialization, the spread of epidemic diseases, the diffusion of the horse, expansion of the fur trade, and increased pressures from advancing European populations are all essential factors in understanding the historical situations of specific native peoples, the perspective developed above is also fundamental. This perspective seeks to understand social change in terms of the creative responses of native peoples rather than viewing the situation purely in terms of domination by colonizers, their technologies, and their cultural values. Native peoples struggled to interpret the meaning of what was happening to them, sought to relate in creative ways to alien cultural forms even if that creativity was often expressed in terms of resistance. In this sense, peoples in the Americas were agents within a larger historical process that finally engulfed both them and the European settlers.

Present trajectories

These perspectives on the role of religion in both continuity and change are helpful for interpreting twentieth- and twenty-first-century social realities among Northern Plains peoples. During the late nineteenth and early twentieth centuries, enormous social pressures were placed on indigenous peoples in the US. In 1887 the US Congress passed the General Allotment Act, also known as the Dawes Act. This legislation was aimed at breaking up tribal land holdings by allotting parcels to individuals and families. Often the reservation land that was left over after allotment was opened up for white settlement. Accompanying the General Allotment Act were attempts to coerce Native American peoples to give up their languages, forms of dress, ceremonial life, and oral traditions. The federal and private boarding schools created during this period were intended as powerful instruments of social changes that would lead to assimilation and the full Americanization of indigenous children.

Early twentieth-century announcements that Native American cultures would disappear either through assimilation or through internal disintegration have clearly been proven wrong. At the same time that people on the Northern Plains were being subjected to repressive acculturation policies there were individuals and groups engaged in resistance and cultural preservation. Ironically, the production of massive ethnographic and linguistic studies during the late nineteenth and early twentieth centuries also functioned to preserve materials to which later generations of Native American people could return to reconstruct aspects of their cultures and languages. While many groups on the Northern Plains and elsewhere were reduced to poverty and became marginal ethnic groups within the larger North American society, they continued in many instances to preserve their oral traditions and ritual processes. These oral traditions and ritual processes were dynamic realities that were reinterpreted through time, but they functioned to mediate a sense of identity to many Native American peoples. The oral traditions and ritual processes described in this essay are the sources out of which many contemporary Northern Plains peoples have constructed their individual and social identities. While responses to the forced acculturation policies of the late nineteenth century in North America ran from resistance to assimilation, and it is also true that some groups did not survive this trauma, the vitality of specific Native American cultures that did survive reappeared in surprisingly vigorous ways. The present time in history, at the beginning of a new millennium, is a moment when these cultural expressions are again very visible.

Non-indigenous people are more or less aware that Native American competitive dancing on the Powwow circuit is a very prominent reality on many reservations. Among Native American groups who do not live on reservations, these gatherings may also hold some importance as well. Powwows include many activities besides dancing, such as marketing of crafts, art, music and foods, and are open to non-indigenous participation. These gatherings are important institutionalized settings for the maintenance of a modern Native American ethnic identity as well. They are not, however, the most important religious occasions and one must look more closely to bring into view the religious traditions and rituals that are again becoming quite visible on many reservations.

Among the Blackfeet in the contemporary US, for example, the Okan or Sun Dance ritual is again being enacted with increasingly regularity. The same observation can also be made about other groups who have similar ritual processes, such as the Crows and the Lakotas. And among the Cheyenne people, both those who now live in the state of Oklahoma and those who live in southern Montana, the ritual of the Sacred Arrow bundle is still of central cultural significance. Among other Northern Plains groups, bundle ownership and ritual use of these sacred objects also seems on the increase. Among these groups, the practice of piercing has returned and is a visible part of many Sun Dance rituals on the Northern Plains. While the historic Sun Dances involved most or all in the society in the encampment, modern ceremonies are often smaller and associated with particular religious specialists and even extended families. What is striking about these rituals is their continuity with elements of past traditions and their creative adaptability in response to elements of the modern world. While many Native Americans may visit Western-trained physicians for specific ailments, they may also participate in a Sun Dance for the purpose of healing as well. In these rituals appeal is often made to transcendent powers, such as Sun and Moon, in symbolic continuity with a longer past. As in traditional times – but also in continuity with modern alternative spiritual beliefs – healing is viewed in a holistic manner, involving both the body and the spirit.

In continuing ritual processes that involve sweating and the opening of bundles one can again observe continuities at the level of ritual form and oral tradition. One can also observe creative adaptations and in many instances, cultural innovation as well. For example, rather than being associated with hunting and agriculture as some of the bundle rituals had been in the past, contemporary needs for individual and social health are often addressed in the ritual processes. In continuity with older forms, the frame of modern sweat lodges is often built out of willow branches constructed over a central fire pit. Unlike

previous times when the willow frame would be covered
with buffalo robes, contemporary structures are covered
with blankets or whatever material happens to be
available. In these lodges contemporary Native American
people sing, pray, and consult the spirit world while
enduring the intense heat and steam the that are released
when water is sprinkled on the glowing rocks in the fire
pit.

Figure 10.5 A sweat lodge frame

Sweat lodge rituals precede the contemporary
Blackfoot Okan as well as Lakota and Crow Sun Dances. Native American persons in prisons regularly
request that they be allowed to express their religious lives not only through smoking ceremonial pipes,
wearing eagle feathers and opening bundles, but also by engaging in sweat lodge ceremonies. Among
many Northern Plains groups, the sweat lodge ritual has preserved some of its older significance while
at the same time the ritual and oral traditions have often been adapted to new circumstances.
Psychological and physical healing, for example, are prominent features of present practice. These ritual
practices often focus on destructive behaviour such as alcohol abuse and domestic violence. At the same
time, there are also prayers for power that will enable the entire group to flourish.

Another ritual practice of continuing importance across the Northern Plains is the ceremonial use
of sage, sweetgrass, tobacco and animal or bird body parts. Sage is often burnt continuously during the
course of a four-day Blackfoot Okan ceremony. This plant is understood by the participants to be very
powerful, and persons who participate in the ritual regularly seek its comfort and power by passing
their bodies through the smoke that arises from burning sage. Sweetgrass is often used as a plug to
secure tobacco in ceremonial pipes. This plug is removed before smoking and buried in the ground.
Braids of sweetgrass are also burnt to create a sacred smudge that people believe is good for both body
and spirit. Eagle wing fans and other animal body parts often appear in connection with a bundle
opening, again in continuity with a longer past.

In addition to more traditional religious expressions, any interpretation of contemporary Northern
Plains religions must take into account the extent to which Native Americans have appropriated
elements of Protestant and Roman Catholic Christianity. Renewal of cultural forms, oral traditions
and ritual processes connected with indigenous motifs deriving from a longer past does not tell the
entire story. Untold numbers of Native Americans became Christians in response to the missionary
movement although it is difficult to tell exactly what 'conversion' meant in many instances. What is
certainly true is that all groups in North America have been influenced in one way or another by
Christianity, and may synthesize their oral traditions and rituals with various elements of Christianity.
For example, the Native American church in North America is an extension of a much older form that
involved the ritual ingestion of parts of the peyote cactus, a plant that has psychedelic properties.
Although this religious practice originated in Mexico and moved into North America, the Native
American church appropriated images and beliefs from Christianity. In many peyote ceremonies, for
example, the figure of Jesus Christ is quite prominent.

The encounter with Christianity has also produced communities of Native American Christians.
These communities are to be found all across the US and often reflect encounters early in the history
of European conquest and settlement when ancestors of present people were converted to Christianity.
Like the missions themselves, Native American Christianity often reflects the many denominational
and doctrinal affiliations characteristic of wider American society. Within Protestantism, for example,
some of these Native American Christians are liberal, some are conservative and some are
fundamentalists. And among Catholics the spectrum runs from post-Vatican II Catholicism to more

traditional and conservative forms of Catholicism. This portrait would be incomplete, however, without recalling the circumstances of forced acculturation mentioned earlier in this essay. In many instances, Protestant and Catholic churches were the *loci* where social pressures were initially applied in the attempt to assimilate Native American peoples. Tragically, some of the tensions associated with conversion to Christianity still trouble some Native American people, creating rifts within the extended families on some reservations.

Additional conflicts and violence continue to occur in relation to the imaginative appropriation of native peoples by non-Indians. For example, in North America images of Native American people have been readily available as cultural fodder for films and television. Before this, Native American graves were also looted, skeletal remains taken for scientific study and ritual objects collected for display in museums in both the US and Canada. Clear examples of cultural appropriation by non-Indians of what are believed to be Native American views often occur as well in connection with discussions of contemporary environmental issues. For example, Native American religion and culture are currently viewed by many in North America as sources of ecological wisdom. This popular appropriation of Native American religions by non-natives is, for the most part, a fundamental distortion of earlier indigenous views of animals, plants and the earth. These earlier views were supported by culture-specific symbolic universes within which animals, plants and natural forces, such as wind, and objects, such as the sun, were experienced as persons. Ritual processes related the people to these powerful others in ways that embodied specific cultural meanings and sensibilities. Contemporary environmental problems generated by modern societies are specific to the technologies and science of the West and cannot, without distortion, be directly addressed through the symbolic universes of past native peoples. Even so, many expressions of New Age and popular religion in the US lay claim to such indigenous wisdom and seek to appropriate it as their own. Those who see this as an extension of cultural colonialism are may well be correct in their judgement.

Despite these negative features which continue to distort Native American traditions, the signs of indigenous religious innovations indicate that many Native American peoples still possess cultural vitality. Given the violent experience of conquest, the decimation of populations by epidemic diseases and the history of forced acculturation and mission that have characterized their experience in North America, it is remarkable that so many aspects of Native American cultures have survived. The dominant culture has been unsuccessful in completely extinguishing Native American religions, their oral traditions and their ritual processes. Native American people continue to exist, some occupying a significant land base, and continue to define themselves as peoples with specific cultural identities. In many instances, such as the case of the Crows, the Blackfeet and the Lakotas the recovery of language is a part of this total picture of continuing vitality. And, as this chapter has highlighted, religion continues to play a central role.

Summary

- Northern Plains peoples provide a case study that illustrates how important religion was for enabling these groups to respond constructively to the pressures of modernization, including disease, conquest, missions and government policies of forced acculturation.
- Religious traditions and rituals established symbolic boundaries that have enabled native people to achieve a distinctive identity and at the same time provided resources for interpreting their encounters both with each other and with Europeans.
- Religious traditions and rituals still enable present Native American peoples to maintain some

continuity with their historical past while they struggle, often creatively, with the continuing pressures emanating from the dominant North American society.

▪ Because religion has been such a powerful force in both past and present American Indian experience, Native American ethnic identities remain a rich and important part of North American social landscape.

▪ Key terms

Arapaho   The Arapahoes are an Algonquian-speaking group that migrated to the Northern Plains from what is now the state of Minnesota. The descendants of these people now live on reservations in the states of Wyoming and Oklahoma.

Arikara   Along with the Mandans and Hidatsas, the Arikaras were early migrants to the Northern Plains. They lived in earth lodge villages on the Missouri River near the border between the present states of North and South Dakota. Although they formed a separate group, they were once kinsfolk of the Pawnees and were of Caddoan linguistic stock. Desendants of these people now live on the Fort Berthold Reservation in North Dakota.

Blackfeet   The Blackfeet (or Blackfoot) are presently located on reservations in the state of Montana in the US and the province of Alberta in Canada. They are of Algonquian linguistic stock and were historically divided into three groups, the Northern Blackfeet (Siksika), the Bloods (Kainah) and the Piegans (Pikuni).

bundles   widespread ritual objects on the Northern Plains and elsewhere in North America. A bundle contains many diverse items such as face paints, animal body parts, skins, and plant materials wrapped in animal skins. Bundles arose as a consequence of a vision experience and were believed to bring their possessors power to accomplish important life activities such as hunting, gardening, making war, or healing.

cardinal directions   For many Native American peoples, the cardinal directions were associated with primordial personal powers. In some Cheyenne traditions, for example, Winter Man was associated with the north and Thunder with the south. In other Native American traditions the east and west are associated with the sun's path. Almost always associated with specific colours, the symbolism of the four directions is still widespread in Native American ritual processes.

Cheyenne   The Cheyennes are an Algonquian-speaking people who lived, in the seventeenth century, in the present state of Minnesota. Driven from these homelands by the Sioux and other peoples pushing west, the Cheyennes migrated towards the Northern Plains. Some of these people settled for a time on the Missouri River near the Mandans and Hidatsas. There they raised gardens, hunted buffalo and lived in earth lodge villages. Eventually they moved further west towards the Black Hills of South Dakota, becoming in the process fully nomadic tipi-dwelling buffalo hunters. Descendants of these people presently live on reservations in the states of Montana and Oklahoma.

Crow   The Crows are a Siouan-speaking people who lived in earth lodges along the Missouri River in North Dakota. In the eighteenth century they split from the Hidatsas and moved west towards the

Yellowstone River country of Montana. There they became tipi-dwelling buffalo hunters sharing with others the traits of Plains culture. Their descendants presently live on a reservation in the state of Montana.

culture hero   In the anthropological literature on Native American peoples, the term 'culture hero' usually refers to a powerful individual who brought the people important gifts, such as bundles, that are associated with major ritual processes. These individuals are prominently represented in the oral traditions of Northern Plains peoples.

earth lodge   Earth lodges were round structures built around a central four-post frame and were covered with sod. They were long lasting, energy efficient dwellings that were constructed by peoples, such as the Mandans, Hidatsas and Arikaras, who lived in fortified villages on the Missouri River.

Hidatsa   The Hidatsas were closely associated with the Mandans on the Missouri River in North Dakota. They occupied earth lodge villages at the mouth of the Knife River and engaged in a very successful dual economy that included extensive gardening and buffalo hunting. Some of their descendants presently live on the Fort Berthold Reservation in North Dakota.

Lakota   The Lakotas were a part of the larger Siouan-speaking group of people who migrated to the Northern Plains from their homelands in Minnesota. Like other migrants to the area, some of these people became fully nomadic, horse mounted, tipi-dwelling buffalo hunters. Of all the Siouan people, the Teton Lakotas are perhaps the most well known among non-Native Americans due in part to the fame of the holy man Black Elk, whose autobiography was published under the title *Black Elk Speaks*.

Mandan   The Mandans were a group of Siouan-speaking earth lodge dwellers who lived in the Heart River area of North Dakota near present-day Bismarck, North Dakota. Some of the ancestors of these people may have migrated to the Northern Plains as early as 1100 CE. They created a very successful way of life that depended on extensive gardening and hunting buffalo. The Mandans were almost exterminated by the smallpox epidemic of 1837 and some of the descendants of these people still live on the Fort Berthold Reservation in North Dakota.

Old Man/Old Woman   Figures in the Blackfoot creation accounts who gave rise not only to the earth but also to important features of human life. As a consequence of a discussion between these two figures, for example, the roles of men and women were established and the order of life and death was determined.

okan   A Blackfoot term for a ritual more commonly referred to as the 'Sun Dance.' Held during the late summer, this ritual involved the entire Blackfoot nation in a ceremony that was focused on the renewal of the buffalo and, indeed, of the entire world. Prominent among the features of this ritual was the male practice of piercing flesh in the chest area, inserting wooden skewers into the cuts and dancing tethered to the centre pole with leather thongs until the skin broke loose.

okipa   A complex Mandan ritual that recapitulated the history of the group and involved the renewal of the animals that were hunted for food. The ritual was held in an earth lodge that was usually larger than normal and included the spectacular suffering of individuals who were suspended inside the lodge on thongs attached to skewers thrust into cuts made in their chest or back muscles.

Pawnee   The Pawnees were a Caddoan speaking group of people who lived in the area of the present state of Nebraska. Their ceremonial life was based on a series of powerful bundles, the most important of which were focused star traditions, such as the Morning Star, which involved the yearly sacrifice of a young woman. The Pawnees were kinsfolk of the Arikaras and their descendants now live in the state of Oklahoma.

sacred arrows   This was a widespread motif in Northern Plains cultures. The Cheyennes, for example, had a sacred arrow bundle that was given to them by their culture hero, Sweet Medicine. Two of the arrows in this bundle were powerful for war making and two were powerful for hunting.

trickster   This term was developed by historians of religion and anthropologists to describe the ambiguous yet powerful figures that populated the oral traditions of Native American peoples in North America. These figures were often represented as foolish, sexually predatory and destructive yet they sometimes engaged in powerful transformations of the world. Trickster traditions are still widely told on reservations across the Northern Plains.

FURTHER READING

General

Howard Harrod: *Renewing the World: Plains Indian Religion and Morality* (Tucson, AZ: University of Arizona, 1987); Howard Harrod: *Becoming and Remaining a People: Native American Religions on the Northern Plains* (Tucson, AZ: University of Arizona, 1995).

Native American peoples

Alfred Bowers: *Hidatsa Social and Ceremonial Organization* (Lincoln, NE: University of Nebraska Press, 1992) offers a very detailed study of the history and ethnography of the Hidatsa people. Alfred Bowers: *Mandan Social and Ceremonial Organization* (Chicago, IL: University of Chicago Press, 1950) presents the history and ethnography of the Mandan people. Raymond Bucko: *The Lakota Ritual of the Sweat Lodge: History and Contemporary Practice* (Lincoln, NE: University of Nebraska Press, 1998) offers an overview of the Lakota sweat lodge showing how contemporary forms are both continuous and discontinuous with the past. John C. Ewers: *The Blackfeet: Raiders on the Nortwestern Plains* (Norman, OK: University of Oklahoma Press, 1961) is still the best single overview of Blackfoot history and culture. George Bird Grinnell: *The Cheyenne Indians: Their History and Ways of Life*, 2 volumes (Lincoln, NE: University of Nebraska Press, 1972) presents a comprehensive view of the Cheyenne people. Alfred Kroeber: *The Arapaho* (Lincoln, NE: University of Nebraska Press, 1983) offers an overview of Arapaho culture and religion.

Beliefs and rituals

Lee Irwin: *The Dream Seekers: Native American Visionary Traditions of the Great Plains* (Norman, OK: University of Oklahoma Press, 1994) offers an excellent overview of dream and vision experiences on the Great Plains as a whole. William K. Powers: *War Dance: Plains Indian Musical Performance* (Tucson, AZ: University of Arizona Press, 1990) provides an overview of Plains music and dance which shows how contemporary expressions represent both cultural innovations as well as the preservation of older cultural traditions.

Gender

Will Roscoe: *Changing Ones: Third and Fourth Genders in Native North America* (New York, NY: St Martin's Press, 1998) is a fine study of the 'berdache,' both male and female, in Native American societies. Mark St Pierre and Tilda Long Soldier: *Walking in the Sacred Manner* (New York, NY: Simon & Schuster, 1995) provides reflections by a Lakota woman on women healers, dreamers and medicine persons.

Mission and colonization

Studies of the impact of the missionary movement on native peoples in both North and South America are legion. For examples, see Luis N. Rivera: *A Violent Evangelism: The Political and Religious Conquest of the Americas* (Louisville, KY: Westminster/John Knox Press, 1992); George E. Tinker: *Missionary Conquest: The Gospel and Native American Cultural Genocide* (Minneapolis, MN: Fortress Press, 1993); Homer Noley: *First White Frost: Native Americans and United Methodism* (Nashville, TN: Abandon Press, 1991); James Axtell: *The Invasion Within: The Contest of Cultures in Colonial North America* (New York, NY: Oxford University Press, 1985); and Howard L. Harrod, *Mission among the Blackfeet* (Norman, OK: University of Oklahoma Press, 1971, 1999).

American Indian Christians

For analysis of some of the contemporary issues associated with the appropriation of Christianity, see Jace Weaver (ed.): *Native American Religious Identity: Unforgotten Gods* (Maryknoll: Orbis Books, 1998) and James Treat (ed.): *Native and Christian: Indigenous Voices on Religious Identity in the US and Canada* (New York, NY: Routledge, 1996). Christopher Vecsey has produced a massive study of Roman Catholicism among Native Americans. See his three volumes in the *American Indian Catholic Series: On the Padre's Trail*: Vol. I (Notre Dame: University of Notre Dame Press, 1996), *The Paths of Kateri's Kin*: Vol. II (Notre Dame: University of Notre Dame Press, 1998), and *Where the Two Roads Meet*: Vol. III (Notre Dame: University of Notre Dame Press, 1999).

Primary sources

Percy Bullchild: *The Sun Came Down: The History of the World as My Blackfeet Elders Told It* (San Francisco, CA: Harper & Row, 1985) is a fascinating contemporary rendering of traditions and rituals by a respected elder of the Blackfoot nation. Raymond J. DeMallie (ed.): *The Sixth Grandfather: Black*

Elk's Teachings Given to John G. Neihardt (Lincoln, NE: University of Nebraska Press, 1984) provides a rich context for interpreting Black Elk, the famous Lakota holy man associated with the immensely popular book *Black Elk Speaks* (Lincoln, NE: University of Nebraska Press, 1961). *Yellowtail: Crow Medicine Man and Sun Dance Chief* (Norman, OK: University of Oklahoma Press, 1991) is a very illuminating autobiography of an important Crow spiritual leader, as told to Michael Oren Fitzgerald. Clark Wissler and D. C. Duvall: *Mythology of the Blackfoot Indians* (Lincoln, NE: University of Nebraska Press, 1995) is a collection of oral traditions gathered on the Blackfeet Reservation in Montana between 1903 and 1907 by a cultural anthropologist and a native speaker.

CHAPTER 11

New Age religion

Wouter J. Hanegraaff

▌ INTRODUCTION

New Age is not so much a religion as a buzzword that achieved popularity chiefly in Europe and the US during the 1980s. The wide and often vague use of the term, and the amorphous nature of the phenomena it refers to, make it impossible to gain any accurate impression of the numbers involved. For reasons which will be explored below, it is most influential in modern (industrial and post-industrial) societies, particularly North America, Europe, Australia and New Zealand – though pockets of influence may also be found in cosmopolitan cities worldwide, from Rio de Janeiro to Bombay.

As a buzzword, New Age refers to a wide array of spiritual practices and beliefs which share as their most common denominator the fact that they are perceived as 'alternative' from the perspective of mainstream Western society. To many observers during the 1980s, the increasing visibility of its representatives in the media and popular culture conveyed the impression of something radically new: the birth of a grass-roots movement of social and spiritual innovation, prophesying a profound transformation of Western society that should, in due course, culminate in a vastly superior culture – the 'Age of Aquarius' (Ferguson, 1980). Actually, what came to be known as the 'New Age movement' has its immediate roots in the *counter-culture* of the 1960s and some of its immediate predecessors, but its fundamental ideas can be traced much further back into history. As will be seen, New Age religion is neither something completely new, nor just a revival – or survival – of something ancient. It has ancient roots, which need to be taken into account in order to understand the movement that grew from them; indeed, from one perspective New Age may be seen as merely the contemporary manifestation of the traditional alternative religiosity of the West. But perceived from another perspective, New Age religion is radically new: a manifestation *par excellence* of postmodern consumer society, the members of which use, recycle, combine and adapt existing religious ideas and practices as they see fit. In order to understand the New Age movement and its role in the modern world, we therefore need to understand its historical foundations as well as its specific modernity.

The chapter will proceed by first distinguishing two senses of New Age – a wide and a strict sense – before going on to consider its historical roots in esoteric and occult traditions in Christian culture. The impact of modernity is considered in two stages: first, the impact of Enlightenment and early post-Enlightenment modernity (the rise of the natural and psychological sciences being particularly important); second, the impact of later capitalist, consumerist modernity.

New Age in a wide and in a strict sense

FLYING SAUCERS AND UTOPIAN COMMUNITIES

The immediate roots of the New Age movement may seem surprising at first sight. Shortly after the Second World War, popular curiosity was attracted by unexplained phenomena in the sky referred to as Unidentified Flying Objects (UFOs). In various places in Western Europe and the US, study groups were formed by people who wanted to investigate these phenomena, and some of those groups rapidly proceeded to take on 'cultic' characteristics. Typically, such groups believed that the UFOs were in fact spaceships inhabited by intelligent beings from other planets or other dimensions of outer space. Representing a superior level of cultural, technological and spiritual evolution, they now made their appearance to herald the coming of a New Age. The earth was entering a new evolutionary cycle that would be accompanied by a new and superior kind of spiritual consciousness. However, since the present cultures of humanity were thoroughly corrupted by materialism, they would resist this change. As a result, the transition to a new cycle of evolution would necessitate the destruction of the old civilization, by violent causes such as earthquakes, floods, diseases and the like, resulting in global economic, political and social collapse. Those individuals whose consciousness was already in tune with the qualities of the new culture would be protected in various ways, and would survive the period of cataclysms. In due course they would become the vanguard of the New Age, or Age of Aquarius: an age of abundance, bliss and spiritual enlightenment when humanity would once again live in accordance with universal cosmic laws (Spangler, 1984).

These beliefs were inspired by occultist teachings of various provenance, but especially by the writings of the Christian Theosophist Alice Bailey (1880–1949) and, in some respects, the anthroposophical metaphysics of the German visionary Rudolf Steiner (1861–1925). In 1937, Alice Bailey 'channelled' a spiritual prayer known as 'The Great Invocation', which is still being used by New Age adherents to invoke the New Age.

▌THE GREAT INVOCATION

From the point of Light within the Mind of God
Let Light stream forth into the minds of men.
Let Light descend on Earth.

From the point of Love within the Heart of God
Let Love stream forth into the hearts of men.
May Christ return to Earth

From the centre where the Will of God is known
Let purpose guide the little wills of men –
The purpose which the Masters know and serve.

From the centre which we call the race of men
Let the Plan of Love and Light work out.
And may it seal the door where evil dwells.

Let Light and Love and Power restore the Plan on Earth.

These lines illustrate the pronounced Christian elements that still informed the occultist *millenarianism* of the early New Age movement. These elements would remain prominent during the second, counter-cultural stage of its development. During the 1960s, the basic belief system and millenarian expectations of the UFO groups were adopted by various utopian communities, the most famous of which is the Findhorn community in Scotland. The members of these communities were trying to live in a new way, in tune with the universal laws of nature and the universe. They were trying, in the spirit of the 'Great Invocation', to be 'centres of light' or focal points in a network from which spiritual illumination would eventually spread out and encompass the globe. In the attitude of these early New Agers, represented by popular spokesmen such as David Spangler (b. 1945) or George Trevelyan (1906–96), an important change took place compared with the perspective of the UFO groups of the 1950s. Whereas the pronounced *apocalypticism* of the latter entailed an essentially passive attitude of 'waiting for the great events' that would destroy the old civilization and usher in a New Age, utopian communities of the 1960s, such as Findhorn, increasingly emphasized the importance of an activist, constructive attitude: 'Instead of spreading warnings of apocalypse, let Findhorn proclaim that the new age is already here, in spirit if not in form, and that anyone can now cocreate with that spirit so that the form will become manifest' (Spangler, 1984: 34–5). This became the perspective typical of the New Age movement of the 1960s and its sympathizers in later decades.

THE CULTIC MILIEU

This early New Age movement, born in the context of the postwar UFO cults and flowering in the spiritual *utopianism* of the 1960s and 1970s, was only one particular manifestation of the counter-cultural ferment of the times. More generally, this ferment found expression in a widespread 'cultic milieu' (the term comes from

Figure 11.1 David Spangler was born in Columbus, Ohio, in 1945. He spent much of his childhood in North Africa where he had a number of spiritual experiences which led him to an awareness that humanity is entering a new cycle of evolution and stands at the threshold of a New Age. In 1964 he began lecturing on human and planetary transformation in the United States and Europe. He was a co-director of the Findhorn Foundation community in northern Scotland for three years before returning to the United States and becoming a founder–director of the Lorian Association

Campbell, 1972) in Western society: a diffuse phenomenon consisting of individuals who feel dissatisfied with mainstream Western culture and religion, and are looking for alternatives (see also Chapter 15). This cultic milieu proved to be fertile soil for a plethora of New Religious Movements of various provenance. Some of these movements took the form of relatively stable social entities, including an internal hierarchy of power and authority, definite doctrines and rules of conduct, clearly defined boundaries between members and non-members, claims of exclusive truth, and so on (see Chapter 12). Other movements were more ephemeral and fluid, functioning as client cults with relatively few demands on members, and an inclusive and tolerant attitude. The latter type of cultic group may come into existence quickly and vanish as quickly again, and its membership may sometimes be very small. Members may participate in several such groups at the same time – displaying an activity known as 'spiritual shopping' – without feeling committed to making a choice in favour of the one at the expense of the other. This type of spiritual activity is most characteristic for the development of the 'cultic milieu' that spawned and supported the New Age movement of the 1980s.

It is helpful to distinguish the latter movement from the original New Age movement described above. The spiritual perspectives associatied with the UFO cults of the 1950s and the utopian communities of the 1960s and 1970s may collectively be referred to as the 'New Age movement in a strict sense' (Hanegraaff, 1996: 94–103). This movement is characterized by a broadly occultist metaphysics (with special prominence of the deviant forms of *Theosophy* founded by Alice Bailey and, to some extent, Rudolf Steiner), a relatively strong emphasis on community values and a traditional morality emphasizing altruistic love and service to humanity, and a very strong millenarian emphasis focusing on the expectation of the New Age. This New Age movement in a strict sense still exists, but its membership is rather strongly dominated by the baby boomers generation and tends to be perceived as somewhat old-fashioned by new-generation New Agers. By the end of the 1970s, this New Age movement in a strict sense came to be assimilated as merely one aspect within the much more complex and widespread phenomenon that may be referred to, by way of contrast, as the 'New Age movement in a general sense'.

THE NEW AGE MOVEMENT

This New Age movement in a general sense may be defined as the cultic milieu having become conscious of itself, by the end of the 1970s, as constituting a more or less unified movement. (As indicated above, it is not a New Religious Movement in the normal sense of that word, since it lacks a tightly bound organizational structure.) In other words, people who participated in various alternative activities and pursuits began to consider themselves as part of an international invisible community of like minded individuals, the collective efforts of whom were destined to change the world into a better and more spiritual place. The American sociologist Marilyn Ferguson referred to this phenomenon as the 'Aquarian conspiracy': a 'leaderless but powerful network' working to bring about radical change (Ferguson, 1980: 23); and the physicist Fritjof Capra saw it as the 'rising culture' destined to replace the declining culture of the modern west (Capra, 1983: 419). But eventually what they were referring to came to be known as the New Age movement: by the late 1970s and early 1980s the term 'New Age' was adopted from the specific occultist–millenarian movement known under that name, and came to be applied as a catch-all term for the much more extensive and complex cultic milieu of the 1980s and beyond. This is how the New Age movement in a strict sense was absorbed by the New Age movement in a general sense.

This development has been a cause of concern for some representatives of the original movement, who perceived in it a cheapening of the idea of a New Age. While the original New Age movement had been carried by high minded idealism and an ethic of service to humanity, the movement of the 1980s quickly developed into an increasingly commercialized spiritual marketplace catering to the tastes and whims of an individualistic clientele. While the original movement had espoused a reasonably coherent Theosophical metaphysics and philosophy of history, the movement of the 1980s seemed to present a hotch-potch of ideas and speculations without a clear focus and direction. While the excited expectation of a radical New Age dominated the earlier movement, this expectation ceased to be central to the movement of the 1980s which, in spite of its name, tends to concentrate on the spiritual development of the individual rather than of society. The development might also be described in terms of cultural geographics: while the original movement was England based and relied upon occultist traditions that had long been influential there, the new movement was dominated by the so-called metaphysical and New Thought traditions typical of American alternative culture. The move from community-oriented values to individual centred ones is a reflection of that development.

Indeed, the New Age movement in a general sense has been dominated by American cultural and spiritual ideas and values, and the most important spokes(wo)men have been Americans. While many names could be mentioned, two stand out as symbolic of the 1980s and the 1990s respectively. During the 1980s, the most vocal representative of the New Age idea may have been the film actress Shirley MacLaine. Her autobiographies published between 1983 and 1989, in which she describes her spiritual quest, and the television mini series 'Out on a Limb', based upon the first of these books, encapsulate the essential perspective of the New Age movement of the 1980s. For the 1990s, the same thing may be said of the best sellers of James Redfield: *The Celestine Prophecy*, with its accompanying *Celestine Workbook*, and a succession of follow-up volumes capitalizing on the success of the first one. While MacLaine's autobiographies were certainly easy to read, Redfield's books carried the New Age perspective to a new level of simplicity, thereby broadening the potential market for New Age beyond the audiences already reached by earlier authors.

These developments contributed to the fact that, by the beginning of the 1990s, more and more people attracted to alternative spirituality began to distance themselves from the label New Age, perceived by them as loaded with unwanted associations. During the 1980s it was still possible to investigate the New Age movement (in a general sense) simply by questioning people who identified themselves as involved in New Age; during the 1990s, participants have increasingly refused to identify themselves as such, preferring vague and non-committal terms such as 'spirituality'. It is a mistake to conclude from this, as has sometimes been done, that the New Age movement is declining or vanishing. Rather, the movement is showing signs of moving away from its traditional status as a counter-culture that proclaims the New Age in a gesture of rejecting the values of the old culture. Attempts to replace the term 'New Age' by a term such as 'spirituality' fit within a new strategy of adaptation and assimilation instead of rejection and confrontation, as a result of which the New Age movement is now securing its place as an increasingly professionalized 'spiritual' wing within the cultural mainstream.

Figure 11.2 Shirley MacLaine was born in Richmond, Virginia, in 1934. She has written autobiographies during the 1980s describing her spiritual quest. Her website (www.Shirleymaclaine.com) discusses her views on topics as broad as spirituality, health and stress reduction, UFOs, prophecy and psychics, reincarnation, transformational travel, karma, divination, ageing, relationships and dreams

Figure 11.3 James Redfield was born in 1950 and grew up near Birmingham, Alabama, eventually training as a therapist and working with abused adolescents. He self-published *The Celestine Prophecy* in 1992 and has since sold the rights to Warner Bros. The book has been on the New York Times bestseller list for more than three years

Sources and resources

Origins: esoteric currents in Jewish and Christian culture

We have been referring to various occultist movements that provided the early New Age movement with its basic metaphysics, as well as to the metaphysical and New Thought movements in American culture that were equally important to the New Age movement in a general sense. These various expressions of an alternative and popular Western spirituality have a long history. While earlier scholarship tended to interpret them in exclusively sociological terms, as an irrationalist and essentially regressive reaction to the *secularization* and rationalization of society (for example, Tiryakian, 1974), more recent generations have come to consider such an approach unhistorical and misleading (Bednarowski, 1989; Hanegraaff, 1996). The occult in contemporary Western society is merely the most recent manifestation of religious currents and traditions that existed long before the processes of secularization and rationalization began to have their impact, and which should be taken seriously as religious movements in their own right. Furthermore, it turns out to be highly simplistic to imagine the more recent representatives of these currents as irrationalists and conservatives who are fighting a rearguard battle against secularization and rationalization. Rather, historical research demonstrates that their attitude to modernity has always been highly complex and ambiguous: occultists have typically been adapting and reinterpreting ancient traditions so as to make them relevant to the modern world, while simultaneously hoping for a transformation of society along occultist lines. In order to understand the co-existence of 'tradition and modernity' in modern occultism and New Age religion, we first need to explore their historical foundations.

Hermetic gnosis

Human thinking and behaviour is far too fluid and complex to be caught in neat theoretical categories; but provided that this fact is clearly recognized, such categories can nevertheless be of service for providing some rough orientation through the jungle of history. It is useful to distinguish between three general strategies which have been followed in Western culture in order to find truth (Van den Broek and Hanegraaff, 1998). The first one relies on human reason, observation and argumentation: this is the strategy of rational philosophy and scientific research. The second one relies on the authority of divine revelation, which transcends merely human wisdom: this is the approach of established religion and doctrinal theology. The third one, finally, relies on the authority of personal spiritual experience or inner enlightenment: this approach may conveniently be referred to as *gnosis*, and has always had a problematic relationship to the first two approaches. The fact that its adherents look for truth 'beyond reason' has made them look like obscurantists in the eyes of rationalist philosophy and science; and the fact that they believe to have personal access to divine revelation has evoked the suspicion that they are bypassing the authority of established religion and its collectively recognized sources of revelation. In short: the representatives of this third approach tend to be suspected of irrationalism and excessive individualism, while they in turn blame their opponents for relying on religious authoritarianism and excessive rationalism.

Undoubtedly the most famous manifestation of this third perspective in antiquity is known as *Gnosticism*. But far more important for our present purposes – although less important from the perspective of early Church history – is a second movement relying on *gnosis*, and known as Hermetism. This religious current has its origins in Hellenistic Egypt, and flourished in the second and third centuries CE; its name refers to a mythical and quasi-divine founder, Hermes Trismegistus (the 'thrice-greatest Hermes'). Among the many writings attributed or linked to Hermes, most important and influential are the collection known as the *Corpus Hermeticum*, and a longer text entitled *Logos Teleios* but known in its Latin translation as *Asclepius*. The *Asclepius* was known in the Latin West throughout the Middle Ages; but the *Corpus Hermeticum* only became widely known after it had been translated by the Florentine neo-Platonic philosopher Marsilio Ficino in 1463 (printed in 1471).

RENAISSANCE HERMETICISM AND WESTERN ESOTERICISM

Ficino's translation proved to be of pivotal importance for the development of alternative 'esoteric' spiritualities in modern and contemporary Western society. Renaissance thinkers such as Giovanni Pico della Mirandola and Ficino himself saw in Hermes one of the earliest and hence most authoritative sources of a *prisca theologia* or ancient theology. This primordial wisdom had supposedly been revealed by God to Adam, but had declined after the Fall. It was kept alive, however, by a succession of divinely inspired sages, beginning with Zoroaster and Hermes Trismegistus. Since this primordial wisdom had been revealed by God himself, it was necessarily consistent with the most profound mysteries of the Christian faith and could be seen as a prophetic announcement of it. This in itself accounts for the great spiritual authority attached to the *Corpus Hermeticum*, and that authority was enhanced further by the suggestion that the teachings of the Egyptian Hermes had been a source for Moses as well as for Plato: accordingly, the Hermetic philosophy might be seen as a means to reconcile philosophy and Christianity, reason and faith. An important corollary of the authority attached to 'Hermes' was a new appreciation of the so-called 'occult sciences': magic, astrology and alchemy. The *Corpus Hermeticum* contains a spiritual philosophy with very little reference to occult sciences; but since these sublime teachings were supposedly written by the same author to whom had long been attributed a wide array of magical, astrological and alchemical writings, the latter were bound to be perceived in a new and more positive light. As a result, the 'Hermetic philosophy' of the Renaissance came to be linked from the very beginning with a revival of the occult sciences. In the writings of authors such as Cornelius Agrippa, Francesco Giorgi da Veneto, Giordano Bruno, Paracelsus, and many lesser figures, the outlines appeared of a new type of religious syncretism: a mixture of Christianity, neo-Platonism, Hermetism, Magic, Astrology and Alchemy, as well as an important new phenomenon: Christian reinterpretations and adaptations of the Jewish *Kabbalah*.

During the sixteenth century, a basic 'referential corpus' of writings came into existence which, in spite of variations and divergences, clearly displays a common direction. While the Hermetic writings are certainly not its only source, the authority attached to 'Hermes' is more than sufficient to refer to this new *syncretism* as 'Hermeticism' in a general and encompassing sense (as distinct from 'Hermetism', which refers specifically to the teachings of the *Hermetica* and its commentaries). This phenomenon of Renaissance Hermeticism is the foundation of what is commonly referred to as 'Western esotericism': a distinct current of 'alternative' religion and religious philosophy, the history of which can be traced from the Renaissance through the succeeding centuries, and indeed up to the New Age movement. As the main modern and contemporary representative of the 'third component' referred to above, its representatives emphasize the importance of personal religious experience or *gnosis*. More specifically, its world view has been defined in terms of four intrinsic characteristics: a belief in invisible and non-causal 'correspondences' between all visible and invisible dimensions of the cosmos, a perception of nature as permeated and animated by a divine presence or life force, a concentration on the religious imagination as a power that provides access to worlds and levels of reality intermediate between the material world and God, and the belief in a process of spiritual transmutation by which the inner man is regenerated and reconnected with the divine (Faivre, 1994: 10–15).

In 1614, the Swiss scholar Isaac Casaubon provided conclusive proof that the *Corpus Hermeticum* dated not from a remote antiquity but from the first centuries after Christ, thereby exploding the Renaissance myth of Hermes Trismegistus. However, while this discovery eventually weakened the authority of the Hermetic writings among intellectuals, it did not prevent religious currents originating in Renaissance Hermeticism from continuing during the seventeenth century and beyond. Most important in this respect is the so-called Rosicrucian furore caused by the anonymous publication, in Germany and beginning in the very same year as Casaubon's book, of several manifestos claiming to be messages from a mysterious brotherhood of the Rose Cross. The brotherhood in effect announced a transformation of society and the coming of a 'New Age', in the context of a religious ideology wholly founded on Western esoteric (and particularly *Paracelsian* and alchemical) premises. Due to the excited discussions caused by these pamphlets, the image of a 'Rosicrucian brotherhood' took hold in the popular imagination, and eventually (from the eighteenth century on) actual movements were founded that claimed to be its representatives. Side by side with the Rosicrucian manifestos, the writings of the great visionary philosopher Jacob Boehme (1575–1624) laid the foundations for another highly influential Western esoteric current, known as Christian Theosophy, the influence of which would continue through the seventeenth and eighteenth centuries and into the heart of the German Romantic movement. The existence and influence of a popular and learned Hermeticism during the Age of Reason, partly linked to Freemasonry and the general surge of secret societies in this period, has recently begun to receive more attention from historians, and challenges received ideas about the nature and history of the Enlightenment (see Neugebauer-Wölk, 1999).

INTERACTIONS WITH MODERNITY

The impact of modernity

Western esotericism emerged as a syncretistic type of religiosity in a Christian context, and its representatives generally were Christians until far into the eighteenth century. From about the middle of that century, however, the complicated historical processes that may be referred to under the general heading of 'secularization' began to have their impact on Western culture and religion generally, and they naturally affected esotericists as well. If we understand the term 'secularization' as referring not to a process in which religion declines or vanishes but, rather, to a process of profound change and transformation of religion under the impact of a combination of historically unprecedented social and political conditions (Hanegraaff, 1999a), we may speak not just of a 'secularization of religion' but also, more specifically, of a 'secularization of esotericism' during the nineteenth century. The result of this process was a new type of religiosity that may be referred to as 'occultism', and that comprises 'all attempts by esotericists to come to terms with a disenchanted world or, alternatively, by people in general to make sense of esotericism from the perspective of a disenchanted secular world' (Hanegraaff, 1996: 422).

OCCULTISM

The first signs of a secularization of Western esotericism may be perceived in the perspectives of the Swedish visionary Emanuel Swedenborg (1688–1772) and the German physician Franz Anton Mesmer (1734–1815), both of whom have exerted an incalculable influence on the history of esotericism during the nineteenth and twentieth centuries. *Theurgical* practices, spiritual manifestations and psychic phenomena of a type already present in some esoteric societies of the later eighteenth century as well as in the popular practice of 'magnetic healing' achieved mass popularity in the second half of the nineteenth century, in the occultist movement *par excellence* known as Spiritualism. Spiritualism provided a context within which a plethora of more or less sophisticated occultist movements came into existence. Among these manifestations of alternative religiosity, the Theosophical Movement founded in 1875 by the Russian Madame Helena P. Blavatsky (1831–91) is certainly the most important in terms of its influence, and the basic metaphysical system of modern Theosophy may be considered the archetypal manifestation of occultist spirituality at least until far into the 1970s. In addition, popular practices of 'magnetic healing' also referred to as 'Mesmerism' reached the US as early as 1836 and spread widely in the following decades, eventually providing a popular basis for the emergence of the so-called 'New Thought' movement of the later nineteenth century. Each one of these various currents – Spiritualism, Modern Theosophy, and the American New Thought movement – has taken on a multitude of forms, and their representatives have mingled and exchanged ideas and practices in various ways. The result of all this alternative religious activity was the emergence, during the nineteenth century, of an international cultic milieu with its own social networks and literature. Relying on an essentially nineteenth-century framework of ideas and beliefs, this cultic milieu has continued and further developed during the twentieth century, eventually to provide the foundation after the Second World War for the emergence of the New Age movement.

SECULARIZED ESOTERICISM

The occultist milieu of the nineteenth and twentieth century differs from traditional Western esotericism in at least four key respects, and these are of crucial importance for understanding the nature of New Age religion (for further discussion of these areas of difference see Hanegraaff, 1996). First, esotericism was originally grounded in an 'enchanted' world view where all parts of the universe were linked by invisible networks of non-causal 'correspondences' and a divine power of life was considered to permeate the whole of nature. Although esotericists have continued to defend such an enchanted holistic view of the world as permeated by invisible forces, their actual statements demonstrate that they came to compromise in various ways with the mechanical and disenchanted world models that achieved cultural dominance under the impact of scientific materialism and nineteenth-century positivism. Accordingly, occultism is characterized by hybrid mixtures of traditional esoteric and modern scientistic–materialist world views: while originally the religious belief in a universe brought forth by a personal God was axiomatic for esotericism, eventually this belief succumbed partly or completely to popular scientific visions of a universe answering to impersonal laws of causality. Even though the laws in question may be referred to as 'spiritual', nonetheless they tend to be described according to models taken from science rather than religion.

Second, the traditional Christian presuppositions of modern Western esotericism were increasingly questioned and relativized due to new translations of oriental religious texts and the emergence of a comparative study of the religions of the world. Oriental religions began to display missionary activities in Western countries, and their representatives typically sought to convince their audience by using Western terms and concepts to present the spirituality of religions such as Hinduism and Buddhism. Conversely, since occultists had always believed that the essential truths of esoteric spirituality were universal in nature and could be discovered at the heart of all great religious traditions East and West, it was natural for them to incorporate oriental concepts and terminology into already existing Western occultist frameworks. One excellent example is the concept of 'karma' that was adopted by Blavatsky from Hinduism, as a welcome alternative for Christian concepts of divine providence, whereas Blavatsky's essential understanding of reincarnation depended on Western-esoteric rather than oriental sources.

Third, the well-known debate between Christian creationism and the new theories of evolution became highly relevant to occultism as well, and in this battle occultists generally took the side of science. But although popular evolutionism became a crucial aspect of occultism as it developed from the nineteenth into the twentieth century, and although this evolutionism was generally used as part of a strategy of presenting occultism as scientifically legitimate, the actual types of evolutionism found in occultism depended less on Darwinian theory than on philosophical models originating in German idealism and Romanticism. The idea of a universal process of spiritual evolution and progress, involving human souls as well as the universe in its entirety, is not to be found in traditional Western esotericism but became fundamental to almost all forms of nineteenth- and twentieth-century occultism.

Finally, the emergence of modern psychology (itself dependent partly on Mesmerism and the Romantic fascination with the 'night-side of nature') has had an enormous impact on the development of occultism from the second half of the nineteenth century on. While psychology could be used as an argument against Christianity and against religion generally, by arguing that God or the gods are merely projections of the human psyche, it also proved possible to present Western-esoteric world views in terms of a new psychological terminology. Most influential in this respect was the Swiss psychiatrist Carl Gustav Jung (1875–1961), whose spiritual perspective was deeply rooted in the esoteric and occult currents of German Romantic *Naturphilosophie* but whose theories could be used to present that spirituality as a 'scientific' psychology. Apart from Jung, the 'pop psychology' of the American New Thought movement has been a major influence on the mixtures of occultism and psychology typical of New Age spirituality.

Postmodern spirituality: the religion of the self

To the four main aspects of the 'secularization of Western esotericism', perhaps a fifth one may be added that became dominant only after the Second World War, and is fully characteristic of the New Age movement of the 1980s and 1990s: the impact of the capitalist market economy on the domain of spirituality. Increasingly, the New Age movement has taken the shape of a spiritual supermarket where religious consumers pick and choose the spiritual commodities they fancy, and use them to create their own spiritual syntheses fine-tuned to their strictly personal needs. The phenomenon of a spiritual supermarket is not limited to the New Age movement only, but is a general characteristic of religion in (post)modern Western democracies. Various forms of New Age spirituality are competing with more traditional forms of religion (including the Christian churches as well as other great religious traditions such as Islam or Buddhism) and with a great number of so-called new religious movements, popularly referred to as 'cults'. However, in this universal battle for the attention of the consumer, the New Age movement enjoys certain advantages over most of its competitors, which seem to make it the representative *par excellence* of the contemporary 'spirituality of the market'. Whereas most other spiritual currents that compete for the attention of the consumer in modern society take the form of (at least rudimentary) organizations, enabling their members to see themselves as part of a religious community, New Age spirituality is strictly focused on the individual and his/her personal development. In fact, this individualism functions as an in-built defence mechanism against social organization and institutionalization: as soon as any group of people involved with New Age ideas begins to take up 'cultic' characteristics, this very fact already distances them from the basic individualism of New Age spirituality. The stronger they begin to function as a 'cult', or even as a 'sect', the more will other New Agers suspect that they are becoming a 'church' (i.e., that they are relapsing into what are considered old-fashioned patterns of dogmatism, intolerance and exclusivism), and the less acceptable they will be to the general cultic milieu of New Age spirituality. Such a group then takes up a life of its own as a 'new religious movement', which may share many basic beliefs with the New Age movement but should no longer be considered a typical representation of it. Within the present social context of a democratic free market of ideas and practices, the New Age's strict emphasis on the self and on individual experience as the only reliable source of spiritual truth, the authority of which can never be overruled by any religious dogma or consideration of solidarity with communal values, thus functions as an effective mechanism against institutionalization of New Age religion into a religion. This essential individualism makes the New Ager into the ideal spiritual consumer. Except for the very focus on the self and its spiritual evolution, there are no constraints *a priori* on a New Ager's potential spiritual interests; the fact that every New Ager continually creates and re-creates his or her own private system of symbolic meaning and values means that suppliers of the New Age market enjoy maximum opportunities for presenting him or her with ever-new spiritual commodities (see Hanegraaff, 1999b).

> You never knew how beautiful you were, for you never really looked at who and what you are. You want to see what God looks like? Go look in a reflector – you are looking God straight in the face.
>
> (JZKnight, *Ramtha: An Introduction* [back cover])
>
> (JZKnight is one of the most famous channelling mediums of the 1980s. She channelled Ramtha, an 'entity' identifying himself as a warrior from ancient Atlantis who achieved enlightenment during his first and only life on earth.)

As indicated above, that New Age as a spiritual supermarket caters to an individualistic clientele primarily interested in personal growth and development is not only a fact of social observation but also reflects beliefs that are basic to the movement. At the symbolic centre of New Age world views, one typically finds not a concept of God but, rather, the concept of 'the (higher) self', so that New Age spirituality has indeed sometimes been dubbed 'self religion' (Heelas, 1996). The basic symbolism of the self is linked to a basic mythology, that narrates the growth and development of the individual soul through many incarnations and existences in the direction of ever-increasing knowledge and spiritual insight (Hanegraaff, 1999b). Strict concentration on personal spiritual development rather than on communal values is therefore not considered a reflection of egoism but, rather, of a legitimate spiritual practice based on 'listening to your own inner guidance': only by following one's inner voice one may find one's way through the chaos of voices that clamour for attention on the spiritual supermarket, and find one's personal way to enlightenment.

LOOKING TO THE FUTURE

For quite some time now, it has been claimed by scholars and critics that the days of the New Age movement are numbered, that the New Age is over, or that the movement has already yielded to a follow-up phenomenon sometimes referred to as the 'Next Age'. Whether this is true depends very much on one's definition. There are indeed clear signs that New Age religion is losing its status as a counter-cultural movement and is now increasingly assimilated by the mainstream of society (Hanegraaff, 1996: 523). Such a development is anything but surprising: rather, it may be seen as the predictable result of commercial success. From one perspective, the fact that New Age is developing from a distinct counter-culture to merely a dimension of mainstream culture may indeed be interpreted as 'the end of the New Age movement as we have known it'; but from another perspective, it may be seen as reflecting the common-sense fact that New Age is developing and changing, just as any other religious movement known from history.

In any case, we should beware of optical illusion. There are indications that the phenomenon of specialized New Age book shops is declining; but at the same time one notices a substantial increase of spiritual literature on the shelves of 'regular' book shops. Likewise one may predict that specialized New Age centres for 'healing and personal growth' will become less necessary to the extent that at least parts of their therapeutic services are becoming more acceptable in mainstream medical and psychological contexts. One might well interpret such developments as reflecting not the decline of the New Age movement but, precisely, its development from a counter-cultural movement set apart from the mainstream to a significant dimension of the general spiritual landscape of contemporary Western society.

One thing is clear: whether or not the label 'New Age' will eventually survive, there is no evidence whatsoever that the basic spiritual perspectives, beliefs and practices characteristic of the movement of the 1980s and 1990s are losing popular credibility. Quite the contrary: all the evidence indicates that they are becoming more acceptable to many people in contemporary Western society, whether or not the latter choose to identify themselves as New Agers. Again, the phenomenon is anything but surprising, for the highly individualized approach to spirituality traditionally referred to as 'New Age' simply accords too well with the demands of contemporary consumer culture in a democratic society where citizens insist on their personal autonomy in matters of religion.

Finally, that the social dynamics of postmodern consumer society happen to favour a particular type of religion (referred to above as 'secularized esotericism') is a fact of recent history, but once again it is not a surprising one. That traditional forms of religion – the Christian churches and their theologies – are in decline at least in the contemporary European context is a generally known fact. The vogue of postmodern relativism indicates that the 'grand narratives' of progress by science and rationality are losing credibility as well. If more and more people feel that traditional Christianity, rationality and science are no longer able to give sense and meaning to human existence, it can be expected *a priori* that a spiritual perspective based on personal revelations by means of *gnosis* will profit from the circumstances. As long as the grand narratives of the West fail to regain their hold over the population and no new ones are forthcoming, and as long as Western democratic societies continue to emphasize the supreme virtue of individual freedom, the type of 'self religion' traditionally known as New Age will remain a force to be reckoned with.

SUMMARY

- New Age in a strict sense is the movement born in the context of the post-Second World War UFO cults and flowering in the spiritual utopianism of the 1960s and 1970s.
- New Age in a wide sense is the general 'cultic milieu' of alternative religion which flourished after the 1970s and has become increasingly 'mainstream' since. Dominated by American spiritual values and ideas, it is more individualistic and 'self' focused than New Age in a narrow sense.
- The roots of New Age are to be found in (a) Renaissance Hermeticism and Western esotericism, which themselves draw on earlier pagan, Jewish and Christian sources; and (b) occultism, which represents the early 'secularization' of esotericism under such pressures as the Enlightenment and the rise of science.
- Recent New Age has been influenced by a consumerist, market-led cultural economy, leading to a focus on 'spiritual shopping' and spiritual self-development.
- The success of the New Age lies in its rapid assimilation into more mainstream culture, and its congruence with the values of the latter.

KEY TERMS

Alchemy   A practical and speculative tradition focusing on the transmutation and spiritual purification of material substance, either or not interpreted in a mystical sense.

apocalypticism   The expectation of a cataclysmic event that will radically change the world.

counter-culture   The 1960s movement of young people revolting against the values of the Western establishment.

gnosis   Greek term for 'knowledge', referring to personal spiritual experience or inner enlightenment leading to true knowledge of God and the self.

Gnosticism   Movement of late antiquity characterized by a reliance on gnosis and a negative view of the created world as a 'prison of the soul'.

Kabbalah   Medieval Jewish mysticism.

millenarianism   The traditional hope for a 'thousand year' reign of peace.

Paracelsianism   A Western-esoteric tradition referring to the ideas of the sixteenth-century physician Paracelsus (1493–1541).

secularization   The historical processes by which the Christian churches and their theologies have lost their central position in Western religion and have been reduced to the status of competitors on a pluralistic religious market. (See Chapter 13.)

syncretism   The phenomenon of two or more religions or religious traditions intermingling so as to produce new religious syntheses.

Theosophy   Has two primary meanings. It refers to an important Christian–esoteric current represented by the Silesian mystic Jacob Böhme (1575–1624), his followers and later traditions inspired by them. It also refers to the perspectives of the Theosophical Society (founded in 1875) and its offshoots.

theurgy   A type of ritual practice in late antiquity (particularly in the context of neo-Platonism), by means of which the soul was believed to be raised to the divinities.

utopianism   The hope for an ideal society.

FURTHER READING

Sociological approaches

Early publications have mostly emphasized a sociological approach at the expense of a historial one; a representative example is E. A. Tiryakian (ed.): *On the Margin of the Visible: Sociology, the Esoteric, and the Occult* (New York, NY: 1974). Of fundamental importance for later research has been a classic article by Colin Campbell: 'The cult, the cultic milieu and secularization'. In *A Sociological Yearbook of Religion in Britain* 5 (1972, pp. 119–36). The best recent sociological study of New Age is Paul Heelas: *The New Age Movement: Celebrating the Self and the Sacralization of Modernity* (Oxford and Cambridge, MA: Blackwell, 1996).

Historical approaches

For a historical rather than a sociological approach, pioneering work has been done by Robert S. Ellwood: *Religious and Spiritual Groups in Modern America* (orig. 1973), revised edition with Harry B. Partin (Englewood Cliffs, NJ: Prentice-Hall, 1988), and J. Gordon Melton: see especially James R. Lewis and J. Gordon Melton (eds): *Perspectives on the New Age* (Albany, NY: SUNY Press, 1992). One of the first authors to emphasize the importance of analysing New Age beliefs and their context in intellectual history was Mary Farrell Bednarowski: *New Religions and the Theological Imagination in America* (Bloomington and Indianapolis, IN: Indiana University Press, 1989). An encompassing analysis and interpretation of New Age beliefs from the perspective of the history of ideas is Wouter J. Hanegraaff: *New Age Religion and Western Culture: Esotericism in the Mirror of Secular Thought* (Leiden: E. J. Brill, 1996) [US paperback: Albany, NY: SUNY Press, 1998]. In two later articles, the same author has proposed additional frameworks for interpreting the relation between New Age and the secularization of religion in contemporary Western society: 'Defining religion in spite of history'. In Jan G. Platvoet and Arie L. Molendijk (eds): *The Pragmatics of Defining Religion* (Leiden: E. J. Brill, 1999a, pp. 337–78) and 'New Age spiritualities as secular religion: a historian's perspective, *Social Compass* (46 (2) 1999b, 145–60).

Primary sources

For primary sources of New Age, see numerous references in Hanegraaff *op.cit.* (1996). The authors and books specifically mentioned in the text are: Marilyn Ferguson: *The Aquarian Conspiracy: Personal and Social Transformation in the 1980s* (orig. 1980) (London: Granta, 1982); Fritjof Capra: *The Turning Point: Science, Society, and the Rising Culture* (London: Fontana, 1983); David Spangler: *The Rebirth of the Sacred* (London: Gateway Books, 1984); Shirley McLaine: *Out on a Limb* (Toronto: Bantam Books, 1983); David Redfield: *The Celestine Prophecy* (New York: Warner Books, 1993).

Sources and antecedents of New Age

For the historical roots of New Age religion in Western esotericism and the emergence of a 'secularized esotericism', see Hanegraaff, *op.cit.* (1996). On Western esotericism generally, see Antoine Faivre: *Access to Western Esotericism* (Albany, NY: SUNY Press 1994) and Roelof van den Broek and Wouter J. Hanegraaff (eds): *Gnosis and Hermeticism from Antiquity to Modern Times* (Albany, NY: SUNY Press, 1998). Groundbreaking research on the relation between Western esotericism and the Enlightenment is presented in Monika Neugebauer-Wölk (ed.): *Aufklärung und Esoterik* (Hamburg: Felix Weiner Verlag, 1999).

CHAPTER 12

New Religious Movements

Elisabeth Arweck

INTRODUCTION

New Religious Movements (NRMs) – or cults, as they are popularly known – emerged as a new phenomenon in the late 1960s and early 1970s. They are mainly associated with Western societies and with the counter-culture of the 1960s, and include movements such as the Unification Church or UC (its members are generally known as the 'Moonies' – in reference to the founder, the Reverend Sun Myung Moon), the Hare Krishna movement (ISKCON), the Rajneesh Foundation (now Osho movement), and the Church of Scientology. Although countries in the West, notably the US, proved to be fertile soil for the germination of NRMs, numerous new religions have also appeared in other countries across the world such as Japan, Latin America, the Caribbean, and Africa. The answer to the question what kinds of religious groups and movements should be considered 'New Religious Movements' depends very much on the standpoint of the particular observer – a topic to which we shall return later in the chapter. As to the question of how many NRMs there are in any given country or globally, the simple answer is that we do not know. No reliable statistics exist and what figures we have are rough estimations or indications from NRMs themselves. The continually changing picture as well as the fluidity of membership make it difficult to be precise about the numerical importance of NRMs – in fact, we shall see that the social importance of NRMs has been disproportionately large in relation to their actual membership. The issue of the number of NRMs and their membership will also be discussed further below.

Generally speaking, a wide range of groups can be subsumed in the category of NRMs. They may be divided into different families as follows:

1   Those inspired by Eastern traditions (e.g. ISKCON, Sathya Sai Baba, Sahaja Yoga, Friends of the Western Buddhist Order or FWBO, Brahma Kumaris, Transcendental Meditation or TM).
2   Those arising from a Christian context (e.g. UC, Worldwide Church of God, Jesus Army, Church of Christ, COG/The Family).
3   Those originating in a particular country, such as the Japanese new religions (e.g. Sōka Gakkai, Institute for Research in Human Happiness).
4   Those derived from esoteric teachings (e.g. Eckankar, Beshara, Gurdjieff and Ouspensky schools).
5   Those which may be referred to as 'self-religions' (e.g. *est*/Centres Network, Life Training, Silva Mind Control).
6   Those focusing on extra-terrestrial entities and 'ufology' (e.g. Raël movement, Heaven's Gate).
7   Those with links to the New Age movement (e.g. Church Universal and Triumphant or CUT).

For the purposes of this chapter, NRMs are defined as religious groups and movements which have emerged mainly since the Second World War and which have come to prominence in Western societies in the late 1960s and early 1970s. The years before that can be described as a formative or dormant period: founders/leaders underwent formal education or a kind of spiritual apprenticeship or they gradually gathered followers. Most NRMs (at least) started as social organizations which were largely community based, drew clear boundaries between themselves and the wider society, developed hierarchical structures, and had a distinct set of beliefs and teachings formulated by the leadership and put down in writing. These teachings were on the whole of a syncretic and eclectic nature, drawing from various traditions and belief systems. This was one of the important aspects which distinguished NRMs from previous 'new' movements, which had often arisen from dissenting or schismatic processes within an established religion or denomination.

The topic of the 'newness' of NRMs will be pursued in more detail later in this chapter, but one other aspect of this newness that should be pointed out here concerns the way in which NRMs have engaged with the 'modern' society from which they originated. In some ways, NRMs can be seen as a reaction to modernity and its concomitants, as a protest against materialism and capitalism and as a sign of the self-limiting process of secularization. From this view, new religions appear anti-modern in that while elevating individual and personal spiritual growth, they support a simple lifestyle which is community-oriented and free of drugs or alcohol, and thus provide an alternative to the way of living available in mainstream capitalist society. In other ways, however, NRMs can be seen as embracing modernity. This is evident in the way in which they have made use of modern means of communication and technology for the dissemination of their ideas and for the organization of international networks. Looked at from yet another perspective, NRMs can be seen as part and parcel of modernity. As will be shown below, those who joined were young people from a modern background: they came from relatively affluent homes, were well-educated, and enjoyed the opportunity to travel. Further, while NRM members rejected established or mainstream institutions, authorities and lifestyles, they created their own institutions, subjected themselves to the authority of their leaders and, to some extent, relied on wider society to support them, for example by buying their goods and services.

The overlap between some NRMs with New Age spirituality and self-religions, which was mentioned, raises the question of whether the New Age movement (and neo-paganism) should be regarded as NRMs. While NRMs and the New Age movement share common roots in the 1960s counter-culture and the *Human Potential movement* and have thus drawn their membership from a similar cultic milieu, a distinction needs to be made between them, if we adhere to the working definition of NRMs given above. First, the New Age movement gained its momentum slightly later than the NRMs, namely in the 1980s. Second, its mode of organization is quite distinct from that of the NRMs. Although there are some New Age communities (such as Esalen or Findhorn), the New Age movement is a network of groups which do not recognize a central authority or leadership or share a set of common teachings – hence Gerlach and Hine's model of the SPIN, which describes New Age as a 'segmented, leaderless (or multi-headed) and networked' movement (York, 1995: 324–7). It can be argued that the 'spiritual consumerism' or 'pick and choose mentality' prevalent in the New Age movement is evidence of its affinity with postmodernity rather than with modernity, but opinions on this topic differ. However, given the differences between NRMs and the New Age movement, a separate chapter in this volume deals exclusively with New Age religion (see Chapter 11).

In order to show the social importance of NRMs and how they have interacted with various sections of society, this chapter provides an outline of the perceptions which have shaped the view taken of them by the public and the media. The question of which movements are to be considered NRMs will then be taken up again, complemented by a section on both the variety and similarity which characterize them. The issue of the importance of NRMs in terms of their number and membership is addressed in more detail and the controversies associated with them are discussed. The question of NRMs as a new phenomenon is then explored in greater detail, as is the construction of the notion of NRMs by different social agents who have been dealing with NRMs within their distinctive remits. An outlook towards the future of NRMs concludes this chapter.

▌ MOVEMENTS AND LEADERS MENTIONED IN TEXT

Aum Shinrikyo Also known as Aum Supreme Truth. Founder: Shoko Asahara.

Brahma Kumaris Officially Brahma Kumaris World Spiritual University. Founder: Dada Lekh Raj (Brahma Baba).

Branch Davidians Leader: David Koresh (Vernon Howell).

Church of Christ The parent church is the Boston Church of Christ, offshoots: Central London Church of Christ, Birmingham Church of Christ, etc. Founder: Kip McKean.

COG (formerly) Children of God, now The Family. Founder: David Brandt Berg ('Moses David', 'Mo').

CUT Church Universal and Triumphant (formerly Summit Lighthouse). Founder: Elizabeth Clare Prophet ('Guru Ma').

DLM Divine Light Mission, now Élan Vital. Founder: Shri Hans Ji Maharaj. Leader: Maharaji (Prem Pal Singh Maharaj).

Eckankar Founder: Paul Twitchell, current leader: Sri Harold Klemp

est Erhart Seminar Training, now the Centres Network, offshoot: the Hunger Project. Founder: Werner Erhart.

Falun Gong Founder: Li Hongzhi.

Fraternité Blanche Universelle Founder: Omraam Mikhaël Aïvanhov.

FWBO Friends of the Western Buddhist Order. Founder: Maha Sthavira Sangharakshita (formerly Dennis Lingwood).

Heaven's Gate Founders: Marshall Herff Applewhite ('Do') and Bonnie Lu Nettles ('Ti').

Heimholungswerk Officially Heimholungswerk Jesu Christi. Leader: Gabriele Wittek.

Institute for Research in Human Happiness or Kofuku no Kagaku. Founder: Ryuho Okawa.

ISKCON International Society for Krishna Consciousness or the Hare Krishna movement. Founder: A.C. Bhaktivedanta Swami Prabhupada.
Jesus Fellowship Also known as Jesus Army; businesses: House of Goodness, Skaino Services Ltd. Leader: Noel Stanton.
People's Temple Founder: Jim Jones.
Raëlian movement or Raëlians Leader: Raël (Claude Vorilhon).
Rajneesh Foundation also known as the 'Orange People', now Osho movement. Founder: Bhagwan Rajneesh/Osho (Rajneesh).
Sahaja Yoga Founder: Nirvala Devi ('Sri Mataji').
Sathya Sai Baba Founder: Sai Baba.
Scientology Officially Church of Scientology; offshoots: Narconon (drug rehabilitation programme), the Citizens Commission for Human Rights ('to expose psychiatric criminality and oppression'), Applied Scholastics (educational programme). Founder: L. Ron Hubbard.
Sōka Gakkai Officially Soka Gakkai International (SGI), also Nichiren Shoshu UK (NSUK). Founders: Tsunesaburo Makiguchi and Josei Toda, current leader: Ikeda Daisaku.
Solar Temple Also Order of the Solar Temple (*Ordre du Temple Solaire* or OTS). Leaders: Luc Jouret and Joseph di Mambro.
TM Transcendental Meditation. Founder: Maharishi Mahesh Yogi.
UC Unification Church, also known as the 'Moonies'; officially The Holy Spirit Association for the Unification of World Christianity, now Family Federation for World Peace and Unification (FFWPU), offshoots: CARP (Collegiate Association for Research of Principles), ICF (International Cultural Foundation), ICUS (International Conference for the Unity of Sciences), CAUSA (Confederation of the Association for the Unification of the Societies of America); businesses: machine tools and ginseng. Founder: the Reverend Sun Myung Moon.
Worldwide Church of God (WCG) Also Armstrongism. Founder: Herbert W. Armstrong, current leader: Joseph W. Tkach.

PUBLIC AND MEDIA PERCEPTIONS OF NRMs

When the New Religious Movements (NRMs) emerged in the late 1960s and early 1970s, the proverbial man or woman in the street would have been unaware of these new religious groups except when being approached in public places by members of some movements, such as the UC or ISKCON, who would offer books, candles or flowers for sale, or ask for a donation for a charitable cause. Those who became acutely aware of the existence of NRMs at that time were the parents and relatives of young people who joined such movements. Typically in their late teens or early twenties, these young people tended to drop out of university courses or give up their jobs or career prospects, move into a communal setting, hand over their possessions to the group, and devote themselves completely to the affairs of the movement. This intense commitment, in some cases combined with geographical distance, led to strains and tensions in some families: parents could not comprehend this conversion as it seemed to be so sudden and to result in such a radical transformation in their children's appearance and behaviour.

NRMs entered the public consciousness in a significant way with the events in Jonestown, Guyana, where, in November 1978, 922 followers of Jim Jones apparently committed suicide. The mass suicide of the People's Temple has shaped the public's perception of NRMs in a significant and lasting way: it

Figure 12.1 Jim Jones, Leader of the People's Temple. This undated file photo accompanied the news story of 19 November 1978 which revealed that a Californian congressman, Leo Ryan, three American journalists and an unidentified woman, were killed the day before in a jungle ambush while seeking information on Jones's religious cult which maintained a temple in Georgetown, Guyana

has come to represent the culmination and confirmation of what by that stage had become controversial and negative about 'cults' (the term generally used by those opposed to NRMs and by the media).

Allegations have ranged from cults using 'brainwashing' and 'mind control' in order to recruit and retain members, exploiting members (and thus being detrimental to their physical and mental welfare), 'breaking up families' (alienating young people from their parents), to promoting totalitarian (exclusive) world views and autocratic leadership, deceiving the public (*heavenly deception*), and seeking to undermine the general social and political order. In 1999, assertions of this kind were again levelled at the Chinese movement Falun Gong.

The events in Jonestown came to represent the worst possible outcome for those involved in cults: violent death, brought about, it seemed, by the adherents' submission to a powerful leader. Jonestown was proof that NRMs could harbour the seeds for, and actually steer towards, violence and destruction. In some circles, notably in the so-called *anti-cult movement* or *ACM* (the umbrella term for groups which formed in opposition to NRMs), it was feared that any NRM could turn violent at any time and this was used as another argument to warn against the 'danger' of cults. Such fears have been vindicated and fuelled by subsequent events which involved NRMs and violence or (self-)destruction, as in the cases of the Branch Davidians and the Solar Temple.

Media coverage and with it public awareness of NRMs levelled off in the aftermath of Jonestown, that is from the early to mid-1980s onwards, although in Britain, the libel case brought against the *Daily Mail* by the UC in 1980 over the allegation of breaking up families maintained public interest into the early 1980s. However, cults caught the attention of the media again in the late 1980s, when the controversies surrounding the Satanism scare received widespread coverage, not least because of the issue of child abuse. In the 1990s, a number of movements, which had hitherto not featured prominently in the concern of observers, came into the media spotlight: in 1993, the compound of the Branch Davidians in Waco, Texas, was raided by the BATF (Bureau of Alcohol, Tobacco and Firearms) and subsequently besieged by the FBI. In 1994, over 50 members of the Solar Temple were found dead in Switzerland and Canada, with further deaths ('transits' to another world) following in 1995 and 1997. In 1995, Aum Shinrikyo was found responsible for the sarin attack on the Tokyo underground. In 1997, the bodies of thirty-nine members of Heaven's Gate were discovered at Rancho Santa Fe in California – they had died voluntarily in order to progress to what they believed to be a higher level of being. In their terms, it had been time to abandon their 'earthly containers' in order to be carried off by a UFO, believed to accompany the comet Hale Bopp, to a new home at 'the evolutionary level beyond human' somewhere in the galaxy. In late 1999, the impending millennium fostered fears that millennial groups might commit violent acts. Consequently, members of Concerned Christians, a Christian group from Denver, Colorado, were evicted from Jerusalem.

Most of the above incidents occurred without prior warning or anticipation and therefore seemed all the more difficult to explain, especially for those unfamiliar with the recent thinking of the leadership and/or inner circle of membership. Some events, in particular those connected with the Solar Temple and Heaven's Gate, involved intricate rituals and ceremonies which called for explanations. Heaven's Gate had a connection with the Internet – the group designed sophisticated web pages and used the Internet to communicate with followers as well as spread its message. This reinforced the public perception of cults as 'sinister'. The mixture of curiosity and fear in the wake of the Heaven's Gate deaths arose from a coincidental confluence of mistrust of both Internet technology and cults.

Judging from recent events, it is impossible to rule out similar loss of life in NRM related contexts, although it is well nigh impossible to predict such occurrences. However, there is a widely held consensus among the academic community in this field that as much as possible should be learnt about NRMs. The following section provides a summary of academic findings about NRMs. It needs to be stressed that a considerable amount of the scholarly appraisal of NRMs as a phenomenon has occurred with the benefit of hindsight.

WHAT ARE NEW RELIGIOUS MOVEMENTS?

The term New Religious Movements comprises a wide range of groups and movements of alternative spirituality, the emergence of which is generally associated with the aftermath of the 1960s counter-culture. Using a historical or chronological criterion, Clarke defines those groups and movements as NRMs which have formed since the Second World War and came to prominence in North America and Western Europe in the late 1960s and early 1970s (see, for example, Clarke, 1997). Some scholars concur with this broad definition (for example, Beckford and Levasseur, 1986; Barker, 1999).

The foundation of some NRMs occurred before 1945. For example, Soka Gakkai, a Japanese new religious movement, was founded in 1930 by Tsunesaburo Makiguchi and Josei Toda, and Divine Light Mission (now Élan Vital) was founded in the 1930s by Shri Hans Ji Maharaj in India. The Brahma Kumaris World Spiritual University was founded in 1937 in Karachi by Dada Lekh Raj. The origins of Rastafarianism lie at the beginning of the twentieth century, when Marcus Garvey started the Back-to-Africa movement. Some of the spiritual roots of the New Age movement can be found in movements which originated in late nineteenth-century America, namely the Transcendentalist movement, Theosophy and New Thought. The date of foundation however, does not invalidate Clarke's definition; the important point about NRMs is that they are movements which have come to prominence in North America and Europe since the Second World War.

It can be said that a significant number of NRMs spread from the US to Britain, and from there to Continental Europe. Although some had been founded or started in other countries before coming to the US, it is in the US where they came to prominence. The UC or ISKCON are cases in point. There are, however, notable exceptions, namely movements which have successfully recruited members both in their country of origin and abroad, for example Soka Gakkai. There are groups and movements which are indigenous to a particular country and some of them have not found a significant membership elsewhere, for example, the Jesus Fellowship (or Jesus Army) in Britain, the *Heimholungswerk Jesu Christi* in Germany, or the *Fraternité Blanche Universelle* in France. As research progressed, it was found that numerous NRMs had formed in other countries, for example in Japan ('new' and 'new, new' religions), Melanesia (cargo cults), Latin America (Umbanda), the Caribbean, Africa (Aladura), Indonesia (Subud).

A number of NRMs have offshoots and branches of a secular and/or charitable nature, which the ACM generally refers to as 'front organizations'. The UC has a wide array of such branches, for example *CARP*, a youth organization, *CAUSA*, a political organization, and *ICF*, a cultural foundation. Scientology has set up Narconon, a drug rehabilitation programme, the Citizens' Commission for

Human Rights ('to expose psychiatric criminality and oppression'), and educational programmes, such as Applied Scholastics. *est* (now the Centres Network) founded the Hunger Project to eradicate hunger in the world. Some NRMs have commercial enterprises, such as the UC which owns machine tool and ginseng businesses or the Jesus Fellowship which operates community owned businesses (House of Goodness, Skaino Services Ltd).

Having looked at the broad spectrum of NRMs, we shall now explore a number of aspects which show the extent to which NRMs vary, and the extent to which they share similar features.

Variety and similarity of aspects

There is great variety in the kinds of movements subsumed under the term NRMs with regard to a number of aspects which characterize religions or religious movements, such as leadership, authority, concepts of the individual, the family and gender, origin, teachings, organizational structures, size, engagement with the world, and so on. On the other hand, some NRMs share certain traits. The variety and similarity of features have presented a challenge to social scientists in their attempts to classify NRMs by means of a comprehensive system of criteria. The range of academically constructed typologies illustrates the intellectual efforts involved in identifying common features and general characteristics (Arweck, 1999 provides an overview of such typologies). Academics have sought to accommodate the general tendencies of NRMs in 'ideal types', with NRMs of a particular type sharing a number of, although not all, attributes. In order to give some idea of the range of NRMs and their distinctness, some of the aspects mentioned are addressed here in more detail, namely leadership and authority, authoritative texts, the idea of family and the role of women.

Leadership and authority

Regarding leadership and authority within NRMs, some observers speak of a predominance of male charismatic leaders who are often supported by hierarchical, patriarchal structures and reinforced by female devotion (Puttick and Clarke, 1993). However, some leaders have been surrounded by a powerful female elite, for example Jim Jones and Rajneesh. There are also examples of charismatic feminist leaders who require extreme devotion and submission from their followers. The New Age movement on the other hand promotes equality and egalitarianism, placing the locus of authority with the individual as the final arbiter of what is right and true and only recognizing 'authorities' as guides or teachers. (However, some New Age groups and communities, such as Findhorn, can be shown to have hierarchical structures.)

The leadership structures of some NRMs are described as pyramidal, with the leader at the peak, lower leadership ranks arranged in descending levels, and the base formed by grass-roots members. Such structures are associated with shepherding or discipling movements, such as the multiplying ministries movements and (at some stage in its development) the COG/The Family. Changes in leadership structures can occur at the behest of the leader (as in the COG) or at the death of the leader (as in ISKCON where power and authority are diffused among the members of a governing body, the Governing Board Commission or GBC).

Charismatic leadership often involves the individual's surrender to the will of the leader; this is the case, for example, in movements which espouse the path of devotion (*bhakti*), such as the Brahma Kumaris and the Rajneesh movement. Here, meditation is used as the way to know the essential self beyond the socially conditioned ego. In the New Age movement, a range of therapies are used to dissolve the 'ego' and allow access to what lies within. The idea of surrender to a leader involves trust, and where this is abused or misunderstood, disciples are vulnerable to exploitation. In some NRMs, betrayals of trust have occurred through sexual misconduct and abuse of power.

Authoritative texts

A variety of texts and documents form the canon of an NRM's belief and teachings. Leaders may build on existing texts by adding new interpretations and/or revelations. In Christian groups, the Bible may be used in this way. The core text in the UC, for example, is *Divine Principle* which presents a particular interpretation of the Old and New Testaments and adds the revelations of Moon. The *Heimholungswerk*, another Christian group, is based on the revelations received by the leader Gabriele Wittek. In this case, the leader acts as a medium or channel or prophet for 'a higher (divine) source'. In the Brahma Kumaris, female members act as mediums for the teachings of the leader, as they did at some stage in the Rajneesh movement. 'Channelled' teachings are also common in some strands in the New Age movement. In Eastern groups, Hindu or Buddhist scriptures, such as the *Veda* or the *Bhagavad Gita* (both ancient Hindu scriptures), may be used. A. C. Bhaktivedanta Swami Prabhupada, the late leader of ISKCON, provided his own commentary on the *Bhagavad Gita*.

The writings or speeches of leaders usually contribute to the body of authoritative documents. Scientology's (late) founder, L. Ron Hubbard, produced an extensive collection of writings, the principal being *Dianetics* (1950). In The Family, the collection of the (late) leader's letters (known as the 'Mo' letters in reference to 'Moses David' Berg), contains their teachings, although some of these (notably the controversial practice of *flirty fishing*) have been revised in recent years. In some cases, writings may be published in the leader's name, although they are in fact compiled by members, as is the case with Rajneesh.

The idea of family

In some NRMs, the group is the 'true family' (hence also 'The Family'), with the leader considered the 'true' father/mother and members addressing each other as 'brother' or 'sister'. For example, Moon and his wife are considered the 'true parents', the founder of the Brahma Kumaris is known as 'Brahma Baba', Elizabeth Clare Prophet, the leader of the CUT, is referred to as 'Guru Ma', and Nirvala Devi, the leader of Sahaja Yoga, as 'Shri Mataji' (divine mother). In the Rajneesh movement, female members were addressed with the prefix 'Ma', as in Ma Anand Sheela, to point to their nurturing qualities, while Rajneesh, the leader, was considered to be 'beyond gender'.

The idea of the group representing the 'true family' reflects the understanding of some NRMs and their members that they are distinct from the world: they have knowledge and insights which others do not have. They are therefore an elite which is called upon to impart their knowledge to the world and save it or at least offer it the possibility of 'salvation'. Alternatively, those who leave are considered condemned for throwing away a unique chance or as traitors of the group's cause.

The idea of the group as the family may involve living in communal settings, like the first disciples of Christ, sharing resources and facilities. It may also involve members consulting leaders or 'elders' before making important decisions, such as choosing marriage partners. In the UC, Moon matches prospective couples by photograph. The wishes or needs of the individual are subjected to the

Figure 12.2 Hare Khrishna followers chanting in procession down Oxford Street, London, near their temple in Soho

commonweal of the community and put in the service of the group's mission. This sometimes justifies the frugal and simple lifestyle of grassroots members.

The issue of children in NRMs has hitherto remained largely under-researched by social scientists, mainly due to the methodological difficulties involved. Academic research to date points to manifold patterns of parenting and to a wide range of approaches to children and child rearing in NRMs. There are groups with no age distinctions and groups with elaborate rule bound age sets, groups which have little time for children and groups which foster charismatic qualities in young people or consider them endowed with special qualities (Palmer and Hardman, 1999). Further research in this area may well show similarities in child rearing practices between NRMs and comparable religious movements in the past, just as parallels have been drawn with regard to other aspects (see also below).

The role of women

Regarding the role of women, NRMs have, on the one hand, challenged mainstream society in terms of sexual–gender arrangements, while on the other hand reinforcing traditional patterns of gender roles. There is an argument that the instability of gender roles in mainstream society has created a situation in which women are attracted either to NRMs with traditional patriarchal expectations, or feminist spiritual groups in which there is 'equalitarian' participation and leadership (Robbins and Bromley, 1992). Women's conversion to unconventional religions can be interpreted as a response to the rolelessness resulting from dramatic upheavals in the structure of society (Palmer, 1995).

Some argue that feminism had a strong influence on American Buddhism and in neo-paganism generally, but has hardly had an effect on other movements, notably more conservative Christian and Eastern-based movements. Even where the theology is liberal, the social organization may be sexist. Others refute the notion that NRMs tend to be conservative and promote traditional values of sex and the family, the Rajneesh and Raëlian movements being cases in point (Palmer, 1995).

In the Brahma Kumaris, the exaltation of 'feminine' qualities (love, service, humility) makes women fit for leadership and high status. Female members have been encouraged to practise marital chastity, usually reserved for male renunciates, and this has caused controversy. With regard to the issue of women and power, women may be guides and spiritual leaders, but may not have institutional and

Figure 12.3 Two women in saris. Western devotees of the guru Rajneesh can surrender their given names and adopt a new name bestowed by the leader of the movement. Converts often adopt the robes of the movement, such as the sari

administrative leadership positions. However, where the latter has been the case, women have shown that they, too, may abuse their positions of power. Ma Anand Sheela of the Rajneesh movement is a notable example. In neo-paganism, the empowerment of women is not in terms of domination or destruction, but in terms of rejecting the social conditioning of women and reclaiming women's spirituality.

Scholarly studies of women in NRMs have tended to focus on the links between gender roles and sexuality. In the case of some movements, gender and sexuality are intricately linked, as for example in the COG/The Family and its (now defunct) policy of 'flirty fishing' or sharing of partners, or the practice of 'free love' in the Rajneesh movement until the fear of AIDS led to stringent precautions. Some NRMs have strict regulations concerning gender and sexuality: the sexes may be segregated, marriage partners not freely chosen, marital relations regulated or celibacy upheld as a condition for deeper spiritual growth. The views on gender and sexuality are also relevant regarding the concepts of family and children.

Causes for controversy

Some of the aspects described above have caused friction between NRMs and various sections of society. The controversial aspect of NRMs has already been mentioned in the section on public and media perceptions of NRMs. However, it should be pointed out that in their formative stages, NRMs were not immediately perceived as problematic or controversial. Some, for example, the COG/The Family, collaborated with local churches on account of their seemingly Christian beliefs. The UC sought to establish relations with political leaders in the early 1970s. It is also important to note that not all groups which are referred to as NRMs have become controversial or have become controversial to the same degree. Controversies have arisen over issues involving the allegations mentioned above which, in sociological terms, can be largely subsumed under divergent or deviant behaviour, ranging from claims to divinity by some leaders to experimental communal lifestyles and abusive treatment of grass-roots members and children.

It should further be pointed out that controversial aspects related to particular NRMs tended to be generalized and applied blanket fashion to any NRM. In this way, ACM groups and the media tend to speak of 'cults' and 'cultic' behaviour, implying that all NRMs show the same kind of behaviour and practice. In this respect, it was the UC which has become the 'cult *par excellence*', with its practices and teachings assigned to other groups which appear similar. Hence, for example, the allegation of 'heavenly deception' mentioned above.

The debate about the controversial aspects of NRMs has tended to lose sight of the actual numbers of people involved in NRMs, a topic with which the next section is concerned.

NUMBER OF NRMS AND MEMBERSHIP

Estimates regarding the number of NRMs vary greatly. On the one hand, this is due to the way NRMs and the notion of membership are defined, on the other hand this is due to the specific period considered. No definitive figures are available, but some data can be provided to give a general idea.

Melton, using the broad definition of a social scientist, speaks of 5–6 hundred alternative religions in the US, of which over 100 are 'primarily ethnic bodies confined to first and second generation immigrant communities' (Melton, 1992: 7). The second edition of the *Encyclopedia of American Religions* covers 1,350 groups, 'ranging from Adventists to Zen Buddhists' (Melton, 1987: ix). According to the ACM in the US, the number of NRMs is much higher: in the early 1980s, it suggested that 3–5 thousand cults operated in the US (Melton, 1992: 6) and in 1999, Dr Margaret Singer – a psychologist who has become closely associated with the ACM stance – was reported to put the number at between 2–5 thousand.

Clarke estimates that 400–50 new religions have emerged in Britain since 1945 and that many of these, and others, are to be found in the rest of Western Europe (Clarke, 1984). He considers the figure to be very much higher for North America and points to the thriving NRMs in postwar Japan – actually, estimates by Japanese scholars range from 800 to a few thousand (see Chapter 5). Barker extrapolates from the 2,600 groups on file at *INFORM* (a 'cult-watching' organization set up in 1989 by Barker): she states that the majority of these might be called NRMs and that over 2 thousand discrete groups could exist in Europe (Barker, 1999). Using the definition of NRMs by Clarke (see above), Barker considers that the number of NRMs '. . . is likely to be in the order of four figures (two or more thousand) in the West and five figures (probably somewhere in the lower tens of thousands) worldwide'.

The question of membership size hinges on the definition of 'member'. Generally speaking, NRMs have a core membership of fully committed or full-time members, and part-time or affiliated members. NRMs can be associated in various ways with supporters or 'friends'. Some NRMs, including 'audience cults' and 'client cults' (Bainbridge and Stark, 1980), do not have any kind of formal membership (*est*, for example, counts 'graduates'); some have a fluctuating membership, such as New Age groups; some allow dual or multiple membership. The membership of a number of NRMs could be described as a set of concentric circles, with the core membership forming the innermost circle, showing the greatest degree of commitment, and subsequent circles illustrating weaker degrees of commitment for part-time members, affiliated members, friends, and sympathizers (Arweck, 1999). Further, membership status can be flexible in that members can belong to different membership circles at different times, switching between different degrees of commitment. For example, Scientology members can alternate between periods when they are 'on staff' (working as residential staff for the organization full-time) and periods when they take Scientology courses while leading a 'secular' life. Members who are toying with the idea of leaving gradually move towards the outer circles or margins of the group before they make the final break.

Membership status and figures have been affected by the development of NRMs over time, through changes in organization and teachings. For example, in its early stages, the membership of the UC consisted of a highly committed, full-time core membership which lived communally. However, after the introduction of the 'Home Church Programme', members were sent into the wider community where they continued their mission on a part-time basis, while perhaps having a job and raising families. Moonies engaged in 'witnessing' and 'fundraising' tended to be single and live communally in 'centres', but after couples had been blessed in *mass wedding* ceremonies and were allowed to live as man and wife, the communal lifestyle was no longer appropriate.

The membership of the Rajneesh movement has also been affected by changes: the most committed members lived communally, in the ashram in Poona, India (set up in 1974), then in Rajneeshpuram in Oregon, in the US (started in 1981), and in communes around the world; however, the majority lived non-communal lives. In September 1985, coinciding with the demise of Rajneeshpuram, the leader Rajneesh officially disbanded the movement. The changes involved made Poona the main centre again where the most loyal members joined Osho Rajneesh, as he became known since the return to India until his death in 1990, while former members reorganized and continued Osho's legacy on their own, some establishing movements in their own right.

The nature and size of membership is thus influenced by a number of factors, including relocation, the death of the leader, changes in recruitment strategies, high turnover rates, changes in policy and/or doctrines, and the arrival of subsequent generations.

Membership figures vary according to different sources. There tends to be a discrepancy between membership figures as claimed by NRMs and educated guesses (guestimates) by 'experts'. Some NRMs tend to quote optimistic figures, sometimes counting even enquirers as members; others keep membership records secret or do not keep any membership records at all. The media tend to quote inflated figures. Most observers point to the difficulty in establishing accurate figures, or to the lack of reliable statistics.

Clarke has suggested that NRM membership must be estimated in the millions rather than thousands, but that less than 1 per cent of the population in the US and Europe were involved long term, that is more than two years (Clarke,1984, 1992). However, his survey of 1987 of NRM members in Europe seems to correct his estimate of 1984: the figures quoted suggest membership figures in the thousands rather than millions (Clarke, 1987). In 1999, Dr Singer was reported to suggest that 10–20 million were involved in cult activities in the US. Melton believes that '. . . a more reasonable total membership estimate for the several hundred prominent new religions of the last decades would be 15,000 to 200,000', with most NRMs counting only a few hundred members and spending most of their energy just surviving (Melton, 1992). Only some movements, such as the UC and ISKCON, could count their members in four figures. While over 1 million people in the US have taken the basic course in TM, only a minority actually joined (10–20 thousand). Cults grew appreciably during the 1970s, but constitute a numerically small part of the American religious scene. In the mid-1980s, some observers considered NRMs to be on the decline, while others saw steady growth and consolidation, and still others saw full-time commitment on the wane and part-time membership on the increase.

As to more recent figures in Germany, the survey commissioned by the *Enquête-Kommission* of the German Parliament indicates that at least 8–9 million people consider themselves members of a non-mainstream religious group, with *c*.1.2 million participants in various courses. By comparison, the Swedish Government Report of 1998 puts the overall membership figure in Sweden between 50,000–60,000, excluding New Age and related groups. Interestingly, the outcome of the German survey showed that previous estimates of membership (over 2 per cent) had been too high. For some observers, the figures confirm the view that NRMs in Germany constitute a relatively constant, but certainly not a marginal or negligible, social phenomenon, while others do not seem to share this view.

For example, *REMID*'s statistics, although not providing an overall membership figure, appear to point towards a lower membership total, recording the largest membership figures of NRMs in the lower thousands (REMID, 1999).

Estimates of the number of NRMs and membership can be shown to vary significantly, depending on how the terms 'NRMs' and 'membership' are defined, depending on which sources of information are used, and depending on which periods of time are considered. Although it is important to know just how many NRMs and NRM members there are in order to be able to grasp the demographic proportion of this phenomenon, the discrepancy between actual numbers and the amount of attention paid to NRMs suggests the importance of underlying social issues. Some of these have been related to the newness of NRMs, an aspect which was mentioned in the introduction and which will now be explored further.

NRMs AS A NEW PHENOMENON

Although NRMs are called 'new', there are a number of respects in which they are not 'new'. The appearance of new forms of religion was not in itself new – the history of religion provides an account of innovative developments in the course of time, and documents new religious groups, communities, orders, heresies, fellowships, societies, and schisms. A sizeable part of the academic literature on NRMs has been concerned with showing the parallels with historical religious groups and social reactions to their emergence. The fact that NRMs were emerging in Western societies was found not to be a really new aspect either. As mentioned, other parts of the world have experienced the formation of new religious groups, including Latin America and Africa where Pentecostalism – in new forms – has made significant inroads (see Chapter 7 and Chapter 14).

Equally, the newness of NRMs does not consist in the fact that their teachings were completely new. Some NRMs refer to religious traditions and practices of the past and place themselves deliberately and distinctly in the line of venerable traditions or teachers. ISKCON, for example, considers itself as part of Vaishnava Hinduism, in the tradition of the Chaitanya movement of Bengal, which developed from the teachings of the sixteenth-century monk Chaitanya Mahaprabhu (see Chapter 1). Sōka Gakkai is a lay organization associated with Nichiren Shoshu, one of several Nichiren sects which lay claim to the teachings of the thirteenth-century Japanese monk Nichiren Daishonin. Further, NRMs have not been new with regard to the ways in which their members have congregated, arranged or organized group life. Throughout history, people, motivated by strong religious beliefs, have experimented with different forms of communal living, and historical precedents can be found for the variety of communal lifestyles, ascetic behaviour, ritual practices, and attitudes towards the rest of the world observed among NRMs.

Nonetheless, there are a number of aspects in which NRMs are distinctly 'new': the way in which they have combined ideas and practices for their teachings; the kinds of people attracted to them; their visibility; the kind of opposition which they have encountered; the attention which they have received from the academic community; and their responses to views about them. These aspects will now be considered in greater detail.

The combination of ideas and practices

NRMs have been new in the way in which they have combined ideas and practices in their teachings and this has been important for the development of their organizations. NRMs display 'idiosyncratic *structures* of both the belief systems and the practices', and 'the particular combinations of items that are selected, and the rhetoric in which they are packaged' (Barker, 1985: 37–8, emphasis in original). NRMs have drawn on a variety of elements from different religious and cultural traditions and can thus be described as syncretic. For example, while drawing on traditional sources, including forms of Buddhism, *self-religions* – a term coined by Heelas (1988) – use psychological techniques to uncover the 'god within'. Some strands of the Human Potential movement have been classified as NRMs and have fed directly into other groups, in particular the Rajneesh movement.

NRMs have drawn from a wide range of Christian, non-Christian and esoteric/occult sources to which people living in the global village can have access. The process of globalization has facilitated the movement of people and ideas. Since the 1960s and 1970s, various geographical locations have become Meccas for the spiritual seekers, such as Goa in India and Cusco in Peru. It is therefore not surprising that the Rajneesh ashram in Poona attracted spiritual seekers from the West who soon outnumbered their Indian counterparts. In recent years, the Internet has opened new avenues of exchange and created new locations in virtual spaces. Heaven's Gate used the Internet as a source for income and as a resource for reaching out to potential recruits. Through a process of acculturation and inculturation, different cultural contexts have led to specific adaptations of NRM teachings and to variations within movements according to geographical location and cultural conditions. For example, Mahikari, a Japanese movement, has adapted its teachings to European cultures. The syncretic and eclectic aspect of NRMs could be described as postmodern – a question which has been debated in particular with regard to the New Age movement (see, for example, Chapter 11).

Types of members

NRMs have been new with regard to the kinds of people attracted to them in their formative years. A number of studies have shown that members of NRMs have tended to be relatively young, well-educated, idealistically minded, of a largely middle class background, with a concern for religious or spiritual questions, from largely intact families. Before the emergence of NRMs, social scientists considered members of 'unorthodox' or 'deviant' religions as deprived in some way, for example, of social status or economic means, and this explained why people joined such groups.

The arrival of subsequent generations and changing recruitment strategies have, however, resulted in a more varied age range in the membership of NRMs in recent years. For example, in The Family, members who joined the movement in its formative years have moved towards middle age and 'households' now tend to include quite a number of children, some the result of the previous policy of flirty fishing. Other movements, such as the Rajneesh Foundation, attracted a more mature membership in the first place.

Visibility

NRMs have been new with regard to the great visibility which they have achieved through the effective use of modern means of communication, such as the media (printed and broadcast), systems for processing information, modern transport, and – more recently – the Internet. Their visibility has been enhanced by the attention of the media, which, as already mentioned, have played a major part in shaping the public's view of NRMs. However, as already indicated, the attention of the media has been disproportionate with regard to the number of people involved in NRMs.

Opposition to NRMs

NRMs have become distinctive with regard to the kind of opposition which they have encountered; a movement (a 'single-issue movement'), generally referred to as 'anti-cult movement' or ACM (the groups subsumed under this label show variety, just like NRMs), has sprung up whose aim has been to counteract NRMs (in particular their efforts to recruit members), to support families affected by cult membership, and to assist former members. The principal means by which the ACM has sought to achieve this have been the dissemination of information, counselling and lobbying relevant agencies of the state. In the mid-1970s, a radical practice – 'deprogramming' – began to be used against NRM members to reverse the effects of 'brainwashing'. The coercive nature of this practice raised controversies in its turn and the legal implications have led to court cases. Some ACM groups, especially in the US, are said to have referred parents to deprogrammers, while other ACM groups (among them FAIR) have expressly distanced themselves from it. Since the late 1980s, there have been moves away from deprogramming towards 'exit-counselling', although in some circles, the terms are used interchangeably.

The first ACM groups formed in the US in the early 1970s, such as *FREECOG, CFF, CAN*, and *AFF*. Similar groups in Western Europe started to be organized from the mid-1970s onwards, some using their American counterparts as models, for example, *FAIR* in Britain, *ADFI* in France, and *Elterninitiative zur Hilfe gegen Abhängigkeit und religiösen Extremismus e.V.* in Germany. The initiative came largely from parents affected by cult membership and from individuals sympathetic to such parents. Local groups gradually linked up with one another to form a national and international network, with a view to mobilizing concern and action in the media, the mainstream churches and public authorities. The ACM can be seen as having assumed the role of a 'moral entrepreneur' who aims to enlist the support of other agencies. The reports by governments across Europe and bodies of the European Union illustrate the varying degrees to which the ACM has been able to mobilize these agencies; they illustrate also the progression in the perception of NRMs by these bodies and the strategies they have proposed to be put in place. The same can be said with regard to the responses of the mainstream churches: variations between the different social responses are closely linked to differences in the religious cultures, including the nature of the relationship between state and church.

Groups opposed to NRMs reject the label 'ACM', preferring the terms 'cult-watching', 'cult-observing' or 'cult concerned' organizations. However, these terms are also used for other organizations which focus on the phenomenon, such as academic institutes or research centres (for example, INFORM), not all of which necessarily share an 'anti-cult' agenda.

NRMs and the academic community

NRMs have been 'new' with regard to the attention which they have received from the academic community. NRMs started recruiting from the cultic milieu of the counter-culture, drawing in the kinds of young people who could be (and were) children and students of academics. Some academics thus had direct experience of NRM membership and realized that NRMs were a 'new' phenomenon, different from existing forms of religion in terms of their teachings and organization and challenging existing social scientific theories. Academics needed to develop new theoretical frameworks and concepts to account for the emergence of NRMs and their apparent success, while being confronted with the framework which the ACM had developed to account for conversion and recruitment into cults, a framework which centred on the notion of 'brainwashing'.

The distinct differences between NRMs were part of the early findings of the sociological study of the new phenomenon: although they were found to share similar features, they were also found to differ significantly from one another. Therefore, social scientists have refrained from making sweeping generalizations about NRMs, as each movement presents its own distinctive way of developing its doctrine and tenets. This has caused friction with the ACM which tends to deal with the notion of 'cult' as a categorical type, often in association with a set list of characteristics (the 'marks of a cult'). The implication is that all cults respond to these features and can thus be lumped together. This is distinct from an academic view which would see a particular NRM engaging in particular activities and compare them with those of other NRMs, without however considering them as being exactly the same. Hence the attempts at constructing 'ideal types' mentioned above.

The response of NRMs to views about them

Finally, NRMs have been new in their responses to the way the world around them, including academics, has perceived them. Instead of acting like subjects who could be studied like a tribe, they set mechanisms in place which presented their views on what was written or said about them. Just as the parents of NRM members were articulate and organized to set up groups to oppose them, their children proved equally articulate and organized, both in the way in which they presented themselves and in the way in which they joined in the debate about them, for example in disputing the view that they were brainwashed or exploited. This brought a new aspect to the work of researchers, as their findings now came under the scrutiny of the very people about whom they were writing.

This has been significant for a wider context, namely the paradigm clash in the sociology of religion and anthropology, brought about by a shift in the relative power and status of the scientific observer and of his/her subject matter. The shift has affected both the status of the researcher and the methodology of research. It has questioned the idea of objectivity and has made the gathering of data a two-way, interactive, negotiated process. NRMs have been able to stipulate conditions before allowing researchers access and to control the extent to which researchers have gained knowledge about them.

Since the mid-1980s, NRM members have become schooled in the academic discourse, with increasing numbers going through undergraduate and postgraduate university programmes and co-operating in academic projects. Thus the academic community has been confronted with 'subjects talking back' and questioning, if not disputing, theories and views about them. On the other hand, NRMs have used academic findings when making representations to the state or public authorities, for example in applications for charitable status.

THE CONSTRUCTION OF NRMs AND CULTS

As already indicated, there are differences in the use of the terms 'NRMs' and 'cults', depending on context and/or speaker. The term, NRMs' is generally used by academics, because, first, it is considered to be neutral and value-free, unlike the terms 'cult' or 'sect', which have assumed negative connotations in popular usage, especially when combined with adjectives, such as 'bizarre' or 'destructive'. They imply that groups with that label can be subsumed under one heading and thus share a set of characteristics, an implication which academics working in this field have sought to counterbalance. Second, in the sociology of religion, 'cult' and 'sect' are used as technical terms to describe types of religious groups which are distinct from NRMs. Some argue, however, that the term 'cult' has become unusable for social scientists because it has become lumbered with baggage and politicized. Finally, academics want to use a language which reflects their understanding of the phenomenon – in this sense, the term 'NRM' has political implications. However, some social scientists have used the term 'cults' in reference to NRMs. For example, Beckford does so to 'preserve the character and feel of popular sentiment . . . whenever I report or paraphrase popular usage' (Beckford, 1985: 12), as do some academics when addressing a non-academic audience.

NRMs themselves reject being labelled as 'cults', mainly because of the implication that they can be lumped together. In Continental Europe, NRMs are often referred to as 'sects' and classified together with the religious groups which were the 'new religious movements' of their period, such as the Jehovah's Witnesses (JW) or the Church of Jesus Christ of the Latter-Day Saints (Mormons). The prevalence of the term 'sect' in Continental Europe is due to the persisting influence of the Roman Catholic church which has used it to describe non-mainstream forms of religion. Unorthodox religions have naturally been the subject of study within the mainstream churches, as they have an obvious interest in following schismatic or sectarian trends within the Christian faith. A number of established sects, although by no means all of them, have arisen against the background of Orthodox Christianity. Some, for example JW, have been successful in recruiting members in recent years and membership in such groups has created social problems similar to those experienced by families affected by 'cult' membership. Sectarian tendencies within established sects have resulted in splinter groups which may be considered NRMs. The Branch Davidians, for example, were formed in the 1930s as a breakaway group from the Seventh-Day Adventists. Alice Bailey's Arcane School/World Goodwill, which arose in the early twentieth century, is an offshoot of Theosophy.

In Germany, the term *Jugendreligionen* (youth religions) was coined by Pastor Haack as early as 1974. He used it as a category for five 'new' movements: the UC, Scientology, COG, Divine Light Mission, and ISKCON, to which he added TM in 1977. Haack realized that these groups were different from other non-mainstream religious groups: they had three features in common, summarized as 'world-saving formula', 'saved family' and 'holy master'. Also, they seemed to originate in the US and to attract young people in particular. Haack refined his notion of *Jugendreligionen*, as the emergence of NRMs unfolded in Germany in the late 1970s and 1980s. The term came to be used interchangeably with the terms *Jugendsekten* (youth sects) and *destruktive Kulte* (destructive cults). The term *Jugendreligionen* also entered the academic language in Germany, often qualified with quotation marks or with the

Figure 12.4 The Mount Carmel compound near Waco, Texas, where heavily armed Branch Davidian cultists had been surrounded by federal agents for 51 days, burning on the afternoon of 19 April 1993

addition of 'so-called'. The term 'sects' (*sectes* or *sette*) is also commonly used in France and Italy, together with *phénomène sectaire* (the sectarian phenomenon) and *i nuovi culti* (the new cults). Similar terms are used in the other European countries.

Government agencies and public authorities have faced difficulties in finding appropriate terms for NRMs in their concern for finding legal instruments to preclude abuses under the guise of religion, without jeopardizing the constitutionally enshrined basic right to religious freedom of the individual or impinging on the status of established religions and churches. Some ACM groups, for example FAIR, see their work related to such concerns and in the service of human rights.

When the European Parliament debated the Cottrell Resolution – one of the early initiatives which sought to address the problematic aspects of NRMs on a Europe-wide level, the term 'NRMs' raised objections: it was considered too all-embracing, raising questions as to which movements should be considered 'old' or 'new', and provoking the fear of restriction of religious freedom. In 1994, the same concern exercised the Committee of Ministers of the Council of Europe, which resorted to the rather unwieldy definition of 'certain sects and religious movements of a non-traditional character'. On the other hand, the report of the Council of Europe of 1999, still mindful of safeguarding religious freedom, acknowledged that there is no accepted definition of 'sect' (or religion) and actually no need to define what constitutes a 'sect'. It recommends the adoption of 'a more descriptive approach' by concentrating on the acts committed in the name of religious beliefs, instead of on the beliefs themselves (anti-cult circles take this approach in determining whether a group is to be considered a cult) and suggests the term 'groups of a religious, spiritual or esoteric nature'. However, the report uses this term interchangeably with the word 'sect'. In its final report, the *Enquête-Kommission* of the German Parliament calls for greater differentiation among NRMs and suggests that – given its negative connotations – the term 'sect' should be avoided.

The variety in definitions and usage of terminology shows that the phenomenon of NRMs has different labels, depending on the speaker or writer and on the purpose for which s/he speaks or writes. As indicated, different terms are used in popular parlance and in academic language. Despite a broad definition of NRMs, there is no consensus about which movements exactly should be considered 'NRMs' or 'cults'. For example, some academics include the People's Temple; others do not. Some consider Scientology an NRM, others treat it as a form of magic, as a 'manipulationist sect', or as a form of modern, secular religion. Some have questioned whether the term 'religion' should be applied to (some) NRMs at all.

Such questions are complicated by the fact that some NRMs started in a different guise, such as a therapeutic group. Scientology's precursor in the 1950s, Dianetics, offered a 'modern science of mental health'. *est* (Erhard Seminar Training) offered four-day seminars to enhance personality in the 1970s, with one of its offshoots, Exegesis, operating until the mid-1980s. Synanon started as a therapy group for alcohol and drug rehabilitation under Chuck Dietrich.

In anti-cult circles, too, there is some uncertainty about which groups should be subsumed under the heading 'cult'. Generally speaking, the concern of ACM groups has focused on practices and methods rather than beliefs and doctrines and this has guided their categorization. FAIR, for example, has tended to treat those groups and movements as 'cults' or 'cult-like' groups which have given rise to complaints or which have attracted the attention of the media.

While the discussions of definitions and terms may be literally 'academic' when conducted in scholarly circles, they assume great importance in contexts where legal consequences are involved, such as charitable status. In Germany, for example, some authorities have declared Scientology a commercial enterprise and deprived it of its charitable status. In Britain, Scientology's application to the Charities Commission was turned down in 1999. In these cases, the definition formed by the authorities clashes with the way in which a particular group defines itself and wishes to be perceived. However, the case of Scientology also shows different approaches in different countries: in the same year (1999), Scientology was granted tax exempt status in Sweden and the Supreme Court in France ruled that it may be regarded as a religion.

Some NRMs, like Scientology, claim to be religions and want to be recognized as such, while others claim to be secular, for example TM. Questions of this kind are often linked to legal status and ensuing privileges, such as charitable status or access to institutions, such as schools or prisons. In some cases, the very existence of a group may be in question, as has been the case for NRMs in Russia after the introduction of new legislation in 1997 or for Falun Gong, banned by the Chinese authorities in 1999. When public authorities engage in a consultation process with different observers or 'cult-observing' groups (academics and/or ACM groups), they are faced with this variety of approaches.

THE FUTURE OF NRMs

Regarding the question of how NRMs will develop in the future, it is difficult, if not impossible, to make any firm predictions. It is safe to say that some NRMs will decline and/or disappear, while others will thrive and prosper, that some will establish themselves firmly in the religious landscape, while others will remain at the margins of society.

If we look at the future of NRMs in terms of success or failure, Stark's ten criteria may supply some answers (Stark, 1996), although these have so far not been applied to NRMs. However, the notion of success or failure may mean different things: from an outsider's view, the growth or decline in membership could be indicators for success or failure, while from an insider's view, they may not. Further, what to the outside world appeared as the demise of Heaven's Gate was for its members the final step in a trajectory towards a higher plane.

The violent and destructive conclusions of the NRMs mentioned above came as a surprise, even to those who had knowledge of them. Some were not well known or well studied, as, for example, the Solar Temple: the lectures of Luc Jouret, one of its leading figures, had attracted the attention of a cult-observer in the late 1980s, but he did not come away with any sense of foreboding disaster. Another case is Aum Shinrikyo which was seen as an eccentric but idealistic movement preaching asceticism and renunciation. Scholars who had contact with the movement reported nothing untoward. Some even defended it against criticism. However, both the Solar Temple and Aum Shinrikyo had given cause for public concern before the fatal events occurred, in connection with illegal arms and toxic gases, respectively. In these cases, occurrences preceded the violent outcome, which in retrospect looked like warning signals.

Anticipating future developments in NRMs is largely an exercise in conjecture, because, on the one hand, observers are not always apprised of all the facts – for example, Aum Shinrikyo did not, for obvious reasons, show researchers their chemical laboratory – and, on the other hand, events can be triggered in the interaction between a group and the outside world, if the group's beliefs and attitudes predispose it for such action, as illustrated by the events in Jonestown and Waco. What we do know – usually with the benefit of hindsight – is that NRMs may bring about their own demise because of factors inherent to their beliefs and because of their attitude towards the world: the People's Temple and Branch Davidians believed that the outside world, or at least parts of it, were intent on their destruction, while Aum Shinrikyo harboured destructive motives against the world. If a group considers the outside world as hostile or threatening, it feels the need to set up high fences or secure defences and may interpret any negative dealings with the outside as evidence for persecution.

Wessinger distinguishes three types of millennial group which become involved in violence: (1) groups which are attacked because they are thought mistakenly to be dangerous; (2) fragile groups which initiate violence in response to a combination of internal weaknesses and external cultural opposition in order to preserve their ultimate concern; (3) revolutionary groups which seek to overthrow the existing order to establish their millennial kingdom (Wessinger, 2000). A violent reaction is not necessarily proportionate to the objective degree to which a group is attacked, but to the perception by the group. Also, the perception of being attacked can be used by the leadership to convince themselves and their followers that violent action is justified. The Solar Temple would fit the first category; it perceived itself under assault and thus felt forced to leave the planet. However, it is not easy to determine exactly which factors lead to violence. The idea of the 'transit' emerged in the months and years following the first serious internal dissent in the Solar Temple.

However, despite the role of ideological or other factors, the psychology of the leader plays an important part in the evolution of a group towards violence. The leader is a major imponderable factor, as the unpredictable and mercurial element in his/her pronouncements is crucial for the maintenance of charismatic leadership. NRMs usually do not have apocalyptic or cataclysmic scenarios at the very outset. Such hopes or anxieties develop over time and undergo refinement and reinterpretation. The unfolding of such notions generally occurs in the leadership circles; grass-roots members are generally not privy to the preparations of violent or criminal activities and would therefore find it hard to believe that such things could be contemplated by the leadership. (This is one of the reasons why reports by former members may not provide the whole picture about a group.) The 'transit' of the Solar Temple can be interpreted as a 'drastic solution' to counter the 'loss of charisma' as well as a supreme witness to the world.

Regarding the future of NRMs as a phenomenon, it can be assumed that there will always be 'new' religions in an ever changing combination of ideas and organizational structures. The trend of 'believing without belonging' and multiple membership may spread to alternative religions – the diffuse nature of the New Age movement could point to this already. As to individual NRMs, attempting to foresee their future needs careful consideration of what we know about them, but will always involve a certain amount of speculation and thus leave open the possibility of entirely unexpected turns of events.

SUMMARY

- NRMs are perceived as a phenomenon coming to prominence in the late 1960s and early 1970s.
- NRMs have mainly been associated with Western societies, but the formation of new religions has been found to be a global phenomenon.
- There is no one accepted definition for the terms 'New Religious Movements' or 'cults'.
- There are no reliable or exact statistics on the number of NRMs or the number of NRM members.
- The beliefs and teachings of NRMs are derived from a range of religious traditions.
- There is great variety among NRMs and a great variety of the aspects which characterize them.
- There are a number of aspects which characterize NRMs as 'new'.
- Some NRMs have given rise to controversies which have dominated the public debate about NRMs in general.
- NRMs have evolved and changed over time.
- The future of NRMs is difficult to predict, but may hinge on the level of commitment required of members.

KEY TERMS

AFF (American Family Foundation) Founded in 1979 as a 'research center and educational organization to assist ex-cult members and families'.

ADFI (*Association de Défense de la Famille et de l'Individu*) First 'anti-cult' group in France, founded in 1975 by Mr and Mrs Champollion in Rennes. Since 1982, this organization operates as an association of groups in different parts of France, with the headquarters in Paris.

anti-cult movement or **ACM** Umbrella term for a variety of organizations which share the common aim of counteracting cults or NRMs. Like the term 'cults', the term 'ACM' lumps together a range of groups and has a pejorative connotation. Just as NRMs do not want to be referred to as 'cults', 'anti-cult' groups reject this label and prefer to be referred to as 'cult-watching', 'cult-observing' or 'cult concerned' organizations.

Bhagavad Gita Literally 'the song of the lord', probably the most popular book of Hindu scripture. It is part of the great epic the *Mahabharata* (thought to have been composed *c.* second century BCE to second century CE), and represents for most Hindus the essence of their religion.

CARP (Collegiate Association for Research of Principles) The youth organization of the Unification Church which recruits on university and college campuses.

CAUSA (Confederation of the Association for the Unification of the Societies of America) A political arm of the Unification Church which has been active in Latin America.

CAN (Cult Awareness Network) Founded to educate the public about the harmful effects of 'mind control' used by 'destructive cults'. It resulted from the association of small grass-roots groups across the US, but was forced to file for bankruptcy in late 1995/96.

CFF (Citizen Freedom Foundation) Resulted from the association of thirty-one parents' groups in twenty-six states in 1979, with headquarters in Los Angeles.

FAIR (Family Action and Information Resource, formerly Family Action and Information Rescue) The first ACM group in Britain, founded in 1976.

FREECOG (Free of Children of God or The Parent's Committee to Free our Sons and Daughters from the Children of God Organization) Founded in 1971 in San Diego at the instigation of Ted Patrick who has become notorious as the 'father of deprogramming'.

flirty fishing A former recruitment practice of the Children of God (now The Family) through which female members offered sexual favours to potential new (male) members.

heavenly deception An expression taken from the Unification Church to describe the practice of street recruitment teams presenting themselves as conventional Christians and used (mostly by ACM) as a blanket allegation for deceptive fundraising and recruitment practices.

Human Potential movement   An umbrella term comprising a range of psychotherapies, for example, encounter groups, primal therapy, bioenergetics, rebirthing.

ICF (International Cultural Foundation)   A cultural branch of the Unification Church which organizes cultural events, such as performances by The Little Angels (a Korean ballet troupe) and ICUS (International Conference for the Unity of Sciences) to which academics and scholars from all over the world are invited to attend conferences.

INFORM (Information Network Focus on Religious Movements)   A 'cult-observing' organization set up in 1988 by Professor Eileen Barker to provide 'objective, balanced, and up-to-date' information about NRMs.

mass weddings   Members of the Unification Church have become married in mass wedding ceremonies. These started as early as 1961, and until the early 1980s they were held in Seoul, South Korea, with the number of couples increasing with every ceremony. The first mass wedding in the West was held in 1982 in New York, involving 2,075 couples from 50 countries.

REMID (*Religionswissenschaftlicher Medien- und Informationsdienst e. V.*)   Set up in Germany in 1989 by a group of academics to provide the public with more and better information about religions and religious movements, including NRMs.

self-religions   A term coined by Paul Heelas to describe movements which focus on the inner self as the source of true divinity.

Veda   Often (inaccurately) referred to as 'the Vedas', the Veda are the oldest collection of hymns (older than the *Bhagavad Gita*) which – as the Sanskrit word 'Veda' indicates – refer to the 'sacred knowledge' of the Hindus.

FURTHER READING

Reference works

J. G. Melton: *Encyclopedia of American Religions*, second edition (Detroit, MI: Gale Research Company, 1987). A comprehensive collection of information about religious groups in North America, including non-mainstream groups.

J. G. Melton: *Encyclopedic Handbook of Cults in America* ([1986, 1st. ed.] New York, London: Garland Publishing, 1992). Provides short descriptions of many 'established sects' and NRMs and includes sections on the anti-cult movement, the New Age movement and violence and the cults. The introduction discusses the definition of a 'cult' and the lifestyle of its members and makes an assessment of the emergence of cults.

Introductions and overviews

Eileen Barker: 'New religious movements: their incidence and significance'. In Bryan R. Wilson and J. Cresswell (eds): *New Religious Movements: Challenge and Response* (London, New York: Routledge, 1999, pp. 15–31.) This recent chapter shows in what way the phenomenon of NRMs is different from the emergence of comparable movements in the past, how varied NRMs are, how they have changed over time and how their statistical significance relates to their social and cultural significance. The contributions in this collection explore a variety of aspects in NRMs as well as the interaction between NRMs and various social institutions.

P. B. Clarke: 'New paths to salvation. *Religion Today* 1 (1) 1984, 1–3. A brief introduction to the issues discussed in connection with the new religions and a consideration of some concepts recurrent in the teachings of new religions.

P. B. Clarke: 'New religious movements'. In I. Harris *et al.* (eds): *Contemporary Religions: A World Guide* (Harlow, Essex: Longman, 1992, pp. 57–66). A more expanded introduction to the issue of NRMs and the range of aspects related to them, such as their emergence in the West, in what sense they are new, attempts of classifying them, their sources of recruitment, the response of the wider society, membership and their future.

P. B. Clarke: 'Introduction: change and variety in new religious movements in Western Europe, *c.*1960 to the present'. In E. Arweck and P. B. Clarke (eds): *New Religious Movements in Western Europe: An Annotated Bibliography* (Westport, CT: Greenwood Press, 1997, pp. xvii–xliii). An extended introduction to the emergence and impact of NRMs in Western Europe. Explanations for their rise, a historical overview of development in individual countries, membership and social composition, social responses, and the prospects of NRMs are discussed in some detail. The bibliography provides a comprehensive collection of material published on the topic.

T. Robbins and D. Bromley: 'Social experimentation and the significance of American new religions: a focused review essay'. In M. Lynn and D. Moberg (eds): *Research in the Social Scientific Study of Religion* (Greenwich, CT: JAI Press, 1992, pp. 1–28.) A review of the ways in which NRMs challenge mainstream society and display experimentation with alternative lifestyles, with particular reference to the North American context.

Themes and Topics in NRMs

S. Palmer: *Moon Sisters, Krishna Mothers, Rajneesh Lovers: Women's Roles in New Religions* (New York, NY: Syracuse University Press, 1995). This volume examines the question of why women join NRMs and explores the kinds of roles which are open to women in such groups.

S. Palmer and C. Hardman (eds): *Children in New Religions* (New Brunswick, NJ: Rutgers University Press, 1999). This is the first collection of essays by academicss which examines how children in NRMs have been raised and educated and to what extent the second generation of members has changed NRMs.

E. Puttick and P. B. Clarke (eds): *Women as Teachers and Disciples in Traditional and New Religions* (Lewiston, Queenston, Lampeter: The Edwin Mellen Press, 1993). One of the first books to examine the role of women in traditional and new religions. The collection presents a range of traditions and approaches (Eastern and Western, old and new, scholars and practitioners) in order to show the variety of roles women have played in religious communities.

NRMs and society

Elisabeth Arweck: 'Responses to new religious movements in Britain and Germany, with special reference to the anti-cult movement and the churches'. Unpublished PhD Thesis. London: King's College London, University of London, 1999. This work compares and contrasts social responses to NRMs in the UK and in Germany by tracing the development of institutional responses in both countries. The focus is on the interaction of the ACM and the churches with other agencies involved in the debate of NRMs, such the media, the state, the NRMs themselves, and the academic community.

James A. Beckford: *Cult Controversies* (London: Tavistock, 1985). This volume examines the complex issues of causes, effects and social positions surrounding NRMs and the people who have been involved with them as insiders and outsiders. It provides the background to the controversies associated with cults and the responses to them by the ACM, the media, former members, the state, etc.

James A. Beckford and M. Levasseur: 'New religious movements in Western Europe'. In J. A. Beckford (ed.): *New Religious Movements and Rapid Social Change* (London: Sage, 1986, pp. 29–54). This chapter demonstrates how some young adults have responded to the rapidly changing Western world by joining a cult and compares cults to similar movements in the late nineteenth and early twentieth centuries. It shows that demographic, social and cultural changes have provided a specific audience for the NRMs. The public response to the NRMs in France is described.

C. Wessinger: 'Introduction: the interacting dynamics of millennial beliefs, persecution, and violence'. In C. Wessinger (ed.): *Millennialism, Persecution and Violence: Historical Cases* (New York, NY: Syracuse University Press, 2000, pp. 3–39). This essay explores the interaction of beliefs and persecution in millennial groups which leads to violence and presents patterns of responses arising from specific contexts. The chapters in the volume demonstrate variations in the experiences and perceptions of being persecuted among the believers of a range of religious groups.

Typologies and theories

W. S. Bainbridge and R. Stark: 'Client and audience cults in America'. *Sociological Analysis* 41 (2) 1980, 137–43. Presents one of the attempts at classifying NRMs in three categories: cult movements, client cults, and audience cults, together with examples.

Eileen Barker: 'New religious movements: yet another great awakening?' In P. E. Hammond (ed.): *The Sacred in a Secular Age: Towards Revision in the Scientific Study of Religion* (Berkeley, CA: University of California Press, 1985, pp. 36–57). The essay examines the question whether the NRMs of the 1970s represent a true religious revival. The collection of essays in this volume are mainly concerned with the secularization hypothesis.

Rodney Stark: 'Why contemporary religious movements succeed or fail: a revised general theory'. *Journal of Contemporary Religion* 11 (2) 1996, 133–46. The article refines and expands the author's theory of 1987 on the reasons why NRMs succeed or fail. The revised model refers to religious movements in general and consists of ten propositions which specify conditions for success or failure.

Statistics

P. B. Clarke: 'New religions in Britain and Western Europe: in decline?' In P. B. Clarke (ed.): *The New Evangelists: Recruitment, Methods and Aims of New Religious Movements* (London: Ethnographica, 1987, pp. 5–15). The introduction to the volume presents the result of a Europe-wide survey of NRM membership in order to assess how successful NRMs are in recruiting members. The contributions in the volume present the recruitment strategies of some NRMs.

REMID: Religionsgemeinschaften in Deutschland: Mitgliederzahlen. Obtained from the Internet http://www.uni-leipzig.de/~religion/remid.htm 1/12/1999. The site provides an overview of membership figures for religious groups and movements in Germany, ranging from established to non-mainstream groups, including NRMs.

New Age

Michael York: *The Emerging Network: A Sociology of the New Age and Neo-Pagan Movement* (Lanham, MD: Rowman & Littlefield, 1995). Based on the author's PhD thesis, this volume is one of the first accounts of the New Age movement and neo-paganism. It provides a survey and interpretation of the two movements within a sociological framework.

Self-religions

Paul Heelas: 'Western Europe: self-religions'. In S. Sutherland *et al.* (eds): *The World's Religions* (London: Routledge, 1988, pp. 925–31). The author coined the term 'self-religion' and provides in this essay a survey of groups which fall into this category. He traces their origin, the influences that have shaped them and establishes the link between self-religions and the business world.

PART II
Themes and trends

CHAPTER 13

Secularization and de-secularization

Peter L. Berger

SECULARIZATION THEORIES

Since its inception, presumably to be dated in the classical period of Durkheim and Weber, the sociology of religion has been fascinated by the phenomenon of *secularization*. This term, of course, has been endlessly debated, modified and occasionally repudiated. But for most purposes it can be defined quite simply as a process in which religion diminishes in importance both in society and in the consciousness of individuals. And most sociologists looking at this phenomenon have shared the view that secularization is the direct result of modernization. Put simply, the idea has been that the relation between modernity and religion is inverse – the more of the former, the less of the latter. Different reasons have been put forward for this relation. Most often it was ascribed to the ascendancy of modern scientific thinking, making the world more rationally comprehensible and manageable, and thus, supposedly, leaving less and less space for the supernatural. This interpretation was eloquently expressed in Weber's phrase of 'the disenchantment of the world'. Other reasons have been cited – the progressive *differentiation* of modern institutions (this was Parsons's favourite paradigm), the severance of the linkage of state and church in modern democratic regimes making religious affiliation a voluntary matter, and last but not least the massive modern processes of migration, urbanization and mass communication that undermined traditional ways of life. By the time I started my own work in this area, there was a body of theory and empirical work that could reasonably be called (and was so called) secularization theory.

It is worth noting that this understanding of the place of religion in the modern world was not necessarily driven by an anti-religious ideology. Durkheim can probably be described as philosophically inclined towards atheism, but Weber was, if anything, an agnostic with religious nostalgias, and the assumptions of secularization theory were shared by those who deplored and those who welcomed the alleged decline of religion. Not least among the deplorers were theologians of both major Christian confessions, and some theologians even managed to join the welcomers. The central drama of Protestant theology at least since the middle of the nineteenth century has been the question of how one can cope intellectually and practically with the necessity of living in a secular world. In somewhat different form this drama was replicated in the Roman Catholic church, with reactions ranging from defiant resistance against secularity to a cautious adjustment to it (*aggiornamento*). I continue to be impressed by the widespread assumption in religious circles to the effect that we are indeed living in a secular world (and not only in Europe, where this is understandable, but in America, where ordinary experience would make this assumption rather questionable).

A good example of this is provided by the development of so-called *sociologie religieuse* in Catholic Europe in the 1930s. In painstaking empirical research the decline of religious practice and belief was mapped, consciously in the service of fashioning a strategy by which the church might cope with this situation. Thus in one of his numerous works Gabriel LeBras, the father of *sociologie religieuse*, studied the effect on their religion as people migrated from Brittany (then the most Catholic region in France) to Paris – a quite devastating effect. LeBras does not make for lively reading, but in one of his more eloquent passages he mentions the Gare du Nord, the railway station in which Breton migrants would arrive in Paris, and suggests tongue-in-cheek that in this station there must be a magical piece of pavement – as soon as one steps on it, one ceases to be a Catholic. The strategy to cope with this was aptly caught in a Catholic publication shortly after the Second World War *France – Pays de Mission –* 'France, Mission Territory'. If today we have good reason to be sceptical of the old secularization theory, the work of LeBras and many others like him serves to remind us that the theory was not without empirical foundations (and, incidentally, it serves to reassure those of us, including myself, who once held to the theory and later gave it up, that we were not altogether foolish in our younger years!).

SECULARIZATION AND DE-SECULARIZATION

It is fair to say that the majority of sociologists dealing with religion today no longer adhere to the equation of modernity and secularization. Some still do (bravely so, I would say), among them Bryan Wilson, who continues to make significant contributions while adhering to a feisty version of secularization theory. In my own thinking about the sociology of contemporary religion, the major change of mind has been, precisely, the abandonment of the old secularization theory – not, I would like to emphasize, because of some philosophical or theological change, but because the theory seemed less and less capable of making sense of the empirical evidence from different parts of the world (not least the US). But, as I like to tell my students, one of the advantages of being a sociologist (as against, say, being a philosopher or theologian) is that one can have as much fun when one's theories are shot out of the water as when they are supported empirically.

As I see the evidence the world, with some notable exceptions (of which more in a moment), is as religious as it ever has been, and in some places is more religious than ever. This, however, does not mean that there is no such thing as secularization; it only means that this phenomenon is by no means the direct and inevitable result of modernity. It thus becomes an important task for the sociology of religion to map the phenomenon of secularization – both geographically and sociologically – not as the paradigmatic situation of religion in the contemporary world, but as one situation among others. I cannot possibly draw such a map in any detail here. It seems clear that in much of the world there are extremely powerful upsurges of religious movements, some of them having far-reaching social and political consequences. Paramount among these are two – the widely noted resurgence of Islam, both throughout the Muslim countries and in the Muslim diaspora – and the less widely noted explosion of Evangelical Protestantism, especially in its Pentecostal version, over wide regions of the developing world, most dramatically in Latin America (I would refer here to the work of David Martin). However,

Figure 13.1 Charismatic Christian in the US raises his hands in song and praise. The rapid spread of Charismatic Christianity around the globe in the twentieth century and beyond has confounded secularization theory which had predicted the demise of religion at the level both of individual practice and of social and political influence

these two cases are not unique (though, arguably, they are the most important). There are powerful revitalization movements in all the other major religious communities – among Roman Catholics (especially in developing countries), Eastern Orthodox Christians (quite dramatically in Russia), Jews (in Israel and the diaspora), Hindus and Buddhists. Put simply, most of the world is bubbling with religious passions. And where secular political and cultural elites have been established, they find themselves on the defensive against the resurgent religious movements – for example, in Turkey, in Israel and in India – and, last but not least, but in the US!

MAPPING SECULARITY

Where, then, does secularity fit on this map? I would say, in two places. First, there is a thin but very influential stratum of intellectuals – broadly defined as people with Western-style higher education, especially in the humanities and social sciences. They constitute a secular internationale, whose members can be

Figure 13.2 Alongside Charismatic Christianity, resurgent Islam is the most vital, vibrant and growing form of religion in the world today. Here around 200,000 worshippers gather on Temple Mount, Jerusalem on the second Friday of Ramadan, 2 February 1996

encountered in every country. Again, I cannot here go into the question of why this kind of education has secularizing effects (I suspect that it is mainly because of the corrosive insight into the relativity of beliefs and values). But I would point out that this peculiar internationale helps to explain the continuing plausibility of secularization theory among many Western intellectuals: when they travel to, say, Istanbul, Jerusalem or New Delhi, they almost exclusively meet with other intellectuals – that is, people much like themselves – and they can then jump to the conclusion that this faculty club faithfully reflects the cultural situation outside – a fatal mistake indeed! (Need I add that it would be equally mistaken to believe that, say, the Harvard Faculty Club reflects the place of religion in American culture?) There is also, second, a geographical exception to the pulsating ubiquity of religion in the contemporary world – and that is Western and Central Europe. This is, I think, the only major part of the world in which the old secularization theory continues to be empirically tenable. The question of why this is so is tantalizing.

Indeed, I would propose that this is the single most interesting question for the sociology of religion today: 'Is Europe religiously different, and if so why?' The question posits a *European exceptionalism*. It has often been observed that, in contrast to Europe, the US is a very religious country. But that is not exceptional; in this, America conforms to what is the worldwide pattern; Europe is, or seems to be, the big exception. And once one accepts the ubiquity of religion in the modern world, one becomes interested in secularization in a new and very intriguing way – secularization, not as the modern norm, but as a curious case of deviance that requires explanation. In recent years, for understandable reasons, there has been much scholarly interest in the phenomenon labelled *fundamentalism*. Leave aside here the point that this refers to a specific development in the history of American Protestantism and can be very misleading when applied elsewhere; in common parlance, the term is used to describe just about any militant religious movement with a claim to authority and certitude. To be sure, it is interesting to ask, for example, why and how militant Islam came to power in the Iranian revolution at a particular time. But the phenomenon as such, in this or that form, has always been around. It is the exception, not the norm, that invites scrutiny. In other words, sociologists of religion should pay less attention to Iranian mullahs, and more to Harvard professors and to ordinary people in London or Paris.

How does European secularity manifest itself empirically? It does most clearly in behaviour related to the churches. Throughout Western and Central Europe, there has been a dramatic decline in people's participation in church life, in the influence of religion in public life and in the number of people choosing religious vocations. But it also manifests itself in the declining number of people who profess traditional religious beliefs. What is also interesting is that this cultural constellation, which in an earlier period (say, up to the 1960s) was concentrated in Northern Europe (both in Protestant and Catholic religions), subsequently spread rapidly and massively into Southern Europe – most dramatically in Spain (especially after the demise of the Franco regime), but also in Italy and Portugal. Some conservative Catholics in those countries have blamed this development on the alleged subversion of church authority by Vatican II and the reforms that followed. But exactly the same phenomenon can be observed in Greece, whose Orthodox people could not care less about changes in the Roman church! Rather, there seems to have arisen a distinctive Euro-secularity, part and parcel of a cross-national European culture that simply carries it along with the rest of the package. This is what happened as the Pyrenees ceased to be a barrier between Spain and all those (from Franco's point of view) northern aberrations. Most recently, it has been happening dramatically in Ireland and in Poland. Curiously enough, it also happened in Quebec (an odd case of what might be Europeanization at a distance).

There is not much dispute about these facts, but the interpretations vary. There is a group of analysts who dispute the description of the European case in terms of secularization. Prominent among them is Danièle Hervieu-Léger in France, Grace Davie in Britain and Paul Zulehner who focuses on the German-speaking countries. They view the situation as a shift away from the traditional churches (already in the 1960s some German analysts used the term *Entkirchlichung* –'de-churchification' – to describe this shift), with large numbers of people defining and practising their religiosity in non-traditional, individualized and institutionally loose ways. This obviously constitutes a serious problem for the churches; it should not dictate the perspective of sociologists. The latter should instead concentrate on studying these new forms of religiosity, rather than doing (as it were) negative market research for the churches.

Let me say that I have not been fully persuaded by these arguments; I still think that the European case can be subsumed under the category of secularization. But even if one agrees with Hervieu-Léger and others that the category fails to grasp the European situation, it is still the case that Europe is different from any other major region in the world, and that this difference calls out for explanation. We need a more detailed topography of the people who, paraphrasing the title of Davie's recent book on religion in Britain, 'believe without belonging'. We also need a more detailed analysis of how churches, despite empty pews and a shortage of clergy, can continue to be privileged institutions in the public sphere. José Casanova has analysed this phenomenon, which, turning around Davie's phrase, one could describe as 'belonging without believing'.

In any revised sociology of secularization the comparison between Europe and America is, obviously, very useful. The comparison makes the equation modernity/secularization extremely difficult to sustain. America is so much more religious, but can hardly be called less modern, than Europe. Why, then, is there the difference? Let me admit that I have no answer to this question. An answer will almost certainly require a collaboration between sociologists and historians; I believe that the secularizing process began in Europe in the nineteenth century (of course with different starting points and trajectories in different countries). My assumption would be that no important historical development has a single cause, thus a number of factors must have gone into the creation of Euro-secularity. The most commonly mentioned factor is political – a close relation between church and state (in contrast to America), with the result that political opposition often contained an anti-clerical component. Another factor which, I would hypothesize, helps to explain the difference between the two continents – may have to do with education. In most of Europe public education has been mainly in the hands of the state, which sends out teachers into all corners of the land; many of these teachers were, so to speak, foot soldiers in the army of secular enlightenment. When primary and secondary education became compulsory, many parents had no way of shielding their children from the secularizing influence of the school. Until very recently a vastly different situation existed in the US – the schools were under local authorities, and thus much more amenable to the wishes of the parents. Put simply, European parents had to put up with the teachers sent by the educational authorities; American parents – however unenlightened – could fire the teachers. A plausible explanation? Maybe, maybe not. But I would suggest that this question could launch a hundred doctoral dissertations!

One important element of American religion that is quite negligible in Europe is Evangelical Protestantism – the millions of Americans who define themselves as 'born-again Christians'. These too are not a homogeneous group, but that point cannot be pursued here. However, there is an interesting similarity that opens up another important issue for the sociology of religion – the strong presence of what Robert Wuthnow has called 'patchwork religion'. In one study after another in America, not only by Wuthnow but by others (notably Wade Clark Roof and Nancy Ammerman), one finds people who put together an individualized religion, taking bits and pieces from different traditions, and coming up with a religious profile that does not fit easily into any of the organized denominations. Many of them assert that they are not 'religious' at all, but are pursuing a quest for 'spirituality'. Very similar data come up in European research. Hervieu-Léger uses Claude Levi-Strauss's term *bricolage* to describe this form of religiosity – people putting together a religion of their own like children tinkering with a lego set, picking and choosing from the available religious 'material'. It is important to note that such people can be found both inside and outside the churches, both among those who claim to be orthodox in terms of their institutional affiliation and among those who admit to heterodoxy. There is a significant difference, though. In America this group is much more frequently affiliated (thus providing another instance of the American proclivity for association, which incidentally serves to put in question the myth of American 'rugged individualism' – but that is another story).

PLURALISM AND SECULARIZATION REVISITED

This brings me to another important area for the sociology of religion today – a fuller understanding of the dynamics of *pluralism*. If I look back on my own work, I think that I understood this quite adequately a long time ago; what I misunderstood was the relation of pluralism and secularization. Let me put this in the form of two simple propositions:

1 Modernity pluralizes the life-worlds of individuals and consequently undermines all taken-for-granted certainties.
2 This pluralization may or may not be secularizing, depending on other facts in a given situation.

If these propositions are taken as hypotheses, a fascinating area of empirical research opens up. And, again, the comparison between Europe and America is likely to be fruitful, with America a 'lead society' of modern pluralism, yet lagging far behind Europe in the matter of secularization.

There is no great mystery about the causes of modern pluralism – these are the classical processes of modernization – urbanization, migration, mass education, the mass media of communication, all of these gaining additional potency under democratic conditions where the state refrains from trying to impose a monopolistic world view. Social psychology has demonstrated the importance of social support for an individual's definitions of reality; where this support is weak or divided, the definitions of reality lose their taken-for granted status in consciousness and become a matter of individual choices. I continue to think that the most useful way of incorporating these social psychological insights within sociology is through Arnold Gehlen's theory of institutions. Be this as it may, however, to say that religious beliefs are chosen rather than taken for granted is not the same as saying that these beliefs are no longer held. Put simply, I would propose that pluralism affects the 'how' rather than the 'what' of religious belief and practice – and that is something quite different from secularization.

SUMMARY

▮ Since its inception, secularization has been a main preoccupation of sociology of religion, and a range of theories have been developed to explain the link between secularization and modernization.
▮ The fact that the world continues to bubble with religious passions appears to undermine the view that secularization is an inexorable and inevitable process.
▮ Rather than being the norm, secularization now appears to be the exception, found chiefly: (1) amongst an international intellectual and cultural elite; and (2) in Western Europe.

▌ Europe's distinctive political and educational history may help explain European exceptionalism, but further research is required on this topic.

▌ In the light of contemporary sacralization, it seems necessary to revise the belief that there is an inevitable connection between pluralization and secularization.

▌ KEY TERMS

differentiation (sometimes called 'social differentiation') The distinctively modern process whereby social activities become split between different institutions.

European exceptionalism The unique secularity of Europe compared with the US and the rest of the world – a case of deviance which still requires explanation.

fundamentalism In a strict sense, the term refers to a specific development in the history of American Protestantism, but in a much looser sense it is used in common parlance to describe just about any militant religious movement with a claim to authority and certitude.

pluralism The simultaneous existence in a single social arena of a number of different world views. Pluralism is characteristic of modern societies and is brought about by processes like urbanization, migration, mass education, the mass media of communication, all of which gain additional potency under democratic conditions where the state refrains from trying to impose a monopolistic world view.

secularization The process in which religion diminishes in importance both in society and in the consciousness of individuals.

▌ FURTHER READING

Introductory

Linda Woodhead and Paul Heelas (eds): *Religion in Modern Times. An Interpretive Anthology* (Oxford, UK, and Malden, MA: Blackwell, 2000, pp. 307–41 and 429–74) draws together classical and contemporary readings on secularization and sacralization.

Secularization

Peter L. Berger: *The Sacred Canopy. Elements of a Sociological Theory of Religion* (Garden City, NY: Doubleday, 1967). In the course of a wider discussion of the relation between religion, society and knowledge, Berger develops the influential argument that pluralization is the missing causal link which explains the connection of secularization and modernization.

Steve Bruce: *Religion in the Modern World. From Cathedrals to Cults* (Oxford and New York: Oxford University Press, 1996) offers a spirited defence, a strong version of the secularization thesis.

Grace Davie: *Religion in Modern Europe. A Memory Mutates* (Oxford: Oxford University Press, 2000) examines European exceptionalism and the ways in which religion maintains a vicarious and precarious presence in Europe.

Sacralization

Peter L. Berger (ed.): *The De-Secularization of the World. Essays on the Resurgence of Religion in World Politics* (Washington: Ethics and Public Policy Center; Grand Rapids: William B. Eerdmans, 2000) considers how contemporary religious resurgence counts against universal theories of secularization.

José Casanova: *Public Religions in the Modern World* (Chicago and London: University of Chicago Press, 1994) offers an analysis of the ways in which religion retains public and political significance in the modern world.

This chapter is an extract from a longer paper, 'Reflections on the sociology of religion today', by Peter L. Berger, which was originally delivered as the Paul Hanly Furfey Lecture at the 2000 gathering of the Association for the Sociology of Religion. The full paper appears in *Sociology of Religion* 62 (4): 2001, pp. 443–54.
© Association for the Sociology of Religion, Inc., 2001. Reprinted by kind permission of the Association for the Sociology of Religion.

Religion and globalization

David Lehmann

INTRODUCTION

This chapter argues that contemporary theoretical accounts of religion and globalization are misleading. They are misleading because they are enslaved to a model of globalization as the inexorable spread of a homogenous, rationalized, standardized 'modern' culture. This model is generated when the spread of global capitalism is taken to be the model for all globalization. As a result, the globalization of religion tends to be understood in terms of two interconnected processes: (1) the spread of standard, homogenized forms of religion across the globe and (2) the assertion of local religious identities in reaction to such globalization.

Against these theories, this chapter is based on a contrasting view in which religion is seen to be the 'original globalizer'. It distinguishes two forms of religious globalization. First, 'cosmopolitan' globalization, which is characteristic of erudite and institutionalized forms of religion, and which involves attempts to introduce into the clash of religious systems a historical and contextualised 'theory' of other cultures, such as when the bishops and intellectuals of the Catholic or Anglican churches try to come to terms with local culture. This pre-dates modernity, though it is still active in the modern world. Second is the much more disorganized form of globalization which is characteristic of the contemporary forms of religion which are often labelled 'fundamentalist' or 'charismatic'. Such religion is driven not by elites but by a mass of independent actors, who pick and choose elements from different cultures (modern and premodern) without regard to the constraints of a regulating, official religious hierarchy.

The idea that religion is 'the original globalizer' destabilizes the more common assumption that markets are the primary force for globalization. It also stands in contrast to the assumption that globalization abolishes frontiers and leads to homogeneity. In economics globalization does mean homogenization in the sense of drawing far-flung agents into a competitive world market, and although that notion also needs a great deal of refinement, we can take for granted that it does pull down barriers to trade and competition. By contrast, religion breaks through frontiers and in the same process throws up new frontiers because religions ancient and modern, monotheist, polytheist and totemic, with their apparatus of ritual practices and internal, proprietorial, self-sufficient codes, are demarcators and markers of difference rather than similarity and homogeneity.

Thus religion is redrawing old frontiers all the time, and in the process drawing new frontiers, because ritual or religious communities cannot exist without drawing frontiers. In this spreading, almost promiscuous, propagation of religious forms across the globe in all sorts of directions (not only, by any means, from the rich countries to the poor, indeed perhaps not even principally in that direction), the resources of modernity are powerful dynamic vehicles. Modernity offers the indispensable tools of this propagation: fast long-distance transport and communications, the availability of English as a global vernacular of unparalleled power, the know-how of modern management and marketing. This does not mean that impersonal rationality is the content of globalization; rather it serves as an instrument which may be used and translated in different ways and in diverse contexts.

RELIGION AND BOUNDARIES

One way of thinking of modernity is in terms of the use of rational, impersonal criteria to decide, allocate, adjudicate and evaluate (see the Introduction to this volume). Religion can also take rationalized forms, as when it consists of belief based on doctrine, principles and texts, and when it is regulated by official institutionalized authorities. For most people, however, religion is not a set of beliefs at which they arrive by rational reflection from first principles, but rather a set of symbolic systems which confer identity and mark out social, ethnic and other boundaries. Equally, most religion involves *rituals* which mark crucial moments in the lifecycle, and in the daily, weekly and annual cycles, as well as providing powerful emotional and meta-social mechanisms for the resolution of psychological and social tension, and for coping with ill health.

In many societies, both forms of religion exist side by side. In England, for example, we see that the institutions of the Church of England have been shaped by the rationality of modern democratic (and bureaucratic) culture. However, unlike the state, which has retained a monopoly on the rule of law and the use of force, the nominally established Church of England has not succeeded in attaining a monopoly of the ritual life of British society. Here, as in all societies, undercurrents or counter-currents of 'popular' religion take care of the sacred in a manner which does not fit in with the impersonal culture outlined above. In these counter-currents authority is embodied in persons to whom special powers are attributed: they are not Anglican clergy, but charismatic leaders who have sprung as if from nowhere, and who exercise the prerogatives of their office not so long as a church recognizes (and pays) them, but so long as they retain a following. Popular forms of religion can also survive and flourish within the formal framework of the major institutionalized churches, organized perhaps around the devotion to particular saints or shrines to which supernatural powers are attributed, especially powers to heal and powers to dispel misfortune (see Chapter 9 and Chapter 17).

Once we understand that ritual cycles and the symbolic representation of the forces of health and illness, good fortune and misfortune, are markers of identity and difference separating peoples, ethnic groups and primary collectivities in general, and if we also allow that rituals and symbols are the outward manifestations of embodied, as distinct from impersonal, authority, we can begin to see why it is that conquest and colonialism have almost invariably been associated with religious expansion and conflict. For to establish domination it is necessary to embody power, and to do so in a form which is comprehensible to the subject people. That much is evident enough from the history of all the great empires of the past. Since conquerors have no legal–rational grounds for legitimizing their power over the conquered, religious/symbolic methods, which confer authority on their persons independently of a set of principles, are a useful resource for the imposition of their power.

But what then of that contemporary form of conquest and colonization known under the deceptively peaceful word of globalization? For unlike the empires of the past, we have here a process in which all manner of frontiers (political, economic, cultural, religious) are apparently breached and even reduced to nothing in the creation of a seamless web of market relations and of the legal and humanitarian institutions of capitalist democracy. In a globalized world of democratic capitalism, all authority is expected to be rational and impersonal, all economic agents to be optimizing automata, while religion is considered to be a matter of private personal choice experienced in an institutional setting governed by the same democratic principles as the state itself.

Although this image of globalization commands a vast following, it overlooks the processes whereby ritual and symbolism, which are at the heart of popular religion redraw boundaries all the time, and forms of popular religion straddle or violate cultural, ethnic and national frontiers despite the encroachments of legal–rational forms of modernity. Globalization therefore does not mould all the cultures which meet within its dynamic into a single homogeneous whole. Indeed it is almost as if the contrary were true: globalization may bring about the unpacking of local cultural complexes, but in the process it creates multifarious local identities and criss-crossing frontiers, so that diversity comes to rule more than ever before, even if similarities across social and spatial distances also become ever more evident.

An example helps to illustrate the point. In the nineteenth and twentieth centuries millions of Africans came under the influence of English, Scottish and American missionaries. But this did not mean that Anglo Saxon versions of Christianity obliterated the pre-existing religio-cultural landscapes, and that Africans simply exchanged one religious package for another. On the contrary, the packages themselves were reshaped, not only in Africa but in the West as well. That is why African Christianity, even when it is brought back to the colonial metropolis by postcolonial migrants, is so different from any British religious institution – as witness the numerous Caribbean *Pentecostal* churches, Nigerian 'Aladura' churches or branches of the Zimbabwe Assemblies of God Africa in Britain.

When religion crosses frontiers or breaks through barriers, even when it does so in the most violent manner, the outcome is not the abolition of one set of religious beliefs and practices by another, but the creation of new boundaries. If the phrase 'religion as globalizer' is to have any analytic force, it must be underpinned by a concept of globalization which, as sketched above, evokes not homogenization

Figure 14.1 (a) and (b) Good Friday procession in a Philippine village

but rather the rearrangement, and the multiplication, of social boundaries in ways which, at any particular point in time and space, criss-cross inherited borders and barriers, re-inventing them, removing them or indeed violently destroying them.

'COSMOPOLITAN' RELIGIOUS GLOBALIZATION

As mentioned above, religion has often been a natural accompaniment of conquest and colonization. Religion can legitimate the power of a conquering people over their new subjects, and serve as a resource in the imposition of power. Yet this is not a one-way process, for the transmission of religion is often accompanied by a will to appropriate and even domesticate the powers and virtues of the conquered (or invading) 'other'. This requires a 'theory' about who the 'others' are, where they come from and whence they derive their powers or their uniqueness. A conquering people is made aware that those with whom they enter into alliance or confrontation have a place in history and a location in space; they are made aware of this in relation to themselves as well. In short, some theory of history is required – and a concept of history, of origins and of social causation is, of course, a feature of modernity. The generation of such a theory about the position of a dominant power in relation to the 'other' is a defining feature of the cosmopolitan variety of religious globalization.

It is above all Roman Catholicism which embodies a 'cosmopolitan' version of religious globalization, in which a religious culture, identity and institution expand across cultural and political frontiers accompanied by a 'theory' of the other. Such globalization involves the very modern idea that religious practices are embedded spatially and temporally, that they express the location of a people in time and space, and that changing others' beliefs requires an understanding of that embeddedness. The Roman Catholic church has even, in the late twentieth century, developed a theology of inculturation (see Chapter 7) which argues for the explicit recognition and incorporation of non-Western rituals and symbols in Christian celebration among non-Western peoples.

It is extremely important, also within Catholicism, to relate the dialectic of the erudite and the popular within its vast and elaborate institutional edifice to its evident global reach. Ever since the sixteenth-century Counter-Reformation, which represented a response to Luther and Protestantism but coincided with the final stage of the Reconquest of Spain (retaking the kingdom of Granada where Islam had had such a glorious history) and with the conquest of the Americas, the culture of Catholicism has had to deal with 'the other', and the result has been quite different from the corresponding experience of Protestantisms of all kinds, even though Protestantism has also been intimately bound up with colonialism, especially in Africa.

Catholic expansion accompanied the Spanish and Portuguese conquest of the Americas which began in earnest in the sixteenth century. But the church did not always acquiesce with violent conquest. From a very early stage dissidents within the church spoke out against the brutality of conquest and the economic and social subjection of the indigenous peoples, the majority of whom perished as a result of epidemics of diseases against which they had no immunity. Futhermore Western Christianity was not simply imposed upon these territories in a way which left it untouched, nor did it totally eliminate what had gone before. As the Catholic church established its institutional presence in the Americas, the conversion of indigenous peoples produced a vast array of festivals and local organizations under whose auspices there developed cults of saints not dissimilar from those which already existed in the Iberian peninsula. In addition, beliefs in spirits, in supernatural entities governing peoples' lives, inherited from pre-Columbian civilizations in the Andean countries and in Mesoamerica, persisted. Catholicism tried to make sense of this, retaining the idea that a people's identity was encapsulated in their own religious life, and dissidents within the Church claimed that if different peoples practised different religions, maybe this was their way of worshipping the same universal God. The greatest of all 'defenders of the Indians', the Dominican friar and bishop Bartolomé de las Casas (1484–1566), had gone so far as to say that the indigenous Mexicans' practice of human sacrifice, far from work of the devil, was their way of worshipping the same God as the Christians, and he denounced the Spanish conquerors who massacred them in the name of Christianity as violators of God's laws.

A century later in 1648 the Mexican church invented what was to become the most popular and deeply rooted cult in the Americas, that of the Virgin of Guadalupe, based on the apparition of the Virgin to a humble Mexican Indian, said to have taken place in 1531, in the immediate aftermath of the conquest of Mexico (1519–21). The core of the story of Juan Diego's vision of the Virgin of Guadalupe is twofold: that the Virgin appeared not to a bishop or priest or to a Spaniard, but to an unlettered Indian who was able to show evidence of a miracle to the Archbishop of Mexico (at that time a very powerful secular figure as well as the head of the church in the vast colony of New Spain) and convince him to erect a church in the place

Figure 14.2 An enactment of Jesus carrying the cross in Mexico City

where she had appeared. The Indian overcame the Spaniard and the illiterate overcame the educated, in a story which has several hallmarks of a myth of origin: extreme brevity, the establishment of a quasi-kinship relationship between a human and a divine being, through the frequent use of the words 'mother' and 'son' in the standard version of the story, and both the contestation and the confirmation of a politico-religious institution. This is the founding myth of the Mexican church – one of the most thriving churches in the world in terms of the devotion and religious participation of its followers – as well as the Mexican nation. What is more, the Virgin of Guadalupe has even been declared 'Queen and Patron of the Americas' by papal authority.

In 1648 the Mexican elite was startled to learn that the image of the Virgin Mary venerated at the 'hermitage' of Guadalupe, situated on a hill-side outside the city, had a miraculous origin. Over a century ago, so the story ran, on Saturday 9 December 1531, a poor Indian from Cuautitlán named Juan Diego heard sweet music as he was passing the hill of Tepeyac on his way to the Franciscan church at Tlatelolco. He then saw a young lady radiant with brilliant light who told him that she desired to have a chapel built in her honour at Tepeyac, so that she could show herself to be a merciful mother to Juan Diego and his people and to all faithful who might seek her assistance. The Virgin commanded him to speak with the Bishop of Mexico and obtain his permission to build the chapel. But when the Indian went to see Juan de Zumárraga he was rebuffed. The next day he again saw the

Virgin at Tepeyac and again he went to the bishop, who refused him permission. A third time the Virgin appeared and a third time the bishop rebuffed him, on this occasion demanding that some sign be offered that it was indeed the Virgin Mary and not some devil who had appeared. On the fourth day, by now discouraged, Juan Diego decided to go to Tlatelolco to find a priest for his uncle, Juan Bernardino, who was dying of the plague. But on his way the Virgin appeared to him and commanded him to climb the hill at Tepeyac so as to pick flowers. Despite the winter month, Juan Diego found the hill covered with roses and other flowers which he gathered into his cape, a simple mantel woven from cactus fibre. The Virgin told him to take the flowers to Zumárraga. Sure enough, when he opened his cape before the bishop, the flowers fell to the ground, only to reveal imprinted on the coarse *ayatl* cloth a likeness of the Virgin Mary. Awed by this miracle, the bishop fell to his knees in adoration and then had the image placed at the cathedral until it could be taken with all due ceremony to the chapel which was to be built at Tepeyac. Meanwhile, the Virgin had also appeared to Juan Bernardino, cured him of the plague, and told him that her image was to be known as the Holy Mary, Virgin of Guadalupe. Once the painting was installed at Tepeyac, it soon attracted the veneration of pilgrims and travellers and miraculous cures were performed, a sign of its heavenly origin.

(Extract from Chapter 16, 'Mexican Phoenix', in D. A. Brading *The First America* Cambridge: Cambridge University Press, 1991)

Figure 14.3 A taxi driver having a siesta protected by his car and the Virgin of Guadalupe, Mexico City

So Catholicism, for all the church's obsession with dogma, is a plural, multifarious, inclusive culture able to absorb and refashion local cultures worldwide in an unending dialectic of the erudite, or institutional, and the popular. The two feed off one another, borrowing and co-opting elements, while in the process the erudite theorizes, contextualizes and tries to mould or control the popular. In recent times this relationship has been politicized under the influence of Liberation Theology, which arose in the 1960s among Catholic – but also Protestant – theologians in Latin America (see Chapter 7). At first Liberation Theology taught that 'superstition' was a mechanism which blinded the masses to their oppression, but before long theologians of this school began (like Bartolomé de las Casas) to see popular religion as an expression of the untutored devotion of the masses which, because of their innocence, could be understood as a true expression of the divine. In addition, though, Liberation Theologians have added a political element which sees popular religion as a force for social change and popular empowerment. The influence of this current has now had some impact on the official doctrine of the Catholic church, albeit in diluted form, and it was palpable in the campaigns against apartheid in South Africa led by the (Anglican) Archbishop Desmond Tutu.

The cosmopolitan variant of cultural globalization is repeated in a variety of contemporary encounters, and each time the distinctive features of theorizing and contextualizing appear. Examples include the adoption in Europe and North America of Asian religions, with all the accompanying philosophical reformulations, and the creation of Buddhist institutions in the West (and in Asia) in the style of modern institutions (see Chapter 2). The borrowing takes place in the opposite direction as well: the emergence in India of 'Hindu fundamentalism' or, more accurately, Hindu nationalism, could be seen as the institutionalization of a religion which had never before been institutionalized save around village or neighbourhood temples, and which had never before had a doctrine in the Western sense of a coherent, closed philosophical system developed by literate experts (see Chapter 1). Likewise international campaigns to preserve indigenous cultures lead inevitably to their incorporation into the international culture of modernity, as their leaders are incorporated into the life of international institutions and in the culture of *NGOs* (non-governmental organizations), through organizations such as Oxfam, Christian Aid and Survival International, and so adopt the practice of theorizing and contextualizing their own 'other' traditions.

'FUNDAMENTALIST' RELIGIOUS GLOBALIZATION

The term *fundamentalism* carries a wide range of meanings, some of them pejorative. Here it is used to refer to what the French call 'integrism', meaning a religious code which encompasses and governs with its prescriptions the entire private and public life of individuals and the collectivity. The prime examples in the contemporary world are Muslim renewal; the innumerable Evangelical and Charismatic churches, sects and tendencies descended from the Protestant tradition and associated with names such as the Assemblies of God; and Ultra-Orthodox Judaism whose followers are known as *haredim* (those who live in fear of God) or *chassidim* (the pious) (for more on these movements see Chapters 6, 7 and 8). These three varieties of movement represent radical departures from the traditions out of which they have grown – even in the case of the Jewish Ultra-Orthodox who claim to be returning to the practices of their forefathers in every minute detail.

Even though some uses of the term 'fundamentalism' may be problematic, there seem to be enough common features amongst these types of religion to justify its use. Particularly significant is the fact that all can be grouped together as the prime instances of a second main type of modern religious globalization. Unlike cosmopolitan forms of religious globalization, homogeneity (sameness) is a much more striking feature of fundamentalist globalization than heterogeneity (variety). This difference is particularly striking given that this second form of globalization is a popular rather than an elite movement, and is not imposed 'from above' by centralized institutions. Homogeneity is achieved more by reliance on common authoritative texts than on traditions or institutions. Yet despite its universalizing tendencies this second, fundamentalist, form of globalization is also characterized by a remarkable ability to adopt and adapt to local customs, and establish local forms of identity.

Figure 14.4 Images from a Brazilian *umbanda* 'terreiro' in Recife: a crucifix amid veiled images of Brazilian deities of African origin shows the promiscuous borrowing of Brazilian possession cults

Non-cosmopolitan, fundamentalist forms of globalization can thus be characterized in terms of:

- an extraordinary ability to 'plug in' to local cultural practices and to incorporate them into their ritual and symbolic procedures, but without 'theorizing' them (in the manner of the cosmopolitan forms of globalization)
- an ability to provide a framework for coping with serious social ills among marginal or impoverished populations, again in a wide variety of cultural contexts
- an ability to jump over existing political, linguistic and ethnic frontiers and to create transcultural communities of individuals without regard to these prior attachments
- an obsessive attention to the control of sexuality, especially female sexuality
- a belief in the literal ('inerrant') truth of every word in the holy text
- an emphasis on conversion as a crisis and rupture in the life of individuals.

These features are very evident in each one of the three forms of religion mentioned above: Pentecostal/Charismatic Christianity, resurgent Islam and Ultra-Orthodox Judaism. It is, however, important to draw a distinction in principle between fundamentalist movements – whose central focus is on the inerrant word-for-word truth of the sacred text, and charismatic movements which, though, they also support textual *inerrancy*, pay little attention to the contents of holy texts and pay far more attention to 'gifts of the spirit' such as healing, speaking in tongues and inspired oratory. In practice of course, these are overlapping catagories. Nevertheless, Pentecostals are more charismatic, while Ultra-Orthodox Jews (for example) are more text centred.

Pentecostal churches are a movement, not a centralized international organization, yet no observer can fail to be struck by the extraordinary degree of similarity of liturgy, organization, ideology and ethic among Pentecostal churches in the most widely varying contexts – from Chile to China. This sounds as if it fits some ideas about globalization very well, yet it raises as many questions as it answers: it is much less surprising that commercial firms exhibit such similarities across cultural frontiers, because they operate in a 'seamless' world market, but religion is supposed to 'fit in' with inherited cultural traits. Sometimes mass conversions, especially in poor countries, are attributed to the persuasive power of global organizations ('cultural imperialism'), but it is now widely recognized that such explanations are too simplistic and do no justice to the vast proportions of the phenomenon, and to Pentecostalism's long history of cross-cultural transplantation.

Even in its early days, in what was then the seething frontier town of early twentieth-century Los Angeles, Pentecostalism was a multicultural, multi-ethnic movement, drawing on black Americans, and the Mexican, European and Asian migrant communities for its following. Today one of the most striking features of the movement worldwide is that in some countries (such as Nigeria and Ghana) it seems to appeal more to middle class groups; in others it is most visible among the poor and the very poor, but in all cases this is a matter of degree and the appeal is visible across the class spectrum. Pentecostalism in Latin America, and also in the Philippines (also a former Spanish colony with a strong Catholic identity) is particularly successful among the urban poor and among indigenous peoples, and this represents a very profound change after five centuries during which Catholicism has had an almost complete monopoly.

In Islam and Judaism the attachment to the inerrancy of the sacred text is similar especially in contemporary fundamentalist movements and communities. Both of these cultures – and their many sub-cultures and variants – have a past in which an erudite strand of learning has coexisted with a proliferation of healers and seers, especially in Islam. Modern Jewish fundamentalists are over-whelmingly focused on texts, however, and although their heritage in Eastern Europe (the *chassidim* or 'pious ones') has a strong element of ecstatic prayer, that has tended to take second place in the post-Holocaust era to an institutionalization of learning, and of lifelong devotion to learning. There is also within Judaism a mystical strand of more or less *kabbalistic* inspiration, which was revived in Eastern Europe in the eighteenth century. In Islam, likewise, the renewal movements, led usually by lay people not by clergy (except in Iran), focus on the text of the Qur'an and are hostile towards the mystical–magical heritage of *Sufism*.

The international network of Pentecostalism operates in many ways: world-famous preachers, sometimes accompanied by 'road show' publicity and attracting enormous crowds to highly orchestrated rallies, travel the globe building up a mediatic presence for their practices of healing, exorcism and mass conversions. Churches use common manuals and texts for training preachers and pastors, and send missionaries away for long periods to establish branches in other countries. There is also now a growing pattern whereby local churches based or originating in countries such as Brazil, Mexico, Nigeria, Zimbabwe establish missions and then churches in other countries, often following migrants but often also extending their reach well beyond migrant communities – as to the US, where it is claimed (by an admittedly committed source) that there were recently 16,000 full-time missionaries from Africa, Asia and Latin America. This requires a more elaborate type of organization than that usually associated with Pentecostal churches and their characteristic grass-roots approach to growth and organization.

Although Pentecostals preach a similar message worldwide, they have shown a remarkable ability to use imagery and symbolism drawn from local cultures, especially *possession cults*. In Brazil and West Africa this is particularly in evidence. The relationship is complicated by the fury with which Pentecostals attack the cults, branding them the work of the devil and predicting that their followers are condemned to eternal damnation, even while they borrow their ideas about possession by devils, and the language and imagery with which they depict this possession, from the cults themselves. Where the cults deal with possession by spirits and entities who dictate a person's life, and with elaborate esoteric cures and procedures to summon or dispel spirits of varying kinds, the Pentecostal preachers will conduct procedures to deliver people from these same spirits. This is not to say that both are 'the same', for they are not, but it does show that these Pentecostals recognize the efficacy of those spirits, and that from being possessed by spirits to having the Holy Spirit descend upon a person is not such a long step. The difference is that the Pentecostals, like other Evangelicals, call upon individuals to change their lives, to adopt a life of austerity and devotion to the church – by, for example, attending church daily, giving up drinking, smoking and 'licentious living' – whereas in possession cults the medium or sorcerer retains control of the communication between the spirits and the humans whose destiny they determine.

Pentecostals happen to be the fastest-growing contemporary branch of Evangelical Christianity, but they should be thought of as a tendency within a wider multinational and multicultural Evangelical culture – even to call them a movement would give the impression that it is more organized than it is (see Chapter 7). The culture of Evangelical Christianity was carried first by missionaries from England and Scotland to Africa and the US in the nineteenth century and from the beginning this transfer was marked by continuing attempts on the part of indigenous leaders to wrest the emblems and meaning of their symbolic and ritual apparatus away from missionaries and colonial authorities: for example, indigenous Africans, impressed by the medical skills of missionaries, preferred to cast them in the role of healers – much to the dismay of some missionaries who saw their medicine as the application of science and wanted converts to be convinced of the truth of their message. But the missionaries had, so to speak, only themselves to blame, as they propagated the Bible and its innumerable stories of visions, miracles, Virgin Birth, incarnation, resuscitation from the dead and so on.

For indigenous Africans conversion also represented an upward social move and an aspiration to join the colonials' society, yet they found themselves barred from high office in the church. It is not surprising therefore that in the early twentieth century they established their own Christian or semi-Christian movements, either in messianic form in which rituals and taboos from the Old Testament were incorporated (as in the South African Zionist churches) or in churches inspired by American missionaries. Pentecostalism in Africa fits into this heritage even though it could not be said to be descended from it – but the briefly sketched background draws attention to the porosity of boundaries between ritual and symbolic systems: curiously, although Evangelicals are very concerned to draw lines between themselves and 'the world' (the 'world' of earthly concerns and temptation) they also show themselves to be undogmatic and open in matters of liturgy and doctrine – matters to which they pay little attention.

The Islamic revival obviously does not share all these features with Pentecostalism. In particular, there is little sign of the capacity to 'plug in' to far-flung traditions in popular religion. However, resurgent Islam is clearly able to leap across cultural and national frontiers. It too is 'polycentric', lacking any global centre of power, yet exhibiting strikingly common features across frontiers. Islamists, as its promoters are also known, are poised between the spheres of private morality (with emphasis on the regulation of sexual contact and the criminal law by religious authorities) and politics (emphasizing the establishment of Islamic states). Islamists are in rebellion against religious authorities which have occupied positions of power for centuries, through co-operation with the state, and they share with Evangelicals a dissidence or antagonism to the cultural elite.

Another important pattern to note is the growth of Islamism in Western Europe among second and third generation immigrants from North Africa and South Asia, often in rebellion against secularized parents. Here we note patterns in common both with Evangelicals – who are particularly strong in the African and Afro-Caribbean communities in Britain – and Ultra-Orthodox Jews whose parents or grandparents came from Eastern Europe who are now gaining adherents among the children of secularized Jewish families worldwide. Further similarities can be noted between Ultra-Orthodox Jews and Islamists, including tight regulation of the rhythms of daily life (punctuated by prayers at particular times), of dress and of sexual relations.

The Ultra-Orthodox Jews may be divided into a variety of sects, but each sect is grounded in a multinational network bound together by kinship, by marriage and also by flows of funds to support educational institutions and missionary activities. With their self-consciously anachronistic apparel and obedience to an infinity of minuscule regulations of everyday life, Ultra-Orthodox Jews may appear extremely provincial and inward-looking, yet, like the Islamists, their reach is more multicultural and multinational than more cosmopolitan and purportedly more 'modern' versions of Judaism and Islam (which of course are themselves losing their mainstream credentials as these more dynamic fundamentalist movements gain ground, carve out territory and place often irresistible pressure on governments, especially in the Middle East). It is particularly noticeable that Ultra-Orthodox Judaism is now penetrating the deprived and marginalized population of North African and Oriental origin in Israel, even though the type of intrusive institutionalized regulation of daily life adopted by post-Holocaust Ultra-Orthodoxy is quite alien to the tradition of their *Sephardi* forebears. In this relatively new development we may be seeing another case of fundamentalist religion appealing to the outcasts of society.

In the long run dissident religious movements, if they are to survive, tend to institutionalize and to accommodate, though not before they have brought about sometimes earth-shattering changes in society, culture and at the level of individual lives. There are already signs of such a process in all three of the traditions discussed here: the Jewish Ultra-Orthodox have already gained control over physical territory in Israel, as well as over certain institutions of the state – especially in the regulation of marriage and conversion and also in education. They have also managed to impose their rules on numerous aspects of everyday life in Israel, such as the enforcement of Sabbath observance in public services, and the certification of food served to members of the Israel Defence Force.

Islamists likewise have been gaining much respect among the middle classes. In Egypt, for example, a drift towards stricter observance of everyday rules of conduct is noticeable, and Islamists there have also successfully pressured states in the Middle East to align with them in the governance of private life. They have however been less successful in seizing even small parts of the state apparatus – for governments, as in Algeria and Egypt, have responded to them with systematic, and sometimes extremely violent, repression. Pentecostals, despite their totally apolitical tradition, have become increasingly successful politically in Africa and Latin America, countries where no social movement or initiative, secular or religious, can hope to make much headway without building bridgeheads in the state.

Finally we come to the importance of the conversion experience in such globalizing forms of fundamentalism, especially in *charismatic movements*. This is particularly evident in Pentecostal churches, where it is usually accompanied by a personal – but fairly standardized – narrative of healing, perhaps of a disease but also more broadly of fractures in families. Such healing may involve recovery from depression and the abandonment of a dissolute lifestyle – something which has evident echoes of the centrality of healing in indigenous religion in Africa and Latin America, and also confronts the searing social problems of disease, alcoholism and poverty which afflict so many in those continents. In Islam and Judaism conversion – not among outsiders but among secularized members of the community – may be less sudden, but clearly also involves a radical shift in lifestyle, from lax identification to stringent observance of the minutiae of rules of everyday life. In each case, there is a clearly marked transition from an 'old' to a 'new' life.

CRITIQUE OF EXISTING APPROACHES TO RELIGION AND GLOBALIZATION

This chapter began by looking at how, from the time of the first European colonial venture, religion has been indissolubly intertwined with the redrawing of frontiers of all kinds. The term 'cosmopolitan' was used to describe how the theme of difference, and the shaping of difference, has been central to the expansion of the great monotheistic traditions across the globe. Then attention shifted from difference to sameness, from movements and cultures which theorize and contextualize 'the other' to contemporary movements which seem to transcend the popular–erudite dialectic which underlies such cosmopolitanism to construct truly global religious cultures. Although this tendency fits in with globalization as it is most commonly conceived by sociologists, the approach adopted here still diverges from the dominant approach in sociology, and it is finally necessary to explain that divergence in more detail.

The most representative writing in sociology on the relationship between globalization and religion is that of Roland Robertson and Peter Beyer. The following features of their work are the most relevant:

- the understanding that globalization is an extension across national boundaries of the process of modernization as that has been experienced in the West
- the assumption that societies are basic units of analysis whose boundaries coincide with those of nation states
- the assumption that religious revivals are an expression of traditional identities and a reaction against modernity, and that only within the culture and self-understanding of a modern society can there exist a concept of tradition
- the assumption that there is a distinction between private and public religious spheres in all modern societies
- an understanding of the task of sociological analysis as a broad-brush characterization of the prevalent habits, values and structures in societies.

Because it does not deal with points of friction, conflict and interweaving, this approach does not describe or explain how the changes brought about by globalization can be qualitatively different from those which sociologists throughout the twentieth century have equated with modernity. Even when he attempts to deal with the specific relationship between religious change and globalization, Robertson resorts to broad generalities, referring for example to the 'cultural pluralism which is itself a constitutive feature of the global circumstance' (1992: 61). His reference to the adoption of 'culturally protectionist strategies' which 'may at least appear "fundamentalist"' is not elaborated, and although he writes at some length about 'the rise of wilful nostalgia' as a consequence of globalization, he treats it as almost a mood, rather than as the source or symptom of changes in identity and in ethnic or other boundaries, with their attendant consequences for conflict and social structure. There is no account of the sorts of ambiguity and mechanisms of domination and resistance which I have tried to deal with in drawing the contrast between popular and erudite religion and explaining the dialectic which binds them, nor of the sometimes devastating changes which the clash and mutual assimilations of religious practices and rituals have wrought over the long history of colonialism and in today's postcolonial world.

Beyer for his part assumes that 'in premodern societies there was a close association between moral codes, group membership and religion', in other words that those societies have been solidary, unified and unchanging over centuries (1994: 84), and although he recognizes the co-existence of 'great and little traditions' and of 'religion and superstition' in 'more complex older societies', he treats them only as offshoots of the more unified moral/cosmological/religious framework of the elites. The conception of such a unified social order is another version of the monolithic, unchanging notion of 'traditional society' which has long plagued sociology, and there is not even an allowance for *syncretism* – itself a contestable concept – let alone for the sort of dialectic described in the account of the 'popular-erudite' in this chapter. Furthermore, the notion of traditional society ignores a vast corpus of anthropological work on religion in premodern societies as well as in colonial societies. This literature shows that such societies are hard to fit into the traditional–modern dichotomy – a significant finding given that they are, after all, the locus of the expansion of Christianity and Islam across the globe in the nineteenth and twentieth centuries, and thus of the shaping of today's worldwide religious arena.

The division between private and public religious spheres, which is central to Beyer's account, also raises all sorts of difficulties. At its core lies the view that religion is a set of moral and cosmological beliefs, and that the translation of these beliefs into the practice of everyday life is a proper object of sociological analysis. By contrast, this chapter proceeds on the understanding that religion exists only in the public sphere; religion has to be thought of in terms of the ways in which family life and lifecycles are moulded, of ritual and symbolism and, most importantly in the context of globalization, of the demarcation of collective identities which have no necessary relationship with the boundaries of nation states. The corresponding distinction drawn by Beyer between (private) 'function' and (public) 'performance' is difficult to sustain, for one function of religion is performance, and religious belief is expressed in performative ways – such as collective recitations of prayers and doctrinal formulae. This is borne out by the sociologist Grace Davie who describes the English as possessing a 'vicarious' religion in the Church of England: they may not believe, they may not attend services, they may not know prayers or biblical stories, but they remain attached to the Church of England as an institution, as a focus of ritual on important occasions, and a source of moral guidance.

Analytically speaking, the approach adopted in this chapter differs from that of the major sociologists of globalization by its focus on the creation, reproduction and recreation of boundaries, especially between ethnic groups and religious collectivities, as well as the overcoming or transcendence of boundaries. By focusing on boundaries we focus on the encounters where the cultural pluralism evoked by Robertson is translated into real social relationships and real conflicts, over how to rule, how to heal, what authority to obey – and much else besides.

In order to understand boundaries we must, within reason, avoid prejudging them: this is why national boundaries are not a suitable starting point, and why racial, ethnic and evidently religious boundaries should not be described as if they were ready made and to be taken for granted. Ready-made categories such as 'Christian' or 'Jewish' conceal vast differences, while similarities between religious activities operating under different 'titles' can be very striking – witness, for example, the convergence between Catholic Charismatics and the deeply anti-Catholic Pentecostals, who, broadly speaking, come out of the Protestant tradition. Whatever differences one might rightly find between them they are as nothing compared with the differences between a Charismatic celebration and a mainstream Mass, or between a Pentecostal service and a mainstream Anglican Sunday service. The knowledge that in Africa, in the Caribbean, and in Latin America, Pentecostals far outnumber mainstream, or 'historical', followers of Protestants, and that the growth of the Charismatic renewal is currently being likened to a hurricane thundering through the ranks and churches of Catholicism worldwide shows us that these changing boundaries do make a difference.

SUMMARY

- Globalization is not only about sameness, or about homogenization and the destruction of cultural boundaries; on the contrary it generates a proliferation of new and reformulated and cross-cutting boundaries in the spheres of culture, ethnicity, language and religion – and religion plays a prominent role in this process.
- There is at the same time also a spread of homogenized cultural forms across pre-existing boundaries, as witness the market economy, consumption habits and much else besides.

▌ Religious change reflects both these tendencies: 'cosmopolitan' forms of cultural globalization, which have been in existence within Catholicism worldwide since the sixteenth century, involve a dialectic between erudite and popular forms of religious observance, within which there is an awareness of difference and a 'theorizing' of the other, while contemporary fundamentalist forms ignore the dialectic and succeed in making inroads in the most variegated cultural contexts without paying any conscious attention to difference – yet at the same time appropriating all manner of local ritual and symbolic practices and meaning into their own rituals.

▌ Although these movements and communities share a hostility to the permissiveness and moral dissolution they see as rampant in modern society, this does not mean to say they are not modern. On the contrary, their ability to communicate across cultural boundaries and their mercurial entrepreneurship, especially of charismatic sects and their leaders, shows that to be fundamentalist and especially to be charismatic is, indeed, to be modern.

▌ KEY TERMS

charismatic movements   Religious communities and churches which attach much importance to trances, extra-sensory states and incomprehensible utterances (*glossolalia*), all of which are proclaimed to be manifestations of the descent of the Holy Spirit into a person, and thus the conferment upon that person of *charisma* – the Greek for the gift of grace. Although Charismatic Christians profess a belief in the inerrancy of the sacred text, they use the Bible more as a source of quotations and instructional or devotional stories than as text to be respected in every minute detail.

glossolalia   Derived from the Greek word for 'tongue' (*glossos*) – hence speaking in tongues. It refers to a passage in the Acts of the Apostles Chapter 2, which states that when, seven weeks after the death of Christ, 'the day of Pentecost was fully come' the Apostles were gathered together and 'cloven tongues as of fire' appeared before them, whereupon they 'were all filled with the Holy Ghost and began to speak with other tongues' and went out to preach the Gospel 'multiculturally', as we might say today. Christian churches which regard these experiences as a central feature of their ritual and of the lives of their followers are known as Pentecostal.

fundamentalists   They confer overriding importance on sacred texts, namely the Bible, the Qur'an and, in the case of Jews, the Talmud, a vast corpus of commentaries written from the third century until today by rabbinical authorities. (The Talmud consists of commentaries on texts written in Jerusalem and Babylon, but there is in an infinity of later texts which are studied in varying detail by different Jewish communities – see Chapter 6). Fundamentalist Christians – who owe their identity to a series of publications on 'The Fundamentals' published in the US in 1906 – believe in the absolute truth of every word in the Bible and will have no truck with trances, possession, exorcism, glossolalia, gifts of the Spirit and the like.

inerrancy   The fundamentalist view as in 'biblical inerrancy' that there is no error in a sacred text. Fundamentalists also read messages 'into' the text, by finding esoteric correspondences and combinations based, for example, on numbers. Thus Jewish fundamentalists make calculations with the numerical value of the letters of words, since in Hebrew, as in Latin, the letters of the alphabet are also numbers.

NGOs   Non-governmental organizations, and the 'NGO movement' refers to the myriad of local, national and international civic organizations worldwide devoted to the fight against poverty, the defence of the environment and of human and indigenous rights, and similar causes.

Pentecostal   Derived from the feast of Pentecost, fifty days (Greek *pentekonta* means 'fifty') after the Jewish Passover (when Christ was crucified) and has been adopted by Charismatic churches which believe in glossolalia. These churches have grown and spread out from small beginnings in California at the beginning of the twentieth century to the point where they now more or less cover the entire globe.

possession cults   These deal with possession by spirits and entities who dictate a person's life, and with elaborate esoteric cures and procedures to summon or dispel spirits of varying kinds.

ritual   The central element in religious life: it is characterized by regular occurrence at fixed moments in the daily, weekly, monthly and annual cycles, or in the domestic cycle (christenings, marriages and funerals); by the symbolic nature of the acts it prescribes; and by the prescribed and performative nature of its execution. When we characterize a religion, it is more relevant to do so by reference to its rituals than by reference to its beliefs, for most followers are not familiar with the religion's doctrine except in the vaguest manner, and their perception of religious identity is marked by the rituals it prescribes.

Sephardi   Literally 'Spanish'; refers to the Jews of the Mediterranean, and alludes to the mass emigration of Jews from Spain in 1492.

Sufism   The Islamic mystical tradition dating back to the earliest times of Islam. It stands broadly in conflict with modernist and fundamentalist Islam which focus on the reconstruction of society rather than mystical contemplation.

syncretism   Now an unfashionable term, but for a long time it has been used to refer to rituals and symbols which mix elements drawn from different religions. The contemporary sensibility, though, is acutely aware that within religious traditions there are wide variations in practice and belief and that the history of religions is replete with cross-fertilizations and borrowings between religious traditions or communities. The notion therefore of a 'pure' version with a single origin, which is essential to the notion of syncretism, is no longer defensible. It is for this and other reasons that the present chapter insists so much on the multiple and cross-cutting character of boundaries.

umbanda   A generic word for Brazilian possession cults. It was coined by middle class Brazilians in the early twentieth century who were trying to create a distinctive non-African Brazilian religion based on indigenous practices and spiritualism brought from Europe.

FURTHER READING

The best way to deepen understanding of this subject is to read history and anthropology, since they provide a sense of real social processes behind or beyond more general or theoretical pronouncements about religion. The following texts are particularly stimulating:

For a historical and anthropological account of the religious encounter between colonialism and African indigenous culture, and the subsequent interweaving of them:

J. Comaroff: *Bodies of Power, Spirits of Resistance: The Culture and History of a South African People* (Chicago, IL: University of Chicago Press, 1985).

B. Sundkler: *Bantu Prophets in South Africa* (London: Oxford University Press, for the International African Institute, 1961).

For Latin American studies of Pentecostalism:

D. Lehmann: *Struggle for the Spirit: Religious Transformation and Popular Culture in Brazil and Latin America* (Oxford: Polity Press, 1996).

D. Martin *Tongues of Fire: The Pentecostal Revolution in Latin America* (Oxford: Blackwell, 1990). Despite the apparent concentration on Latin America, this also offers the best panoramic account of the spread of Evangelical Christianity across the globe from its English nineteenth-century origins.

Accounts of Ultra-Orthodox Judaism tend to be written in ways that are not easily approachable for outsiders, but the following are good ethnographies:

M. Friedman 'Jewish zealots: conservative versus innovative'. In E. Sivan and M. Friedman (eds): *Religious Radicalism and Politics in the Middle East* (Albany, NY: SUNY Press, 1990).

J. Mintz: *Hasidic People* (Cambridge, MA: Harvard University Press, 1992).

M. Shokeid: 'The religiosity of Middle Eastern Jews'. In S. Deshen, C. Liebman and S. Shokeid (eds): *Israeli Judaism* (New Brunswick, NJ, and London: Transaction Books, 1995, pp. 213–37).

H. Soloveitchik: 'Rupture and reconstruction: the transformation of contemporary Orthodoxy' (*Tradition* 28 (4), 1994: 64–129).

An interesting presentation of the internationalization of Cuban possession cults (*santería*) is found in:

J. Murphy: *Santería: an African Religion in America* (Boston, MA: Beacon Press, 1988).

The standard sociological approach to globalization and religion is to be found in:

P. Beyer: *Religion and Globalization* (London: Sage, 1994).

R. Robertson: *Globalization: Social Theory and Global Culture* (London: Transaction, 1992).

A readable set of texts on the transnational reach of particular religious cultures and communities is:

S. H. Rudolph and J. Piscatori (eds): *Transnational Religion and Fading States* (Boulder, CO: Westview Press, 1997).

A readable survey of fundamentalism, especially in Islam is:

G. Kepel: *The Revenge of God* (Oxford: Polity Press, 1994), while a down-to-earth account can be found in A. Bayat: 'Revolution without movement, movement without revolution: comparing Islamic activism in Iran and Egypt' (*Comparative Studies in Society and History* 40 (1)1998: 136–69).

A similar exercise by the doyen of religious studies in the US on Pentecostalism is:

H. Cox: *Fire from Heaven: The Rise of Pentecostal Spirituality and the Reshaping of Religion in the Twenty-First Century* (London: Cassell, 1996). Note the similarity in title to David Martin's volume.

The University of Chicago Press and the American Academy of Arts and Sciences undertook a massive Fundamentalism Project in the 1980s which published a series of very comprehensive volumes consisting of well-written and well-informed articles by authoritative experts in the field. These volumes are very useful for basic information on a very wide range of topics:

M. Marty and R. S. Appleby: *Fundamentalisms Observed* (Chicago, IL: University of Chicago Press, 1991).

M. Marty and R. S. Appleby: *Fundamentalisms and Society: Reclaiming the Sciences, the Family and Education* (Chicago, IL: University of Chicago Press, 1993).

M. Marty and R. S. Appleby: *Accounting for Fundamentalisms: The Dynamic Character of Movements* (Chicago, IL: University of Chicago Press, 1994).

M. Marty and R. S. Appleby: *Fundamentalisms Comprehended* (Chicago: University of Chicago Press, 1995).

The theoretical basis for the present chapter can be found in:

D. Lehmann: 'Fundamentalism and globalism' (*Third World Quarterly* 19 (4) 1998: 607–34 and D. Lehmann: 'Charisma and Possession in Africa and Brazil' (*Theory Culture and Society*, 2001: forthcoming).

CHAPTER 15

Religion and politics

Jeffrey Haynes

▌ INTRODUCTION

Though it will glance back as far as the nineteenth century, the focus of this chapter falls on the recent past, particularly the latter part of the twentieth century. The period has been characterized by particularly interesting developments in the relations between religion and politics across the world, developments still in train at the start of a new millennium. The 1980s and 1990s were, globally, an era of fundamental political, social and economic change. Many changes stemmed from, or were at least galvanized by, the ending of the Cold War (involving the Soviet Union and the US from the late 1940s to the late 1980s). Others were associated with the multifaceted processes known collectively, if somewhat vaguely, as 'globalization' (for clarification of the term see Chapter 14). Key developments in the period included not only the consolidation of a truly global economy and, some would argue, the gradual emergence of a 'global culture', but also a number of fundamental political developments including the steady if uneven advance of democracy – from Latin America to Eastern and Central Europe, Asia and Africa. There have also been myriad examples of the political involvement of religious actors around the world – to the extent that some claim that a global religious revitalization, a 'de-secularization' of the world, as a third characteristic of the period (see Chapter 13). As this chapter will show, this does not imply only an apolitical respiritualization, but also widespread contemporary interaction of religion and politics.

This interaction between religion and politics has not been uniform across the globe. Religious actors with political goals were especially prominent in – though not restricted to – Third World countries. Encouraged by the Iranian Islamic revolution of 1978–9, widespread Islamic militancy developed in the Middle East and elsewhere. Turning to Asia, an explosion of militant Hinduism in officially secular India helped to transform the country's political landscape. During the 1990s Hindu fundamentalists, focused in the *Bharatiya Janata Party*, were politically highly important. In Thailand, new Buddhist groups and parties emerged with political concerns, while in Africa there were numerous examples of religion's political involvement, including in Nigeria (a country politically and socially polarized between Muslim and Christian forces), in Somalia (which may well soon have an Islamist government), and in Sudan (a nation politically divided between Muslims and non-Muslims).

Figure 15.1 Hindu fundamentalists celebrate atop the Babri Masjid Mosque, Ayodhya, 6 December 1992. The mosque was reduced to rubble at this disputed holy site in the city

The list of examples could be extended, but hopefully the point is clear: at the beginning of the twenty-first century it is rather difficult to find a country, especially in the Third World, where religion is not somewhere near the top of publicly expressed sociopolitical concerns, even in states that have followed secular principles and practices for a long time.

This chapter will examine the extent and nature of religion's interaction with politics, and assess its contemporary political significance across the globe. It will look at the interaction of religion and politics in both Western and non-Western areas in the twentieth century, following a brief discussion of colonization and its impact upon the current political scene in the Third World. It will also discuss the concept of secularization and its relevance for an understanding of the interaction of religion and politics around the world.

CHURCH–STATE RELATIONS

To begin to understand the current political importance of religion, it is useful to start from an understanding of what religious actors say and do in their relationship with the state. Here more is meant than mere government when referring to the state: it is the continuous administrative, legal, bureaucratic, and coercive system which aims not only to manage the state apparatus but also to structure relations between civil and public power and within civil and political society. Almost everywhere, modern states have sought to reduce religion's political influence, to privatize it and hence significantly reduce its political and social importance. But this has not been the whole story. In countries at differing levels of economic development – for example, rich Western countries, such as the US, economically middle-ranking countries, like Israel and Poland, and poor Third World countries including Nigeria, Tanzania, Indonesia, and Burma – states have also recognized the importance of religion for politics by seeking to create 'civil religions' that is, bodies of state-designated religious dogma. The purpose was to engineer consensual, corporate religious forms that could claim to be guided by general, culturally appropriate, societally specific religious beliefs, not necessarily tied institutionally to any specific religious tradition. The development of civil religion was often part of a strategy not merely to avoid social conflicts but also to try to promote national co-ordination in countries with serious religious and/or ideological divisions. But seeking to develop civil religions had a danger: minority religious persuasions tended to perceive it as part of an attempt to perpetuate the hegemony of a dominant religious tradition at their expense.

Whilst the interaction of church and state has historically been tense and problematic in many Western countries, to compare the situation with non-Christian contexts necessitates some preliminary conceptual clarifications – not least because the very idea of a prevailing state–church dichotomy is culture bound. Not only is the concept of 'church' a Christian rooted notion; the modern understanding of 'state' is also deeply rooted in the post-Reformation European political experience. In terms of their specific cultural setting and social significance, the tension and the debate over the church–state relationship are uniquely Western phenomena, present in the ambivalent dialectic of 'render therefore unto Caesar the things which be Caesar's and unto God the things which be God's' (Luke 21:25). The consequence is that because they are heavily rooted in the West's cultural history, the two concepts cannot easily be translated into non-Christian terminologies.

Among Third World regions, it is only in Latin America that it is pertinent to speak of church–state relations along the lines of the European model. This is because of the historical regional dominance of the Roman Catholic church in that region, and the widespread creation of European-style states after colonization. However, the traditional Eurocentric Christian conceptual framework of church–state relations appears alien within and with respect to nearly all African and Asian societies. Some religions – notably, Hinduism – have no ecclesiastical structure at all; consequently there cannot be a clerical challenge to India's secular state comparable to that of, say, Buddhist monks in Southeast Asia or Shi'ite mullahs in Iran. On the other hand, political parties and movements energized by religious notions – particularly those of Hinduism and Sikhism – are of great importance in India.

The differences between Christian and other cultural conceptions of state and church are well illustrated by reference to Islam. In the Muslim tradition the mosque is not a church in the European–Christian sense of the word. As a concept, the closest Islamic approximation to 'state' (*dawla*) has the sense of a ruler's dynasty or administration. Only with the specific stipulation of 'church' as the generic concept for 'moral community', 'priest' for the 'custodians of the sacred law', and 'state' for 'political community' is it fully appropriate to use these concepts in Islamic and other non-Christian contexts. On the theological level, the 'command–obedience' nexus that constitutes the Islamic definition of authority is not demarcated by conceptual categories of religion and politics. Life as a physical reality is an expression of divine will and power (*qudrah'*). There is no validity in separating the matters of piety from those of the polity; both are divinely ordained. Yet, although both religious and political authorities are legitimated Islamically, they invariably constitute two independent social institutions. They do, however, regularly interact with each other.

Until recently it was widely believed that modernization would, ineluctably, lead both to religious privatization and to a more general secularization of society. But when Iran's Islamic revolution erupted it suggested not only that there was more than one interpretation of modernization, but also that religion might play a leading role. Since then, religion in politics seems to be everywhere. What have been the political consequences of religion's intervention? The short answer is: they are variable. Religion sometimes appears to have had a pivotal influence on political outcomes – for example, when leading church figures strongly urged the introduction of democracy in Latin America and Eastern Europe in the late 1980s and early 1990s. However, elsewhere – for example, when Algerian Islamist party the *Islamic Salvation Front* (FIS) won a convincing electoral victory and the government nullified it and then banned the party from political activity – religion seemed unable definitively to influence political outcomes (despite a civil war in Algeria in the 1990s which cost as many as 100,000 lives).

DEFINING THE 'WEST' AND THE 'THIRD WORLD'

The West

A dictionary definition of the term states simply: 'Europe, or Europe and America'. However what is commonly meant by the term implies more than a statement about geography. It is also about science and ideas. In the guise of the Enlightenment the modern West was arguably born as a reaction against religious and cultural diversity (which had led to war across Europe) in the face of which absolute, universal truths were upheld in scientific, philosophical and religious domains. In the West, science came to provide the model for modern rationality in the form of abstract and general axioms, principles and theories. In this development there seemed little room for historical religion. Consequently, it is surprising to many that religion's political involvement continues to occur in at least some Western areas – that is, where it was long thought to have left the public arena.

Recent examples abound. In Europe, a region long thought to be inexorably secularizing, civil war in the early 1990s in Bosnia-Herzegovina between Croats, Serbs and Bosnian Muslims was a *de facto* religious conflict. Each combatant identified religious and cultural (not ideological) allies, respectively, in Germany, Russia and the Arab–Muslim world. In the late 1990s civil war in Kosovo was fought between ethnic Albanians and Serbs, a conflict between Muslims and Christians, with the former allegedly aided by co-religionists from the Middle East. In the US, sustained attempts by a *New Christian Right* to mould and drive the political agenda underlines religion's growing sociopolitical significance. In Israel, the growing political significance of religiously orientated groups, such as the Ultra-Orthodox Shas Party, is manifested in their appearance in the ruling coalition government. There has also been a political role for religion in former communist Eastern Europe. In Poland Catholic priests achieved considerable political importance in the late communist and post-communist order, while the Pope, a Pole, has involved himself in political and social issues, such as the campaign to reduce Third World

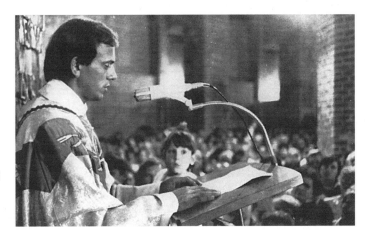

Figure 15.2 Fr Jerzy Popieluszko, pro-Solidarity priest, delivering a sermon in Gdansk at St Brygida's Church during a Mass on the eve of the fourth anniversary of the beginning of the August 1980 strike which gave birth to Solidarity. The pro-Solidarity priest was subsequently murdered in November 1984

debt, as well as in fierce denunciations of birth control. In Russia, the Orthodox church emerged from communism as an actor of major social and political importance, while various constituent republics, including Chechnya and Dagestan, have been subject to serious attempts at *Islamicization* from Islamist radicals, fought against by the Russian government which devoted thousands of troops to try to thwart them.

The Third World

The term Third World, a shorthand expression embracing more than 100 non-Western countries, was invented in the 1950s to refer both to the large group of economically underdeveloped, then decolonizing countries in Africa, Asia and the Middle East, as well as to Latin American states; the latter were mostly granted freedom from colonial rule in the early nineteenth century, but were still economically weak over a century later. However, despite a shared history of colonization there are notable differences between Third World states. For example, such economically diverse countries as the United Arab Emirates (GNP per capita of US$ 18,220 in 1998), South Korea (US$ 7,970) and Mozambique (US$ 210), or politically singular polities such as Cuba (one-party communist state), Pakistan (military dictatorship from October 1999), and India (multi-party democracy), are all classified as Third World countries. To many observers the economic and political – not to mention cultural – differences between such countries outweigh their purported similarities.

While the blanket term 'Third World' obscures important cultural, economic, social and political differences between states, it does however have certain advantages over alternatives like 'the South' or 'developing countries'. The expression 'the South' is essentially geographic and ignores the fact that some 'Western' countries (Australia, New Zealand) are in the geographical South. The idea of the 'South' does, however, have the advantage of getting away from the connotation of developing towards some preordained end state or goal which is explicit in the idea of 'developing countries'. It is by no means clear, however, what the idea of a 'developed' state looks like: does it connote only a certain (high) degree of economic growth or is there an element of redistribution of the fruits of growth involved? And what of widely divergent social conditions in a 'developed' country? In this chapter I will (somewhat hesitantly) use the term Third World in the absence of a clearly better alternative.

SECULARIZATION

Secularization, implying a significant diminishing of religious concerns in everyday life, is seen by many as one of the main social and political trends in Western Europe since the Enlightenment (1720–80). It was long believed that as a society modernizes it inevitably secularizes and differentiates – that is, in becoming more complex, a division of labour emerges in society whereby institutions become more highly specialized and, as a consequence, are increasingly in need of their own technicians. To many, secularization was the most fundamental structural and ideological change in the process of political development, a global trend, a universal facet of modernization. As Western societies modernized there would be a demystification of religion and a gradual yet persistent erosion of religious influence. The end result of secularization, a secular society, is where the pursuit of politics takes place irrespective of religious interests.

Secularization has gone hand in hand with separation of power between church and state in much of Europe. This situation developed over time, an important symbolic moment being the 1648 Treaty of Westphalia, an agreement which not only brought to an end the Thirty Years War between Protestants and Catholics, but also saw the end of religious wars which had followed in the wake of the Reformation. The Westphalian settlement established the rule that it was for secular political leaders to decide which religion would be favoured in their polity. What this amounted to was that the emerging states of Western Europe often tended to become more or less monopolies of one religion or another, as well as increasingly the homes of self-conscious national groups. Autocratic rulers saw religious conformity as an essential underpinning of their rule, necessary to maintain the existing social political order in their favour.

The tendency towards rulers' absolutism and the growth of nationalism were both greatly affected by the French Revolution of 1789. In France itself the Catholic church, which had retained much of its wealth, social influence and political power after the 1648 treaty, came under attack from the radicals and revolutionaries. The division between them and the church was not bridged during the nineteenth century, and by the end of that period the rise of socialism and communism helped to diminish further the church's influence in the political battles fought between socialists, social democrats and conservatives in Western Europe. While this simplifies a complex situation (for example, the church retained much power in Italy, Ireland and elsewhere), the overall effect of the growth of nationalism and secular political mobilization in Europe was effectively to diminish the church's political power in relation to secular rulers.

COLONIALISM

As the institutions of church and state separated in Europe during the nineteenth century, the region became increasingly involved in colonizing Asia and Africa. As a result, the vast majority of countries constituting the contemporary Third World underwent the experience of European colonial rule. Now, however, virtually no such colonies remain. By the Second World War (1939–45) there were a few European colonizing countries and a large number of colonized areas. The colonizers were not especially interested in the nature and characteristics of the areas that they ruled, despite the diversity of political and social systems, other than in terms of quiescence at their rule and maximization of economic gains.

Most colonies, including some with large populations and extant religious conflicts (for example, India, Indonesia and Nigeria), became independent after 1945. In South Asia there was a rush to independence shortly after the Second World War, while in Africa there was a similar movement towards independent statehood around the year 1960. Other former colonies have been politically independent for much longer: most Spanish and Portuguese colonies in Latin America achieved independence in the first quarter of the nineteenth century. In some former colonies, however, political independence was attained by European communities which continued to dominate populations of non-European descent. In this way a colonial situation was both internalized and until very recently 'frozen' in, for example, South Africa; at an earlier period the independence of Brazil and other South American countries may be seen in a somewhat similar light. To this day, there is a sociopolitical hierarchy in much of South America and the Caribbean, even in socialist Cuba, in which one's skin colour is often an accurate guide to one's status. This situation is a legacy of European colonialism.

To many Europeans, the spreading of Christianity was an important element in the extending of Western civilization to supposedly godless, benighted native populations; as a result, Christianity made substantial headway in many Third World areas in the nineteenth and twentieth centuries. However, the post-1945 emergence of the Third World, the contemporaneous decline of war-weakened European powers and serious rivalry between the nuclear weapons-endowed superpowers, the US and the Soviet Union, emphasized the changing nature of the international system.

RELIGION AND POLITICS SINCE THE 1960S

To take the analysis further it is convenient to divide the world into three parts, on the one hand, the West (especially North America and Western Europe) and, on the other, the former 'second world' (the erstwhile Soviet Union and its Eastern European communist allies) and finally the Third World. The second world is treated apart from the West not least because of attempts at state imposed secularization in the former during the communist era (typically, from the late 1940s to the late 1980s/early 1990s).

The West

Two phenomena are simultaneously taking place in many Western countries at the current time, and both challenge prevailing theories of inexorable secularization: (1) an increase in various forms of spirituality and religiosity (see Chapter 17) and (2) more readily and openly than in the recent past, mainline churches articulate their views on political and social issues. It seems that the latter is occurring because churches are no longer willing to be sidelined as states' jurisdictions have expanded into areas historically under their sole control. In relation to the first issue, the question is: are people becoming personally more religious while their societies are becoming collectively more secular? Three main arguments have been offered in support of this contention: (1) religion is replacing secular ideologies which have lost appeal for many people; (2) religion achieves enhanced popularity cyclically; and (3) new religious movements are a response to the impact of modernity and/or postmodernity. Let us look at each argument.

First, people are said to be turning to religion in response to a decline in the attraction of secular ideologies such as communism and socialism. As people need to believe in something, especially in the context of the post-Cold War 'new world disorder', the decline of radical secular ideologies has meant that people have (re)turned to religion to (re)discover a religious dimension of group identity, for example the US. While superficially attractive, the main problem with this explanation is that religion has not returned only in the 1990s. Rather, in some countries (the US is the archetypal example) politicized religion has been important since the 1960s.

Second, some argue that a periodic collective thirst for religion is a cyclical phenomenon. That is, religion has been a significant factor in a number of sociopolitical mass movements in the West over the last thirty years, including the American civil rights movement, the Northern Ireland struggle for dominance between Loyalists and Nationalists, and the so-called 'moral majority' in the US. To many people, it is claimed, this-wordly answers to the meaning and purpose of life periodically appear alienating and unsatisfying and, as a result, religious beliefs intermittently find fresh relevance and power, perhaps within new structures and patterns of belief. However, what needs to be explained is why religion should enjoy a periodic resurgence? What set of factors needs to be in operation to trigger this development? These questions are difficult to answer and are not satisfactorily dealt with by the proponents of the cyclical theory of religious resurgence.

Third, the contention is that Western people are becoming more religious, not less; that is, secularization is being reversed. The argument here hinges partly on surveys purportedly showing both growing attendance at religious services as well as increased sales for religious books. It is also dependent on the fact that large numbers of new religious movements have emerged, including the fast growing 'charismatic' Christian phenomenon unattached to any strong doctrinal tradition. (*Charismatic Christianity* is a widespread non-denominational tendency offering devotees spiritual excitement, with belief in divinely inspired gifts of *glossalalia* (speaking in tongues), healing, and prophecy; see Chapter 8.)

While, for many charismatics, religion and politics should be kept separate, they are not alone in eschewing political involvement. Various manifestations of new religious and spiritual phenomena, such as sundry kinds of New Age spirituality (Chapter 12), sects, including the Scientologists (Chapter 13), 'exotic' Eastern religions like the Hare Krishna cult, 'televangelism', renewed interest in astrology, and so on, may not be particularly relevant for the social and political sciences and the self-understanding of modernity insofar as they do not present major problems of interpretation. For in many ways they seem to fit within sociological expectations and can be interpreted within the framework of established theories of secularization. The point is that such religious manifestations are normal phenomena, examples of private religion which do not challenge – nor do they wish to – dominant political and social structures. Because such religious phenomena are, typically, rather apolitical, all they really show is that many people are interested in spiritual issues at the present time. In sum, it is correct to stress that the contemporary multiplicity of extant religious phenomena belie the claim that there has been a widespread loss of interest in religious meaning, even in apparently highly secular countries, and that innovative religious forms are gaining ground, often at the expense of traditional religions. But from a political perspective new religions are rarely very important.

The new christian right in the USA

The 'New Christian Right' (NCR) in the US attacks liberalism as the engine of moral decay. The NCR is dominated numerically by white Protestants – around 20–2 per cent of the adult population, that is, some 35–40 million people. There has been a remarkable upsurge in the disaffection and politicization of such theologically conservative Protestants over the last 30 years; many seem to act on their beliefs – especially in relation to attempts to prevent legal abortion – with growing militancy. It is the voice of theologically conservative Christians, united by a shared 'born-again' experience, who regard America's travails (Vietnam, abortion, drug addiction, etc.) as punishment for alleged departure from traditional Judaeo-Christian morality. The Christian conservatives strive to uphold what they perceive as desirable 'traditional values', regarding as anathema manifestations of unwelcome liberalism – legal abortion, the absence of prayers in state-run schools, and science teaching which adopts a rationalist, as opposed to a 'creationist' perspective (that is, one believing explicitly in the literal truth of the biblical creation story).

Figure 15.3 Revd Pat Robinson addresses a Christian Coalition faith rally to highlight conservative issues during the Republican Convention in Philadelphia, August 2000

The non-Western world

Given that one of the areas in the throes of an apparent religious revival, Eastern Europe, is a region where religion was, until recently, strongly controlled and reduced in importance by the state, it is perhaps unsurprising that once the state's restraints diminish it would assume a higher profile than before. However, does it mean that religion necessarily assumes a higher political profile simply because there are more openly religious people than before? Not necessarily: for example, the Russian Orthodox church does not involve itself extensively in political controversies at the present time despite a popular shift to religion in Russia in the post-communist era. In other words, Russian society may now be highly religious at the level of individual belief, but this has not led to an institutionalized political role for the Orthodox church. This may be because the church has not found it easy to change its behaviour after an eighty year period when it was in thrall to the communist state. During communist domination, the Russian Orthodox church was compelled to withdraw to its core area of expertise: the spiritual realm.

Before the overthrow of communist governments, the countries of Eastern Europe were characterized by church-state relations where the latter dominated the former. Following the example of the Soviet Union, after the Second World War the new communist regimes made serious attempts to reduce drastically the social status and significance of religion. Such regimes were 'anti-religious polities', making serious attempts to throttle religion. No religious organizations had the right to be actively engaged with matters of public concern or to play a role in public life. Churches were to be confined to liturgical institutions alone, that is, their only permitted role was the holding of divine services. The point is that the communist regimes saw that it was impossible to get rid of religion completely so they begrudgingly allowed people to retain their religious beliefs – but only as a private concern. On the one hand, this constituted a kind of promise that the authorities would respect the privacy of people's religious faith and practice. On the other, it was normally no more than a camouflage for a policy of aggressive religious privatization.

Before the democratic revolutions of 1989–90, church–state relations fell into two broad categories – 'accommodative' and 'confrontational'. Church and state were in confrontational mode when they argued over the premiss for their mutual relations and operated in the absence of a *modus vivendi*; neither side felt able to make serious compromises. In this situation, state hostility towards religion was overt and scarcely disguised. Consequently, churches would often be thrown into postures of defensive defiance. Czechoslovakia and Poland offer perhaps the best examples of prolonged confrontation between state and church. In Czechoslovakia, after a communist led coup d'état of 1948, there was bitter confrontation between the state and the Catholic church. In Poland, the authorities had to proceed with considerable caution against the church because it enjoyed a great deal of popular support: over 90 per cent of Poles are Catholic.

The accommodative style, on the other hand, involved compromise on both sides; in other words, there were rules of the game to which each side adhered. One important factor on the part of the church was that religious officials would strive to avoid criticizing government policies in order to be left in peace. Another aspect was that the majority of priests and high ranking church officials (with the exception of Poland and to a degree Hungary) consistently failed to confront the state on a variety of issues. Some religious officials actively collaborated with state security.

More frequently, however, state–church relations oscillated between confrontation and accommodation. For example, in East Germany they were confrontational from 1948 until 1971; after that there was more accommodation. In the USSR, the Russian Orthodox church also experienced periods of both accommodation and confrontation. State policies of repression were apparent between 1917–43, 1958–64 and 1975–85. They were interspersed with periods of relative church–state harmony.

Turning to the Third World, opinion surveys over time indicate that there is a high proportion of religious believers in such countries. It is sometimes argued that social upheaval and economic dislocation, connected to the processes of modernization, have stymied the development of secularization. In particular, the 1980s and 1990s were, for many people, a prolonged period of social, economic and political transition. The consequence, it is claimed, is that many Third World peoples are rediscovering the religious dimension to group identity and politics. There is, in other words, a contemporary 'return' to religion which may be the consequence of various developments, including: (1) inconclusive or unsatisfactory modernization; (2) disillusionment with secular nationalism; (3) problems of state legitimacy; (4) political oppression and incomplete national identity; (5) widespread socio-economic grievances; and (6) perceived erosion of traditional morality and values. It is the simultaneity of these crises that is said to provide an especially fertile milieu for the growth of religion with political goals.

Such factors no doubt provide an enabling environment for religion's political prominence in many Third World countries. Put another way, such unwelcome developments no doubt prod many people to look to religion to provide answers to existential angst. However, it could be argued that religion has often fulfilled such a role; it is highly unlikely that there is 'more' religion now than in the past. Why then do religious groups with political goals seem more common? It is possible that they are simply more visible due to the global communications revolution? Put another way, there are not necessarily more of them, perhaps we can observe them, and their consequences, more easily than before.

It is important to understand that there were numerous historical examples of political religion in the Third World, especially during and after Western colonization. During colonization European rulers often sought to introduce secularism which, in many cases, led to a religious backlash with Hinduism, Buddhism and Islam, in various countries, all exhibiting periods of intense political activity. Before and after the First World War (1914–18), for example, religion was widely employed in the service of anti-colonial nationalism in Africa, Asia and the Middle East. For example, political Islam was the spearhead of anti-colonial activism in various parts of Africa, as in El Hadj Oumar's campaign against the French in West Africa. Later, for example, in India, Hindu appeals and symbolism popularized the nationalist message, as it did among Buddhists in Southeast Asia. The end of the colonial era was also marked by a political role for religion. For example, Pakistan was founded as a Muslim state in 1947, religiously and, to some extent, culturally distinct from Hindu dominated India. In addition, Buddhism was of great political importance in Burma and Vietnam in the struggle for liberation from colonial rule. During the 1960s in Latin America, Christian democracy and Liberation Theology were also of widespread political significance in many regional countries. Political religion was also of great importance in Iran, Afghanistan and Nicaragua in the 1970s and 1980s. What this all points to is that political religion in the Third World has a long history of opposition to unacceptably secular regimes; it is not *ab initio* in the contemporary period. It should be understood as a series of historical responses to attempts by the state to reduce religion's (political) influence.

In the aftermath of independence, modernizing politicians, often influenced by Western ideologies, filled the void left by colonial administrators. However, the modernization process promoted by nationalist leaders, such as Kwame Nkrumah in Ghana or Sekou Toure in Guinea, did not bring the degree of development they looked for. Instead, modernization, also involving secularization, resulted in the attempted transplantation of alien Western institutions, laws and procedures which collectively aimed to erode, undermine and eventually displace traditional, holistic religio-political systems. Because putative modernizers saw their countries as politically, socially and economically backward they believed that what was needed was to emulate the secular model of progress pursued so successfully by Western countries. Consequently, policies and programmes of modernization were pursued. However, over time, the credibility and legitimacy of both secular socialism and secular capitalism often became seriously undermined. This was because such ideologies widely failed to deliver on promises of economic and political development and national integration.

Poorly implemented modernization programmes proved incompatible with traditional religious practices, as growing numbers of people left rural areas for urban locales because of land and employment shortages. While the social, political and economic impact of displacement and urban migration is extensive and complex, it is highly likely that dislocations of large numbers of people from rural communities, and the reforming of personal relations in urban areas, opened the way to renegotiation of allegiances to traditional institutions. Where modernization was particularly aggressively pursued, for example in Iran, India, Thailand, Egypt, Algeria, and Brazil, religious backlashes occurred.

Figure 15.4 Ayatollah Khomeini speaking from a balcony of the Alavi School in Tehran during the country's revolution in February 1979

In summary, postcolonial governments often followed policies of nation building and expansion of state power, equating secularization with modernization. However, by undermining traditional value systems, often allocating opportunities in highly unequal ways, modernization produced in many ordinary people a deep sense of alienation, stimulating a search for an identity that would give life some purpose and meaning. Many believed they might deal with the unwelcome effects of modernization if they presented their claims for more of the 'national cake' as part of a group. Often the sense of collectivity was rooted in the epitome of traditional community religion. The result was a focus on religiosity, with far reaching implications for social integration and political

IRAN'S REVOLUTION

Because of Islam's pivotal role, the overthrow of the Shah of Iran in 1979 was one of the most spectacular political upheavals of recent times. The outcome of the revolutionary process was a clerical, authoritarian regime. The Shah's regime was not a shaky monarchy but a powerful centralized autocratic state possessing a strong and feared security service (SAVAK) and an apparently loyal and cohesive officer corps. Unlike earlier revolutions in other Muslim countries, such as Egypt, Iraq, Syria, and Libya, Iran's was not a secular, left-wing revolution from above, but one with massive popular support and participation. The forces which overthrew the Shah came from all urban social classes, the different nationalities and ideologically varying political parties and movements, but an Islamic Republic was eventually declared. Shi'a religous leaders (*mujtahids*) organized in and by the Islamic Republican Party came to power, established an Islamic constitution and dominated the post-revolutionary institutions.

Iran's revolution was internationally significant in a number of ways. It was the first since the French Revolution of 1789 in which the dominant ideology, forms of organization, leading personnel, and proclaimed goals were all religious in appearance and inspiration. The guide for the post-revolution Iranian state was the tenets of the Muslim holy book, the *Qur'an*, and the *sunna* (the teachings of the Prophet Muhammad and those of the twelve Imams). While economic and political factors played a major part in the growth of the anti-Shah movement, the leadership of that movement (the clerics) saw the revolution's goals primarily in terms of building an Islamic state in which Western materialism and political ideas would be rejected. Over time, this was to be of major importance in the context of Iran's generally poor international relations with the West .

The radicals within Iran's ruling post-revolution elite began to lose ground following the death of Ayatollah Khomeini, the revolution's charismatic leader, in June 1989, just months after the end of the bloody Iran–Iraq war (1980–8). As it became clear that Iran's government was in dire need of Western investment, technology and aid to help build its revolution, the pragmatic state president Hashemi Rafsanjani and his political allies seemed to gain ascendancy. The lesson of this was that even a successful Islamic revolution cannot succeed in splendid isolation. Iranians, like people everywhere, hoped for improving living standards and were not content with increased Islamicization of state and society, which many perceived as little more than political and social repression behind a religious facade.

stability. This was not just a 'return' to religion, but the mobilization of religious belief in pursuit of social, political and economic goals.

A consequence has been that most states in the Third World have sought to prevent, or at the least make it very difficult for, political religion to organize. In most Muslim countries, for example, Islamist parties are either proscribed or, at least, infiltrated by state security services. Algeria's Islamic Salvation Front (FIS), the Islamic Tendency Movement of Tunisia, Hamas and Islamic Jihad in Palestine, the Islamic Party of Kenya, and Tanzania's Balukta were all banned in the 1990s. Others, including the Partai Persatuan Pembangunan of Indonesia, the Parti Islam Se Malaysia and Egypt's Muslim Brothers, were controlled or infiltrated by the state. On the rare occasions when Islamist parties were allowed openly to seek electoral support they were often reasonably successful. Examples include the FIS's electoral victories in 1990–1 and that of Turkey's *Welfare Party* (*Refah Partisi*). The latter won the largest share of the vote (21 per cent) of any party in the 1995 election. Later, in 1996, Refah achieved power in coalition with a right-wing secular party, the True Path. Parties like the FIS and Refah are electorally popular because they offer the disaffected, the alienated and the poverty stricken a vehicle to pursue beneficial change.

On the other hand, in India, there is strong electoral support for Hindu nationalist parties – and not only from the poor and marginalized. Shiv Sena jointly rules Bombay (Mumbai) and Maharashtra state with the Bharatiya Janata Party (BJP). Nationally, the BJP has emerged as the largest political party in recent years, eclipsing the country's traditionally dominant Congress (I) Party. In Buddhist Thailand, on the other hand, a Buddhist reformist party, Santi Asoke, had some electoral success in the early 1990s. The point is that parties like Shiv Sena, the BJP and *Santi Asoke* all have a wide appeal as viable alternatives to ruling parties characterized as both corrupt and inefficient. In sum, when people lose faith in the transformatory abilities of secular politicians, religion often appears a viable alternative for the pursuit of beneficial change. It has widely re-emerged into the public arena as a mobilizing, normative force.

▮ THE BHARATIYA JANATA PARTY (BJP)

The Hindu nationalist Bharatiya Janata Party (BJP) is the most successful contemporary political party in India, the mainstay of various coalition governments from the mid-1990s. This was surprising to many observers as, during the 1960s and 1970s, Hindu nationalism was merely one of the diverse currents in the ebb and flow of Indian politics. However, by the late 1980s electoral support for the BJP was rising swiftly: between 1989–91 its share tripled to 20 per cent. Many observers linked the rise of the BJP to India's economic turmoil during this time, with popular support for the BJP at least in part a manifestation of ordinary people's disquiet at unwelcome economic developments under the aegis of various Congress (I) governments.

By 1991, it had become the strongest official parliamentary opposition to the Congress (I) Party. Between 1990–5 the BJP won power in the National Capital Territory of Delhi and in six of India's twenty-five states – four in the Hindi-speaking belt of north India and two on the west coast. Of the 119 BJP members in the 545-seat Lok Sabha (Parliament) in 1995, 106 came from these areas, while only eight of the 220 seats in the eastern and southern regions of India were held by the party. On the other hand, the fact that the BJP's share of the vote in the1996 general election did not increase much above the 1991 figure, only to 23.5 per cent, suggests that there were definite limits on its appeal. Nearly a quarter of the popular vote was, nevertheless, enough to give it and its allies 188 seats, that is, more than one third of the total on less than a quarter of the vote.

The 1996 result confirmed both the BJP's rise and a steady polarization of Indian society. The traditionally dominant Congress (I) Party (the party of Indira Gandhi and her son, Rajiv) lost seats heavily in the north, west, and south, although it managed to maintain its position in the east of the country, hanging on to thiry-six seats. The result was that the share of the vote for Congress (I) declined from 48 per cent in 1984 to just over 28 per cent in 1996. The fading of Congress (I) was hastened because of the failure of India's Muslims to do what they traditionally did: vote for the Party. In the 1995 round of state elections, most Muslims voted against both the BJP and Congress (I) – in favour of candidates or parties with secular credentials. This helps explain the rout of the ruling Congress Party in 1996 and again in 1999: many Muslims identified the party with pro-Hindu sentiments, particularly because of the demolition of the mosque in Ayodhya in 1992 (see Chapter 2).

However, this was not enough to prevent the BJP's relentless electoral progress. But, like Christian Fundamentalists in the US or Islamists in Turkey, the BJP was not able to achieve power on its own. The BJP's chief difficulty lay in persuading those unimpressed by its nationalistic agenda that its political aims had a wider applicability in India's pluralist society. The BJP failed to stitch together a coalition government, with the result that the second largest party – Congress (I) – managed to put together a ruling coalition that survived into 1997.

The late 1990s saw the electoral dominance of the BJP: it now dominates the political landscape of north and west India. In these regions, its communalistic programme, perceived by many Indian secular intellectuals as the expression of primordial sentiments indicative of the underdeveloped nature of the people concerned, was nevertheless highly appealing to millions of Indians. On the other hand, the BJP found the south and west of the country a tougher nut to crack. This is because it is widely regarded in these regions as a northern dominated party, intent on imposing its own narrow version of the Hindu tradition, at the expense of alternative regional traditions. The result was that the BJP and its allies only managed to acquire a handful of seats in the south and east in elections in the late 1990s. The point is that the geographical unevenness of the Hindu nationalist support reflected the plural character of the Indian political scene. For example, many Muslims and Christians found it hard to support the BJP because of its uncompromising message of Hindu domination.

CONCLUSION

Globally, the recent political impact of religion falls into two, not necessarily mutually exclusive, categories. First, if the mass of people are not especially religious, as in many Western countries, religious actors seek a renewed public role believing that society has taken a wrong turn and, as a result, requires an injection of religious values to put it back into equilibrium. In other words, religion will try to deprivatize itself, so that it has a voice in contemporary debates about social and political direction, aiming to be a significant factor in sociopolitical deliberations. Religious leaders seek support from ordinary people by addressing certain crucial issues, such as the perceived decline in public and private morality and the insecurities of life, the result of an undependable market where, it is argued, greed and luck appear as effective as work and rational choice. In sum, religion's return to the public sphere is moulded by a range of factors, including the proportion of religious believers in society and the extent to which religious organizations perceive a decline in public standards of morality and compassion.

In many Third World societies, on the other hand, most people are already religious believers. Attempts by political leaders to pursue modernization led religious traditions to respond. Following widespread disappointment at the outcomes of modernizing policies, religion serves to focus and co-ordinate opposition, especially, but not exclusively, that of the poor and ethnic minorities. In the Third World religion is often well placed to benefit from a societal backlash against the perceived malign effects of modernization.

And what of the future? If the issues and concerns that have helped stimulate a return to religion continue (sociopolitical and economic upheavals, patchy modernization, increasing encroachment of the state upon religion's terrain) – and there is no reason to suppose they will not – it seems highly likely that religion's political role will continue to be an important one in many parts of the world. This will partly reflect the onward march of secularization – which will continue in many countries and regions, perhaps linked to the spread of globalization – which will be fought against by religious professionals and followers, albeit with varying degrees of success.

SUMMARY

- During the 1980s what was both new and became news was the widespread, and simultaneous, refusal of the so-called world religions (Christianity, Hinduism, Islam, and Buddhism) to restrict themselves to the private sphere.
- Religious organizations of various kinds seem openly to be rejecting the secular ideals dominating most national policies, appearing as champions of alternative confessional options and challenging both the legitimacy and autonomy of the main secular spheres: the state, political organization and the market economy.
- Refusing to be condemned to the realm of private belief, religion is once again reappearing in the public sphere, thrusting itself into issues of moral and political contestation.

KEY TERMS

Bharatiya Janata Party   India's leading Hindu nationalist party.

Charismatic Christianity   A widespread non-denominational tendency offering devotees spiritual excitement, with belief in divinely inspired gifts of speaking in tongues (glossolalia), healing and prophecy.

Islamic Salvation Front   During the late 1980s and early 1990s, the Islamic Salvation Front was a popular political party in Algeria.

Islamicization   This occurs when a political party or the state wishes to introduce or impose an array of values in society which are ostensibly linked to what are described as Islamic values.

New Christian Right   The voice of theologically conservative American Christians, united by a shared 'born-again' experience.

Qur'an   The holy book of Islam.

Refah Partisi (Welfare Party)   Turkey's now-banned Islamic party.

Santi Asoke   A Buddhist reformist party in Thailand.

secularization   When the pursuit of politics takes place irrespective of religious interests. The end result is a secular society.

sunna   The traditions of the Prophet Muhammad, comprising what he said, did and approved of.

FURTHER READING

Introductory

Jeffrey Haynes: *Religion in Global Politics* (Harlow: Longman, 1998) surveys the contemporary importance of religion around the world.

Secularization and sacralization

José Casanova: *Public Religions in the Modern World*, (Chicago and London: The University of Chicago Press, 1994) examines the issue of religious deprivatization in the contemporary world.

Carl Hallencreutz and David Westerlund: 'Anti-secularist policies of religion'. In D. Westerlund (ed.): *Questioning the Secular State. The Worldwide Resurgence of Religion in Politics* (London: Hurst, 1996, pp. 1–23) is a useful contribution to the debate about secularization.

The West

S. Coleman: 'Conservative Protestantism, politics and civil religion in the United States'. In D. Westerlund (ed.): *Questioning the Secular State. The Worldwide Resurgence of Religion in Politics* (London: Hurst & Co., 1996, pp. 24–47) offers a useful survey of the sociopolitical importance of the Amercian New Christian Right.

The Third World

J. Chiriyankandath: 'Hindu nationalism and regional political culture in India: a study of Kerala' (*Nationalism and Ethnic Politics* 2 (1) 1996: 44–66) is a very useful summary of the political appeal of the Bharatiya Janata Party and its attempt to make inroads in the southern Indian state of Kerala.

H. Dabashi: 'Symbiosis of religious and political authorities in Islam'. In T. Robbins and R. Robertson (eds): *Church–State Relations* (London: Transaction Books, 1987, pp. 183–203) examines the relationship between church and state in Muslim contexts in a comprehensive manner.

Paul Gifford: 'Some recent developments in African Christianity' (*African Affairs* 93 (373), 1994: 513–34) is a useful survey of recent developments in African Christianity, and includes an assessment of its political role.

Jeffrey Haynes (ed.): *Religion, Globalization and Political Culture in the Third World* (Basingstoke: Macmillan, 1999) examines the impact of globalization on various religions in a number of countries. The collection is written by experts on politics and religion in the Third World.

M. Z. Husain: *Global Islamic Politics* (New York, NY: HarperCollins, 1995) identifies a global Islamic resurgence and seeks to explain it.

E. Sahliyeh: 'Religious resurgence and political modernization'. In E. Sahliyeh (ed.): *Religious Resurgence and Politics in the Contemporary World* (Albany, NY: SUNY Press, 1990, pp. 1–16) assesses the importance of, and reasons behind, the contemporary religious resurgence.

P. J. Vatikiotis: *Islam and the State* (London: Routledge, 1987) is a very useful history of the relationship between religion and politics in Islam.

Women and religion

Linda Woodhead

▌ A GENERAL THEORY OF RELIGION AND GENDER

Until very recently the topic of gender has been almost absent from the agenda of the study of religion. The situation has changed partly as a result of the impact of the so-called 'second wave' feminism which developed after the 1960s, and whose perspectives and analyses have gradually influenced many of the disciplines which make up the study of religion – from history to anthropology. Whilst this represents a significant advance, a less helpful legacy from feminism has been the tendency to approach the study of religion and gender in terms of a single problematic: is religion a 'good' (liberating) or a 'bad' thing for women? Does it reinforce patriarchy or undermine it?

There are a number of problems with this way of approaching the topic. One is that the question is too broad and too blunt to do justice to the hugely varied forms of religion on the ground, or to the subtle, complex and highly specific ways in which women indwell, subvert and negotiate them. Another is that the criterion of goodness or badness (often equated with liberation and oppression) is equally blunt, and rides roughshod over cultural as well as historical difference. It is not at all clear that what a modern Western woman would count as 'liberating' is a very illuminating category when applied, for example, to the actions of a rural Hindu woman who visits a local shrine to ask the goddess for success for her daughter in her first exams. Since the notion of liberation is often cashed out in terms of autonomy, the result tends to be that all forms of religion are judged and found wanting. What is more, given the evident and continuing attraction of religion to women all round the world, the condescending conclusion would seem to be that a majority of the world's women are prey to false consciousness.

Given the manifold problems of this feminist-influenced approach to the topic of religion and gender, the temptation may be to abandon the attempt to formulate any general theory of women and religion altogether. Better, perhaps, simply to stand back and look at the diverse ways in which women's religious lives unfold in different times and places. In the last couple of decades, an important and highly illuminating body of literature has developed from this starting point, much of it shaped by a broadly anthropological–ethnographic methodology. Studies of women in Christian Fundamentalist churches and lay organizations, in Orthodox Judaism, in forms of resurgent Islam, in Buddhist and neo-Hindu monasteries – for example – yield rich and fascinating information. However, it may still be helpful to reflect on the broader findings of such studies and their more general implications for our understanding of women and religion. This chapter attempts to do just this, drawing on the data yielded by such studies, as well as the observations on religion and gender offered in the chapters which make up this volume.

The most general conclusion which emerges can be stated very simply: that women's involvement in religions has less to do with false consciousness than with the ways in which religions offer social spaces for the articulation and, in some cases, the realization, of women's desires. This is not to suggest that these desires are uniform or natural, nor that they are not themselves shaped by sociocultural contexts of which religion is one. It does not exclude the possibility that in some cases religions may not serve this function, or that alternative social spaces may better serve it. Nor does it deny that women may have to subvert, appropriate or reinterpret religions before they become spaces in which they can articulate their lives and desires.

If this initial observation about women and religion is true, then it would seem that the key variable that affects women's participation in religion is the nature of the social spaces available to them for the articulation and realization of their desires. In modern societies, what will therefore be key will be the nature and extent of *social differentiation*: the ways in which social activities are split between different institutions, the way in which religion relates to this division, and the nature and extent of women's participation in these different spheres or institutions. Broadly speaking, it seems possible to discern two main patterns:

1 Advanced industrial/highly differentiated/Western societies: from at least the nineteenth century industrialization was generally accompanied by the drawing of a clear distinction between private and public life. Women's proper sphere was the former – the family and domestic life. Men dwell in both spheres, but their natural realm is the rationalized, impersonal, secular sphere of public life. Throughout the twentieth century and beyond women have increasingly won the right to move into the public sphere, but the latter remains masculinized and male dominated. Religion in the nineteenth century was itself pushed into the private realm, and tended to reinforce women's domesticization by becoming the guardian of private life and family values. Consequently, religion became a natural environment for the articulation of the lives and desires of women whose lives centred round home, family, children and husband. Women who move into public life by (for example) entering one of the professions, however, may experience tension between traditional religious values and the values of their public/professional lives. This tension may be found to be creative, or it may lead to an abandonment of traditional religion, and/or the creation of new spiritualities.

2 Differentiating/non-Western/postcolonial societies: have been subject to different (though related) patterns of modernization from the advanced industrial West. In relation to *differentiation*, many of these societies are not, or have not yet become, as highly differentiated as Western societies, and the distinction between public and private is not always as clear or as sharply drawn. In addition, religion is often more central and integral to the modernization process than was the case in Western societies. These differences are closely related, and are due in part to the pressures to create independent national identities which do not simply imitate the West and its pattern of secular modernization. In relation to women and gender, one consequence has been a confinement of women to a domestic sphere, in order that they may become the chief markers and bearers of a traditional identity, whilst the rest of

(male dominated) society modernizes around them. More often, however, women have been able to use religion as a means of easing their way into the new social spaces and opportunities created by non-secular forms of modernization.

Though it is still too soon to be sure, a third pattern of de-differentiation may also be emerging. This is related to a shift to postindustrial societies in which the nation state and politics become less important drivers of change than the global economy. New patterns of work emerge which privilege creativity and individuality over discipline and deference, and small groups over the factory and mass production. These developments begin to break down the private–public distinction, and to blur the boundaries between different social institutions. New opportunities are created for both women and religion as a result: religion maybe revitalized and offer new work ethics focused on individual empowerment and/or effective relationality; women's values and ways of working and relating attain a new 'public' relevance and an economic value. This may be occurring in Western and non-Western societies.

In practice, of course, these patterns prove far more complex and overlapping than in theory. All three are explored in what follows, though particular attention is given to the first two patterns.

WESTERN/HIGHLY DIFFERENTIATED SOCIETIES

Gender, the family and social differentiation

Most modern Western societies are characterized by a high level of social or functional differentiation. Differentiation is the process whereby social activities become split between different institutions. Thus in modern states such activities as political governance, law, education, welfare, health care, and productive work become specialized functions carried out by autonomous and differentiated institutions and agencies. The process is related to the division of labour, whereby tasks which were once performed by a single individual are divided between many specialized workers. Thus even a housewife or househusband in the modern West will normally leave tasks such as baking bread, growing vegetables, making clothes, educating children and dealing with their physical (and perhaps mental) health to others. One consequence is the pluralization of lifeworlds: instead of inhabiting just one or two social institutions (the family and the church, for example), modern men and women now inhabit many different ones – domestic, educational, legal, political, medical, economic, religious. Such institutions are often referred to as the *primary institutions* of society in which most people (or at least most men) participate, and they can be contrasted with *secondary institutions* which tend to be smaller, voluntary, more face-to-face, and less governed by rules, laws or traditions.

Sociological theories of social differentiation are often gender blind, and fail to distinguish the different ways in which men and women are involved in and affected by the process. Whereas most men have participated across the different social spheres of modernity, many women have been excluded from participation in public spheres like the law, the workplace, politics. Many would argue that women are still excluded from equal participation with men in these spheres. Without doubt, there are still many women whose primary sphere of existence is the home and the family, and whilst this has become more of a voluntary option during the course of the twentieth and into the twenty-first century, it still tends to be socially and culturally reinforced. The choice by men to opt out of participation in the workplace remains a much more unusual and controversial choice.

Some scholars argue that the distinction between public life and private life, and the alignment of women and the family with the latter, is a product of modernity. They suggest that the distinction was not as clear in traditional, premodern societies and that this lack of differentiation was related to the fact that women had more involvement in public life in pre-industrial societies. Women might, for example, be involved in such activities as cultivation, animal husbandry, spinning and weaving as well as in more narrowly defined domestic duties. As such they played a greater and more publicly acknowledged role in economic and social life. Likewise, many men lived and worked in and around the home, and they too may have drawn a less clear distinction between the public and the private.

If this is true, then one important effect of modernization was to confine women (particularly middle class women) more to the private and domestic realms than had been true in less differentiated, earlier societies. Their sphere of independent action would have been correspondingly diminished. It would not be surprising to find that the one sphere in which they were socially free to participate – religion – would have assumed greater personal importance as a result. At the same time, the process of differentiation was stripping religion of its public roles like education, governance and welfare, and it too was becoming more privatized. Thus a natural alliance between the primary institutions of religion and family took place, as religion became more feminized and domesticized and championed family values, whilst women and children found a natural home from home in religion (which in the West generally meant the Christian churches). To a limited extent religion could still offer women some entrée into public life, through voluntary social and charitable activities, or – more dramatically – by way of religious orders and/or mission work at home or abroad.

Some nineteenth-century feminists (both male and female) observed and deplored the restriction of women's lives in this way, and their writings and campaigns had some effect – most notably changes in legislation allowing women to own property and to vote. The real change, however, came later in the twentieth century as a result of wider material and social changes. This 'silent revolution' has opened greater opportunities for women to participate in a range of primary institutions on more – though still not fully – equal terms with men. The revolution has come about as a result of many converging factors: both World Wars allowed women more of a role in public life; the impersonal and unregulated effects of a competitive market have undermined protectionist strategies which favoured male employment; the massive expansion of non-manual occupations and the rise of a new knowledge class has opened up new opportunities for women; and the invention of more effective forms of contraception has given women a new control over their reproductive lives.

The silent revolution has been given voice, and reinforced, by the *second wave* of feminism which developed after the 1960s. To some extent this has continued the agenda of *first wave* nineteenth-century feminism, which tended to stress women's equality with men and campaign for equal rights. In this way, feminism appropriated a broader modern cultural turn (the turn to the self) and its concern with the dignity, freedom and autonomy of the individual. However, second wave feminism has also placed emphasis on the difference between men and women and the necessity of reshaping society in ways which are less *androcentric* and more oriented to the distinctive needs, strengths and characteristics of women.

Traditional forms of religion

In the context of rapidly modernizing societies religion in the West often adopted a reactionary posture. For much of the nineteenth century, for example, the Roman Catholic church opposed modern secular states and ideals of individual liberty and democracy. Unable to control the increasingly autonomous spheres of economics and politics, the church was, however, forced to wage its wars in the realms of culture and domestic/private life (see Chapter 7). One very important result was the reinforcement of the role of the church (both Catholic and Protestant) as a defender of the family and family values.

Thus traditional religion became increasingly identified with the family and with women. This would appear to have had two main effects so far as women's participation in traditional Western religion is concerned: to reinforce the commitment of women who are primarily engaged in domestic life, whilst challenging that of women who have moved out to inhabit other social spheres. This is entirely explicable in terms of our general theory, since differentiation means that traditional, family focused, forms of Christianity have clearly been highly successful in providing social spaces in which women can articulate and realize their desires, whilst many women who have rejected defining domestic roles have found that the church is unable to fulfil the same function for them, or less able that other non-Christian spheres of social existence. Some may abandon religion, whilst others may seek new forms which generate less internal tension in their lives. This can be illustrated by studies of women and conservative forms of Judaism and Christianity in the West.

DOMESTIC SPACE: ORTHODOX JUDAISM IN THE US

In the modern world, conservative wings of Judaism, Christianity and Islam have all arisen in direct opposition to modernity and to more liberal forms of religion (see, for example, Chapter 6 on Judaism). One feature of such religion is an assertion of difference not only between God and the world, but between men and women. The divine hierarchy is taken to be a reflection of the (proper) social hierarchy, in which woman obeys man, just as humanity obeys God. This re-inscription of hierarchical difference tends to be bound up with a reassertion of the value of the traditional family, which is seen as a bulwark against the secularizing forces of modernity.

Given that such re-inscription of difference is directly opposed to the values of much modern culture, the ethos of a capitalist economy, and the ideas of feminism, it has surprised some commentators to find not only that women continue to participate in such religion, but that some even convert to it. The explanation seems to be that women whose status as wives and mothers has been disrupted and undermined by the forces of modernization find here a congenial social space in which they have a clear and respected role and status. This may be particularly true in Judaism where, since the home has long been the primary locus of religion, the domestic sphere has even more status and significance than in Islam or Christianity. In her study of women who convert to Orthodox Judaism in the US, for example, Lyn Davidman (1991) found that such religion offered wives and mothers considerable status and a role that was considered to be truly 'equal but different' to that of men. Their exclusion from public life did not seem a loss, given that major religious rituals take place in the home, and given the power and prestige of the home in the Orthodox scheme of things. What is more, women benefited from the fact that Jewish men are taught to be closely involved in home and family, and deeply respectful of their womenfolk. As a result, a number of women – largely from socially and culturally disadvantaged backgrounds – converted to Orthodoxy. Here we have a clear example of the way in which differentiation between religious and secular values in modern times can serve to reinforce women's participation in religion. Secular modernity may leave many women feeling homeless; religion offers a social space in which nobodies become somebody.

POWER THROUGH POWERLESSNESS: EVANGELICAL AND FUNDAMENTALIST CHRISTIANITY

A number of studies of women in *Evangelical* and Fundamentalist forms of Christianity have also appeared which explore the question of why and how women participate in such apparently male directed forms of religion. Both forms of religion place heavy emphasis on the authority of scripture, the sovereignty of (a male) God, and divinely commanded male leadership both inside and outside the home. Yet study of such religion on the ground shows that in practice women have been able to open up significant spaces for the articulation and realization of their lives and desires in such religion. This is true first in relation to the family, where women not only turn Evangelical respect for its God-given status to their advantage (as in Orthodox Judaism), but also employ strategies for maximizing their power and influence in the domestic realm. Whilst they give formal acknowledgement to male authority in the home, in practice they often exercise considerable power over their menfolk – as Nancy Ammerman discovered in her study of a Christian Fundamentalist church in the US (1997). The fact that men are enjoined to respect and cherish wives, children and home, and to honour Christian values of love, peaceableness, faithfulness, cleanliness, decorum, sobriety and relationality, can easily be turned to women's advantage.

In addition, Evangelical Christianity may offer women a space for the articulation of desires and frustrations in wider, more public settings – not only in churches, but in small groups and para organizations linked to the church. Evangelicalism may prohibit women from teaching in public (teaching men), but it offers them free access to the holy scriptures and the Holy Spirit. What is more, there is no prohibition on their teaching one another. Thus many Evangelical women belong to some form of small group – for Bible study, prayer, healing, and so on. Such groups have characterized Evangelicalism from its origins in the seventeenth and eighteenth centuries, and have flourished in recent times. They seem particularly well suited to women since they make possible the intimate, face-to-face relationality in which women still tend to be socialized from the earliest age. They offer a safe space in which women can articulate their deepest desires and concerns – prayer groups, for example, are a natural setting in which to share fears, hopes, desires and personal experiences. Such secondary institutions offer a forum for healing not only by God, but through the love and support of one's sisters.

An important example of a small group movement with international reach is the *Charismatic–* Evangelical 'Women's Aglow' which is the subject of a study by Griffith (1997). Griffith finds that meetings are indeed dominated by women's concerns, concerns that they would probably be unable to articulate in other social spaces, particularly with men present. Appropriating the traditional genre of the Evangelical testimony in which an individual describes in public how being born again as a child of God has effected a break between their past (unredeemed) and their present (saved) lives, women in Aglow meetings spend a great deal of time describing domestic strife and woes – childhood abuse, unhappy marriages, unresponsive husbands, wayward children. They then go on to testify to the way in which surrender or yielding to God has effected dramatic change for the better. In other words, their religion provides a means by which their apparent powerlessness is turned into power; by obeying the injunction to obey God and their husbands they actually win what they desire. Likewise, by praying and talking together about their suffering and powerlessness, these women are empowered. Interestingly, Griffith notes that since the 1980s, the stress in Aglow literature has been shifting away from submission to men, to more active partnerships with men. Equally, more emphasis is being given to the power of prayer in relation to the world as a whole and not just to domestic settings. This is most evident in the way in which Aglow meetings now devote time to praying for the conversion of particular parts of the world, and for victory over the powers of evil. Women are waging spiritual warfare, and becoming aware of their spiritual power. This religion of the powerless thus offers woman a power they might not otherwise have, and increasingly it is offering possibilities for exercising it (at least in spiritual forms) in public as well as private.

■ WOMEN'S AGLOW: POWER THROUGH SUBMISSION

Women's Aglow Fellowship provides support, education, training, and ministry opportunities to help women worldwide discover their true identity in Jesus Christ through the power of the Holy Spirit. We believe that:

- All women and men are created equal in the image of God, each with dignity and value
- God has a unique purpose for all of us and equips us for that purpose
- We can reach our full potential only after finding identity and restoration in Jesus Christ.

(Affirmation of faith, Women's Aglow)

Jesus, thank You for showing me that housework is sacred. Help me to realize while I am cooking and cleaning that I am doing them for You because You are living here and my husband is Your representative.

(Sacred housework, from *Aglow in the Kitchen*, a cookbook for Christian wives)
(Both passages cited by Griffith, 1997, pp. 64, 182)

LIVING WITH TENSION: PROFESSIONAL WOMEN IN TRADITIONAL RELIGION

Both the case-studies above provide examples of how the tension which exists for women caught between traditional, family orientated religion and other primary institutions of modernity may be lessened by religions which help situate women firmly in the former, providing the social space which allows the articulation of their suffering and desire, and allowing them to relate to the public world on superior terms. The latter is viewed as an unredeemed realm in need of the nurturing and transforming spiritual powers that these women can harness.

The situation is rather different for professional women whose working lives are spent in the public world amongst men, but who also participate or are raised in traditional, hierarchical and family orientated, religion. For them the tension can be acute. One remedy is simply to leave the church. Though there has been little research on this topic, there is some evidence that this has indeed been happening in Western societies. For example, the sociologist Andrew Greeley (1990) has found that Roman Catholic women who identify themselves as feminists are 17 per cent less likely to attend church regularly than those who do not. He also discovered a negative correlation between women who attended college and church attendance, but the greatest negative correlation of all was between those who attended college and whose mothers did not work during the first six years of their daughter's lives (40 per cent less likely to attend church). Greeley's conclusion is that this is a function of the conflict which college educated women perceive between their image of themselves as women, and the image of woman observed in their mothers. Another sociologist of religion, Penny Marler (1995), has also observed that many Christian congregations cater disproportionately for older couples whose children have left home, and younger couples with children – the former often assisting the latter. Such churches often model themselves on a family, and speak of themselves as families. As a result single people and couples without children are marginalized and under-represented.

Clearly, however, there are still many women who participate on more or less equal terms with men in the workplace and continue to participate in traditional forms of religion. In the absence of research, it is only possible to guess that such women will tend to experience more tension in this situation than do their male counterparts, not least because the autonomy, power, choice and leadership which professional women enjoy at work are contradicted by the denial of these in church, synagogue or mosque (where male leadership continues to be the norm). Some women may, however, find the tension creative. Their religious participation may, for example, allow them to give expression to a female identity which they have to suppress at work. It may offer a balance with the harsh, competitive pressures of the market and its iron cage rationality, and allow them to mediate between different aspects of their lives. Alternatively, they may be defecting in place, as one recent study suggests – women stay in the churches because they believe that they are their institutions as much as men's, but try to change them from within. In Christian theology this position has been championed by reformist feminist theologians like Rosemary Radford Ruether (see Chapter 7). A final possibility is that some women (and men) may simply keep religion and the rest of life in quite separate compartments in their lives – thus confirming the sociological thesis of the privatization of religion.

Modern forms of religion

Western women who find that that the conservative wings of traditional religions offer little or no space for them to articulate their fears, sufferings and desires may turn to – or create – more congenial forms of religion and spirituality. Indeed, the desire of women to forge new social spaces may be a major, though much neglected, factor in the evolution of new religious forms in modern times.

EGALITARIAN/LIBERAL/RELATIONAL RELIGION

Given that many women who have carved themselves out a space in the primary institutions of education, the workplace and so on have done so under the banner of equality with men, it would not be surprising to find that more egalitarian forms of religion prove congenial to them. Most of the world's religions have liberal wings, characterized not by strongly inscribed difference between God and humanity, man and woman, parent and child, but by a flattening of this hierarchy. Such religions tend to be humanitarian, both in the sense that they emphasize the value of human beings and their natural affinity with the divine, and place stress on what is common to human beings rather than what differentiates them. Both elements may be very appealing to women: the latter because it allows them to compete on equal terms with men, and the former because it reinforces their esteem in a way that religions which only affirm male divinity may not. In addition, liberal forms of religion tend to have a strongly ethical and relational stress: humanitarian deeds – particularly loving kindness – are more important than dogma (also appealing to women who have traditionally been excluded from theology). Not surprisingly, it tends to be the more liberal wings of traditional religions which have been the most willing to grant women leadership roles – as in Reform Judaism, and the more liberal Protestant Christian denominations (see Chapter 6 and Chapter 7). For all these reasons, such religion tends to lower the tension between religion and other spheres of modern existence, particularly for women.

As yet, however, research has not been carried out to determine whether or not liberal forms of religion attract professional women to a greater degree than conservative forms of traditional religion. What research has shown, however, is that women tend to favour more relational and less steeply hierarchical understandings and pictures of God, that they value community and connectedness in

Figure 16.1 Women and men gather to campaign outside a General Synod meeting which is deliberating whether women should be ordained in the Church of England, 12 November 1992. The first women were ordained in 1994

Figure 16.2 All the consecrated women bishops in the Anglican communion gather at the Lambeth Conference 18 July–9 August 1998. The first Anglican woman Diocesan Bishop, Penny Jamieson, Bishop of Dunedin, New Zealand, is second from the left in the back row

religion, and that their religion often has a relational flavour. Thus Ozorak (1996) found that women's responses to religious community depended heavily on the extent to which they found it to be 'supportive, cooperative, and emotionally open', and that satisfaction in these areas more than compensated for dissatisfaction with male dominated leadership and organization. Whilst Ozorak was concentrating on organized forms of religion, it seems likely that many women in the modern West also satisfy their need for sacralized relationality both inside and outside institutional religion. For example, Princess Diana forged a personal religiosity which combined a Christian emphasis on love and charity with a humanitarian stress on care for others, whilst at the same time drawing on teachings and techniques from the more alternative/New Age wing of things. Judging from the reaction to her death, many of those who mourned her shared a similar affective relational religiosity – a 'religion of the heart' (Woodhead, 1999).

The sacralization of the feminine

Turning to this more alternative or complementary fringe of modern religion (alternative or comple-mentary, that is, to traditional religion), we also find new forms of religion and spirituality which are created by women with the explicit intention of creating spaces for the articulation and realization of their desires. These range from the more individualized, like that of Princess Diana, to the more socially organized. By their very nature, the more individualized or personalized forms of spirituality are obviously extremely well adapted to the needs of the women who create them (see Chapter 17). They may well be resourced and reinforced – given a social dimension – by workshops, reading, attendance at occasional meetings or worship events. Whilst they do not belong to a formal religious institution then, women who develop personalized forms of spirituality are normally plugged into larger spiritual networks.

At the more organized end of the spectrum, feminized forms of spirituality often give a central place to the goddess, and may well draw on pagan and Wiccan traditions which allow a central place to women (even though it is often acknowledged that many of these traditions are in fact fairly recent creations). Such religion is usually highly reflexive, with practitioners openly acknowledging that the worship of a female divinity is necessary to enhance women's lives and self-esteem in the here and now, and to counteract the damaging results of *patriarchal* religion and society. The limited research which has been carried out on feminist forms of spirituality suggests that the women involved tend to be middle class, educated to degree level and often that they have or have had some form of prior traditional religious involvement.

▌ GODDESS RELIGION

The second night out was a full moon and we waited impatiently for the moon to crest the tall pines so that the ritual could begin. Finally, we saw two flames winding down the mountain path. As they neared, we saw that these were torches, held by priestesses in silver gowns which caught the light from the flames and glittered like pieces of the moon herself. The priestesses paused in the south, and then I noticed the enormous shadow thrown against the hill. It is Diana who comes behind them. Rationally, I know it is Hypatia [a witch and priestess], but I also know it is Diana. A heavy green cape is swept over her shoulders and matches her baggy pants. Her huge breasts are bare, and her chest is crossed with the leather straps that hold her cape and the quiver of arrows on her back. She carries a large bow and her face is hidden behind a mask of fur and dried leaves. Deer horns spring from her head. There is no face, not a human one, anyway . . . The Goddess pauses between the torches and fits an arrow to the bow. She draws it back and with a 'twang' shoots it into the darkness. The sound is like a catalyst. We are released like the arrow and begin to cheer.

A description of a ritual performed by a coven of feminist witches in North America, 24 August 1991

(Wendy Griffin: 'The embodied goddess: feminist witchcraft and female divinity'
Sociology of Religion 56 (1) 1995: 35–48)

Women have also been attracted to the various New Religious Movements (NRMs) which have come to prominence in modern times. As Chapter 12 indicates, such movements tend to be much more tightly organized and institutionalized than alternative spirituality more generally (closer in that respect to traditional forms of Western religion). As Chapter 12 also shows, the role of women in such movements has been important, as has the significance of gender – though in widely varying ways. Some NRMs, like the Jesus People, Hare Krishna and Unification Church (Moonies), have tended to reassert traditional roles. Others have provided space in which women have been able to explore their (gendered) identities much more freely than in traditional religion (and, perhaps, more easily than in feminism). Palmer (1994) argues that NRMs offer women the opportunity to occupy a whole range of gender roles – from the conservative to the radical – thereby developing a more mature gendered identity than might otherwise be possible (an identity which often takes them outside of NRMs later in life). In this way, religion may offer women more choices than can be found in a secular realm which is often found to be restrictive so far as women's gendered and sexual identities are concerned.

NON-WESTERN/SEMI-DIFFERENTIATED SOCIETIES

As Chapter 15 suggests, the language of First and Third World countries must be used with caution, but it does help point out some important distinctions. One is that between countries that colonized other parts of the world in modern times, and territories which were colonized. Another is the distinction between advanced industrial societies and societies with other – or mixed – forms of socio-economic organization (in Rwanda, for example, 91 per cent of the workforce is in agriculture, compared to 2.3 per cent in the US). Often these differences are linked: thus colonizing countries (including the US and Japan) have become fully industrialized, whilst those they colonized have not. Most of the latter are in the Southern hemisphere (including China, India, most of Africa, some of Latin America), whilst most of the former are in the north.

Both clusters of difference have important consequences for religion and gender. Being at different stages of industrialization, Third World societies tend to be less differentiated. Consequently, the social spaces which women can indwell may be different from those in the West, and different tensions may exist between them. Colonization is also significant; in its wake almost all non-Western countries have developed into independent nation states, but in many cases these have fragile and contested boundaries, and religion and gender are often implicated in their defence and negotiation. Many of these countries are also attempting to modernize without Westernizing – again with implications for religion and gender.

Despite the usefulness of the Third World/First World distinction, it must also be borne in mind that there is considerable diversity within and between so-called Third World countries. For example, whilst agriculture remains the main economic activity predominantly rural forms of economy often exist alongside rapid urbanization and industrialization and the creation of an affluent, urbanized middle class. As a result, extremes of wealth and poverty exist side by side. Equally, there is great diversity between different Third World countries, with some being much more technologically advanced, more wealthy, more integral to an increasingly global economy. Indeed few if any countries are now wholly untouched by the latter. What is more, many countries – in Latin America, and the Middle East, for example – do not fit easily into categories of First, Third, or even Second World at all.

Traditional forms of religion

NEGOTIATING SOCIAL CHANGE: INDIGENOUS RELIGIONS

In minimally differentiated societies, both premodern and contemporary, religion tends to infuse all aspects of social life. It provides the means by which individuals are integrated into wider society and by which that society's values are articulated and reinforced. In addition, it marks boundaries between (for example) one society and another, one social group and another, different genders, and different stages of life (on these functions see Chapter 14). Since such societies range from chiefdoms to less hierarchical and non-centralized communities, it is hard to generalize about religion and gender, but in most cases the official religion of a tribe or society could be expected to support existing hierarchies of power. For example, as Chapter 9 shows, ancestor worship often underpins the authority of (normally male) elders, who ritually mediate on behalf of the ancestors through their closer proximity in terms of age. Likewise, the institution of kingship in some African societies is often closely bound up with ancestor worship, with the ruler's ancestors representing the ancestors of the entire kingdom.

However, as Chapter 9 also shows, indigenous religions do not just support the *status quo*. They can also serve as effective resources on which less powerful members of society (including women) can draw, and they may be potent agents of social change (see also Chapter 10 on Native American religions). Because such religions tend to have oral rather than written traditions, and because they focus upon living relations between the spirit world and the human world, they have considerable flexiblity and potential for change – in many ways they may be more flexible than tradition- and text-bound world religions. Moreover, precisely because such religions exist in societies which are not highly differentiated, they have considerable social and political importance and are not rendered ineffectual by being relegated to a private realm. Indigenous religion may therefore be a very potent resource for women, who may, for example, derive considerable authority from their ability to act as spirit mediums. For example, as Chapter 9 shows, Tonga women who are constrained within a domestic environment may be possessed by marginal non-ancestral spirits known as Masabe who demand and are satisfied with gifts bought out of the wages of their husbands from a cash economy from which they would otherwise be excluded. Likewise, Kalabari women of the Niger delta gain much influence through divining, in which they are possessed by water spirits that reside in the creeks and which bring economic success in return for human devotion. Many women have achieved considerable freedom in economic, and sometimes political spheres as a result. In these examples, religion helps women adapt in advantageous ways to new money based trading economies, whilst keeping them within the ambit of existing society.

Of course, religion may also serve to conceptualize and control the ambivalences of women's power. This may occur in relation to women's sexual and reproductive power, which may be ritually controlled in both indigenous religion and the world religions (for example, by moral and ritual laws surrounding sexual intercourse, menstruation and childbirth). Equally, witchcraft may serve both as a form of female power (the threat of witchcraft activity being a way in which society is regulated, and a disincentive to the infliction of injuries, wrongs and inequalities), and as a way of controlling that power (the accusation of witchcraft and the sanctions used against it serving as a powerful form of control). As the following reading shows, witchcraft today often has close connections with the tensions generated by modernization.

▌ WITCHCRAFT AND THE TENSIONS OF MODERNITY

Africa has been drawn inexorably into the world of capitalist production. And while it has hardly been made over entirely in European image, it *has* been subjected to forceful social change – of which the marginalization of the domestic, the rural, the 'primitive', and the female has been a crucial, if complex component. This process of marginalization has many sides to it. Perhaps the most poignant is the fact that those displaced along the way quickly tend to become signs and ciphers with which others

> make meaning. [. . .] In its late twentieth century guise, witchcraft is a finely calibrated gauge of the impact of global cultural and economic forces on local relations, on perceptions of money and markets, on the abstraction and alienation of 'indigenous' values and meanings. Witches are modernity's prototypical malcontents. They provide – like the grotesques of a previous age – disconcertingly full-bodied images of a world in which humans seem in constant danger of turning into commodities, of losing their life blood to the market and to the destructive desires it evokes. But make no mistake: these desires are eminently real and mortal. And some people are indeed more vulnerable than others to their magic allure. Nor, it should be stressed again, are witches advocates of 'tradition', of a life beyond the universe of commodities. They embody all the contradictions of the experience of modernity itself, of its inescapable enticements, its self-consuming passions, its discriminatory tactics, its devastating social costs.
>
> (Jean Comaroff and John Comaroff: 'Introduction'. In Jean Comaroff and John Comaroff (eds): *Modernity and its Malcontents. Ritual and Power in Postcolonial Africa*, Chicago and London: University of Chicago Press, 1993, pp. xxviii–xxix)

DEFENDING NATIONAL AND SEXUAL INTEGRITY: RELIGIOUS NATIONALISM IN INDIA

Whilst nationalism in the West is often viewed as a defining feature of secular modernity (the secular nation state refuses to ally itself with religion, which it relegates to the private sphere), the latter part of the twentieth century saw the rise of religious nationalisms in several parts of the world. The Indian subcontinent offers a good example (see Chapter 1 and Chapter 15). Despite having a nominally secular state, Hindu nationalism has become a powerful force in India, as has Islamic nationalism in Pakistan. The vitality of such neighbouring nationalism can be related – in part – to the fact that both nation states are attempting to define and defend themselves not only over against once another, but over against the West which had colonized the region until 1947.

This situation has powerful repercussions for gender. In religious nationalism, women often become living symbols of the integrity of the defended faith and nation. Women are often spoken of in highly exalted terms by male leaders of these movements. They are the guardians of the purity of the nation who raise children in the faith, and guard the sanctity of the home. Such women may be contrasted with Western women who are seen to be libertarian, sexually loose, morally degraded, and lacking in essential femininity. Just as it is necessary for men to guard and protect the integrity of the nation state against its enemies, so it is necessary to protect female bodies. Thus in Pakistan, the institution of female seclusion and veiling (*purdah*) becomes the sign of the integrity of both women and the nation. It is preserves honour and protects against violation. Here women are firmly located within a private realm, and dissuaded from entering into the male spheres of religion and politics. Though presented as traditional, this actually represents a recent Islamic response to modernizing forces and the rise of the nation state. Differentiation is partially resisted – men are allowed to participate in economic and political modernity on Islamic terms, and women must remain in the private realm, thus safeguarding and upholding traditional Islamic society. The position is well set out in the following extract by Mawdudi (1903–79) (for more on Mawdudi see Chapter 8).

▌MAWDUDI ON THE POSITION OF WOMEN IN ISLAMIC SOCIETY

Mawdudi was a major theorist of the Islamic movement in Pakistan, and his writings influenced the development of Islamism more generally. He developed a systematic sociopolitical programme for Islam. As this extract shows, he believed that women should be largely confined to the domestic sphere in modern Islamic society. What is also notable, however, is that Mawdudi gives women a central place in his programme: he is well aware that successful social reform cannot take place without their co-operation.

> Family is the first cradle of man. It is here that the primary character-traits of man are set. As such it is not only the cradle of man but also the cradle of civilisation. Therefore, let us first consider the injunctions of the *Shari'a* (Islamic law) relating to the family.
>
> A family consists of the husband, the wife and their children. The Islamic injunctions about the family are very explicit. They assign to man the responsibility for earning and providing the necessities of life for his wife and children and for protecting them from all the vicissitudes of life. To the woman it assigns the duty of managing the household, training and bringing up children in the best possible way, and providing her husband and children with the greatest possible comfort and contentment. The duty of the children is to respect and obey their parents, and, when they are grown up, to serve them and provide for their needs.
>
> To make the household a well-managed and well-disciplined institution, Islam has adopted the two following measures:
>
> a The husband has been given the position of head of the family. No institution can work smoothly unless it has a chief administrator . . . There must be someone as head of the family so that discipline can be maintained. Islam gives this position to the husband and in this way makes the family a well-disciplined primary unit of civilisation and a model for society at large.
> b The head of the family has responsibilities. It is his duty to work, and do all those tasks which are performed outside the household. Woman has been freed from all activities outside the household so that she may devote herself fully to duties in the home . . . Women have been ordered to remain in their houses and discharge the responsibilities assigned to them . . . Islam therefore effects a functional division of labour between the sexes.
>
> But this does not mean that the woman is not allowed to leave the house at all. She is, when necessary. The law has specified the home as her special field of work and has stressed that she should attend to the improvement of home life. Whenever she has to go out, certain formalities can be observed [. . .]
>
> Outside the pale of the nearest relations between whom marriage is forbidden men and women have been asked not to mix freely with each other and if they do have to have contact with each other they should do so with *purdah*. When women have to go out of their homes, they should wear simple dress and be properly veiled . . . Through this directive Islam aims to cultivate in its followers a deep sense of modesty and purity and to suppress all forms of immodesty and moral deviation.
>
> (Abu al-Ala Mawdudi *Towards Understanding Islam*,
> The Islamic Foundation, pp. 108–9, 112)

A SAFE ROUTE INTO PUBLIC SPACE: ISLAM

It would be wrong to think that the veil in Islamic societies has just one meaning. Whilst it can be used to symbolize and enforce the seclusion and restriction of women, it can equally be appropriated by women and used to negotiate their way in social space. Thus in many Islamic societies today, veiling is understood by women as an option which allows them to avoid both libertarian Westernization on the one hand, and a traditionalism which would confine them solely to the domestic realm on the other. Far from being merely reactionary and traditional, the veil and its meanings are being reinvented in order to allow women new freedoms in modernizing societies. The veil is literally reinvented in the form of the *hijab*, a scarf that covers head and neck and retains echoes of traditional forms of dress, but without their restrictions. It is also reinvented and reinterpreted in ways which allow women to cross from the domestic sphere into the public sphere safely and without a dramatic break with the past or Islam. Those who wear the *hijab* are often daughters of first-generation immigrants to the city, cutting free from traditional roles and seeking social advancement. Analysis of their views suggests that they desire education to the highest levels, along with jobs and political rights; they divide only on the issue of gender equality in marriage.

For these reasons, it is possible to argue that contemporary *Islamism* serves many Muslim women as an indigenous form of feminism – not a Western borrowing, but an indigenous liberation movement. Indeed, it may be viewed as a superior option to what is available in the West, where women can enter the public world only on male and rationalized secular terms, and are forced to leave behind vital aspects of their identity including religion. Some Muslim 'feminists' thus interpret the veil as a revolutionary sign, for it symbolizes the entrance of the previously marginalized (women and the poor) into spheres which were previously closed to them (see, for example, Ahmed 1992). It marks the triumph of the urban and rural poor over a Westernized elite, and a system of inclusion over one of exclusion. For many, the veil represents an attempt to combine religious belief and values with desired social change. It is part and parcel of the process in which Muslim women have become catalysts for change, entering the professions and public life, becoming scholars and spokespersons for Islam, and establishing women's professional and campaigning organizations.

∎ THE VALUE OF THE VEIL

We became Muslims not to follow previous values, but to follow our new values. And we are not forcing anybody to follow our values – we will not impose them on Christians, on Western life . . . What I say is right, they will say is wrong. I say that this dress is to protect my dignity as a woman; Simone de Beauvoir will say that it is an attack against women and a violation of her dignity. I will not go and force Simone de Beauvoir to put on Muslim dress. And I refuse Simone de Beauvoir to tell Imam Khomeini with rudeness, 'Don't apply this Muslim rule on Muslim women.' By God, this is very strange.

[Simone de Beauvoir was a pioneering French feminist writer and philosopher]
(Safinaz Kazim, Egyptian journalist and drama critic. Quoted in Francis Robinson (ed.): *Cambridge Illustrated History of the Islamic World*, Cambridge: Cambridge University Press, 1996, p. 204)

The entrance of women into public life in Islamic countries is, however, occurring at different rates, and it inevitably generates its own tensions. Being a text based tradition, Islam is constrained by its

Figure 16.3 Palestinian Muslim women bow in prayer on the steps leading to the Dome of the Rock, Jerusalem, Ramadam, 17 February 1995. The act has considerable political significance, since sovereignty over the site is disputed between Muslims and Jews

sacred teachings regarding the sexes and relations between them, and despite strong egalitarian aspects, these teachings tend towards a hierarchical view of the relation between men and women. Concern about women's sexual power over men, and the social disruption which it could cause, is also a significant factor – albeit one which the veil is designed to address. However, countervailing forces include the fact that both men and women have been actively involved in the resurgence of Islam in the postcolonial world, and in the urgent task of restructuring societies and nations along Islamic lines. In these activities, it has often been hard to draw a clear line between the public and the private – for example, women played an active role in the Iranian revolution of 1979. Unlike the West, where modernization was a process internal to society, and was primarily driven by men (in scholarship, the arts, science, technology, business and commerce, law and politics), modernization in Islamic societies has become a shared task of whole peoples, both male and female, and is pursued with the conscious desire to follow an Islamic rather than a Western path.

ENTERING SACRED SPACE: BUDDHIST AND HINDU MONASTIC TRADITIONS

An important traditional form of religious space for both men and women is the monastic community. Characteristic of several of the world's religions, monasticism persists in the modern world. Early industrialization, particularly in the nineteenth and early twentieth centuries, saw a dramatic increase in monastic vocations in Roman Catholic Christianity in the West, amongst women as well as men. From the origins of Christian monasticism in the third century CE, women had always been attracted to the movement. Though nominally under male celerical supervision, separate women's monastic orders offered women considerable autonomy. Not only did they free them from the necessity of marriage, childbirth and domesticity, they offered them protected opportunities for education, leadership, prayer, devotion and independent action which would not otherwise have been available. This continued to be true in the nineteenth century, when opportunities for women to enter the public sphere were, as we have seen, perhaps even more restricted than in previous centuries.

In the West, this situation has slowly changed over the course of the twentieth century and into the twenty-first. Not only are the primary institutions of society now much more open to women, but increasing affluence has freed many women from economic dependence on a provider (whether a spouse or an institution like a monastery). These changes are undoubtedly an important factor in the decline of Christian monasticism, which has been most dramatic in advanced industrial societies. In addition, the posture of monasticism – obedience, subservience, self-sacrifice, renunciation of the world – sits uncomfortably with the wider values of these societies (which tend to encourage the exact opposite).

In other societies and other parts of the world, however, monasticism remains an option for women, albeit one which is not untouched by the pressures of modernization.

Interesting examples are furnished by Hindu and Buddhist monasticism. Though solitary asceticism is a traditional (and prestigious) element of Hinduism, social monasticism represents a modern development in the tradition. So too does the option of asceticism/monasticism for women: since the traditional sannyasi (renouncer) was one who controlled his sexual desires and harnessed the energy which would otherwise be dissipated by the release of semen, and since he wandered freely in the public world, renunciation was only an option for men. An influential form of modern monasticism in Hinduism is that founded by Swami Vivekananda (1863–1902) the modern Hindu monk (see Chapter 1). Vivekananda founded a monastic order and mission named after his teacher and guru, Ramakrishna. The Ramakrishna Math and Mission was a central part of his drive to revivify Hinduism and turn it into an agent of indigenous modernization. Monasteries were founded for women as well as men, since Vivekananda recognized women's supreme social importance in Indian society.

Whilst these women's monasteries continue to exist in contemporary India, a recent study shows that some are struggling to attract and retain nuns (Sinclair-Brull, 1997). At the time of independence some flourished, since their aim of charity and uplift was supported by high caste families, and they provided a social space for women who were unable to find a suitable husband (perhaps because their families could not afford the dowry (bride price) which must be paid to a bridegroom's family). But modernization has engendered a crisis in the monastry studied by Sinclair-Brull: in an increasingly affluent society in which middle class women are now expected to be educated and to have jobs, the appeal of the ascetic ideal has waned considerably. Where once monasticism offered women who might not otherwise have a choice an option about the course of their lives, such women are now offered many choices. What is more, modern middle class Indians are also increasingly alienated from the strongly hierarchical order of the monastery, which is seen as a relic of a hierarchical caste and gender system with which many are now dissatisfied. The traditional duties of a woman (*stridharma*) such as loyalty to husband, self-sacrifice, and forbearance in the manner of the goddess Sita may be waning in influence, and with them the value of deference more generally. Forms of Hinduism which offer immediate satisfaction and help for the individual in the here and now are increasingly favoured over communal forms which ask for submission and self-sacrifice and promise only intangible rewards.

The situation in Buddhism appears to be rather different. In part this is due to the important structural difference that monasticism has always been integral to Buddhism, in a way it has not to Hinduism (equally, Buddhism has not sanctified the family and women's role within it, in contrast to Hinduism and many other world religions). As Chapter 2 shows, the Saṅgha (monastery) is the key social space in which the Buddha's teachings can be followed. Set free from worldy concerns, monks are thought to be in a privileged position to concentrate on the path of enlightenment. In both theory and practice, the Saṅgha exists in close relationship with both nuns and lay people. Reciprocal duties exist between the two: nuns and lay people are to serve the material needs of the monks, whilst the monks will in turn nourish them with spiritual teachings and enable them to attain better rebirths through their merit making activities. The monastery also serves an important social function by providing education and social mobility for the bright and ambitious, especially from rural areas.

Just as Buddhist teachings on the place of women are ambiguous, so to has been women's position in relation to monasticism. Unlike Hindu yogic asceticism whose theory and practice excluded women, the Buddha's diagnosis of the ills of human life and their spiritual remedy apply equally to men and women. Stories of Buddhist nuns date from the earliest phases of the religion. Yet the organization of the sangha formally relegates women to a subservient status, and restricts them from taking part in the decision-making processes of the Buddhist community. Given the continuing importance of the Saṅgha

Figure 16.4 More than 80 per cent of Buddhist nuns in Burma come from villages. By entering a Buddhist monastery they are not only pursuing a religious vocation, but achieving a social and educational advancement which would otherwise be impossible (compulsory state education ends at puberty). These girls may continue as nuns and/or become established teachers. The option of 'postgraduate' study will depend upon finding a learned monk willing to act as an instructor. Nunneries in Burma have only educated girls since the nineteenth century. In Thailand, most Buddhist nuns are still not educated

in Buddhist societies, it is not surprising that the modern period has witnessed campaigns and attempts to raise the status of women's monasticism and to introduce or revive women's monastic orders (*bhiksuni* Saṅgha) alongside and on equal terms with men's. As Chapter 2 shows, these campaigns have had some success in both northern and southern Buddhism, but have also had to contend with considerable opposition. Such opposition has come not only from Buddhist monks, but from lay nuns who are not fully ordained – and whose ambivalent status gives them a freedom and power they fear would be lost if full ordination brought them under the control and direction of monks.

Modern forms of religion

RENEGOTIATING GENDER IDENTITIES: CHARISMATIC CHRISTIANITY

It is hard to draw a sharp distinction between traditional and modern forms of religion in semi-differentiated modernizing societies, since – as the previous section shows – even the most apparently traditional are often significantly reshaped in modern contexts. Resurgent Islam, for example, represents a mobilization of tradition to meet the challenges of a postcolonial era of nation states. Charismatic Christianity outside the West, the next most vital form of late modern religion, perhaps tips the scale even further in the direction of the modern. With its roots in the Pentecostal movement of the beginning of the twentieth century, Charismatic Christianity combines an Evangelical emphasis on the authority of scripture (the Word) with an emphasis on the authority of direct experience of the Holy Spirit. As such, it is more orientated to individual than collective empowerment, and lacks Islam's strong political dimension. (For more on Charismatic Christianity see Chapter 7 and Chapter 14.)

Like resurgent Islam, however, Charismatic Christianity has proved highly attractive to women in industrializing countries, and is helping them to negotiate their position in rapidly-changing environments. For a start, it empowers each individual without distinction or caveat, offering them the most precious of all gifts – the gift of the Holy Spirit. Since the Spirit confers authority, it gives women considerable scope to receive gifts of healing, prophecy, speaking in tongues, and so on on equal terms with men. What is more, it frees them from the bondage of past failures, fears, sufferings, and invalidations and gives them the courage and momentum to change their lives and grasp new possibilities. All this is of particular relevance for women who find themselves moving from less differentiated, rural forms of life into the dislocating and impersonal world of an industrial city, for example. Charismatic Christianity not only offers safe passage from the old world to the new, but the spiritual courage to face new socio-economic worlds, the moral guidance to cope, and the cultural and material resources necessary to compete – from education to welfare.

For all these reasons, Charismatic Christianity may be viewed – like some forms of resurgent Islam – as an indigenous feminist movement. Yet its form is very different from Western feminism, and its respect for traditional authority, including the authority of men, much greater. Rather than asserting women's rights, equalities and radical freedoms in opposition to patriarchal oppression, Charismatic Christianity attracts both men and women by affirming some elements of traditional, patriarchal religion and society (male leadership, a sovereign male God, women's domestic roles), whilst at the same time subjecting them to the transforming powers of charismatic rebirth. Under the influence of the Holy Spirit, all that was solid can melt into new forms. Traditional hierarchies and gender roles undergo a gentle revolution, as a social world is partially recast. Thus the male, authoritative, transcendent, divine 'Word' of God is complemented by the insinuating influence of the gentle, loving, dove-like 'Spirit' of God. Such emphases serve not only to exalt the feminine, but to challenge machismo. Space is created for women not only by offering them divine power, but by converting men to less macho postures. The validation of male leadership in church, world and home may persist. But the process whereby men take more responsibility for their families, and learn Christian virtues of love, gentleness, kindness, faithfulness, leaves women as major beneficiaries. Both the home and the church become spaces in which women can place their fears and sufferings into the hands of God, and fulfil their desires for a new life of divinely inspirited power and love.

INDIVIDUAL EMPOWERMENT: NEW RELIGIOUS MOVEMENTS

An emphasis on divine spirit, and on individual empowerment in this life, are also features of many of the most obviously modern religious movements of industrializing countries. Though they can be categorized together under the very broad headings of 'New Religious Movements' or *spiritualities of life*, these labels conceals huge variety on the ground (see Chapter 12 on NRMs in the West, and Chapter 17 on spiritualities of life). A feature of religious life in the West for over a century, such religions are also becoming prominent in other parts of the world, particularly those affected by capitalist modernity. The rise of such religions is clearly related to differentiation and to the expanding importance of the market. As individuals are cut loose from traditional societies and their supporting religions, they find themselves in need of more personalized, individualized forms of religiosity to support them in the stresses and strains of modern life, and to help them integrate and steer a course between its different spheres. This need may be pressing for women in particular, since the journey into public, male dominated worlds is a new and hazardous one which requires considerable personal resources.

Drawing only on examples mentioned in this book, we find examples of empowering spirit religions in both highly differentiated and in differentiating societies. An example of the latter is provided by the growth of the Mama Wati cult in West and Central Africa. As Chapter 9 shows, Mama Wati is a new deity: fair skinned, long haired, fast living, seductive and beautiful. Seen as the bestower of great wealth on those she possesses, she is often depicted with the trappings of material success, including sunglasses and fast cars. Her success can be explained, in part, by her appeal to single women who tend to be marginalized by religions like Christianity and Islam with their legitimations of domestic space. Unlike their male deities, Mama Wati 'underlines and legitimates control of modern women's individual sexual, reproductive and economic capacities and frees them from being determined by kinship or marriage, while at the same time sanctioning the personal pleasures of modern urban consumption' (Chapter 9).

At the other end of the socio-economic spectrum, we find examples of this-worldly, life empowering modern religiosity with a special appeal to women in the new religious movements of Japan. Chapter 5 shows how many New Religious Movements in Japan took communal and nationalistic forms in the nineteenth and into the twentieth centuries. Their egalitarian and communitarian stress opened them to both men and women, and encouraged a solidarity which not only legitimized nationalism, but eased the transition from rural to urban society. In the long run, however, the most successful have not been the nationalistic cults but those which have developed an optimistic view of human nature, an emphasis on self-cultivation and practical techniques for the attainment of worldly blessings, both spiritual and material. Women have played an active and central part in the upsurge of such practical religion, much of which addresses the particular strains and stresses imposed upon them in a society in which their traditional domestic roles can be simultaneously affirmed by culture and undermined by socio-economic developments. Different New Religious Movements can serve a range of functions: empowering women to make their way in modern society; helping them to cope with the pressures of traditional domestic roles in modern society; and healing the afflictions which result from both wealth and its loss or lack – particularly relevant in times of economic recession.

CONCLUSION

This chapter offers an overview of religion and gender in the modern world, paying particular attention to women's participation or lack of participation in religion. Starting from the premiss that women participate in religion because it allows them the social space to articulate their lives, fears and desires, the chapter considers how the increasingly differentiated social terrain of modern societies affects women's participation in religion and spirituality.

It is suggested that:

1   In highly differentiated modern (usually Western) societies, traditional religion is often used to legitimate and resource the domestic sphere, and that this allows women who remain in that sphere to participate more easily (with less experienced tension) than women who are trying to make their way in the interlocking spheres of the public and male dominated world beyond the family.
2   Such societies are also characterized by the rise of modern forms of religion (including liberal, relational, and life-oriented religions and spiritualities) which are more adaptable in resourcing the lives of women both within, outside and betwixt-and-between domestic and public spheres. These religions tend to be individualized, or to take social form as secondary rather than primary institutions.
3   The situation for women tends to be different in semi-industrialized societies (mainly non-Western), which are generally less differentiated, and in which the imperative of national identity formation in a postcolonial situation is an important pressure. In many of these societies religion tends to be more central to the process of modernization than it has been in the West, and women's position is affected by this. Whereas in the West feminist movements tended to reject religion because it was identified with the private and domestic sphere, in these non-Western societies religion may itself become the site and the resource for the articulation of indigenous feminist movements.

4   Outside as well as within the West, the rise of religions and spiritualities focused on this-worldly, life enhancing goals are also providing a resource for women entering new and often alien social spaces. Often focused on spirit possession, these new religions tend to be focused on the empowerment of the individual. Women are often highly visible.

Other conclusions follow:

5   In terms of women's participation, two types of religion appear to be doing well across the globe: (a) conservative hierarchical forms which affirm women's domestic and private versus men's public roles; (b) radical new religions and spiritualities which offer individual empowerment to women. Both are doing well because they offer social space to women for the articulation of fears and desires – albeit to very different constituencies of women, and in different ways.
6   At the same time, those forms of religion are doing well (particularly outside the West) which break down (or do not set up) a clear differentiation between public and private. As such, these religions offer women the chance to enter the public sphere without abandoning gendered identity and domestic responsibilities, loyalties and virtues. They may represent a new, religious rather than secular, form of feminism.
7   A related form of de-differentiation may also be taking place, whereby the boundaries between public and private and between different spheres of social existence are beginning to break down. This development is closely related to changing patterns of work, in which large-scale, impersonal factories and offices are giving way to smaller-scale enterprises (even within large corporations), team-working, and home working. In this process 'home becomes work, and work becomes home'. This change may offer women new opportunities, and make the option of home or work less absolute – with important consequences for religion. Increasingly seen as a means of resourcing work as well as personal life, new holistic spiritualities of life proclaim their ability to integrate the different aspects of an individual's identity. Interestingly, such spiritualities tend to be highly feminized, not only in their imagery and ethos, but also in their forms of organization and leadership.

Finally, if anyone still doubts the importance of the topic of women and religion, it should be enough to point out that the religions which are going to survive and flourish in a new millennium will be those that are most successful in attracting women and providing the social spaces for the articulation of their fears and desires in a rapidly changing world. The social and political repercussions of their success will also be significant (Muslim women, for example, now comprise one-tenth of humankind). One of the reasons the widespread religious upsurge at the end of the twentieth century took so many sociologists and commentators by surprise, and upset so many theories of secularization, was that they had failed to pay sufficient attention to the gender factor.

SUMMARY

- Women participate in religions because these offer social spaces for the articulation of their lives, fears and desires.
- Modernization in the West involved the process of differentiation in which a private/domestic sphere was separated out from other public social spheres. Since religion aligned with the former, it catered well for women in the domestic sphere, but less well for women attempting to enter public life.

New forms of religion catered better for the latter, including liberal/egalitarian forms of religion and (more recently) spiritualities which sacralize the feminine.

Outside the West, the process of differentiation between public and private has often been less stark. Equally, modernization has often been as much a religious as a secular development. This has meant that religion has not been as 'privatized' or 'domesticized' as in the West, and consequently that women have not had to choose between (traditional) religion and entry into public life. On the contrary, religion can serve to mediate between the private and public in creative ways.

KEY TERMS

androcentric Focused around the male; taking men and masculinity as the norm.

Charismatic Christianity An offshoot of Evangelicalism which has spread rapidly across the world throughout the twentieth century. Places particular emphasis on the gifts of the Holy Spirit.

Evangelical Christianity A pan-denominational movement within modern Protestant Christianity which emphasizes the authority of the Bible and experience of the Holy Spirit.

first wave feminism Nineteenth-century feminism which championed the equal rights and dignity of women on the grounds of their common humanity with men.

differentiation (social or functional) The process integral to modernization whereby social activities become split between different institutions.

Islamism The militant attempt to make contemporary society and politics conform to Islamic law.

patriarchy An overarching concept used by feminists to refer to a system of male dominance which extends to both social and ideological spheres, and which ensures a hierarchical ordering of society in which men dominate women.

primary institutions The most wide-ranging and powerful social institutions in a society – educational, legal, political, economic, domestic.

second wave feminism The resurgence of feminism after the 1960s which continued to campaign for women's equal rights, whilst developing a critique of androcentric and patriarchal society, and placing more stress on male–female difference and the importance of reform which takes account of gendered difference.

secondary institutions Social groups which tend to be smaller, voluntary, more face-to-face, less powerful, and less governed by rules, laws or traditions than primary institutions.

social differentiation See *differentiation.*

spiritualities of life Spiritualities which emphasize this-worldly empowerment of indviduals' lives and which often have a holistic emphasis.

FURTHER READING

General/Introductory

Ursula King (ed.): *Religion and Gender* (Oxford, UK, and Cambridge, MA: Blackwell, 1995). Contains a range of essays which consider how feminism and women's studies have affected the study and practice of religion.

S. S. Sered: *Priestess, Mother, Sacred Sister. Religions Dominated by Women* (Oxford and New York: Oxford University Press, 1994). Presents research on women across the world who have reinterpreted or broken tradition to take control in the religious realm.

Arvind Sharma (ed.): *Today's Woman in World Religions* (New York, NY: SUNY, 1994). A useful introductory book with chapters on the place of women in aboriginal religions, Hinduism, Buddhism, Chinese and Taiwanese religions, Judaism, Christianity and Islam. Also contains a wide ranging bibiliography.

W. H. Swatos, Jr (ed.): *Gender and Religion* (New Brunswick, NJ, and London, UK: Transaction, 1994). A collection of articles on gender and religion drawn from the journal *Sociology of Religion*. Mainly deals with women in the West, particularly the US.

Linda Woodhead: 'Feminism and the sociology of religion: from gender-blindness to gendered difference'. In Richard K. Fenn (ed.): *The Blackwell Companion to the Sociology of Religion* (Oxford, UK and Malden, MA: Blackwell, 2001, pp. 67–84). Surveys the sociological literature dealing with women and religion, and its changing interests.

Women and religion in Western/differentiated societies

M. Adler: *Drawing Down the Moon: Witches, Druids, Goddess-Worshippers, and other Pagans in America Today* (Boston, MA: Beacon Press, 1986). Offers a vivid portrayal of new religions and spiritualities which sacralize the feminine.

Nancy Ammerman: *Bible Believers. Fundamentalists in the Modern World* (New Brunswick, NJ, and London: Rutgers University Press, 1987). Influential and informative study of a Christian Fundamentalist congregation in the US, which keeps a close eye on gender issues.

Lyn Davidman: *Tradition in a Rootless World: Women Turn to Orthodox Judaism* (Berkeley, CA: University of California Press, 1991). Sociological study which asks why American women convert to Orthodox Judaism.

Ann Douglas: *The Feminization of American Religion* (New York, NY: Albert A. Kopf, 1978). Considers, from a literary point of view, the way in which the churches became feminized or domesticized in early industrial society.

Andrew Greeley: *The Catholic Myth. The Behaviour and Beliefs of American Catholics* (New York, NY: Charles Scribner's Sons, 1990). Contains comment on professional women's defection from Roman Catholicism.

Wendy Griffin: 'The embodied goddess: feminist witchcraft and female divinity' (*Sociology of Religion* 56 1995 (1): pp. 35–48). A description of two feminist spirituality groups in North America, their beliefs and practices.

R. Marie Griffith: *God's Daughters. Evangelical Women and the Power of Submission* (Berkeley, CA: University of California Press, 1997). Sympathetic, closely observed and theoretically interesting study of the Evangelical Women's Aglow movement.

E. W. Ozorak: 'The power but not the glory. How women empower themselves through religion' (*Journal for the Social Scientific Study of Religion* 35 (1) 1996: 17–29). Argues that women look for relational and connective satisfaction in religion.

S. J. Palmer: *Moon Sisters, Krishna Mothers, Rajneesh Lovers: Women's Roles in New Religions* (Syracuse, NY: Syracuse University Press, 1994). Study of women's roles in new religions which shows how they allow women to explore different sexual identities.

M. T. Winter, A. Lummis and A. Stokes: *Defecting in Place: Women Claiming Responsibility for their own Spiritual Lives* (New York, NY: Crossroad, 1994). A survey-based study of middle class, mainly feminist, women in North America, which finds that despite considerable dissatisfaction some may continue to worship in church, whilst others participate in women's spirituality groups.

Linda Woodhead: 'Diana and the religion of the heart'. In Jeffrey Richards, Scott Wilson and Linda Woodhead (eds): *Diana: The Making of a Media Icon* (London: I. B. Tauris, 1999, pp. 19–139). Argues that both Princess Diana and the reaction to her death provide evidence of a relational turn in contemporary Western religion.

Women and religion in less differentiated/non-Western societies

Leila Ahmed: *Women and Gender in Islam. Historical Roots of a Modern Debate* (New Haven, CT, and London: Yale University Press, 1992). An informative discussion which argues that the veil has become a symbol of class and gender assertion in many contemporary Muslim societies.

Salvatore Cucchiari: 'Between shame and sanctification: patriarchy and its transformation in Sicilian pentecostalism' (*American Ethnologist* 18, November 1991: 687–707). A highly original and influential article which shows how Charismatic Christianity has become a crucible for the forging of new gendered identities, both male and female, and how this favours women.

J. S. Hawley (ed.): *Fundamentalism and Gender* (New York, NY: Oxford University Press, 1994). A collection of essays which – in its own words – 'sets out a range of materials that will enable readers to understand the strength of the tie between fundamentalism and a conservative ideology of gender'. The book looks at Christian, Islamic, Hindu and Japanese fundamentalism as well as wider theoretical issues.

Penny Long Marler: 'Lost in the fifties: the changing family and the nostalgic church'. In Nancy Tatom Ammerman and Wade Clark Roof (eds): *Work, Family and Religion in Contemporary Society* (New York and London: Routledge, 1995, pp. 23–60). A study which reveals the continuing alliance between congregations in the US and family values.

Bernice Martin: 'The Pentecostal gender paradox: a cautionary tale for the sociology of religion'. In Richard K. Fenn (ed.): *The Blackwell Companion to the Sociology of Religion* (Oxford, UK and Malden,

MA: 2001, pp. 52–66). A discussion of women in Pentecostalism which frames the latter as 'a modernizing egalitarian impulse'.

Wendy Sinclair-Brull: *Female Ascetics. Hierarchy and Purity in an Indian Religious Movement* (London: Curzon Press, 1997). Study of a Ramakrishna monastery for women in Kerala, India.

CHAPTER 17

The spiritual revolution: from 'religion' to 'spirituality'

Paul Heelas

▌ INTRODUCTION

In many parts of the world, religious traditions are thriving. Authoritative beliefs and practices informed by *tradition* hold sway – whether it be Buddhism and Hinduism in Sri Lanka or Islam in Pakistan. The situation is very different, however, in the great majority of late modern advanced commercial societies. Here institutionalized traditions (most especially the churches, chapels and cathedrals of Christianity) have been eroded by the forces of *secularization* (see Chapter 13). *Life* after tradition, it is often claimed, is therefore taking the form of atheism, agnosticism or simply indifference to what the religious realm has to offer. *Religion*, it is claimed, is giving way to secularity.

But the evidence supports another interpretation. Whilst it shows that institutionalized religious traditions are not faring well under the conditions of late modernity, there has not in fact been a great surge in the numbers of atheists, agnostics and the indifferent. And not all forms of institutionalized religion are faring badly. The explanation suggested here – and the argument developed in this chapter – is that rather than the religious giving way to the secular, the religious (for God) is giving way to the spiritual (for life). 'Religion' can be defined in terms of obedience to a transcendent God and a tradition which mediates his authority; *spirituality* as experience of the divine as immanent in life. Whilst the former is under threat, it will be shown that the latter is thriving. And it is doing well in two spheres: (a) amongst those who are not involved with institutionalized religion (church, chapel, mosque, temple) – which helps explain why numbers of atheists, agnostics and the indifferent are not increasing as rapidly as might be expected given the overall decline of tradition; and (b) within the field of traditional religion itself – which explains why not all forms of the institutionalized are faring badly.

Finally, by way of introduction, it should be emphasized that the shift from religion to spirituality would 'appear' to be associated with advanced industrial society. I emphasize 'appear' since it could be the case that the shift has also taken place elsewhere, but has not been studied to the same extent as – say – with regard to the US or Northern Europe.

CHARACTERIZING AND LOCATING 'RELIGION' AND 'SPIRITUALITY'

Before providing a more detailed account of how spirituality is flourishing in territories beyond institutionalized traditional religion as well as those within the traditional frame of reference, more needs to be said about the widespread shift from 'religion' to 'spirituality'. What, more precisely, is to be understood by these two terms? How, more exactly, is the decline of 'religion' and the growth of 'spirituality' to be mapped with regard to what is happening to beliefs (from the religious to the atheistic) under conditions of advanced commercial society?

Characterizing religion and spirituality

The distinction between 'spirituality' and 'religion', and therefore what these terms have come to mean for many people, has been long in the making. And the distinction has come into greater prominence during and since the 1960s.

'Religion', as defined by the *Concise Oxford Dictionary*, involves 'belief in a superhuman controlling power especially in a personal God entitled to obedience and worship; expression of this in worship; a thing that one is devoted to'. 'Religion' is here very much God-centred, with no mention of any affirmation of life in the here-and-now. Furthermore, especially since the 1960s, 'religion' has increasingly come to be seen as that which is institutionalized: involving prescribed rituals; established ways of believing; the 'official', as regulated and transmitted by religious authorities; that which is enshrined in tradition; the ethical commandments of sacred texts; the voice of the authority of the transcendent. For many, it has also come to be associated with the formal, dogmatic and hierarchical, if not the impersonal or patriarchal.

One of the people interviewed during a study carried out by Robert Wuthnow (published as *After Heaven*, 1998) says, 'Religion is something outside of yourself. There's somebody in the pulpit telling you things, but I needed to know from the inside.' And this leads us to the key characteristics which have come to be associated with 'spirituality'. 'Spirituality' has to do with the personal; that which is interior or immanent; that which is one's experienced relationship with the sacred; and that wisdom or knowledge which derives from such experiences. At heart, spirituality has come to mean 'life'. The equation is Spirituality = Life = Spirituality = Life, 'Life' being taken to mean the spiritually-informed, personal, intimate, experiential, existential, psychological, self and relational-cum-self depths of what it is to be alive: rather than life as led in terms of what the stresses and strains, ambitions and configurations of capitalistic modernity has to offer. Life, rather than what transcends life, becomes God (thus contemporary spirituality may more precisely be termed 'spirituality of life').

The following two extracts serve to illustrate the contrast between 'religion' and 'spirituality'. The first is from G. K. Chesterton's *Orthodoxy*. The second is from the Introduction to Count Hermann Keyserling's best known work, *The Art of Life*. (Keyserling was the founder of the School of Wisdom in Darmstadt, which operated at the beginning of the twentieth century.)

▌ ILLUSTRATING 'RELIGION' AND 'SPIRITUALITY'

'Religion':

> That external vigilance which has always been the mark of Christianity (the command that we should *watch* and pray) has expressed itself in typical Western orthodoxy: [it] depends on the idea of a divinity transcendent, different from ourselves, a deity that disappears. Certainly the most sagacious creeds may suggest that we should pursue God into deeper and deeper rings of the labyrinth of our own ego. But only we of Christendom have said that we should hunt God like an eagle upon the mountains: and we have killed all monsters in the chase. . . .
>
> By insisting especially on the immanence of God we get introspection, self-isolation, quietism, social indifference – Tibet. By insisting on the transcendence of God we get wonder, curiosity, moral and political adventure, righteous indignation – Christendom. Insisting that God is inside man, man is always inside himself. By insisting that God transcends man, man has transcended himself.
>
> (G. K. Chesterton: *Orthodoxy*, Glasgow: Collins Fontana Books, 1961 [1908], p. 131)

'Spirituality':

> *The Art of Life*, Keyserling's latest work, is a collection of essays wherein the author develops the central idea that living is something entirely different from the multifarious activities in which men so readily immerse themselves; that it involves the effort to master the raw material of experience and transform it into a harmonious and complete expression of the Self.
>
> (Hermann Keyserling: *The Art of Life*, London: Selwyn & Blount, 1937, from the dust jacket)

Locating religion and spirituality

If indeed a shift has taken place from religion to spirituality, perhaps amounting to a spiritual revolution, where has it taken place? Having discussed how religion and spirituality have come to be understood by many in advanced commercial societies, this shift is now explored by reference to 'maps' of beliefs in three countries: Sweden, the US and Britain. All indicate that although the numbers involved in institutionalized traditions in the great majority of cultures of advanced modernity (the US apparently being the main exception) are relatively small, and often declining, the numbers of atheists or agnostics are also relatively small, and not increasing significantly. There seem, therefore, to be a lot of people in the middle ground who are neither involved in traditional religion but do not identify themselves as atheist or agnostic. This suggests that if a spiritual revolution is underway, it could well be located among this sector – a majority who may believe in 'something' (in that they are not atheists or agnostics) but who are not obviously religious in the traditional sense.

As Tables 17.1 and 17.2 show, the *numerical evidence* supports the idea of a 'middle territory' betwixt-and-between regular attendees and atheists/agnostics in both Sweden and the US. In Sweden, regular attendance of traditional religion is on the point of total collapse. Yet only some 15 per cent of the population identify themselves as atheist or agnostic. In the US, the great majority 'believe in God' (whatever that might mean). On first sight, institutional attendance is also very much higher than Sweden, at 42 per cent. However, this figure (derived from people being polled about attendance) drops to 20 per cent when congregational size is assessed. If this is true, the middle territory amounts to 74 per cent of the population rather than the 52 per cent suggested by less reliable self-reporting.

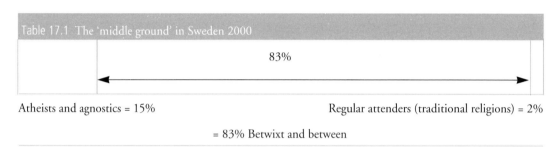

Table 17.1 The 'middle ground' in Sweden 2000

83%

Atheists and agnostics = 15%   Regular attenders (traditional religions) = 2%

= 83% Betwixt and between

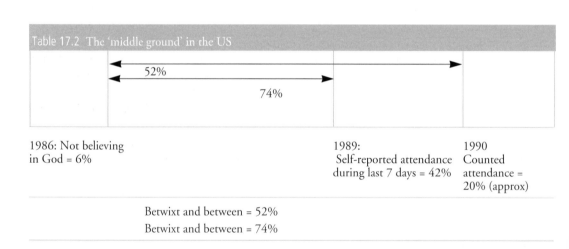

Table 17.2 The 'middle ground' in the US

52%

74%

1986: Not believing   1989:   1990
in God = 6%   Self-reported attendance   Counted
                                        during last 7 days = 42%   attendance =
                                                                   20% (approx)

Betwixt and between = 52%
Betwixt and between = 74%

Table 17.3 introduces a longitudinal dimension to what is happening in Britain. The figures show the numerical growth of the middle territories – betwixt-and-between regular attenders of traditional religion and atheists or agnostics. The key thing to note is that there has been a much larger decline of regular attenders than there has been an increase in atheists or agnostics. There has thus been an 18 per cent increase in the betwixt-and-between population during the period under consideration.

All this evidence (and much more could be included) raises the question: what is going on in these territories among those who are neither atheists/agnostics nor regular attenders? The first thing to say is that a very considerable variety of beliefs and practices may be present. Drawing on evidence from a range of sources, these might include: non-attending traditionalists (for example Bible readers in old peoples homes); nominal Christians; rites of passage Christians (who only go to church for ceremonial purposes); those who believe in some sort of spirit or life force (three in ten of Western European populations, according to 1992 findings (and see below)); those who believe they have a soul (also

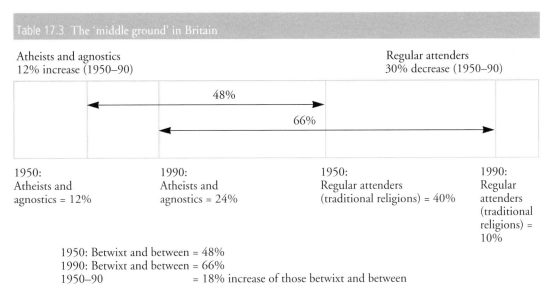

Table 17.3 The 'middle ground' in Britain

Atheists and agnostics
12% increase (1950–90)

Regular attenders
30% decrease (1950–90)

48%

66%

1950:
Atheists and
agnostics = 12%

1990:
Atheists and
agnostics = 24%

1950:
Regular attenders
(traditional religions) = 40%

1990:
Regular
attenders
(traditional
religions) =
10%

1950: Betwixt and between = 48%
1990: Betwixt and between = 66%
1950–90   = 18% increase of those betwixt and between

below); those who believe in the paranormal (figures for astral influence on personality include 26 per cent in Sweden, 50 per cent in France and 59 per cent in Latvia, a figure which rises to 63 per cent in Britain according to a 1998 survey); those who experience the sacred in nature (the 63 per cent of Finns who get in touch with God through nature); those who hold the 'There are more things in heaven and earth . . . than were dreamt of in your philosophy' outlook (for example British cultural commentator Ekow Eshun with his 'I want to discover what more there is to life beyond what's in front of me'; or consider an off the street into a focus group survey which has been held in Nottingham, the typical response being along the lines of, 'I'm not religious . . . I definitely believe in something'); belief in angels (with very high figures indeed being reported from the US); and out-of-the ordinary experiences (figures for self-attested religious or spiritual experiences being in the order of 30 per cent to 40 per cent).

Given this range of activities and beliefs, is it possible to argue that a spiritual revolution is under way within the territories between institutionalized religion and atheism/agnosticism? I believe so, for my very strong hunch – not enough research has yet been done for this to be conclusive – is that a very great deal of what is taking place in the territories beyond institutionalized-cum-traditionalized religion has been indeed to do with life-cum-spirituality.

NEW AGE SPIRITUALITIES OF LIFE

The most visible expression and articulation of a spirituality of life is the New Age movement (see also Chapter 11). Here, more than anywhere, we might look for evidence of a spiritual revolution. Here we find a vivid and influential example of life-cum-spirituality-cum-life. Yet (it will be argued below) the New Age is not only of significance in itself – just as importantly, it can be viewed as a symptom of something wider, a spiritual revolution more broadly conceived and more widespread in mainstream culture. The New Age may be just the most visible tip of the iceberg.

Portrayal

New Age life-spirituality (or self-spirituality) is characterized by three basic themes.

First, life lived out of the 'ego' or 'lower self' does not work. Life at this level is mechanistic, distorted, malfunctional. It is replete with neuroses, irritations, unsatisfactory accomplishments, bad habits, good habits which in fact do not work. Life at this level of existence is life lived in terms of what we all are by virtue of socialization, education, parenting – in sum, of what we are by virtue of what has been imposed on us since our birth.

Second, the experience of those involved with *New Age spiritualities of life* is that from birth (if not before) our true essence is of a spiritual nature. Our life, that is to say, is entirely bound up with, integral to, a spiritual realm which is entirely distinct from that which is acquired from the institutions, structures and values of society and culture. And life lived out of what lies within – the 'higher self', 'source' or goddess/god – is as perfect as this life can be.

And third, spiritual disciplines are experienced as providing the key to effecting a transformational 'shift' from the lower to the higher realm of being. The great cry is: practise, engage, find 'what works for you', experience it.

In sum, New Age spiritualities of life are all about realizing one's inner, true life. Such spiritualities are (albeit to varying degrees) *detraditionalized* (in this regard they must be distinguished from more traditionalized New Religious Movements, as Chapter 12 on the latter indicates). Ultimately, life can only be experienced through one's own inner-directed life. One has to be able to live one's own life, express one's own life, experience the wisdom inherent in one's own life. Traditions, with their supra-self, externally sustained frames of reference and injunction, can have little or no role to play. New Age spiritualities provide diagnoses of what is wrong with a life solely informed by the externals of mainstream culture and society. Maintaining that spirituality is the same thing as one's true inner life; the New Age then provides all those countless disciplines whereby one can transform one's life – if only for short periods of time – by liberating oneself from the hold of the ego in order to experience the life within.

▌ ILLUSTRATING LIFE IN SPIRITUALITY

Shelley 'the god of my own heart; 'the divinity of man's own nature'; the 'divine beauty of life'.

Tolstoy 'Life is everything. Life is God. Everything changes and moves in that movement is God. And while there is life there is joy in consciousness of the divine. To love life is to love God. Harder and more blessed than all else is to love this life in one's sufferings, innocent sufferings.'

Tagore 'A poet's religion'; *jibansmriti* ('deity of my life').

Hilma af Klint (Swedish mystic painting at the beginning of the twentieth century) 'Life in the spirit of love'.

Martin Goodman (illumined by contemporary mystic, Mother Meera) 'I will be a Filament of Life but an Affiliate of No one.'

Growth of New Age spiritualities of life

But are New Age spiritualities of life a growing force? And, if so, do developments add up to a spiritual revolution?

Cutting a long story short, until the 1960s New Age spiritualities of life were largely – although by no means entirely – the concern of professional people, often from the upper middle classes. During the 1960s, however, the quest for inner spirituality shifted from being the concern of (relatively) small numbers of a cultural elite to being the concern of much greater numbers of younger people. With the counter-culture, the inner quest entered the campus and became adopted by many of that generation of baby boomers who were then coming of age and going to university or college.

As for what has happened since the 1960s, there is little doubting the fact that New Age spiritualities of life have continued to increase in numerical significance. It might be objected that this is unlikely, given the fact that the counter-culture (the 'home' of spiritualities of life during the 1960s and earlier 1970s) has largely withered away. However, the New Age has become more mainstream. And it is in connection with the mainstream that one finds growth.

Consider, for example, the expansion of *new spiritual outlets*. These are comprised of individual practitioners, or small(ish) groups led by practitioners, who cater for the spiritual quest: typically of those who live mainstream rather than counter-cultural lives. Practitioners offer any number of practices

Illustrating new spiritual outlets:

Figure 17.1 Just off the Cowley Road, Oxford

Figure 17.2 A healing centre, the Cowley Road, Oxford

Figure 17.3 Eastern fare, the Cowley Road, Oxford

Figure 17.4 Magical empowerment, Newark Airport

in order for participants to experience healing, empowerment, growth, wholeness, tranquillity, vitality or, for example, power. And there is pretty conclusive evidence that new spiritual outlets have grown. One can think, for example, of the adverts which appear in that key institution of the New Age, namely all those publications which direct people to new spiritual outlets. The magazine *Common Ground*, covering the Bay area of San Francisco, provides a good illustration. A 1979 issue contained 300 adverts for spiritual services; the 1997/8 issue contained something in the order of 1,500 new spiritual outlets. And much the same pattern appears in many other places: from Rio de Janeiro to Stockholm.

Together with new spiritual outlets, which involve face-to-face experiential practice, we can also think of new spiritual outlets which provide material to be taken home. This is material which can then be drawn upon by oneself, in (relative) solitude such as the book, music, the video, the magazine; or indeed, the material that can be found at home by way of the Internet. Considering just one of the ways of providing (potentially) spiritually enlightening material, namely the book, it would be hard to refute the claim that growth has taken place. From 1993 to 1997, for example, there was a 75.5 per cent increase in the UK of 'New Age/occult' publications.

Then there are those new spiritual outlets which operate directly within the mainstream of society: directly in that they aim to replace existing institutional arrangements with those which are more enlightened. The hospice movement, for example, whilst by no means entirely being encompassed by spiritualities of life, has certainly grown in Britain and other countries, and is very much focused on spiritually informed meanings of life. Or think of schools, in particular at the primary level, with classes on 'RE' or personal and social 'values' dwelling on shared (supra-traditional) spirituality, not least in order to find common ground in an egalitarian but pluralistic world: a common ground to avoid excluding minority faiths. Only fifty years ago schools taught Christianity, and by rote; in Britain at least, there is little of this left today. And consider the fact that new spiritualities of life have increasingly entered the very heartlands of capitalistic modernity, namely big business. Company after company has entered the ranks of those who provide trainings or seminars to transform what it is to be a manager.

A recent survey in Britain finds that 39 per cent have tried or experienced 'alternative medicine', with 22 per cent having practised meditation. Figures such as these do not of course demonstrate serious involvement with New Age spiritualities of life ('alternative medicine' could simply mean, for example, buying aromatherapy at a major pharmacy). But they are suggestive. What is more, a major study carried out in the US finds that 31 per cent of baby boomers (those born after the Second World War) say that 'People have God within them'. And as we shall see below, there would appear to be 14 per cent in the US who identify themselves as 'metaphysical believers and seekers'. In Holland, 16 per cent of youth claim to have been influenced by New Age or Eastern religions.

SPIRITUALITIES OF LIFE IN MAINSTREAM CULTURE

The evidence above suggests that a New Age type spirituality of life is no longer confined to the New Age – that is to the relatively small proportion of people who are willing to accept this label. Rather, New Age spiritualities are a growing force in mainstream culture. Indeed, in some localities (such as Marin County, north of San Francisco) it could well be the case that the spiritual revolution has taken place in that more people are now engaging in the face-to-face encounters provided by new spiritual outlets than with the congregations of tradition. (In passing, it can also be noted that there are recorded instances of New Age spiritual outlets buying church and chapel properties.) It would be rash, though, to conclude that New Age spiritualities of life have overtaken traditionalized religion in the population at large. There is simply not enough evidence to support such a conclusion. But there is another way of arguing that a spiritual revolution is under way. This involves pointing to evidence that spiritualities of life – of a more indeterminate, inchoate, if not mysterious nature than is to be found in explicit New Age circles – are widespread in the culture, there also being evidence of growth relative to traditional beliefs.

Consider, in this regard, surveys which show that belief in a spirit or life force has overtaken the traditional (theistic) belief in a personal God. Thus figures provided by the sociologist of religion Steve Bruce show that 45 per cent of Britains in 1947 believed in a personal God, the figure for 1987 being 37 per cent; whereas in 1947 39 per cent believed in some sort of spirit or vital force which controls life, the figure for 1987 being 42 per cent. Consideration can also be paid to a very recent (2000) survey, carried out for the BBC's 'Soul of Britain' series. Involving detailed telephone interviews with 1,000 people, the survey shows that whereas 26 per cent express belief in a personal God, 44 per cent believe in some kind of spirit or life force or that 'there is something there' (27 per cent declaring that they do not have a clear belief in God at all, with only 8 per cent 'convinced atheists'). Gill, Hadaway and Marler add credence to this picture when they report belief in God as personal as having declined from 43 per cent during the 1940s–50s to 31 per cent during the 1990s, with 'God as Spirit or Life Force' having increased from 38 per cent to 40 per cent during the same period of time. As for Europe, the overall picture (for the 1980s) is that 32 per cent believe in a personal God, 36 per cent in a spirit or life force.

Supporting evidence also comes from figures concerning belief in the 'soul'. Drawing again on the Soul of Britain survey, respondents were asked, 'Do you consider yourself solely to be a biological organism, which ceases to exist at death, or is there another existence after death?'; 52 per cent replied 'No, another existence after death'; 31 per cent answered 'Yes, a biological organism, which ceases at death', and 17 per cent said 'Don't know'. In response to another question (with multiple answers allowed), concerning a range of beliefs, 69 per cent claimed belief in the soul, 62 per cent in God; 51 per cent in life after death. It can be added that the 62 per cent believing in God have fallen from the 76 per cent of 1980, whereas those believing in the soul have risen from 59 per cent in 1981 to the current 69 per cent. And turning briefly to Europe, figures gathered during the 1980s suggest that the overall picture is of some 60 per cent believing in the soul.

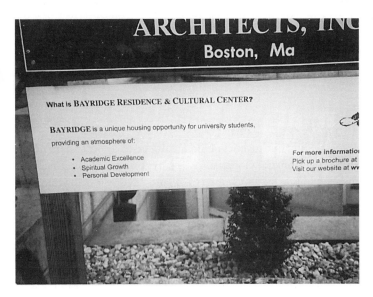

Figure 17.5 Spirituality within the culture. A housing development for students, Boston

It is presumably the case, of course, that Christians believe in the soul. But given the fact that so many in the population at large believe in some sort of spirit or life force, it is highly likely that the soul-figures which have just been presented indicate that very considerable numbers of people (somehow) link their souls with some sort of spirit or life force. Furthermore, it is highly likely that many equate their lives – better, their '*being* alive' – with spirituality when they say they believe they have a soul. And then there is the consideration that 51 per cent (or 52 per cent) believe in life after death: presumably reflecting the fact that they believe that they have a soul, a soul which transcends what it is to be a mere biological organism and which therefore can live on once biological life ceases to exist. And many of these do not belong to a traditional religion.

THEISTIC SPIRITUALITIES OF LIFE

Evidence of widespread belief in a life force, a spirit and a soul provides support for the spiritual revolution thesis, and there is also the evidence of growth in New Age quarters. But there is also another cluster of evidence that supports the thesis of a spiritual revolution: the fact that spiritualities of life are also a growing force within the sphere of institutionalized, traditional religion. In other words, the shift from religion to spirituality is even taking place within religion.

Theistic spiritualities of life combine belief in a transcendent personal God and other components of traditional (particularly Christian) belief with themes more commonly (and obviously) found in New Age spiritualities of life. Thus belief in biblical authority (traditional) may well be combined with a stress on the importance of experiencing the indwelling and life-transforming power of the Holy Spirit (spirituality of life). Theistic spiritualities of life thus combine or mix the traditionalized (the authority of tradition) with the detraditionalized (the authority of one's own spiritually informed experience).

■ ILLUSTRATING THE GROWTH OF LIFE-SPIRITUALITY THEMES WITHIN TRADITIONAL RELIGION

More than any other, it is the experiential face of religion that takes on current prominence: in story after story the quest is for something more than doctrine, creed, or institution, although of course these are usually involved. What is sought after has to do more with feelings, with awareness of innermost realities, with intimations of the sacred – what amounts to the very pulse of lived religion.

(Wade Clark Roof , *Spiritual Marketplace*, 1999)

Many manifestations of what I am calling 'theistic spiritualities of life' are discussed under such headings as 'Pentecostalism', 'neo-Pentecostalism', 'Charismatic Christianity', many forms of 'Evangelicalism', and 'born-again Christians'. Since these are discussed in Chapters 7, 9 and 14, I will here look more closely at the more detraditionalized forms of Christianity in the West which cater for 'life'. As we shall see, they are a growing force.

Donald Miller's *Reinventing American Protestantism. Christianity in the New Millennium* (1997) offers a vivid portrayal of the phenomenon in the US. Miller is looking at 'new paradigm churches' otherwise called 'megachurches', 'post-denominational churches', even the 'postmodern traditionalist'. More specifically, he is looking at Calvary Chapel, Vineyard Christian Fellowship and Hope Chapel, together numbering over 1,000 congregations in the US and growing rapidly. In some ways these denominations are strongly traditionalized. Clergy, for example, insist on biblical authority, even literalism. At the same time, however, the detraditionalized is also well in evidence. What participants call 'purity of heart' is taken to be more important than what they think of as 'purity of doctrine'. Time and time again, it is emphasized that personal conviction counts for more than doctrine. Above all, detraditionalization is in evidence in the way in which the Holy Spirit has become more important than external tradition. For it is the Holy Spirit which plays a key role in providing direction for daily life. First hand experience of the Holy Spirit rather than tradition *per se* serves as the key source of authority in guiding believers' lives. Furthermore, and more generally, new paradigm worship provides direct access to an experience of the sacred, an experience which addresses the deepest personal or therapeutic needs of participants: thereby transforming their lives here and now.

New paradigm churches are thus detraditionalized in the sense that personal experience – directly informed by the Holy Spirit – serves as the key source of authority. Even the way in which biblical tradition is understood is being detraditionalized, as shown below:

■ ILLUSTRATING NEW PARADIGM RELIGIOSITY:

In spite of their relatively conservative ['fairly literal'] reading . . . new paradigm Christians do not see the Bible as a legalistic 'rule book' so much as an instrument through which the Holy Spirit speaks to them. For new paradigm Christians the Bible is God's way of communicating to humans, and it is in meditating on scripture that individuals receive guidance and instruction for their lives. When they read the Bible, they claim, the Holy Spirit speaks to them regarding the things they should change in their lives, people they should nurture and care for, and new directions they should take in their career or service to God.

Donald Miller (*Reinventing American Protestantism. Christianity in the New Millennium*)

So new paradigm churches provide a 'spirituality' (a favoured term) of the 'heart' (another favoured term). They cater for life. They address deepest personal needs or quests. They have a strong therapeutic dimension. And as indeed Miller argues, one of the key reasons for their growth lies precizely with the fact that they cater for life – a key value for many of those attracted to this form of religiosity. In addition, however, and to add somewhat to Miller's analysis, a related reason for the success of new paradigm churches seems to be that they provide a relatively traditionalized or organized frame of reference for exploring, nurturing, what it is to be alive. That is to say, rather than leaving participants floundering with their own, relatively inchoate experiences, they provide guidance.

The success of new paradigm churches is significant enough, Miller writing of a 'revolution' transforming American Protestantism. The success of what Robert Wuthnow calls 'small groups' or 'support groups' is even more remarkable. The story is told in his *Sharing the Journey. Support Groups and America's New Quest for Community* (1994). Little in evidence prior to the 1960s, some 80 million Americans had become involved in small face-to-face groups by the early 1990s. According to Wuthnow, small groups that meet regularly and provide caring and support for those who participate in them now have such social significance that they amount to something which has become at least as important to understand as the economy or the political system.

Whether or not this is overstating things is open to debate. What is clear, however, is that the small group movement – two thirds of which is underpinned by religious tradition – is very much orientated towards life, more exactly, the life of the soul. For these are intimate, egalitarian groups which provide an opportunity for participants to discover what it means to become more fully human and more deeply in tune with their own spirituality and with God (see below). Quite literally, the groups provide an opportunity for participants to share their journey through life by discussing interpersonal relationships, emotions, matters to do with self-identity or personal morality.

For the majority of groups where religion is important, scripture serves as a point of reference; as something to be discussed and interpreted. The widespread view is that people must pursue their own unique spiritual goals (for no one else can live one's own life), sharing insights with one another on the basis of unique life experiences rather than relying on any absolute, universal truths. Small groups, in other words, might often have a Christian frame of reference, but they are quite strongly de-traditionalized. So, like the new paradigm churches, there is a degree of tradition-input, but tradition does not stand in the way of allowing participants the freedom to explore and express their own (and relational) lives.

▌ SMALL GROUPS IN ACTION

Group members feel their spirituality being deepened by the emotional experience of being a party to caring in their group. Caring was often described as a feeling – such as warmth, closeness, togetherness, or well-being – and this feeling in turn made people sense, quite often intuitively, that God was somehow more real, alive, present, or available to them than before. In other words, spirituality was deepened not so much by an event that motivated people to go out the next day and live better lives; it was deepened by a sense of divine presence, a sense that one was accepted by God or perhaps submerged in God's love.

This heightened awareness of God was very decisively influenced by the group process. As people shared their problems or just their thoughts, and as they empathized with others, they ceased feeling so alone. Rather than feeling they were distinct individuals, they momentarily dropped the boundaries separating themselves from others and felt more a part of something larger than themselves. There seemed to be a kind of spirit in the group that they were participating in, but one that was more powerful than they.

The example that perhaps stands out most closely among all the people we talked to was the observation of one woman in a twelve-step group who described how she felt at a recent meeting. 'When I sit amongst the group and I listen to what people have to say,' she mused, 'I feel very strongly a movement of my own spirit, so it's I suppose what one would call a meditation, but I have a very strong sense of God being present for me in that context.' Emphasizing that this sense occurs at the heart level and that it involves a realization of the fullness of life, she continued: 'I have a very strong awareness of the presence of God in that context, so it's a spiritual experience for me. One could say that God is there whether you're aware of it or not, but my awareness of that presence for me makes it happen at the heart level. And not every time. This past time in particular I found that everything people said was just kind of like going through my whole body. I thought "Holy Smokes." I feel I'm opening up a lot more to feeling things than I did before.'

(Robert Wuthnow, *Sharing the Journey. Support Groups and America's New Quest for Community*, 1994, pp. 263–4)

Looking more generally at theistic spiritualities of life then, there is little doubting the fact that combinations/transformations of the more traditionalized and the more detraditionalized, of the authority of tradition and that of experience – of what might be called 'traditionalized experience', is a potent force. As well as the examples above, one might think of the success of Pentecostalism in South America: on the one hand a (relatively) traditionalized Christian frame of reference; on the other the immediate and experienced authority of the empowering and life-transforming Holy Spirit, by-passing tradition by virtue of its transmission by way of personal experience. Or again, one might think of the success of some forms of Evangelical, Pentecostal or Charismatic Christianity in Britain: doing better than other (liberal or strongly traditionalized) forms of Christianity by holding their own against the forces of secularization, or actually growing. The evidence is widespread.

THE SPIRITUAL REVOLUTION AS A CULTURAL FACT

To summarize so far, this chapter has been arguing a controversial thesis, namely that a spiritual revolution has taken place in that more people now favour the language of life-spirituality to that of traditional religion. And the conclusion to be drawn is that if people in advanced industrial–commerical societies today are going to be spiritual or religious, they will tend to favour the former. More controversially, the conclusion might also be that spirituality is a growing force both within and beyond institututionalized religion. The thesis is contrary to that of those secularization theorists who see both religion and spirituality fading away. It is supported by three main arguments (and associated batteries of evidence):

- First, that New Age spiritualities of life are growing. (Although it has to be accepted that this, alone, does not amount to a widespread revolution.)
- Second, that less clearly articulated beliefs about life spirituality – often articulated in terms of 'soul', 'life force', 'spirit' – are widely pervasive within mainstream culture. (And there is some evidence to suggest that they are expanding in some settings.)
- And third, that within the territories of traditionalized–institutionalized religion, much suggests that theistic spiritualites of life are doing well, if not very well indeed, in some countries.

There is also supporting evidence of the turn from religion to spirituality in the work of two major sociologists of contemporary religion, Robert Wuthnow and Wade Clark Roof. Although Wuthnow does not deal with the issue systematically, his *Sharing the Journey* contains example after example linking the success of the small group movement to the attention it pays to spirituality (life, the personal or psychological, the therapeutic, the intimate concerning the relational). Roof's more systematic analysis, based on a large-scale study which he organized and which is reported in his *Spiritual Marketplace*, breaks his sample down into the following categories: dogmatists (totalling 15 per cent), born-again Christians (33 per cent), mainstream believers (26 per cent), metaphysical believers and seekers (14 per cent) and secularists (12 per cent). The dogmatists (traditionalist religions of the text) are those who say they are religious, not spiritual. The born-again Christians (broadly equivalent to what we are here calling theistic spiritualities of life), mainstream believers (liberal religion) and metaphysical believers and seekers (broadly equivalent to our New Age spiritualities of life), however, are reported as being spiritually minded, indeed, in the throes of spiritual reawakening and ferment. This means that 73 per cent of those surveyed (or more) prefer to use the language of 'spirituality' rather than 'religion'. But that is not all. Rather strangely, it transpires that one half of the people in the secularist category claim that God lies within the person. This means we can add 6 per cent to the 73 per cent already arrived at: 79 per cent of Americans, it follows, are spiritually minded.

EXPLAINING THE SPIRITUAL REVOLUTION

This chapter is primarily about the spiritual revolution and the highly charged question as to whether or not it has taken place. But it is also interesting to consider – albeit briefly – why spirituality has apparently grown in significance relative to religion.

The 'HS' factor

To pave the way for exploring why New Age and theistic spiritualites of life are a growing force, the first step is to see what they have common. For if shared features can be ascertained, it is reasonable to infer that similar (if not identical) sociocultural factors are at work with regard to growth in both cases.

Both New Age and theistic spiritualities of life involve what can be abbreviated as the 'HS factor'. In New Age spiritualities of life, the 'HS factor' is the 'higher self', the aim of such spiritualities being to perfect one's life by escaping from the stranglehold of the 'lower self' in order to experience the spirituality of the higher plane of being. On the other hand, in (many) theistic spiritualities of life the 'HS factor' is the Holy Spirit, that 'giver of life' as it says in the New Testament; or, as in Wuthnow's small group material, the 'personal saviour', the 'Christ in my heart'.

What is interesting is that although the Holy Spirit is grounded in a transcendent realm in a way which is not true of spiritualities of life, it functions in much the same way as the higher self of New Age spiritualities of life. That is to say, the typical aim of (many) theistic spiritualities of life is to 'give up' or 'surrender' one's fallen or imperfect self (functionally equivalent to the lower self of spiritualities of life) in order to let the Holy Spirit 'take up residence'. Then one serves the 'God' within.

So both New Age and theistic spiritualities of life involve a remarkably similar dynamic. Both address life by promising release from the wrong kind of selfhood (lower self – sinful, fallen or imperfect self) and, conversely, promising the best possible life (and self) in the here and now. And this leads to the hypothesis that the success of these two forms of spirituality must surely be bound up with the fact that they cater for what many today are most interested in: their own intimate and personal (and their relational) lives. In other words, the success of these two forms of spirituality of life – New Age and theistic – is bound up with a widespread cultural concern with 'life', in particular the interior life.

This way of explaining the popularity of spirituality-cum-life, it can be added, is given further credence by the fact that forms of religion which do not cater for life are not doing as well as those which do. Conservative–traditional forms of religion, such as Roman Catholicism in Britain, are in decline. By telling people how to live in a particular way in order to prepare for the next (true–higher) life, rather than catering for people's desire to develop and express their own lives here and now, such religions of difference have not been able to benefit (it can be argued) from the cultural turn to life. As for liberal forms of religion, typical of many Church of England congregations for example, the argument is that their decline (at least in some measure) is due to the fact that they seldom have much to say or offer with regard to the problems, possibilities and promises of a person's own life. Liberal denominational religiosity is not exactly renowned for its ability to enable people to experience their spirituality (or the spirituality of the Holy Spirit), to enable people to 'feel alive', to empower, to address life problems, to heal, to facilitate expression and creativity.

The 'cultural turn to life'

But is there a wider cultural demand for spiritualities which cater for life? And can or should the spiritual revolution be explained in relation to this? It is widely assumed that the key values of advanced commercial cultures are freedom, equality and the like. Mention is rarely made of what is surely the central value (or valued state of being), namely 'life'. But there is significant evidence to support the greater centrality of life.

First, life plays itself out in various ways within Western cultures. One might think of the massive investment in scientific research, attempting to 'create life' or to 'understand life' (as the media often puts it) or to manipulate life at the genetic level. Or one might think of the massive investments in prolonging life, not simply with regard to scientific methods but also with regard to the very considerable percentages of people in many countries who turn to alternative/complementary forms of medicine and healing. Then there are the huge investments in improving the quality of personal life, whether it be way of consumer activities or therapies, training, travel and exploring nature, and so on.

And second, the importance of 'life' is also shown by the fact that the ethic of humanity – which lies behind so much law and international relations, all the specifics of human rights legislation, the specifics of equal opportunities programmes, harassment procedures and so on – may well be the dominant ethical 'complex' or 'matrix' of our times (certainly in terms of social and political policy). The ethic of humanity is premissed on the value ascribed to human life. Furthermore, the vitality of this ethic is seen in the fact that the so-called 'culture wars' are battled out over the conflicting implications and values of the ethic, for example human 'life' (for the anti-abortionists) versus 'freedom' (for the pro-abortionists). The vitality and importance of the ethic is also seen in how 'life' is as it were extending into nature, in the sense that it comes to provide the basis of animal (and other) rights.

And so to the sense of 'life' which is of most relevance to explaining the (relative) success of New Age and theistic spiritualities of life. Writing during the last century, the sociologist Georg Simmel claimed that 'life' has increasingly become the true meaning or value of our existence. (See Simmel on the turn to life, below.) This is 'life' in the sense of that 'inner' realm, which – ultimately – belongs to the individual alone, and which has to do with one's emotions, experiences, subjectivities, consciousness, psychology, personal ethicality, authenticity, the value of being true to oneself, the importance of finding out what one truly is and is capable of becoming, one's sense of being 'alive' and in the here-and-now, drawing on memories and expectations to enhance the present whilst neither diminishing the quality of life – now – for the sake of obeying the past nor investing too much for the future.

Furthermore, this 'life' is not *life as* – that is as constituted and regulated by the roles, duties and obligations of the institutional order, the 'given' or 'traditional'. Indeed, it has been argued that this is a 'life' that has come into prominence precisely because 'life as' a traditionalist Christian, family member, businessperson, or 'public man' has proved unsatisfactory. 'Life' in the sense we are discussing has come into prominence precisely because capitalistic modernity has resulted in significant numbers becoming disillusioned with what the 'primary' institutions of society have to offer with regard to 'the meaning of life'. 'Life as . . .', that is, as constituted by the roles and promises of primary institutions (like church, political parties, workplace), has increasingly had to compete with 'life itself' as the key source of significance: the ultimacy of 'feeling alive'; of self exploration and growth; of getting in touch with as much as possible of what life has to offer; of experiencing 'the quality of life'; indeed, of staying alive for as long as possible. Or, to amend a fashionable injunction, in 'getting oneself a life'.

It is of course true that great swathes of the population remain firmly locked into various forms of 'life as . . .' which take life into roles, duties, obligations. Having said this, however, the fact remains that 'life itself' has become so much more significant. Fewer today than in the past are convinced by that great traditional, overarching canopy, namely life in the hereafter; many more are convinced by the value of what the here-and-now, the immediacy of experience, the breadths and depths of consciousness, have to offer.

And so back to New Age and theistic spiritualities of life. Quite simply the argument is that the cultural turn to life is widespread, and explains why if people are to be spiritual or religious they are much more likely to practise forms of spirituality or religiosity which cater for the immediacies of their lives in the here-and-now than they are to be involved in forms of traditionalized religion which are either God-focused whilst paying scant attention to individual lives *per se*, or which are life denying in that they emphasize this life as a disciplined preparation for the true life to come. Furthermore, those intent on exploring their own lives are much more likely to adopt detraditionalized forms of spirituality (which illuminate, fulfil and express what it is to have a life of one's own) than they are to turn to those traditions which dictate what kind of (traditionalized) life one should have. For if one is living out one's own life, with what right and with what knowledge of the intimacies of one's unique existence is anyone else in the position to tell one how to live? The dictates of the tradition-informed past are simply not in order in relation to life-focused cultural assumptions and priorities.

Thus detraditionalized New Age and theistic spiritualities of life seem to succeed because they pay attention to what it is to be alive in the expressive, creative, therapeutic, life-affirming here-and-now. Such spiritualities facilitate diagnoses of what is wrong with one's life; they offer practical remedies, to be experientially tested to see whether they can help to fulfil what one's own life has to promise. They promise the great therapeutic, miraculous, healing, life-enhancing and empowering shift. That is, from an old life (due to the contaminations of modernity, the Fall, or both) to the new life (resting with intrinsic spirituality, the salvational coming-to-dwell of the God from without, or both). Liberation, healing, the release of potential, all contribute to make the most of one's own life in this world.

▮ SIMMEL ON THE TURN TO LIFE

. . . this emotional reality – which we can only call *life* – makes itself increasingly felt in its formless strength as the true meaning or value of our existence.

. . . the change to the religious shaping of life itself, and to the spiritual reality that, in philosophical terms, one could call the self-consciousness of the metaphysical significance of our existence – the change by which all otherworldly yearning and dedication, bliss and rejection, justice and mercy, are no longer found in the lofty heights above life, as it were, but in the depths within it.

(Georg Simmel, *Essays on Religion*, 1997)

LOOKING TO THE FUTURE

'Church may die in 40 years' or 'The Empty Pews' are common newspaper headlines. They are almost certainly on the right lines, but what they neglect are those forms of religion which are doing well in catering for 'life-needs'. This chapter argues that spirituality is doing well – both within religious traditions and the territories beyond tradition – and is holding its own against secularization, with evidence of growing numerical strength.

Broadly speaking, it would appear that New Age spiritualities of life are predominantly catering for those de-institutionalized 'free spirits' who have no faith in the personal God of theistic religion, whereas theistic spiritualities of life are predominantly catering for those (perhaps not quite so 'free') who retain faith in the personal God of theism. And as has been suggested in this essay, the turn to life – more exactly the turn to the unique, expressive inner life of the autonomous free spirit – goes a long way in explaining the growth of New Age and theistic spiritualities of life; that 'flight from deference' (as Linda Woodhead calls it) seen among those who favour detraditionalized spiritualities catering for one's 'own' life, rather than what traditionalized religions, with their demands that you live your life 'as' a member of tradition, have to offer. Traditionalized religions might be fine when what matters is affirming and regulating existence as a member of an established order. But this is by no means so relevant a function when what matters is exploring one's unique, expressive life.

Grounding his argument on material gathered from the World Values Surveys, Ronald Inglehart adds another dimension to the turn to life thesis. He argues that with economic development attention shifts from the imperatives of making a living to the project of maximizing individual well-being, a form of well-being which is very much associated with subjective, 'quality of life', factors. The shift from being a 'materialist' (life being gauged by success in the material world) to being a 'postmaterialist' (life being gauged by success in the 'life' world) is quite naturally associated with increasing emphasis being attached to 'meaning and purpose of life' questions. (The Soul of the Nation survey suggests that such matters are now firmly on the agenda in Britain.) People have the time, security and energy to pursue 'meaning'. Hence Inglehart's prediction – informed by survey data – is that spiritual concerns will become more widespread. To which it can be added that (free market) economic development is typically associated with the development of beliefs in the value of the autonomous person – this also fuelling faith in life-spiritualities rather than in the constrictively traditionalized.

Looking to the future, to the extent that the turn to life retains momentum, it can reasonably safely be predicted that the spiritual revolution will continue apace. What is of special interest is that established trends strongly suggest that the declining realm of insitutionalized religion as a whole will be increasingly 'taken over' by theistic spiritualities of life. The reason is simple – these spiritualities are holding their own (or doing better) than other forms of religion in this declining area.

Finally, and turning all too briefly to international considerations, if indeed Inglehart is correct in arguing that economic development fuels 'meaning of life and life-cum-spirituality' concerns, then clearly economic development in huge areas of the globe could well have profound implications for the religious–spiritual landscape. One fascinating aspect of this is that countries like India and Japan already have immense resources in the form of mystical 'traditions' which can readily be deployed to serve those wanting to shift from religion to spirituality. Several of the chapters in this volume

Illustrating old spiritual outlets:

Figure 17.6 South of Madras: the Foundation for Self Knowledge

Figure 17.7 South of Madras: back to nature

Figure 17.8 South of Madras: the Sri Jagmnath Spiritual Cultural Complex

provide evidence (see for example, Chapters 1, 5, 6, on Hinduism, Japanese religion, Judaism). Figures 17.6 to 17.8 illustrate 'old' spiritual outlets just to the south of Madras in India in which Hinduism comes to serve 'life'. If what has been argued is correct, outlets of this kind will be expanding in places like India (as the world's largest middle class gets yet larger) for much the same reasons that newer outlets are expanding in the West.

And then there are theistic spiritualities of life in, say, Brazil. There is a great deal of evidence of a Brazilian spiritual revolution, from religions which do not pay much attention to the subjective life of the person to those which do. Figure 17.9 offers an example in relation to Charismatic Christianity. Holding huge 'warehouse' events in a building named 'Terco Bizantino' (Byzantine Rosary), Roman Catholic Father Marcelo brings God into the emotions: 'Joy is in the heart of those who know Jesus'.

A worldwide spiritual revolution?

Figure 17.9 Theistic spiritualities of life in Brazil: Father Marcelo Rossi celebrates Mass with 70,000 people in São Paulo

SUMMARY

First, New Age spiritualities of life are growing. This does not in itself, however, amount to a widespread spiritual revolution.

▌ Second, less clearly articulated forms of spiritualities of life – articulated in terms of soul, life force, spirit – are much more widely abroad within mainstream culture. And there is some evidence to suggest that such forms are expanding in some countries.

▌ And third, within the territories of traditionalized religion, much indeed suggests that theistic spiritualites of life are doing well, if not very well indeed in some countries.

▌ The conclusion of this chapter is that a spiritual revolution is under way, a turn from tradition to life, and from religion to spirituality.

▌ Key terms

detraditionalization   The shift of authority from faith in, or reliance/dependency on, that which lies beyond the person to that which lies within. 'Voice' is thus displaced from the establishments of traditions to the creativities of the spiritually/religiously inspired self.

life   Life experienced as intensely personal.

life as   Life experienced as directed by that which transcends personal life, whether this transcendence involves overarching religious tradition, or the secular establishment.

New Age spiritualities of life   Spiritualities which equate spirituality with the life which we are born with, and all the potentials which this is experienced as possessing.

new spiritual outlets   Outlets (centres, homes, shops) which cater for those seeking spirituality in a (relatively) non-authoritative – that is in a facilitory, self-help journey fashion – rather than in an impositional, 'THIS is the way to lead to your life' manner.

religion   A term which has come to mean life informed by 'supra-self' tradition: 'supra-self' in that traditions are sustained by vehicles (especially books) which have existed before any particular person has been born and which will continue to exist after they have died.

secularization   The processes whereby religion (or spirituality) either disappears from the public realm of the institutional order, or disappears from the lives of individuals, or both.

spirituality   A term which has increasingly come to mean the sacralization of life.

theistic spiritualities of life   Increasingly popular forms of religious activity (it appears) which combine use of tradition with reliance on what the Holy Spirit (or similar inspirers or transformers) have to offer with regard to the salvation of life in the here-and-now.

tradition   See *religion* above.

▊ FURTHER READING

Characterizing and locating 'spirituality' and 'religion'

The two (albeit recent) classics concerning the ways in which spirituality and religion have come to operate in the culture are by Wade Clark Roof: *Spiritual Marketplace. Baby Boomers and the Remaking of American Religion* (Princeton, NJ: Princeton University Press, 1999) and Robert Wuthnow: *After Heaven. Spirituality in America since the 1950s* (Berkeley, Los Angeles and London: University of California Press, 1998). For detailed figures concerning Britain, bearing on the significance of the territories 'betwixt and between', see R. Gill, C. Hadaway and P. Marler, 'Is religious belief declining in Britain?' (*Journal for the Scientific Study of Religion* 37 (3), 1998: 507–16).

New Age spiritualities of life

The portrayal given in this section is drawn from Paul Heelas: *The New Age Movement. The Celebration of the Self and the Sacralization of Modernity* (Oxford, UK, and Malden, MA: Blackwell, 1996). See Wouter Hanegraaff's essay (Chapter 11, New Age religion) in the present volume for additional material concerning the characteristics of this kind of spirituality. Chapter 4 of Heelas's *The New Age Movement* provides a more extensive discussion of the significance of New Age spiritualities than can be given here.

Spiritualities of life in mainstream culture

For figures concerning the shift from 'a personal God' to 'some sort of spirit or vital force which controls life', see Steve Bruce: *Religion in Modern Britain* (Oxford: Oxford University Press, 1995) and 'Religion in Britain at the close of the twentieth century: a challenge to the silver lining perspective' (*Journal of Contemporary Religion* 11 (3), 1996: 261–75). See also R. Gill *et al.* (*op cit.*). For figures concerning Europe, see Grace Davie: 'Unity in diversity. Religion and modernity in Western Europe'. In John Fulton and Peter Gee (eds): *Religion in Modern Europe* (Lewiston: The Edwin Mellen Press, 1994).

Theistic spiritualities of life

Donald Miller's *Reinventing American Protestantism. Christianity in the New Millennium* (Berkeley, Los Angeles and London: University of California Press, 1997) provides an excellent account of such spiritualities; so does Robert Wuthnow in his *Sharing the Journey. Support Groups and America's New Quest for Community* (New York and London: The Free Press, 1994). See James Davison Hunter: *Evangelicalism. The Coming Generation* (Chicago and London: University of Chicago Press, 1987) for what he calls 'subjectivization' amongst Bible Belt Evangelicals. Linda Woodhead and Paul Heelas discuss what are called experiential religions of difference in their *Religion in Modern Times* (Oxford UK, and Malden, MA: Blackwell, 2000).

The spiritual revolution as a cultural fact

Wade Clark Roof's *The Spiritual Marketplace* (*op. cit*) is a useful place to go in order to explore the extent to which the US has become spiritualized. See especially Chapter 6.

Explaining the spiritual revolution

To the best of my knowledge, Georg Simmel was the first sociologist to really advance the thesis concerning the turn to life. Most of his key essays bearing on this theme are to be found in his *Essays on Religion* (New Haven, CT, and London: Yale University Press, 1997). A useful contemporary volume is Jonathan Rutherford (ed.): *The Art of Life* (London: Lawrence and Wishart, 2000), which includes an excellent essay, 'The sacred life', by Madeleine Bunting.

Looking to the future

For Ronald Inglehart's evidence and predictions, see his *Modernization and Postmodernization. Cultural, Economic and Political Change in 43 Societies* (Princeton, NJ: Princeton University Press, 1997).

Acknowledgements

Linda Woodhead and Ben Seel have provided invaluable suggestions with regard to the development of this chapter.

Index

Note: References to illustrations and tables are indicated by *italics* (*64*, *70t*). Definitions of key terms are in **bold** type (**301**).

Erasmus, Desiderius 167
Eshun, Ekow 359
esotericism, Western 256–8
ethic: Buddhism 42; of humanity 371
Ethiopia 208
Europe, Eastern 324–5
European exceptionalism 175, 294–5, *297*
Evangelicalism 170–3, **178**, 196, 224, *224*, 308,
    336–8, **353** *see also* Pentecostalism
Evans-Pritchard, E. E. 218

FAIR (Family Action and Information Resource) 278,
    281, **284**
Falun Gong 101–2, 266, 268, 282
Family, The *see* Children of God
Family Action and Information Resource *see* FAIR
feminism 332–3, 335, 346, **353**
fengshui 92, 103, **104**
Ferguson, Marilyn 252
Fernandez, James W. 222
Ficino, Marsilio 255
Findhorn community 251
Findhorn Press *11*
Finland 361
five Ks 73, **83**
flirty fishing 271, 273, 277, **284**
Florovsky, Georges 165
flying saucers 250–1, 252, 268
Fortes, Meyer 211
France: ADFI (*Association de Défense de la Famille et de
    l'Individu*) 278; *Fraternité Blanche Universelle* 266,
    269; New Religious Movements (NRMs) 269,
    281; religion and secularization 175, 321, 361;
    Roman Catholicism 158; Scientology 282
Frankel, Rabbi Zachariah 136–7
Fraternité Blanche Universelle 266, 269
FREECOG (Free of Children of God/Parents'
    Committee to Free our Sons and Daughters from
    the Children of God Organization) 278, **284**
Freemasonry 256
fundamentalism 294, **297**, 305–9, **312**; Christianity
    171, 172, **179**, 306, 307–8, 309, 336–7; Hinduism
    316–17 (*see also* Hinduism: nationalism); Islam
    195, 307; Judaism 307

Gabon 222
Gabriel 185
Gandhi, Indira 24, 31, 80
Gandhi, M. K., 'Mahatma' 23, 24, 27, 28, 31–2,
    33
Gandhi, Rajiv 24
Gandhi, Sonia 24
Ganjin (Chinese Chien-chen) 112
Garvey, Marcus 269
Gautama, Siddhārtha 42
Gehlen, Arnold 296
Geiger, Abraham 135
Geluk 47, **67**

gender and religion 8–9, 332–4, 351–3; Africa
    211–13, 215, *216*, 219, 342–4, 350–1; androcen-
    tric **353**; Buddhism 46, 49, 54–6, *55*, 61–2,
    348–9, *349*; Charismatic Christianity 175,
    349–50, **353**; Chinese religions 94, 97–8, 102;
    Christianity *168*, 170, 171, 175, *176*, 177, 336–7;
    Conservative Judaism 143, 144, 145–6; differenti-
    ation 333–5, **353**; egalitarian/liberal/relational
    religion 339–41; Evangelicalism 171, 336–8, **353**;
    feminism 332–3, 335, 346, **353**; Fundamentalism
    336–7; Hinduism 20, 21, 25, 30–2, 348; Indian
    religious nationalism 344; indigenous religions
    342–4; Islam 200–1, 225, 344–7, *347*, 352;
    Islamism **353**; Japanese religions 120, 122, 351;
    Judaism 135, 140–1, *141*, 143, 144, 145–6,
    148–9, 336; key terms **353**; monastic traditions
    347–9, *349*; Native American religions 235–6,
    236–7; New Religious Movements (NRMs) 270,
    271, 272–3, *273*, 341–2, 350–1; non-
    Western/semi-differentiated societies 333–4,
    342–51; Orthodox Judaism 148–9, 336; patri-
    archy 102, **105**, **353**; primary institutions 334,
    335, **353**; professional women 338–9; Reform
    Judaism 140–1, *141*; Roman Catholicism 160,
    338; sacralization of the feminine 341–2;
    secondary institutions **353**; Sikhism 72, 73, 74,
    77, 78, 81, 82–3, *83*; Southeast Asia 55–6;
    spiritualities of life **353**; third gender 236; Tibet
    61–2; traditional Western religions 335–9;
    Western/highly differentiated societies 333,
    334–42; witchcraft 341, 344–5; 'Women's Aglow'
    337–8 *see also* marriage
Germany: anti-cult movement (ACM) 278; East
    Germany 324; New Religious Movements
    (NRMs) 269, 275–6, 280, 281; Orthodox Judaism
    136; Romantic movement 167; secularization 295
Ghana 206, 211, 325
Ghosananda, Maha 52
ghosts 94, 96
Gifford, Paul 226
Gill, R. et al. 365
Giorgi da Veneto, Francesco 255
globalization 299–300, 311–12; and authority
    300–1; Charismatic Christianity 173–5, *174*, *293*;
    charismatic movements 312; Christianity 163–4,
    176–7, 302–4; 'cosmopolitan' religious globaliza-
    tion 299, 302–5; existing approaches 309–11;
    'fundamentalist' religious globalization 299,
    305–9, **312**; glossolalia 312; inerrancy 312; key
    terms **312–13**; and New Religious Movements
    277; NGOs (non-governmental organizations)
    305, **312–13**; Pentecostalism *306*, 306–8, 309,
    313; possession cults 307–8, **313**; religion and
    boundaries 8, 300–2, 311; ritual 300, 301, **313**;
    Roman Catholicism 163–4, 302–4; sufism **313**;
    syncretism 310, **313**
glossolalia 173, **312**
gnosis 254–5, 256, **261**

HUC-JIR (Hebrew Union College-Jewish Institute of
    Religion) 140, 141
Human Potential Movement 265, **285**
human rights 8, 164, 371
Humanae Vitae 160
humanism 168
humanity 8, 371
Hungary 135–6, 324

Ibn Taymiyyah 191
ICF (International Cultural Foundation) 269, **285**
identity 300, 301, 303; Native American religions
    239, 240, 241; Sikhism 77–8, 81; Yoruba 220
ijtihad 191, 192, **202**
Imams 187–8, **202**
immortals **104**
imperialism 6
India 320; Ayodhya mosque 22, 24, 26, 33, 34, *317*;
    Bajrang Dal 34; Bharatiya Janata Party (BJP) 24,
    33, 34, 327–8, **330**; brahmans 16, 18, 22, 33;
    British rule 16, 22, 23; caste system 16, 20, 21,
    32, 74; Christianity 24, 34; communalism 33;
    Congress Party 24, 328; Deobandi movement
    195; as goddess 18; 'Hinduness' 34; Hindus (*see*
    Hinduism); independence 23, 33; Kashmir 24;
    Mother India (Bharata Mata) 23, 34; Muslims 16,
    22, 23–4, 34, 189–90, 194, 195–7; national
    anthem 23; nationalism 22–3, 24, 25, 26, 27,
    33–4, 305, 325, 327, 344–5; partition 22, 23–4,
    79, *79*; politics 24, 34, 318, 327–8; post-partition
    24–5; Punjab 70, 71, 74, 75–6, 79, 80; Rajneesh
    Foundation 275, 277; Rashtriya Svayamsevak
    Sangh National Volunteer Association (RSS) 34;
    religious nationalism 344–5; Sangh Parivar 34;
    Shiva Sena 34, 327; spirituality *373*, 373–4, *374*;
    Tamilnadu 33; *Vande mataram* 23; Vishva Hindu
    Parishad (VHP) 34; women 344–5
Indonesia 269, 327
inerrancy **312**
INFORM (Information Network focus on Religious
    Movements) **285**
Inglehart, Ronald 373
intellectualism 293–4
International Cultural Foundation (ICF) 269, **284**
Internet 269, 277
Iran 183, 191–2, 194, 198–200, 318, 325, 326,
    326–7, 347
ISKCON (International Society for Krishna
    Consciousness/Hare Krishna movement) 267, 269,
    270, 271, *272*, 275, 276, 280
Islam 182–4, 201–2; 18th century 190–2; 19th
    century 192–4; Africa *199*, 204–5, 208, 209–10,
    219–20, 221, 225; Akhbaris 192; Ali 186, 187,
    188; Allah 182, 184, 185, 191; authority 186–8,
    188, 198, 199, 318; banking 197; China 88, 90;
    and Christian mission 193–4; 'church–state'
    relations 318; and colonialism 192–4; community
    186–90; Deobandi movement 195; din 182, **202**;

Egypt 182–3, 195–7, 198, 309, 327; fundamental-
    ism 195, 307; Gabriel 185; gender 200–1, 225,
    344–7, *347*, 352; globalization 308; *hadith* 184,
    185, 191, 196–7, **202**; *hajj* 188, **202**; *hijab* 346;
    ijtihad 191, 192, **202**; *Imams* 187–8, **202**; India
    16, 22, 23–4, 34, 189–90, 194, 195–7; influences
    on 186, 194; Iran 183, 191–2, 194, 198–200;
    Islamism 308, 309, 346, **353**; Isma'ilis 187; *jihad*
    188, **202**; key terms **202–3**; *khalifa* 186, **202**;
    marriage 197, 200, 201; Mecca 182, 188, 190,
    200; Medina 182, 186, 190; miracles 196;
    modernist reform 195–200; and modernity 184,
    192–5; mosques *193*, *196*, *199*, *317*, 318;
    Mouride brotherhood 221; *mujtahids* 188, 194,
    198, **202**; *muslim* 182; Muslim world 182–4, *183*;
    Muslim World League 198; nationalism 193,
    344–5; number of adherents 182; Pakistan 197,
    199, 344–5; and politics 191, 194, 316, 318, 327,
    326, *347*; present trends 200–1; Prophet
    Muhammad 182, 185, 186; public interest 197;
    Qur'an 182, 184–6, *187*, *189*, 196, 197, 200;
    Ramadan 188, *293*; *rasul allah* 188, **202**; *salat*
    188, **202**; *sawm* 188, **202**; scripture 184–6;
    secularization 194; and the self 188; *shari'a* 186–7,
    197, **202**; Shi'a 187–8, 191–2, 198–200; Sufism
    (*tasawwuf*) 186, 188, 190, 191, **202**, **313**; *sunna*
    184, 185, 186–7, 197, **202**, **330**; Sunni 182,
    186–7, 191, 192, 195–8; *taqwa* 188, **202**;
    tasawwuf (see Sufism); Traditions of the Prophet
    184, 186, 196–7; *ulama* 185–6, **202**; *umma*
    183–4, 186, **203**; Usulis 192; Wahhabi 225, 228;
    Yan Izala movement 225; *zakat* 188, **203**
Islamic Salvation Front (FIS) 319, 327, **330**
Islamicization **330**
Islamism 308, 309, 346, **353**
Israel 130, 131, 135–6, 143–4, 147, 194, 309, 319
Italy 281

Jacobson, Israel *134*, 134–5
Jainism 16, 20
Jamieson, Penny *340*
Janamsakhi 73, **84**
Janzen, John M. 216, 221
Japan: colonialism 109; cultural superiority 117,
    120–1; gender 122, 351; histories 111; Imperial
    Rescript on Education 118; modernity 109,
    116–19; nationalism 109; New Religious
    Movements (NRMs) 269, 274, 276, 277, 351;
    spirituality 373–4; urbanization 121–2; Yasukuni
    Shrine 118–19 *see also* Japanese religions
Japanese religions 108–10, 125; Agonshū 122–3;
    Amida 114; ancestor rites 108, 109; ascetics
    112–13; Aum Shinrikyō 109, 123–4, 266, 268,
    282; *bodhisattava* 113, **125**; buddha nature 113,
    125; Buddhism 63, *110*, 110–11, 112–16, 118,
    121, 124; Christianity 108–9, 112; Confucian
    texts 111–12; *daimoku* 115, **125**; Dōgen 115;
    Eisai 114–15; festivals 119, *122*, 124; funeral rites

sacred arrows 237, 241, **246**
sacred kingship 217–18
sacrifices 16, 26, 238
sages 88, **105**, **151**
Sahaja Yoga 267, 271
saizei itchi 118, **126**
Sakya 47, **68**
Sakyamuni 93, 110
salat 188, **202**
Samantabhadra's aspirations 43–4
Samkhya 20, 37
samsara **37**
Sande society 213, 214, 215
Saṅgha 45, 46–7, 49, 50, 52–4, 65, **68**, 348–9
Sanskrit 19, **37**
Santi Asoke 54, 327, **330**
Saradamani 30
Sarasvati, Jayendra 26
Sarit Thanarat 53
Sarkar, P. R. 29
Satanism 268
Satchidananda 29
Satguru Sivaya Subramuniyaswami 27
Sathya Sai Baba 18, 29, *30*
sati (suttee) 17, 25, 28, 31–2, **37**
Savarkar, V. D. 33–4
sawm 188, **202**
Schechter, Solomon 137
Schleiermacher, Friedrich 167
Schneerson, Rabbi Menahem Mendel 147–8
science and technology 24–5, 26, 27
Scientology 264, 269–70, 271, 274, 280, 281–2
scriptures: authority of 10; Buddhist 43, 45, 46,
   60–1; Christian 154–5, 172, 173, 220, 318, 367;
   Hindu 18–20, 23, 26, **37**; Islam (*see* Qur'an); Sikh
   71, 73, 77
secondary institutions **353**
sects 259, 279, 280, 281
secularization 256–7, **261**, 296–7, **297**, **330**, **375**;
   Christianity 175–6, 292, 294; European exceptionalism 175, 294–5, **297**; fundamentalism 294,
   297; intellectualism 293–4; Islam 194; key terms
   297; mapping 293–6; pluralism and 296, **297**;
   politics and 320–1, **330**; and sacralization 10–12,
   292–3, 357–8; theories 291–2; United States of
   America 175
self, turn to the 9–10, 139, 161, 177 *see also* 'HS
   factor'
self-religions 10, 259, 277, **285**
Senegal 221
Sephardic Jewry 129, 147, **151**, **313**
Serbia 166
Seventh-Day Adventists 280
Seymour, William Joseph 174
SGPC (Shiromani Gurdwara Parbandhak Committee)
   78, 80, 84
Shaiva 17, 35, **37**
Shakta 17, **37**

Shakti 27, 29, **37**
Shankara 18, 19
shari'a 186–7, 197, **202**
Shelley, Percy Bysshe 362
Sheppard, William 209
shinbutsu bunri 117, **126**
Shinto 113, 116–19, 124
Shiromani Gurdwara Parbandhak Committee *see*
   SGPC
Shiv Dayal, Swami 27
Shiva 17, 18, 19, 26, 29, **37**
Shivananda 28
Shri Hans Ji Maharaj 267, 269
Shulkhan Aruch 130, **151**
Sierra Leone 208, 213, 214–15
Sikhism 70–1, 75, *76*, 83; 3HO 81; activism 79–80;
   Adi Granth 73–4; *Akali Dal* 78, **83**; Amritsar 73,
   80; authority 74, 76–7, **83**; colonial challenges
   75–6; and colonial modernity 76–8; community
   71, 72, 73, 74, **83**; diaspora 70, 70*t*, 80, 82; five
   Ks 73, **83**; formative phases *74*; future trends
   82–3, **83**; gender 72, 73, 74, 77, 78, 81, 82–3, **83**;
   Granth 71, 73, *73*, 81, 82, **83**; *gurbani* 72, 82, **83**;
   gurdwara 72, 78, **83**; *Gurmukhi* 73, 78, **84**; Guru
   Arjun 73; *Guru Granth Sahib* 73–4, 77; Guru
   Nanak 71, *72*; Guru Panth 74, 77; *Harimandir*
   73, *80*; identity 77–8, 81; influences on 71;
   influences on Hinduism 27; Janamsakhi 73, **84**;
   key terms **83–4**; Khalistan 79, 80, **83**; the Khalsa
   73–4, 75, 77, **84**; marriage 78; Namdhari sect
   76–7; the Nanak Panth 71–3; neo-orthodoxy
   80–2, **83**; Panth 71, 73, **84**; postcolonial world
   79–82; *rahit* 74, **84**; Rahit Maryada 80–1; Sants
   71; scriptures 71, 73, 77; self 74, 82, *83*; SGPC
   78, 80, **84**; Sikh Dharma 81; Singh **84**; Singh
   Sabha 77–8, 79, **84**; Tat Khalsa 77, 78, **84**;
   temples 72, 73, 78, *80 see also* India
Simmel, Georg 371, 372
Singer, Margaret 274, 275
Singh **84**
Singh Sabha 77–8, 79, **84**
Sita *26*, 31, **38**
small group movement 367–8
Sobrino, Jon 162
social differentiation *see* differentiation
social encyclicals 160, **179**
social relationships: and Buddhism 66; Confucianism
   88; Hinduism 20–1, 35; Islam 188; Sikhism
   71
sociologie religieuse 292
Sofer, Rabbi Mosheh 135–6, 146
Soka Gakkai 63, 121, 267, 269, 276 *see also* Nichiren
sokushin jōbutsu 113, **126**
Solar Temple 267, 268, 269, 282, 283
Somalia 317
soul 365
'the south' 320
South Africa 206, 217, 226, 321

The Library
SOUTH TRAFFORD COLLEGE
Altrincham Centre
Manchester Road
West Timperley
ALTRINCHAM
Cheshire WA14 5PQ